HELEN

OUR FIRST AMBASSADOR TO CHINA

AN ACCOUNT OF THE LIFE OF
GEORGE, EARL OF MACARTNEY

WITH
EXTRACTS FROM HIS LETTERS, AND THE NARRATIVE
OF HIS EXPERIENCES
IN CHINA, AS TOLD BY HIMSELF

1737-1806

Elibron Classics
www.elibron.com

Elibron Classics series.

© 2005 Adamant Media Corporation.

ISBN 1-4021-4906-9 (paperback)
ISBN 1-4212-8019-1 (hardcover)

This Elibron Classics Replica Edition is an unabridged facsimile
of the edition published in 1908 by John Murray,
London.

Elibron and Elibron Classics are trademarks of
Adamant Media Corporation. All rights reserved.

This book is an accurate reproduction of the original. Any marks, names, colophons, imprints, logos or other symbols or identifiers that appear on or in this book, except for those of Adamant Media Corporation and BookSurge, LLC, are used only for historical reference and accuracy and are not meant to designate origin or imply any sponsorship by or license from any third party.

OUR FIRST AMBASSADOR TO CHINA

THE LIFE AND CORRESPONDENCE OF
GEORGE, EARL OF MACARTNEY,
AND HIS EXPERIENCES IN CHINA
AS TOLD BY HIMSELF

Macartney

Portrait in the possession of C. G. Macartney, Esq.

OUR FIRST AMBASSADOR TO CHINA

AN ACCOUNT OF THE LIFE OF
GEORGE, EARL OF MACARTNEY

WITH EXTRACTS FROM HIS LETTERS, AND
THE NARRATIVE OF HIS EXPERIENCES
IN CHINA, AS TOLD BY HIMSELF
1737—1806

FROM HITHERTO UNPUBLISHED
CORRESPONDENCE AND DOCUMENTS

BY HELEN H. ROBBINS

WITH ILLUSTRATIONS

LONDON
JOHN MURRAY, ALBEMARLE STREET, W.
1908

TO

MY BROTHER

CARTHANACH GEORGE MACARTNEY

IN AFFECTIONATE REMEMBRANCE OF

MANY HAPPY DAYS OF CHILDHOOD

AT LISSANOURE

PREFACE

THE present time is one of reawakened interest in the countries and peoples of the Far East. In divers ways and in various places there is manifest a strong indication of the growing feeling among the population of Asia that there has been more than enough of Western interference and domination, and that the East should be for the Easterns. In China this movement has of late been very apparent. Among other things, the changes in the administration and control of the customs point to the doctrine of China for the Chinese, and a new order of affairs in that country has set in. It appears to me not improbable that some, at any rate, of the reading public may, therefore, be interested in the account of the first British Embassy to China, given in his own words by the man who conducted it, and written down on the spot while the impressions he received were fresh upon his mind.

To the student of history much of the information contained in these pages is already familiar, and the book is intended to appeal not so much to the expert as to the ordinary reader, who has probably not had the description of such a mission as that carried out by Lord Macartney brought before him in any detailed manner.

In order to make the book more complete, I have incorporated a short memoir of the Ambassador himself, giving an account of the various positions he had previously occupied, and the reasons which led to his having been selected for so important and delicate a task.

In 1797 Sir George Staunton published the account of

Lord Macartney's famous Embassy to Pekin, and ten years later Sir John Barrow gave to the world some account of the public life and writings of the Ambassador. The first-named work has long been out of print, and Sir John Barrow's ' Life ' laid no claim to being a complete biography, as much of the existing material was not accessible to him, nor had the time come for making it public. Barrow, indeed, expressly says he ' thought it right carefully to avoid all private anecdote and correspondence, and forbore to ask for any papers which might be·considered to fall under this description.'

I have had before me the original copies of the Chinese journals, and rough notes upon them, and the numerous letters and papers in the possession of my brother, Mr. C. G. Macartney, as well as the ' Proceedings of the Select Committee of Fort St. George ' and the manuscripts which are to be found in the British Museum. I am also greatly indebted to Mrs. Godfrey Clark, who kindly lent me many of Lord and Lady Macartney's private papers and notebooks, and to the Hon. James Home for the extracts from Lady Mary Coke's unpublished diaries. The contemporary history of India has been so frequently dealt with that I have touched but lightly on that part of Lord Macartney's career, confining my attention principally to the personal side of his mission and relations to those with whom he was brought into contact.

Macartney's life was a full and varied one ; I therefore hope that his character may be found sufficiently attractive to interest the reader in his doings and experiences in the West Indies, in Ireland, and at Verona, to which latter place he went on a confidential mission from George III. to Louis XVIII. His account of this undertaking is now made public for the first time.

The design on the cover of the book is one adapted from a sprig of the original Macartney rose, growing in the North of Ireland. Lord Macartney brought this distinct species of evergreen rose back with him from China, and it has been known by his name ever since.

PREFACE

In conclusion, I wish to record my grateful thanks to all the friends who in various ways have helped me so kindly in my task, especially Mons. J. Gennadius, to whom the book owes much of the idea of its existence, and who has assisted me with criticism and advice.

Last, but by no means least, I wish to express my affectionate thanks to my mother, whose constant sympathy and interest in the undertaking have been of the greatest help and stimulus.

HELEN H. ROBBINS.

CONTENTS

CHAPTER I

EARLY DAYS AND MISSION TO RUSSIA

History and origin of the Macartney family—Descent from the Macarthy More—Removal into Scotland—Return to Ireland in seventeenth century—'Burgesse' and 'Soveraigne' of Belfast—Lord Macartney's grandfather—Birth of Lord Macartney at Lissanoure—Childhood in the North of Ireland—School outfit and education—Enters Trinity College—Macartney goes over to London—Acquaintance with Edmund Burke, Dr. Johnson, and Sir Joshua Reynolds—Travels abroad—Visit to Voltaire—A *mésalliance* in Piedmont—Acquaintanceship with Stephen Fox—Gratitude and interest of Lord and Lady Holland—Macartney's appearance and manners—He stands for Parliament—Is appointed envoy to Russia—Hopes entertained that his charms may fascinate the Czarina—The treaty of commerce—Macartney is knighted by King George III.—Arrival in Russia—Lord Buckinghamshire's kindness—First interview with the Empress—Diplomatic speech and its results—The cultivation of Panin—His character and influence—Letter from Macartney to Lady Holland—Description of Court and Czarina—The masquerades and entertainments—Prevalence of use of rouge among Russian women—The Empress's jewels; fondness for diamonds—Love affairs, and Macartney's reflections on them - - - - - 1-25

CHAPTER II

MISSION TO RUSSIA

The treaty of commerce—Russia's plans and projects—Catherine's annoyance with the French Court—Sir George's difficulties with Panin and his own Government—The Russian Commercial Commissioners are spiteful—Macartney signs the treaty without first sending it to England—His

CONTENTS

reasons for this action—Displeasure of the English Cabinet —The wrangle over the 'Navigation Act' clause—Opinions of the English merchants in Russia—Panin's irritation with the English Ministry—Difficulty in soothing his ruffled feelings—Inflexibility of the Empress—She determines to break off all negotiations—Macartney's difficulties and discouragements—He has a sudden inspiration—Panin and the Empress finally agree to a treaty, which is at length ratified by England—Mr. Stanley is appointed as Ambassador—Macartney's unpleasant position—The Russian Court leaves for Moscow—Letter from Macartney to W. Burke—Letter to Mr. Conway—Letter to Mr. Stanley —Letter from Panin—The Empress's farewell gift—Letter from the King of Poland—Order of the White Eagle— Macartney's return to London—Resignation of Mr. Stanley —Macartney's appointment and refusal of it—His expenses and disinterested conduct - - - - - - 26-48

CHAPTER III

MARRIAGE, PARLIAMENT, IRELAND

Marriage of Sir G. Macartney and Lady Jane Stuart—Lord Bute and his influence at Court—Lady Jane's appearance and character — Lady Mary Coke's comments on the engagement—Wedding and honeymoon—Account of a visit to Lady Jane Macartney—Sir George Macartney loses £100 at cards—The non-success of the Stuart marriages— Reasons why the Macartney marriage was not altogether a particularly happy one—Lady Louisa Stuart to Lady Caroline Dawson—Her appreciation of Macartney's integrity and uprightness — Macartney and Sir James Lowther stand for Parliament—Resignation by Macartney of English seat, and election to the Irish House of Commons —Changes contemplated in the system of government in Ireland—Lord-Lieutenants—Undertakers and patriots— Irish and Anglo-Irish—Lord Townshend's appointment— Macartney's appointment as Chief Secretary—His hopes of obtaining Ambassadorship at Madrid—Letters from Lord Townshend — Difficulties with Undertakers and patriots—Sir George Macartney's first visit as Secretary to Ireland—Lord Townshend's satisfaction at the failure of the Madrid project—Private letters from permanent officials at the castle—Arrival of Sir G. and Lady Jane Macartney in Ireland—Letter from Lady Bute—Macartney as Chief Secretary—His good temper and firmness - 49-70

CONTENTS

CHAPTER IV
CHIEF SECRETARY FOR IRELAND

Letters from London—Sir George Saville's speech in the House of Commons—Mr. Wilkes and his debts—Debate on American affairs—The remonstrance—Reports of differences between Lord Townshend and Sir G. Macartney—Scene in the House of Lords—The liberty of the press—Comments on Irish affairs—Riot at the Guildhall entertainment — Mr. King's book — Lord Cathcart and his daughter's love affair—Princess Dashkoff's mischief-making—Dedication of Mr. King's book, and presentation of it to the King and Queen—Denmark and 'The Queen of Tears'—Appreciation of Macartney by the Irish—Macartney made Knight Companion of the Bath—Retires from Chief Secretaryship of Ireland—Lord Townshend's recall—Arrival of Lord Harcourt—Letters from Ireland to Sir G. Macartney — Denunciations against Lord Townshend — Conflicting opinions about Colonel Blaquiere - - - - - 71-93

CHAPTER V
GOVERNOR OF GRENADA

Appointment as Governor of Grenada—Elevation to the peerage of Ireland—Reason for not changing his name on this occasion—Journey to the West Indies—Fear of meeting American privateers—Reception at Grenada—First impressions—Difficulties, and Mr. Staunton—Account of the latter—Voyage to Tobago and Round Island—Amount of salary as Governor — Duel between Mr. Young and Mr. Franklyn—Administration of the islands—Rumours of a French war—Visit to Barbadoes—Increasing rumours of French invasion—Precautions for defence of the island—Taking of St. Lucie—Attack upon Grenada by Count d'Estaing — Gallant attempt at defence — Letters from Mr. Staunton and Lord Macartney upon the taking of Grenada by the French—Ill behaviour of Count d'Estaing—Loss of all Lord Macartney's effects—Lady Macartney's departure, and loss of papers—Address from the inhabitants of Grenada to the ex-Governor—Mr. and Mrs. Staunton go to France—Letter from the latter—Macartney's exchange—Confidential mission to Ireland—Election as member for Beeralstone - - - - - - - - - 94-115

CHAPTER VI

MADRAS

The East India Company's selection of a President for the province of Madras—Reasons for preferring an 'outsider' —Macartney's speech, and general fitness for the post— His letters to Mr. Staunton—Macartney's arrival at Madras —The war with Hyder Ali, and the difficulties from disaffection and lack of money—The taking of the Dutch settlements on the coast—Fruitless attempt to make peace with Hyder Ali—Sir Eyre Coote's objection to the attempt to capture Negapatam from the Dutch—Successful accomplishment of the plan by Macartney—Transactions with the Nabob of Arcot—Engagements between French and English fleets—Inhumanity of the French naval commander—Account of the misery of Hyder Ali's captives— Difficulties with Sir Eyre Coote and Warren Hastings— Death of Hyder Ali—Difficulties with General Stuart—Death of Sir Eyre Coote—Arrest of General Stuart, and his deportation to England—Behaviour of Sir John Burgoyne— Negotiations with Tippoo Sahib—Macartney's anxiety, and subsequent satisfaction—The release of the prisoners, and their gratitude—Bengal Government disapprove of terms of peace—Macartney adheres to his line of conduct—His resignation in consequence of orders from England—Affidavits on his retirement—He decides to visit Bengal—Offer of the Governorship of Bengal, and reasons for refusing it—Quarrel and duel with Mr. Sadleir—Macartney's return home   116-152

CHAPTER VII

INDIA, LONDON, IRELAND

Lady Macartney's reasons for not accompanying her husband to India—Her ability in managing his affairs—Her anxiety about his health, and her doubts as to what course of action to pursue—Letters to her sister, Lady Portarlington— Macartney's return to England—Interview with the Chairman of the East India Company—Macartney's ideas on the subject of the Governorship of Bengal, and unwillingness to take up the office—Fox's speech in Parliament, and Pitt's reply—Macartney asks for an English peerage— Reason for Government's refusal of this demand—Lord Cornwallis appointed Governor-General—Marks of appreciation of Macartney's services from the East India Company—General Stuart's resentment—Account of the

CONTENTS

duel between him and Lord Macartney—The King interposes to prevent a renewal of hostilities—Macartney's visit to Ireland—He and his relations-in-law find each other mutually improved—Move from Charles Street to Curzon Street—Marriage of Macartney's niece—Visit to Lissanoure—Lady Macartney's dislike of the place—Macartney as a landlord and country gentleman—Reasons for an Embassy to China—Macartney accepts the office—Preparations and search for an interpreter—Departure from Spithead - 153-179

CHAPTER VIII

JOURNAL OF EMBASSY FROM LONDON TO CHINA

Departure from London—Members of the Embassy—Arrival at Madeira—Visit to the Governor—Dinner and ball at Val Formosa—Dinner-party at the Governor's house—Music on board the *Lion*—Teneriffe—The Governor's civilities—Religion—Reluctance of women to enter convents—Expedition up the Peak of Teneriffe—St. Jago—Lord Macartney struck with its poverty—The line is crossed—Lord Macartney has an attack of gout—Arrival at Rio Janeiro—Description of town and people—Free and friendly manners of the women—Tristan d'Acunha. The *Lion* drops anchor—Preparations for an expedition—Are unable to land—Sea-lion and albatross—Unfortunate fate of the latter—Island of Amsterdam and its inhabitants—Exploration of the island, and scientific observations—Hot soil—Accident to several members of the party—Lord Macartney's reflection on cures, progress of modern science, and age of the world 180-210

CHAPTER IX

STRAITS OF SUNDA AND BATAVIA

Arrival in the Straits of Sunda—Dutch claims, and Sir Erasmus Gower's reply—Welcome to Batavia—Reception of Lord Macartney — Mr. Wiegerman's hospitality — Ball at the Governor's house—Dress of the ladies—Indisposition of Lord Macartney—Treachery of the Malays—Murder of a sailor—Sufferings from heat—Description of Batavia and its population—The deadly upas-tree—Scarcity of physicians in Batavia—Insects, floating islands, and thunderstorms—A Cochin Chinese village, and its fear of the Embassy—Departure from Pulo Condore, and accident on board the *Hindustan*—Arrival in Turon Bay—Visit from several Portuguese and Chinese Mandarins—Dinner-party, and

CONTENTS

importunate hosts—Present from the Governor—Market—
Letter from the King of Cochin China—State visit to the
Great Mandarin—Chinese play and dinner—Mr. Jackson's
unplesant adventure—Departure for China   -   -   211-243

CHAPTER X

A JOURNAL OF THE EMBASSY TO CHINA IN 1792-1794

First glimpse of China—Loss of one of the interpreters—Difficulty of procuring pilots—Governor's assistance in the matter—Visit and present of food from the Governor of Tenchoufou—Arrival at the mouth of the Yellow River—Chinese expectations from the Embassy—Visits from Mandarins—First appearance of Van-ta-gin and Chou-ta-gin—Transport of presents to junks—Lord Macartney and suite leave the *Lion*—Visit from the old Viceroy—Return of the Macao missionaries—The Embassy proceeds up the river—First appearance of the Tartar Legate—Crowds of natives—Sufferings from mosquitoes—Tainted provisions—Summary justice—Conversation on Court ceremonies—Great hospitality—The Embassy carefully and jealously watched—Arrival of the presents at Yuen-min-yuen—The Tartar Legate's ill-humour — Death of Henry Eades — Departure of the Embassy for Pekin—Arrival there, and poor accommodation—Visits from European missionaries—Attempt to make Macartney consent to 'kow-tow' to the Emperor—Visit from Father Raux—Information from him as to the Emperor's family and habits—Chinese pride—Satisfaction of the Emperor with the conduct of the Embassy - - - - - - - - - 244-291

CHAPTER XI

EMBASSY TO CHINA

Journey to Gehol—Van-ta-gin and Chou-ta-gin delighted with the post-chaise—The Great Wall of China—Difference between Tartars and Chinese—Entrance into Gehol—Visits from the Tartar Legate to the First Minister—Disgrace of the Tartar Legate—Difficulties as to the ceremonial of presentation—The matter finally settled—Visit to the Emperor—Dress and ceremony—Presentation of gifts to and from the Emperor—Conversation and banquet—Visit to the Park of Gehol—Introduction to Sun-ta-gin—Lord Macartney's endeavours to talk of business are frustrated—Jealousy and suspicion of the Chinese—Ceremonies on the occasion of the Emperor's birthday—Departure from Gehol—Presents

CONTENTS

for King George III.—Arrival at Pekin—Disposal of the presents to the Emperor—Arrival of the Emperor at Pekin—Indisposition of Lord Macartney—Chinese anxiety to get rid of the Embassy—Minister avoids discussion of business—Interview with the Colaos—Their stiffness and unsatisfactory answers—Father Amyot's opinions—Date of departure fixed—Arrangements for the journey—Lord Macartney's reflections - - - - - - 292–338

CHAPTER XII

EMBASSY TO CHINA

Departure from Pekin—Conversation with Sun-ta-gin on the subject of Ambassadors and the Embassy—Great attention shown to the wants of the travellers—The Emperor is pleased with the accounts of the journey—The Yellow River—Soldiers and their uniforms—Bridge of one hundred arches—Visit from the new Viceroy of Canton—His good wishes and favourable disposition—Letter from Sir Erasmus Gower—Departure of Sun-ta-gin—Conversation with the Viceroy on trade and the grievances of the English merchants — Ambassadors from the Liev Kiev Islands — Overland journey for three days—Conversation started by a match-box—Visit to the Temple of Pusa—Description of the Emperor and his manner of life—Arrival at Canton—Entertainment by the Viceroy—Lord Macartney's regret at having to depart—Visit to the interior of Canton—Farewell to Van-ta-gin and Chou-ta-gin and their regret—Departure of the Embassy—Notes from Appendix—Two distinct nationalities — Ceremonies and Court character—Houses, furniture, dress, and manners—Advantages to China from the Embassy—Small feet and comparison between English and Chinese fashions — Religions and missionaries in China—Constitution of China—The Tartar conquest—Laws—Rank—Science—Printing—Trade with foreign nations, and conclusion - - - - - 339–412

CHAPTER XIII

MISSION TO VERONA

Lord Macartney's return to England—Illness and death of Lady Bute—The confidential mission from George III. to Louis XVIII.—Macartney's journey and arrival at Verona—Visit from the Maréchal de Castries—First interview with the French King—Rumours of peace between France and Spain—Letter from Lord Bute—The Empress of Russia favours Louis' recognition—The Maréchal de Castries is anxious for the prompt action of Great Britain in the matter—Lord Macartney's reasons for caution and slowness—King Louis' proclamation to the French people—Long interview with the King—He objects to residence in Rome or Gibraltar—The French King's poverty, appearance, and character—Description of his Court and chief Ministers—Letter to Louis from the Empress of Russia—Macartney visits Padua and Venice—Austria's schemes with regard to Madame Royale—The King's annoyance, and wish to see her—Conversation on compensation expected by friendly States — Macartney is worried by impecunious French refugees—Letter from Sir William Hamilton—Difficulties of finding a suitable place of residence for Louis, and reasons against continuing to live at Verona—Conduct of Spain, and Louis' indignation thereat—Letters to Sir George Staunton and Lord Grenville—Journey of Madame Royale to the Austrian capital — Lord Macartney visits Naples, Rome, and Florence — Letters from Sir William Hamilton—The Venetian Republic notify to Louis their wish for his speedy departure — The King's reply and departure—Macartney's regrets, and comments on the situation to Lord Grenville - - - - - 413-440

CHAPTER XIV

GOVERNOR OF THE CAPE, AND LAST DAYS

Macartney appointed Governor of the Cape—He is unwilling to accept the appointment—Voyage out—Success of his administration—Mutiny among the English sailors—Macartney's failing health — Appointment of successor, and return home—Lord and Lady Macartney settle at Corney House—Illness and death of Sir George Staunton—Lord Macartney's letters to his son—Monument erected to Sir G. Staunton in Westminster Abbey—Final illness and death of Lord Macartney—His appearance at Lissanoure on the evening of his death—Obituary notice in the *Morning Post*—His burial and tomb at Chiswick—Lord Macartney's will—Death of Lady Macartney—Sale of his library in 1854—Lord Macartney's scholarly tastes and fondness for literature — His ideas on party politics — Assertions as to the failure of the Chinese Embassy—Some account of the Dutch Embassy—Macartney's reflections upon Mrs. Montagu—Summary of his character - 441-466

INDEX - - - - - - - - - 467-479

LIST OF ILLUSTRATIONS

	TO FACE PAGE
LORD MACARTNEY WEARING THE ORDER OF THE WHITE EAGLE OF POLAND (Photogravure) - - *Frontispiece*	
'BLACK' GEORGE MACARTNEY (SOVERAIGNE OF BELFAST)	4
From the Portrait in the possession of C. G. MACARTNEY, ESQ.	
GEORGE MACARTNEY (ÆTAT. 21)	12
From the Portrait in the possession of C. G. MACARTNEY, ESQ.	
LORD AND LADY MACARTNEY (Photogravure)	52
From Miniatures in the possession of C. G. MACARTNEY, ESQ.	
MRS. BALAQUIER (SISTER TO LORD MACARTNEY)	86
From the Portrait in the possession of C. G. MACARTNEY, ESQ.	
GEORGE, EARL OF MACARTNEY, AND HIS SECRETARY, SIR GEORGE LEONARD STAUNTON, BART.	120
From the Picture in the National Portrait Gallery.	
JANE, LADY MACARTNEY, 1786 (Photogravure)	156
From the Portrait in the possession of C. G. MACARTNEY, ESQ.	
LISSANOURE CASTLE AND LOUGH GUILE	170
From the Picture in the possession of C. G. MACARTNEY, ESQ.	
THE VISCOUNT MACARTNEY	196
From an Engraving by C. TOWNLEY, *after* S. DE KOSTER.	
GEORGE, EARL OF MACARTNEY	238
From an Engraving by HENRY HUDSON, *after* M. BROWN.	
ONE OF THE EMBASSY YACHTS	264
From the Drawing by WILLIAM ALEXANDER *in the British Museum.*	

LIST OF ILLUSTRATIONS

	TO FACE PAGE
VAN-TA-GIN (THE WAR MANDARIN WHO ACCOMPANIED THE EMBASSY)	290
By WILLIAM ALEXANDER, 1793. *In the British Museum.*	
THE APPROACH OF THE EMPEROR OF CHINA TO RECEIVE THE BRITISH AMBASSADOR	304
From a Drawing by WILLIAM ALEXANDER *in the British Museum.*	
TRACKERS FOR THE YACHT CONVEYING THE AMBASSADOR	342
From a Drawing by WILLIAM ALEXANDER *in the British Museum.*	
THE EMPEROR TCHIEN-LUNG	374
From a Drawing by WILLIAM ALEXANDER *in the British Museum.*	
CHOU-TA-GIN (THE CIVIL MANDARIN WHO ACCOMPANIED THE EMBASSY)	390
By WILLIAM ALEXANDER, 1793. *In the British Museum.*	
LORD MACARTNEY	418
From the Drawing by BARTOLOZZI *in the British Museum.*	
ROOM AT MESSRS. COUTTS' BANK, SHOWING THE WALL-PAPER BROUGHT BY LORD MACARTNEY FROM CHINA	442
ELIZABETH HUME (NIECE AND ADOPTED DAUGHTER OF LORD MACARTNEY)	456
From the Portrait in the possession of C. G. MACARTNEY, ESQ.	

MEMOIR OF THE
LIFE OF THE EARL OF MACARTNEY

CHAPTER I

GEORGE, EARL OF MACARTNEY, diplomatist, statesman, and first Ambassador from England to China, was born on May 14, 1737, at his grandfather's residence, Lissanoure, in the county of Antrim.

It is usually of interest to know something, however slight, of the descent and parentage of any prominent person. Much truth is contained in the idea that the life of every man is, to some extent, written before he is born. An acquaintance with ancestral and racial influences is, therefore, often an aid to the just appreciation of character, as well as a knowledge of the surroundings and friendships which play so important a part in the formation of it.

The family of Macartney is an ancient one, said to be descended from that of the MacCarthy More, one of whose sons went over to Scotland in the beginning of the fourteenth century, and was the progenitor of the family.[1]

The Irish Celts, who had been for some time very impatient under the English yoke, were encouraged by the defeat of Edward II. at Bannockburn to try and rid themselves of it. They invited the Bruces, who were descended

---

[1] It seems evident that the MacCarthys, or MacCartneys, have the same origin, as their armorial bearings have ever been the same, with the exception of the bordure used by the latter, which would appear to mark them as a younger branch of the same family.

from the Celtic chiefs of Galloway,[1] on their mother's side, to undertake an expedition into Ireland. Accordingly in May, 1315, Edward Bruce landed in Ulster with about six thousand men, accompanied by the Earl of Moray and several other Scottish commanders. He was immediately joined by a number of the Irish chieftains, and, taking possession of Carrickfergus, Coleraine, and Dundalk, was crowned King of Ireland at the hill of Knocknemelan, not far from the latter place.

Barbour, Archdeacon of Aberdeen, who lived in the reign of King David, and received a pension for writing a life of his predecessor, Robert Bruce, says that two of the chiefs, Mac-Cartney and Mac-Gocilchone, subsequently deserted, and laid an ambush for Bruce at the Pass of Endnellane, but were defeated by the Earl of Moray.

One of MacCartney's sons, Donough or Daniel, went over to Scotland after the death of Edward Bruce,[2] and serving his brother, King Robert, in his wars, obtained from him a grant of lands in Argyllshire. His descendants, being ousted from their possessions in that county, removed into Galloway, and settled upon certain lands there, to which they gave their name. The family eventually divided into three branches: Mac-Cartney of Mickle-Leathes, Mac-Cartney of Blacket, and Mac-Cartney of Auchinleck. Of the last-named branch was George Mac-Cartney, who in 1522 married Margaret, daughter of Godfrey MacCulloch of Fleet Bank, Kirkcudbright. His descendant George, born in 1626,

[1] 'All the things of Lesser Scotland (Scotia Minor) have drawn their blood from Greater Scotland (Scotia Major)—*i.e.*, Ireland—and retain in some degree our language and customs,' wrote Donald O'Neill, a chief of Ulster to the Pope. It was therefore very natural they should have called upon the Bruces to aid them in their struggle for freedom.

[2] Edward Bruce, who was brave and rash, was eventually killed in battle, and his body quartered and set up as trophies in the chief towns of the English colony in Ireland. His head was sent to England, and presented to Edward II. Barbour, however, declared that the head was not that of Bruce, but of a devoted follower who had worn his armour upon that day.

BURGESSE AND SOVERAIGNE OF BELFAST

removed into Ireland in 1649, and settled near Belfast, where he subsequently acquired a large estate.

This ancestor of Lord Macartney seems to have been a man of capacity and energy. His name is frequently to be met with in the records of the town meetings in Belfast from 1659 to 1681. He figures there first as 'Burgesse,' and then as 'Soveraigne,' offices equivalent to those of Lord Mayor and Alderman at the present day.[1] He was also a Captain of Horse, Surveyor-General of the Province of Ulster, and in 1678 served as Sheriff for the county of Antrim.

In Benn's 'History of Belfast' it is stated that George Macartney, sometimes called 'Niger' or 'Black' Macartney, was the ablest man of his time in that city; 'and it may be said, without exaggeration, that at no period has the town contained a citizen of more ability. . . . Belfast was the home of his affections and the field of his labours; he was Collector of the Customs, and a merchant of repute . . . shipowner, miller, sugar-refiner, possibly . . . also a worker in woollens. He was chief magistrate, and . . . there was no project for the public advantage of which he was not the originator or promoter.' The population of Belfast having much increased, it was found necessary, in 1678, to provide the town with a fresh water-supply. 'George Macartney, ever alive to the public wants, engaged in this laudable object . . . agreed with workmen, and brought clean *holesome* water in wooden pipes underground into Belfast . . . for the supply and general good of the inhabitants, partakers of the comforts of the same.'

At the revolution of 1688, Macartney, at the head of his troops, proclaimed Queen Mary and King William in Belfast.

---

[1] At an assembly houlden 1659 William Leathes, 'gent[l] sofferaigne, L[t] Thomas Theaker, M[r] George Martin, M[r] Hugh Doake and Capt[n] Francis Meake and Burgesses of the Borrough afforesaid then p[r]sent, George Mac-Cartney gent was sworne one of the Burgesses of the said towne according to y[e] ellection and order at y[e] court, holden the 17[th] Sep. 1659, and toke y[e] oath of a Burgesse according to y[e] use and custom of the said Towne and Corporation.—WILLIAM LEATHES, 1659, Sov[ne]. THOS. THEAKER. GEORGE MARTIN. HUGH DOAKE (his mark).—From 'The Town Book of Belfast.'

Shortly after the town was occupied for King James,[1] and Macartney obliged to fly to England. He was attainted in King James's Parliament held in Dublin in 1689, but being restored on the settlement of Ireland,[2] he returned to Belfast, where he died shortly after. By his will, dated April 22, 1691, he directed that his body should be buried in the church of Belfast, and left £40 for the benefit of the poor of that parish. To his eldest son, James, he left his estate of Auchinleck in Scotland,[3] and after making ample provision for his younger children, constituted his wife executrix and guardian of her sons Chichester and George.

The younger of these two boys (George) received his education at Christ Church College, Oxford, removed to the Middle Temple, and was called to the Bar in 1700. He subsequently sat for upwards of fifty years in the Irish House of Commons, and at the time of his death, October, 1757, was the oldest member of it. He also was a Deputy-Lieutenant and Colonel of Militia Dragoons for the county of Antrim. By his first wife he had three sons, two of whom died without issue. The second one, George, married Elizabeth, daughter of the Rev. John Winder, Prebendary of Kilroot, and Vicar of Carmony in County Antrim, and became, by her, father of the subject of the present memoir.

George, Earl of Macartney, as previously mentioned, first saw the light at Lissanoure in May, 1737. He appears to have been a boy of lively and inquiring disposition, and early showed promise of the quickness of perception and retentive memory which were so remarkable in after-life.

---

[1] By 'six companies of Colonel Cormack O'Neal's regiment, and a troop of dragoons in Malone and the Fall, and they were kept to strict discipline.'—From 'The Town Book of Belfast.'

[2] The Duke of Schomberg occupied Belfast August 17, 1689. 'While the Duke staid at Belfast, there came a letter to him by a trumpet from the Duke of Berwick, but it was returned unopened, because it was directed for *Count* Schomberg.'—From 'The Town Book of Belfast.'

[3] With restrictions against alienating the same, it having been in possession of the ancestors of his own name for many generations.

'BLACK' GEORGE MACARTNEY
SOVERAIGNE OF BELFAST
From the Portrait in the possession of C. G. MACARTNEY, ESQ.

THE HOME AT LISSANOURE

The early years of his childhood were spent at Lissanoure, much in the same manner as those of most children of his class and time. Throughout life he retained a strong affection for his northern home, and always returned to it with pleasure.

The country surrounding Lissanoure is somewhat bare and desolate, but the place itself picturesque and lovely with lakes and woods, the effect of which is heightened by the manner of approach. After a long, uninteresting drive, the road drops down a steep wooded hill upon the lake, and suddenly brings the traveller into an entirely different region. The castle, now, alas! in ruins, stands on gently rising ground overlooking Lough Guile, which lies at its feet, smiling and sparkling when the sun shines and skies are fair; at other times dark and frowning when clouds are heavy and lowering, and the plentiful grey mists of Ireland are wrapping it about. One solitary wooded island, long since the abode of a colony of herons, stands in the middle of the lake. It is said by some to be the remains of a crannog, or lake dwelling, and traces of similar antiquities are to be found also in other places in the neighbourhood. A tower,[1] dating from the twelfth century, stood directly behind the castle, under which, so legend relates, are dungeons. A tale is also told of treasure lying safe within the muddy fastness of the lake's embrace, swift and dire disaster being prophesied as the portion of any adventurous spirit who should attempt to search for it.

In this romantic and lonely spot little George Macartney passed many happy and uneventful moments of existence till July, 1745, when, being eight years old, he took his first important step in life, and went to school. His grandfather, who appears to have taken much pride and interest in the child, thus records the fact: 'My grandson George Macartney went to Mr. Thompson's school at Leixlip on Thursday, 18th July, 1745. Dr. Obbins in company with Dr. T.' The charges for his board and tuition

[1] This tower was, unfortunately, pulled down in the early part of the last century.

there sound ridiculously small to modern ears, and run as follows :

'The particulars of a quarter's note, contingencies excepted:

	£	s.	d.
Board and school	5	15	0
Writing-master	0	10	0
Barber	0	3	6
Washing	0	3	3
Taylor	0	1	0
French	0	15	0

Admission Fees, Three Guineas.

' Two pair of sheets, six napkins, a silver spoon. They who learn to write and dance pay the writing master half a guinea entrance, and the dancing master a guinea.'

' A list of linen, cloathes, books, etc., left with my grandson, George Macartney, at Leixlip school with Mr. Thompson on Thursday, 18th July, 1745, the day he was placed there. Also a memorandum where to direct and convey letters or other things to be sent to him.'

Memorandum, not in the same handwriting :

' To send to Mr. Labelios, Bookseller, Damack Street, anything you want to have conveyed to Leixlip school.'

The list of little Macartney's things, taken by both mother and grandfather, give an amusing insight into the sort of school outfit considered necessary at that period for a child. It runs as follows :

' 12 new shirts all marked and numbered from 1 to 12. And one of them ruffled. 5 old shirts ruffled only at the breast and neck. 6 night caps. 5 pair of course worsted stockings. 1 pair thread ditto. 6 pocket-handkerchiefs. 2 new pocket-handkerchiefs, bought of Mrs. Clarke at 0—1—4 each. A piece of cloath left of his shirts to neck and wrist them when they shall want. A piece of blue shag which was left of fronting his britches. 2 wigs a new and a old one (the grandfather's list gives three wigs). 2 hatts. One pair of shoes and a pair of pumps. 2 pair of britches of figured Druget. New scarlet Camblet waistcoat. One shute of cloathes which is on him. His green morning habit, blue rug, big coat and brush bag, 3 yards of black ribbon and pair of gloves. Pair of silver shoe buckles, and pair of state knee buckles. Piece of scarlet single, and piece of figured Druget to mend his cloathes.

2 pair of sheets, 6 napkins, and silver spoon. One Bible, one Whole Duty of Man, one Common Prayer Book. A grey cap for a green head. Puffindorf's Whole Duty of Man, Sherlock upon Death, his copy and ciphenie book, Steele's Christian Hero, A Week's Preparation for the Sacrament, Bishop of Sodor and Man on the Sacrament, and letter case.'

How long young Macartney remained at Leixlip School is uncertain, and though such a complete record is left of the clothes and literature he took with him, there are no details of his life there. Among his papers are two lists of the boys at the school, taken at different times, containing many well-known Irish names. Barrow states that Macartney's education was at first conducted by a private tutor of the name of Dennis; but whether he was a master at the school, or whether, as would seem more probable, Macartney went on to his care from that of Dr. Thompson, does not appear. Mr. Dennis was possessed of a library, consisting for the most part of theological works. There happened, however, to be among them a collection of curious old tracts on chronology, genealogy, and heraldry which young Macartney's fondness for books led him to study, in default of others more calculated to attract a boy's attention. He was probably referring to this library when in after-life he stated that 'the events, dates, and other facts gleaned up when a boy were of great service.'[1] When quite young, he appears to have thought of medicine as a profession, but 'accidentally coming across certain curious old tracts on chronology, his ideas became enlarged, and ambition changed his first design.'[2] Throughout life he retained a grateful memory of Mr. Dennis, and in later years, when it was in his power to do so, rewarded his tutor's care and instruction by the gift of the benefices of Clane and Dunmore.

At what seems to us now the early age of thirteen Macartney was admitted a Fellow-commoner of Trinity College, Dublin, where in 1759 he took the degree of M.A., then,

[1] From little manuscript account of Lord Macartney, in possession of C. G. Macartney, Esq.   [2] *Ibid.*

proceeding to London, entered as a student of the Middle Temple. The charm of manner, ability, and good looks with which the young Irishman was endowed soon procured him friends and acquaintances. He quickly became on intimate terms with various clever and rising young men of the day, among whom may be mentioned Edmund Burke, the great orator and political writer. Burke was born in Dublin in 1729, and was therefore several years older than Macartney; but both were Irish, and graduates of the same University.[1] They also felt alike on many subjects, and had ideals in common, which formed an opening for the friendship which existed between them from this time throughout life. Macartney was also much attached to Burke's distant cousin and great friend, William Burke.[2] To Burke, Macartney probably owed his first introduction to Sir Joshua Reynolds, and most likely formed one of the crowd of Irish whom Burke was in the habit of introducing to that great man's hospitable house.

Although he entered as a student at the Temple, Macartney had no intention of being called to the Bar, and remained there but a short time while completing his arrangements for a prolonged tour on the Continent. He resolved to spend several years abroad, visiting the various Courts and countries of Europe. This, he considered, was one of the essential preparatives for the public career which he intended to adopt on his return to England, and decided to begin it by endeavouring to secure a seat in the House of Commons.

Switzerland was naturally one among the countries visited, and Macartney was so charmed with its scenery and inhabitants that he determined to remain there for some little time.

[1] Edmund Burke, who had been a fellow-student of Goldsmith's at Trinity College, came to London in 1750, and formed a warm friendship with Sir Joshua Reynolds, Johnson, and Garrick.

[2] 'Whether Edmund Burke and William Burke were relations or not, and if so in what degree, neither of them ever knew; they believed that their father sometimes called one another cousins, and that was all they had to say on the subject. But they were as intimate as brothers.'—Morley's 'Edmund Burke.'

While at Geneva, he was introduced to Voltaire, who invited him to his house. He spent several days there, greatly delighted with the society of this extraordinary man, with whom he is said to have kept up a correspondence after his return to England. Captain Robert Jephson, writing to Macartney in 1775, asks him to forward a copy of his tragedy, 'Braganza,' to Voltaire, ' whom you have cultivated more than any of our countrymen since his retirement,' further adding :

'I cannot so entirely suppress the partiality of an author as not to wish you may add a word or two of undue influence to your old acquaintance of Ferney, to recommend the play to his perusal.'

At the time of Macartney's visit Voltaire had not long been settled on his estate at Ferney, on the Lake of Geneva, to which part of the world he came with his niece, Madame Denis, after the flight from the Court of Frederick the Great with the famous Œuvre de Poésie. It is not difficult to understand the attraction Macartney must have felt towards this remarkable man, who to many brilliant gifts and vivacity of temperament joined a keen sense of truth and honesty. Voltaire's quick susceptibility to every form of beauty, both moral and intellectual, must have appealed strongly to the young imaginative Irishman, the keynote of whose long and varied public career was integrity and uprightness. Throughout his life there are traces of the intellectual influence exerted upon him at this impressionable period by the philosopher of Ferney.

While in Savoy, Macartney visited the Château de Vèry, which stood in a romantic position surrounded by snow mountains. He described the building as being more like an English gaol than the seat of a man of quality. The Vèry family were poor, but of very ancient lineage. The then owner of the château had sought to retrieve his fortunes by marriage with an heiress whose family was descended from Speed the tailor, and author of the 'Chronicle.' This was regarded as a great *mésalliance* by the Court of Turin, which was much displeased at the marriage. Macartney remarks that there is no place where matches of that sort were more disapproved of than at Turin, and tells his correspondent a story of

'a Piedmontese nobleman of great talents and virtue, but reduced to a very low fortune, who endeavoured to repair it by marrying a rich oilman's daughter at Lyons, and soon after appeared at Court in a manner suitable to his quality. The only notice the King took of him was by saying: "Hé bien, Marquis, comment va l'huile?" He answered: "Hélas! sire, sans l'huile ma lampe était éteinte," and then retired, convinced that his marriage had ruined all his hopes of favour or preferment.'

To the same correspondent Macartney wrote of the Duke of Wurtemberg and his brother, whose acquaintance he also made about this time:

'The Duke is an odd fish, and so are all his family. . . . I was particularly intimate with his brother, Prince Louis, who is a Lieutenant-General in the French service, and has the *cordon bleu*. He made a *mésalliance* with a Mademoiselle Byclinck, and seemed to have been given up by the world on that account. If that was the case, he said, he would give up the world in revenge, and so he retired with his *chère épouse* to a small château near Lausanne. I first met with him at Voltaire's, and he invited me to visit him, which I did, and saw him and Madame very frequently. As for her, she had few attractions either of mind or person, and he told me he thought so, but that he had a *fantasie* for her, and that with him a *fantasie* was just as strong as a passion. He was much admired at Vienna, and was once very near marrying an Archduchess. His figure was handsome and his conversation very agreeable. He had not much literature, but what he had he made every advantage of by a very lively voluble jargon, which he had the art of adapting to almost all subjects whatsoever, so that, *étant* Prince, he often imposed on people much more knowing than himself, and passed for a savant and philosopher. . . . I have passed many very pleasant days with him.'

During the course of his travels Macartney made the acquaintance of Stephen Fox, eldest son of the first Lord Holland, whose romantic clandestine marriage with Lady Caroline Lennox in May, 1744, had convulsed the society of the day. Stephen Fox, who was delicate,[1] appears to have spent much of his time abroad, being apparently as much addicted to gambling as his brother, the celebrated Charles Fox.[2] Indeed, both were encouraged thereto by Lord Holland, whose method of education[3] was to initiate and encourage his sons in every form of vice and extravagance, and they were constantly in debt and difficulties.

To Stephen Fox, Macartney was able to render some important service[4]—in all probability helped him out of a serious scrape, and so gained the gratitude and confidence of Lord Holland, and the friendship of the younger members of the family. On his return to England he became an inmate of Holland House.

At this time Macartney was considered one of the handsomest and most accomplished young men of the day. In person he was somewhat above middle height, powerfully built and athletic, although inclining to stoutness as years went on. The expression of his face was placid, his bearing easy yet dignified, and his manners engaging. To other accomplishments he added a taste for music and poetry,

---

[1] Lord Holland's one-time intimate friend Rigby says in a letter: 'I dined at Holland House, where, though I drank claret with the master of it from dinner till two o'clock in the morning, I could not wash away the sorrow he is in at the shocking condition his eldest boy is in . . . a distemper they call San Vitos' dance. I believe I spell it damnably.'

[2] Stephen Fox had large debts. Lord Holland paid at least £200,000 for debts for his two elder sons.

[3] Lord Shelburne says 'he educated his children without the least regard to morality, and with such extravagant indulgence that the great change which has taken place among our youth has been dated from the time of his son's going to Eton.'

[4] 'At this time Mr. Macartney rendered his friend [Stephen Fox] some very essential service; what it was we do not pretend to state, but it was of a nature to awaken the most grateful sentiments of the then Lord Holland, who, though he was not popular as a public character, had many private virtues; and among them may be numbered a never-failing spirit of remuneration for good offices to himself, or any branch of his family. He therefore became the warm patron and friend of Mr. Macartney, whose qualities and talents justified that partiality.'—From the *Gentleman's Magazine*, 1806.

and in conversation was extremely entertaining and brilliant, yet without show of assurance or undue familiarity. He possessed all the dignity of the old school without its stiffness, and in matters of attire seems to have been of a conservative disposition, as the fashion of his dress remained unchanged for the last forty years of his life. He was also well read, a good linguist,[1] and told a story with genuine good-humour. His memory being exceedingly retentive and well cultivated, he managed to recollect the date as well as the circumstances of any event of importance. And, above all, he possessed the invaluable faculty of obtaining information from those with whom he talked, even where they might really be indisposed to bestow it.

Macartney was a member of Dr. Johnson's literary club; Barrow, indeed, says he was an original member, but this does not appear to have been the case. He, however, joined the club in the early stages of its existence, and was intimate with Dr. Johnson, Burke, Hume, and the rest of the literary and artistic circle who met at Sir Joshua Reynolds' house. He probably was often present at the dinners where 'there were frequently more guests than seats, but never a lack of hospitality.'[2] Two or three portraits were painted of him about this time (1763-1764), one of which was by Sir Joshua.

Shortly after Macartney's return to England he was introduced by the Holland family to Lord Sandwich, then Secretary of State for the Northern Department. He and Lord Holland decided to bring Macartney into Parliament as member for Midhurst. This borough, one of the most comfortable of constituencies from the point of view of a candi-

---

[1] Charles Fox, writing to him from Florence in August, 1767, says: 'At present I read nothing but Italian, which I am immoderately fond of, particularly of the poetry. You who understand Italian so well yourself will not wonder at this. As to French, I am far from being so thorough a master of it as I could wish—I want such an example as yours to make me conquer my natural idleness, of which Lady Holland will tell you wonders. Indeed, I am afraid that I shall never be anything but a lounging fellow.'

[2] 'Sir Joshua and his Circle,' Fitzgerald Molloy.

Robert Hunter, pinxit

GEORGE MACARTNEY

ÆTAT. 21

From the Portrait in the possession of C. G. MACARTNEY, ESQ.

To face p. 12

date, was afterwards represented by Charles Fox. The election rights rested in a few score of small holdings, all of which had been bought up by Viscount Montague. At the time of an election he assigned a few of them to his servants, with instructions to nominate the member, and then make back the property to their employer.[1]

However, just as Macartney was about to commence his parliamentary career, circumstances occurred in Russia which Lord Holland considered Macartney's various acquirements rendered him peculiarly well fitted to cope with. He thought that the young Irishman's talents might be employed with greater advantage to the public at the Court of St. Petersburg than in the House of Commons. He gave expression to this opinion in a letter, of which the following is an extract:

'*May 22, 1764.*

'DEAR MACARTNEY,

'Lord Buckingham leaves Russia; there is business there which will not be transacted with success by his lordship, but which it is hoped will be by his successor. Your character will be that of Envoy Extraordinary, and I can answer for everything in Lord Sandwiche's power to make your station agreeable and useful to you. Lady Caroline bids me put you in mind that the Empress is about the age you like, not a slim woman, and, I add, growing older every day, and when she passes the turn of perfection you will be coming away.'

For some time past Russia had been presenting an interesting and puzzling problem to the statesmen of Western Europe. The Empire of the Czars had stepped into the position of a first-class Power, under the guidance of an energetic man and a clever, ambitious woman, whom a successful revolution had unexpectedly placed on the throne. Macartney was one of the first to form a just appreciation of the position, and to define it in these memorable words:

[1] In the year 1794 the number of burgage holders at Midhurst was reduced to one. By that time Lord Egremont had acquired the burgage holds at the cost of forty thousand guineas.

'Russia,' he said, 'is no longer to be gazed at as a distant glimmering star, but as a great planet that has obtruded itself into our system, whose place is yet undetermined, but whose motions must powerfully affect those of every other orb.'[1]

For England at that moment an alliance with Russia was desirable on many considerations, especially from a commercial point of view. Fears also were entertained of the undue ascendancy of French interest and influence at the Russian Court. Russia's old treaty of commerce of 1734 with England had expired by its own limitations, and the Empress Elizabeth, though unwilling to renew it, had acquiesced in the continuance of the regulations thereby established. But scarcely was Catherine seated upon the throne than this *laissez-faire* attitude was altered. A flat refusal was given to Lord Buckinghamshire,[2] who, as well as his predecessor, Sir Robert Keith,[3] had been engaged in attempting to negotiate a treaty with the Russian Cabinet. The reason assigned for this refusal was that Russia did not intend to enter into any exclusive engagement with any foreign Power. The situation was therefore peculiarly one in which penetration, discretion, and vigilance, joined to agreeable manner and address, were more than usually important. Lord Holland considered these qualities were to be found united in Macartney, and suggested his employment to Lord Sandwich. Nor were the hopes entertained of him destined to be disappointed. He was well informed as to the interests of our trade with Russia, and had thoroughly studied the public records of all that had been done and attempted since the opening of diplomatic relations between that country and Great Britain. His con-

[1] J. Barrow, 'Life of Earl Macartney.'
[2] Lord Buckinghamshire was Ambassador at the Court of St. Petersburg for two years, and, in spite of good looks, pleasant manners, and plenty of money, does not seem to have been successful in his intercourse with the Empress and her Ministers.
[3] Sir Robert Keith was English Ambassador at St. Petersburg for fourteen years, and had been a convivial favourite of the unfortunate Peter. He retired in 1762.

ARRIVAL AT ST. PETERSBURG

summate tact, coolness, and patience enabled him to overcome the difficulty of obtaining access to the Empress, which had discomfited the previous envoys, and his charm of manner and personal appearance made an easy conquest of that astute but highly susceptible lady.

On August 22, 1764, Macartney was appointed Envoy Extraordinary to the Court of Russia, being at that time twenty-seven years of age. The October following he was knighted by King George III. All preliminaries having been arranged, he set out on his mission in November, and arrived in the Russian capital before the close of the year.[1]

He was received with great kindness and attention by Lord Buckinghamshire,[2] and stayed as a guest in his house during the short time the ex-Envoy remained in St. Petersburg. This gave Sir George a chance of making himself acquainted with the ins and outs of Russian politics, and of estimating the character of the people he would have to deal with. In Lord Buckinghamshire's opinion, the Russian Chancellor and Vice-Chancellor were men wholly incapable of directing the affairs of so great a nation, and he considered the former possessed no great friendship for England. Panin, Governor of the Grand Duke, and Minister for Foreign Affairs, he thought better qualified than most of the Russian Ministers to hold the first place. He also enjoyed the confidence of the Empress. Catherine herself,

[1] Barrow says: ' When he [Macartney] passed the Hague, on his way to S. Petersbourgh, Sir Joseph Yorke, then Minister at that place . . . invited all his brother Ministers to meet Sir George Macartney at dinner. The conversation turned . . . on the affairs of Europe, and although some of the company were pretty well hackneyed in the diplomatic service, and Sir George but just entering upon his career of public life, yet it was observed that he was much better informed with regard to the respective Courts of Europe than . . . the Ministers . . . who represented them.'

[2] Years after Macartney wrote of Lord Buckinghamshire to a friend: ' He was Ambassador at St. P. when I was there, and tho', as he wished to have stayed, you may imagine I could not be very welcome to him, yet . . . he received me not as a stranger or as a rival, but as a friend and an equal. Indeed, his whole conduct was so noble and so kind that while I live I can never forget it.'

as far as he could see, was in every way superior to those around her. She was, however, too much taken up with trifling amusements, combined with intense application to the concerns of her Government. Her plans were numerous and extensive, but her means inadequate. She was, in addition, much hampered by the obligations she owed to those who had been instrumental in placing her upon the throne. Much dissatisfaction had been aroused by the favours lavished on Gregory Orloff, who was hated, and considered an upstart, even by those who had been engaged with him in the late revolution. In consequence of all these complications Catherine had hardly yet ventured to act for herself. He also told Sir George that of all the foreign Ministers, he had guarded against the Spanish one, as the most insinuating, and at the same time the most zealous to promote the objects of his Court and their connections.

Macartney had his first public audience of the Czarina on January 11, 1765. It is said that he gained her consideration on this occasion by a piece of diplomatic flattery. Having first assured her that his master, King George, had an inviolable attachment to her person, and a constant regard for her interests, he added:

'And forgive me, madam, if I here express my own particular satisfaction in having been chosen for so pleasing and so important an employment. By this means I shall have the happiness of more nearly contemplating those extraordinary accomplishments, and those heroic virtues, which make you the delight of that half of the globe over which you reign, and which render you the admiration of the other.'[1]

To this speech the Czarina herself returned a most gracious extempore reply[2] instead of delivering one through her

[1] Charles Fox, in a letter to Macartney, thus eulogized his address to the Empress Catherine: 'I think your speech to the Czarina is one of the neatest things of the kind I ever saw; and I can assure you Edmund Burke admires it prodigiously.'—J. Barrow, 'Life of Earl Macartney.'

[2] 'Having laid before the King your letter enclosing a copy of your speech to the Empress of Russia, upon presenting your creden-

Chancellor, which action occasioned much comment on the part of her courtiers and Sir George's diplomatic brethren. The same day the Earl of Buckinghamshire had his audience of farewell.

The retiring Ambassador seems to have been popular in Russian society, and Macartney wrote:

'Did you know how much you are regretted, it would almost tempt you to make another tour to Russia.... Votre chère Sophie (who loves you, I believe, too much to be very happy) and her sister supped with me some time since on the occasion of a ceremony which was lately performed here. It was the christening my negro. It seems all good believers cried shame against me for not having him sooner sprinkled with the Gospel. Many people thought I had but little religion.... So to save my character and avoid scandal I had him received into the bosom of the Church and the congregation of the faithful. This, however, was very near proving fatal to him, for he was so frightened at the awfulness of the ceremony that he fell sick the next day, and had like to have died of regeneration.... I meet with the same obstacles here that your lordship did, and know not when they will be removed. I must trust to accident, which is often a very good friend to our profession.'[1]

Macartney lost no time in cultivating the acquaintance of Panin, whom he soon discovered was in reality sole Minister of the Russian Empire, and high in favour with Catherine. His political ideas coincided with hers, and he firmly supported her opinion on every occasion. He was undoubtedly honest and upright, but exceedingly obstinate, and attached to his own opinions. Though not brilliant, he was an excellent man of business when in his ordinary groove, along which he proceeded slowly and steadily.

---

tial letters, I have the pleasure to acquaint you that His Majesty entirely approved of the manner in which you acquitted yourself upon that occasion, and was extremely pleased with the marks of friendship and attention which the Czarina showed in the distinguished reception of his Minister.'—Letter from Lord Sandwich (Stowe Manuscripts).

[1] Lord Buckinghamshire's correspondence.

But once put out of his usual routine, he became confused and embarrassed. He therefore adopted certain fixed notions, and a system of conduct to which he rigidly adhered.

'He is certainly an uncorrupted man, and though not without many faults ... he is, in my opinion, by far the properest person in this country for the great employment with which he is honoured,' wrote Macartney to a brother diplomat.

'Prince Gallitzen, the Vice-Chancellor, is extremely polite and well bred, but has neither inherited great talents from Nature, nor taken much pains to cultivate those few which she gave him. He was several years Envoy in England, but I do not look upon him as very hearty in his good wishes towards it. Happily for us, he has but little credit, and is a Minister rather of parade than of confidence. The Empress herself is a most extraordinary woman ... infinitely superior to any of her subjects. Count Orloff is her chief favourite, and seems lately to have taken a resolution worthy of a much wiser man, which is to meddle very little in public affairs, and not at all in foreign ones, but quietly to enjoy his good fortune and present happiness.'[1]

To conciliate and gain the friendship and good opinion of Panin, Sir George exerted his best endeavours, and had the satisfaction of perceiving they were not in vain. An intimacy, such as is not often the result of diplomatic intercourse, sprang up between him and this wary statesman.

During all the lengthy and trying negotiations with the Court of Russia, Panin invariably treated him with esteem and regard. He frequently spoke with admiration of Macartney's acquirements and knowledge, remarkable in so young a man, and freely acknowledged he was indebted to Sir George for much information respecting the various Courts of Europe. He had even been enlightened on points regarding Russian commerce with Great Britain, Macartney having drawn up a general view of it, which he presented to Panin for his private use.

Some time after Macartney's departure from Russia, Panin

---

[1] Letter to Sir Andrew Mitchell (Mitchell Papers).

sent him a message, through Mr. Shirley, expressive of the sincerity of his regard and attachment : ' Dites lui, combien je suis sensible à son amitié, et que je conserverai le souvenir, toute ma vie avec un plaisir infini.'[1]

In the spring of 1765 the Princess Dashkoff,[2] who had lived a very retired life since her husband's death, left St. Petersburg and went to Moscow. ' She had been forbid the Court long since, but as she was to leave, perhaps for ever,' the Empress consented to see her before she left. Her reception was, however, cold and ungracious.

'Everybody seems pleased she is no longer here; tho' scarce twenty-two years old, she has been already in half a dozen plots. The fifth succeeded, but not being considered or rewarded, as she imagined, according to her services, she engaged in new conspiracies which were abortive, and was punished by a total loss of her mistress's favour. She is a woman of an uncommon strength of mind, bold beyond the most manly courage, and of a spirit capable of undertaking impossibilities to gratify any predominant passion — a character highly dangerous in a country like this, especially when joined to an engaging behaviour and a beautiful person. For notwithstanding the general ferocity of the inhabitants, women here seem to have as much sway as among the most civilized nations.'[3]

From the following extracts from his writings it would appear that Macartney did not entertain a very favourable opinion of the Russians:

'I don't find the people here in general either polite or engaging among themselves, and with regard to strangers

[1] Letter-book of H. Shirley.
[2] Princess Dashkoff, a sister of Peter's favourite Elizabeth Woronzoff, and niece of the High Chancellor, had originally been drawn to Catherine by a common love of literature and philosophy. High-spirited and ambitious, the Princess felt much sympathy with Catherine, and espoused her cause with warmth. Princess Dashkoff was one of the most active and energetic of the conspirators who assisted to place Catherine on the throne, but entertained a very exaggerated view of her services in the matter, and by her arrogance, jealousy, and imprudence, made herself generally intolerable.
[3] Private letter to Lord Sandwich (Stowe Manuscripts).

they are downright barbarians. The kindness and affability of Mons. Panin and the uncommon civility of Count Cheremetew entitle them, however, to an exception in their favour.'[1]

He considered the Russian nobles were depraved in disposition and perverted as to judgment. Conscious and jealous of foreign civilization, they affected to despise it.

'They are vain, petulant, light, inconsequent, indiscreet, and changeable, . . . incapable of true friendship, and insensible to all the nobler movements of the soul. . . . Luxurious, effeminate, and averse to corporal activity . . . they have no passion for sports of the field, but prefer the more tranquil amusements of cards or billiards, in which they are extraordinarily proficient. Many sleep their time away, insensible of the charms of refined conversation. Their natural parts are tolerably good, but they universally want the distinguishing faculty, and fall into the most absurd imitations of foreign life and manners, and, abandoning the common sense of nature, adopt fashions and customs totally contrary to their climate and troublesome to themselves. The Russian gentlemen are certainly the most ignorant of all others in Europe; the chief points of their instruction are a knowledge of modern languages, particularly French and German, which they usually speak with very great facility, tho' incapable of writing either of them with the smallest degree of precision or propriety. . . . Their ridiculous imitation of foreign manners stifles every original spark of genius. . . .'

Among the ladies the most profligate manners and unbounded libertinism prevailed. Their education was entrusted to French governesses, as the instruction of the boys was carried on by French adventurers.

'They are vain and light, greedily following any shadow of new and untried amusement. Bold and adventurous in the pursuit of pleasure, equally regardless of danger and dishonour, shameless on detection, and hardened against reproof.

'The people are barbarous, the clergy ignorant, and the nobility is but half civilized. The two first can scarcely be said to have any education at all, and the latter had better

[1] Lord Buckinghamshire's correspondence.

have none than that which they have. . . . Vast sums of money go out of this country to France, the return of which is made in silks, velvets, ruffles, pompons, etc.; for the Russians are as fond of trifling toys or gaieties as the wildest Indian or most barbarous American.'

Despite their want of civilization, Macartney described the lower orders as being patient, hospitable, and kindly, and considered it was a rare occurrence for a Russian peasant to perform an intentionally cruel action.

'They are a nation of inconsistence and paradox. . . . Hating the stranger, they copy him, affecting originality; they are the slaves of imitation; magnificent and slovenly, irreligious yet superstitious, rapacious and prodigal.'[1]

About this period Sir George wrote a long letter to Lady Holland, giving an account of the doings at the Russian Court and a description of the Empress:

'*February*, 1766.

'It is now high carnival, but, indeed, differs very little from the rest of the year, except with regard to the masquerades. There are two kinds of these—one at a public room kept by an Italian adventurer, where everybody pays for admission; the other at the Palace, where the entry is free to every one that can procure a ticket—a point by no means difficult, as there are generally five or six thousand distributed on these occasions. One of our privileges as foreign Ministers is to have as many as we think proper to send for. These Court masquerades are highly magnificent, being held at the Palace, where all the great apartments are thrown open. The wainscot of the great room is coloured green, and the flowers and mouldings richly gilded. On one side are fifteen great windows, to which on the other correspond an equal number of glasses, whose dimensions are of the largest size that ever were made. The ceiling is finely painted with emblematical figures. . . . The whole floor is covered with an infinity of masks all in motion, dressed in the richest habits, and divided into a variety of quadrilles and parties. The illuminations of the apartments are finely distributed, no less than ten thousand tapers being lighted at the same instant. There are a number of smaller chambers

[1] Manuscript account of Russia by Sir George Macartney.

for dancing and for gaming, the furniture of which is equally splendid and elegant. In one of these rooms the Empress usually plays at ombre or picquet till about ten o'clock. She then retires, and appears again at the masquerade, sometimes half a dozen times in the same night, in different disguises; and the ball seldom breaks up sooner than three or four o'clock in the morning.

'We have three comedies here—the French and Russian, which are maintained at the expense of the Crown; and the German, where one pays for admittance. The theatre where the French and Russian plays are represented is a very fine one, and such a profusion of gilding as would induce one to think that Mexico was transported to Petersburg.

'There is a regular Court every Sunday evening, besides those which are held on the grand festivals. The Empress generally stays two or three hours, during which time she either converses with us or plays picquet. The foreign Ministers, the ladies of State, or the great men of the Court usually compose her party. Nothing can be more noble than the appearance on these occasions, there being seldom less than two thousand persons assembled there, the flower of the youth of both sexes commonly attending. The ladies belonging to the Court alone contribute not a little to the brilliancy of the assembly. They possess the art of dress to an eminent degree, and not only that, but they possess the air of repairing beauty beyond any I have seen. Every woman here, of what rank soever, from the Empress to the peasant, wears rouge, and they are so fond of it, and think it so becoming, that a red woman and a beautiful one are synonymous terms in the Russian language. Those of the better fashion usually paint white, and one of the greatest ladies of the Court is thought to be a most accomplished artist in that way, for she not only lays on the common colours of red and white, but intersperses blue in the proper places. For my part, I think her hideous; yet so much is the Russian taste depraved in this respect that she is looked on as a beauty of the first class, is in high favour with Her Majesty, and passionately beloved by one of the finest men in the empire.

'The dress of the ladies is extremely magnificent, and generally well fancied; but the quantity of diamonds here is astonishing. I have seldom seen a woman any ways known that has less than five or six thousand pounds' worth of jewels. These they wear at all times and on all occasions, never appearing either at home or in public without them. Many of the ladies are so fond of their jewels that it is said they make them a part of their night dress.

'Of all the Sovereigns in Europe, I believe the Empress of Russia is the richest in diamonds. She has a kind of passion for them; perhaps she has no other weakness. Her crown is certainly superior to the famous one of the Great Mogul, of which travellers give so magnificent a description. When I first saw her jewels I was almost struck blind with astonishment; indeed, it is impossible to behold them without being dazzled. She has shown infinite taste in the manner of setting them. . . . The star of her order is one of the finest pieces of workmanship in the world. Her dress is never gaudy, always rich, and yet still more elegant than rich. She appears to great advantage in regimentals, and is fond of appearing in them. . . . Her air is commanding and full of dignity. Her eye might be called fierce and tyrannical, if not softened by the other features of her face, which, though not regular, are eminently pleasing. I never in my life saw a person whose port, manner, and behaviour answered so strongly to the idea I had formed to myself of her. Though in the thirty-seventh year of her age, she may still be called beautiful. Those who knew her younger say they never remember her so lively as at present, and *I very readily believe it.*

'It remains now to speak of her in another light, where it will be more difficult to do her justice. Her talents are certainly of that kind which border on the extraordinary and marvellous. . . . In the particular incidents of her life the firmness and resolution of her temper and the calmness and resignation of her mind render her worthy of admiration. The courage and intrepidity of her spirit alone wrought that miracle which elevated her to the dignity she now possesses. Whatever melancholy circumstances that great event was attended with, I am persuaded that she was entirely innocent of them. Her nature is benign; I know the softness of her character and the clemency of her disposition.[1] It is inconceivable with what address she mingles an ease of behaviour with the dignity of her rank,

---

[1] 'She certainly did not order him [Peter III.] to be put to death. Those who did put him to death had as much interest in his death as she could have, and they were too good courtiers to ask whether they should do what she could not disapprove.'—Extract from one of Lord Macartney's notebooks.

with what facility she familiarizes herself with the meanest of her subjects without losing a point of her authority, and with what astonishing magic she inspires both respect and affection. Her conversation is . . . perhaps too brilliant, for she loves to shine in conversation, and does so to an uncommon degree. It is almost impossible to follow her, her sallies are so quick, so full of fire, spirit, and vivacity. Her manner of treating every subject is peculiar to herself, equally lively and entertaining. She is perfectly well read, and mistress of almost every kind of literature.

'Most of the modern languages are familiar to her. She has Hume's " History of England " by heart, and is fond of speaking on the subject. She admires him exceedingly, yet is by no means blind to his defects, and has often astonished me by the propriety and solidity of her remarks upon our constitution. . . . All this is nothing more than the literal truth unheightened by exaggeration.

'I hasten to speak of the other amusements which the city affords me. When the weather is not excessively cold, a common diversion during the winter is to drive about in sledges, and 'tis inconceivable the rapidity with which one is whirled about in those machines.

'The English merchants give a ball and supper once a fortnight, where your humble servant has the prerogative of always figuring in the first couple. I attend constantly, dance always with the most *agreeable*, though not the youngest, woman of the assembly, and, considering myself as the greatest person there, must, as Ste and Charles[1] will tell you, be vastly happy.

'I at first intended to have figured in the carousal, but, upon better thoughts, have renounced all intention of it. Enclosed is my device[2] as it should have been had I appeared in the list.'

Macartney thus concludes his long letter :

'I don't recollect whether there be enough of ermine to make a complete petticoat. If not, please to let me know, and I will send it by the first messenger.'

While in St. Petersburg he appears to have formed a strong attachment to a Russian lady. In a commonplace

[1] Stephen and Charles James Fox.
[2] Device : A lady fishing, and a fish caught on the hook. *Je meurs où je m'attache.*

book, among numerous notes and remarks on the books he had been reading, occurs the following passage under the heading of ' Notes for My Life ':

' I purposely avoid ever speaking of my amours, but this affair is so connected with the history of my life and fortunes that I can't avoid saying a few words. Madlle. Keyshoff was of a great family, but neither young, handsome, nor clever. She had neither beauty nor wit to engage, to captivate, or to retain. Her only merit in my eyes was a passion which she either had, or affected to have, for me.'

This rather cold-blooded dissection of his lady-love, and the reasons for his passion, do not sound as if Macartney was capable of being carried away by the fervour of a lover at any period of his existence. Whatever may have been the possibilities of romance which existed in his nature, they turned more towards principles and ideals of conduct than to personalities. That he had early decided his career should be moulded by reason and ambition is clearly indicated by the following extract taken from the same notebook :

' With the spirit of a man I broke the bonds of effeminate love, and reason quelled the swelling passion. My reason and my reflection have been, however, my faithful guides, and though I have sometimes wandered from their paths, I never let them out of view ; after a short sally I rejoin them always, shake hands, and proceed in good earnest. They have drawn me from ——, and brought me at last triumphant to the gates of ——.[1] Now I must plant new passions in my breast, and instead of glowing with desire and love, must be in future a British person with a Roman soul, and an admiration of what I wish myself to be. . . . When we let ourselves be carried away by some particular affection, the pursuit of it makes us incapable of anything else.'

[1] These blanks are in the original.

CHAPTER II

WHEN Sir George Macartney began to treat of the principal object of his mission to St. Petersburg—namely, the conclusion of a treaty of commerce and alliance between England and Russia—Panin listened to him with great attention. He then, in return, unfolded the projects he had formed for the aggrandizement of his own country, to which schemes he intended to devote his life. To effect a confederation of the northern Powers, with Russia as the centre of it, was his great object. The first step towards the furtherance of this end was to make common cause with England and Denmark against the French interest in Sweden, and for this purpose it would be necessary to subsidize a majority in the Swedish diet. Money would be wanted, and if England entered into his plans she must be prepared to pay liberally. Denmark, in the case of a war with Turkey, had bound herself to pay to Russia a subsidy of five hundred thousand roubles a year, in quarterly payments. She had also promised, by a secret article, to disengage herself, as soon as might be, from all French connection, and further the views of Russia in Sweden.[1] Panin spoke frequently of the strong desire felt by the Empress for an alliance with Great Britain, that being the surest way of disappointing the views of the Courts of Vienna and Versailles, against

---

[1] '£15,000 per annum on our part would be sufficient to support our interest, and absolutely prevent the French from ever getting at Stockholm again.'—Private letter from Sir George Macartney to Lord Sandwich (Stowe Manuscripts).

THE TURKISH CLAUSE

which she was greatly irritated.[1] But this alliance could only be brought about by England's assent to the Swedish project, which he hinted would be expensive. She must also agree, by a secret article, to pay a subsidy in case of a Turkish war, as Denmark had done. If England consented to enter into an alliance on these terms, he observed that the treaty of commerce would grow with it *passibus æquis*.

From this conversation Macartney became well aware of the difficulties he would have to encounter in the course of his negotiation, as it would embrace points which did not depend upon him. In fact, every subsequent conference began and ended with Sweden. The Turkish clause was the next point. Panin complained bitterly that plans for a treaty of alliance sent to London in Lord Buckinghamshire's time had not been accorded proper notice. He also observed that, had England been sincere in her professions, she would have acted otherwise than she had done. To this Sir George replied his predecessor had proposed certain alterations which had been rejected by Russia; that he would furnish them with other proposals in a day or two, provided the Turkish clause was abandoned, which he knew England would never agree to insert in any treaty. But every effort was in vain, and it became quite obvious that the obnoxious clause would be a *sine qua non* in every negotiation with the Court of Russia. Indeed, Sir George found that a treaty containing it had been concluded with Russia, on the understanding that the same terms were to be included

---

[1] The irritation felt by Catherine seems to have been chiefly due to the fact that the King of France had refused to give her the title of *Majesté Imperiale* in his Ambassador's credentials, on the ground that it was contrary to the idiom of their language. The Russian Ambassador at Paris, having complained of this, received as answer that the French Court had no objection to allowing the Imperial title to the Crown of Russia, but that they could not possibly use the expression *Majesté Imperiale* in writing. The Duc de Choiseul is said to have remarked: ' Qu'il ne pouvoit pas introduire dans la langue Françoise un barbarisme en faveur de la Russie.' The effect which this sarcasm made on the sensitive pride of the Russian Court was, as may be imagined, not a favourable one.

in any subsequent alliance with any other Power, the Prussian Envoy having orders to remonstrate in the strongest manner if this was not carried out.[1]

Macartney had less difficulty in promising the co-operation of his Government in the matter of undermining the French influence with the northern Powers. But the progress made in the treaty of commerce was slow. Finally, he urged that the matter should be settled between himself and Panin without reference to the Russian College of Commerce. To this Panin consented, provided the arrangement was agreeable to the Empress. Catherine, who was fully aware of the incapacity of the Commissioners, suggested that the points should be settled by Panin and the British Minister, the Commissioners being empowered to sign the treaty to save appearances. This gave rise to much illfeeling and resentment on the part of these latter. In revenge they managed that Macartney should not receive an invitation to the dinner given by Catherine on the anniversary of her accession to the throne. The Vice-Chancellor having received orders to invite all the foreign Ministers to the banquet, his absence was noticed by the Empress, and Macartney contrived to let her know the real reason for it. On the following Sunday, when he appeared at Court, Catherine took special notice of him; all the foreign Ministers were present, but Macartney was the only one she addressed that day.

After a close negotiation of some months a treaty of commerce, holding good for twenty years, was concluded; the terms, it was hoped, being such as would prove accept-

[1] 'I can assure your Lordship that a Turkish war, in an article in the body of the treaty, or a secret article, will be a *sine qua non* in every negotiation. The Prussian King had consented to the proposal, only inserted in the hopes of destroying the negotiation entirely, by Count Bestuchef, who was the King of Prussia's mortal enemy. But he was mistaken; the King of Prussia immediately consented to the proposal, on condition that Russia should make no alliance with any other Power but on the same terms. Count Solms came to visit me, and told me that if this Court had any intention of concluding an alliance with ours, without such a clause, he had orders to oppose it in the strongest manner.'—Private letter from Sir George Macartney to Lord Sandwich (Stowe Manuscripts).

DISAPPROVAL OF THE CABINET

able to both sides. Those obtained for England were more advantageous than the Government had anticipated, and the merchants concerned in the trade were quite satisfied. Thereupon Macartney signed the treaty, being anxious to take advantage of the moment, and fearing the result of any delay in the matter. It never occurred to him to doubt receiving the approbation of the Cabinet for having done more than they had expected, and which three former Ministers had failed to effect. He did, in fact, receive a letter, dated September 17, written by the order of the Duke of Grafton, then Secretary of State for the northern department. This letter acknowledged the treaty, and stated that he and the rest of the Ministry were pleased with it. But twelve days later Macartney received another communication from the same source, informing him that the Ministers were dissatisfied he should have taken on himself to sign a treaty of commerce before sending it to England for the King's approbation. They also took exception to the following clause in the fourth article of the treaty :

'Mais alors on se réserve de la part de la Russie, en réciprocité de l'acte de navigation de la Grande Bretagne, la liberté de faire dans l'intérieur, tel arrangement particulier qu'il sera trouvé bon, pour encourager et étendre la navigation Russienne.'

The words 'en réciprocité de l'acte de navigation de la Grande Bretagne' they considered as a reservation in favour of Russia. They also took exception to them as an infringement of the Navigation Act, the bare mention of which should be carefully avoided in all treaties.[1]

Macartney replied he had been aware the objection might be made. But he considered that by admitting the reservation in favour of Russia (which he knew she could

---

[1] 'The Duke of Grafton sent him a copy of the Navigation Act, and Macartney, after thanking the Duke for his kind intention, assured him he need not have given himself so much trouble, for he had the Navigation Act by heart many years ago.'—J. Barrow, 'Life of Earl Macartney.'

make no use of) he had obtained an equality of duty upon exports, and better terms than had been anticipated. The merchants, who were always the first to complain, were well satisfied with the terms he had procured. They also had made no objection to the wording of the clause, although they were enthusiastic supporters of the Navigation Act. He had already been threatened that if the treaty were not signed, a ukase would be issued depriving the English factory of their privileges, and putting them on an equal footing with other traders. The Court was highly dissatisfied with the conduct of England in regard to Sweden, considering it parsimonious. Gregory Orloff[1] and Panin were on the worst of terms, and if the former got the better of Panin there would be an end to the treaty. Taking all these circumstances into consideration, Macartney thought it better to conclude the business at once, and not risk a delay—in his own words, 'preferring the public service to his own private security, and daring a fault which success might convert into a virtue.'

The Duke of Grafton was annoyed at the disapprobation of the treaty expressed by some of the Ministers. He therefore thought it would be advisable to obtain the opinion of the Russian company in London upon the obnoxious clause. They laconically expressed themselves as adverse to it. Macartney, however, did not consider the company well qualified to give an opinion, and pointed out to the Duke that not a third of the court of assistants had ever been in Russia or carried on trade there. But as the Duke had thought fit to refer the matter to them, Macartney considered it would be right to hear the ideas of the British Company in Russia on the subject. They

[1] Gregory Orloff, who, together with his brothers, was mainly instrumental in placing Catherine on the throne, held the position of her principal favourite for ten years. He was fine-looking, tall, and handsome, but a man of little education and no culture. In addition, his manners were brusque and his temper stormy. He managed, however, to retain his hold over the Empress's affections for a longer period than any of his predecessors or successors.

constituted a body of men not only capable of giving a thoroughly good opinion, but were also deeply interested in every sentence of the treaty of commerce between the two countries. He therefore desired the Consul to assemble the merchants, read the treaty, and inquire whether there appeared to them any material objection to the whole or part of it. Especially were they to notice the fourth article, which had been disapproved of. As a result of the meeting he received a letter, drawn up and signed unanimously by the merchants resident in Russia.

In this letter they expressed their thanks for having been allowed to see the new treaty of commerce previous to its final ratification, and were sensible that the Envoy must feel great satisfaction at having accomplished his task in so full and perfect a manner. They accorded entire and unreserved approbation to every article in a treaty so advantageous to the trade and navigation of Great Britain. In conclusion, they stated that they were more particularly pleased with that part of the fourth article whereby an equality of duty on exports between the British and Russian merchants was established, and congratulated Sir George on having obtained such a favourable explanation of the succeeding clause. This was a declaration, signed by Panin, respecting the clause which had alarmed the British Cabinet. But the declaration did not satisfy the Ministers. They required it should have the signatures of the four plenipotentiaries who had signed the treaty; also that new powers should be granted by the Russian Court authorizing them to do so. Upon hearing this Panin flew into a violent rage, saying

‘ he would have Sir George Macartney know, and he wished to inform the Duke of Grafton, that he himself was Minister, and he alone. That a distrust of a letter written by him at the Empress's command, as therein expressed, was a kind of affront he could not be insensible of. If His Majesty's Ministers thought him or his Court capable of breaking their word or departing from their engagements in that form, it was very unlikely that any declaration would bind them, were it ever so solemnly made or unequivocally worded.’

He concluded by saying he would advise the Empress to do no more. She was thoroughly tired of the subject, and Russia objected to his having done so much, and thought her interests had been sacrificed. If Great Britain did not like the treaty with the explanatory letter, she might take her own measures. But if the signatures were annulled, the English company should immediately be put on the same footing as the merchants of other nations.

Macartney did all he could to soothe Panin's ruffled feelings and carry the point which the English Ministry laid so much stress on. But every effort was futile. He even addressed the Empress herself upon the subject, and almost went down on his knees to induce her to comply with his request. But he found her, as he expressed it, 'inflexible even beyond a woman's obstinacy.' He quite saw it would be as difficult to persuade them to give the required declaration as 'to count the billows of the Baltic, or number the trees in the forest of Onega.' Still, he persevered in his disagreeable task, until he discovered that Panin had really received orders to cancel the signatures and put an end to the treaty. This step was immediately followed by a revocation of the declaration in favour of the British merchants, given by the Empress Elizabeth. It required the use of all Macartney's powers of persuasion to induce Panin to delay the execution of this violent measure. He then proposed that the objectionable words 'en réciprocité de l'acte de navigation de la Grande Bretagne' should be omitted, and the treaty written and signed afresh. Panin thought the Empress would not object, as the omission made no alteration in the terms, Russia being left free to make what laws she pleased respecting her own commerce. The Ministry had taken alarm at the mention of the Navigation Act; it could not be supposed they could object to the omission of it. The treaty was therefore rewritten, leaving out the obnoxious words, and dispatched to England. But the obstinacy of the English Cabinet quite equalled that of Russia. They insisted that not only the objectionable words, but the entire clause, should be expunged. Thus three times they refused to ratify the treaty, and sent back fresh proposals.

Catherine now began to consider the conduct of England so trifling and indifferent to her more cherished schemes that she determined to break off all negotiations. She directed that as soon as the first English ship arrived at Cronstadt a ukase should be published revoking the declaration in favour of British merchants. Vainly did Macartney point out to Catherine and her Minister the advantages Russia must derive from a close alliance with England. They were immovable.

'No art,' wrote Sir George, 'has been left untried, no argument unenforced, and no effort unexerted. All that my own ingenuity could inspire, the nature of the subject furnish, or the circumstances of the times suggest ... I have employed with the most ... unceasing diligence and ... assiduity. But this Court has listened to me with the most provoking phlegm and the most stoical indifference.'

The situation had now become so painful that in another letter he observes:

'Nothing on this side of heaven could bribe me to pass the last six months over again. Mortified and dejected ... I have long since disclaimed the least hopes of applause for any Ministerial endeavour, however judiciously conducted or fortunately concluded. . . . Nothing is more dangerous than to do more than is commanded. . . . He alone is secure and happy who entrenches himself within the bounds of duty, unambitious of the renown which arises from enterprising boldness or successful temerity.'

Still he persevered, and though often rebuffed, returned to the charge. At length it occurred to him, during a conference with Panin, that the same inveterate objection might not be made against the remodelling of the clause as against its omission. He took a sheet of paper, and folding it in half, drew up on one side the clause as it originally stood, and on the other the clause as he now suggested it. He was surprised to find Panin thought the alteration admissible, but would say nothing till he had seen the

Empress. Six weeks later he returned the paper, proposing it should be altered as follows :

Clause as proposed by Russia.	Clause as proposed by Great Britain.
' Mais alors chaque haute partie contractante se réserve pour elle la liberté de faire dans l'intérieur de ses états tel arrangement particulier qu'elle trouvera bon pour encourager sa propre navigation.'	' Mais alors on se réserve de la part des deux hautes parties contractantes la liberté de faire dans l'intérieur tel arrangement particulier qu'il sera trouvé bon pour encourager et étendre leur navigation respective.'

In this the pride of Russia sustained itself to the last. Panin was inflexible, and there being no alteration in the sense, Macartney thought it well to give way to the vanity and obstinacy which suggested the change as to the wording. He asked for new powers for the plenipotentiaries, but was refused. It was useless to contend, knowing it would be as easy for him ' to heave Pelion upon Ossa as to persuade them to a new power to the Commissioners.' Considering, therefore, the ill consequences of delay, Macartney ' put his own safety on the cast for the public service, and signed the treaty a second time.'[1]

The management of the northern department had now devolved upon Mr. Conway, from whom Macartney at length received the ratification of the treaty, but with it a notification to the effect that Mr. Stanley had been appointed as Ambassador to the Court of St. Petersburg. No intimation was, however, sent as to whether he was to continue in office as Minister until Mr. Stanley's arrival.

Indeed, from August, 1766, to the following March Macartney was left in complete ignorance as to what was going on at home, and his own destination. To this was added the mortification of perceiving he had lost the Ministerial confidence of Panin. The latter's personal feelings, as well as those of the Empress, remained unchanged, and they were as friendly as before. Catherine,

[1] J. Barrow, ' Life of Earl Macartney.'

indeed, entertained a sentimental regard for the good-looking young Irishman, and presented him with a miniature of herself.

To Lord Buckinghamshire, Macartney wrote as follows:

'I fear you will think me equally lost to friendship and good manners for having so long delayed to answer your most obliging letter. . . . But I was really so hurried, so busied, and so tormented by the damned negotiation of the treaty of commerce that for a considerable time it was impossible for me to attend to any other object. I have now at last happily got over every difficulty that retarded the completion of that affair, and have worked it through in the teeth of every opposition. . . . I flatter myself my Ministerial labours are now at an end. . . . Mr. Stanley is long since appointed Ambassador here, and will, I hope, by his abilities and address, accomplish every object which his predecessor leaves imperfect. Between ourselves, I do assure you most sincerely that nothing ever gave me more real pleasure as his nomination, as by that means I am withdrawn from the most disagreeable in nature. Your lordship knows better than anyone what negotiating is at this Court, and how much a man is to be pitied that is charged with such a commission. The labour, trouble, and vexation which I have suffered for these two years past would absolutely have overturned a mind less steady than mine. Besides, neither honour nor advantage attend even success on this walk of life. I therefore quit it with infinitely more pleasure than ever I entered upon it. . . . Several marriages are settled to take place immediately . . . the most magnificent wedding of all will be that of young Lapuchin . . . to Mdlle. Panin, which is to be celebrated next week . . . according to all the ancient Russian ceremonies. The Empress gives her 50,000 roubles. . . . As for myself, I have had an intrigue here that no man but myself would ever have dreamed of. But I reserve it for you when we meet in England. I think . . . that you'll have the pleasure of laughing at me for it at least four-and-twenty hours.'[1]

The Grand Duke Paul, accompanied by Panin, set out for Moscow on February 18, 1767. On the day of his departure the Minister saw Sir George, who had been laid up with

[1] Lord Buckinghamshire's correspondence.

'a most severe cold, fever, and sore throat,' and spoke to him on public affairs with kindness and candour. He said it was a sort of farewell speech, and Macartney might absolutely rely on the sincerity and truth of it. He was ready to conclude a firm alliance with Great Britain at that moment without the interposition of any other Power, but which the Powers of the north might be invited to accede to. He insisted on the Turkish clause, and said he was inflexible upon that article. A treaty with England could be of no use to Russia except in case of war with the Ottoman Porte, whereas England had every advantage to reap from a Russian alliance. On Sir George seeming to be somewhat doubtful on this point, Panin asked whether in common sense he could suppose that another Minister would find him more tractable; and that even if England scattered millions as well as declarations in Sweden and Poland, which former she did not appear inclined to do, it could not alter his opinion upon the Turkish point.

To Sir Andrew Mitchell, Macartney wrote:

'I must not omit to tell you in confidence that nothing can equal the contempt in which not only the Empress and her Minister, but even all the diplomatic body, hold British politics. For however wise judged, or necessary, the frequent changes in the administration may be supposed at home, it is certain that they render us ridiculous, nay despicable, abroad. I have given a hint of this in my private letters, but never ventured to insert it in my public dispatches, being assured from good hands that our Ministers are so torn with factions and divisions that they give themselves very little trouble about what foreign Powers may think of them. You will scarcely believe me serious when I assure you that I have not yet received orders relative to my own destination, and am still ignorant whether I ought to go to Moscow or wait for Mr. Stanley here, and yet . . . I have repeatedly entreated Mr. Conway to send me His Majesty's commands upon that point. . . . I am convinced that Mr. Panin will never recede from the principle he first set out upon of including a Turkish war in the *casus fœderis*. He is irritated against us for our refusal of this

WORRY AND ANXIETY

condition, more than I venture to express to the Office, in so much that he makes no scruple to declare publicly that, seeing the conduct of our Court, he consented to sign the treaty of commerce at last, merely from personal consideration and friendship for me.'[1]

The long strain of worry and anxiety, added to the vexations and disappointments of his position, had told upon Macartney's health, and he entreated that a recall to England should relieve him from his embarrassing situation. He had pointed out that the Russian Court was preparing to depart for Moscow, where all the foreign Ministers were to attend it. After its departure he would be of no further use in St. Petersburg, and he left in a disagreeable, and for a public Minister in a most ridiculous, situation. Notwithstanding these representations, he received orders to remain at St. Petersburg.

What his feelings were will best appear from the following letters:

Letter from Sir George Macartney to William Burke, dated St. Petersbourg, August 24 (September 4), 1766.

'Believe me, my dear Burke, I am highly sensible to all your instances of friendship, and believe me too, that on all occasions you will find me eminently grateful.

'I am very particularly obliged by your letter of the 27th July. . . . The nomination of Mr. Stanley did not at all surprise me. The only thing that surprises me is, that since they chose to put a slight upon me, they did not turn me out without further ceremony. It is true, I have happily accomplished a very laborious and a very difficult negotiation, and brought to a conclusion a treaty of commerce which, but for my zeal, industry, and activity, I will venture to say would have been lost to us for ever. I will make no scruple, neither, to own to you, that in my opinion my first treaty was preferable to my second. Probably I may be called on one day or another to defend it, and I think I have irrefragable proofs to support my opinion. I must add besides that to me alone is the treaty owing. It was extinguished and dead, to all intents and purposes, till I

[1] Mitchell Correspondence.

revived it. By indefatigable labour, and at a considerable expense, I worked it through in the teeth of every opposition. Mr. Panin here makes no scruple publicly to say that no other man could have obtained so much as I have done. And seeing the conduct of my Court in this and in other objects, it was merely from personal consideration to me that he concluded it at all. Mr. Stanley I know not. But I respect his character and abilities. If he were my enemy I could not wish him a greater punishment than his present commission. Were he my friend, I could not wish him a greater happiness than to be relieved from negotiating with this Court. Had he been informed of the real situation of things here, I am persuaded he would have declined so disagreeable an employment. Had the gentlemen at home known the footing I am upon with the Empress and her Ministers, they never would have dreamed of appointing another in my place. I am by no means, however, mortified at it. When I accepted this commission, which you know I gave value for (having resigned a seat in Parliament for it), I resolved to execute it with cheerfulness, however disagreeable I might find it. Had not Mr. Stanley been named to succeed me, I should have persevered till I had fulfilled every object of my instructions. But the affair being now settled otherwise, I cannot avoid expressing to you how very well pleased at it I am. To be sure, the proceeding is extraordinary, to turn a man out, if I am turned out, immediately after he had finished a treaty which had been the object of nine years' negotiation; which the other contracting party declares could be finished by nobody else, and which the gentlemen concerned in the trade have thanked me for in such terms as I blush to repeat. But some people tell me I am not turned out. No matter. I cannot in honour continue here whilst Stanley is in Russia. Because, in the language of a great Minister, I should not wish to be responsible for measures which I am not permitted to guide. Or, supposing I met with success in conjunction with him, I should certainly get no thanks for it. For, to borrow the expression of a minister of the Gospel, as I have just now done that of a Minister of State, "When we have done all that we can we are unprofitable servants," and, what is worse, unprofited too, I assure you. I know at least I have found it so. For not to speak of the expense of living here, which is very great, I have spent above a thousand pounds of my own money for secret service. This I never mentioned before, nor do

I intend to speak of it to the Office, though upon my honour it is true. Though I have got no thanks for my service, yet, since it has been of use to the public, I do not regret it. For these reasons I have demanded leave to return to England, at least while Stanley is here. I have another, which perhaps you may think better than all. I have an ambition of sitting in the next Parliament, where I hope I shall be able to serve both my Sovereign and my country with more approbation and with better success.

'I must entreat that you will use your interest with Mr. Conway for my leave to return home this winter. Also beg that proper instructions may be given to Mr. Stanley to inform himself in the most particular manner of my conduct here as a Minister. Especially, whether what I say of Mr. Panin's yielding to the treaty merely from personal friendship to me be true or not. In short, let the flat question be put to Mr. Panin himself. Seeing by the General's last dispatches that I have not the confidence of the present administration, I am reduced to the mortifying reflection that it is possible my veracity may be questioned, and to the necessity of having that veracity justified. Stanley is a man of honour, and will nothing extenuate, nor set down aught in malice. And his report, I will venture to say, will be that no man ever served his King and his country with greater zeal, nor with a more unblemished reputation, than I have done. It is in vain to say, as possibly some may do, that no dissatisfaction is meant to me by naming an Ambassador. Certainly there is, otherwise would they have named one without being sure whether it was agreeable or not to this Court? And as it happens, it is not. This letter, my dear Burke, will appear a very vain one. But called upon by this occasion, I am obliged to speak a great deal of myself. I have this satisfaction, however, that whatever I have said is literally true.

'I am much mortified at missing Ned's letter.[1] But hope he will find some method of forwarding it to me. I have made very ample collection of everything relative to this country, and shall with infinite pleasure impart to you and Ned all my stores.

'Adieu, my dear friend; be assured of the highest sentiments of esteem and regard, etc., etc.

'GEORGE MACARTNEY.'

---

[1] Edmund Burke.

Letter to the Right Hon. Hans Stanley, dated St. Petersbourg, September 1 (12), 1766.

'SIR,

'It seems to me very happy for the public that Administration did not entertain such favourable sentiments of me as you are pleased to do. For had their opinion, either of my abilities or address, been in any degree answerable to the flattering expressions of your letter, in all probability the care of His Majesty's affairs here would never have been transferred to your able hands.

'Though it must give me some pain to leave a Court which has distinguished me by such uncommon marks of attention and regard, yet I shall certainly do it with less regret when I consider that your Excellency is to be my successor. If you think it is in my power to be of the smallest use to you here during the interval that remains till your arrival, I beg you will freely lay your commands on me. I shall esteem myself extremely happy in being honoured with them, and I shall execute them with infinite pleasure. And as you are so obliging as to offer me your services in England, I take the liberty of entreating you to employ your good offices in obtaining for me the King's immediate permission to return home for a few months, during the winter, for the recovery of my health, which is in a very declining state. In doing this you will confer upon me the highest obligation, and on all occasions you may depend on finding me eminently grateful.

'I beg leave to conclude this letter by assuring you, without any compliment, how much I respect your character, how much I honour your abilities, and (whatever may happen in the revolution of public affairs) how ambitious I shall always be of your private friendship.

'I am, etc.,
'GEORGE MACARTNEY.'

Letter to the Right Hon. Henry Seymour Conway, dated St. Petersbourg, November 16 (27), 1766.

'SIR,

'I am honoured with your very obliging letter of the 24th October. Considering the accounts which the Ministry here received from all hands, particularly the communications of Mr. Gross;[1] considering that they saw an Ambas-

---

[1] The Russian Minister at the Court of London.

sador named over me, supposed to be charged with a commission not judged proper to be entrusted to me, and that they knew also how I had been reprehended for consenting to the only method by which it was ever possible to conclude the treaty of commerce, it was natural enough for them to suppose that I could not enjoy any great share of favour or confidence at home. Nor, indeed, did I presume to have much; for till I was honoured with your letter of the 30th September (which letter I did not receive till three months after Mr. Stanley's appointment) I was left entirely ignorant of my own destination, and, therefore, whenever questioned upon the subject, always declined giving any explicit reply. I continued, however, to walk on as before in the Ministerial track without deviation. I endeavoured to do my duty to the best of my abilities, and equally resigned myself to the obedience of whatever orders I might receive, whether depressive of my hopes or flattering to my wishes. I take the liberty of mentioning to you, sir, these particulars solely in the intention of destroying every suspicion which might be entertained of me as if I was in any degree discontented. Disappointed I possibly might have been, but I am not discontented. I feel too much gratitude for His Majesty's gracious permission of returning home for the recovery of my health to suffer the slightest ill-humour or peevishness to intrude upon my sentiments or behaviour, and I have such confidence in your generosity and good nature that I am persuaded, if any such ideas have been imbibed to my prejudice, you will not refuse to contradict or remove them.

'And here, sir, I must entreat you to accept my sincerest thanks for the very obliging expressions of your last letter. Your good opinion must be particularly flattering to me, and I might justly be vain on this occasion were I not humble enough to know that the best Minister, even when, like the best Christian, he has done all that he can, is, after all, but an unprofitable servant.

'Nothing can be more just than what you are pleased to observe ought at present to be the objects of attention to a British Minister residing at this Court. Ever since I have had the honour of being employed here I have been watchful of every circumstance of every kind, whether productive of foreign negotiation or domestic intrigue; but I laid it down as a rule never to communicate anything to you the truth of which I had not the strongest reason to rely upon, and particularly endeavoured to avoid swelling my dispatches with dissertations or conjectures. For these reasons the private broils of the Court and the silly squabbles of the bedchamber, unless attended, or likely to be attended, with serious consequences, have seldom found a place in my letters. It is true that we are frequently alarmed with accounts, at some times of smart repartees and at others of sullen quarrels between the Empress and her favourite, either arising from *her* excess of sensibility or *his* excess of presumption, but I have never found them of any great violence or duration. It has often happened besides that reports of such misunderstandings have been purposely spread and artfully propagated merely to sound the opinion and temper of the public. This is so much suspected that if a serious quarrel was to happen, perhaps it would be regarded with less attention than it really deserved. I have, therefore, avoided sending you relations of this nature, generally persuaded that the history of to-day's dispute would vanish before the account of to-morrow's reconcilement.

'The report of the late misunderstanding which you allude to has no real foundation, but took its rise merely from a hunting-party which Count Orloff went upon some time since, and which occasioned his absence from Court for eight or ten days. His favour with the Empress seems rather increased than diminished, and he is in appearance on the best terms with Mr. Panin, who, perhaps, would be sorry to see a minion of genius or ability in his place.'

Letter to the Right Hon. Henry Seymour Conway, dated St. Petersbourg, January 26 (February 6), 1767.

'SIR,
 'I resume my pen to answer your letters of the 19th December last, and to assure you that though I am persuaded my residence at this Court in my present situation can be of very little use to public affairs, yet, since your commands are such, I shall most certainly remain here and drag on a miserable existence till I am relieved either by the arrival of my successor or by natural dissolution.

'Since you are pleased to mention the late season of the year as a reason for Mr. Stanley's delaying to set out from England, I cannot but regret how unfortunate it was that I did not sooner inform him that the months of December,

January, and February are by far the most agreeable and undoubtedly the most proper for travelling in this part of the world, as the greater half of the journey—that is to say, from Dantzig to this city—is then performed by sledgeway, and in a much more expeditious manner than can possibly be done at any other season upon wheels. I remember that I was ordered to set out on the 1st November, exactly two months after my nomination, and the Earl of Buckinghamshire left this in the middle of January. I do not recollect that either of us suffered any great inconvenience from the coldness of the weather or the congelation of the roads.

'I do most sincerely agree with you in your opinion of the absurdity of Russia's inflexibility, and have done all in my power to engage her to agree with us both; but I might as well dream of governing human society by the laws of Plato's republic as of working upon this Ministry either by the common rules of negotiation or the principles of our ancient engagements. And at this moment I should think a treaty of alliance with the Empress of Russia (during Mr. Panin's Ministry) as distant and unlikely to be brought about as a league with Prester John or the King of Bantam. I mean as long as no method can be hit upon for removing the fatal, the only, difficulty that remains between us.

'And here, sir, lest you should look upon this Court's sending an Ambassador to London as a favourable omen, I must put you on your guard, and assure you that it arises merely from a sense of propriety on the part of the Empress, who will not in this instance suffer herself to be outdone in politeness or civility. If I might presume to know this Court from a very attentive perusal of two years, I would give my opinion by declaring that we flatter ourselves with the vainest hopes if we imagine that either the late advances on our side, or the return on hers, will, in the present sentiments of this Court, have the smallest effect in bringing about a closer union between us.

'We have no credit here at present, the whole of it lying between Mr. Asseburg and Count Solms.[1] What these gentlemen may have to negotiate together beyond the terms of private friendship I am at a loss to conjecture; but certain it is they see one another of late much more frequently than formerly, and that too in a sort of mysterious manner, avoiding as much as possible the appearance of any great connection in public. In so much that, though Mr. Asseburg goes generally four or five times a week to

[1] The Danish and Prussian Ministers.

Mr. Solms' house, and that usually, like Nicodemus, by night, yet, either being afraid of his brother Ministers, or for some other reason, he conceals this intimacy very carefully even from his own family. These gentlemen, being both Prussians, have talked to Mr. Panin, I believe, pretty much in the same style upon the subject of our alliance; and as the King of Prussia intends, if possible, to monopolize the friendship of Russia to himself without suffering any other Power to share it that he can hinder, I dare say that even supposing the present impediments to our union with this Court removed, he would find means to throw other *remoras* in the way; so far from his forwarding or assisting us, he has been all along, ever since my residence here, the grand enemy of our interest; and I do really believe that the Mufti of Constantinople might with as much probability expect a blessing from the Pope as the Court of London flatter itself with hopes of assistance from the Court of Berlin in any Russian negotiation.

'Your sentiments upon our affairs here, as expressed in your last letter, are entirely mine, and I have at every favourable opportunity endeavoured to impress them upon Mr. Panin. I have been answered, perhaps, of late in gentler terms than formerly, but always with the same meaning and determination of never yielding the point relative to Turkey. My own opinion is that this Court has long since resigned all thoughts of bringing us into the system, and therefore endeavours to compose it as well as she can without us. The Empress seems of late to give much less attention to foreign politics than formerly, and at present chiefly to turn her thoughts to the interior government of her dominions. She sets out in a few days for Moscow; from Moscow she goes to Yeroslaff; from Yeroslaff to Kasan; from Kasan to Astrachan; and from Astrachan Heaven knows where the genius of travelling may conduct her.

'When these peregrinations are over, another grand object will claim her attention—I mean the convention of the States of the Empire, in order to compose and establish a new code of laws. Now, as these States are to consist of a number of deputies, perhaps eleven or twelve hundred, chosen out of all ranks of people, and out of all nations under the Russian dominion, whether Christian, pagan, or Mahommedan, it is not to be expected that the proceedings of so tumultuous an assembly should be very regular, or their decisions very speedy. These circumstances, together with many others too tedious to be here enumerated, will probably blunt the edge of every appetite for foreign politics, and during a considerable time totally engross the attention of the Empress, of her Ministers, and of her people.

'The only chance we have of this Court's abating her inflexibility upon the Turkish clause is that, from the dissatisfaction of Sweden, or from the convulsions in Poland (if France exerts herself in the one and Austria intermeddles in the other), some incidents may arise which will render our alliance necessary to Russia on her own terms.

'I conceive that it would be of infinite service to His Majesty's affairs if I was permitted to return home immediately, that I might give to Administration and to Mr. Stanley a clearer, more accurate, and more particular account of things here *viva voce* than I can possibly do by letter, and which being delivered to both at London would certainly be of more utility than if communicated separately to each at different times and at different places. But this I submit with every sentiment of deference to the wisdom of my superiors, assuring you, however, at the same time that, until the Ambassador arrives, your office-keeper could perform the functions of a Minister here, not only to as good purpose as myself, but as well as a man of much higher abilities in my situation. Let me, therefore, once more entreat you, sir, to interpose in my favour for permission to return, and be convinced that as soon as my health is re-established I shall with uncommon readiness and pleasure obey His Majesty's orders, whenever and wherever he is pleased to command me.

'I am, etc.,
'GEORGE MACARTNEY.'

Letter from Mr. Conway.

'LONDON,
'*March* 13, 1767.
'DEAR SIR,
'I cannot help adding to the public letter I have the honour of writing to you by this post one word more to assure you of my very sincere regret and concern for the disagreeable account you give of the state of your health, and of the anxiety you have for some time suffered from other circumstances in your situation, the continuance of which for so long, and the uncertainty you have been left in, could not but in some measure appear chargeable to the

person filling the office I hold. Yet I can assure you nobody could enter more deeply into the distress of the situation, nor have been more desirous to relieve you from it. In respect to the long indecision on the departure of Mr. Stanley, it arises from a variety of circumstances—the illness and absence of His Majesty's Ministers, and from his own personal situation. I hope to have the pleasure of seeing you soon in England, and having a better opportunity of explaining things to you.

'Your most humble and obedient servant,
'J. S. CONWAY.'

As there was not the smallest hope of negotiating a treaty of alliance without the Turkish clause, and other reasons given in the letter to Mr. Conway, Macartney was at length given permission to return to England for the sake of his health; but even then he did not receive any letter of recall or intimation that Mr. Stanley was about to proceed to Russia. Having sent his secretary to Moscow, he left St. Petersburg and proceeded to Gothenburg, from whence he took passage to England.

Previous to his departure from Russia Catherine sent him a magnificent gold snuff-box, richly set with diamonds, valued at about £600, as a token of her regard. It was accompanied by the following letter from Panin, written by command of the Empress, who was at that time at Moscow:

'Dans le moment ou je lui (l'Imperatrice) ai présenté vos homages en vous congédiant de sa cour, j'ai reçu pour vous, Monsieur, les assurances les plus positives de sa bienveillance; et je vous les transmets avec un contentement qu'il vous sera facile de vous representer. Sa Majesté Imperiale ne veut point que vous partiez, sans en emporter une marque distinguée. La manière dont vous vous congédiez sans produire des lettres de rappel, nous engageant à vous considérer toujours comme ministre actuel auprès de notre cour, vous n'êtes pas encore dans le cas de recevoir le présent d'étiquette que nous faisons aux ministres, et nous le renvoyons au tems ou il doit avoit lieu. Mais independamment de ce présent, sa Majesté m'a ordonné de vous envoyer la boëte que j'ai l'honneur de joindre ici, comme un témoinage de son approbation et de l'estime qu'elle a jugé que vous meritez. Trouvez bon, Monsieur, que mes sentiments particuliers s'expriment tous dans la satisfaction avec laquelle je vois ceux de ma souveraine. Je vous demande avec empressement la continuation de votre amitié et je vous prie de croire que l'attachement que je vous ai voué est aussi sincère qu'inviolable.'

During the period of Macartney's residence at St. Petersburg he had on several occasions rendered service to the King of Poland by counteracting the schemes of the King of Prussia with regard to that country. Stanislaus Poniatowski, singularly handsome and refined, with graceful manners and a cultured mind, had formerly been one of Catherine's lovers. He was elected King of Poland in 1764, chiefly through her influence. His stormy reign there came to an end in 1793. As an acknowledgement of Macartney's good offices, Stanislaus sent him, in 1766, the insignia of the order of the White Eagle, accompanied by the following letter :

'VARSOVIE,
'*ce* 31 *Mai*, 1766.'

' MONSIEUR DE MACARTNEY,
' Il m'est bien agréable et bien flatteur de retrouver d'une façon si efficace dans un homme de votre mérite et de votre distinction les mêmes sentimens de bonne volonté, dont j'ai le plaisir de recevoir les preuves de tant de vos compatriotes. Ma reconnoissance et mon affection particulière pour votre nation est connue ; je souhaite que la mienne pour vous personellement le soit autant. C'est ce que me determine a vous conférer, Monsieur, l'ordre de l'Aigle Blanc, dont le Compte Rzewuksi, mon envoye extraordinaire et plenipotentiare à la cour impériale de Russie, est chargé de vous remettre les marques. Je vous prie d'y reconnoitre l'estime parfaite et l'amitié sincère dans laquelle je suis veritablement, Monsieur de Macartney,
' Votre très affectionné,
'STANISLAS AUGUSTE ROY.'

Shortly after Macartney's return to London, Mr. Stanley, perhaps alarmed by the difficulties awaiting him, sent in his resignation. Sir George was immediately appointed to succeed him in Russia as Ambassador Extraordinary and

Plenipotentiary. Possibly the Cabinet of St. James may have reflected on the impolicy of removing a Minister who, in the words of the King's speech from the Throne at the opening of Parliament, had concluded 'a just and satisfactory treaty of commerce,' and who stood, moreover, high in the estimation of the Court with which he had had to treat; but for various reasons Macartney considered it best not to take up the appointment.

On his return from Russia he voluntarily delivered up the warrants for silver-plate, equipage money, and other emoluments usually granted to Ambassadors, and which his predecessor, who had never left England, retained to the value of some £10,000.

He acted in this unusually disinterested manner despite the fact that he had spent several thousands out of his own pocket[1] in maintaining the dignity of his position.[2]

The only advantage he received from his appointment was the portraits of the King and Queen, which he particularly requested he might be allowed to keep.

[1] 'In Russia I sustained my character by involving myself in a debt of £6,000.'

[2] 'I took the earliest opportunity after my arrival of laying before Lord Sandwich and Mr. Greville the very great expenses of living at St. Petersburg, and that there appeared to me a real necessity of augmenting your appointment, but was sorry to find that for the present there is no prospect of so reasonable a proposition being attended to.'—Letter to Sir George Macartney (Buckinghamshire correspondence).

CHAPTER III

NOT long after Macartney's return from Russia a marriage was arranged between him and Lady Jane Stuart, second and favourite daughter of John, Earl of Bute, and his wife Mary, only daughter of Edward and Lady Mary Wortley Montagu. This match seems to have been brought about by Lady Holland, who took a warm interest in Sir George and his affairs, and considered the connection would be eminently helpful to an ambitious and rising young man.

Although he had been obliged to resign the office of Prime Minister some years previously, and his political influence was no longer what it had been, Lord Bute was still very powerful at Court. He had found places there for many of his friends and dependents, having, indeed, been unpleasantly noted for the patronage of his Scotch relatives and connections. He had great influence with the King through his mother, the Princess of Wales, whose confidential adviser and friend Lord Bute had been for many years. Lady Jane was at this time about twenty-seven, and in appearance somewhat resembled her father, but without the good looks which he is said to have possessed. She was sharp-featured and not attractive, having a prim and rather cold expression, and the unpleasantly striking characteristic of different coloured eyes, the right being blue and the left brown. She suffered from deafness, which increased as years went on, and was neither clever nor entertaining, but good, kind, religious, and thoroughly conscientious.

Lady Hervey was much attached to Lady Jane, and, it is said, greatly wished to arrange a match between that lady and her son, the Earl of Bristol, but it came to nothing.

Lady Mary Coke, in her diary, thus records the announcement of the engagement:

'*Thursday, December* 24, 1767.—Lady Betty Mackenzie[1] asked me if I had heard of the marriage in the family. I said I supposed it was Lady Jane Stuart and Sir George Macartney, as I had seen it in the newspapers. She said it was, and commended Sir George extremely. I told her I knew him very well, and thought him a very pretty man, but I feared his fortune was but small, though he had at present a great employment;[2] that I hoped she liked a cold country, as she was to go to Russia. Lady Betty told me that Sir George Macartney talked of going to Russia by sea, and that Lady Jane had no objection. If she knew what it was to be sick, she would not have given her consent so readily.'

The wedding took place on February 1, 1768, by special licence, at Lord Bute's house in South Audley Street. Immediately after the ceremony the newly-married pair left London, and proceeded to Parkhurst, a country place recently acquired by Sir George, in the neighbourhood of Dorking.

In those days weddings were family affairs, and not the public show which is now the prevalent fashion. Apparently even a small gathering was unusual upon such occasions, as in a letter to a friend written a few years later Macartney says:

'Last week the long-expected wedding in Berkeley Square was celebrated. There were several persons present, and afterwards a supper of three-and-twenty persons. I suppose so much ceremony is a sort of etiquette in the Beaufort family. Everybody pitied the poor young lady who was to go through it.'

[1] Sister to Lady Mary Coke.
[2] At that time Macartney had not definitely declined the Russian appointment.

The Macartney honeymoon was not a lengthy one, and they were soon back again in London. Lady Mary Coke, in a letter to her sister, mentions her first visit to the bride:

'*Tuesday, February* 9.—I went to Lady Jane Macartney, and found her at home; the Duchess of Ancaster was sitting with her. 'Twas a cold, damp day, and, unluckily for me, one of her windows was half open, to prevent, as I suppose, the room smoking; but as I never inquire after an imperfection, I did not ask the reason, though I was obliged to be exposed to a terrible cold wind, the Duchess having the best place in the room. Lady Jane seemed in very good spirits. I must now asknowledge myself in the wrong: Sir George does not go to Russia; but I am told 'tis as yet a secret, so don't mention it. The circumstance that perhaps will surprise you is that he quits the Embassy without any place in lieu of it. All that is said is " 'Tis hoped in time he will have one." '

A few days later Lady Mary notes in her diary:

'Went to the Duchess of Bolton's, where there was a very small party. I played at lu, and lost nine guineas. Sir George Macartney was of the party, and lost a hundred.'

The Macartney marriage does not appear to have been a particularly happy one. It had been entered into more from motives of convenience on the one hand, and ambition on the other, than from mutual affection. Lord Bute did not consult his elder daughters' inclinations in the matter of husbands, and their matrimonial affairs, with one exception, do not appear to have been very satisfactory.

Lady Louisa Stuart, the only one of the sisters who remained unmarried, was a voluminous and entertaining letter-writer. She remarks, in one of her numerous communications to her youngest sister, Lady Caroline Dawson, afterwards Lady Portarlington:

'It gives me such comfort to think of you and Mr. Dawson at your happy fireside, in comparison to the rest of the family, that I am drawing the picture to myself every day.'

It is to be inferred from this remark that Lady Caroline's marriage must have been the only really successful one among the Bute family of that generation.

But the Macartney marriage was by no means openly unhappy, as were those of the Duchess of Northumberland and Lady Lonsdale, which were notoriously so. It was more that they were not particularly well suited, though each entertained a profound respect for the other. Lady Jane was good, kind-hearted, and well-intentioned, but straight-laced, conventional, and somewhat *bornée* in her views. She belonged to a restricted circle of the fashionable London society of the day, and being neither clever nor artistic, was unable to appreciate her husband's literary and Bohemian friends and acquaintances, or find pleasure in their society. His Irish ways must often have sorely tried and puzzled her, and many of the friends and companions of his youth been hopelessly uncongenial, but she always tried to do her best and perform what was required of her.

To Lady Jane, devout, narrow, and religious, which combination not unfrequently implies a lack of humour, Macartney's free-thinking and satirical turn of mind must have been both trying and incomprehensible, and though she profoundly admired his integrity and ability, she must often have deplored many of his views, which in some ways appear to have been in advance of his time. Macartney had no domestic tastes, and possibly was not always very considerate. Ambition and his career occupied the foremost place in his life, and though he had to a large extent the capacity for friendship, lacked that touch of deep feeling and emotion which makes the lover. He respected his wife deeply for her many good qualities, but she had neither the charm of mind nor appearance which would have been necessary to inspire a man of his type with a deep affection for any woman. However, they always addressed each other most affectionately in their letters, and Lady Macartney, writing to a relation some months after his death.

Lord & Lady Macartney

From Miniatures in the possession of C. G. Macartney, Esq.

'sends two little curious purses . . . which were brought to her from China some years ago. Lady Macartney wishes them to be looked upon as keepsakes to the memory of her dear Lord Macartney.'

Perhaps, like many other couples, they were fonder of each other in theory than in practice, and most harmonious in their relations when apart.

From various remarks scattered throughout Lady Louisa Stuart's correspondence it is evident that she was not particularly attached to her brother-in-law, and she occasionally spoke with some contempt of Irish people. But that, in spite of her dislike, she appreciated his sterling qualities can be seen from the following extract from one of her letters written long after his death :

'. . . every letter he [Lord Macartney] received while Governor of Madras. I just looked into each, and as they amounted to many hundreds, it was curious to see what a number of worthy and excellent people went to seek their fortunes in India.

'. . . When one saw them gathered into that amazing heap, it did strike one that if a twentieth part had spoken truth India would have received in its bosom the choicest characters of Great Britain, and been a paradise, instead of the sink of iniquity which a letter to him from thence calls it. . . . For, give him his due, he was the first who reformed its abuses, and set the example of coming away with perfectly clean hands.'[1]

Macartney's refusal of the appointment of Ambassador to Russia had been partly due to the fact that he considered a parliamentary career would afford wider scope for his talents and ambition. Previous to his marriage it had been decided that he should stand as candidate for Cockermouth in the following March.

Lady Mary Coke says in her diary :

'*Monday, March* 14.—I called on Lady Betty Mackenzie, and while I was with her Sir George Macartney came in, saying he was to set out in half an hour, with Sir James

[1] 'Letters to Miss Clinton from Lady Louisa Stuart,' edited by Mrs. Godfrey Clark.

Lowther,[1] for the North, to be chose, as I understand, for Cockermouth. I asked if the report of Sir James carrying all his elections was true. They told me for the two counties he was sure ... and added it had cost Sir James Lowther a very great sum of money.'

Accordingly, in April, 1768, Sir George was chosen as one of the representatives of Cockermouth in the English House of Commons. He thought, however, that it would be possible to serve his country and advance himself more effectually in the Irish Parliament, so resigned his seat almost immediately, and in July was elected member for Armagh.

About this time considerable changes were contemplated in the system of government for Ireland. It had long been customary for the Lord-Lieutenant to go over about once in two years, and while there to concern himself but little with public affairs. He convened a Parliament which lasted a few months, lived in a state of great magnificence, provided for his dependents, ' received freedoms, gold boxes, and complimentary addresses, and then hurried back to England with the utmost precipitation.'[2]

At his departure the Government was vested in a commission, usually composed of the two principal members of the Church and the Law, together with the Speaker of the House of Commons. These individuals were usually appointed Lords Justices, but in Ireland were better known by the title of ' Undertakers.' The power, patronage, and influence they possessed was very great, and gave them almost unlimited control over the internal government of that kingdom. They considered themselves so important and necessary to the Crown in transacting what was termed the King's business that they were generally able to dictate their own terms to the English Administration.

In all these transactions with the Government of England it is necessary to bear in mind that the people concerned in

[1] Sir James Lowther, afterwards Lord Lonsdale, married Lady Mary Stuart, eldest daught'r of the Earl of Bute.
[2] Sir George Macartney, An Account of Ireland.'

them were not really Irish. A good many of them were the descendants of the colonists of 1691, when, after the suppression of Tyrconnel's rising in favour of King James,[1] much of the land was confiscated, and the original inhabitants treated with harshness and severity as outlaws and savages. The extensive forfeiture of the lands of the Catholic Irish, and the grant of these lands to Protestant natives of Great Britain, became a fresh source of hatred between the irreconcilable factions of Catholic and Protestant.

Thus the Protestant ascendancy began its rise, and the Catholics, who composed the greater part of the population, groaned under the oppression of the penal laws.

The Anglo-Irish had towards the native Irish much the same feelings as the American colonists entertained towards the Indians, and regarded them as an inferior race, being averse to much intercourse with them. They also objected to employing the Irish Catholics about their persons or in their houses, a feeling which is, alas! not even yet extinct, and among a certain class still obtains to a large extent.

But the peasantry were gradually beginning to take heart, and practically resent their spoliation and ill-treatment. The Anglo-Irish were also bitterly discontented with the mother-country, and with reason. The commercial policy pursued towards them by England was not unlike that pursued towards America, and they found their attempts at trade and commerce thwarted and restricted for the benefit of the English merchants. All these causes combined, therefore, to produce an atmosphere of struggle and dissatisfaction.

At the change of English Ministry in 1766, one of the first measures settled by the Cabinet was that Ireland should no longer be left to the discretion of the Undertakers.

---

[1] Tyrconnel was a Catholic gentleman of English extraction. His object was the erection of Ireland into an independent Catholic State, under the protection of France, in event of the English crown being again on the head of a Protestant. King James landed in Kinsale in March, 1689.

In future the Lord-Lieutenant was to reside constantly in the country, and hold the reins of government in his own hands. The Earl of Bristol was first appointed under the new régime, but never took up office in consequence of the resignation of his political friend, the great Lord Chatham. Lord Townshend, who immediately went over to Ireland, was nominated as his successor in 1767.

Macartney did not take up residence in Ireland immediately on his election. Lady Mary Coke mentions a party at her sister's house on September 28, 1768, and says: 'Lady Jane Macartney was at Lady Betty's; Lady Jane is deafer than ever,' and later, in November of the same year, remarks :

'Lady Percy told us Lord Mountsteuart and Sir George Macartney had both spoke in the House of Commons. 'Twas upon the petition against Sir James Lowther, who, I imagine, they thought they ought to support. Lord Mountsteuart, I was told, spoke with great warmth; Sir George Macartney was cooler, but, according to my information, more parliamentary. . . . Sir George Macartney, I believe, expects something, but I should think he is not likely to get anything so considerable at first till it is seen what use he can be to the Government.'

From which it would appear that, although elected member for Armagh, Macartney was still in evidence in the English House of Commons.

In the autumn of 1768 Sir George was made Chief Secretary for Ireland, but by Lord Townshend's wish the public appointment did not take place till January 1, 1769.

On March 30 following he was sworn a member of the Privy Council there, but apparently did not take up office in Dublin till the autumn. He was indeed anxious to obtain the appointment of Ambassador to the Spanish Court, and for a time had good hopes of it,[1] which were, however, doomed to disappointment.

[1] 'LONDON,
'*October* 12, 1770.

'. . . I heartily wish you were now at Madrid, as the interposition of a person of your talents might be of essential service; but I am

THE SPANISH APPOINTMENT

'*July* 18, 1769.—I'll tell you a secret, but pray say nothing of it till you hear it from some other person. Sir George Macartney does not go to Ireland; he expects a better office. The Duke of Grafton has, I believe, promised to send him Ambassador to Spain.'

'*Tuesday, August* 15.—'Tis now publickly talked of that Sir G. M. is to go to Spain. A circumstance that I think very hard upon Lord Townshend is that the Duke of Grafton intends to name his new secretary, which I don't think any Ministers ever took upon them to do before.'

'*Friday, September* 1.—I asked Lady Townshend who was to be secretary to her son in Ireland, but I found she did not know. It may be Sir G. M. at last, for I am told he is not to go to Spain, which will be a great disappointment, as he had mentioned it to several people.'[1]

Amongst Macartney's correspondence are numerous letters to him from Lord Townshend dealing with Irish affairs, and as time went on, expressive of his wish for Macartney's presence at Dublin Castle.

'DUBLIN CASTLE,
'*November* 25, 1768.

'DEAR SIR,
'I had answered your obliging letter before, but the wind which you know generally blows three weeks in four from the west hath, as usual, cut off our communication with England.

'It gave me a most sincere pleasure to have this opportunity to express my respect for those who have brought us better acquainted together; at the same time, I am persuaded that I shall derive every advantage for the King's service, as well as my own particular, from your abilities and assistance.

'The situation of affairs here and the conduct of the Leading People must naturally make me wish to have the earliest and fullest communication with you, and that we

---

not enough in the secrets of administration to be able to say whether any arrangement is made with regard to the appointment of an Ambassador in the room of Mr. George Pitt.
'Your most obedient and humble servant,
'SANDWICH.'

(Letter to Sir G. Macartney from the Earl of Sandwich.)
[1] Lady Mary Coke's diary.

could go over this large and interesting field in the most confidential manner together ; but your reasons for wishing to stay in England are too cogent for me to desire you to be absent one moment from the King's service there at such a crisis to English government and, indeed, to the British Empire.

'Lord Frederick Campbell was so good some time before his intention to quit this situation were known to undertake to forward the conclusion of some very important points he had begun with the Duke of Grafton. I fear he will not be in town before the 20th of next month. For these reasons I flatter myself you will approve of my wishing you may not be publickly declared my Secretary until these matters shall be brought to a conclusion.

'Lady Townshend desires I shall express at the same time with my own, our ambition to make this situation agreeable to Lady Jane and yourself, and our desire to be charged with any commissions you may have either side of the water in which we can be useful.

'I have the honour to be, with the truest regard and esteem,

'Your most Obed^t Humble Ser^t,
'TOWNSHEND.'

'DUBLIN CASTLE,
'*December* 11, 1768.

'DEAR SIR,
'I am this morning favoured with your letter of the 5th December, and hope you will believe I feel most sensibly the obliging attention you express on my sentiments relating to the period of your appointment, which assuredly arose from no other motive than a conviction of the great benefit it will be to the King's service here to bring those points Lord Fred. Campbell hath so largely discussed with the Duke of Grafton to as speedy a conclusion as possible. There is another motive too much connected with this circumstance for me to omit. It is an apprehension that, should your Notification in form here take place whilst Lord Frederick was in conference with the Duke of Grafton in town, some *Circumstance of Delicacy* might possibly arise that might interrupt the present depending business, and fling us back so as to make our subsequent proceedings more difficult than you can conceive.

'In short, my dear sir, I will leave it to your judgment how far you will think it prudent to risk these interesting points for the consideration of passing the short time you propose here, which I assure you will hardly enable me to communicate to you that large field of business which I am anxious to put you in fullest possession of. I think myself greatly obliged to you for the candid and confidential light in which you view the particular circumstances attending your appointment.

'I am with great esteem, Dear Sir,
'Your faithful Servant,
'TOWNSHEND.'

'LEIXLIP,
'*February*, 1769.

'DEAR SIR,

'Having no hopes of seeing you, I took my intended trip into the interior parts of this Kingdom. . . . I wrote very fully to the Duke of Grafton lately upon the situation of things here, as far as I could then form an opinion, and I have no reason to alter it. I have no communication with those Powerful Men whose weight in this Kingdom has enabled them to defeat the measures of the Crown. It does not appear to me essential to the success and dignity of Government that I should express any anxiety about their future conduct, and, indeed, the distance at which they hold themselves, and the neglect of the common civilities to my station, would deprive me of any intercourse except where His Majesty's immediate service required it. At the same time be assured, Sir, that I have never suffered, nor ever will, any marked neglect or incivilities to me in my publick Station to interfere with the most circumspect and firm conduct in pursuit of His Majesty's service.

'Before I quit this subject I must just say a word upon a report I hear is propagated in London that I have had a quarrel with the Duke of Leinster and Lord Tyrone, which, if occasion require, you may affirm on my authority to be entirely without foundation. I have the pleasure to live on the most polite and friendly footing with the first. He is my neighbour here, and it would be tedious to instance the civilities that have passed. . . . Your Letters gave me hopes of a favourable determination upon Revenue business. Perhaps I may be excuseable for some Degree of Anxiety upon this Subject, as it is the source from whence all the Difficulties to the measures of the Crown, the distress of Successive Chief Governors, and the Dominion of Party in this Kingdom hath flowed. . . . The influence of the Board, as it is at present exercised, the power of creating or increasing salaries, the doling out of £116,000 every two years, chiefly in jobs, with the operation of their party branching over the whole face of the Kingdom . . . is a weight greatly superior to the . . . Patronage of a Chief Governor ! . . . These servants of the Crown ransack even the sick beds of their Dependents to defeat a measure . . . having first provided for their friends by their demands, or rather Exactions from my Predecessors. They have now expelled from their Burroughs such who dared to be grateful to the Crown, leaving them a dead weight upon Government, and have brought in such as can perplex it most. . . . They boast they shall open the next Session with near forty Majority against Government. . . . It is from you, Sir George, that I hope . . . such a system on the part of Government as shall prevail over . . . such citizens as these. . . .

'. . . Let me observe how advantageous the augmentation of the number and salaries of Judges would be to this Kingdom. . . . It is certain that a sufficient following must in this as in all countries be held by Government to carry on business. . . .

'I have some hopes you may now have time to read this long letter, as I flatter myself you have e'er now compleated in your House that work so necessary to maintain good order and peace in every part of H.M.'s Dominions.

'I am, Dr Sir,
'Most respectfully Yours,
'TOWNSHEND.

'Pray present Lady Townshend's with my best respects to Lady Jane. You see what cursed paper. We have desired Sir Robert to order your supply over from England.'

'DUBLIN,
'*February* 24, 1769.

'DEAR SIR,
'I have received y^r favour of the 15th Inst., and esteem your openness and sincerity. I wrote to you on the 7th and on the 20th Inst., and you will judge from those letters what confidence I repose in your fidelity, and what opinion I entertain of your Abilities. I would not press you

to come over whilst so many important Matters were depending in Parliament, but now, as you inform me that publick business is drawing to a conclusion, I desire I may have the satisfaction of seeing you as soon as you can conveniently set out. I wish you to stay here about a Month or Six Weeks, and then return to London. I have many points of Importance to communicate which are too voluminous for Letters, and which I mean you should lay before the Duke of Grafton in person, upon your return. . . . If you could bring over his Grace's decision upon the Revenue Points, . . . it would be of the highest Importance at this moment, when the Influence of that board has been exerted in a most striking manner in support of a gentleman whom I dismissed from my Family for opposing the King's Measures, and who is now amply provided for in the Revenue for his attachment to those who defeated them. . . . I hope you are by this time acquainted with Lord Tyrone and Mr. Beresford. . . . They are well worth cultivating, and the sooner you are on an easy footing with the former the better; you will then understand him best. I dare say you are well with Mr. Conolly. He is a most sincere, amiable Man, and if he talks of Ireland at all will speak in a most frank, undisguised manner. . . .

'With truest regard, etc.,
'TOWNSHEND.'

The change in the system of government previously alluded to had made, as was only to be expected, strong and opposite impressions on the different political parties in Ireland.

'The people, ever fond of novelty, were rejoiced beyond measure at the happy tidings. Those who had been long in leading-strings, but had never been led to what they looked for, felt new hopes rise in their bosoms, and flattered themselves that the day of enfranchisement had come. Golden visions of profit and of honour opened on the eyes of every patriot. He who had disdained the thraldom of an Undertaker was ready to wear the livery of a resident Viceroy, and the most inveterate Republican became a convert to the new theory of government. All was rapture and reformation. . . .

'The Undertakers, against whose usurpation this scheme of residence was levelled, immediately took the alarm, and strenuously used all their endeavour to defeat it. They knew, indeed, that opposition, if steadily resisted, must soon smoulder into insignificance; but they flattered themselves that no Lord-Lieutenant would long persevere in the new plan. If he should, they were resolved to omit nothing on their part to make his situation as uneasy and as unpleasant as possible.'[1]

In this state of the public mind Lord Townshend had arrived at his new government, and was immediately beset, as all his predecessors had been, by the patriots on one hand, and the Undertakers on the other.

Both parties suggested many conflicting measures, which they assured him would render him personally popular and assist his government. The wildest schemes were proposed, which, if adopted, would have been ridiculous or an encroachment on the revenue. In places where no commerce could exist it was proposed to make roads to facilitate it.

'One day a bounty on fish, fishing busses, and whale-catching was desired. The establishment of county hospitals and public coal-yards was another day mentioned. A Septennial Bill, a Judges Bill, a Habeas Corpus Bill, premiums for corn preserved upon stands, and for corn brought to Dublin coastways, were all asked in their turns. Nay, what will scarcely be believed, a proposal was seriously made that the *land carriage* bounty should be paid for all corn and flour brought to Dublin *by the new canal*. . . . A Lord-Lieutenant new in his government, perhaps new in business of any kind, unacquainted with the people and constitution of Ireland, and desirous of carrying on his administration with popularity and good-humour, probably at first did not apprehend any danger or inconveniency from adopting these schemes. He perhaps seemed to approve them, and his seeming approbation was immediately sworn into a positive promise, the performance of which he was afterwards either soothed or frightened into, according to the features of his character and the circumstances of the times.'[2]

Lord Townshend soon discovered that by conceding a few points he was every day harassed with greater and more extravagant demands. He determined in future to

[1] Sir George Macartney, 'An Account of Ireland.'   [2] *Ibid.*

IRISH PATRIOTS

act upon his own observations, and rid himself at once of both patriots and Undertakers. The demands of these latter were outrageous and extravagant.

'One was only to be satisfied with half a dozen peerages for his friends, another preferred some great reversion for himself. Those who had not pensions wished to have them, those who had . . . desired an addition, and almost all who were already in good employments agreed in asking for better ones. Lord Townshend's hesitation to comply with these extraordinary requisitions was highly resented. Thus, these gentlemen, instead of being grateful for past favours, were enraged at the refusal of new ones, turned the power of the Crown entrusted to their hands against the Crown itself, and endeavoured to extort by faction and opposition what was meant to be the reward of loyalty and service.'[1]

The first great object of Lord Townshend's administration was to crush this growing aristocracy of Ireland, and rid the country of an evil injurious alike to people and Government. Their ingratitude to the Crown eventually hastened the destruction of their power. Among the Bills framed in the Irish Council and sent over to England in the usual manner was a money Bill. This was rejected, the Duke of Leinster, Lord Shannon, Master of the Ordnance, Mr. Ponsonby, the Speaker, and all the strength of the Undertakers having on this occasion mustered against the Government. The Lord-Lieutenant protested, and by the prorogation of Parliament put an end to the session. Lord Shannon and Mr. Ponsonby were dismissed from their employments, it being very evident their opposition arose from interest and not from principle. After this they combined with the Duke of Leinster and the patriots, and proceeded to harass the Government by every means in their power. All kinds of spiteful resolutions were proposed in the House, and the Dublin press teemed with scurrilous libels. Lord Townshend, who was much worried, wrote to Sir George Macartney as follows:

[1] Sir George Macartney, 'An Account of Ireland.'

'DUBLIN,
'*February*, 1769.

'DEAR SIR,
'I wrote to you by last post expressing how much I wished to see you now, if King's business would admit of your coming over. Since that time Captain Tottenham's appointment, as I am told, makes a great noise, and the best friends of Government look upon it as the crisis to the Lord-Lieutenant or the Speaker's power. . . . If any of His Majesty's servants in the Revenue who have defeated the King's measures shall be at liberty to reward their followers in opposition to the Chief Governor (who has from duty mark'd their conduct), it needs no further comment to describe the situation of the Chief Governor, nor direction to the road men are to pursue.

'I believe I mentioned to you that Captain Tottenham was dismissed from being one of my aidecamps on account of having followed the Speaker's party during the session, particularly on the great affair of the augmentation.[1] He is now amply provided for in the Revenue for his attachment to those who defeated the King's measures.
'Yours, etc.,
'TOWNSHEND.'

Macartney went over to Ireland for a short time in March, and before returning to London paid a visit to his Scotch relations.[2] From Lord Townshend he heard as follows:

'DUBLIN,
'*April*, 1769.

'I hope you had a pleasant journey to Scotland, and that it will prove a prosperous one. . . . I have no news to send you from hence, but that you and I had a monstrous quarrel, and that you went away the next morning in the highest displeasure. This has given great hopes to the silly party. . . . I hear the Speaker has complained much of

---

[1] Bill for increasing the number of soldiers in the Irish regiments, making them equal with those in England. Part of the measure was also concerned with the disposal of the forces throughout the kingdom.

[2] In March, 1770, Sir George received a letter from his cousin Catherine Macartney, informing him that her father had left him absolutely 'the little Scotch estate, and all arrears of it due at his death.'

your categorical style. He is a man . . . incapable of secrecy, as such a man must be who seeks for his politics at a club, and canvasses for friends by whispering what a man in his station should reserve.'

'April, 1769.

'. . . When you have cast your eye over Mr. Ponsonby's letter and mine, pray seal and forward the latter. I believe you think it extremely civil, and such as it ought to be, on this occasion especially. I remember a Grenadier once observed in the line, as Prince Ferdinand was going along and nodding to the soldiery, how *extraordinarily civil* the Prince was. "Yes," replied another; "I observed it too, and be damned to him! You'll find he always is so before we are to be damnably peppered."'

'June, 1769.

'. . . There is a report to-day you are not to come back. I shall be infinitely mortified and disappointed if you leave me, for I know your knowledge of men and things here is to my success. It will be a matter of triumph to Mr. Ponsonby to have you leave me; I'm sure the King's service will suffer by it. If you are thought of for an Embassy of the first moment, you might, however, extend and confirm the weight of Government here in the interim. . . . From the King's birthday to this hour I have known nothing but rain and rheumatism, and the next day rheumatism and rain again.'

'August, 1769.

'. . . The idea of your removal to Spain hath, I assure you, greatly shaken our credit, as Mr. Ponsonby and his agents have so proscribed you. It has given them exceeding credit for the moment. . . . Nothing can be more detrimental . . . to the King's affairs than that you should not open the session. Without flattery, sir, a very early and perfect esteem fixed my wishes with respect to your assistance and friendship. If you had been more consulted in England, and sooner back here, I am confident things would have worn a better aspect. There is a general respect for the moment towards English government.'

'August, 1769.

'. . . I am happy to hear you do not go to Madrid. I should have been exceedingly mortified to have lost your assistance and friendship here. Although I never mentioned it, it was talked of publicly here to the great mortification of our friends.'

The following extracts are taken from the letters of Mr. Waite, one of the permanent officials at Dublin Castle, to Sir George Macartney:

[*Private.*]

'*June*, 1769.

'. . . I hear with great pleasure from my Lord-Lieutenant that you are in perfect health, that you write in good spirits, and that your letters are full of wit and humour. . . . You will have seen by the copy . . . of my Lord-Lieutenant's letter to Lord Weymouth that his Excy's and your sentiments correspond as to the Money Bill and the augmentation.

'If he be supported with proper powers, and has your assistance in the exercise of them, I can have no doubt of success. But I must tell you freely that he cannot go alone; management will be necessary, and for that the Ministry must depend upon you.

'The principal difficulties which you will have to combat against will arise from his own irregularities. The sooner, therefore, you break him to your subjection the better. I hope the moment the great point of his continuance here is determined that you will set out and make your preparations for the ensuing campaign. . . . Mr. Jackson is a most worthy and religious man, but he is very timorous in his disposition, and wants the courage that is necessary for a Minister. I think that the prospect that lies before you is as fair a one as you could desire, and the termination of it will depend upon your own Prudence. Let not your noble courage be cast down.

'But we are told by some Persons that you are to go immediately to Madrid; by others that you are shortly to be appointed sub-Governor to the Prince of Wales. All in good time, and I am sure that these Honors will not blush upon your head, but first make a campaign in Ireland. You cannot go to a Better School for reading Men and Characters. There is great Reputation to be gain'd here at present, and you have abundant abilities to acquire it, and without much trouble. . . .

MILITARY SCHEMES

'... His Excy has not yet fixed his Day for setting out upon his Military Survey of Munster. ... I wish you would give him a small hint not to write such voluminous letters to the Duke of Grafton. He has this moment a scheme in agitation for building a Riding House at East Barrack, where the Cavalry are quartered, the Expense whereof will amount to Ten Thousand Pounds at least. Is this political at a time when you wish to obtain some Alterations of Economy in our Military Establishment to smooth the way for the augmentation ? and why are such Riding Houses particularly necessary now ? The Cavalry have done very well without them hitherto. But his Excy's ideas are all Military, and the officers think of nothing but what they please to want.

'I am, dear Sir, with great truth.'

[*Most Private.*]

From Mr. Waite to Sir George Macartney.

'DUBLIN CASTLE,
'*July*, 1769.

'Yesterday I received a Letter from Mr. Jackson, who seems to be greatly alarm'd at my Lord-Lieutenant's having transmitted the Alphabetical List of the House of Commons. He says ... he had found reason to wish that it had not been sent over. ... It has given ample Room to People in London to draw conclusions ... that may be turned to my Lord Lt's Disadvantage. ... So far Mr. Jackson, which I give you in the utmost confidence, and hope I may depend upon your never saying anything to Him of what I have done. ... If the Ministers have made it [the list] publick ... or suffered those under them to talk of it, or give ... extracts from it, it becomes a very serious affair. ... I submit it to you, therefore, whether you will not take some notice to Lord Weymouth of what you have heard ... that it has been left open to the view of low people. ... I hope that Mr. Jackson, who sees every object of terror thro' a multiplying as well as a magnifying glass, has made more of the matter than it deserves. But at all events it is for you to take the alarm, and to recall the list into your own possession. ...'

[*Private.*]

From Mr. Waite to Sir George Macartney.

'July, 1769.

'... There is no doubt that Lord Townshend wishes to remain here, but it does not appear to me that he has undertaken the Business, or that he ever meant to undertake but upon terms.... If administration has pledg'd itself to support him, it is high time they should let him know it in express words.... I am heartily sorry that you are not here upon the spot to assist him with your advice....

'In the utmost confidence I may tell you that his Excy has received two letters from General Burgoyne mentioning that you was shortly to go to Madrid, and thereupon offering his services to succeed you.... Your presence here is of infinite consequence, and therefore for Heaven's sake come over as soon as you can. I am very confident that your abilities and dexterity work out our salvation, that Mr. Jackson may bottle up his terrors, and make a present of them to Mr. Conway. But a great deal of management will be necessary, and of such management I know you to be a complete master.... You cannot bring over anything of greater importance to his Excy's service than yourself, and the sooner that is done the better.'

From Mr. Waite to Sir George Macartney.

'DUBLIN CASTLE,
'*September* 11, 1769.

'I received this morning your favour of the 4th inst. from Tunbridge Wells, acquainting me of your intention of being at Holyhead by the 30th inst. at farthest, and desiring that the yacht may be ordered thither to receive Lady Jane and you on the 29th.... We expect His Excy to-morrow. He has by all accounts passed his time very agreeably in Munster, and met with particular marks of attention and respect from the County and City of Cork. I cannot say whether He has seen Lord Shannon and Mr. Ponsonby. I know he expected it, and the world says all unkindness has been settled over a cup of mild ale....

'... I have not been backward in hurrying your workmen, and I have this day put them into convulsions by telling them that I expect Lady Jane and you next Sunday.

BAD WEATHER

This will have some good effect, and you will have your Parlour below, and your Drawing Room above, ready for your reception; but as to the rest, you will find everything in woeful condition. . . .

'Terrible weather in this part of the world. The new Comet has almost overwhelmed us with a deluge.'

Sir George and Lady Jane Macartney went over to Ireland on the last day of September, 1769, and took up their residence in Dublin Castle. Lord Townshend wrote to greet them, saying he was glad they had 'reached Ireland with no more inconvenience than Lady Jane's fatigues.'

Part of the summer of 1770 they spent in the north of Ireland at Lissanoure, and Lady Jane also visited her parents at Luton, in Bedfordshire, but was unaccompanied by her husband.[1]

For upwards of three years Macartney filled the somewhat thankless office of Chief Secretary for Ireland, and carried through three stormy and difficult parliamentary sessions there.

The Lord-Lieutenant, being English, was represented as an enemy to the real interests of the country, while his secretary, for the opposite reason, was said to be no true friend to Ireland, in spite of the fact that he possessed large estates there, and might be likely to have an interest in its prosperity. No suggestion was too wild to put forward,

---

[1] 'LUTON PARK,
'*June* 5, 1770.

'MY DEAR SIR GEORGE,

'I am sorry you thought it necessary to make any excuse for not accompanying Lady Jane in her intended visit to her dear Father and me. I'm sure neither of us could have thought of, or expected, such an attention even from her. I have wrote to Lady Jane to let her know if the difficulties of her journey do not appear so formidable to you and her, as I own they do to me. I hope she will follow her inclination; as her company is the sincerest pleasure to me, no consideration could have made me decline it, but my Regard for her Health and Convenience.

'I am, with very great Regard,
'Your affectionate Humble Servant,
'M. W. BUTE.'

and it was hinted that he had probably become a Papist from having passed so much of his time abroad.

'During the whole course ... Mr. Ponsonby ... the Duke of Leinster ... and the patriots gave all possible opposition. ... For the first four months the House of Commons ... very frequently sat several hours after midnight Scarcely a day passed without an attack upon the Castle.'[1]

But Macartney maintained an imperturbable calm under this constant hailstorm of abuse and reprobation. To violent speeches he returned good-tempered and well-reasoned replies, and opposed the numerous absurd propositions with invariable good-humour, spirit, and firmness.[2]

The Undertakers soon found that they were losing influence in proportion as the Government for the first time broke down their power, and regained its authority. As a consequence of the change, various wise and salutary measures were carried through, and the finances of the kingdom retrieved, and placed upon a better footing.

[1] Sir George Macartney, 'An Account of Ireland.'
[2] '... During the sessions he acquitted himself with great credit in the different speeches which he made, and in every other respect, his conduct and behaviour were such as proved him to be a very judicious knowing man, and perfectly the man of business.'— Letter from Lord Townshend to Lord North (J. Barrow, 'Life of Earl Macartney).

CHAPTER IV

DURING his term of office in Ireland Macartney received many letters from friends in England. A small selection from the most interesting of those preserved is given here:

From Mr. T. Allen to Sir George Macartney.

'LONDON,
'December, 1769.

'DEAR SIR,
'I was yesterday at Court, where the conversation of the day ran upon the state of matters in Ireland, our rejecting the money bill sent from here, and adopting another. I explained this to as many and as often as I could, but of my hearers, or rather inquirers, at least two-thirds remained as uninformed as before.... I dine to-day with Mr. Rigby, where I am to meet Lord Weymouth. I write this before I go, for I should not be very fit to write after.
'Your most obedient, hm^{be} servant,
'T. ALLEN.'[1]

From Mr. T. Allen to Sir George Macartney.

'December, 1769.

'... In the evening after my return from Lord North's, I found a letter from Ireland with the particulars of the debate, but no explanations.... In this uncertainty I was called on to attend the Cabinet Council.... The news of the city to-day is that the French Ambassador, who has left Berlin, had, whilst there, been endeavouring to create disturbances at Petersburg. That the French are wanting to raise a hundred million by a lottery, and the Spaniards

[1] Mr. Allen was a member of the Irish House of Commons, and a man of property.

raising money by annuities at nine per cent. The Bill of Rights men have lost carrying an alderman, and are rather down. Four Dutch mails last night enlivened us a little. The Princess of Orange got the small-pox; the Princess of Dessau dead. The general rendezvous of the Russian fleet to be at Leghorn; the two Orloffs are at Pisa, and are to have the direction of the Russian operations.'

From Mr. T. Allen to Sir George Macartney.

'*January*, 1770.

'... The conversation of the town is taken up with a speech of Sir George Saville's on Wednesday, totally unexpected, and from what motive people are at a loss to find out. He began by making a short preface, then said that if a steward concealed from his master the true state of his affairs, the world, when informed of it, must declare him to be knave. But if he did more than this, and represented the situation of his affairs to be in a prosperous, when they were really in a ruinous, condition, he would be deemed a still greater knave.... That to call that House corrupt and misrepresenting would but ill become that decency of character he had ever striven to support. But to say that the House of Commons in which he then stood had betrayed the Important Trust committed to their care by their constituents was a fact that he dared to affirm, and would with his latest moments support. He then sat down. The House were in amazement for some time; no one offered to speak. At last Mr. Jenkinson got up, spoke very favourably of Sir George—uncorruptible, his great property, connections, amiable publick and private character—and apologizing for the Indecency of the charge against the House as the effect of warmth and zeal for his country, promised himself that upon reflecting he would explain himself to the satisfaction of the House. Charles Fox then rose, and did not treat him in that style, but plainly said he supposed the honourable gentleman wished to add to his popularity by being sent to the Tower. Mr. Burke and General Conway spoke palliating, and tending to soften what Sir George had said. He heard them all very patiently, then got up and said "... that while he lived he would maintain that the present House of Commons had betrayed," etc.

'The House continued some time in confusion, and then adjourned, and next day, when they came to consider what was to be done, they found they could do nothing.'

MR. WILKES

From Mr. T. Allen to Sir George Macartney.

'LONDON,
'*February*, 1770.

'... Lord North gains ground daily; the Opposition give it up for this Session. To-morrow the Committee on the state of the nation sit again.... The only news we have, the French have stopt payment of the Interest of all their Extra Funds to the amount of about twelve millions, which has occasioned great Bankruptcies in Holland; several expected here.... The gentlemen of the London Tavern are out of humour with Mr. Wilkes. It seems they had desired a list of his debts, which he sent, amounting to sixteen thousand pounds, which they have paid or compounded for; when they expected he would be ready to make his appearance abroad, he has sent them a list of seventeen thousand pounds more.[1] ... My Lord North spoke to me at Court on Sunday, and told me he was determined as soon as the hurry of the Session was over to make a close Inspection into the Revenue of Ireland, and to put it on a proper footing.'

From Mr. T. Allen to Sir George Macartney.

'LONDON,
'*March* 6, 1770.

'... I find from the active part I took that I am not so well received at some places as I was before, but it gives me no concern.... The debate on American Affairs opened yesterday by reading a Petition from the Merchants of London, praying a repeal of the last Acts taxing America Lord North opened by stating the situation of the different provinces, showing that the Combinations against the

[1] John Wilkes, an alderman of London, noted for the violence of his political conduct, was imprisoned for the publication of a libel, and then outlawed. In 1768 he returned from France, as he had been elected M.P. for Middlesex, but was prevented from taking his seat and committed to the King's Bench prison, which occasioned serious riots in St. George's Fields. He was four times re-elected for Middlesex, but still kept in prison. His friends and admirers raised a large subscription to pay his debts. In 1774 he was chosen Lord Mayor of London, and about the same time again elected for Middlesex. This time he was permitted to take his seat without further opposition.

Importation of British Commodities was nearly at an end, that they had quarrelled among themselves, those of New York accusing the Bostonians of breaking the agreement. . . . General Mackay gave an account how he found affairs when he commanded at Boston. . . . In his detail he happened to say that had Mr. Grenville known as much of America as he did, he never would have attempted the Stamp Act. This called up Mr. Grenville, who vindicated himself, and did not speak long, but extremely well. General Conway then rose and attacked Mr. Grenville . . . he was answered by Mr. Wedderburn, who mauled him without mercy. . . . The Livery met to-day to agree on a Remonstrance, when they were all of one side, as out of the twenty-six Aldermen, there was only the Lord Mayor, Sir W. Stephenson, Alderman Trecathick, and the two Sheriffs. . . . The Sheriffs are to go to Court to know when the King will be attended.'

From Mr. T. Allen to Sir George Macartney.

'LONDON,
'*March*, 1770.

'. . . We have no news here but the Remonstrance,[1] which puzzles both Court and City, and will end in nothing. There was very high words in the House on Thursday between Mr. Ed. Burke and Mr. Rigby on the Carmarthen election, exceedingly gross on both sides; the former in better language, the latter very plain, said he was a scoundrel, and had been kicked downstairs. The House and Speaker interfered, and Mr. Rigby was ordered first to explain himself, which it seems implies that he was most in fault. I was not there, and cannot give you rightly what passed. . . . It is now said the Opposition will not take any notice of what has passed in Ireland this winter. . . . To-morrow the Sheriffs go to St. James' with their Remonstrance, and I suppose will be attended by all the Black Guards in Town, and probably a riot. I enclose you a note from an old Temple Acquaintance of yours. If you are inclined to subscribe to his Matrimonial Letters, it will be kindly received.'

[1] *Petition to the King for the Dissolution of Parliament.*—' There is a time when it is clearly demonstrable that men cease to be representatives. That time has now arrived. The House of Commons do not represent the people.'—Green's ' History of the English People.'

THE KING'S REPLY

From Mr. T. Allen to Sir George Macartney.

'LONDON,
'*March* 14, 1770.

'... The Lord Mayor with only two Aldermen, the two Sheriffs, and a parcel of the Livery, who made a very shabby appearance, were this day at St. James's, and presented their Memorial or Remonstrance.

'The King received them on his Throne. His answer, which was delivered with great precision and dignity, was distinctly heard in every part of the Room, to this effect. That he was ever open to hear the complaints of his subjects, but that he looked on this Remonstrance as disrespectful to himself, injurious to his Parliament, and not agreeable to the Constitution of this Country, which he had ever made his study to maintain, and had no doubt he would be supported in, by his subjects.

'The Remonstrance, which was very badly read, is almost word for word the same as in the papers, and is said to be disapproved by Lord Rockingham. They kissed the King's hand, and went off not quite satisfied with their reception.'

From Mr. T. Allen to Sir George Macartney.

'LONDON,
'*April*, 1770.

'... Reports have been spread here of a difference between his Excellency and you. ... Every day brings some new plague to Ministry. The riot at Boston is now the subject of conversation; by the fairest accounts the soldiery were not to blame. ... Sir Jos. Mawbey said in the House that it was Mr. Wilkes' intention to come and demand his seat.'

From Mr. T. Allen to Sir George Macartney.

'LONDON,
'*May*, 1770.

'... I wrote you a few lines on Tuesday. I mentioned in a former letter the report that had been spread here of a difference between his Excellency and you. I took a great deal of pains to trace from whence it took its rise, and have found it arose from a letter wrote by a man who lives at Broomfield, near Luttrell's Town, to a Mr. Chamberlayne here. I am exceedingly happy it is without foundation; it was first mentioned to me by Lady Townshend. Your intention of being in the North with Lady Jane, which she had heard of at Lady Bute's, confirmed her.... Lord North is exceedingly polite to me, sees me whenever I call, which is very seldom.... Lord Chatham moved his resolution to-day in the House of Lords that the King's answer to the City Remonstrance was Unconstitutional, and highly improper to be given to an address directed to the Father of his people, able and ready to hear and redress the grievances of his subjects.... I dined to-day with Lord Halifax at Hampton Greene, where Sir George Osborn came and brought us the news of the King of Prussia's death; how true I will not pretend to say.

'There were two gentlemen just arrived from Boston, where affairs are in a very critical situation.... Lord Holland is expected about the 20th. The town have strange stories about Mr. Stephen, that he has raised very large sums payable on his father's death.... I am exceedingly happy at your intention of being here, and most heartily wish you were here now, as Lord North has directed me to attend him ... on Irish business.... You will find things in another sort of situation than when you left this. A steady attention to business, a punctuality whenever promised. It is really unconceivable the number of friends Lord North has made among the Opposition.

'The citizens went up to-day with the address on the birth of the Princess.[1] At Temple Bar the mob let the Lord Mayor's coach pass, then shut the gates, and attacked Mr. Hartley, and forced him out of his Chariot into an Ale-House, happy in saving his life; and the two patriotic Sheriffs quietly looking on, without attempting to protect him or to seize any of the mob.'

From Mr. T. Allen to Sir George Macartney.

'December, 1770.

'... The plain fact I believe to be Ministry would wish to avoid meeting the Irish Parliament.... Your idea of the matter may be a just one; they never think of us but when drove to it by dire necessity.... About a fortnight ago Mr. Bradshaw sent for me late of a Sunday night.... After some conversation ... he begged I would tell him if

[1] The Princess Elizabeth, third daughter of George III.

SCENE IN THE HOUSE OF LORDS

you were not on bad terms with Lord T. . . . I replied that from a residence of two months . . . with his Excellency and you, I could with safety say you were not on bad terms with Lord T. ; that you had given most constant attendance. . . . Lord T. was, and wished to be understood, his own Minister. . . .

'. . . I have got some India pickles, which I am told are very good. I have sent a Box directed for his Excellency, and in it a jar of mangoes, and another of Bamboos for you. . . . Since writing so far I am come from a most extraordinary scene in the House of Lords. . . . It was on a motion of Lord Gower's to clear the House of all strangers, members of the House of Commons included. Lord Chatham and the Duke of Richmond endeavoured to speak on it, but could not be heard by the cry of " Clear the House !" After a noise for a full half hour, Lord Chatham and fifteen or sixteen more Lords of the minority walked out of the House and left us, are to protest and the Lord knows what. The most compleat riot you ever saw.'

From Mr. T. Allen to Sir George Macartney.

'*December*, 1770.

'. . . On Sunday night there was a Cabinet on Irish affairs, at which I was ordered to attend. . . . Lord Rochford sent for me in the morning, and kept me about two hours. . . . His chief secretary is the proudest, most disagreeable man I ever had to do with. From Lord Rochford's I went to Lord North. . . . He spoke of your desire to go to Spain, and added he believed a man of the first rank here must be sent. Spoke of you with much respect, and said he knew nowhere so profitable for you as your present situation, and appeared surprised when I told him there was not a sixpence to be saved in it.'

From Mr. T. Allen to Sir George Macartney.

'*January*, 1771.

'I have yours of the 12th inst. I am sorry to say it, but it does not give me pleasure. I most sincerely wish things were on another footing between you and his Excellency. I am convinced every endeavour of yours will be exerted for the publick service. We shall want them all. . . . We do hear much talk of the starving condition of the manufacturers in Ireland, where your Patriots are as absurd as they are here. . . . The City is dissatisfied with the terms agreed to with Spain. Stocks have rose considerably by orders from Holland.'

From Mr. T. Allen to Sir George Macartney.

'*April*, 1771.

'. . . I went to Court last Wednesday with Lord Rochford, and was presented to His Majesty, who very graciously asked me several questions relative to Ireland. . . . There was a report that Lord North intended resigning; the reason given that he had not been consulted on the arrangements made for the Prince of Wales. No truth in it. . . . The only news we have is the French Ambassador's Secretary is a lame duck, and has taken in . . . several in the city. The Ambassador suspected his secretary was a jobber, and drew him in by giving him false information. . . . I stated your situation, and difficulties you had about engaging another session to Lord Rochford. . . . I think you are deficient to yourself if you do not make a trip over here as soon as our session is over. . . . Everything in the city as quiet as possible. Even the Executions on Tower Hill hardly draw a mob together.'

From Mr. John Campbell to Sir George Macartney.

'LONDON,
'*October*, 1769.

'. . . Here we are on this side the water in the same state of tumult and confusion that you left us. . . . Saturday last was the birthday of the Grand Incendiary, which was properly distinguished by bonfires, illuminations, and ringing of bells, particularly in the City. All possible methods are used to keep up popular disaffection. . . . In my own opinion, we are still sound at heart, and . . . I think . . . may have rational hopes, that we shall see these popular storms subdued. . . . Faction has indeed triumphed . . . but that a moonshine Opposition should get the better of King, Lords, and Commons, in a country the inhabitants of which are allowed to have common sense is beyond my comprehension. . . .

'The great source of all our disorders is what we, very

THE LIBERTY OF THE PRESS

falsely, call the Liberty of the Press. A liberty never indulged till now, and . . . upon very false Pinciples. *Vox Populi Vox Dei* makes this species of madness now thought sacred, and yet I am old enough to remember a poor Printer's Boy (one John Shephard) who for printing a Pamphlet with this title was hanged, drawn, and quartered at Tyburn. . . . The Earl of B. [Bute] has been very much indisposed to my very great Grief. I made constant enquiries, as was my Duty, till he went to Luton. I dined with Lord Holland the Day before he left England; his Health was better than his Temper, harassed with Mischief, Foreign and Domestick, and not having Lady Holland with him, he was excusably peevish. The treatment he has received is abominable, and upon my Word I think I feel it as much as he. . . . The Duty and Affection of all this family wait upon you, and that likeness of her Father, Lady Jane. Mrs. Campbell has a great opinion of your good Fortune, and begs you will send her a single ticket in the Irish Lottery. The Russians have succeeded to my wish; the Ottoman Empire have received a Blow they will never recover. The first Grand Vizier, who was a wise man, would have saved the Empire, if they would have let him, but they have disgarnished his shoulders of a Head, the best furnished in their Dominions.'

From Mr. John Campbell to Sir George Macartney.

'LONDON,
'*November*, 1769.

'. . . People affect to be very doubtful in respect to the Existence of the present Parliament. The Minister is reserved, and that is the tone. Like my Lord Oxford's Porter, they can't so much as tell you what it is O'clock for Fear of betraying a secret of State. . . . There are not four counties in the Kingdom that sincerely desire a Dissolution. In Norfolk, Sir Edward Astley, attended by his friends, galloped from one Races to another, in order to propose a Petition. But he always met with a Devil in the shape of black Charles Townshend with a stronger squadron. At length a friend of his told him, "Sir Edward, you spent some thousands to get in for the County of Norfolk, and you had but a scrimp majority. In case of a Dissolution you must think of some other Place, for I assure you myself and many of my Friends will never vote for you again."

This for the honour of that County; if the same spirit had been shown elsewhere, the Royal Eyes had never been insulted with the Subscriptions of Grooms and Ostlers in the Guise of Freeholders.... I will tell you (I hope without offence) what People say is the state of things on your side of the Water; which is that His Excellency has not been well or wisely dealt with here. It is said that if he had had the necessary Powers when he asked them, the forming a factious Opposition might have been prevented. It is also said that they are now granted when too late. But I hope not.... The language of the Populace is much in the same Tone, though a little louder than when you left us. The City Monarch had as much of this as he could desire, but it was a little embittered by the conduct of the Magnates and the Magi of London. For, except Stephenson, not one of the Aldermen above the Chair, and none of the City Law Officers assisted; so that in fact his mob not only accompanied him to, but at Dinner, which his Pride could not help feeling, and which with all his natural insolence he could not conceal. The Entertainment added to the Play at the Guildhall was truly ridiculous. Shuter the Comedian, overheated with Wine and Politicks, threw a bottle at a Gentleman's Head, which Compliment was returned, and in a short space of Time there was a very regular Engagement in which several Persons were wounded, Clothes spoiled, Ladies treated with the greatest indecency, and what you cannot but think very extraordinary, tho' at the same time it is strictly true, there were some Persons actually robbed.

'The famous Trial against the Earl of Halifax came on last Friday, when there was such a Display of modern Liberty, that the worthy Chief Justice threatened to adjourn the Court. At length a verdict was found for £4,000 Damages, and perhaps very wisely; for large as this Sum may appear, it was so far from giving satisfaction to the Mob, that the Jury were glad to escape with their lives.... All this for the Honour of the Liberty of the Press and as a full Proof of the Freedom of our Courts of Justice has been published with Triumph in the Newspapers.... I have heard this Day by a letter from Lady Holland that the life of Lady Cecilia was not expected for more than a few hours. But notwithstanding this my Lord Holland is not likely to return before April.'

From Mr. John Campbell to Sir George Macartney.

'LONDON,
'*December,* 1769.

'. . . I have received your acceptable Favour with the tickets enclosed. . . . I cannot but wonder that the people of Ireland seldom form a just opinion of their Lord Lieutenants till they have lost them; and then they are very ready to deplore the Indignities they have offered them, and drink their Healths in Token of Repentance. . . . If, instead of this, they made it a Point to treat their Lord Lieutenants with rather more complacency, they would establish a Number of respectable and useful Friends in the Court and Council of Britain. . . . Instead of this they seem studious to make those who have gone through this great office either indifferent or indignant.

'The present L. Lᵗ. is most undoubtedly a Person of whom they may make as much advantage as of any that ever was sent them. He is a man (unless he is much changed) of an open, flowing, generous Disposition, ready to do anything that can reasonably be asked. . . . At all times it is in the Power of the People of Ireland to pursue a Conduct, that would effectually recommend them to the Government of Great Britain. . . . But what they are to get by crossing, embarrassing, and perplexing Government I confess I am at a loss to learn. . . . At this juncture they have a peculiar . . . circumstance in their favour. . . . We are overrun with Faction here. It is a Truth that cannot be concealed. This then is the Time for the People on your side . . . to express their good sense . . . their . . . Patriotism . . . and their political Abilities by the steadiness of their Loyalty. . . . This would secure the Favour . . . of Government . . . and be a sure Path to all they reasonably desire. For what, in our circumstances, could be refused to so just and prudent a conduct ? I do not know how far you relish these kind of hints, but I know from your Regard to me will forgive them. Things have an untoward Aspect at present, but they will mend if you will have Patience, for nothing is lost to Men who do not lose their Temper.'

The following extracts are from letters from Mr. J. C. King, a clergyman, whose acquaintance Macartney made in Russia. In the autumn of 1770 he came to London, being extremely anxious to publish a book on the Greek Church, with an account of its Rites and Ceremonies, and also, if possible, to find employment in England.

'*November*, 1770.

'... I ... pleased myself with the hope of seeing you in England by this time, but hearing that Lady Jane is some time since returned to Ireland, I fear that hope must be given up. I know not what to do without seeing you. ... I want your opinion of the book you made me write. ... I would gladly come over to you for a fortnight or three weeks ... therefore if you will permit me I will ... make you a visit at Dublin. ...

'... I am astonished to learn how very few persons in administration understand the affairs of the North, and how little pains they take to be informed of them. I was recommended by Lord Cathcart,[1] as knowing a little of these matters, and yet scarcely one man has thought it worth while to ask me a single question. ...

'... I see Mr. Shirley sometimes ... he is really clever, and gave great application to business when with Lord Cathcart, who kept him to it. I suppose you know the real reason of his leaving, as the ostensible one is seldom the real: but as it is nothing which makes against him, I'll tell it you. It was on account of Miss C., who is a fine bouncing lass of sixteen or seventeen, and from constitution naturally fell in love at that age, and having no other object, fixed her affections on him. He was not to be blamed for that, and indeed L^d. and Ly. Cathcart conducted the affair with the greatest prudence; for I believe they never let either of them know their sentiments.

'I have got a pair of earrings of the Great Stone, which I intend to beg Lady Jane to do me the honour to accept, when she comes to London. I mean the great stone on which Falconet's statue is to be placed.[2] ... It is ... arrived at St. Petersburg: the Empress had earrings made of it for herself, and gave a pair to Lady Cathcart, and, if I mistake not, to the Queen.'

[1] British Ambassador at St. Petersburg.
[2] The celebrated monument to Peter the Great, by the French sculptor Falconet. It stands close to the Neva, being mounted on an enormous block of granite, the transportation of which to St. Petersburg was then a great feat of engineering.

From Mr. J. C. King to Sir George Macartney.

'*January*, 1771.

'... I have great hopes of getting tolerably through the subscription [to the book]. A great many persons of fashion, particularly Lady Sussex and Lady Frances Coningsby, have been so obliging as to promise to help this poor bantling into life; for as they have heard the Empress read part of it, they think it will be a ladies' book. I long to see you.... If you had not forbidden me, I should have been tempted to make you a visit in Ireland... tho' I assure you I should have thought myself well repaid if... only to take an early morning's walk with you.... I this morning waited upon Mr. Ed. Burke; he asked me if I was much acquainted with you in Russia. He said you was his intimate friend, and spoke of you as every one does who knows your talents and abilities....

'... You once said you would... find out a patron for my work ... do you think I might offer it to Lord North? ...'

From Mr. J. C. King to Sir G. Macartney.

'*February*, 1771.

'... I must tell you the Princess Dashkoff, who presented me at Spa to all the English of distinction as a man of genius and erudition beloved and esteemed by everybody in her country, when she came to London blackened me all in her power, and said ... that I was *l'homme le plus perfide, et que je passe à Petersbourg pour le plus grand menteur*, etc.— you know her character, and talents to speak ill; and tho' every one despises and detests her, yet I am afraid and have reason to fear what she said has made some impression on the minds of several persons, particularly on the Bp. of P——, with whom she was much acquainted; for tho' he is civil, he is not friendly. It seems the cause of Madam's resentment, and the reason why she calls me *un menteur*, is, that she had heard at Spa that I had said some truths which offended her, or were made offensive by the Lady, a country woman of yours, as I suspect, who repeated, or rather misrepresented, what I said. I assure you I was very cautious on that subject; but while one thought she was banished, others that she was a spy, and all were questioning me, I was necessitated to say something; yet from her civilities to me there, I was disposed to speak as favourably as possible. However, the thing was, as I apprehended, Prince Lobhowitz, the Imperial Minister, happened to be at Spa at the same time, and as you know, he is not very cautious or delicate in his terms. Half what he said has been fathered upon me: for she did me the honour to join his name and mine together in her abuse; of which I have written this post to acquaint him.

'I have thought of taking my Doctor's degree either in Divinity or Laws; perhaps it will give some persons a better opinion of my work.'

'... Dining the other day at your friend Mrs. Greville's,[1] she told me ... that you were seeking a country house, and would not come to England this summer.... If it is true, pray let me know. ... I took my Doctor's degree in Divinity at Oxford ... as the University of Cambridge made difficulties I thought ridiculous.'

'*October*, 1771.

'... I am extremely obliged ... for ... your letter, with one enclosed to Lord Rochford. ... Last Saty. I had the favour of a note from him to let me know that the King was graciously pleased to permit me to dedicate my book to His Majesty.'

'*January*, 1772.

'... I finished the dedication ... and last week presented it to the King at the Levée, and yesterday to Her Majesty at the Drawing-room. I had the honour to be very graciously received by both, very graciously indeed by the Queen, who asked many questions about Russia and my situation there.... The book[2] is to be presented to H. R. H. the P. Dowager of Wales, and to the Princess of Brunswick. To the former by Lord Boston, for the Princess D. sees nobody; but whether or no I am to carry it to the latter I don't yet know.

'Have I no chance of seeing you in England before I return to Russia in April? ... but be assured as long as I live, wherever I am and whatever I am, I shall always love and esteem you. Adieu, Adieu, Dear Sir.'

[1] Frances Macartney, cousin of Lord Macartney, was wife of Fulke Greville, Envoy Extraordinary to the Elector of Bavaria. Mrs. Greville was mother of the beautiful Mrs. Crewe, and wrote poems, being the authoress of the 'Ode to Indifference.'

[2] 'The Rites and Ceremonies of the Greek Church in Russia.' Still regarded as a standard work upon the subject.

THE QUEEN OF DENMARK

From Mr. R. Wilmot to Sir George Macartney.

'ST. JAMES'S, 1772.

'... News came yesterday morning of a revolution in Denmark. I mean with respect to Parkes. The Queen has of late had the power. The King has now recovered it. The Doctor, I suppose, is executed before this time, and Her Majesty in prison.[1] St. James's is in great trouble about it. It comes at an unseasonable time. The Princess Dowager will read all the papers. His Majesty, being apprehensive that the affair might be inserted in a disagreeable manner, was so humane as to make a visit to his Mother with the Queen (which prevented the levée, and caused a little alarm) in order to break this unlucky event to Her Royal Highness as easily as possible.[2] You may imagine that His Majesty's thoughts are pretty much taken up at present.'

From Mr. R. Wilmot to Sir George Macartney.

'*February*, 1772.

'There is more secrecy observed with respect to the Danish affairs than I ever remember in any other case. I have, however, made all proper enquiry after Count Osten, who was esteemed a friend of Struensee, and if he has not found it necessary to temporize and turn about. He is in all probability involved in his ruin, at least under disgrace. ... The marriage bill has gone through the Lords, much to the satisfaction of the Queen's House.'

[1] Queen Caroline Matilda, youngest sister of George III., was married in 1766 to Christian VII. of Denmark and Norway. Her marriage was a very unhappy one, and in 1769 one Struensee, a doctor, obtained a great influence over her. The Queen and Struensee ruled the kingdom for two years, the King being in a state of semi-imbecility. Their power came to an end in 1771; Struensee was beheaded, and Queen Caroline Matilda, after five months' captivity in the fortress of Kronborg, was sent to Celle, in her brother's territory, where she died in May, 1775, aged twenty-three. Great efforts were made by the English Court to suppress as far as possible all public scandal and gossip about the matter.

[2] There seems no doubt that this sad tragedy and scandal hastened the end of the Princess Dowager of Wales.

From Mr. R. Wilmot to Sir George Macartney.

'*March*, 1772.

' My Lord Townshend has carried his point surprisingly ... and much for his own honour as well as for the benefit and credit of government. His Excy. stands in the highest estimation on this side for his conduct, and every body agrees that you have done your part.'

From Mr. R. Wilmot to Sir George Macartney.

'*May*, 1772.

' The Queen of Denmark is to be at a Hunting Box of the King's, not far from Hanover, is to be served as a Queen, and to have one lady of the Bedchamber.'

By the Irish in general Macartney was, on the whole, greatly esteemed, and though frequently obliged to disappoint many of their expectations, usually contrived to dismiss them in good-humour. On his part, he had a true regard for the country of his birth and education, and towards the close of his term of office remarked in one of his speeches :

' If I have merited the approbation of my countrymen, I shall rejoice not only as a servant of the Government, ... but as an Irishman, as a man who thinks it an honour to have been born among you, ... and who has a heart that feels warmly for the interests and liberties of his country. May she be happy ! .... But to be happy she must listen to the voice of moderation and take wisdom for her guide ; and the paths of wisdom are the paths of peace.'

In 1772 Macartney's office in Ireland came to an end. In the June of that year he was made Knight Companion of the Bath, and installed, by proxy, at Westminster on the 15th of that month.

It had hitherto been usual to make provision for the Chief Secretary of Ireland on the resignation of his office. The appointment of Muster-Master General was the only one then vacant which would have been at all suitable

MRS. BALAQUIER

SISTER TO LORD MACARTNEY

From the Portrait in the possession of C. G. MACARTNEY, ESQ.

for Sir George to accept; but he gave it up, in order to accommodate the Lord-Lieutenant.[1]

In 1774 he was, however, made Governor and Constable of Toome Castle, with a nominal salary of £1,300 a year. This he disposed of in order to pay off some of his debts.

The next twelve months appear to have been spent by Macartney in comparative quiet, and he busied himself with drawing up his accounts of Ireland and Russia.

Lord Townshend, who had taken to dissipated habits,[2] was for that, combined with political reasons, recalled to England in 1772, and Lord Harcourt appointed to succeed him.

The following extracts are from letters from the permanent official at the castle, previously mentioned, and give an account of the arrival of the latter and the handing over of the Sword of State:

From Mr. Waite to Sir George Macartney.

'DUBLIN CASTLE,
'*September*, 1772.

'... I hope this will find you and Lady Jane arrived safely in London.... I do not hear that his Excy has lately received any intimation from the Secretary of State when the yacht is to be at Holyhead to receive Lord Harcourt; but it is understood that his Lordship means to be here on the 20th of next month.... You are out of conceit with your adventures in this Kingdom, and all things considered, I do not wonder you should complain. But you are now on the road that leads to

[1] 'The conduct of Sir George Macartney is very meritorious; I am sure it must appear so to the King. He will never want an advocate there whilst your humble servant is able to bear to his merit the testimony which is due to it.'—Extract of a letter from Lord North to Lord Townshend, April, 1772 (J. Barrow, 'Life of Earl Macartney').

[2] 'My Lord is most happily engaged with everything but business, which of course takes its own progress. There is a hope spread thro' the people that you are not about to desert us utterly.'—From the unpublished correspondence.

fortune, and be assured that your campaign here will exceedingly help you on your way. The first time you rise to speak in the English House of Commons you will feel yourself stronger upon your legs than you ever was before in that place, owing to your practice and experience in Ireland. . . . My Lord L⁺ says He is glad that He is so soon to leave us, but I do not believe him, and it is said about Town that his acquaintance with Miss Anna Montgomery[1] will make him cast many a longing lingering Look behind.'

From Mr. Waite to Sir George Macartney.

'November 30, 1772.

'. . . Lord Harcourt embarked on board the yacht at Holyhead last Saty night, and after a most tempestuous passage . . . arrived in this Harbour about 2 o'clock this morning. His Lordship, Col. Blaquière,[2] etc., landed about four at the Pigeon House and *walked* from thence to the Castle, where they arrived safe and in good health about seven. His Lordship was sworn in council about three this afternoon, and then received the Sword of State from Lord Townshend, who behaved with the utmost propriety. You would have been exceedingly pleased with his behaviour. . . . Your Emoluments and Privileges as Secretary cease this day.'

The following letter, from another friend, gives a more detailed account of the arrival of Lord Harcourt :

'December 2, 1772.

'. . . Last Monday morning about two o'clock, Lord Harcourt arrived in the Bay, landed at Kingsend about four, and left that about six o'clock, and walked up to the Castle, where He arrived at seven. He sent on his arrival for a Coach and Pair of Horses, but a doubt arising with Mercer whether he could actually be a L. L. without approaching in State, they debated the point so long that his Lordship appeared walking through the Castle yard by the light of a lanthorn before the carriage set off. At two o'clock in the afternoon Lord

[1] Lord Townshend married his second wife, Anne, daughter of S. W. Montgomery, M.P. for Ballinahill, on May 19, 1773.
[2] Lord Harcourt's Irish Secretary.

Townshend went into his levee, and being seated in the Chair of State, Lord H. was introduced, and presenting His patent, the two Viceroys withdrew, with all present, to the Council Chamber, where Lord T. sitting and Lord H. standing, the patent was read with the power to the Primate to administer the oath. Lord H. being then sworn, the Sec. of State read the King's letter directing Lord T. to deliver up the Sword of State, as being the Ensign of Government: which being done Lord T. returned to the Levee Room with all who were not of the Privy Council, and Lord H. with the Priv. Councillors followed soon after, when we were all presented. Lord Kildare . . . Sir Lucius O'Bryen and others in the opposition were present. . . . Lord Townshend is to live at the Castle whilst He remains in the Kingdom, and neither Lord Harcourt nor He will accept an invitation until his departure.'

December 14, 1772.

'. . . Lord Townshend embarked on Friday last. He was attended to the boat's side by Lord Harcourt with all the honours belonging to a Lord Lieutenant's grand Procession. He received as great marks of applause from the People as I have ever known given to any man in Station, however looked up to for popularity. . . . May peaceful and happy days for the remainder of his life recompense him for the difficulties and miseries of his arduous Administration. . . . Lord Harcourt received me very politely. . . . I sate also with Col. Blaquière, and found him extremely pleasant as well as vastly civil.'

Regarding the recall of Lord Townshend and appointment of Lord Harcourt, Macartney wrote as follows:

'A strange fatality seems to have attended most of Lord North's measures. If he stumbles on a good one it is soon defeated by the next that follows. The dismissal of Lord Townshend was certainly a wise, indeed a necessary, measure. Neither the spirit of the people nor the interest of the Crown could any longer bear such caprice, absurdity, and wildness. But the appointment of his successor was as injudicious as the other was prudent. The merit of T.'s recall was destroyed by the nomination of H. This poor old gentleman, whose reigning passions are to be thought descended from a grand Norman family, to look like an old French militaire, to live long in an Hotel . . . and to die rich, was unfortunately appointed to the Government of a country which was formerly easy enough to govern, but which is now become almost impossible to manage. His assistant a person of low birth, of a garrison education, of mean abilities and extravagant presumptions. . . .'

On his part Lord Townshend appears to have always entertained a real respect and friendship for his one-time Secretary. Many years later he was the friend who induced the King to interpose his authority in the affair of the duel between Macartney and General Stuart, which took place in consequence of the conduct of the latter while in India.

There is an amusing comment of admiration, by Lord Townshend, on the back of a letter drawn up by Macartney, addressed to a man named Armstrong, who had offered his support to the Lord-Lieutenant on condition that a friend of his received promotion. Macartney forwarded the draft, and wrote on the back of it:

'If the enclosed sketch . . . is such as you think proper, your Excellency will please to write *Probatum* underneath and return it to me, as no time ought to be lost.'

Lord Townshend wrote:

'*Probatum*, and I wish to God I had learnt how to say half so much to a man who says nothing.—T.'

Extract from a Letter from Lord Townshend to Sir G. Macartney.

'DUBLIN CASTLE,
'*October* 21, 1772.

'. . . Ld Harcourt will I hope be here soon to relieve me from . . . an endless thankless task wherein I most devoutly wish he may find more ease and gratitude than I have. I am . . . at this moment . . . like a wreck on the coast which is supposed to have some kegs of brandy on board, assailed every moment and trampled by a most rapacious crew. We have had nothing but challenges and rencontres in the streets lately, and mobs following the combatants about every public place. Daly . . . extricated himself well from a very complete rascal and bully, and left a huge mark of a cudgel on his front. Arthur Browne challenged the same man again, but he has proved shy, so it is hoped the tempest will subside among the Galileans.'

Macartney spent part of the summer of 1773 in the North of Ireland. His Dublin correspondents, at this time, differed in their opinions regarding his successor in office, some entertaining a favourable estimate of him, and others not.

From Mr. Waite to Sir George Macartney.

'*June*, 1773.

'. . . Your faithful commissioner Waller inform'd me yesterday morning of your arrival at Lissanoure, where I hope this will find you and Lady Jane in perfect Health and spirits. . . . The state of things here is very alarming and distressful. The Revenue is so much fallen that for some months past, they have had enough to do at the Treasury to pay the monthly subsistence of the Army. If the Judges have received their Quarter's Salary due last Xmas, it is within a Fortnight only. . . . You told me . . . you believ'd Col. Blaquière would do vastly well in his new employment. Every day evinces the justice of your observation. . . . We expect to have a busy winter. Great denunciations are made against "the tyrant Townshend," as he is called. A thousand enquiries are to be made into the Distribution of the Revenue under his Administration, and He is to be censured until he is all over black and blue. But amidst the Changes and Chances of this mortal life, don't be surprised if before the winter is over you should hear him toasted as the only patriot Lord Lieutenant since the days of Lord Chesterfield. . . . Miss Montgomery is to be married to Mr. Gardiner next Monday.'

COLONEL BLAQUIÈRE

From Mr. Waite to Sir George Macartney.

'DUBLIN CASTLE,
'*October*, 1773.

'... This day sen'night the campaign opens, and I hear of many horrid denunciations against Lord Townshend and his measures. With regard to Lord Harcourt, there seems to be as favourable a disposition towards him, as his Friends could wish, but you know that the weather in this climate is so uncertain that in the Winter we are never sure of sunshine for an Hour. The Duke of Leinster is come to town extremely out of order with a Dropsical complaint, and your friend the Provost is obliged to flee for life to a warm climate.... I hope we have established ourselves perfectly with Lady Jane, as Stables has sent off the Pickles and blue by a carrier ... also two pieces of Cheese, the one Cheshire the other double Gloster.... I am much pleased that you like the Grey Horse.... I am of opinion he is cheap. I hope when you become used to him you will not find his shyness ... inconvenient.'[1]

From another Correspondent.

'... You never knew a man so detested by all parties as your successor. You had political enemies but no real natural ones, and your conduct to men is now contrasted to his misbehaviour.'

' B. [Col. Blaquière] is sole governour of Ireland, and his influence is absolute and he feels his consequence. He is as great an adventurer as the Duke de Ripperda; his head is full of schemes. He paid addresses to a girl of sixteen with an estate of £1,200 per an., and he flattered himself she was as much in love with him as his Master is. But she, after being countenanced at the Castle and taken much notice of for his sake, gave him a short and peremptory denial as to an old battered weather-beaten coxcomb. It is not to be expressed how exceedingly obnoxious B. is to all ranks.... Men of birth and fortune can't brook being sent to him by the Chief Governor, who defers all to him, and then to be treated as inferiors.... I speculate that it will not be long before you ... will grow tired of your retreat. You are no more calculated for the raw unripened meridian of the North, than a sunflower is for the shade.'

[1] On leaving Ireland in 1772, Macartney had sold his horses at a great loss.

From another Correspondent.

'*March*, 1773.

'... Lord H. acts with so much unaffected politeness, and yet with so much unoffending reserve, that the old speculating politicians don't know what ground they stand upon. Patmore is drinking into secrets, but Blaquière can discharge the bottles without divulging any.'

'... B. is indefatigable in his office and obliging in his manner and address.... He is warm in his temper, I think, therefore he can't do with a coadjutor.... He pays the greatest deference to the House.... This procedure has begot much goodwill to him.... I have no news to send you but that I hear the women say Lord Bellamont behaves very coolly to Lady Emily Fitzgerald, and that after all it is much to be doubted whether it will be a match.'

'*November*, 1773.

'... The Levee on Sunday was the fullest I ever saw, made up of the most violent Patriots ... the reason ... the demolition of the Excise Board.... Mr. Ponsonby still talks of opposition, but I do not believe him sincere.... They say at the Castle that the Absentee Tax is not a measure of Government, but that Lord North has promised to carry it through in England.... Lord Bellamont is quite wild about that, as he is about every thing else. Lord Mountmorris is come over, nobody knows in what temper. ... On Tuesday and Wednesday the Attorney came in a brown coat, but on Thursday He did not even appear.

'My Wife is very uncomfortable, for We lost our second girl this morning, and I am obliged to conclude ... a little sooner than I otherwise would that I should go to her.'

While the Macartneys were in Ireland, there was a rumour in the family that Lady Jane had prospects of becoming a mother, and one of Sir George's cousins wrote in 1770 :

'I hear Lady Jane is in a way to fulfil the Scripture, "increase and multiply." I hope she will take care to bring her good works to perfection, both for the sake of her health, and that it would make me exceedingly happy to congratulate you on the birth of a son.'

These hopes, however, were not fulfilled.

CHAPTER V

In October, 1774, Sir George Macartney was elected member for Ayr, Irvine, Rothesay, Cambleton and Inveraray, in the English House of Commons.

The December following he received the appointment of Captain-General and Governor of Grenada, the Grenadines, and Tobago in the West Indies.

Shortly afterwards he was elevated to the peerage of Ireland under the title of Lord Macartney, Baron of Lissanoure, in the county of Antrim.

Apropos of his accession to this dignity he wrote to a friend:

'Perhaps you may be of opinion that I might have changed my name upon this occasion, for one of a more harmonious combination of syllables. But as I had passed through several employments, and was pretty well known everywhere as Macartney, I thought it better not to alter it, at this time of day.'

He appears to have quitted England and his parliamentary career with great regret. But being much embarrassed pecuniarily (having, among other things, never recovered from the expenses of his Russian mission), he hoped that a residence of three or four years in the West Indies might enable him to save sufficient to pay off all his debts and start afresh, cleared from all encumbrance.

Lady Macartney also did not enjoy the prospect of several years' exile from England and the separation from her family, to the different members of which she was deeply attached.

They set sail from Plymouth on March 4, 1776, on board a vessel of some 300 tons, freighted from London with

VOYAGE TO GRENADA

Macartney's 'family and equipage, and commanded by a very intelligent and obliging captain.'

As information had been received that the Americans were sending out privateers, and it was not impossible they might fall in with them, the vessel was fitted with six carriage-guns and a few swivels. These, it was hoped, together with their small arms, would prove sufficient to protect them from anything they were likely to meet with.

Macartney also took the precaution of insuring his plate, furniture, books, etc. They met, however, with no adventures of a warlike nature, as the expedition they had entertained fears of had come to an end before they started. It was said the commander was full as anxious to get back to Philadelphia as they could be to reach Grenada.

Macartney much preferred travelling in this manner to being on board a man-of-war, and expressed himself thus to a correspondent who had asked a question relative to his future plans:

'It is my intention to certainly return home in the same manner I came out. In a merchant ship a man is, as it were, in his own house, master of his own time and motions. But in a King's ship there must always be some degree of gêne and constraint in spite of every effort to avoid it.'

The voyage lasted forty-one days, and Macartney gives the following account of it:

'Sailed with a fair wind which in less than a fortnight brought us into the latitude of Madeira. All our passengers were sick for the first week; they then gradually recovered, and seemed as much habituated to the ship, and to mind her rolling as little as the sailors themselves. Monday 1st April was . . . the most delightful day . . . the air pleasant . . . the sun bright but not burning. . . . We celebrated the day in the usual manner, made fools of as many as we could, and were as merry, perhaps merrier, than people on shore. This indeed is generally the case at sea. Every one knows that on shipboard it is in vain to be peevish, or to complain. There is no remedy but good humour, and good humour is so necessary, that even those who have but a small stock, generally are wise enough to contrive that it shall last for the voyage. We therefore endeavoured to draw amusement from everything about us, and to divert ourselves as well as we could. Sometimes we played at whist, and sometimes at chess and backgammon. There were two or three flutes and fiddles among the crew, so we had balls by the sailors on the quarter deck, who endeavoured to entertain us to the best of their power by a variety of marine gambols and nautical pantomines. Husslecap, hotcockles, hunt the slipper, and storming the castle had each its turn of succession and amusement. Thus we passed our time till the 13th, on which day we crossed the Tropic, which event was celebrated with the usual ceremony of ducking, or fining, those who had never crossed it before. We were now got into the finest climate in the world, but the ennui of the voyage began to grow stronger every day, and I cried out a hundred times . . . "Ye Gods! annihilate space and bring me to Grenada." . . . At last on the 1st May we got sight of Barbadoes, and ranged close alongside of it for several hours, near enough to fling a biscuit on shore. The next morning we made St. Vincent's, and steering between it and Begunia we run down, within view of a string of thirty-three small islands called the Grenadines, and part of my government, till ten o'clock at night, when we came to an anchor under Fort Royal in this harbour [Grenada].

'On the 3rd of May I landed, and was immediately sworn into the Government.'

The inhabitants greeted the new Governor and his wife with much friendliness, and gave them a warm reception. Immediately after his arrival Macartney wrote to the same correspondent, a lady for whom he entertained a great and romantic friendship, and to whom he wrote constantly and freely during most of the time he was in the West Indies.

'I have been in a constant round of bustle, hurry and parade, ever since my landing, and shall I fear continue so for a fortnight or three weeks. For my baggage is not brought on shore, my house is not in order, no establishment yet made, in fact nothing of any kind arranged. Till these matters are settled we are entertained by the gentlemen of the Island, at their different houses, which, though very

WEST INDIAN FEUDS

kind, is extremely hurrying, and leaves us scarcely a moment of leisure. We have been received with great cordiality, the fruits of which I hope to see in a short time.'

Macartney's first impressions of his new surroundings seem to have been that everything relative to the climate and appearance of the island was contrary to the ideas usually entertained of them in England. He wrote enthusiastically of the scenery and healthy atmosphere after he had been but forty-eight hours at Grenada, and evidently found the place more agreeable in reality than his anticipations of it had been.

He soon discovered, however, that the island was distracted by party quarrels and ill-feeling, which had materially tended to obstruct its welfare and diminish its prosperity.

The population was a very mixed one, consisting of English, Scotch, Irish, French, Creoles, and Americans. With a few honourable exceptions they appeared to him as '. . . a strange discordant mass of heterogeneous animals . . . easily irritated to do mischief, and but seldom to be roused to do good.'

The most bitter feuds were those between the French and Scotch inhabitants. The former hated the latter as intruders, and the Scotch on their side were fiercely intolerant of the French Catholics. They had even gone so far as to threaten the destruction of all the French churches in the island, so desperate was their religious zeal and hatred of ' Popery.'

The new Governor was assisted in his endeavours to obtain a thorough grasp of the situation by Mr., afterwards Sir George, Staunton, a man of moderation and integrity, whose wise counsels had already prevailed on several occasions, and prevented the contending parties from proceeding to violent extremities.

His collaboration in business with Macartney, and the mutual liking and esteem arising from it, laid the foundation of a firm and lasting friendship between them, which existed from that time until the death of Sir George Staunton in 1801.

And here it may not be amiss to insert a short account of Mr. Staunton, as, from this time on, his fortunes were intimately connected with those of Macartney, whose devoted and disinterested friend he remained for so many years.

The Staunton family, one of some importance in the county of Galway, had settled in Ireland in 1634. They were always on the moderate side, and steady advocates of milder measures towards the Catholics. George Staunton was the same age as Lord Macartney, having been born in April, 1737. He was delicate as a youth, and, showing symptoms of consumption when about seventeen, was sent abroad, where he remained for some years, and decided to take up medicine as a profession. He returned to England in 1760, and, taking up literary work, formed an acquaintanceship with various writers, including Dr. Johnson. It is quite probable he may have met Macartney at that time, but there is no record of his having done so.

Staunton then proceeded to the West Indies, and for a short time practised as a doctor there. He acquired a considerable fortune, which he invested in the acquisition of a sugar plantation, and later on held various official positions of more or less importance, being for a time secretary to the Governor of Dominica.

During a visit to England in 1770 he married a Miss Collins, who returned with him to Grenada, where he had purchased an estate.

Staunton's character and influence were of great help to Macartney, and his support and co-operation in the administration of the islands proved a valuable assistance to the new Governor.

Macartney had intended visiting Tobago as soon as the session in Grenada was over, but a variety of unavoidable accidents caused him to postpone his visit until December.

Towards the latter end of that month, accompanied by Lady Macartney, he embarked on board the Government sloop, which was kept for the purpose of conveying the

ROUND ISLAND

Governor to the other islands under his jurisdiction on his annual visits to them.

Owing to the constant rumours of rebel privateers cruising in the neighbourhood, they were obliged to go fully armed. They also thought it wise 'to make assurance doubly sure,' and to go under the convoy of H.M.S. *Pelican*, an armed brig, 'but as he was a bad sailer we very soon run him out of sight and followed our own course without him.'

They first dropped anchor in Lee Bay at Round Island, where Mr. Irwin,[1] the proprietor, entertained them for two days, 'rendered very cheerful and agreeable by the hospitality and good-humour of our landlord.' Macartney made the tour of the island 'once on foot and once on horseback, and gathered new pleasure at every step.' Every cultivable inch was cultivated, and game was abundant. The sea all round abounded with the finest fish, and 'the beef, mutton and kids were excellent to a proverb.' There were three white persons and about one hundred and fifty coloured inhabitants, and Macartney thus concluded his description:

'Here then Mr. Irwin commonly lives, to all appearance one of the happiest men in the world. And he ... might be so in reality ... but he is of an active not to say unquiet disposition, constantly forming new projects of future opulence ... which induce him from time to time to quit his delightful solitude for the busy haunts of Grenada, in search of what it would probably be much better for him never to find there.'

[1] Mr. Andrew Irwin was the younger son of a good family which had a moderate estate in Leitrim. He was bred a surgeon, and entered the navy; then settled at Antigua, where he acquired a large fortune, and lost it through the dishonesty of his agent. He then removed to the Danish land of Santa Cruz (the King of Denmark being anxious to encourage English settlers upon it), where he became a considerable person. After the cession of Grenada to Great Britain, Mr. Irwin removed over there, and engaged in several large purchases, which he afterwards relinquished or resold, with the exception of Round Island.—Macartney's Letters from Grenada.

On the third day of their stay at Round Island, Lord Macartney was joined by his aide-de-camp, whom he had 'left sick at St. George's,' and immediately set sail for Tobago, which they reached on a Sunday morning. The moment their flag was perceived the signal battery gave notice of the approach of their vessel, and in less than two hours the whole island was aware of it.

'The militia was drawn up on the beach, and we landed in Courland Bay at two o'clock in the afternoon, midst guns, drums, blunderbusses, and thunder. We rested about an hour at a gentleman's house near the shore, and then proceeded, Lady M. in a phaeton, and I on horseback, to Mr. Fairholme's house at Orangehill, which was our headquarters whilst we stayed at Tobago.... We made almost the whole tour of the island, and passed our time in a continued round of jollity and feasting all day, and dancing all night, at the different houses where we visited. It is curious to observe what a number of people are brought together here by various accidents who, one would imagine, were never intended to see each other's faces. It puts me in mind of a story they tell at White's. A Mr. St. Leger, who was an *étourdi* of the first order, being at dinner there, in endeavouring to dissect a fowl, let it slip from his fork into a dish of turbot, and bespattered the old Duke of Devonshire all over with the sauce. Instead of making any apology to the Duke, Mr. St. Leger apostrophized Lord Montford, who was present, in this manner: "I hear, my Lord, that you are a great adept in the doctrine of chances, and superior to most men in the judgment of a bet. Pray, now, when that turbot was feeding at the bottom of the German Ocean and that capon was pecking at the barn door of an Essex farmer, what were the odds they should ever meet at White's, and play at loggerheads on the Duke of Devonshire's plate?" There are to be seen here to the full as singular rencontres, such a concourse of jarring atoms, as no imagination could ever suppose to assemble together. Yet necessity, *le besoin mutuel*, and common interest, make them to go on tolerably well, in hopes like good Christians, and your humble servant, after their time of probation to reach the Paradise which is to make amends for all their labours and misfortunes.... In short, the mixture is so great, and the inhabitants so chequered in respect to birth, breeding, colour, and consideration, that the contemplation of them is to me a highly philosophical entertainment.'

The Governor spent the business part of his time in visiting the batteries, meeting the Houses of Legislature, and receiving their addresses.

Hitherto the inhabitants of Tobago had not given salaries to their Governors, but they now voted one to Lord Macartney of £800 a year.[1]

That, together with his salary as Governor of Grenada (which was £1,000 a year more than his predecessor had received), the home salary, and fees of office, amounted to £6,000 per annum. As his expenses were about £2,000, he hoped to save annually about £4,000 towards the payment of his debts.

'A very short time indeed at that rate would pay them off,' he wrote, 'but a considerable part of them is on annuities, which eat up sixteen per cent. However, I am getting rid of them as fast as I can. . . . I have been informed my predecessors made considerably more of this employment than I am sure I shall.'

Two days after Macartney's departure from Tobago, Mr. Young, the Lieutenant-Governor of the island, arrived from London, and promptly called out Mr. Franklyn, the collector of customs. It was said he had received tidings of this official while in England, which had occasioned his precipitate return to the West Indies. Mr. Franklyn declined the meeting as long as was consistent with his honour, but eventually it took place, and he shot his antagonist through the body, killing him on the spot.

This affair caused Macartney much concern, and he deeply regretted he had not known of the quarrel in time, so as to have interfered in the matter, or at least prevented it from happening within his government.

In February of this year Macartney was, for the first time, laid up with a sharp, though short, attack of gout. He

[1] £800 currency, equivalent to 500 pounds sterling.

suffered considerably from this complaint during his later life, and eventually it was the cause of his death.

By this time the Governor and his wife had moved into a house other than the one occupied upon their first arrival. It had not been intended as a permanent residence, but suited them so well that Macartney decided to remain in it for the whole period of his stay at Grenada. He describes it as 'an old barrack, just under the guns of the battery, about a hundred feet above the sea. Very dry and breezy, and considered to be the healthiest spot in the island.'

At first the Governor found his administration no easy task. He, however, reflected philosophically that it was almost impossible for anyone employed for the Crown in a distant colony not to meet with many difficulties. In these critical situations it was better to maintain authority by conciliating affection than by employing force, which was only to be used when gentleness proved ineffectual. One of his invariable rules was never to allow a man's attitude towards himself to affect his judgment of that man's worth and ability, and never to admit private feelings into public concerns. Gradually the unswerving rectitude of his conduct, and his just and impartial decisions, uninfluenced either by importunity or intimidation, inspired all parties with confidence, and as time went on he contrived to pass several measures which added greatly to the public welfare and the prosperity of the colony.

He had found the island in a very defenceless state, the troops few in number, batteries dismounted, and guns without carriages. In the course of time most of these matters were set right; but his measures for the formation of a regular militia met with a good deal of opposition, especially from the French inhabitants, who found means to ensure the rejection of the Bill in the Assembly after it had passed the Council.

Through the exertions of several of the private gentlemen on the island, a body of men, about one hundred strong, was raised, and formed into a very effectual company of volunteers. Later on they contributed, in no small

SKIRMISHES WITH PRIVATEERS

degree, to the gallant manner in which the garrison stood upon its defence when attacked by the French under Count d'Estaing.

About this time Macartney had vague hopes that he might be offered the Governorship of Jamaica. This would have greatly assisted his efforts to pay off what he owed, and 'emerge on the billows of independence.' But it came to nothing, and he does not appear to have really regretted it. It is difficult to realize now that in those days of sailing vessels the passage from Jamaica to Grenada took from six to seven weeks on account of the winds.

In 1777 began an exciting time for the inhabitants of Grenada. There were constant rumours of war with France, and consequent fears of a French invasion of the island. Was the mail-packet late, surmises were rife as to her fate and those of her cargo. There were constant skirmishes with privateers, and on one occasion, to the great satisfaction of the inhabitants, an American ship, the *Oliver Cromwell*, was taken, after an engagement which lasted upwards of an hour, and in which she lost thirty-one men and had many wounded. She was brought into the harbour of St. George's by the sloop *Beaver*, who only had three men wounded and none killed.

Macartney said he had a thousand good reasons for believing France would avoid seriously breaking with England, though no doubt she would give all the assistance in her power to America. But he added that his fine reasons might not prove worth a farthing, 'car le probable n'arrive jamais,' and it was a great mistake to judge of what people will do by what we imagine it to be their interest to do.

He deeply deplored England's differences with America, and considered the war as most disastrous to our true interests.

'If we adopt this Tartar kind of war,' he wrote, 'we can never hereafter resettle those countries, for we shall find those enraged people at our backs much more dangerous and implacable than the untutored Indians which our first colonists had to deal with.'

In the autumn of this year Macartney paid a visit to Barbadoes. The Governor, Mr. Hay,[1] was an old friend, having been Minister in Portugal when Macartney was at Lisbon. He embarked on board the *Fly*, sloop-of-war, and after a tedious passage of eight days reached Barbadoes. On the way there they gave chase to every vessel that they saw, one in particular giving them a good deal of trouble. She was a good sailer, and stood from them with all the canvas she could carry. All on board the *Fly* were in the highest spirits, believing her to be an American with a valuable cargo. The decks were cleared for action, and no doubts entertained as to her ultimate capture. In the midst of an exciting chase, and as they were gaining on the prize, the wind dropped and gradually settled into a dead calm. Nothing daunted, the captain sent out the longboat and pinnace, fully manned and armed, to continue the chase. They came up with the vessel, and found, to their exceeding mortification, that she was a large Barbadoes ship bound for Tobago.

Macartney stayed for a week at Barbadoes, his headquarters being with Governor Hay, whom he found greatly changed and broken since they last met in Portugal.

The principal inhabitants of the island called to pay their respects, with the exception of Sir John Gay Alleyne. This gentleman, having had a tiff with the Governor, felt it would be inconsistent with his dignity to appear at Government House, and sent Lord Macartney a polite message of excuse.

Macartney was delighted with Barbadoes, which he described as a garden. He made the tour of the island, to the astonishment of its inhabitants, who could not understand such energy and indifference to exertion and fatigue. They declared he had seen more of the island in a week than they had done during the whole course of their lives. Macartney on his part thought the descendants of the first settlers had degenerated a good deal, and remarked

[1] Brother of the Earl of Kinnoul.

'that the inhabitants of the other West Indian islands did not scruple to say that in half a century more the Barbadians would be ranked in the monkey class by naturalists.'

From thence he proceeded to Tobago, where he met the Council and completed his business expeditiously and satisfactorily. In one of his letters he said he felt not a little partial to Tobago, 'for they appear the most public-spirited people of the West Indies, and have shown uncommon alacrity on every occasion,' the following being an instance of it: One night as they were sitting at supper, about ten o'clock, all were alarmed by the sudden and dismal noise of shells blowing to windward. The party immediately set out on horseback in the direction of the noise, which they found proceeded from the town, about two miles distant. There they found the militia under arms, the batteries manned, and every person capable of service in his proper position. All this took place in about twenty minutes with great spirit and alertness.

The cause of alarm was the approach of an armed vessel, whose movements and appearance excited suspicion, but she proved to be only a privateer from Grenada.

During the spring and summer of 1778 there were increasing rumours of a French invasion. Martial law was proclaimed in the island upon the news of the taking of Dominique. One-sixth of the male inhabitants, without distinction, were constantly upon duty night and day, and all of them assembled upon a general alarm. To prevent, as far as possible, any discontent, the Governor took part himself in all the precautions, allowing also his horses and servants to be used in the public service, and frequently visiting the various posts at night. This produced a very good effect upon the inhabitants, and Macartney was, in consequence, able to pass several measures which he had been endeavouring to do for nearly two years and had almost despaired of. These were a new Militia Bill, a Bill for granting an aid to the Crown for the establishment of a dockyard, a Battery Bill, and another authorizing the raising a large sum of money for the payment of the public debts. The moment of danger seemed for the time being to stifle private animosities, and permit all exertions to be turned to the public defence.

The fate of the island was mainly dependent upon the movements of Byron's and d'Estaing's respective squadrons. According to the accounts received, the latter was at Boston, his motions being carefully watched by the former, who was stationed at the mouth of the harbour.

On December 18, 1778, the Governor happened to be standing by a window looking seawards, when he observed an advice-boat, flying English colours, sail into the harbour with great alacrity and cast anchor just below the fort. It turned out she came from Santa Lucia, a French island at open war with England, and had brought several letters. One of them informed the Governor that Admiral Hotham's squadron of five battleships and seventy-two transports, having on board General Grant and five thousand troops from North America, had arrived at Barbadoes a few days before. They were joined there by Admiral Barrington, and three days later sailed for Santa Lucia. The troops were landed, and took possession of the town, Government House, barracks, and strong posts, with the loss of one man. The day following, while they were congratulating themselves on this easy conquest, and were taking measures to secure it, a French squadron of twelve ships of the line and nine frigates appeared in view. This proved to be the Count d'Estaing, who had escaped from Boston Harbour, owing to the dispersal of Admiral Byron's fleet by a violent storm, in which he lost two ships. D'Estaing got safely to Martinique two days prior to Hotham's arrival at Barbadoes. Having refitted his squadron, and taken a large body of troops on board, he was about to proceed against Grenada and St. Vincent, when he received the news of the taking of Santa Lucia by the English. This induced him to alter his course and proceed to that island. He publicly announced his intention of making a short breakfast of the English fleet and army, and taking possession of all the

British colonies in that part of the world.[1] He was, however, mistaken in this, for his twelve ships were repulsed with great loss and disgrace by Admiral Barrington's little squadron.[2]

General Grant announced the fact to the Governor in the following dispatch:

'ST. LUCIE,
'*December* 26, 1778.

'MY LORD,
'We fortunately effected a landing and got possession of this island a few hours before M. d'Estaing appeared with a superior fleet and army, which were destined for the reduction of St. Vincent's, the Grenadines, and, some of the prisoners add, Barbadoes. M. d'Estaing has made two unsuccessful attacks upon Admiral Barrington's fleet. ... Having failed in his attempt upon the fleet, M. d'Estaing made a spirited attack upon the Grenadiers and light infantry. ... We had ten men killed and thirty wounded; the French were repulsed with the loss of fifteen hundred men killed and one hundred and thirty wounded. ... Provisions of all kinds would come to a good market. ... We remain blocked up by a superior fleet, but we look out every hour for Admiral Byron.
'I have the honour to be, etc., etc.,
'JAMES GRANT.'

The long-expected attack upon Grenada did not actually take place until six months later. On receiving reliable information as to the movements of the French fleet, Macartney sent a message to Admiral Byron. But the latter thought fit to proceed to St. Vincent's, telling the

[1] D'Estaing and M. de Bouillé actually landed 11,000 men at St. Lucie; General Grant had barely 5,000.—Macartney's letters from Grenada.

[2] 'MY LORD,
'The Count d'Estaing having made his appearance here with a force superior to the squadron under my command, I think it not unlikely that he may pay you a visit. ... I dispatch this that your Excellency may be prepared for the worst. ... I am not without hopes of seeing Vice-Admiral Byron with his fleet in a few days.'—Admiral Barrington to the Governor (Macartney's letters from Grenada).

Governor that if the island were attacked he would immediately proceed to his assistance.

On July 2, 1779, Count d'Estaing appeared before Grenada with a powerful fleet, and landed a large body of troops. As the fort was incapable of holding out for any length of time, the defending force retired to Hospital Hill. This was the strongest position, inasmuch as it commanded the town, fort, and harbour. The French commander sent a flag by an aide-de-camp with a peremptory summons to surrender.

To this the Governor, who hourly expected assistance from Admiral Byron, made the following reply:

'Lord Macartney is ignorant of Count d'Estaing's force; he knows his own, and will defend the island to the utmost of his power.'[1]

Next day the enemy commenced operations by cannonading the town and fort. A large body of troops at the same time attacked Hospital Hill. After a brave and obstinate defence, which astonished the invading force by its steadiness and gallantry, the hill was taken by storm. The British inhabitants retreated into the fort, where a council of war was called, and an unconditional surrender agreed upon as the least possible evil. It seemed hopeless to expect assistance, and nothing could justify further waste of life in a continuance of useless hostilities.

In one of his letters Mr. Staunton gives the following account of the taking of the island:

'July 14, 1799.

'The island of Grenada was invested and attacked the 2nd inst. by the forces of Count d'Estaing. He summoned the Governor to surrender under severe menaces. The Governor endeavoured, though in vain, to gain time. He expected every instant to see Admiral Byron and General Grant come to his relief. They knew of his danger. Admiral Byron had returned . . . to St Lucie the 1st inst. If he could have sailed from thence that day, or even the next, this island might still be English. Count d'Estaing

---

[1] Egerton Manuscripts.

THE FRENCH CAPTURE GRENADA 109

lost no time in his attack, and our chief place of strength was taken by storm. After a resistance applauded by our conquerors, the Governor sent me to the Count d'Estaing to treat on the terms of a capitulation. But all negociation was vain, for the Count had his terms ready prepared long since ... and would not deviate from them. The chief English inhabitants who were consulted unanimously preferred a surrender at discretion rather than by subscribing to such terms to put their lives in danger.... Their properties are confirmed to them under the French laws. I mean what remains of them; for many have been totally pillaged and ruined. I am among the chief sufferers, my plantation being close to the place of debarkation, and attracting the immediate attention of all the freebooters following the fleet and army. Lord Macartney has employed himself to the utmost in favour of all the English. His conduct during the siege and negociation, however unsuccessful, has been unanimously acknowledged by the principal people here since the business has been concluded. It is possible that I may be sent to France as a hostage by Count d'Estaing, chosen from my knowledge of the country, and its inhabitants, French and English.'[1]

Macartney wrote an account of the taking of Grenada to Lord George Germaine, Secretary of State for the Colonies, and with regard to the capitulation says as follows:

'As the place was absolutely untenable ... there was nothing left for me but to endeavour to obtain such a capitulation as might be honourable to His Majesty's troops and advantageous to the inhabitants of the island.... I sent my aide-de-camp, Mr. Staunton, with articles founded on the capitulation of St. Lucie and Dominique, as a basis of negociation. But ... the Count peremptorily refused to enter into any treaty, rejected my propositions *in toto*, and instantly transmitted to me a letter ... which will appear to your Lordship the most extraordinary project that ever entered the mind of a general or politician.... It required no deliberation in me to declare that I would never put my hand to such conditions, and all the principal proprietors of the island ... preferred to surrender at discretion rather than subscribe ... to terms which were not merely unprecedented and humiliating, but so ensnaring and uncertain in their nature, extent, and aim that they might at any time

[1] 'Life and Family of Sir G. L. Staunton.'

supply a pretext for taking away the lives, together with the fortunes, of the capitulants. Thus, having neither the means of resistance nor possibility of relief, determined never to consent to the capitulation offered to us, yet unable to obtain a better, we found ourselves reduced to the hard necessity of yielding up the island without one. . . . An assurance has been given that the inhabitants shall retain quiet possession of their estates, and that during the present war they shall not be obliged to bear arms against His Majesty. . . .

'M. d'Estaing would on no account consent to any exchange in the West Indies, or to our going on parole to a British, or even a neutral island. The remains of the . . . 48th regiment, the recruits of the artillery, together with the officers and myself, are, I understand, to embark for France in a few days."[1]

The conduct of Count d'Estaing throughout the whole affair showed him to be a man of mean and ungenerous disposition. He allowed his troops to pillage the British quarters, and they carried off everything belonging to the Governor, leaving him literally nothing but the clothes he stood in. His furniture, books, plate, and wearing apparel were seized, and most of his effects publicly sold in the market-place of Grenada for the benefit of the French soldiery. Mr. Staunton also lost everything of which he was possessed, and, together with his wife, was sent to France as one of the eight hostages from among the principal inhabitants of the island which Count d'Estaing was pleased to order off to that country. Lord Macartney was sent there also, the Count having refused him permission to proceed on parole to any of the other British settlements in the West Indies.

Possibly the last-named gentleman judged of the sense of honour in others by his own, which would appear to have been almost non-existent. He had twice been taken prisoner of war by the English some years previously, had broken his parole after the first occasion, and subsequently taken Fort Marlborough in the East Indies.

[1] Letter to Lord G. Germaine (Egerton Manuscripts).

MACARTNEY'S LOSSES

When Macartney was in Paris in 1761, d'Estaing was sent thither by George III., who signified to the French King that he left d'Estaing to the discretion of his own Sovereign; but instead of receiving reprimand and punishment, he was immediately promoted, and taken into high favour.

Macartney met his misfortunes with composure and dignity, but the loss of his plate and property, for which he never received the least compensation, must have been a great blow to his hopes of being able to free himself from debt.

The day after the attack on the hill the French commander sent him an invitation to dinner. This he accepted with his usual courtesy, merely remarking that he hoped the Count would overlook the style of his dress, as the French soldiers had made a little free with his wardrobe.

They had, in fact, not left him a second coat.

Some months previous to the capture of the island, foreseeing the likelihood of such an event, Macartney had thought it better for his wife to return home. A passage was taken for her in the supply storeship, and duplicates of all Macartney's papers sent in her charge to England. The ship stopped for a few days at St. Kitts, and the passengers went on shore. Lady Macartney debated in her mind whether it were wiser to take the precious box of papers with her, or leave them on board ship. Unfortunately she finally decided to adopt the latter course. On the third morning, as the passengers were about to reembark, the storeship was discovered to be on fire. Despite all efforts to subdue the flames, it was speedily consumed, and Lady Macartney lost not only the papers, but every article of value, and nearly all her clothes, having nothing left but the few changes of linen she had taken on shore.

The injury Macartney suffered to his private fortune was thus further augmented by the loss of all his papers. The original documents fell into the hands of the French, and could never be recovered.

Therefore, it may be said, he had returned from every

public appointment he had hitherto held in worse circumstances than when he entered upon it.

Before leaving Grenada the ex-Governor had the satisfaction of receiving an address presented to him by the principal inhabitants of the island. In this they most warmly expressed their sense of gratitude for the wisdom and justice of his government, the vigilance and ability with which he had constantly endeavoured to provide for their security, the skill he had shown in the defence of the island, and his personal courage and coolness during the attack.

Mr. Staunton also lost all his property, and was compelled to begin the world anew. He remained several months in France, and while there negotiated Macartney's exchange with the French Government.

This he carried through to the entire satisfaction of the person chiefly concerned, who wrote that this object had been carried through with an ability and address that he could never do justice to.

Had Macartney merely been liberated as a prisoner on parole, he would have been unable to accept the post of Governor of Madras, which was offered to him the following year.

The time which elapsed between her unfortunate journey to England and the return thither of Lord Macartney was one of great anxiety for his wife.

'*October* 15, 1779.

' Hearing Lady Bute was come to town, I went to see her.[1] She seems in great uneasiness about Lord Macartney, who they have never heard from but once: Lady Macartney has taken a house in Queen Street, Berkeley Square. She is, I am told, excessively wretched. Never was anybody so ill treated as Lord Macartney has been. Had not the people of Grenada (in gratitude I suppose for his mild government while in command of the Island) given him some necessary linen, he would not have had a shirt to put on. Everything was plundered, and all done by the express orders of

[1] From Lady Mary Coke's Journal.

D'Estaing, who is now gone with twelve ships of the line to North America, and I fear we have not above five or six in that country. . . .'

'*Thursday, October* 20.

' I went to town to see Lady Bute and Lady Macartney. They have heard from France that Lord Macartney has leave to come to England upon his parole. . . ."

'*Saturday, October* 30.

' Lord Macartney is not yet arrived, but expected at the beginning of the week. . . .'

'*Wednesday, November* 3.

' . . . Lord Macartney is arrived, and is of opinion that the French mean that the combined Fleets should engage ours, which is the best news I've heard, as I think we shall certainly obtain a victory which will make a great change in our affairs.'

Mrs. Staunton seems, on the whole, to have rather enjoyed her enforced residence in France, and in one of her letters to her mother gives the following account of a visit to the French Court:

'*January*, 1780.

' . . . Mr. Staunton, with a view of getting his leave, has waited on the Minister at Versailles.

' He took that opportunity of letting me have a sight of that famous palace ; but the weather was so cold for a West India constitution, that I did not enjoy the grandeur that surrounded me. I was besides in a habit which I found from an officer in the French Guards, the Count de Lardenoy, who had promised to show me the Court, was a dress not suitable to the place. However, I had a peep at the Queen, who is indeed quite a woman, for she seems perfectly to enjoy her beauty ; she is very handsome, and her state is magnificent. My dress and English appearance caught her eye, as she passed by me to go to Chapel, and many a courtier seemed to envy me the look she cast upon me. Her train was borne by a lady. . . . She walked very fast through a long and magnificent gallery decorated with statues, paintings, and lustres : the ladies, embarrassed with large hoops and long trains, could scarcely follow her. The Comtesse d'Artois, and Madame married to the King's brother, and Madame Elisabeth the King's sister, were also in the procession. Their trains were borne by gentlemen, but they were otherwise confounded in the crowd. While I was employed in satisfying my curiosity Mr. Staunton was at the Levee of the Minister; and it seems he must be there pretty often, before he can accomplish his purpose.

'We have been visited and handsomely entertained by many families of fashion.

'It is the ladies here who constantly invite. When first I received a card from the Countess de Rochard, to dine with her, I supposed her husband must have been in the country, and was surprised to find him at table confounded among the guests. The person to whom the greatest compliment is intended is put at the head of the table, and as a stranger that honour has been frequently conferred upon me. The lady of the house sits at the middle of the table.

'There are generally three courses, of which the dessert is constantly the most costly. At Monsieur Darlincourt's, a former general of the King's revenues, we had dessert knives and forks, and spoons, richly gilt, and everything else in proportion.

'The rooms are exceedingly lofty, and generally hung with rich silk or handsome tapestry, and adorned with looking-glasses of great height between the windows, which are nearly level with the floor. All the genteel houses have courts with large gates to them, through which the carriages drive in.

'It is chiefly men who are employed, instead of chambermaids, which is very disagreeable to an Englishwoman.

'The servants of the meanest rank are commonly seen with ruffles, bags, and muffs; nor could I observe any ill-dressed persons even in the upper galleries of the play houses.

'The other evening I was at the first exhibition of a play called "The English Lord and the French Knight." You may guess who was rendered the ridiculous character. The English servant was represented speaking broken French, swearing, and getting drunk. The lord was exhibited full of insolence and pride: but I must do the audience the justice to say that they did not seem much to relish national reflections.

'Whenever I am able to go out Mr. Staunton takes me to see some of the curiosities of this place, but the severity of the winter will not allow me to go very often abroad. You will find me, I fear, much altered from the many troubles[1] and climates I have gone through, and especially from this jaunt that Count d'Estaing has given us. Though Mr. Staunton could not be in a very good humour with him, he thought it prudent to pay him a visit on his arrival at his country seat, near this city.

'The Count received him with vast civility, and kept him to dinner. We were that day engaged abroad: and therefore ... I found myself obliged to face alone a large French company. The name of Count d'Estaing was an ample apology for my husband, who gratified the company, when he came in the evening, with some account of the conqueror of Grenada and other persons of the first rank whom he had met that day.

'The embarrassment I had been in was quite surprising here, where women often go into company alone, and scarcely ever with their husbands. When first I arrived, I found it necessary to conform to the practice among the ladies of embracing each other on meeting, but was very near getting into a scrape, and borrowing some paint from a lady's cheek, when I luckily took notice that kissing on the *chin* is the contrivance now adopted to avoid such accidents....

'Of the churches, I was most anxious to see that of Notre Dame. Among the first things which struck me on entering it were the colours taken at poor Grenada hanging up there in triumph. But there is no comparison between this building and our St. Paul's, or even, in my humble opinion, Salisbury Cathedral.'[2]

Macartney had spent but a short time in France as prisoner of war before he received permission to return to England, where he was immediately exchanged.

In the summer of 1780 he was sent to Ireland by Lord North on a secret and confidential mission, which Barrow says he accomplished equally to the satisfaction of his Majesty's Ministers and that of the Lord-Lieutenant.

On his return to England he stood as candidate for Beeralstone in Devonshire, and was elected to represent that borough in September, 1780.

[1] The Stauntons lost two children in 1775 in the West Indies—a little girl of three, and an infant son. Their only other child was born in 1781, during Mr. Staunton's absence in India.
[2] 'Life and Letters of G. L. Staunton.'

CHAPTER VI

THE directors of the East India Company had for some time been casting about for a suitable candidate to fill the office of President of Madras. Great abuses in the government of India had been on the increase for years, and corruption prevailed in almost every department. The Government of Fort St. George was involved in confusion and disgrace, and it was felt the services of a man of no ordinary capacity and intelligence were needed to restore order to the distracted affairs of the Carnatic.

There were many who thought that the post should be given, as had hitherto been the case, to one who had already been in the employment of the Company, and who, being connected with India, might be supposed to know more of its affairs.

But among the directors there happened to be several who felt it was important for the honour of the nation, as well as the prosperity of the Company, to appoint a man of rank and reputation totally unconnected with its affairs. They considered it was not so much knowledge of local customs which was required as general experience, education, capacity for business, and an unprejudiced mind.

The suggestion of the appointment of an outsider met, as might naturally be expected, with the most strenuous opposition; but the reforming party among the directors was strong enough to carry the point, it being felt that some attempt must be made to stem the torrent of abuses.

Macartney was thought of by several as being very

SUSPENSION OF MR. WHITEHILL

suitable for the position, and was easily prevailed upon to come forward as a candidate.

His principal opponents were soon reduced to two—Mr. Russel, formerly a store-keeper and commissary, one of the principal creditors of the Nabob of Arcot; and Colonel Call, surveyor and engineer. Both men had amassed considerable fortunes in the service of the Company, and Colonel Call was son-in-law to Lord Pigot, who had lately terminated his life in confinement.[1]

The Court of Proprietors were in the habit of recommending their selection of Governors to the Court of Directors, and heated debates on the subject took place.

In 1780 the government of Madras was for some months in the hands of Mr. John Whitehill, who, as senior member of that Council, had succeeded Sir Thomas Rumbold as President, on the return of the latter to Europe. Mr. Whitehill showed himself very inefficient in the capacity of Governor, doing everything in his power to irritate Hyder Ali, and make certain of war. He had, moreover, retained possession of the district of Guntur after the receipt of orders from Hastings that it should be restored. On October 11, 1780, the Bengal Government resolved that Mr. Whitehill should be suspended from his office, as he was unfit to be entrusted with the conduct of affairs. A letter was accordingly written to the President and Council of Madras, accusing the former of having shown a contemptuous indifference and want of common respect to the Governor-General and Council of Bengal. Sir Eyre Coote, to whom the letter was entrusted, embarked in the ship *Duke of Kingston*, and arrived at Fort St. George on November 5, 1780. Three days later Mr. Whitehill was publicly declared to be suspended from his office, and Mr. Charles Smith, second in the Council, took charge of the

[1] Pigot was appointed Governor of Madras in 1775, and soon found himself at variance with the majority of his Council. After many struggles between the two parties in the Council, he was arrested by Colonel Stuart, and imprisoned about a mile from Madras. He died at Fort St. George a month before he was restored to office by the general Court of Directors.

government, and was proclaimed with the usual ceremonies. Hastings had somewhat strained his powers in the matter, although Whitehill's appointment had not been confirmed at home, and Sir Eyre Coote wrote he thought it not improper to inform the Supreme Council that ideas were entertained of prosecuting it for an illegal act. He also remarked that he was thrown into a distressing and delicate predicament, determined as he was on the one hand to support the Bengal Government, and threatened, on the other, with all the consequences of an illegal dismission of Mr. Whitehill from his Government.

At a meeting of the Court of Proprietors in London on November 23, 1780, notice was given of the resignation of Sir Thomas Rumbold, and it was stated that on November 14 following his successor would be nominated.

General Smith addressed the Court, and moved: 'That it be recommended by the Proprietors to the Court of Directors to appoint as Governor of Madras . . . some person who is or has been in the service of the Company.' Edmund Burke, who was present, proposed an amendment to the effect that 'such servant should have proved himself worthy of their recompense by his obedience and integrity,' and, with his usual eloquence, delivered an address in which he touched on the rapacious and disobedient conduct of the Company's servants in India; the loan to the Nabob of Arcot, for which they received an exorbitant interest; and their contempt for the authority of their employers at home. He said if all the servants of the Company were as he described, he would prefer supporting Lord Macartney's candidature, as a man of worth and ability, whom he highly respected. But if there were any honest and obedient servants, he thought it would be only right to reward that obedience and integrity.

Macartney then came forward, and in his address disclaimed connection with any particular party, but considered he was possessed of the friendship of all. He stated it would be his endeavour to serve the interests of both Crown and Company, and his aim would ever be so to con-

NOMINATED GOVERNOR OF FORT ST. GEORGE

duct himself on all occasions as to enable him to appear before the Court, on his return, with as little necessity for apology as he had had hitherto in respect to the positions he had filled elsewhere.

His speech was listened to attentively, and a sense of his general fitness for the position seems to have prevailed, with the result that, despite a certain amount of opposition, he was nominated Governor and President of Fort St. George on December 14, 1780, and sworn in next day.

Macartney was well aware that his new post would be no sinecure—in fact, would tax his patience and firmness to the utmost. He would be surrounded with difficulties of every kind, and much opposition and hostility. It was, however, one of his favourite ideas that plain dealing and clean hands would always, in the end, be an overmatch for artifice and dishonesty. He had in view a safe rather than a brilliant government; and knowing how more than usually important it would be to have as secretary a man on whom he could thoroughly rely, he appointed his friend Mr. Staunton to that post.

That they quite realized what lay before them, and had been for some time working together in view of the appointment, may be seen from the following letters:

'BUCKINGHAM,
'*March* 19, 1780.

'. . . I am to acknowledge and to thank you for your several letters. . . . And now, my dear Sir, allow me to express how much I feel obliged to you for your care and attention to my business, which you have accomplished with an ability and address that I can never do too much justice to. . . . I have been confined to my bed for some time past by a severe fit of illness, which prevented me from writing to you by the last post, and I am very sorry it is not yet in my power to write to you conclusively on your own affair. I have sent three letters to Sir William James since Monday last, and have been every day promised a satisfactory answer, but none has as yet come to hand. I am, however, disposed to make great allowance for his situation and that of the other directors, which at this moment is certainly very difficult . . . but I trust that in a very short time the whole will be entirely settled.

'P.S.—Lady M. joins me in many compliments to you and Mrs. Staunton.'[1]

'BUCKINGHAM,
'*September* 18, 1780.

'. . . I propose returning to London on Thursday or Friday at farthest. It will be best for me not to stir from it till my business is decided. Most of the Indians declare against an interloper, as they term me, and are trying to form a strong opposition to my appointment; but I don't think it will signify. I, however, omit nothing . . . to strengthen myself, and I proceed as if I had everything to apprehend. My competitors themselves affect to talk of my success as certain, but would not fail attempting to surprise me if they found me at all off my guard. I must beg you will get all the persons applied to, and secured, whom you mentioned in your letter, together with such as may have occurred to you. I shall hope to see you as soon as you arrive in London, and beg you will believe me to be, with very sincere regard and esteem, dear Sir,

'Most truly yours,
'MACARTNEY.'[2]

On June 21, 1781, after a voyage of four months, the new Governor arrived before Pondicherry, where he found Vice-Admiral Sir E. Hughes with his squadron. From him he first heard of our war with Hyder Ali, his invasion of the Carnatic, and the gloomy appearance of British prospects in every part of India.

The day following Macartney landed at Madras, and the commission of government was read, first to the inhabitants assembled in the Council-room, and afterwards to the troops on the parade. The same day at eight o'clock p.m. he took the chair as President and Governor of Fort St. George.

[1] 'Life and Family of Sir G. L. Staunton.'
[2] *Ibid.*

Lemuel F. Abbot, pinxit

GEORGE, EARL OF MACARTNEY, AND HIS SECRETARY, SIR GEORGE LEONARD STAUNTON, BART.

From the Picture in the National Portrait Gallery

To face p. 120

WAR WITH HYDER ALI

He found the situation of affairs on the coast in a deplorable condition.[1]

Hyder Ali had spread his troops over the country, desolating and plundering it, thousands of helpless peasants being murdered in cold blood. He had possessed himself of several strongholds and garrisons, the disaffection of people and army rendering this comparatively easy, and parties of his cavalry came daily almost to the very gates of Madras.

The town was filled to overflowing with Europeans and natives, who had fled thither for refuge; provisions were none too plentiful, and the supply liable to be cut short at any moment.

But in spite of everything, such was the supineness of Government that no serious attempt appears to have been made to cope with the situation.

The army was inclined to be mutinous, on account of arrears of overdue pay; there was a deficiency in the commissariat arrangements, and a want of animals for the artillery.

No assistance could be hoped for from any of the Indian Princes; they were openly hostile to the English, alarmed at their ambition, and suspicious of ill-faith. Their sentiments may be seen from the following extract from a letter which had been intercepted, and came into Macartney's hands:

From the Nabob Nizam ud Dowlah to Fazel Beg Cawn.

'*September,* 1780.

'... The world is now involved in calamities through the turbulence of the English. The deceits of this wicked nation are spread over the whole empire.... These people, with the greatest inward deceit and treachery under the cloak of sincerity, and professing a strict adherence to their

[1] Three days after his arrival Mr. Staunton wrote as follows to his parents: '... We found all things in confusion and distress, arising from the invasion of the country by a famous Indian Prince named Hyder Ally.'—' Life and Family of Sir G. L. Staunton.'

engagements, have stretched forth their hands over what they . . . at first affected to borrow. A people worse than women . . . have trod under and consumed the honour of the most illustrious families in this country. A handful of people without a head or foundation have possessed themselves of the three richest provinces in the empire.

'A set of merchants without a name, and scarcely known, have engrossed and disposed of the revenues of the Imperial Crown.

'A handful of tradesmen, who in their nature are like foxes, have pretended to put themselves on a footing with tigers.

'Since the necessity of punishing this wicked people is obvious, there is no time to be lost in considering of it; for these shameless people are not able to face the heroes of war or bear their deadly blows. They are indebted to fortune alone; the acquisitions they have made with hostile intentions they conceal under appearances of a friendly correspondence. We owe this to our misfortunes and sins. . . . If the fire of war is not lighted at the very foundation of this people . . . their settlements cannot be destroyed. It was with this view I stirred up the Poonah Ministers and Hyder Ally Cawn. . . .'[1]

The Government of Bengal, who were themselves at war with the Maharattas, had sent reinforcements under Colonel Pearse to assist Sir Eyre Coote; but, for various reasons, this does not appear to have been of much service.

A French fleet, superior to that commanded by Sir E. Hughes, was momentarily expected on the coast; and the Dutch settlements, having been apprized of the outbreak of hostilities between their mother country and Great Britain, prepared to lend their assistance and harass the English still further.

It was at this moment of embarrassing complications and acute distress that Macartney assumed the reins of government of the Carnatic. One of his first efforts was an attempt to secure the Dutch settlements on the coast of Coromandel, to prevent their being of service to Hyder Ali, who possessed no ports there. Within a short space of time Sadras and Pulicat were taken. Macartney also

[1] From Miscellaneous Papers, 1781.

NEGOTIATIONS WITH HYDER ALI

augmented the militia, and placed himself at the head of it.

These successes, and the zeal and activity of the new Government, did not fail to make an impression upon the people. The troops acquired fresh spirit from the immediate attention given to their demands and the small, but welcome, supply of money raised for their relief by Macartney, principally by loans from private individuals. Shortly after this improved condition of things the army, under the command of Sir Eyre Coote, gave substantial proof of its renewed bravery and discipline by an encounter with Hyder Ali, in which he was defeated. He, however, carried off the English guns owing to the lack of cavalry to prevent it.

At this moment of apparent superiority Macartney considered it would be opportune to endeavour to persuade the Indians that the Company did not aim at extending its possessions, and really desired the settlement of its differences with Hyder Ali. In this the Governor was seconded by the Admiral and Sir Eyre Coote. Macartney was the more anxious for this as the India Company had, during the previous year, given positive and express directions to maintain, if possible, a connection with this enterprising chief.

An address to Hyder was drawn up, and enclosed in a letter to Sir Eyre Coote, to whose judgment Macartney left it to forward or suppress the communications as he thought fit. At the same time the Governor expressed himself as ready to abide by the consequences of such an act, and said that no unpleasantness to himself or displeasure from Bengal[1] should prevent him from persevering in any measure conducive to the honour and interest of the Company in which the Admiral and General concurred.

But Hyder returned an evasive answer, and showed no disposition to put faith in the Company's propositions or come to terms with them. He appeared more disposed to enter into communication with the French and Dutch, in

[1] The Bengal Government was alone empowered to conclude treaties and make peace and war with the country powers.

the hopes that their united forces would be able to exterminate the British power in India.

On August 27 another successful engagement with Hyder Ali's troops took place, but owing to the want of sufficient provisions for the English force it was impossible to follow it up.

By the end of autumn most of the Dutch settlements had been captured; there remained as exceptions but Negapatam and Tutucorin. Macartney was anxious to proceed immediately against the former, but Sir Eyre Coote opposed the idea. The Governor still adhered to his original plan, but determined to take the whole responsibility upon himself. He also thought it best not to employ a single officer or man from the main army, since the General was not in favour of the proposal. The attack was successfully planned and carried out, and on November 12 the town and fort surrendered. Besides a quantity of stores and ammunition, a treaty with Hyder Ali was found among the papers, which showed how greatly the English interests might have suffered from the continuance of the Dutch possession there. In fact, the fall of Negapatam restored a degree of security to the country which it had not enjoyed since the beginning of the war.

During all this time the Nabob of Arcot had given no assistance towards the prosecution of a war in which his interests were so immediately concerned, and this in spite of an undertaking that he would do so. The Bengal Government expressed themselves exceedingly surprised and indignant at this neglect of obligations, and were of opinion that the Nabob's behaviour in the matter would justify their demand for the immediate transfer of his country to their hands. Macartney, always loath to proceed to violent extremities, sought by every means in his power to induce the Nabob to alter his course of conduct, and tried to convince him that it would be to his real interest to do so. After much conversation and correspondence the Nabob agreed to assign the revenues of his country to the Company during the continuance of the war, reserving one-sixth part for his own private expenditure, this arrangement to continue in force for at least five years. The revenues were to be managed by the Company, and Macartney endeavoured to appoint only such persons as were agreeable to the Nabob, and understood the finances of the Carnatic. This plan met with the Nabob's approval at first, but later on he affected to consider the arrangement derogatory to his dignity. Perseverance and good temper, however, gained the day, the difficulties were surmounted, and all points gradually carried.

Thus at the close of 1781 the prospects of the Company on the coast of Coromandel had brightened considerably. But the improvement was not one of long duration.

In the beginning of January, 1782, news was received of the loss of Chittoor and the investment of the important fortress of Velloor. The army, under the command of Sir Eyre Coote, immediately proceeded to the assistance of the latter place. Although the General had only just recovered from a violent apoplectic seizure, he nevertheless decided to accompany the army, which accomplished the purpose with which it had set out. On their way back to Madras, after the relief of Velloor, the British troops encountered those of Hyder Ali, and repulsed them with but little loss.

About this time Macartney received the following letter from Edmund Burke:

'*October* 15, 1781.

'MY DEAR LORD,

'... Your appointment has been but too well justified in the call which the distresses of your province have made for great abilities. ... You enter in a province harassed and endangered, which will ... require all your exertions to defend ... and your wisdom to restore it. Your task is difficult, but I have no doubt you will acquit yourself with honour. ... India business had a good share in the last session, but it employed, without much agitating us. ... In my opinion the salvation of that country, and of this too, as far as it depends upon India—and that is a great deal—must depend upon our making an impartial review of our conduct. ... Circumstances did not permit me to have a share in your appointment, but I can say with truth that no man wishes your success more cordially than I do. . . . Our friend Fox desires to be remembered to you. He gains ground daily in esteem and popularity with the nation, and with his constituents. You will have pleasure in hearing that all his debts are either paid or settled, and that he is perfectly at his ease.

'I have the honour to be, with my very sincere affection and high esteem,

'Yours, etc., etc.
'ED. BURKE.'

All through the year there were continual engagements between the French and English fleets, and constant encounters between the respective forces on land. The French commander, M. Suffrein, was an active and indefatigable officer, who would, on emergencies, work for whole days in his shirt-sleeves like any ship's carpenter. But his good qualities as an officer were tarnished by a lack of humanity, which casts a stain upon his memory that no professional merit can remove. He proposed an exchange of prisoners to Macartney, who had already released the French surgeons. There was some slight delay in the conduct of the matter, as Sir Eyre Coote was desirous that the English prisoners then in the custody of Hyder Ali should be included in the exchange. But this arrangement did not suit the purpose of the French commander. Under the pretext that the English had failed to comply with his offers of exchange, and secure in the knowledge that the French captives were in the hands of an honourable foe, he landed his unfortunate prisoners at Cuddalore, and deliberately transferred them to Hyder Ali, who was well known to treat the hapless people who fell into his hands with the utmost brutality and indignity. It is only fair to state that M. Suffrein's ideas were not shared by many of his countrymen. Several of his officers remonstrated with him on the matter, and endeavoured to dissuade him from so barbarous and dishonourable an action, but their efforts were of no avail. By Hyder Ali the prisoners were marched in chains to Bangalore, to what fate the ensuing

MISERY OF THE ENGLISH PRISONERS

extract will serve to show. The following account was written by Lieutenant Melville, whose left arm was shattered during an engagement, the muscles of his right being also severed by a sabre cut. After lying for many hours of suffering on the field of battle, he was carried into a tent, where the wounded were all crowded together, and a short time after was marched with his companions to Bangalore.

'We had looked forward,' he says, 'to the close of our long and painful journey with the cheering expectation that it would cause some mitigation of our woes. But great was our disappointment, or rather our horror, on entering a wretched shed, pervious to wind and weather, the destined place of our captivity, and on beholding the miserable objects by whom it was already tenanted—our brother-officers in chains, whose meagre countenances and squalid forms revealed at once the secrets of the prison house, and ... the welcome provided for its new inhabitants. ... Our wounds were severe and required surgical aid; some were maimed and helpless. All medicine was denied, and it was very difficult to procure it clandestinely, under the strict prohibition of introducing it and the danger of punishment if detected. While our bodies were racked with pain and enfeebled with sickness, our minds became a prey to gloom and despondency. We were sometimes visited as objects of curiosity by men of rank. The contempt and abhorrence with which they in general regarded us were extremely mortifying, and hurt us more than the ignominy of our chains. Our unfeeling guards insulted and tyrannized over us, threatened, and sometimes struck us. Applications for redress were heard ... with contemptuous indifference, and we were often told in plain terms that it was not intended we should survive our imprisonment unless we complied with the infamous requisition of bearing arms against our country. Like felons, we were mustered and examined twice a day, and the severest and most ignominious scrutiny of our persons followed a suspicion that we corresponded with our friends or received supplies of money or necessaries from any quarter. Our couch was the ground, spread with a scanty allowance of straw. . . . The sweepings of the granary were given us in any dirty utensil or broken pot. Swarms of odious and tormenting vermin bred in our wounds; and every abomination to the sight and smell accumulated around us, till its continuance became intolerable to our guards.

'The French officers retained by Hyder Ali had not forgotten in his service the courtesies of civilized warfare. They did as much as they could to mitigate the sufferings of the wounded prisoners, and would have done more had they not been restrained by the tyrant whom they served, and without their assistance many more of the hapless captives might have perished.'[1]

In addition to the difficulties of the Government caused by a toilsome and harassing war, there now began a series of differences between Macartney and Sir Eyre Coote. The successful attack on Negapatam, carried out contrary to his opinion, was disagreeable to the latter, as it proved that, with regard to it, his judgment had been at fault. In the first stress of war with Hyder Ali the late Governor and Committee of Madras had been only too thankful to hand over the whole conduct and responsibility to Sir Eyre Coote, who, ten years previously, had been most successful in expelling the French from the coast of Coromandel. They had invested him with great and peculiar powers, and these he was naturally disposed to maintain, but in a somewhat aggressive and pertinacious manner, which tended to render the Governor's position ornamental rather than useful. He did not appear to realize that Macartney was a man of entirely different calibre to his predecessors, and differed greatly from them. Of higher social rank, wider experience and outlook, he was also greatly their superior in ability and administrative power, and, moreover, entirely free from any taint of self-interest or corruption. His sole object was the welfare of his Government, and from the moment he had landed in India he had perceived and experienced the evils which inevitably arise as a result of the subordination of the civil to the military authority. He had suggested that the Commanders-in-Chief of the King's forces on land and sea should each have a seat and voice in the Select Committees of the different Presidencies, being

[1] Thornton's 'History of the British Empire in India.'

GOVERNOR AND GENERAL

bound, like any other member, by the wishes of the majority. But this arrangement did not fall in with Sir Eyre Coote's ideas. Several collisions took place, but Macartney having much the advantage of his opponent in point of temper, no actual quarrel occurred. The Governor invariably treated the General with punctilious respect and courtesy, and if he occasionally was obliged to make adverse comments on the conduct of military matters, he clothed his remarks in diplomatic and courtier-like language, making due allowance for the General's outbursts of temper, as the result of disappointments, years, and ill-health,[1] all of which was, no doubt, additionally irritating to the irascible and hasty old soldier, whose temper evinced 'mournful evidence of his having outlived some of the most attractive qualities of his earlier character.'[2]

These broils were suspended by the departure of Sir Eyre Coote for Bengal, General Stuart being left as his successor in command. The English Admiral also announced his intention of proceeding thither to refit his ships, regardless of the fact that by so doing the British possessions on the coast of Coromandel were exposed to danger. Macartney opposed the proceeding, but in vain. Shortly after, in consequence of a violent storm, a large cargo of rice, most sorely needed by the inhabitants of Madras, was lost.

[1] 'I never retort any sharp expression which may occur in his letters. In fact, I court him like a mistress, and humour him like a child; but with all this I have a most sincere regard for him, and honour him highly. But I am truly grieved at heart to see a man of his military reputation, at his time of life, made miserable by those who ought to make him happy, and from a great public character worked into the little instrument of private malignity and disappointed avarice. All, however, has been and shall be good humour and good breeding on my part.'—Letter to J. Macpherson, Esq. (Private Correspondence, British Museum Manuscript).

'It is very difficult to keep on good terms with him. He is now no longer what he was. Soured by disappointment, grown old, impaired in health, jealous, and fractious. I begin to think this apoplexy has been hanging about him for a long time.'—Private Correspondence of Lord Macartney while Governor of Madras.

[2] Colonel Mark Wilkes, quoted by Sir Charles Lawson in 'Memories of Madras.'

Famine set in, to which was added the horrors of pestilence. Everything in his power was done by Macartney to relieve the sufferers, and he reduced himself to the barest necessities of life in order to set an example. It afforded him scant consolation to receive a letter from Sir Edward Hughes regretting that the weather prevented his return, which communication clearly showed that he felt his step had been a somewhat incautious one.

In Calcutta the Admiral and Sir Eyre Coote foregathered with Warren Hastings. The latter had, not unnaturally, from the first disliked Macartney as an outsider. He was also probably not uninfluenced by jealousy, and therefore indisposed to give the Governor of Madras the credit due to him. Macartney's action in refusing to accept a large sum of money from the Nabob of Arcot, on his arrival in India, had given rise to much adverse comment. It was felt that such conduct was a dangerous innovation.[1] The custom was one sanctioned by precedent, and Macartney's refusal to conform to it cast unpleasant reflections upon the majority, who found themselves unable to resist the temptation of adding to their (often inadequate) salaries by this method.

The following account of the affair is given in the *Gentleman's Magazine* for April, 1806, in the report of the proceedings in the then session of Parliament:

'A conversation ensued . . . relative to the debts of the Nabob of Arcot . . . which amounted to £4,200,000, of which £600,000 was interest. Mr. W. Keene . . . mentioned the following curious circumstance to elucidate the causes which involved the Nabob . . . in such embarrass-

[1] 'His rigid adherence to covenants and his positive refusal of all presents . . . were matters so new to them that they were totally at a loss to what motive they ought to be ascribed. At one time such conduct was imputed to his ignorance of the mode of governing the black people of India, and at another it was suggested that his avarice might aim at something more than had yet been offered. . . . The embarrassment into which the refusal of £80,000 threw the whole Durbar was extremely amusing to Lord Macartney.'— Sir J. Barrow, 'Life of Earl Macartney.'

ments. He knew Lord Macartney, who was once sent as Governor to Madras. His Lordship told him that he had scarcely reached the seat of his government when he received a message from the Nabob requesting to see him. He went, and was astonished to find it was for the purpose of being presented by the Nabob with a sum of money adequate to £20,000, with proportionate tenders to the officers of his suite. Lord Macartney expressed much astonishment, and declined accepting the money, at the same time wishing to know the motive that induced such an offer. He was told by the Nabob that it was quite a customary present to every new Governor, and had never before been refused; and the offer was repeated with a pressing request to take it, as it was considered a proper compliment to the Head of the British Government, whom, ever since the taking of Pondicherry, he considered as his protectors against the French.

'Lord Macartney, however, still persisted in his refusal, assuring the Nabob of his determination to render him every protection in his power. But this generous integrity was everywhere reviled by the servants of the Company, and every pains taken to slander him for venturing such an innovation upon the system they had so long established.'[1]

Sir Eyre Coote's complaints and dissatisfaction with the new state of things at Madras were listened to with much attention by the Governor and Council of Bengal. They wrote to Macartney to the effect that Sir Eyre Coote's wishes were to be gratified as far as possible, and that he was to be allowed an unparticipated command over all the forces

[1] 'Good God! what is human nature if avarice can degrade it to the point it does in this country? But it is not to be wondered at that men are so little scrupulous, since they may act with so little danger. It is impossible to bring a delinquent to justice. . . . Your sea fish seem to me to be full as fond of money here as any of our land crows. . . . My conduct in this respect is not a flight of heroic virtue, for I do not pretend to it. Men have different passions: one loves wine, another women, a third gaming; money does not happen to be my passion . . . and when a great empire is at stake, it is impossible to throw a thought upon it for a moment.'—Letter to Commodore Johnson (Private Correspondence).

under Macartney's authority in the Carnatic. They added that the officer charged with the conduct of the war, if deserving of confidence, ought to be trusted implicitly; and they finished up by declaring that they did not command, but only recommended.

This letter, Barrow says, was written at the very moment when Mr. Staunton, Macartney's private secretary, was living in Hastings' house, and receiving from him the fullest assurances of his determination to co-operate with and support all Macartney's measures. To this letter the Madras Government replied in such a manner as to alarm the supreme Council, who feared that their interference might result in a movement disadvantageous to themselves.[1] Accordingly they thought well to modify the propositions in their first communication, and entered into an investigation of their own and Sir Eyre Coote's conduct from the time of Macartney's arrival at Madras.

From Mr. Staunton to Lord Macartney.

'CALCUTTA,
'*February* 24, 1782.

'... We went ashore at Mr. Macpherson's country house opposite to Calcutta. He received me with great cheerfulness and welcome, and spoke of your lordship in the strongest terms of affection and esteem.... Mr. Hastings, he said, was very well disposed, and, in general, his sentiments were such that there was nothing but the most perfect cordiality between every member of the board. It was, however, to be acknowledged that Mr. Hastings had suffered his temper to be somewhat affected by the long opposition he had met in council here. He is somewhat irritable, for which Mr. Macpherson is willing to make the more allowance that he thinks it almost wonderful he should have preserved any temper.'[2]

[1] 'We have yielded to Sir Eyre Coote in a number of things, which at another time would have occasioned much discussion. But it is not always that compliance produces the expected satisfaction or precludes further demands.'—Letter from Lord Macartney to Hastings (Warren Hastings Papers).

[2] 'Life and Family of Sir G. L. Staunton.'

DEATH OF HYDER ALI

In the beginning of December, 1782, the death of Hyder Ali took place. It was concealed by his Ministers for several days, as his son, Tippoo Sahib, was absent, being occupied in opposing the British troops on the coast of Malabar. On hearing of his father's death, Tippoo immediately hastened to the camp and assumed the supreme command without any opposition. It was said that Hyder Ali, having been disappointed in the results of his alliance with the French, left a letter desiring his son to make peace with the English, bestowing large bribes amongst the officers.

On the departure of Sir Eyre Coote for Bengal, General Stuart, as already stated, had succeeded to the command of the Madras army. Stuart had seen a good deal of active service earlier in life, and entered the service of the East India Company in 1775. The following year, by the order of the majority of Council, he had been instrumental in the arrest of Lord Pigott.

Macartney did not entertain a high opinion of General Stuart, and was by no means disposed to allow him as free a hand as that granted to Sir Eyre Coote. He assumed direction of all military matters, leaving only to the General the duty of executing his orders. This, as might be expected, was bitterly resented by General Stuart. He showed himself also much indisposed to carry out the Government's plan of campaign against Tippoo Sahib and the French, and seems to have considered it incumbent upon him to reject every military measure proposed by the Governor. The universal opinion of the community appears to have been that the death of Hyder Ali was the moment for a decisive blow to be struck by the English. General Stuart, however, took no notice of the desire for prompt action, and showed himself extremely dilatory in the matter, merely remarking 'he did not believe that Hyder Ali was dead, and if he were the army would be ready for every action in proper time.'[1]

Sir John Burgoyne was also among those who expressed themselves as much dissatisfied with the civil control.

[1] Proceedings of the Select Committee of Fort St. George.

These dissensions greatly embarrassed the Government, and were of serious detriment to the affairs of the Company. At length Macartney and the Select Committee decided that, under the circumstances, they could no longer with safety leave General Stuart in command at Cuddalore.[1] It was agreed that General Bruce be appointed to succeed him, and Stuart be recalled to Fort St. George. Mr. Sadleir, a member of the Committee, and Mr. Staunton were accordingly sent off with a letter of instruction for Generals Stuart and Bruce. They also had authority to carry on negotiations with the French commander for the suspension of hostilities, news having arrived that preliminaries of peace between France and Great Britain had already been signed in Europe.

General Stuart was at first disposed to resist, but eventually complied with his orders and returned to Madras. Here he adopted an offensive and insulting attitude towards Macartney, accusing him of personal hostility and unfairness. He wrote that he considered the minutes bordered upon direct invective, which he hoped to prove without foundation, and spoke sarcastically of the President's 'supposed prodigious memory' and 'old bad humour.' He also addressed a letter to the Court complaining of the injustice and cruelty of his recall, and Macartney's malevolence and groundless insinuations. In conclusion, he begged the members of the Court to believe that "no consideration on earth of power or otherwise ever did, or ever will, influence me to be unfaithful to my trust in their service, where I have, at the age of fifty, cheerfully dropt a bloody limb,[2] while others at their ease are only dropping ink on their paper in black characters.'[3]

[1] 'Resolved that it is necessary . . . from incontrovertible facts, that General Stuart shall be recalled to the Presidency. . . . The General chose to disbelieve the death of Hyder Ali, and when that event could no longer be disallowed, he then declared that the army, which he had a month before assured the committee *might and must move, and be ready in any real emergency*, was not even then ready to move or co-operate at this most real and important emergency.'—Proceedings of the Select Committee of Fort St. George.

[2] General Stuart lost a leg in battle on August 27, 1781.

[3] Proceedings of the Select Committee.

To the accusations of malice the Governor replied that General Stuart was mistaken. His (Macartney's) obligation to censure and recall the General was merely a painful public duty; he disdained personalities, and had acted in the matter without prejudice.

Three months previously, and before matters had reached this acute crisis, Sir Eyre Coote, whose health had much improved, decided to return to Madras. He purported to resume his command there in consequence of the difficulties and disagreements which had arisen between the Governor and his successor,[1] and embarked on board H.M.S. *Resolution* from Calcutta. When nearing Madras she was espied by two French ships of the line, who gave chase; but the *Resolution* outsailed her pursuers and eventually reached Madras in safety. The General's anxiety during the pursuit kept him constantly on deck; the excitement and exposure proved too much for him, and brought on a return of his malady. He died on April 27, 1782, two days after his arrival at Madras.

Sir Eyre Coote was a brave and valiant soldier, and to mark their appreciation of his services, and commemorate the important victories gained by him over the French in Southern India, the East India Company erected a monument to his memory in Westminster Abbey. They also caused a white marble statue of him to be placed in their consultation hall. But they did not bestow any pension upon his widow, who, being in India, was most probably with her husband at the time of his death.

Matters at length reached such a pitch that Macartney considered his only alternative was to get rid of General Stuart. Accordingly he recommended to the Council the immediate dismissal of Stuart from the service, in consequence of the conduct of the latter since his return to

[1] '. . . I have determined to revisit you, and shall embark on the *Media* frigate as soon after her arrival as may be possible, and I hope, and expect, on reaching Madras, to find the army amply equipped and ready in full force.'—Letter to General Stuart from Sir Eyre Coote.

Madras. This conduct the Governor characterized as premeditated, wilful, repeated and systematic disobedience; which was prejudicial to the Company's regular government. The General's fatal misconduct had allowed the French to be in such force in India as might prove of much embarrassment and evil to the Company. The President concluded by recommending the appointment of Sir John Burgoyne, senior officer in the King's service on the coast, to succeed General Stuart, who should be immediately dismissed from the service, 'in virtue of the powers given to the Government in case of the disobedience of any of its military officers.'[1]

But Stuart denied the power of the Government to remove him. He also exercised so much influence over Sir John Burgoyne that that officer declined to take over the command. Then Macartney, mindful of the fate of Pigott, and having good reason to suppose that Stuart meditated some such design with reference to himself, perceived it was incumbent upon him to take immediate action of a decisive character, and to place the General under arrest.

This was accordingly done without loss of time, and in the following manner: Stuart had left the fort, to be from under the control of the Governor, and had retired to his country house. Here he was surrounded by a guard of soldiers, his secretary, and his aides-de-camp. Mr. Staunton, Lieutenant Cooke, and Lieutenant Gomond, Adjutant of the garrison, were ordered to proceed with a party of sepoys to General Stuart's residence, secure his person, and remove him under close arrest to the fort. Orders were also sent to Captain Hughes to collect his battalion and follow, but with little hope of their being in time. It was about eight o'clock in the evening. Lieutenant Cooke and the sepoys stopped at the outer gate; Messrs. Staunton and Gomond were not distinguished by the sentinels from ordinary visitors, and proceeded to the apartment where General Stuart was engaged in drawing up orders with two or three of his staff.

[1] Proceedings of the Select Committee, September 17, 1783.

ARREST OF GENERAL STUART

The arrest came upon the General sooner than he had expected; first he said he would obey it at some future time, and at length seemed determined to resist. The sepoys were called upstairs with their bayonets fixed, and led by Mr. Staunton, sword in hand. The moment must have been tense with excitement. The number of Europeans was equally few on both sides, and the part that would be taken by the sepoys depended on the impression made upon their minds. They had been accustomed to respect and obey the General, his secretary spoke their language fluently, and his aide-de-camp was in the habit of commanding them. A momentary exertion on the part of the General might have transformed them into his protectors. Mr. Staunton, however, took a loud and authoritative tone, and Lieutenant Gomond with equal coolness and firmness repeated to the General he must proceed to execute his commission. But the latter busied himself in destroying his papers, and arguing that there was no written order. He insisted on being removed from his seat, upon which Lieutenant Gomond and two unarmed sepoys touched him. He was then assisted by his own servants, and carried without difficulty to the fort, employing himself on the way there in tearing into minute fragments any papers he foresaw might prove his guilt.

The foregoing account is taken from a memoir of Sir George Staunton, written, for private circulation, by his son.

General Stuart was kept under arrest in the fort for a few days until a passage was obtained for him in a ship which was leaving for England. He was anxious to be sent to Bengal or Bombay instead, and was exceedingly indignant at the arrangements made with regard to his voyage. After his embarkation in what he deemed an unsuitable ship, he wrote to Macartney, saying:

'I have been made to go on this vessel, which you for the occasion call a packet, unfit in every respect for the voyage you propose, however you may have crammed it with pigs and geese; and where I see only one man's face I knew formerly in camp.'

He further complained the ship had a most disagreeable smell, and there was every chance he would lose his life in it.

'After what you have done to me ... this is most probably what you have ultimately in view. If I die on board, or am shipwrecked, it is in direct consequence of what you have done; while living I shall appeal to the records, and others will do me justice after my decease. I do not look for justice or fair dealing at your hands.'

He was also extremely annoyed to find that his correspondence from 'this most disagreeable vessel' was to pass through the Governor's hands, and said: 'This is carrying my distress to the utmost degree of imagination; you cannot go much further, thank God.'[1]

General Stuart, in spite of his misgivings, reached London in safety, nursing a bitter sense of wrong, and determined to exact satisfaction from Macartney on the arrival of the latter in England. The account of the duel which took place between them shortly after the Governor's return home will be narrated in due course.

In consequence of the behaviour of Sir John Burgoyne, the Government decided to pass him over and bestow the command on Colonel Lang. This officer was junior to Burgoyne, but senior officer in the service of the Company on the coast. Sir John remonstrated in a violent manner against the indignity of his supersession by a junior. He wrote that he intended marching with his regiment, and retaining the command of the King's troops in India. But the Company replied that they had no alternative but to supersede him, it being necessary to entrust the command to an officer on whom they could rely with greater confidence than on himself. This answer so annoyed Sir John that the following day he withdrew from the army and applied to the Admiral for protection, which the latter refused to give. Sir John, crestfallen, had to return on shore, and acquaint Macartney with the fact that he had rendered himself liable to arrest for having left his post without per-

[1] From Proceedings of the Select Committee.

MACARTNEY'S FORBEARANCE

mission to do so. He offered to give himself up at once, to save himself from such an indignity; but the Government behaved with leniency, and replied they would not place him under restraint, provided he did not force them to do so by his future conduct. In spite of this mild treatment, Sir John shortly after entered into an acrimonious dispute with Macartney and his Government over what he considered the rights of the officers under his command to compensation for exceptional expenditure. Macartney, who throughout the affair was supported by his civilian colleagues, behaved with great moderation and forbearance. He took little notice of Sir John's expressions of resentment [1] and his complaints that the Governor's rule was 'one uniform plan of tyranny and oppression.' He concluded by writing to Macartney:

'There is scarcely one person whose misfortune it has been to have any transactions with you who has not had reason to curse the hour his ill stars doomed him to have any connection with your Lordship. . . . The time must come, and you know it, when ample justice must be done me, and when divested of the plumes of government you must answer for your conduct.'[2]

Not long afterwards Sir John Burgoyne again fell under the displeasure of the Madras Government. This time he was placed under a nominal[3] arrest,[4] and tried by court-

[1] To this violent abuse Macartney merely replied that he lamented it should have fallen to his lot to conduct the affairs of the Company at so unfortunate a period. He was conscious of the rectitude of his views and intentions, and declared his fixed purpose of never shrinking from public or private responsibility for any one act of his government or his life.

[2] Proceedings of the Select Committee.

[3] 'You know you neither have been, nor are confined at all, and you were particularly told you might go to England whenever it suited.'—Letter to Sir J. Burgoyne from Lord Macartney.

[4] *January*, 1784.

'We have been at last obliged to put Sir John under an arrest, at large. He was determined that it should be so, as he declared to everybody, and he rendered it impossible for us to avoid it.'— Private Correspondence of Lord Macartney when Governor of Madras.

martial, being eventually acquitted. He died in the autumn of 1785, at the age of thirty-nine.

Owing to the treaty concluded between France and England, Tippoo Sahib had been invited to concur in the general pacification, but had hitherto shown no disposition to do so. However, during the summer of 1783 he sent a communication on the subject to Madras, in which he offered certain conditions, and expressed his willingness to send two ambassadors to treat for peace. Two vakeels, or agents, arrived there, accordingly, for that purpose. Later on in the autumn it was decided that Mr. Sadlèir, senior civilian member of Council, and Mr. Staunton should proceed to Seringapatam to confer with Tippoo on the terms of peace. Macartney wished to accelerate the proceedings as much as possible, being anxious for the prompt release of the numerous English prisoners held by that Prince in a barbarous captivity. These unfortunate men had been treated by Hyder Ali with a cruelty which showed an utter indifference for the preservation of their lives. But Tippoo did not scruple to employ direct means to deprive them of existence.

The English Commissioners proposed that all places captured by either party to the east of the Ghauts should be restored; the release [of all the English prisoners to follow; and, finally, that exchanges should be made of all places on the western coast.

But Tippoo's agents demanded that the unconditional surrender of Mangalore should precede the second of these conditions. To this Mr. Staunton refused to agree, as he considered it the only security they had for the speedy release of the prisoners. His colleague, however, was of a different opinion, and ready to yield on that point. In consequence of the differences between them, the military secretary, Mr. Huddleston, was sent to join them, that all disputed points might be settled by a majority of opinion. To Mr. Staunton his chief wrote as follows:

NECESSITY FOR PEACE

'Fort St. George,
'*November* 26, 1783.

' Thank you a thousand times for your letters ... enclosing the draft. Your reasoning is conclusive with me, and it behoves you and Mr. Sadleir to put no confidence whatever in Tippoo that it may be in his power to abuse. Certainly he ought to give up our prisoners before we consent to the delivery of Mangalore, or the other places on the Malabar coast. The refusal seems little short of a declaration of taking every advantage and making the most of it. Both my colleagues are clearly of that opinion. . . . My mind is much affected by the state of things at present. A scarcity of money, and of provision and every difficulty arising from these circumstances, are every moment before my eyes, and occasion very unpleasant sensations. . . . Peace will alleviate, and for that object I look chiefly to your address ; if you have health you will surmount every obstacle. I must in all matters of business rely solely upon you. Be his [Mr. Sadleir's] fancies and vagaries what they may, I would not for a million, that you were not at his elbow.

'Adieu, ever yours,
'Macartney.'[1]

'*December*, 1783.

'Since writing my letter of yesterday I received yours of the 24th, communicating the conduct of your colleague. It appeared to me so unjustifiable, and so dangerous, that not a moment was to be lost in determining upon it. I therefore in confidence informed Mr. D. and General L. of the whole, in consequence of which the letter of this day to you and Mr. Sadleir was agreed upon. . . . Your conduct will do you immortal honour, and that of your colleague would justify us in immediately removing him if, in our circumstances, it could be contrived without more inconvenience than his continuance. By our letter we have put it out of his power to do further positive mischief. . . . I cannot for a moment entertain the idea of your retiring. Upon your judgment, address and integrity I solely rely for the happy accomplishment of this business, on which not only my reputation and future lot of life may depend, but the salvation of the British Empire in this part of the world.

'I am, etc., etc.,
'Macartney.'[2]

---

[1] ' Life and Letters of Sir G. L. Staunton.'   [2] *Ibid.*

'*December 27*, 1783.

'... It is some days since I have written to you, having been prevented by a variety of circumstances, rheumatism, gout, Christmas holidays, and a thousand indispensable avocations. In short, my dear friend, I am really worn down with distemper and fatigue. For God's sake, therefore, make a good peace as fast as you can and return to us.'

'I would with pleasure almost part with a limb for Mangalore, but I know you can have no peace with Tippoo without restoring it to him, and I know peace is an absolute necessity, for we are totally unable to carry on the war. ... For each party to remain as before the war with undiminished possessions respectively will be surely not a dishonourable peace. Perhaps a more brilliant one might be less permanent or safe.'[1]

Throughout the negotiations Tippoo Sahib treated the Commissioners with haughty and arrigant insolence, and they underwent many inconvenience and difficulties on their journey to his camp. Correspondence with their countrymen, in ships off the coast, was restrained and tampered with; and they learned that several of the British prisoners had been murdered by the tyrant into whose hands they had fallen.[2] But the Commissioners were fully aware that it would be worse than useless to show irritation or resentment at this juncture. They clearly perceived the necessity for circumspection, and that nothing short of actual hostilities could warrant offensive measures at this stage when so much was at stake.

How acutely Macartney felt the position of affairs may be seen from the following extracts from letters to Mr. Staunton:

'... I am really very uneasy at the situation with Tippoo. ... For God's sake act with decision. If you and one of your colleagues agree, the third is a cipher and

[1] Private Correspondence of Lord Macartney when Governor of Madras.
[2] 'General Mathewes and his officers were undoubtedly obliged to swallow poison by order of Tippoo, but there are various accounts of the manner in which it was administered. According to some, they were destroyed in separate prisons, and others say that they were invited to an entertainment prepared by Tippoo's orders, and there compelled to drink the deadly draught.'—*Ibid.*

CONCLUSION OF THE TREATY

can do no mischief if you are peremptory. . . . I think really if this business fails I shall not survive it.'

'. . . We have little expectation of supplies from Bengal. Their new treaty with Scindia I look on as little better than moonshine. He is at an immense distance, and is engaged in objects of much more consequence to him than our quarrel with Tippoo. . . . We may expect the definite treaty [between France and Great Britain] very quickly, and with it a large body of French troops from the Cape and the islands. What airs they will give themselves, and what trouble they will be disposed to give us, I need not hint to you, who know them so well. If the war continues I foresee the most serious mischief from them, not because it would be their interest at this time to embroil us, but because a thousand other circumstances would lead them to it. If a safe peace can be obtained upon fair and honourable terms, it is preferable to the most brilliant war; but if it appears to you that Tippoo is not sincere . . . no time should be lost in acquainting us.

'Your plan is equitable; if Tippoo wishes for peace, he can have no objection to that plan. Perhaps, if peace were really made, we should have then little less to apprehend from him than during an open war. I am sick—sick at heart. Your letters of yesterday have not been a cordial, and Bengal has begun again to plague us with letters of reproach.'[1]

The long-pending treaty was at length concluded, and the following letter received from the Commissioners:

'CAMP NEAR MANGALORE,
'*March* 11, 1784.

'MY LORD AND GENTLEMEN,
'We have the honour to inform you that peace is at length concluded between the Company and the Nabob Tippoo Sultan. The treaty was signed and mutually interchanged this evening a few miles from hence. . . .
'(Signed) A. SADLEIR,
'GEORGE LEONARD STAUNTON,
'J. HUDDLESTON.'

On receipt of the news Macartney wrote as follows to his wife:

[1] From 'Life and Letters of Sir G. L. Staunton.'

'FORT ST. GEORGE,
'*March* 22, 1784.

'MY DEAREST LOVE,

'I have this moment received an account from our Ambassadors . . . that peace with Tippoo Sultan, the son and successor of the late Hyder Ali, was concluded, and the treaty signed, sealed, and mutually interchanged by him and them on the 11th inst. in his camp near Mangalore. In about an hour I shall dispatch an express overland to communicate this event to the Court of Directors. You will naturally imagine I have but little time to write to you. I must, however, say a few words to thank you, which I do most sincerely, for your letters by Captain Courtney of the *Eurydice*. . . . He is an extremely pretty young man, and universally approved of here. . . . You will no doubt have received my letters by the *Pondicherry* and *Medea*. Whatever I have written in those letters I still adhere to, and you are to consider them as my present sentiments, unaltered by any subsequent circumstances or intelligence. I shall conclude my government here as I begun it. The first turn of the war was given by the brilliant capture of all the Dutch settlements without any assistance from, and, indeed, against the consent of, Sir Eyre Coote. . . . The war is now concluded with our Indian enemy, and the treaty made by us is the only treaty which has concluded any of our late wars without our suffering some loss or dismemberment of territory. We remain in my Government exactly as we begun. . . . I have infinite difficulties and enemies to encounter, but I doubt not of overcoming them all. The Bengal Government will disapprove, possibly, of the treaty I have made. . . . I depend solely on the rectitude of my actions, and I believe, my dear, that it will be found in the end to have been the wisest part I could have taken. . . . Continue to write to me, but don't send any books or parcels, as I think it highly probable I shall depart hence in October. . . .

'Adieu, my dearest Love.

'Ever yours,
'M.'

Of Indian affairs and Mr. Staunton, Macartney wrote as follows to Charles Fox:

'MY DEAR CHARLES,

'I do not know in what situation this letter will find you, whether in or out of office. But in any situation, your personal weight and opinion will have ... influence.... It appears that you are fully impressed with the value and importance of our Indian Empire; but I fear there are few besides who either feel its value and importance, or ... give sufficient attention to the subject. Should it, however, be much longer neglected, be assured that our possessions here will ... slip from us; and you will then discover that the information given about India has been as deceitful as that which was swallowed so long from America. The only chance of preserving it is the employment of the ablest and honestest men that can be found ... from among the best-informed ... liberal-minded men.

'You ... must be sensible the old system cannot answer any longer, and that what was adapted to the regulation of mere commercial factories cannot now suit the administration of a great empire.

'There may be found some among the Company's servants that are not ill-qualified for continuing in office here, but the number is small. The man in my opinion the most capable of rendering essential service to the State in India is Mr. Staunton.... He is a man of strict honour and uncorruptible integrity and moderate views.... I trust that you will not let slip any occasion that may offer ... for giving Mr. Staunton such a respectable appointment in this part of the world as may enable him to do ... the most essential service to his country and honour to his employers.

'Adieu, my dear Charles. I must refer you to our public dispatches for the *true undisguised* state of this settlement. A private letter would give you but a very inadequate idea of our affairs.

"I am, etc.,
'MACARTNEY.'

Macartney had at various times, though often vainly, done everything in his power to mitigate the sufferings of the prisoners; and after their release the officers presented him with an address expressive of their heartfelt gratitude for his efforts on their behalf. They concluded by saying:

'As men restored to life, as members of society restored to our friends and country, as soldiers restored to profession and honour, permit us, my Lord, with the sincerest and most lively gratitude . . . to assure you that we shall ever retain the deepest sense of the essential protection you afforded us.'[1]

But the peace concluded with Tippoo Sahib did not meet with the approval of the members of the Bengal Government, as Macartney had hinted to his wife. They took exception to the moderate manner in which Macartney had expressed himself to Tippoo, which they chose to consider humiliating. They wrote to say that they could not think of the treaty without the most serious displeasure, and considered it had placed them in a contemptible position in the opinions of the powers of India. A rumour also that gibbets ' with every necessary for service ' had been erected in front of the Commissioners' tents had specially annoyed them. Macartney was able to declare this report an utterly false one, and to state also that the Commissioners had complained of no inattention that could affect the Company or the negotiations.

But for many reasons there never had nor could have been any cordiality of feeling between Hastings and Macartney. The new Governor's caution, the economy he at once adopted in the expenditure of the public money, the power he had been given to correct abuses, and, above all, the firmness and independence of mind showed by him from the moment he took up office, could not fail to have been extremely disagreeable to persons of quite another outlook and point of view.

Macartney vainly attempted to allay the feelings of suspicion and resentment. On his arrival in India, he had endeavoured to assure Hastings that he fully estimated his wisdom and experience, and was quite determined to support his measures.

In letters written shortly after his arrival at Madras, he expressed himself anxious that confidence and friendship might be established between them, and went on to say :

' Though scarcely possible for two persons distant from each other to coincide always exactly . . . minute differ-

[1] Sir J. Barrow, ' Life of the Earl of Macartney.'

ences can never affect our general views, or . . . weaken that union which I most sincerely wish to cultivate and maintain with you. . . . New as I am to this country, and totally devoid of local prepossessions, I cannot have been biassed by any of those rooted and popular prejudices which you foresaw you would have to encounter in other breasts. With me, the general security and promotion of the British interest are the only objects, placing as I do my personal advantage solely in the success of the whole plan, and aiming at no kind of importance from the extent or value of any part which may continue under my immediate care.

'I came to this country under such strong impressions of your experienced wisdom and uprightness that it required no effort to reject imputation against either. India was, indeed, never considered by me otherwise than in a collected view, nor have I had any other ambition than that of contributing . . . towards the general welfare of my new employers.'[1]

But in the essential nature of things it was wholly impossible that these two should have really amalgamated. Constant differences existed between them from the beginning of Macartney's government, and the friction which ensued often resulted in strained relations, which were scarcely conducive to the prosperity of the government of India as a whole.

In the early summer of 1782 Macartney had written in a confidential and conciliatory manner to Hastings about their points of difference. He told him he had early seen and warned Sir Eyre Coote there were men to whose interest it was that the General and Governor should not be on good terms. He thought that from a certain sharpness in the style of Hastings' last letter to the Madras Government it might be imagined that ill impressions had been conveyed of his conduct as President. He therefore told Hastings that, as a private individual, nobody was less interested in the concerns of India than he was, and as a public man nobody more so. He hoped that the fair and unreserved

[1] Private Correspondence of Lord Macartney when Governor of Madras.

manner in which he then wrote would be sufficient to obviate any further prejudices, and concluded this very excellent and straightforward letter by saying :

'I have now opened myself to you with all that frankness which I have ever practised since my first entrance into public life, and which both reason and experience convince me to be the wisest as well as the most honourable system. . . . I do not dismiss this letter from my hands without much hesitation, lest what I sincerely mean as a mark of unreserved confidence may not be taken in the sense it is intended. If I had not conceived ideas of you very different from the generality of men, I certainly should have adopted a very different style, and have addressed you in a manner more suitable to the formalities of common intercourse than to the attention of a great mind occupied only by essential objects, and superior to the intrusion of little ones.'[1]

Hastings'[2] principal objection to the treaty with Tippoo appears to have been that it did not include the Nabob of Arcot. To remedy this the Bombay Government directed a new ratification should take place. This Macartney resisted, and had Hastings been confident in his own stability, serious consequences might have ensued. But Hastings was no longer what he had been. Heavy charges were being brought against him in England, and he had found it necessary to send home an agent to attend to the defence of his character and conduct. On the other hand, Macartney's influence appeared to be a rising one, and he had powerful supporters behind him, notably Charles James Fox, who was

[1] Private Correspondence of Lord Macartney when Governor of Madras.

[2] In November, 1784, Macartney had written to Hastings, apologizing for writing again after so long and unpleasant an interruption to a correspondence which was commenced under the most promising appearances of union and cordiality : 'Although I cannot recede from my opinions in the points from which our public differences have arisen, I can and will most heartily meet you upon every measure that tends to keep the affairs of the Company peaceably and steadily in their course until we can recover in some degree from our numerous difficulties.'—Private Correspondence of Lord Macartney.

MAHOMET ALI

no friend to Hastings. He therefore continued to exercise his authority without interruption until June, 1785, when, in consequence of the action of the home Government, he resigned his appointment. The action referred to was with reference to the reassignment of the revenues of the Carnatic to Mahomet Ali. It will be remembered that the arrangement entered into with his predecessor in 1781 was to hold good for at least five years. The Bengal Government sent orders to Macartney to deliver up the revenues to the Nabob. This he opposed on the ground that from the moment they surrendered the assignment they would cease to be a nation on the coast. The English Government took an opposite view of the matter,[1] and sent out an order for the immediate restitution to Mahomet Ali, thus rendering inevitable Macartney's resignation. By the same packet arrived the nomination of Mr. Holland as his successor in the government of Madras.

Macartney was not in the least surprised by either of these dispatches, being, in fact, quite prepared for both events. He had repeatedly requested the Court of Directors to appoint an eventual successor, and had thought it extremely probable that the assignment might be upset at home. But he felt that it would be utterly impossible for him to carry on the Company's administration under the orders just received. After all that had passed relative to the assignment, and the struggles he had made to keep it against the whole power of Bengal, he expected the Court of Directors would give greater credit to the motives which, contrary to personal interest, induced him to hold fast to the assignment as the great resource for the common preservation of the Company.

Ever ready to do all that he could for the service of his country, Macartney, though at this time in very bad health,

[1] 'The war being concluded, it was deemed expedient by His Majesty's Ministers for the affairs of India to show to the Nabob another instance of the honour and generosity of the British nation, however undeserving he had proved himself of it.'—Sir J. Barrow, 'Life of the Earl of Macartney.'

offered to go to Bengal before leaving India. He hoped that a personal interview with the Council might enable him to impress them with a sense of the difficulties in the conduct of affairs at Madras in consequence of the order for the reassignment. The Board gratefully accepted the offer, and expressed their sincere regret at the President's resignation. They moved a unanimous vote of thanks to Lord Macartney for 'his able and unwearied exertions in the discharge of his public duty, and, above all, for the inflexible firmness and integrity of his personal conduct, by which the authority of the Government has been supported, and the affairs of the Company successfully carried through a scene of the most trying and unexampled difficulties.'[1]

At the time of Macartney's resignation he left in the treasury a larger sum of money than was ever delivered over by any former Governor of Fort St. George to his successor. A great part of the amount consisted of presents and fees as had been usual for Governors to take for their private emolument, but which had rarely, if ever, before been applied to public use.

A few days previous to his departure, and having evidently good cause to suspect that malicious reports of his conduct might be circulated after his departure, he entered two papers upon the records of the Company. One was an affidavit to the effect that he solemnly swore and declared he had never, to the best of his belief, accepted or received for his own benefit presents of any kind, with the exception of two pipes of Madeira from two particular friends, a few bottles of champagne and burgundy, and some fruit and provisions of very trifling value. He further swore that he had strictly confined himself to the Company's allowances, and had never appropriated any part of their moneys and effects. Neither had he engaged in trade or traffic of any kind, but had strictly observed all covenants with the Company, and acted for their honour and interest in all things to the best of his ability.

[1] Proceedings of the Select Committee of Fort St. George.

A FLATTERING OFFER

The second paper was a declaration which had to do with the details of his private fortune and expenditure.

Macartney's errand to Bengal proved fruitless, but while in Calcutta he received a dispatch from England offering him the Governor-Generalship of Bengal, now vacant by the return of Hastings.[1] The offer was a flattering one, the more so as it was entirely unsolicited, and he was unconnected with the political party then in power. But Macartney was by this time seriously ill,[2] and had little inclination for a further stay in India. He had at various times written to his friends that he was worn out with fatigue, labours, and difficulties, and said it was not easy to describe the disappointments he had met with in India. He had expected to find friendship and support, but had experienced nothing but jealousy and counteraction.[3] On hearing a report that he was to be made Governor of Bengal, he had written to Mr. James Macpherson, a member of that Council:

'I do assure you I am by no means desirous of it, for ... I have had full enough of one Presidency to wish trying my hand with another ... and though perhaps I may, and probably do, entertain a higher opinion of myself than any-one else does, yet I confess I think I should not shine to much advantage in your meridian.'

He had, moreover, while in Calcutta, been obliged to fight a duel with Mr. James Sadleir, one of the three Commissioners sent to treat with Tippoo Sahib, and who, it will be remembered, had been ready to surrender Mangalore

[1] Edmund Burke wrote to apprize Lady Macartney of the offer, saying: 'Permit me to wish you joy of this appointment, so pleasant to all your friends and beneficial to the public.'—Private Letters.

[2] Barrow considers that this illness was due to too much walking exercise and exposure to the sun.

[3] 'My inclination, my interest, my system naturally led me to a close connection with Mr. Hastings, but some untoward incidents seemed early to throw impediments in the way. I endeavoured to remove them, and thought I had succeeded, but have found myself mistaken.'—Private Correspondence.

prior to the release of the English prisoners. It appears that on one occasion Mr. Sadleir, whom Barrow describes as 'a fickle, intemperate and unaccommodating man,' opposed a resolution to which he had previously given his consent. It was proposed to grant an additional allowance to Mr. Huddlestone, who had acted as third Commissioner, on account of his services. The entire Board agreed that Mr. Sadleir had formerly assented to the proposal, 'but he persisted in contradicting the assertion of his colleagues in the most positive and provoking manner.'[1] Thereupon Macartney, annoyed by so unjust and illiberal a refusal, gave way to anger, and declared that Mr. Sadleir told a lie. Such a loss of temper, so unusual and uncharacteristic of Macartney, was probably greatly due to the fact of his ill-health.

Mr. Sadleir was informed by his military friends that it was absolutely necessary for his honour to challenge Macartney. He accordingly did so, and a meeting took place between them, in which Macartney was wounded in the left side. On this Mr. Sadleir declared he had received satisfaction, and quitted the ground.

Shortly after this occurrence Macartney left India, and arrived in London on January 9, 1786, after an absence of five years.

[1] Sir J. Barrow, 'Life of the Earl of Macartney.'

CHAPTER VII

LADY MACARTNEY did not accompany her husband when he went out to India. Her principal reason for this appears to have been that her mother, to whom she was devotedly attached, objected to her daughter going so far from home. It may be also that Lady Macartney, who had unpleasant recollections of her voyage from the West Indies, was, at first, by no means averse to being left behind. But as time went on she became more and more torn in two between duty to her husband and affection for her parents. She felt that eight or nine years was a long time for husband and wife to be separated, especially in those days of slow and infrequent communication.

Although in one sense it may be said that 'absence makes the heart grow fonder,' people have a decided tendency to drift somewhat apart and become independent of each other during a long separation, more particularly in the case of a couple whose minds were already not very sympathetic.

That Lady Macartney took an anxious interest in her husband's career and did all she could to further his interests is shown by her letters, and her sister, Lady Louisa Stuart, writing to Lady Carlow, expresses her satisfaction that 'Mr. Dundas[1] is struck with Lady Jane as a remarkably sensible woman.'[2]

Macartney had great confidence in his wife, and left the management of his affairs in her hands,[3] including hospitality

[1] Mr. Dundas, afterwards Lord Melville, was at that time Minister for India.
[2] Mrs. Godfrey Clark, 'Gleanings from an Old Portfolio.'
[3] 'You and Mr. Jackson are my attorneys, and I know you will manage for the best. Whatever you may want for yourself, you know you are to command without scruple.'—Private Correspondence.

to his friends. He was not one of those men who, as they rise in the world, think it necessary to confine their friendships to people of importance whom they think will do them credit, giving the cold shoulder to those earlier ones of a humble position in life. He had many friends in all ranks of society, and always took a kindly interest in his country neighbours from the North of Ireland. That Lady Macartney, accustomed to an orderly and narrow social groove, found their entertainment rather irksome and trying upon occasions, is scarcely to be wondered at.

Lady Carlow, in a letter to Lady Louisa Stuart, thus expresses her sentiments in the matter :

'*October*, 1781.

'... I am very sorry poor Lady Jane is so tormented with those horrid Irish people, especially as I think they are likely to leave her no rest whilst they remain in London, as they are doing exactly what I suppose they would be delighted to have her do with them here, for it is the Irish way to make no difference between friends and strangers, and they are just as fond of you and as delighted to have you the first minute they are acquainted as we should be with an old friend.'

In another letter, after laughing heartily at ' the strange vulgar manners ' of some of her own Scotch country cousins, Lady Carlow goes on to say :

' As to the L——'s, I can't help being out of patience with them, and more so with Lord Macartney for saddling his poor wife with such trumpery people, which I am sure they must be, for there is none even of my Portarlington neighbours that are half as vulgar as you describe them. I shall be delighted to hear that they are tired of London, or rather that their money will hold out no longer, for I fancy that will happen first.'[1]

Lady Macartney appears to have been very anxious as to what might be said about the affair with Sir John Burgoyne, and wrote thus to her sister :

[1] Mrs. Godfrey Clark, ' Gleanings from an Old Portfolio.'

NEWS FROM INDIA

'*August* 2, 1784.

'There is now a ship arrived from Madras which has brought me a letter of the beginning of last February from Lord Macartney. At that time his health was pretty good, but he complains much of his constitution being in general much hurt and weakened by all he has gone through. He gives me no reason to hope he has fixed any time for returning, as he bids me continue to write and send him letters. I have, according to custom, lost some letters in which he says he has given me an account of the arrest of Sir John Burgoyne. If they are not lost they are suppressed, a circumstance very disagreeable, as the other party have their story to tell, and I have no materials to answer them. I cannot find out yet what was the cause of his arrest, or whether it was by order of General Lang or Lord M. Some people tell me Sir John is coming home immediately; others that he is going to wait in India to be tried by a court-martial. I defer my going to Tunbridge till I know what the determination at the India House is with respect to Lord M. in consequence of this new Bill.[1] I think they must finally settle in a short time whether he is to be removed or not.'[2]

The general view taken of the Governor's conduct was a favourable one, and Lady Bute wrote in January, 1785:

'I think I have not seen Lady Macartney so well for several years as she is this winter. The great credit and

[1] About this time Lady Macartney wrote to her husband: 'Mr. Hastings' friends have been trying by every method to keep him in his present office; many of them who promoted your election are now taking a part against you which is very ungenerous, as it can do him no good, and may possibly do you harm. The Duke of Portland, however, says always that whenever the change at Bengal happens, Lord M. is the properest person to succeed.'—Private Correspondence.

[2] *Lady Louisa Stuart to Lady Carlow.*

'*September*, 1784.

'Lady M. is still in London, putting off her going to Tunbridge from week to week, according to the delays of the E. I. Directors, who are about settling the government of Madras. I hope it is almost impossible that they should remove, that is to say disgrace, a man who has deserved so well of them as Lord M.'—'Gleanings from an Old Portfolio.'

reputation Lord Macartney has acquired contribute not a little to her satisfaction, and indeed she has good reason to be pleased with it. I wish the E. I. Company may show their approbation by something more substantial than praise.'

But she was still much torn in her mind as to the advisability of joining her husband in India, being also urged there by Mr. Staunton, who was then in England.

Lady Macartney to Lady Carlow.

'*May*, 1785.

'I think much of India, but God knows whether I shall ever accomplish that scheme. . . . I propose to spend the greatest part of next summer at Tunbridge in order to try to get as much strength as I can, lest I should go to India, though my mother is so entirely adverse to that scheme that I doubt I must give it up. I certainly should not hesitate one moment about it were it not for her, but I owe her so much, and I know her to have so few comforts, that I shall never be able to prevail upon myself to go. If she sees it in the light of an affliction, the situation is surely a cruel one, for I daresay you agree with me, that if one is ever to live with anybody, a separation of eight or nine years is rather too great a trial, particularly when a woman is advancing in life. The time that has passed may be of use, but several years added must estrange people from each other more than would be prudent. And supposing anything was to happen to Lord M. (he has already had very bad health), I should never forgive myself to have remained here. Mr. Staunton is urgent with me to go, and as both he and his wife would, in every respect, be of much more consequence in India, and meet with more attention of every kind if I were not there, I must suppose his advice is totally impartial and disinterested. If I do go it surely would be most desirable for me to take the voyage with them, and not go alone, or with people I am unacquainted with. In short, my dear, it appears to me thus : Shall I go and make my Mother miserable, or shall I stay and totally give up all prospect of cordiality and friendship with Lord M. ? One thing I own makes a great impression upon me : I have never yet met with any person, any common acquaintance, who does not suppose I shall certainly now go to India. I fear if I do not it will be a reproach upon my mind as long as I live, unless he positively sends to forbid me.'

Jane Lady Macartney
1786
From the Portrait
In the possession of C. G. Macartney, Esq.

DRESS FOR THE BIRTHDAY

'*June*, 1785.

'I am going to the birthday, when I wish for you to accompany me, and I am really at a loss without your advice and taste about my gown.

'I thought it would be right for me to go this year, and also to have a gown rather more expensive than a plain lustring, yet I grudge any expense for my dress. I therefore determined to have some sort of trimming made at home, and knowing nothing about the matter myself, and my maid being as ignorant, we have together contrived an ugly thing which costs twice as much as I intended. My head is so confused and taken up by other things that I have quite lost the little genius I had for dress. I received a letter last night from Lord M. dated the 8th January, in which he says he is tolerably well, but has had some severe attacks of rheumatism, and he longs to such a degree to come home, that it makes me hate the thought of the Government-General, and wish that he may not think himself obliged to undertake it. But if he does the circumstance of his health will make me doubly anxious to go to him. However, my dear, I have already said enough to you upon this subject.'[1]

On January 9, 1786, Macartney returned home. Four days after he had a conference with the chairman and deputy chairman of the East India Company with reference to his appointment of Governor-General of Bengal. As a matter of fact, he was not at all anxious to return to India. The hot climate and the worry and anxiety inseparable from his government had told upon his health, and he felt that he needed a prolonged rest. He foresaw much opposition to his appointment and many difficulties, but under certain conditions was willing to take up office. His views upon the necessity of subordinating the military to the civil authority in India were decided; and he felt that he must be certain of a consistent support from the Government at home if the office of Governor-General was to be more than a shadow without substance.

At the opening of Parliament in January, 1786, Fox, when commenting upon the King's Speech, observed that

[1] Mrs. Godfrey Clark, 'Gleanings from an Old Portfolio.'

158   SPEECHES BY FOX AND PITT

'Lord Macartney had acted throughout the whole of his stay in India upon the most upright principles, and had come home with hands perfectly clean and unsullied.' He eulogized the ability and zeal of the late Governor of Madras, also the disinterestedness and integrity of his conduct, and wished it to be understood that what he had said was not 'from any authority derived from his Lordship,' and no more than 'what he, in common with the rest of the public, was well acquainted with.'[1]

Pitt made a reply which was extremely complimentary to Macartney, and in which he dwelt upon the noble and disinterested conduct of the latter. He said that from the whole of his administration at Madras he was perfectly eligible for that of Bengal; and that, with the one exception of the assignment of the revenues of the Carnatic, Macartney's conduct throughout his government 'entitled him to the highest glory and applause.'[2]

But in spite of this approbation of Macartney's behaviour,[3] Pitt showed no disposition to grant any substantial recognition of his services. This Macartney seemed to consider necessary, in order to emphasize the appreciation of government. He therefore asked for elevation to the English peerage. But this moderate demand was somewhat ungraciously refused, under the plea that it established an undesirable precedent. At the close of his interview with Mr. Dundas and Pitt on February 21, Macartney expressed himself as very undesirous of the appointment. He concluded by repeating the opinion often given to the Court of Directors, and hoped their choice would fall upon the

[1] Sir J. Barrow, 'Life of the Earl of Macartney.'   [2] *Ibid.*

[3] 'By what I have heard from time to time of the general state of Indian affairs, and the strong tide of corruption you have had to encounter there from all quarters, it astonishes me how you have been able to stand against it for so many years with such unshaken firmness and perseverance. It could only be surmounted by your uncommon abilities . . . and unexampled integrity; which last quality, I fear, was the source of all your troubles. . . . You have the singular circumstance in your favour of uniting all the political leaders . . . to applaud your conduct.'—Extract from a letter from Mr. Jackson to Lord Macartney.

APPOINTMENT OF LORD CORNWALLIS

most suitable man they could find, and one superior to himself in other qualifications.

Three days later he received the news that Lord Cornwallis had been appointed Governor-General of Bengal. Shortly after hearing this he went on to an evening party, at which Lady Macartney was present, and taking a card from his pocket, wrote on it in pencil: 'I am the happiest man in England at this hour. Lord Cornwallis, I hear, is Governor-General of India.'

The East India Company marked their appreciation of his services by an annuity for life of £1,500 a year. He was also presented with silver plate to the value of £1,600 for the forbearance and justice of his conduct while at Madras, and his great pecuniary moderation.

Some time previously they had granted an annuity of £500 to Mr. Staunton, who had returned to England in advance of his chief. Mr. Staunton was also given an Irish baronetcy as a reward for his distinguished and meritorious conduct in India.

Lady Macartney presented Mrs. Staunton at Court on the occasion of her husband being made a baronet. The following account of her presentation was written by Lady Staunton to her mother, Mrs. Collins:

'SUFFOLK STREET,
'*January* 28, 1786.

'... My brother William gave me the pleasure of hearing that he left you well. He found me occupied in the important business of preparing for Court, where I was going to be presented, upon my husband's being created a baronet. Lady Macartney accompanied me to the drawing-room, and I was presented by Lord Ailesbury to the Queen, and to the King by Lord Fauconberg. According to the ceremony I made a very low court'sey to the King, who raised me up, and saluted me on the left cheek. You may naturally suppose I was in some little flutter: however, His Majesty asked me but a few civil questions, which it was not difficult to answer.... After this I had still to pay my respects to the Queen. To her I likewise made a very low courtsey, on which she held out her hand, which I kissed. She then spoke to me a few words, to which I replied, repeating my courtsey, and then retired, mixing again among the crowd of company that filled the drawing-room. Among those whom I knew there were Lord Barrington and Mr. Pitt, in whose company I had dined the week before.

'Before I left the drawing-room I had an opportunity of seeing the Speaker in his robes and other members of the House of Commons, presenting an address to the King. The Queen's birthday is kept next Thursday, when I understand it is proper I should appear at Court to pay my compliments, and I am therefore now preparing for that occasion.'[1]

During all this time General Stuart had by no means forgotten his resentment and schemes for revenge. The day after Macartney's arrival in London he received a note from General Stuart, informing him that the General had sent a petition to the King contradicting the charges brought against him in Madras, and protesting against their injustice and falsehood. To this Macartney returned an answer, saying he was by no means concerned as to the petition. He had 'long been resigned to the consequences of having filled the duties of his station, and being exposed to the contradictions and opposition of those individuals of whose misconduct he was, in his official capacity, obliged to take notice.' He also intimated his willingness to accept a challenge by informing General Stuart that he would take no further notice of any communication from him, unless made known in direct terms by any gentleman appointed for the purpose. To this General Stuart replied that his first object was the vindication of his honour, which he should proceed to do without loss of time. Having requested that Lord Macartney would observe an absolute secrecy in the matter, he concluded by stating that the friend he intended to employ in the affair was then at Bath, otherwise he would have been the channel of this last communication.

Nothing further was heard of the matter till the night of

[1] 'Life and Family of Sir G. L. Staunton.'

CHALLENGE FROM GENERAL STUART

May 27, when, on his return from a performance at the opera, Macartney found the following note awaiting him at his house in Charles Street :

'Colonel Gordon presents his compliments to Lord Macartney, and wishes to see him when convenient. Saturday, quarter past nine o'clock p.m. No. 20 Charing Cross, Corner of Craig's Court.'

Next day at noon Macartney called on Colonel Gordon, and received from him a packet of papers containing a statement of General Stuart's grievances, and demand for satisfaction.

The preliminaries of the duel were speedily arranged, and the place of meeting decided upon, a spot twenty minutes' drive from the Tyburn turnpike. The following account of the proceedings is taken from the *Gentleman's Magazine* for June, 1786 :

'This morning a duel was fought near Kensington between Lord Macartney and Major-General Stuart, of which the following is an authentic account, as transmitted to us by the seconds, Colonel Fullarton and Colonel Gordon, the former accompanying Lord Macartney and the latter General Stuart. The place and time of meeting having been previously fixed, the parties arrived about half-past four o'clock in the morning, and took their ground at the distance of twelve short paces measured off by the seconds. . . . General Stuart told Lord Macartney he doubted, as his Lordship was shortsighted, he would not be able to see him ; his Lordship replied he did perfectly well. . . . When they had levelled, General Stuart said he was ready ; his Lordship answered he was likewise ready, and they both fired within a few instants of each other. The seconds observing Lord Macartney wounded, stepped up to him and declared the matter must rest here. General Stuart said "This is no satisfaction," and asked if his Lordship was not able to fire another pistol. His Lordship replied he would try with pleasure, and urged Colonel Fullarton to allow him to proceed ; the seconds, however, declared it was impossible, and they would on no account allow it. General Stuart said " Then I must defer it till another occasion," on which his Lordship answered, " If that is the case we had better proceed now. I am here in consequence of a message from General Stuart, who called upon me to give him satisfaction in my private capacity for offence taken at my public conduct. . . . I have nothing personal; the General will proceed as he thinks fit." General Stuart said it was his Lordship's personal conduct to him that he resented; the seconds then put a stop to all further conversation between the parties, neither of whom had quitted their ground. General Stuart, in consequence of his situation, having been under the necessity, from the first, of putting his back to a tree.

'The surgeons . . . who were attending at a little distance, were brought up by Colonel Fullarton. Colonel Gordon . . . assisted his Lordship in taking off his coat, and requested him to sit down, apprehending he might be faint through loss of blood. Colonel Gordon then left the ground in company with General Stuart, and an easy carriage was provided to convey his Lordship home.

'The seconds cannot help expressing that no two persons ever met on a similar occasion who shewed more firmness and composure; and they are happy to add that the ball is extracted which was lodged in Lord Macartney's right shoulder, and that there is every reason to hope for his recovery.'

The duel was not renewed, in spite of General Stuart's wishes. It was understood that the King had himself personally intervened in the matter, it having been brought to his notice by Lord Townshend.

Years after among Lady Macartney's papers was found the following letter, with this inscription, in her handwriting:

'Copy of a letter written by my dear husband just before he went out to fight a duel with General Stuart, and left with Sir George Staunton to deliver to me. The original of this was given to me by Sir G. S. upon Lord M.'s return wounded, and I trust will always be preserved in my family.

'*June* 8, 1786.

'MY DEAREST LOVE,

'When you receive this letter I shall be no more. To leave you is the only pain I feel at this moment, but I trust we shall meet again in a happier world, for, if the step I am now obliged to take be forgiven, I know of no other crime to sit heavy upon me.

THE DUEL

'My will, which Sir George Staunton will deliver to you, will show you that I retain to the last the same affection and confidence which I have ever reposed in you. Let me recommend to your care and friendship my niece Miss Balaquier, Sir George Staunton, Captain Benson, and Mr. Acheson Maxwell. Adieu.

'MACARTNEY.'[1]

The following account of the affair is given by Lady Mary Coke in her (unpublished) journal:

'NOTTING HILL,
'*Thursday, June 8th*, 1786.

'. . . I left London about two o'clock, and am now settled here, though in an uncomfortable way. They tell me there was a duel fought this morning in a field just by here—two officers, one Mr. Corbett, who married a daughter of Lord Bute; he was shot in the body, but the other not wounded.

'*Friday*.—They have just told me Mr. Corbett died of his wounds this morning. Murder in any shape is dreadful, though this method has the sanction of being called honourable. . . .

'*Saturday, June* 10.—Though so near the scene of action, I did not hear the true names of those engaged . . . it was Lord Macartney and General Stewart. The quarrel was in the East Indies, where Lord Macartney thought it necessary, to prevent mischief as Governor, to imprison Stewart, who had frequently been creating disturbances. You may remember, I believe, how ill he treated poor Lord Pigot, and was thought by that treatment to have been the cause of his death. He is certainly a very troublesome person and a very revengeful one, and after having wounded Lord Macartney in the right arm, he wanted to continue till one of them fell, but the seconds interposed and put an end to it, but Stewart said it must begin again. I hope, however, His Majesty (who alone can) will prevent a second duel. Poor Lady Macartney had been ill of a fever, and you may guess what her situation was to have him brought home wounded; however, 'twas lucky she knew nothing of the affair till it was over. He dined at

[1] This letter is now in the possession of Mrs. Godfrey Clark, who kindly allowed the writer to see it.

II—2

home, and, as she says, appeared in perfectly easy spirits. After dinner he went out and settled all his affairs, and then went to a Bagnio, where he slept till four o'clock, and at five they met in a field on the other side of the Acton Road. I've mentioned all these particulars, as they are falsely related in the public papers. I went this morning to town to see Lady Bute, who, added to her fit of the gout, has been much affected with this affair. I called at Lord Macartney's; he is thought to be in a good way, but the wound is not to be opened in three days, so they can't tell as yet whether the bone is touched. . . .

'*Wednesday, June* 14.—. . . Poor Lord Macartney has got the gout in both his feet, and his wound is very painful; the bone is touched, and poor Lady Macartney suffers almost as much as him; 'tis really a pitiable situation. . . .

'*Friday, June* 16.—I called on Lady Bute yesterday evening, and found her a great deal better, but poor Lord Macartney suffers terribly from his wound; a bone has worked out, and perhaps there may be more that are hurt. . . .

'*Thursday, June* 29.—I made a visit to Lady Bute, and found her quite recovered. Poor Lord Macartney yet suffers very much from his wound, but I hope he is in no danger of being pursued any more by the revengeful temper of his adversary, as His Majesty has been so good to interpose, and has ordered them to give their word of honour not to fight again, and if either breaks their word and send a challenge, he is to be prosecuted by the Attorney-General.'

As soon as he had somewhat recovered from the effect of his wound, Macartney went over to Ireland, and before returning to England paid a surprise visit to his sister-in-law and her husband.

Extract from a Letter from Lady Portarlington to Lady Louisa Stuart.

'DAWSON COURT, QUEEN'S CO.,
'*September* 8, 1786.

'. . . You may imagine how agreeably surprised I was in the afternoon to see a chaise drive up to the door and Lord M. in it. I cannot describe the flutter I was in, nor the joy I felt at seeing anybody belonging to the family here. I believe I should have been out of my wits with joy if she had accompanied him. He is not as much altered as I expected, and seems in very good spirits, and I think much more agreeable, as he has left off the sneering way he had. We are going to drive him about the place, so I hope it will be a fine day, for I would wish him to make a favourable report of it. . . .

'Lord M. seemed surprised not to find me altered; I suppose he thought six years and five children would have made an old woman of me. I wonder he did not think I looked ill, as I am without powder. . . . He had a fine romp with the children last night.'

On his side Lord Macartney appears to have been equally impressed with a change for the better in his host and hostess, and told his wife that he was 'much pleased with his visit to Dawson Court.' He thought the place beautiful, the children charming, and Lord and Lady Portarlington grown fat and improved. As to the former, he was quite another man, so much more talkative and sociable than he used to be. 'He gives his Lordship good judgment in many things, and says he and his wife seem uncommonly comfortable together.'[1]

Some months afterwards the Macartneys gave up their house in Charles Street, and moved to 3, Curzon Street. Here Lord Macartney appears to have become more domestic in his habits.

'As for the two people (Lord and Lady M.), they have really lived in a more comfortable style than I have ever known them do; always supping at home for one thing. He is very fond of his fine house and his great room, partly for its convenience and partly for grandeur, and that makes him fonder of home than he used to be. Then we are more at our ease with all his friends and companions, and know better how to manage them. In short, I verily believe he intends doing everything that is right, and there is but one thing he wants—feeling. However, we are not sensible of that failure, or do not own it to ourselves, so it's mighty well. For farther views in the way of ambition, I suppose he has them, and he may very reasonably and

[1] Mrs. Godfrey Clark, 'Gleanings from an Old Portfolio.'

laudably. One cannot expect a man of very great abilities for business, and a very high reputation, to be content to sit still in his chair at scarce fifty years old. I wish he were Secretary of State with all my heart. But I don't know whether I do wish him a good sinecure, or a place at Court, for an increase of income and nothing to do would be likely to make him extravagant. I hardly think there is any probability of his getting anything good enough for his acceptance at present, but there is no immediate hurry.'[1]

During the summer Macartney was laid up with a sharp attack of gout, and was ill for some time. Mrs. Sturt, of Critchell House, Dorset, sent him a present of choice venison, with a letter of condolence on his 'troublesome enemy.' She entreated him not to acknowledge the gift, or 'put pen to paper whilst the gout is flying about, as the mind ought to be kept unemployed, the heart light, and the head not affected by business.' Both Mrs. Sturt and her son Humphrey, who was in India, had reason to be grateful to Macartney, who appears to have been very helpful in the management of their affairs. Humphrey Sturt, writing to Macartney, says he did not intend to come home to be a weight upon his family, though he disliked India, and found the manners and ideas of the people 'very discordant' with his own. He intended to 'worry through with them,' and concludes his letter by describing Macartney's character as 'not only spotless, but shining.'

In October, 1787, Macartney's niece, Elizabeth Balaquier, wrote to announce her approaching marriage with the Rev. Travers Hume, and their projected trip to France. They spent the winter at Pau and the summer of 1788 in the neighbourhood of Bordeaux, to which place they proceeded for the birth of Mrs. Hume's eldest child (a daughter), which took place on October 31, 1788. The following spring the Humes returned to Ireland, and paid a visit to the Macartneys on their way home.

[1] Lady Louisa Stuart to Lady Portarlington, 'Gleanings from an Old Portfolio.'

'CURZON STREET,
'*April* 7, 1789.

'We return to-morrow to Surrey, but shall probably come backwards and forwards till we set out for Ireland, which is still intended the end of May. We expect Mr. and Mrs. Hume here from abroad on their way to Ireland the beginning of next month, and then we must, I suppose, be in town to show them the lions here.

'All sorts of fine things are going forward. The King and Queen are to go in state to St. Paul's; after that it is said there are to be magnificent entertainments given by the French and Spanish Ambassadors to Her Majesty.

'The fine entertainment at Brooks's is to be Wednesday se'nnight. I think we have got off very well, as Lord M. has not been obliged to subscribe either to that or White's.'

'*April* 25, 1789.

'. . . We return again to Parkhurst for ten days, and then come back here to receive Mr. and Mrs. Hume. . . . They will probably remain here a few weeks. Lord M. says we are to stay with them for a fortnight, and after that either to go over to Ireland, or to settle at Parkhurst: his present plan seems to be that we should go to Lissanoure to stay several months . . . or to go over himself for a month, finish his business, and return to Parkhurst. I own I dislike the thoughts of Ireland, both on account of leaving my Mother for so long a time, and the taking of so long a journey is very troublesome and expensive. However, I shall not declare any choice, but leave Lord M. to determine what he thinks best.'

'*May* 9, 1789.

'We are now in town for a fortnight to see Mr. and Mrs. Hume, who arrived from France the day before yesterday. I like her better than I expected; I think she seems sensible. Her manner is now rather genteel—this perhaps she may have acquired by living abroad some months—and both she and her husband appear inclined to a very reasonable domestic plan of life. He is one of the youngest-looking men I ever saw, and she, I think, looks very old of her age; anyone would suppose her to be ten years older than him . . . yet they say he is two years older: there is an appearance of great goodness about him. I am a very bad person to show London to strangers, and I am therefore very glad they seem well satisfied to take the coach and go about by themselves. There is a sister of his living here with Lady Brooke, and they have other Irish acquaintances in town.'

'Parkhurst,
'February 1, 1790.

'I told you in my last that we were only to stay a week in London, and have now returned to this place for some time. Next month we are to go to make a longer stay, and to prepare for our journey to the North of Ireland, which now I think Lord M. seems absolutely determined upon, and says he proposes to set out the end of April or beginning of May. You know how much it will grieve me to go to such a distance from our dear Mother, and there are other very unpleasant circumstances attending a residence there; but I must submit with as much patience and content as I can.'[1]

Macartney suffered severely from several sharp attacks of gout in 1789, and during the summer went to Buxton for a course of the waters there.

Letter from Lord Macartney to Sir George Staunton.

'August, 1789.

'My sentiments seldom vary much upon any subject, but with regard to India it is impossible they should change, and I have long determined never to meddle with that country, unless I could make it a certain instrument of great benefit to the State, and of great honour to myself. Those objects I could not hope to accomplish unless it were manifest that I had the united support of the Company, the Ministers, and the Crown. The want of such support was, as you know, a very strong reason, among others, for my twice declining the Government of Bengal some years ago, and since that time d'ye think the prospect less discouraging? But enough of this.

'. . . Lady M. joins me in a thousand thanks to you for your letter and the hearing-trumpets[2] which accompanied it. . . . She almost despairs of relief, having tried so many

[1] Extracts from letters from Lady Macartney to Lady Portarlington.
[2] The Stauntons had lately been in Paris, and while there heard of a new kind of ear-trumpet.

remedies without success, yet will certainly make a fair experiment of the one you have sent her. I shall be happy to give you a favourable account of it. . . .'

Letter from Lord Macartney to Sir George Staunton.[1]

'*October* 10, 1789.

'In my way from Hampshire I stopped a few days in London, in order to pay my duty at the Levee last Wednesday, where I found almost as great a crowd as used to attend there before His Majesty's illness; but many were, I believe, disappointed, as he made a turn to his left at the door instead of standing to talk to people in the threshold as formerly. However, he did not appear to pass by anyone intentionally, but spoke pretty equally to everybody who was fairly in his way. What he said to me, and what I overheard him say to others, was remarkably proper and guarded. . . .

'The King is perfectly well, but to my eye looked more ruddy and more corpulent than formerly. His manner composed, and much less hurry or precipitation in his address and enunciation than he used to have. . . . A few transient smiles, but not a single laugh that I could observe.

'The news at Court was the Duke of Dorset's appointment to the stewardship of the household, and the Duke of Beaufort's to the government of Ireland.'

The much-dreaded visit to the North of Ireland took place, and the Macartneys remained there for some little time. Lady Bute wrote to her daughter that she hoped they would not stay too long in the country, as a public man is soon forgotten if he does not keep before the world.

It was but natural that Lady Macartney should have disliked the change from the comparative warmth and brightness of the South of England to being, as she must have considered it, buried among the bogs of Antrim. She also dreaded the temptation to her husband of spending more than was strictly prudent on improvements and alterations to his house and grounds. For though extremely cautious in his expenditure of public money, Macartney was apt to

[1] '*Life and Family of Sir G. L. Staunton.*'

be somewhat lavish of his own. Mr. Jackson, a friend of Lord Macartney's, who was in the habit of looking after things at Lissanoure for him, wrote in the autumn of 1789 to Lady Louisa Stuart:

'I returned lately from Lissanoure, where I spent a few days, and took my family with me.'[1] It is a pretty wild place now, and may be pleasant for a few months in the summer, but a most dreary one when the bad weather sets in. He (Lord M.) has lavished a large sum of money on the house, plantations, etc. Considering how many of the great comforts of life are wanting in such a situation, besides many inconveniences and dangers from storms and rains, it seems a wild idea to think of making it a constant residence for a family. This, however, I find is his plan . . . but upon trial I believe it will be found to be insupportable. The house is neat and well aired at this moment, but when that is over a set of unconquerable difficulties will arise, neither foreseen nor thought of. . . . He has all his life filled his mind with numberless schemes and fanciful ideas. . . . If confidence were placed where it ought to be,[2] a new scene of substantial comfort should follow. Few men have that common sense to estimate things as they really are. I wish our dear Friend to look for nothing certain in this world, and if she must suffer to consider it God's will.'

The year following the Jacksons visited the Macartneys at Lissanoure, and Mrs. Jackson, in writing an account of their visit to Lady Louisa, speaks in the warmest terms of Lady Macartney's goodness and kindness, adding, 'Think how she will be refined after these severe trials which she has borne like a Christian,' and concludes by saying that nothing but religion could support her through them. All this sounds, of course, rather exaggerated to our ears in these days of railways and motors, when moving about

[1] Mr. and Mrs. Jackson were ancestors, on the maternal side, of the present owner of Lissanoure. Their daughter eloped with a handsome but penniless young curate, Mr. Alexander, nephew of Lord Caledon, who became in course of time Bishop of Meath. From one of their numerous children the present Macartney of Lissanoure is descended.

[2] The Jacksons were extremely religious people, and devoted to Lady Macartney.

LISSANOURE CASTLE AND LOUGH GUILE

From the Picture in the possession of C. G. MACARTNEY, Esq.

presents no difficulties and distance is annihilated. But there is no doubt that Lady Macartney, as well as disliking climate and surroundings, suffered terribly from social loneliness and being cut off from her family.

A woman of narrow interests, born and brought up in the atmosphere of Court life and society, she can have had little in common with her country neighbours, and doubtless found intercourse with them more irksome than otherwise. She had not even the interest of children to give colour to her life. For her husband it was quite otherwise: he was a native of the place and loved it, knew the people from early childhood, and having knocked about the world, found no difficulty in suiting himself to his company and surroundings. As a matter of fact, he was extremely busy and happy during the time he spent at Lissanoure, and occupied himself with improvements to the estate. He drained large tracts of boggy ground, and made extensive plantations. He rebuilt the village of Dervock, about nine miles from Lissanoure, so that his tenants there might be provided with clean and comfortable dwellings, a sufficiently rare state of things at that time among the Irish peasantry. He had no middleman upon his estate, but managed it himself, letting it out in small allotments, and encouraging the prosperity and happiness of his tenantry as far as he possibly could.

In 1788 he had, for the first time, taken his seat in the Irish House of Peers. Later on he accepted the office of *custos rotulorum* for the county of Antrim, and became one of the trustees of the linen manufacture in Ulster. He also was Colonel of a militia regiment of Dragoons. To Sir George Staunton, Macartney wrote in the winter of 1790 as follows:

'LISSANOURE,
'*December*, 1790.

'I ought to have sooner thanked you for your obliging letter of the 25th October . . . but various accidents and occurrences have, I know not how, constantly intruded upon me, and disappointed my intentions. . . . You are not very fond, I think, of a country life. . . . The taste for it grows upon me wonderfully. Not a moment seems tedious, and so far from time being heavy upon my hands, I am always complaining of its rapidity, and never find it sufficient for the schemes I have of filling it up here. . . . The whole of Mr. B.'s[1] pamphlet on French affairs has been retailed by piecemeal in one of our county newspapers here. . . . An old Presbyterian neighbour of mine, who almost worshipped Mr. B. for his speeches against the American War, for reforming the King's household, and for punishing the enormities of Hastings, was so shocked at what he called apostasy that I had no way of bringing him to himself but by observing that this last book of Mr. B.'s might be a mere *jeu d'esprit*. . . . I assure you, so unwilling was my friend to change his opinion of Mr. B. that he was *half* willing to believe me *quite* serious. . . .'

Towards the close of the year 1791 the exactions and acts of injustice perpetrated by the Chinese on English subjects at Canton had reached such a climax that it renewed the desire of the British Government for an embassy to the Court of China. An attempt had been made some years previously, but had come to nothing, owing to the death, on his way out, of the person entrusted with the commission.

The Chinese being indifferent—indeed, rather hostile than otherwise—to the progress of foreign trade with their country, it followed there was but a slender chance of even common justice being shown towards the people who carried it on. More especially was this the case with the English, who, in the course of their dealings with the Chinese, were subjected to many oppressions and insults to their persons.

The introduction of the English into China for the purposes of trade seems to have been of an unfortunate nature. The first attempt was made by Queen Elizabeth, who, at the close of the sixteenth century, 'sent out John Mildenhall overland from Constantinople to the Court of the Great Mogul, for obtaining certain privileges for the English, for whom she was then preparing a charter. He was long opposed by the arts of the Spanish and Portuguese Jesuits

[1] Edmund Burke.

ENGLISH TRADERS IN CHINA

at that Court; and it was some years before he could entirely get the better of them.'[1] The Portuguese and Dutch, who had established the first commercial relations with China, were naturally averse to the introduction of the English into the country in the capacity of merchants. During the reign of Charles I. an expedition, under the command of a Captain Weddell, set out for China. Those who composed it appear to have been more or less adventurers, but quite willing to trade peaceably. However, through the ill offices of the Portuguese, who spoke of them as thieves and beggars, a quarrel was fomented between them and the Chinese, with the result that, although a seeming peace was patched up at the end, the English continued to be depicted in the most unfavourable manner to the government of the country. This continued for a long time, and the inhabitants of the British Isles were known by the somewhat contemptuous appellation of 'carrotty-pated race.'[2]

It would have required a long course of reserved and cautious conduct on their part to obliterate these unfavourable impressions. This, unfortunately, was somewhat difficult to reconcile with the spirit and freedom of action resulting from the nature of British government. Their conduct, however justifiable, often appeared as presumption in the eyes of the arbitrary mandarins, especially when observed in those of a mercantile profession. The behaviour, too, of the British seamen was often offensive and annoying to a people like the Chinese, whose actions, even to the least important, were controlled by specific regulations.

From these causes, of all foreigners resident at Canton the English were depicted in the most unfavourable light to those at the head of affairs, and often treated with great rigour on the spot. Their complaints were considered as frivolous and ill-founded, and attributed to their unreasonable dispositions. Measures also were taken to avoid the constant repetition of remonstrances by the punishment of those natives who were suspected of having assisted in

[1] Sir G. L. Staunton, 'Embassy to China.'   [2] Ibid.

the translation of their grievances into Chinese. Indeed, to teach them the language at all was found to be a somewhat dangerous employment. Thus they were under the necessity of trusting entirely to the native merchants with whom they had to deal.

The English, however, did not believe that such treatment was authorized by the Emperor of China; possibly, indeed, it was not known to him. The agents of the East India Company urged, therefore, the advisability of sending an Embassy to His Imperial Majesty of China, in the hope that he might look into their grievances, and redress, at any rate, a portion of them. They pointed out that a British Ambassador would be a novelty, and his mission a compliment which would probably be well received. The English were scarcely known at Pekin, and those at Canton, not having been recommended by their Sovereign, might possibly be considered merely as adventurers not entitled to any particular respect. The Court of Pekin was known to be little fond of promiscuous intercourse with strangers. It was inclined to the view that the happiness of its subjects would be best preserved by secluding them as much as possible from contact with strangers and people of different habits and ideas. No one expected that a change in this policy could suddenly be brought about, but it was hoped that a succession of British subjects, of courteous and dignified behaviour, residing at Pekin in a suitable manner, might influence public opinion and gain the confidence of all classes. This, by bringing about a better mutual understanding, would pave the way to a subsequent alliance with the country. Macartney was at once thought of as almost the only person capable of undertaking such a mission with any strong probability of success. When approached upon the matter, he intimated his willingness to accept the office, with this proviso: that he should have as secretary and successor in case of his death his tried and trusted friend Sir George Staunton. This was agreed to without hesitation, and his recommendations were accepted in every other department of the

SEARCH FOR INTERPRETERS

Embassy. Macartney's salary was fixed at £15,000 a year, and he was asked to select any ship of sixty-four guns then in commission to convey him to China, and to name the captain whom he would wish to command her. That captain was also to be allowed to select all his own officers. The East India Company, by whom the expense of the Embassy was to be borne, left to Macartney the selection of presents for the Emperor of China; they also sent, at his request, the *Hindustan*, one of the finest ships in their service, and another small vessel to accompany the Embassy.

The post of interpreter and translator was a difficult one to fill, as no man capable of being employed in that capacity then existed in the British Empire. From what has been stated previously as to the difficulties of obtaining instruction in the Chinese language, it is not surprising that the supercargoes of the East India Company returned home, after several years' residence in the country, still unproficient in the language. It was not advisable to rely upon finding a fit person to act as interpreter in Canton. Some of the natives there, it is true, knew enough of a European language to interpret for foreign merchants in matters of sale or barter, but their linguistic attainments would have been hardly sufficient to carry on a conversation upon any other subject. It was thought best to search on the continent of Europe for a Chinese who had been able to leave his native country, and since then acquired the use of any of the European languages. A college had been founded at Naples for the education of the young Chinese whom the European missionaries from time to time contrived to get out of the country. Sir George Staunton accordingly started forth in quest of a suitable interpreter. After a fruitless search in France he proceeded to Italy. There, through the help of Cardinal Antonelli of the Congregation for the Propagation of the Faith, he obtained letters of introduction to the Italian missionaries in China, as well as to the Curator of the Chinese College in Naples. He found there several young men from China who were being trained for the priesthood and missionary work. A few, having completed their education, were ready to embark as soon as a suitable occasion presented itself. By the help of the English Minister at Naples, Sir William Hamilton, and Don Gaetano d'Ancora, the services of two of these young Chinese were obtained. Both were of amiable disposition and manners, thoroughly conversant with Latin and Italian, and perfectly qualified to act as interpreters. They were also most useful in their suggestions as to the most suitable articles for presentation to the Chinese Emperor. As the Court had already acquired, through private channels, a number of costly mechanical toys of various kinds, known by the name of 'Sing-songs' in Cantonese jargon, it was thought better to restrict the presents to articles of a more solid and scientific nature.

Fearing that the Viceroy of Canton might be somewhat inclined to conceal the news of the projected Embassy from the Emperor, it was decided to announce the fact as speedily and as publicly as possible. Three commissioners were selected by the East India Company from among their most approved employés and entrusted with a letter from Sir Francis Baring, the chairman, expressive of the intention of the Embassy to visit China.

The object of the Embassy was not solely confined to the mercantile affairs of Canton. Lord Macartney had discretionary authority to visit not only China, but any of the adjacent islands. He had ambassadorial powers addressed to the Emperor of Japan and the King of Cochin China, as well as a general commission to the Princes of any States he might happen to touch at in the Chinese seas.

Sir George Staunton, who seems to have had peculiar ideas on the subject of education,[1] stipulated that his son,

[1] Sir George Staunton brought up his son carefully and strictly, and never allowed him to employ an authoritative tone in dealing with inferiors in rank. He was extremely careful that the sentiments and ideas expressed in the child's presence were only those he wished to inspire him with. He carried this to such an extreme that the unfortunate boy was not allowed to associate with companions of his own age, which naturally proved a great disadvantage to him later on. He began to study Latin a few days after he attained the age

then a boy of twelve, should, with his German tutor,[1] accompany the Embassy to China.[2]

This arrangement was much against the wishes of Lady Staunton, who most naturally objected to her only surviving child being taken so far from home, and to such an unknown country as China. Her husband, however, considered this course of action would be of great advantage to the lad in preparing him for a future career, should there be any opening of diplomatic relations between England and China.[3] He endeavoured to point this out to his wife, and at the same time wrote to his brother-in-law to beg him to use his influence to restore Lady Staunton's mind to 'its wonted tranquillity.'

There had been some idea that it might be better for Sir George Staunton to precede the Ambassador, and prepare the way for him, but Macartney was averse to any arrangement of the kind.

---

of four, and was much delighted with Mrs. Barbauld's books. Like most children, he was fond of toys, but one conversation with his father, who explained how foolish such things were, and what a waste of money it was to buy them, sufficed to make him regard both toys and toyshops with disdain.—From a memorandum, in French, on the education of his son, in Sir G. Staunton's note-book,

[1] Mr. Hüttner, tutor to young Staunton, was a good classical scholar, and soon after the return of the Embassy was appointed interpreter to the Foreign Office.

[2] Sir George Staunton's son, a boy of twelve years old, during our passage from England, learned in a few broken lessons from a very cross master, and by his own attention, not only such a *copia verborum* and phraseology as enabled him to make himself understood and to understand others when he arrived in China, but acquired such a facility in writing the Chinese character that he copied all our diplomatic papers for the Chinese Government (the Chinese writers being afraid of their hands being known). And here let me observe that this young gentleman possesses already five languages—English, Latin, Greek, French, and Chinese.'—Lord Macartney, Appendix to Journal.

[3] These hopes were not realized, though young Staunton accompanied Lord Amherst's Embassy to China in 1816. His opinion, also, was asked on the question of trade with China when it came again before Parliament in 1813.

'... The more I read and think, the more I am of opinion that if I am to have the advantage of your assistance (which you may be assured I wish for above all things, if not contrary to your interest), we ought to go together and not be separated on any account. ... If you succeed in the object of your present expedition into Italy, I have little doubt of our making our own way much better by ourselves than by the aid or interposition of the people at Canton. ... I have had many disagreeable things relative to this business, and applications without number to be of our party to China, but I have uniformly resisted, though I fear I have given offence by doing so.'[1]

Everything being now in a state of preparation, on May 3, 1792, Macartney was appointed Ambassador Extra-

[1] Macartney was determined the choice of candidates should be decided by merit and capacity, and not by interest or influence though in one case he appears to have departed from that rule, as the following extract will show :

' Mr. Crewe (I believe a subaltern in the army), a young gentleman hanging loose on society, and a frequenter of the gaming-table, was the son of the celebrated wit and beauty of her day, so beautiful that Madame d'Arblay says "she uglifies everything near her." Admired by George, Prince of Wales, and adored by Charles Fox, she became the standing toast of the Whigs, was consecrated as their patroness by the Prince, who, on some great occasion, gave as a toast—

" Bluff and Blue,
And Mrs. Crewe."

Mrs. Crewe was also a great favourite of Lord Macartney, and she being most desirous of removing her son out of the temptations of London, earnestly entreated his lordship to take him to China. " The only condition," said Lord M., " on which I can possibly allow him to go is a most solemn pledge, on his honour, that he will not touch either cards or dice, or other instruments of gambling, either on board ship or at any place where we may stop. He gave the pledge and broke it—lost to one of the Lieutenants of the *Lion*, it was said, some thousand pounds, not any part of which could he pay. It was also said he had compounded the debt for an annuity of as many hundred pounds as he had lost thousands. My cabin on the passage home was on the lower deck, and scarcely a night passed in which I was not disturbed by the rattling of dice or by Mr. Crewe's scraping on the bass-viol. He was a most gentlemanly, good-natured young man, and was urged on by an old Scotch Lieutenant who ought to have known better.'—Sir J. Barrow, 'Autobiographical Memoir.'

ordinary and Plenipotentiary from the King of Great Britain to the Emperor of China. The same day he was sworn a Privy Councillor, and on June 28 following raised to the dignity of Viscount Macartney of Dervock, in the county of Antrim.

The Embassy sailed from Spithead on September 26, 1792, and the account of their adventures on the voyage out and their doings in China will be given in Lord Macartney's own words in the succeeding chapters.

CHAPTER VIII

JOURNAL OF EMBASSY FROM LONDON TO CHINA

Tuesday, September 11, 1793.—Set out from London to Portsmouth, and arrived at the latter place in eight hours.

Friday, September 21.—I embarked on board the *Lion*, Man of War of sixty-four guns, commanded by Sir Erasmus Gower.

Wednesday, September 26.—The whole Embassy, consisting of ninety-five persons, set sail from Spithead, in company with the *Jackall* brig, a tender attending the Embassy.

Tuesday, October 2.—We saw Ushant this morning at daybreak, five leagues S.E. distant.

Wednesday, October 10.—Arrived off Madeira, and in the evening, whilst endeavouring to get to our anchoring ground in Funchal Road, Mr. Robert Cock, the British Vice-Consul, with Mr. Vetch, Mr. Pringle, and Mr. Gordon, came on board the *Lion*, and Messieurs Vetch and Pringle gave us a very cordial invitation to their house.

Thursday, October 11.—Sir Erasmus Gower sent his first Lieutenant, Mr. Thomas Campbell, on shore this morning, to acquaint the Governor of our arrival, but before his return the Governor's boat came on board us, with his Secretary and his Aide-de-Camp, with a compliment from the Governor offering his house, services, etc., etc., to my command.

I went on shore soon after with Sir George Staunton, Sir Erasmus Gower, and the Vice-Consul, Mr. Cock.

Friday, October 12.—I paid a visit to the Governor, accompanied with all the Gentlemen of my train, dressed in the uniform of the Embassy, and was received with all the honours of the parade. The whole guard turned out, three ruffles, colours, etc., etc. The Governor was as civil in expression and attentive in deportment as possible, and

FESTIVITIES AT MADEIRA

pressed me earnestly to name a day to dine with him before I left the Island. As I wished to be as private as I could, I had declined the Guard, and meant to decline every other ceremony that could occasion trouble or delay. I endeavoured to excuse myself, but he urging his invitation, and the Vice-Consul and British gentlemen of the British factory mentioning to me that it would be very kindly taken, and would add to the harmony now prevailing between him and them, I consented, and fixed a particular day for the purpose. In the evening he returned my visit, attended by ten officers. We played at whist for two or three hours and grew very sociable together.

Saturday, October 13.—We dined at Val Formosa, a country seat of Mr. Murdoch's, which, as we were forty minutes walking, is I suppose about two miles distant from Funchal.

Mr. Murdoch is a very considerable merchant, well bred, gentlemanlike, and hospitable, married to a very agreeable woman, by whom he has a daughter, a fine girl of fifteen, sensible and conversable. In the evening my music attended, and there was a ball, at which Dr. Dinwiddie[1] exhibited as a very capital reel-dancer.

Monday, October 15.—Dined this day at Mr. Smith's, a native of Germany, but a naturalized Englishman, and acting as Imperial and Swedish Consul. The Governor and several Portuguese gentlemen were there, and among them Don John Estachia de Sousa, treasurer of the Island, having both in figure and in countenance a very striking resemblance to Mr. Charles Fox.

We had a ball in the evening at Mr. Smith's, to which several handsome Portuguese ladies came, one of whom, Donna Isabella, sung several songs after supper, in a very superior style. She has a most delightful voice, and performed in a much better taste than I could have expected at Madeira.

Tuesday, October 16.—This day we dined at the Governor's.

---

[1] ' Dr. Dinwiddie was a Scotch philosopher, but of what school I know not; he was also called an experimentalist, and expected to instruct the Chinese in electricity and in flying balloons, but it all ended in smoke. On our return he requested to be discharged and sent to Calcutta, where he meant to deliver lectures. The novelty took, and Dinwiddie is said to have made a little fortune.'—Sir J. Barrow, ' Autobiographical Memoir.'

There was a table of above two hundred covers, well served and attended.[1] All my train was there, also Sir Erasmus Gower and several of his officers ; Lord Mark Kerr, Mr. William Stuart, etc., etc., together with Captain Mackintosh and some of the officers ; the whole British factory and the principal Portuguese gentlemen of the Island. All the honours were extremely well done, and a strong desire shown in every instance to mark a regard for the English nation.

The Governor is called Don Diego Perreira, Forjas, Contino, a little fat, dark-complexioned man, blind of one eye, and about sixty years old. He served a campaign in Portugal, under Burgoyne, and is now a Colonel of Horse, and a Knight of the Order of Christ. Donna Louisa, his wife, who is related to the Chevalier Pinto, has been very handsome, and seems now turned of forty. Being indisposed, she did not appear at table till the dessert, but her place was filled and her functions performed by her daughter, Donna Maria de Monte, a little girl of ten years old, who sat between me and her father, and acted her part to admiration.

The Governor has one son, an officer in Portugal, a young man of great hopes, about twenty-two years old. The Governor himself has been eleven years in the command of Madeira, and expects to be sent to Brazil; but I doubt it. He has a tolerable fortune of his own, and his employment is worth about £2,000 per an.

Wednesday, October 17.—This morning returned on board the *Lion*. Soon after the Governor, attended by a numerous cortège, came on board the *Lion* to wish me a good voyage.

[1] 'This entertainment consisted of three very splendid courses of fifty dishes.'—From 'Narrative of the British Embassy to China,' by Æneas Anderson, body-servant to Lord Macartney.

'The Governor gave a most sumptuous entertainment, and as few nations besides our own exhibit on their tables whole animals, as pigs, grinning, with oranges in their mouths, hares squatting as if about to leap down the throats of the hungry guests, and pheasants with their feathers ready to fly after them, the Portuguese Governor, in compliment to the English taste, had employed English cooks for the occasion—a mark of consideration which I very much doubt if any of the British merchants would have condescended to pay to the Portuguese Governor, as a due respect for the customs and prejudices of other nations is certainly not to be found in the catalogue of an Englishman's good qualities.'—Sir J. Barrow, 'Voyage to Cochin China.'

THE INQUISITION

A handsome[1] collation was prepared for him, with music, drums, salutes, and all military honours, and both he and the gentlemen who came with him seemed highly pleased with our attention.

As soon as they left us we got up our Anchor, and set sail for Santa Cruz, in the Island of Teneriffe.

There are several people of considerable fortunes resident in the Island of Madeira. Don Antonio Fernandez, who has the rank of Colonel in the service, and formerly travelled into Russia, where he is well known, has a good estate here, and is lately married to the Chevalier Pinto's daughter. He usually lives at his chateau a few leagues from Funchal.

Religious bigotry is losing ground very fast here, and the teeth of the Inquisition are now drawn. All persons arrested by its authority may bring their *Habeas Corpus*, insist on their crimes being declared, and enter upon their defence without delay.

As several voyagers, Cook, Foster, etc., etc., who stopped at Madeira have given accounts of it which seem pretty just, I say the less upon the subject. Indeed, unless something really new in arts, sciences or manners should offer, it would be an idle affectation to parade upon beaten ground. Little more can be learned by us here from those whom we had occasion to converse with than has already been learnt and described by our predecessors. More can only be known by a larger residence, and by skill in many things which we have not skill in. Nothing is more ridiculous than a literary tailor, who wants to pass off his worn-out flippery for fresh materials by making it up in a different fashion.

During our passage from Torbay to Madeira we usually had a concert every day, either in the morning or in the evening, when the weather permitted. My band consisted of five persons, every one of whom was master of several instruments. They were all Germans. We had, besides, several gentlemen amateurs on board, some of whom took their share occasionally as performers.

The brig *Jackall*, our tender, whom we lost sight of the

[1] 'The entire forenoon of this day was employed in making preparations for a breakfast in the ward-room, to which Lord Macartney had invited the Governor of the island, the British Consul, and the principal inhabitants. This entertainment consisted of tea, coffee, and chocolate, cold meats of all kinds, with fruits, jellies, and variety of wines.'—From 'A Narrative of the British Embassy to China,' by Æneas Anderson, body-servant to Lord Macartney.

first night of our departure from Spithead, not having joined us at Madeira according to rendezvous, Sir Erasmus Gower left orders for her conduct, in case she should touch here after our departure.

Teneriffe, Sunday, October 21.—Don Antonio Guttieres, the Governor, sent his nephew and another officer on board this afternoon, with compliments to me, and offers of his house, and all service in his power, etc., etc. Mr. Rooney, an Irish merchant residing at Santa Cruz, and partner of Mr. Barry of Port Orotava, accompanied these gentlemen, and I have invited them all to dinner to-morrow.

Monday, October 22.—They accordingly came, and they brought me an invitation from the Governor for dinner the next day, but I excused myself. Sir George Staunton, Dr. Gillan,[1] Messrs. Maxwell,[2] Stronach and Hapton (two gardeners) and Tiebolt (artist) went on shore, intending to try to ascend the Peak of Teneriffe.[3] They were joined by a party from the *Hindostan*.

Tuesday, October 24.—A very hard gale of wind came on this morning, and blew the whole day, by which the *Hindostan* lost two of her anchors.

Wednesday, October 25.—The weather growing moderate, the wine for the crew of the *Lion* was brought on board by the purser.

[1] 'Dr. Gillan was a good scholar, a physician, and, moreover, a Scotch metaphysician. He was selected as a gentleman well calculated to bring home valuable information on all subjects of science and physics. But, in point of fact, his acquirements were rendered nearly unavailing, partly from indolence of habit occasioned by indifferent health.'

[2] 'Mr. Acheson Maxwell had been private secretary to Lord Macartney in India. Being a steady, sedulous, and intelligent gentleman, he received on our return an appointment as Inspector of Public Accounts in the Audit Office.'—Sir J. Barrow, 'Autobiographical Memoir.'

[3] 'We set off on our expedition—to the great surprise of the inhabitants, who bestowed on us very liberally the epithet of *mad Englishmen*. (The season was considered too far advanced for the ascent.) The weather became increasingly unfavourable, and the wind and rain became more violent as we advanced in height, and the mules as obstinate and refractory as the drivers. Dr. Gillan and his mule were carried to the brink of a precipice, and narrowly escaped destruction, and Sir G. Staunton was thrown to the ground at a moment of great danger. We were obliged to return and abandon the project, to our great regret.'—J. Barrow, 'Voyage to Cochin China.'

I went on shore to view the town. The parish church is large and handsome, with several altars highly decorated; one in particular of fine wood, the produce and workmanship of the Island, little inferior to Gibbons' carving.

It seems the ladies here, like those at Madeira, have no vocation to be nuns. I was told at Funchal that no nun had been professed there for above twenty years past. The expense, I was at the same time informed, would amount to £300.

I called on the Governor, who is an unaffected, gentlemanlike man about fifty years old. He wore round his middle a red sash fastened with a gold buckle, which denotes his military rank of Major-General. He spoke French intelligently, and requested me to stay and take a family dinner with him, and said he would give me a better next day. He was communicative in conversation, and unaffectedly answered me upon almost every subject which I wished to be informed of by him.

In the evening the French Consul, Monsieur Fontpertius, with his wife, Donna Isabel, and her sister, and her cousin, a brother, and uncle, came alongside the *Lion* requesting leave to be permitted to see the ship, and were received on board. The women (whose Mother was Irish) it seems were educated during five years at a boarding-school in Hampstead in England. They spoke English perfectly well, and of everything English with rapture.[1]

The Consul is a violent democrat, and expects to be soon recalled, as a war from Spain was probably to be soon declared.

The affairs of France are forbidden to be spoke of at Santa Cruz.

The women said there were no amusements whatsoever except the Almeyda, either at Santa Cruz or at Laguna, which is the capital, and about three leagues distant.

There are a few convents at the latter, but the Nuns are all very old, for of late years nobody like to be professed, or go into a Convent, either for education or devotion. Not

[1] 'On our return to the ship, we found several young ladies, inhabitants of the island, who, having been educated in England, were naturally inclined to visit a ship belonging to that country. They were received with the greatest politeness by Lord Macartney; and the band of music was ordered to play during the whole of their very agreeable visit.'—Æneas Anderson, 'Narrative of British Embassy to China.'

many years ago a young girl brought to be professed ran out of the church door, and declared off in the presence of several hundred people.[1]

Thursday, October 25.—This day the French ship sailed for Brest with a fresh breeze, and carried some letters from us to our friends in England.

Captain Mackintosh, not choosing to risk any more anchors (the ground here being foul), stood off and on during the whole day. I received a letter from Sir George Staunton informing me that on Tuesday morning they had set out from where they had slept the night before and proceeded on their way up the Peak as far as they could persuade their guide to conduct them that evening. Having no tents, they rested themselves under the shelter of a rock, made a good fire, and slept upon the broom, which grew near them in great abundance. In the morning all the party returned to Orotava, except Dr. Gillan and Mr. Barrow, who proceeded up the mountains as far as the cold and the violence of the wind would permit them. They then returned to their companions at Orotava, very much fatigued and indisposed, where they were very hospitably entertained by the English merchants there.

Friday, October 27.—The gentlemen returned on board this evening from their expedition. Laguna is the capital

---

[1] 'The escape of an intended victim to devotion made some noise about this time in Teneriffe. A young lady, during her novitiate, had by uncommon accident the opportunity of seeing a youth, who inspired her with a passion inconsistent with her former views of religious retirement. Notwithstanding the apparent freedom left to novices to alter their intentions, it is, in fact, as unsafe as rare. This young novice manifested no symptoms of reluctance, and preparations were made for—the ceremony.

'When the day arrived which was to resign her for ever to the cloister, her relations and friends assembled, as is usual, to be present on the occasion. In the crowd of spectators was the young gentleman, who was disputing with heaven the fair victim. After solemn exhortations—that now the final moment was arrived when she was to devote herself to God, abandoning all sublunary considerations, as well as all ties of affection, or instantly to quit the holy place she then inhabited for ever—she stretched out her hand to the youth, who advanced quickly to receive it, and, hurrying with her from the church while the priests, the nuns, her relations, and the people stood motionless with astonishment, the happy pair got soon safely to a place where they were married.'—Sir G. Staunton, 'Embassy to China.'

THE ISLAND OF ST. JAGO

of Teneriffe, and there are held the Courts of Justice.[1] It is a pretty town situated on an extensive plain, and inhabited by the principal gentry of the island. The people in general of all ranks are remarkably personable and well looking. I could hear nothing of the tea-tree, nor of the double lemon, which are mentioned in Cook's voyages.

Friday, November 2.—This morning we made for the Island of St. Jago, worked into Praya, and came to an anchor there before noon. No appearance of our brig tender, which made us very uneasy.

Immediately on our coming into the roads, Sir Erasmus Gower sent his first Lieutenant, Mr. Thomas Campbell, to announce the arrival of the *Lion* to the Governor.

He is a native of Lisbon, and called Don Joseph Francisco Texeira Carnero. He has been here three years, and is now returning to Portugal to solicit some command in the Brazils. He is a tall, emaciated figure, much reduced by a consumption, occasioned, he said, by the bad air of Port Praya, which is of late become very unhealthy.[2] This he need not have mentioned to me, as I had already observed an extensive swamp just under the town, stretching to the north and east, so that the trade winds for a considerable part of the year blow all the miasmata that arise from it full upon the fort. The landing-place is close to the swamp; the path up to the gate is steep and rocky, and above two hundred yards in length. Here we were saluted by eleven guns, and half a dozen ragged soldiers with a bit of a drum, turned out to compliment us as we passed. The Governor

[1] 'The jail was by far the most lively part of Laguna. It seemed to be crowded by disorderly females, who were laughing and singing at the iron gratings, and whose joyful countenance wore no indications of their suffering in confinement any very severe punishment for their offences, whatever the nature of them might have been.'—J. Barrow, 'Voyage to Cochin China.'

[2] 'There is nothing inviting in the aspect of the island of St. Jago, when seen from Praya Bay; and it requires only to set foot on shore to be convinced that poverty, and sickness, and pining want, are the constant companions of the greater part of its wretched inhabitants. The only Europeans we saw were the Governor, his Secretary, the Commanding Officer of the troops, a raw-boned Scotch sergeant, six feet high, who had served in the American army, and his wife, a slender, diminutive Irish woman. All these wore an aspect so sickly and wan, and so full of misery and woe, that we could not help considering them as the most deplorable objects of compassion.'—J. Barrow, 'Voyage to Cochin China.'

conducted us to his house, which is a little barrack, pleasantly situated at one end of the town, looking down the valley over a fine coco-nut grove towards the harbour and the shipping; but he offered us no sort of refreshment, which I believe was because he had none to offer, for the place and everything around him seemed poor and wretched to a great degree. His suite consisted of a dozen or more officers, some barefooted, some with shoes but no stockings, scarcely any with both; they were nevertheless all dressed in laced clothes, had laced hats on their heads and handsome swords on hangers in their belts.

There are not above a hundred and fifty houses in the place; a few of them are whitened and have a tolerable neat look, but the rest are miserable hovels. The fort or battery is almost in ruins, and the few guns that are mounted upon it are most of them honey-combed, and scarcely supported by their carriages. We were told that there were three regiments of Militia in St. Jago, and seven or eight hundred men in each. They are chiefly officered by mulattoes or negroes. Not above ten white officers in the whole, one of whom keeps the Inn. The best building is the Jail, and next to it the Church, which is served by a priest who is very dark-coloured mulatto, almost a negro.[1] The greater part of the inhabitants are slaves; the proportion of free people is very small. There has been scarcely any rain in these islands for three years past, which has reduced them to great distress of all kinds; most of their cattle having died in consequence of the drought, and their provision ground having proved unproductive. Bread and clothes were much wanted, and preferred to money in exchange for what the islanders had to sell, which chiefly consisted of salt and fruit. One bushel of flour would purchase fifteen or twenty bushels of salt, and I have heard of a thousand oranges being sold for an old pair of breeches.[2]

[1] 'The clergy were people of colour, and some of them perfectly black. The officers of justice, of the Customs, the troops, the peasantry, and the traders were all black, or so very dark that they would scarcely be supposed to have any European blood in their veins. Yet most of them aspire to the honour of Portuguese extraction, and are proud of it. The Cape de Verde Islands were to Portugal what Botany Bay is to England.'—J. Barrow, 'Voyage to Cochin China.'

[2] 'Several of the men belonging to the corps of the Artillery went on shore to wash and dry their linen; they returned extremely scorched, from standing in the burning sun. Having given my

Sunday, November 18.—We crossed the Line this day at daybreak, with a brisk south-east trade wind. The weather cool and pleasant with a few flying showers. The usual ceremonies on passing the Line were performed on board the *Lion*.

Thursday, November 22.—Seized with a very severe fit of the gout.

Friday, November 30.—This day at noon we came to an anchor at Rio Janeiro, about a mile from the town; Sir Erasmus Gower sent Mr. Campbell, his First Lieutenant, to acquaint the officer commanding there who we were, and from thence to the town, to settle with the Viceroy the salutes and other ceremonies. Everything was soon arranged without difficulty, and with much civility.

Thursday, December 6.—I continued on board till this day, and though still weak and indisposed, I made an effort and went on shore after an illness of a fortnight.

The Viceroy had at different times sent his Minister and some of his counsellors or disembargadoes and officers on board, with repeated compliments to me, and had already provided a house for my reception and that of the gentlemen of my train, when we chose to come on shore. Sir Erasmus Gower and Sir George Staunton had preceded me in the morning, in order to pay their visit in form to the Viceroy, and to tell him of my intention of landing this day. They then returned on board, and accompanied me in the barge from the ship to the wharf stairs.

I was saluted by fifteen guns from the *Lion* on quitting her, and by the same number from the fort of St. Sebastian at my landing, where I was met by the principal officers and people of the place. About three hundred infantry were drawn up under arms. A squadron of fifty Dragoons paraded on the beach to receive my orders, and the Viceroy's chariot attended to convey me to my quarters. Sir Erasmus Gower and I got into it, and, escorted by the Dragoons, drove without delay to the house prepared for me, before which I found a similar guard to that which I had left on the

---

linen to be washed by a man of Prayà, and having reason to apprehend that I might share the fate of the others, who had not found the natives of the country perfectly correct in their returns, I went in quest of my washerman, and was obliged to be content, not only with paying an exorbitant price for what he had done very ill, but the loss of several articles which he could not be persuaded to restore.'— Æneas Anderson, ' Narrative of British Embassy to China.'

beach, drawn up in the same manner. I declined the compliment of detaining them, and only kept two sentinels, which it was afterwards found necessary to increase to four, to keep off thieves and other intruders which soon began to grow troublesome. I had scarcely alighted from the chariot, when the Viceroy sent the Lieutenant-Colonel of the regiment to attend me, and to offer me all sorts of civilities, the use of his horse, carriages, etc, etc., and declaring that it was his wish to do everything in his power to make my stay here agreeable. To this was added, that if I wished to make excursions into the country to any distance, or to go up to the harbour and visit the islands in it, he (the Lieutenant-Colonel) would accompany me, having been selected on purpose as speaking the French lauguage and being particularly desirous of rendering himself useful and agreeable to us.

It had formerly been always the custom to send officers to attend all strangers on shore wherever they went, and with orders never to lose sight of them, but this was soon dispensed with in regard to our people, whose conduct and behaviour were in general so proper and becoming as to impress the Portuguese of Rio Janeiro with a very favourable opinion of them. And this does them the more honour as I took on shore with me the greatest part of my family, a step in a great measure necessary, as several of them had become sickly or listless, and wanted (as is usual with persons not much used to the sea) those reliefs which can only be afforded by the land air and its accompaniments, and which seldom fail in a short time to restore the most languid to health and good-humour. The house provided for me was a spacious building, pleasantly situated opposite the new Alameyda or public walk, with a fine view of the harbour and shipping in front, and in the rear was a large agreeable garden bounded on one side by the great public aqueduct. But this house, though very large, not being quite sufficient to contain my whole train, the Viceroy took care to provide an additional one very near it, that fully answered our purpose.[1]

Sunday, December 9.—Being now somewhat recruited in my health, I paid my visit in form to the Viceroy at the

[1] 'The house provided for the Ambassador was not very clean; there was little in it besides some clumsy, old-fashioned chairs of heavy wood, a few tables, and wooden frames with cane bottoms, intended for bedsteads, but without either posts or curtains. Fortunately, we took on shore our own bedding, the Portuguese not being over nice in this respect.'—J. Barrow, 'Voyage to Cochin China.

A GRANDEE OF PORTUGAL

Palace, an extensive and handsome edifice, forming one side of the great parade near the sea, where I was received with all the proper honours, a company of infantry being drawn up with colours flying, drums beating, trumpets sounding, etc. From the gate a lane of well-dressed officers reached to the stair-board and antechamber, at the door of which the Viceroy met me, and conducted me into the great saloon. Observing, as I looked behind me, that the circle was closed, I desired that it might be opened in order to make way for all my company to come in, as I had brought not only my own train, but most of the officers of the *Lion*, with above twenty young midshipmen belonging to her. Very fine youths, well dressed and of uncommonly elegant and manly appearance, though several of them were not more than eleven or twelve years old. I presented them all to the Viceroy, explaining to him the nature of our naval service, and adding that no wonder we had the first sea-officers in the world at mature age, when we could show such specimens in their childhood.

The Viceroy is called Don Joseph Louis de Castro Count de Rezende, a grandee of Portugal. He has also several other titles. This gentleman seems to be towards forty years of age, is married, and has several children, two of which are good, pretty boys of twelve or thirteen years of age, and were present at our visit. He is a tall, well-looking man, and remarkably fair for a Portuguese. Civil, but slow and uninformed, appears not to have seen much of the world, nor has he the air of having lived in good company. It is now three years since he filled this government, but it is thought he will soon be superseded. He is not liked or esteemed by the people, who accuse him of attending to little but the increase of his fortune, which his situation affords him different methods of doing.

His predecessor, Vasconcellos, who was a man of great address, and, though an enormous peculator, contrived to acquire many friends, raised a fortune of above a million and a half of cruzadas in ten or eleven years (£170,000). I could not learn whether the Viceroy be of the family of the famous John de Castro, Viceroy in the Indies; but I could not avoid remarking that he is almost the only Portuguese gentleman I have ever met with who had only one name. A pleasant story is somewhere told on this subject of a Spaniard who arrived late at night at an inn in France, and knocked violently at the door. When he was asked who he was, he replied, 'Don Joseph Louis Xavier Manuel Henriquez

Fernandez Masones of Luna and Cortez and Navarro and Gova and Nonia,' upon which he was desired to go with his company to some other inn, as there was not room in the house for the half of them.

The Viceroy either is, or affects to be, an invalid, and therefore chiefly resides in the country, at a small house about seven or eight miles from town, where he lives at a trifling expense, and in a private manner. He never invited me, nor any of the gentlemen of my train, either to dinner or any other kind of entertainment—whether owing to awkwardness or economy I know not, but partly, I believe, the former, as he seemed in everything else very desirous of obliging.

Tuesday, December 11.—This day the Viceroy returned my visit in great state.[1] He brought with him not less, I suppose, than one hundred and fifty officers, very sprucely dressed, all of whom he presented to me. He was also attended by a good, intelligent young man called Don Francisco. He was a native of Rio Janeiro, who served as interpreter, having learnt English perfectly well by residing some time in London with the Chevalier Pinto, and by studying medicine in Edinburgh under Dr. Cullen.

It is not many years that Rio Janeiro has been the capital of Brazil. Bahia de Todos or Santo was so till the discovery of the gold and diamond mines about a hundred leagues from Rio Janeiro, whose importance occasioned the removal of the seat of Government to their neighbourhood.

Bahia, though no longer the capital of Brazil, has, nevertheless, a great deal more trade at present than Rio Janeiro. But Rio, if not depressed and smothered by apprehensive jealousy of Portugal, the parent state, will undoubtedly very soon grow to be a most opulent and flourishing country. But the rising spirit of the people, and the late insurrection at the Mines, together with a sort of prophetic sensation, have so alarmed the Court of Lisbon that they seem determined to distress and starve, instead of nursing and promoting their colonies, and to strangle their children in the

---

[1] 'The dress of the Viceroy was scarlet cloth, very much enriched with gold, embroidery, and precious stones. His attendants wore a splendid livery of green and gold, and he had several black running footmen, who were dressed in fancy uniforms, with large turbans on their heads and long sabres by their sides.'—Æneas Anderson, 'Narrative of Embassy to China.'

CONVENTS AND MONASTERIES

cradle, from a dread of their being too strong when they grow up. But it signifies nothing; the Crown of Portugal must either soon transport its seat of Empire to Brazil, or leave Brazil to take its own chance by itself. For, in spite of all political or commercial regulations and restrictions, it must soon burst the bud and unfold and exert its native powers, uninfluenced by the weight and unrepressed by the terror of a distant sceptre.

No gold is suffered to be manufactured at Rio. Not long since a general search was made in the town by the Government, and all the tools and instruments used for such purposes that could be found were seized, and confiscated without redemption. One-fifth of all the gold in the mines belongs to the Crown, the remainder to the owners and discoverers; but if any diamonds are found in a gold-mine it is immediately shut up as a gold-mine, all diamond-mines being the sole property of the Crown.

There is no Holy Office or Inquisition in Brazil, but there are some families belonging to it in different parts of the country, who may have persons of suspected heresy taken up and sent to Lisbon to be examined and judged there; but nothing of this kind has happened there for many years past. Indeed, the people are now much less under the dominion of religious prejudices than formerly, and of late few are found of either sex who prefer the monastic to the worldly life. There are, however, some considerable and wealthy convents, both of men and women, still remaining. The Benedictines alone have a thousand slaves and a good estate inland. The Franciscans are also very rich. These two Convents very hospitably entertained our Chinese during the whole time we stayed at Rio.

There is a very large nunnery dedicated to Our Lady of the Conception, in which there are forty professed nuns, and where a hundred young girls are educated. The Abbess, who is an agreeable, well-looking woman of forty years old, invited me and the gentlemen of my train to visit her at her Convent. We were received with great ceremony and respect, and she and her nuns and her pupils, though behind an iron grating, immediately entered into a very spirited and lively conversation with us, which was maintained for a considerable length of time, and was rather terminated by a respective sense of propriety than from want of topics or disinclination to continue it. They were much pleased with my band of music which I had ordered to attend them, and sent me frequent messages afterwards under various pretences.[1] Dr. Gillan often visited them as a physician, and had several curious conversations with them on the nature of their complaints and the proper method of curing them.

Many of the officers and others who visited us were very inquisitive about the late subversion in France, and appeared in their conversation to entertain no very respectful opinions towards their own Government. The thread of connection between this country and Europe is every day growing more and more slender, and if not spun anew by a skilful hand, will soon snap asunder.

To guard against foreign attacks and domestic insurrection, a considerable military force is kept in Brazil. There is, besides, a large body of people in the town who, though not disciplined, are registered as capable of service, and might be rendered useful as a sort of militia in case of necessity. It is, however, to be considered that, as the white officers and soldiers, who are sent from Europe from time to time, are never changed in regular rotation, but most of them remain here all their lives, they generally become perfect Americans, and consider Brazil as their chief country and home.

The native Indians are not very numerous, and as yet have been scarcely rendered useful as subjects—whether from their own insuperable character, or from want of skill in the Government, I am not sufficiently informed. Wherever they are at liberty and out of the reach of authority, as they still are in many parts of Brazil, they are implacable enemies to the Portuguese, and massacre them without mercy whenever they fall into their hands. A great part of the coast between Rio Janeiro and Bahia is infested, or inhabited, by them, so that there is no regular road or communication by land between the two settlements.

Nothing can be more beautiful than the harbour of Rio; the numbers of large ships arriving, departing, or resting

[1] 'The persons who composed Lord Macartney's suite were indulged with the permission to visit the convent, and the nuns took opportunity to throw out to them a variety of elegant little toys of their own fabric. Nor had even their confined and devoted situation prevented them from knowing the art of manufacturing another kind of article called *billets-doux*. They even applied to Lord Macartney, by the director of the convent, for the use of his band of music, which accordingly performed at several morning concerts within these sacred walls.'—Æneas Anderson, 'Narrative of Embassy to China.'

at anchor, the swarms of pleasure boats and of other small craft constantly passing and re-passing on business or amusement, when viewed from the *Lion*, where she lay at her mooring about half a mile from the shore, presented, I think, one of the most picturesque and striking scenes I had ever beheld in any part of the world.

Being much indisposed for the greater part of the time of my stay at Rio, I was not able to enjoy so much of these charming scenes as I wished, but Sir George Staunton, whose curiosity and attention were awake to everything, and carried him everywhere, could scarcely find expressions to describe the raptures he was thrown into by what he had seen and felt in the course of his excursions.

We were supplied plentifully with beef (which is, however, not good), pigs, goats, fowls, geese, ducks, sweet potatoes, grapes, oranges, limes, and pineapples, but no mutton. On the whole everything was extremely dear, and Rio Janeiro far inferior to the Cape of Good Hope as a place of refreshment. The water was brought to the town from a considerable distance in the country, but I should imagine the stream to be very scanty and insufficient, for I always observed a great number of people at every one of the fountains during the whole day, waiting with their buckets and other vessels to have them replenished. A guard always attends to regulate the distribution.

The common people are thievish and imposing. The shops are well supplied with goods from Europe, mostly English, our cottons, hardware, yellow ware, broadcloth, and serges, and, what surprised me, a great variety of our prints, both serious and caricature.

The public amusements of operas, plays, and masquerades have been discontinued some time past, on account of the Queen's malady. The women very seldom stir abroad until late in the evening, which is the time for their visiting each other; whilst at home they usually sit in their galleries, or behind the lattices, and often throw flowers at the gentlemen passing by, which is considered a fair challenge, especially if the flowers are without stalks. It is not, indeed, infrequent to send invitations to such whose appearance happens to please them. At least some of our young gentlemen were said to have been distinguished by these signals of partiality, and to have received in consequence more substantial favours. I should hope, however, that the roses in these nosegays were without thorns, as well as without stalks, as such presents are sometimes attended with a spice of danger. Dr. Gillan was assured by a reverend gentleman (whose conversation was quite unconstrained with him on such subjects) that—

'Omnes feminæ in Rio Janeiro tam honeste quam inhoneste pronæ sunt, et Veneri deditæ et fere hic venera laborant.'

These were his literal expressions. This worthy minister of the Gospel added that the Abbess and her nuns whom we had visited were so delighted and flattered by such civility and attention to them from us that they could scarcely think of anything else ever since, and 'omnes flagrabant amore nostri' giving pretty broad hints to the doctor of the influence he had in the Convent, and how much he could contribute to our amusement there.

Indeed, a general depravation of manners seems to prevail among both sexes.[1] We were told of many instances of the most scandalous libertinism in the women, and few of the gentlemen took much pains to disguise their false appetites.

Saturday, December 15.—Having now stayed nine days on shore, I returned on board the *Lion* somewhat recovered, but still very weak and languid. From the time of our dropping anchor till our getting to sea, we were eighteen days at Rio.

Tuesday, December 18.—This day we sailed from Rio Janeiro with the *Hindostan* in company. No appearance yet of our brig tender, the *Jackall*. No sooner were we re-embarked in the *Lion*, and the mountains began to recede,

[1] Mr. Barrow did not take so unfavourable a view of the conduct of the ladies at Rio, and says : 'Nor do I believe that their good humour signified by nodding, smiling, and throwing flowers from balconies to passing strangers, after having repeatedly seen the same thing done when the fathers or the husbands were standing by their side, could justly be construed to convey any particular meaning, or bear any other explanation than that of its being a mere local custom, practised without design. It is scarcely fair to decide on the moral character of a whole nation from the occasional occurrences and observations of a few hours in the day during a week's residence. The manners are so different in different countries, and local customs sometimes so extraordinary, that ocular demonstration alone may be easily deceived. And where the character of the fair sex is at stake we ought at least to incline to the favourable side, especially as, in every country, the female part of society owes in a great degree its good and bad qualities—and more particularly the latter —to the character of the men.'—J. Barrow, 'Voyage to Cochin China.'

THE VISCOUNT MACARTNEY

From an Engraving by C. TOWNLEY, *after* S. DE KOSTER

TRISTAN D'ACUNHA

than a fresh object of curiosity engaged our attention, and we directed our course to the islands of Tristan d'Acunha, which, lying in our track to the Straits of Sunda, and having been but superficially observed by former navigators, it was thought that a more accurate knowledge of them might be of use, both in point of geography and of natural history.

The winds and weather were so favourable to us that we calculated that we should see it the next morning, and we certainly should have done so had we not anticipated the object by imaginary possession, for on Saturday evening one of the gentlemen of the quarter-deck, deceived by some cloudy appearances, cried out that he saw the land, and several others adopting the idea, it was thought prudent to lie to during the night.

Next morning, however, we could see nothing of it. We therefore pressed forward all day, and the weather proving very clear and the moon shining out, we stood on during the night under an easy sail, and at daybreak on Monday morning we discovered first the southernmost island called Inaccessible, then Nightingale Island, and soon after that Tristan d'Acunha, which is the most northerly of the three.

Sir Erasmus Gower, as we approached it, sent two of his boats to explore the coast, in one of which was Mr. W., a Lieutenant, and in the other Mr. T., the master. The latter soon returned and informed us that he had found the best anchoring place in thirty-one fathoms, and had fixed a buoy upon it. It was a black sandy bottom, from which grew sea-weeds from eighteen to twenty fathoms long, and we were now in such good-humour with the novelty of the scene that he might have engaged our belief of their size to a still greater extent.

Here we dropped anchor just as the evening closed upon us, yet still affording us sufficient light to observe the romantic situation of our berth, which, though half a mile from the shore, was now quite overshadowed by the dark mass of the island, whose sides on our left hand seemed to rise like a moss-grown wall perpendicularly from the ocean. On the right the elevation was less rapid, and left between it and the sea at the bottom a fine green carpet of some extent, through which a rill of the clearest water had worn its channel, and gushed in a double cascade over a verdant ledge into the sea almost opposite the ship.

We thought we could discover a path leading to the southern extremity, which seemed to be divided by a narrow valley and to open a passage to the upper part of the island.

These appearances flattered our imaginations, and promised such entertainments of various kinds that schemes were immediately formed for exploring the internal country, and Sir George Staunton, whose curiosity and activity are seldom repressed by difficulty or fatigue, thought of little less than visiting, if practicable, the highest pinnacle of the mountain, invited particularly by its volcanic appearance and by the disappointment he had formerly met with at Teneriffe upon a similar project. At all events, he had prepared for acquiring a knowledge of its height, having engaged Mr. Barrow, a gentleman belonging to the Embassy of great mathematical science expertness, to accompany him with proper instruments to measure the angles necessary to be taken for ascertaining altitudes. Dr. Gillan and Lieutenant Parish of the Artillery were also to be of the party, and every arrangement was immediately made for rendering the excursion as useful and satisfactory as possible. Lighton was called upon to attend as a draughtsman, Haxton and Stronach as botanists, and some soldiers with hatchets and pole-axes were appointed to the service of dislodging any seals, sea-lions, or other enemies who might dispute or impede the landing, and also to act on occasion as pioneers for clearing away the reeds, brushwood, or similar obstructions that were likely to occur in the route. Several servants were to be loaden with quadrants, sextants, octants, magnets, theodolites, telescopes, barometers, tin plant-boxes, specimen pouches, and botanical stiff paper, together with all such philosophical accoutrements as seemed requisite for completely equipping the expedition, and as philosophers are no more secure than vulgar mortals from the impertinence of Nature, care was taken to provide hams, tongues, chickens, port, porter and madeira in order to answer her calls, not to mention the resources expected from the skill and exertions of Messieurs Maxwell, Winder, and Baring, who, whilst Sir George and his party were engaged in their more important speculations and researches, proposed to scour the rocks and thickets in pursuit of game, and being, by their own accounts, most capital marksmen, had no doubt of bringing in an additional reinforcement to the provisions from the *Lion*. It was now near ten o'clock at night, and everything seemed to be finally settled. The boats were ordered to be held in readiness, and the party was to disembark at break of day. Just as they were retiring to take a little previous rest, Lieutenant W., who had been despatched in the yawl to make his observations towards the western point, returned on board. He had been several hours absent, during which time he ranged along the coast without being able to find a spot where a boat could land, so violent was the surf; but he found the shore fully inhabited by penguins, seals, sea-lions, and sea-elephants, and the air darkened and the water covered with gulls, boobies, and albatrosses. As he was determined not to return without some trophies of his expedition, he shot a sea-lion, and immediately swam on shore to secure his prey, which he effectually did, and with the assistance of a couple of intrepid sailors who had followed him, he dragged the monster through the surf and hoisted him into the boat. But he was so large and filled so much space that Lieutenant W. was under the necessity of getting rid of him by tumbling him back into the water, which was much regretted, as he was of a most prodigious size, and bore upon his skin many of those marks and scars which the author of 'Anson's Voyages' tells us are the consequence of the severe battles in which a rivalship for female favour frequently engages them. But Mr. W., though disappointed in this particular object, was so fortunate as to succeed in another, for, observing an albatross rising out of the water, he immediately fired at him, and hit him so dexterously as only just to disable him from escaping, without much injuring or otherwise disfiguring him. Mr. W. brought the bird safe on board, where he was much admired for his size and beauty. His wings measured ten feet from tip to tip, and he weighed sixteen pounds, but some of the officers on board who had seen several before looked upon this as a mere chicken, and talked of albatrosses of their acquaintance that weighed above thirty pounds, and whose wings expanded to seventeen or eighteen feet at the shortest. As soon as the examination of this bird was finished we all retired to bed, to dream of the amusements of the following day. But let no man give way too much to the delusions of hope, or trust his happiness to the holding of a ship's anchor; for, unfortunately, the wind freshening in the night, the *Lion* dragged hers for near half a mile before the watch upon deck were aware of it. They were therefore obliged to heave it in as fast as they could, and put before the wind immediately; and when I waked in the morning I found we had lost sight of the island, were above forty miles from it, and going ten knots an hour.

Tuesday, January 1, 1793.—Thus, then, all our projects were blown away in an instant, and we were under the necessity of relinquishing such philosophical treasures as Tristan d'Acunha may contain to the discovery of more fortunate adventurers.

The regret we felt upon this occasion is difficult to describe, and there were some among us who could scarcely have supported the disappointment, had they not been flattered with an indemnification in the treasures of the nature which were expected to be found in exploring the islands of Amsterdam and St. Paul's, towards which we now directed our course.

And now, before I proceed any further, it may not be amiss to say a word or two on the subject of the sea-lion and albatross, which were the principal articles of zoology that we had any opportunity of observing at Tristan d'Acunha.

As to the first, the sea-lion, Mr. W., when he returned on board, seemed to think him a good deal larger than upon recollection afterwards he ventured to affirm. From the idea his description had impressed upon us, we supposed him to be two or three and twenty foot long, and little short of the bulk of an elephant. He was, however, the next day reduced to four or five yards in length, and then dwindled to the size of a middling bullock.

As soon as the albatross was brought on board he discharged upwards of a pint of oil from his stomach on the floor. The wound he had received being found on examination to be a compound fracture, and more serious than we at first imagined, it was intended to have him the next morning killed, dissected, and stuffed, but he obtained a short reprieve by the humanity of young Staunton and a proposition of Dr. Gillan, who, like Podalicus and Machaon[1], and other eminent physicians of remote antiquity, joining the art of surgery to the science of medicine, offered to take charge of the fracture, to saw off the protruding splinter, to treat the remainder *secundum artem*, and in a short while to set the bird on his legs again. By these means we should have been able to preserve him alive—at least, for some time—and to become better acquainted with his person, character, and manners. But here again we met with another disappointment, for it seems the size and beauty of the bird had attracted the particular notice and attention of one of the gentlemen of the ward-room, who happened to be more curious in cookery than natural history; so that before

---

[1] Podalicus and Machaon were sons of Æsculapius, and skilled in the medical art. They were surgeons at the Siege of Troy.

THE SEA-SERPENT

Doctor Gillan could prepare his dressings and instruments the patient was skinned, spitted, roasted, and swallowed by this marine epicure. We had, however, the satisfaction of hearing that he proved very bad eating, and had almost poisoned his devourer. But, however perishable his body was, and unpalatable a dish, it is with pleasure I learn that his skin, which may without profanation be called his immortal part, has been very carefully preserved, and is intended to be properly stuffed and fitted up ; so that the curious ornithologist may probably be one day gratified with an ocular inspection of it among the rarities in the Museum.

Thursday, January 31.—A month was now elapsed since we had been driven from our anchors at Tristan d'Acunha, and three days having passed after the time when by our chronometers and lunar observations we had expected to have seen the islands of Amsterdam and St. Paul's, we began to grow very impatient, and some of our company went to bed that night almost in despair of ever seeing them. Messieurs M., W., and B., however, kept up their spirits, and confiding in the goodness of Mr. Campbell the First Lieutenant's eye, who was persuaded that he had perceived the land early in the morning, continued upon deck ; and the breeze then springing up, and the moon shining out, flattered themselves with hopes of discovering it before midnight. They were disappointed, however, in this particular, but thought themselves rewarded for their vigilance by having the good fortune to see an enormous water-snake, or sea-dragon, almost in contact with the ship. His belly, by their account, was of a shining white, and his back was spotted like a leopard's. They did not, indeed, exactly agree about his size, but from their lowest computation he must have been well deserving of an ichthyologist's inspection. Mr. B. imagined he saw his head, and heard a very distinct sibilation on the weather-bow, whilst his tail was conspicuous a good way to leeward ; so that the ship being near five-and-forty feet beam, and proper allowance being made for the sinuosity natural to animals of this form, he could not in conscience be less than sixty feet long at the most moderate calculation. Mr. M., with the circumspection of any old evidence, did not choose to give a positive opinion upon the matter, but contented himself with hinting that this water-snake might be ten or twelve yards in length, and about three or four feet round the middle. But he added that from the posture of the animal, which to him appeared almost semicircular, he could not take upon himself to be a very accurate judge of the dimensions. Mr. W., however, not quite so cautious, expressed himself perfectly disposed to support his friend Mr. B.'s testimony.

Friday, February 1.—Very early in the morning Mr. O., the Lieutenant of the watch, called out that he could then perceive Amsterdam Island about seven or eight leagues ahead. This intelligence was of too interesting a nature to be heard without strong sensations by all within the reach of it, and Sir George, who was then dozing in his cabin, which joined the quarter-deck, and dreaming of this Promised Land, quickly caught the welcome sound, and starting from his cot, suddenly appeared on the deck in his night-dress, like a ghost just risen from the dead. The after guard started back in consternation, the wheel stood still in the hands of the quarter-masters, and even the gallant young midshipmen upon the poop felt some symptoms of alarm, but impressions of this nature are not considered as in any degree affecting the valour of British seamen; for as they certainly fear nobody alive in this world, it can be no sort of imputation to startle at a spirit from the other. The firmest nerves may be discomposed by an unexpected phenomenon; and when Sir George stalked forth, it was natural to shrink from so formidable a figure. Over his shirt he had thrown a voluminous night-gown which flowed down to his heels in a long sweeping train; on his head he wore a high sugar-loaf night-cap, tied with a scarlet ribbon, which when blown by the wind 'streamed like a meteor to the troubled air.' The ample folds of his *robe de chambre* and the appendages of his head-dress being enlarged, as all objects are, by the haze or mistiness of the dawn, added considerably to his bulk and stature, and rendered his appearance more awful and impressive. But the undaunted Lieutenant O., like Hamlet in the play, was determined to speak to the ghost without flinching, and hailing him in a boatswain's voice exploded through the funnel of a trumpet, demanded what he was, and from whence he came, whether a spirit blessed, or goblin damned, with airs from Heaven, or blasts from Hell. Sir George, who at first was a little surprised with the singularity of such a salutation from an old shipmate, soon, however, comprehended the mistake which his apparition had occasioned, and unscrewed his features with an immoderate fit of laughter which immediately unravelled the mystery and restored the tranquillity of the quarter-deck.

The hour of breakfast being now arrived, we sat down to it, and during its continuance discussed the plan of our intended operations on shore, and made proper arrangements for the purpose, which being much the same as at Tristan d'Acunha, it is needless to repeat them.

We then returned to the deck, and finding that we neared the land very fast, everybody provided himself with a spyglass to explore it under the various shapes which it assumed from every movement of the ship. The yawl was hoisted out, and Mr. T., the master, despatched in her to find out the proper anchorage. Just as she put off, two human figures presented themselves to our view, standing on a little hummock about a hundred yards above the beach, waved their hats to us in the air, and displayed a handkerchief at the end of a stick. As we moved along, we several times lost sight of them, occasioned by the inequalities of the ground; but whenever we recovered them they were observed running upon the cliffs with great speed abreast of the ship. We immediately hoisted our colours, in order to give them the earliest mark of attention in our power, for we imagined them to be some unfortunate people who by shipwreck or other accident had been thrown or deserted on this solitary spot. Our conjectures seemed to be confirmed by our observing that, as soon as they saw Mr. T.'s boat approaching, they stripped off their clothes, and were preparing to swim towards it, but the surf growing uncommonly violent, their efforts were rendered ineffectual. In about an hour after we let go our anchor a little more than half a mile from the land in twenty-five fathoms of water. The *Hindostan* anchored a good way farther out. In the afternoon I went on shore in the twelve-oared barge, accompanied by Sir George Staunton, Dr. Gillan, and Lieutenant Atkins, Sir Erasmus Gower, Colonel Benson,[1] Captain Mackintosh, Messieurs Parish, Maxwell, Winder,[2] and Baring. Lieutenant Whitman, Mr. Jackson, and some other gentlemen soon after followed us, so that this desert island became very populous on a sudden. We were received on landing by five persons, two of whom we saw and recognized to be the same we had seen before. Their chief or superintendent was a Frenchman, about thirty years of age, intelligent and communicative, who gave me the following account of himself and of his companions. He said his name was Perron,

---

[1] 'Colonel Benson was a smart, correct, and active officer, well known to Lord Macartney, and selected by him.'—Sir J. Barrow, 'Autobiographical Memoir.'

[2] Mr. Winder was a distant connection of Lord Macartney.

or Du Perron; that he was born at Brest in Brittany, but, having no relatives, settled at Mauritius. He had been induced to come over there and engage in a house of commerce, a branch of which was the supplying of Canton with skins and furs of different kinds suited to that market; that he and his four companions (two of whom were Frenchmen, and the other two native Englishmen bred up in the British Navy, but now become Americans, and belonging properly to Boston in Massachusetts Bay) had been upwards of five months on the island, being left there for the purpose of procuring a cargo of twenty-five thousand seal-skins, which they hoped to complete in about ten months more, having a stock of near eight hundred already provided. Du Perron himself has a considerable share in the adventure, but the people with him are paid wages proportionately to their expertness. One of them told me he had ten dollars a month, and twenty dollars per thousand skins provided. Another had seven dollars per month, and ten dollars per thousand skins. Nothing but the prospect of great advantage could induce any human beings to live for fifteen months together upon this miserable spot in the manner that M. du Perron and his companions do. The hut they inhabit is of the most wretched materials, being a small square of about twenty feet, the walls of which are built of rough stones piled upon one another, and covered with skins and the rushes or sedgy grass that grow near it. Half of the hut is used as a magazine or store-house for the seal-skins, which exhale such a stench as almost extinguished my sense of smelling for a week after. Indeed, the whole air for miles round is equally infected, for after the skin is stripped off the seal the carcass is left on the ground to putrefy at leisure. The only remedy I had was my snuff-box, which I was obliged so often to apply to that its contents were soon exhausted. The squalor, filth, and dirt of every kind in these people's persons, clothes, furniture, and food perfectly corresponded with their occupation, and show how soon men may be reconciled to nastiness and the savage state.

> 'For some of these had looked on better days,
> Had oft with holy bell been knolled to church,
> And sat at good men's feasts, and wiped their eyes
> Of drops that sacred pity had engendered.'

Disgusted and shocked at what we saw, we returned to our boat, and rowed round the cone in hopes of some amusement to compensate for the offensive scene we had quitted.[1]

Here we found a number of seals and clapmatches sitting on the rocks, several of which were killed by our boatmen as we passed along. We were also shown the carcasses of two sea-lions, which, being animals entirely new to me, I took particular notice of. They were enormous monsters, not less than sixteen or seventeen feet long, and ten or eleven feet round at the shoulder; but they stunk so abominably that we hastened away from them. Indeed, nothing but a very strong curiosity could possibly have induced us to approach them at all. We saw also an infinite number of birds of various kinds, which flew close to us without any apprehension of danger.

We visited the warm mineral spring and the sugar-loaf rock, and collected a few of the plants that grew within our reach. We then returned to the ship, and got on board just as the evening closed, intending to make a more extensive excursion the following day.

During the short time we were at this place our gentlemen appeared to make such uncommon exertions in their several respective departments that I feel myself quite at a loss how to do them justice. Sir George Staunton and Dr. Gillan comprehended every object of curiosity within the sphere of their attention and research. Sir George added to his cabinet such uncommon nondescript plants as the place furnished, and his acquisitions in ornithology were numerous and valuable. Several penguins were brought on board the *Lion*, and remained alive some time.

The dusky petrel is a good deal larger than the other petrels. Valmost de Bomare says that the petrels are so called from St. Peter, whose attempt to walk upon the Lake or the Sea of Galilee there is an account of in the New

[1] 'These poor adventurers, we have since been informed, met with a hard return for the great sacrifice they had been induced to make in the hope of gain. While we were in China the *Lion* fell in with their little vessel; the report of hostilities between England and France having reached Canton, she was captured as French property and sold. Twelve months after the time fixed for her return to Amsterdam the poor fellows, hearing nothing of her, resolved to embark on the first ship that called at the island. It happened to be an American, who took them and their skins on board, and steered for New Holland, where the men were landed, after which she set sail for the Chinese market with her cargo of skins, leaving the proprietors behind to shift for themselves.'—J. Barrow, 'Voyage to Cochin China.'

Testament. But as that holy navigator's want of faith was near sending him to the bottom, and he was obliged to cry out for help (whereas these birds tread the water with great confidence and security), this apostolic appellation does not seem to be very apposite.

Dr. Gillan's travels into the interior of the island gave him an opportunity of examining the nature and properties of the soil, of making many ingenious conjectures with regard to its formation, and of collecting a variety of mineralogical and other specimens, particularly of lava.

Whilst the Doctor was thus employed, Mr. Winder, Mr. Baring and Co. were by no means idle, and what with carbines, fusils, and pocket pistols, did great execution among the sea poultry. Mr. Maxwell, indeed, did not kill two birds with one stone, but he certainly brought down a fish that I may almost say was flying in the air, and with the same shot killed the greedy petrel that was carrying it off in his bill to devour it.

Mr. Parish, Mr. Barrow,[1] and Mr. Jackson took separate measures of the diameter and circumference of the cone and of the depth of its soundings, and though they differed somewhat in the results of their calculations, their performances had very great merit. Mr. Parish was, however, by no means so engrossed by his mathematical and surveying instruments as to neglect the military ones more particularly belonging to his profession as a soldier, which he handled in such a masterly manner, and levelled with so true an aim, that his piece never missed its object, the consequence of which was a most deadly carriage among all sorts of game within the range of his musketry. Mr. Jackson, too, after finishing his survey, made a sporting excursion along the shore in his boat, and returned late in the evening laden with the spoils of the ocean. Of the seals and clapmatches in his collection, one remained still alive and merry, and danced up and down the decks with a spirit and agility that afforded excellent sport to the sailors and other spectators.

But among the various actors of the day Lieutenant W. was by no means the least distinguished, for, though not so fortunate as to find at Amsterdam any sea-lions for riding,

[1] Mr. Barrow, Comptroller of the Household, looked after the property of the Embassy. On the homeward journey to Canton he walked several hundred miles through the heart of the country, and published a long quarto volume regarding China ten years after his return to England.'

ONE-LEGGED PENGUIN

as he had done at Tristan d'Acunha, he met with other adventures almost equally marvellous. Among the different animals which he brought on board from his expeditions were two clapmatches of extraordinary size and of singular beauty, besides silver birds, petrels, cape-hens, and penguins without number. Of these latter we could not avoid particularly remarking a penguin of his catching that had a wooden leg—I mean that ought to have had a wooden leg, having lost one of those which he had brought into the world with him. By what accident it happened, whether it was bitten off by a shark, or otherwise amputated, I know not, but the wound had been long healed, and the animal itself seemed but little sensible of the want of it, for he hopped about upon the stump with such briskness and activity as would probably have enabled him to escape from any other sportsman less keen and determined than Mr. W.

Though the neighbouring island of St. Paul's is said to abound in excellent springs, no good fresh water has yet been discovered at Amsterdam. There is, indeed, a small rill of water which falls into the basin through a channel of an inch and a half diameter hollowed through the rock for the purpose, and which rill, we were told, took its rise on the heights at a considerable distance; but it is a strong chalybeate, and of so disagreeable a taste and quality that it occasioned violent sickness in some of our people who drank of it. It is, nevertheless, the principal beverage of the inhabitants, who fill all their casks with it, and say that it becomes cold and fit for use in a few hours. They are now so accustomed to it that they prefer it to the water they might have from the rain and snow which fall here abundantly through the winter. It issues warm from the rock, and deposits an ochreous sediment upon the stones which it passes over. For culinary purposes they use the salt or brackish water which bubbles everywhere towards the edge of the basin on digging a few inches below the surface into the earth. In this water they boil their fish and other food without any artificial calefaction, it being in itself so hot that an immersion of Fahrenheit's thermometer immediately raises the mercury to 212.

Though the mould seems in most places to be deep and rich, we saw no plants besides those collected by Sir George Staunton. This is owing, I presume, to the heat of the strata, which would probably stifle most kinds of vegetation.

The heat, indeed, is so intense that some of our gentlemen, incautiously sitting down upon the ground, found, before they had time to get up again, that it had already burnt through their breeches and blistered their skin[1] like a flagellation with nettles ; but from this painful sensation they were soon relieved by Dr. Gillan, who prescribed an application of some sanative oils to the part, which ceremony of *unctio in extremis* set everything to rights there like a charm.

At one particular place near the centre of the island the surface is covered six or seven feet deep with a soft hot mud or paste for the space of a couple of hundred yards square. Recollecting upon this appearance a new nostrum introduced into practice by the illustrious Dr. Graham a little before I left England, it occurred to me that this mud or paste might be usefully employed in medicine. If the earth bath has been prescribed with such success as to bid fair for putting the water bath out of fashion, possibly our Amsterdam hot mud or paste, when brought down to a proper temperature and used as an earth bath, may be found as much preferable to any other soil for the purpose as the tepid streams of Buxton or Matlock are to the cold pickle of Eastbourne or Brighton. Should such an idea be approved of and adopted, such is the passion of English people for travelling in search of health that this little island might in time grow into reputation, become, if I may use the expression, a kind of watering-place, and be frequented by whimsical invalids, like Nice, Lisbon, or Montpelier. And no doubt the medical concatenation of physician, surgeon, nurse, and apothecary would soon follow, and practise their arts with the usual advantage, as it is remarked by those who often visit Bath and Tunbridge that the gentry of the Faculty never thrive better, nor are to be seen in greater numbers, than at those places, where one would imagine there ought to be least occasion for them. However ludicrous at first sight the proposition of curing diseases by our Amsterdam discoveries may be, I am persuaded it will be received and considered with candour by the liberal and ingenious of this enlightened age ; especially at a time when, in spite of apparent impossibility, so many other new inventions have been published and practised with success. The art of flying in a balloon is now becoming almost as easy as that of driving in a whiskey, and Dr. Hawes and the Humane Society raise the dead without difficulty by a mechanical operation. No attempt, therefore, for the benefit of the human race and

[1] The original is somewhat more outspoken, after the manner of the times.

the improvement of science should be ridiculed or discouraged, however absurd and uncompromising.

We frequently in the daytime perceived considerable quantities of smoke issuing, as it were, from the fissures in the hills, and at night we in the same places saw flames which blazed violently for some moments and then vanished, or burnt but faintly. These appearances were said by the seal-catchers to be the remains of fires kindled by the sailors of an American vessel which had touched here about a year ago; but I much doubted the accuracy of the observations and the information, for I observed both the smoke and the flames to arise from places inaccessible, or, if accessible, by no means likely to have been climbed by anybody merely for the purpose of setting fire to. From these circumstances, and other particulars which I have mentioned relative to this island, the reader will not be indisposed to believe that it was originally thrown up by some subterraneous, or rather subaqueous, fire. To my understanding this is clearly demonstrated in an accurate and ingenious investigation of the subject by Dr. Gillan. His idea is that Amsterdam is truly an *insula phlegræ*, marked with the strongest evidence of volcanic eruption in every part of it. The cone, or basin, he thinks to have been the mother of the island, and that all the materials of which it is formed have been ejected from her womb at different periods, the earliest of which he would date many thousand years back.[1] The whole treatise is written with

[1] 'In the tour which some of the gentlemen from the *Lion* made of the small but singular island they were accompanied by Perron. When they were preparing for departure, they had the mortification to find he had been despoiled of no inconsiderable proportion of the skins. Whilst he was away from the hut, some persons from the ship, suspected of being above the rank of common seamen, brought spirituous liquors ashore, which was a temptation too strong for the other seal-catchers to resist. They first began to bargain upon reasonable conditions, but when once they had tasted the rum in sufficient quantity to affect the understanding, they lessened the heap of skins with a profusion which knew no bounds, and Perron had to regret his good nature to strangers, and to lament the arrival of English ships at the place of his abode. Sir Erasmus Gower, who felt much indignation when he heard the story, ordered a general search to be made for the skins thus unwarrantably acquired. Some were found, and it was intended to leave them at Canton, for the *Lion* was already under sail from Amsterdam before he could know the fact.'—Sir G. Staunton, 'Embassy to China.'

so much philosophical candour, and in so agreeable a style, that I hope the Doctor may be persuaded to gratify the world with a sight of it. The thing most likely to withhold it from the public eye would probably be his inviolable respect for the Sacred Writings, and his firm persuasion of the truth of Revealed Religion, as there are some passages in it which, if not properly understood, might go near to singe Moses' whiskers and turn the Book of Genesis topsy-turvy. It has, indeed, been long suspected, from a consideration alone of the numerous strata of larva near Etna and the intermediate soil between them, that the world is by no means such a chicken as the Bible would induce us to believe; and from the late wonderful discoveries in chemistry relative to the nature of the elements and the properties of matter, some knowing ones pretend to talk as if the world had never been created at all, forgetting that Moses and Ovid and the Brahmins, and all the cosmogonists of every age and country, all agree in the same story, and begin much in the same manner with ' This is the house that Jack built.'

CHAPTER IX

STRAITS OF SUNDA AND BATAVIA

OUR passage from the Island of Amsterdam (which we left on Saturday night, the 2nd February) till our arrival in the Straits of Sunda afforded but few incidents worth remarking.

On Tuesday the 26th February we got sight of Java Head, but the wind and current being unfavourable, we did not come to an anchor till the next evening.

Whilst we lay here, a Dutch boat from Angora Point with a pendant at her bow came alongside of us. She brought provisions of various kinds, and had an officer on board who presented a book to Sir Erasmus Gower, requesting him to write down the name of his ship, and her destination, and any other particulars he might think proper. This procedure, which, I believe, is of no very ancient standing, seems to be an impertinence of the Government of Batavia, introduced, it has been said, as a sort of foundation for their claiming a right to the regale or passage of the Straits of Sunda. Most of our Indiamen and the country ships submit to it without difficulty, either from motives of private interest, or to avoid contest; but all similar encroachments ought to be resisted in the earliest instance. Sir Erasmus Gower told the officer that he might easily see his ship was an English Man-of-War, but he condescended to no further explanations or particulars.

On the 1st of March we lifted anchor and proceeded a few leagues higher up to our rendezvous at the North Island, where we found the *Hindostan*, which had been separated from us a few days before.

On the same day an American ship, Spanish built, called the *Grand Duke of Tuscany*, and commanded by one Ingram, stopped at North Island. She was laden with sugar, and was bound to Ostend, but meant to call in on her way at St. Helena. We took this opportunity of writing to our friends in England, and put on board her a box of letters directed to Colonel Brooke, Governor of St. Helena, whom we requested to forward them by the first of our India-men that should call at his Island.

Having now recruited our wood and water, we stood on towards Batavia. As soon as we approached the land (which was in the afternoon of the 4th of March), Sir Erasmus Gower despatched Mr. Campbell, his first Lieutenant, to Batavia in his boat, to inform the Governor, as is customary, of our arrival. He was scarcely a gunshot from the ship when Mr. Andriesse, the Dutch Commodore of the Road (a gentleman born at Rotterdam of British parents), came on board the *Lion* to offer us all the services and civilities depending on his department. And the next morning at nine o'clock I was visited by Mr. Titsingh and Mr. Wiegerman, two members of the Council, together with Mr. Van de Weert, the principal secretary, and the before-mentioned Mr. Andriesse, the Commodore. They came with a compliment from Mr. Alting, the Governor, welcoming me to Batavia, inviting me on shore, and requesting to know when I meant to land, that every preparation might be made for receiving me with all proper honours and respect.

Mr. Wiegerman at the same time gave me a very sincere and cordial offer of his house, equipages, and services, whilst I should continue at Batavia. Being much indisposed, I was obliged at that time to defer my going on shore, but signified that I proposed to be at Batavia on Friday, 8th of March, which happened to be the Prince of Orange's anniversary.

The Governor, as soon as informed of my intention, sent the Captain of the Road with two other officers to express his satisfaction at it, to inquire after my health, and to invite me, and all the gentlemen of my train, with the officers of the ship, to a ball and supper which he proposed giving the next evening.

On the Thursday, the 7th March, being somewhat recovered, I set out from the *Lion* on board the twelve-oared barge, at ten o'clock a.m., with Sir George Staunton, Sir Erasmus Gower, and Captain Mackintosh. The gentlemen of the Embassy, and the principal officers of the *Lion* and the *Hindostan*, followed in the other boats.[1] In less

[1] 'In a short time after Lord Macartney had quitted the ship, a Dutch officer of distinction, with several ladies and gentlemen, came on board the *Lion* from Batavia to take a view of her. They were received with all possible politeness by Lieutenant Campbell,

DUTCH HOSPITALITY

than half an hour I landed at the Castle, where I was received, at the gate, as I came out of the barge, by all the members of the Council with the usual ceremonies of saluting, firing of guns, sounding trumpets, and beating of drums. The troops were drawn out under arms, and lined all the avenues and passages which we went through, till we reached the great stairs, where I was met by the Governor, who conducted me thence to the Grand Council Chamber, and seated me in an arm-chair on his right hand, all the Members of the Council at the same time taking their places in due order, each having at his elbow a brazen spitting-jar, of the shape and size of a large china beaker, about four feet high, finely polished and shining like a mirror.

After conversing together about an hour, and drinking a few glasses of excellent Madeira without which no ceremony can be completed nor business transacted, the dinner broke up, and we marched out in the same form as we had entered, till we came to the foot of the stairs, where the Governor took his leave of me. I then proceeded with my excellent landlord, Mr. Wiegerman, in his chariot to his house in the country, through one of the city gates, which is exclusively sacred and appropriated to the use of the Governor and Council, no other person's carriages being permitted to pass that way.

There we found a most sumptuous dinner provided, and a most cordial welcome, Mr. Wiegerman entertaining me and all my train with equal magnificence and hospitality.[1]

---

and appeared to be much satisfied with their reception. A very fine young English lady was one of the party, and enhanced the honour of the visit.

'In the afternoon I went on shore in the launch, having charge of the luggage belonging to the suite, which was, with some difficulty, rowed up the canal, and safely landed before the door of the Royal Batavian Hotel.'—Æneas Anderson, 'Narrative of Embassy to China.'

Royal Batavian Hotel: 'The public regulations of the house and the table which was kept for the Ambassador's suite was very superb. The breakfast always consisted of tea, coffee, chocolate, and cocoa, with every kind of cold meat, broiled fish, and eggs, to which were added jellies, sweetmeats, and honey, with various kinds of wines and confectionery. Both dinner and supper consisted of the most delicate dishes dressed in a superior style of cookery. The servants' table was also supplied with equal propriety and plenty.'—*Ibid.*

[1] Description of Mr. Wiegerman's banquet from J. Barrow's 'Voyage to Cochin China':

THE GOVERNOR'S BALL

When the banquet was ended, we retired for a couple of hours to refresh ourselves with a short sleep, or siesta, as is usual in the tropical countries, and at eight o'clock we adjourned to the Governor's ball, which was as splendid, as sumptuous, and as numerous as his taste, his opulence, and the state of society at Batavia were capable of making it. It was given at his garden house, within a short distance from town, and comprehended all the variety of amusement and conviviality that could be devised by the good-humoured ingenuity of the Governor and his daughter. Just at the entrance of the garden on the right hand was erected a theatre, on which Chinese dramas, both serious and comic, were performed by a set of actors who seemed to execute their parts with great skill and intelligence. On the left was a large booth, in which were represented the humours

---

'We had scarcely set foot in the house when a procession of slaves made its appearance, with wine and gin, cordials, cakes, and sweetmeats—a ceremony that was repeated to every new guest who arrived. After waiting a couple of hours, the signal for dinner was given by the entrance of three female slaves, one with a large silver basin, the second with a jar of the same metal, and the third with towels for wiping them. The company was very numerous, and the weather being remarkably close, the velvet coats and powdered wigs were thrown aside, and their places supplied with short dimity jackets and muslin nightcaps. I certainly do not ever remember to have seen a European table so completely loaded with what Van Wiegerman was pleased to call poison and pestilence. Fish boiled and broiled, fowls in curries, and pillaws, turkeys and large capons, joints of beef, boiled, roasted, and stewed, soups, puddings, custards, and all kinds of pastry, were so crowded and jumbled together that there was scarcely any room for plates. Of the several kinds of dishes there was generally a pair; a turkey on one side had its brother turkey on the other, and capon stared at capon. A slave was placed behind the chair of each guest, besides those who handed round wine, gin, cordials, and beer, all of which are profusely used by the Dutch, under an idea that by promoting perspiration they carry off in some degree the effect of the poison and pestilence. After dinner an elegant dessert was served up of Chinese pastry, fruits in great variety, and sweetmeats. There were not any ladies in the company, Van Wiegerman being a bachelor. A band of Malay musicians played in the veranda during dinner. From table, the Dutch part of the company retired to their beds, in order to recover by a few hours' sleep the fatigues of eating and drinking, and to prepare for those of a far more serious one to follow. The dinner is considered only a whetter of the appetite for supper.'

of a Dutch fair, with its usual diversions. Behind the house opened four long vistas, terminated by picturesque buildings, adorned and illuminated with diaphanous figures and many-coloured lamps. On a given signal, these fabrics expanded into a thousand fireworks, changing their appearance at every moment, and assuming every form and displaying every effort of pyrotechnical art and ingenuity. Here you saw the gigantic shapes of dragons and basilisks, flapping their burnished wings, and vomiting inundations of flame, whilst their arrowy tongues quivered like the coruscations of reiterated lightning. There you beheld the refulgent figure of the bird of Juno, dilating his plumage, spangled with myriads of eyes, rolling round in incessant sparkles, and flashing innumerable fires at every gyration. The whole pageant concluding with a volcanic eruption, which shot up to a tremendous height in the air, and then descended in a blazing shower of suns, moons, stars, comets, and meteors of every imaginable shape, accompanied by such millions of echoes and reverberated explosions as if the solid firmament had given way, and let loose all its magazines of thunder and cataracts of fire.

These illuminations were heightened and enlarged when viewed in the smooth expanse of the numerous canals and basins which adorned the gardens, and produced the effect of so many looking-glasses, reflecting and redoubling *ad infinitum* the brilliant imagery that glittered on every side; whilst the water nightingales that nestled under the banks raised their voices from below, and aided the harmony of the orchestra with the melody of their song.

The intermediate time between the conclusion of this exhibition and the serving of the supper was employed by us in walking through the gardens, playing at cards, viewing the dancers in the ball-room, and assisting at the Governor's conversation in the smoking gallery.

The custom of the Governor and Councillors (with whose gravity dancing would be considered incompatible) is, as soon as the first bows and salutes are over (which ceremony is always performed in a well-powdered periwig, and a well-trimmed suit of crimson velvet), to exchange their coats and waistcoats for a short silver tissue jacket, and their caxons for a calico nightcap. In this Aurelian state these Eastern Magi reposed in their arm-chairs, and inhaled at leisure the fragrance of the nicotian herb.

In the ball-room, the ladies who did not dance sat round the wall in proper state, each having at her foot a female

Malay slave, holding a silver spitting-pot in her hand, for the frequent use of her mistress.

The fair frows who figured on the floor were all most richly habited, and wore their hair dressed in the Batavian mode, except two or three ladies lately imported from Holland, who had not yet worn out their European wardrobe, nor expended their stock of powder and pomatum. All the rest had adopted the Malay mode, which, however admired by some, did not to my eyes at least appear very attractive or becoming.

The hair (which is usually very black and never powdered) is combed smooth back from the forehead, and fastened on the crown of the head with a large diamond bodkin, behind which all their jewels are placed, and disposed in different shapes of braids, chains, stars, crescents, fly-boats, windmills, and butterflies, according to the taste and fancy of the wearer. But whatever different opinion may be entertained with regard to these ladies' artificial ornaments, there seemed to be but one with most of our gentlemen, of their natural beauties.

If their air, shape, or motions did not appear very elegant or easy at their first entrance in the ball-room, they were undoubtedly still less so on their second. A little before supper they retired for a few minutes in order to change their dresses, a measure which the heat of the climate renders not a little necessary after dancing.

They then returned in a different, and what seemed to us a very singular, sort of habiliment. It was literally a shift of silver tissue, which being quite loose about the body above the girdle, discovered at every evolution all the beauties of neck, bosom, and waist which these ladies had to boast of. But I know not how, these loose attires did not appear either very becoming or alluring.[1]

At twelve o'clock we sat down to supper, which was

[1] 'Many of the ladies laid aside their spangled gowns, and appeared in their dimity jackets. These jolly dames took especial care that the strangers should be well pleased and well plied with wine, to which, at the same time, they were by no means backward in helping themselves. Some of the elder sort sat at a table to a late hour, while the younger part returned to the ball-room, where reels and jigs and hornpipes now took the place of country dances. A Scoto-Batavian officer displayed his raw-boned activity in a saraband, to the great amusement of the native dames. So fascinating was the entertainment that it was near four in the morning before the company dispersed.'—J. Barrow, 'Voyage to Cochin China.'

THE GOVERNOR'S DAUGHTER

served with great magnificence and profusion.[1] The number of guests was about three hundred, and there was ample room for them all. I was placed between the Governor and his daughter, who, if not distinguished from the rest by superior beauty, yet certainly outshone them all by the richness of her dress, and the number and size of her jewels.[2] She is married to one of the Edelherrn, or noble Councillors of Batavia, who has passed through most of the lucrative employments of the East India Company in this part of the world.

We drank two-and-twenty toasts in regular order, a manuscript list of which was previously given to the principal guests. They were chiefly political. The health and prospects of the Stadtholder, the States-General, the India Company, the King of England, etc., etc. All these were announced with the stentorian voice of the master of the ceremonies, from behind the Governor's chair, and drank by the Company (as Nebuchadnezzar's image was worshipped) to the sound of the drum, trump, trumpet, sackbut, salt-box, and every kind of music.

[Here are missing fourteen pages of the Journal, which have been cut out.]

Mr. Wiegerman accompanied me when I went to return the visits of the principal persons of the settlement. I also went to view the Church, which is of an octagon shape, and is a handsome building, neatly fitted up within and furnished with a very capital organ. I also visited the Stadthouse and other public edifices, and whatsoever besides was considered worthy of notice in the place, but I was much indisposed during the whole time. Both my mental and corporeal elasticity deserted me, my spirits were sirocco-struck, I felt a secret dread, an inward horror, of falling into

---

[1] 'A little after midnight a magnificent supper was served in the great hall, which, it is almost unnecessary to add, consisted of every delicacy that Europe and Asia could supply. The old Governor, who with the rest of the Dutchmen had hitherto kept on his full-dressed suit of velvet, now threw off his coat and wig, and took his seat at table in a light muslin jacket and a nightcap.'—J. Barrow, 'Voyage to Cochin China.'

[2] 'The Governor's daughter, who by her Mother's side was of dingy extraction, was so bespangled with jewels that, according to the Dutchman's valuation, she was whispered to be worth twenty thousand rix dollars, or about four thousand pounds, as she then stood.'—*Ibid.*

naught, which took away from every enjoyment and diffused over my whole frame such sensations as no language can describe. I soon found that a change of air was my only chance of relief. I therefore made an effort, and fortunately had strength enough to remove and return on board the *Lion*, where I gradually, though very slowly, recovered.[1]

The very extensive tracts of land both in Java and Sumatra, formerly cleared from the original woods and jungle, and now again abandoned to spontaneous vegetation, would naturally infer a population there in remote times much greater than at present. But no excess of devastation can be surprising in a country whose inhabitants live in an almost constant state of hostility, and that this was the case formerly is reasonably deducible from their present manners and customs. Every male inhabitant, though otherwise half naked, goes always armed with a criss. This must be still considered by the people as a necessary precaution, for he that is poor is not likely to purchase what is superfluous, neither will he that is indolent and lazy labour for what is useless, or carry without necessity what in a hot climate and peaceable community would be alarming to others and cumbersome to himself.

The criss is a sharp-pointed dagger, in the use of which the Malays are uncommonly dexterous, and which (in order to render it still more fatal) they are said to envenom with an incurable poison, expressed from the various baneful vegetables which these regions luxuriantly produce. These people (at least those whom we saw) are generally of a low stature, and copper-coloured complexion. They have broad faces, wide mouths, strong, horse-like, black hair, and truculent countenances which indicate no control of the mind over the passions.

Some degree, however, of reflected civilization appeared in a trifling incident that occurred whilst we lay on the coast. Sir Erasmus Gower, previous to our departure from thence to Batavia, ordered a board to be nailed to a post on the shore, which contained his directions to the tender which had separated from us in the beginning of the voyage, and

[1] 'On my return to the hotel, I found, with great concern, that Lord Macartney had been seized with a violent fit of the gout, and was returned on board the *Lion*; so that the various entertainments which were preparing to have enlivened the time of our stay at Batavia were frustrated, by this very unpleasant change in the health of the distinguished person who was the object of them.'—Æneas Anderson, 'Narrative of Embassy to China.'

which he expected speedily to arrive. On our return we found that the board had been taken down, and the nails, which it seemed were of some value to the natives, carried away. Here a mere savage would have stopped, satisfied with the gratification of his own wants, and little solicitous of anything further, equally careless of the board and of the purpose for which it might have been left there. But these Malays, though determined to pursue their own interests, were unwilling to defeat our intentions, for after appropriating the iron nails to themselves they took care to replace the board by fastening it with wooden pegs to the post where they had found it, although from inadvertence or ignorance of our language, they happened to invert it.

I must mention another incident. One of our seamen who was accidentally left on shore by himself with a considerable quantity of linen to be washed, and who unthinkingly strolled to a village at some distance, was hospitably treated and assisted by the inhabitants. Yet such is the precariousness of their manners and the fluctuation of their principles, that the very next day the same people murdered one of our valuable artificers, who went to wash a much smaller and less valuable bundle of linen in the river where our boats usually took in their water.[1]

In the letters we had received from Canton, we were told that we might expect to hear further from the Commissioners there by the *Sullivan* and *Royal Admiral*, two of the Company's ships which would be ready to sail from thence to England in the beginning of March. We therefore determined to wait for their arrival in this neighbourhood. From this circumstance we were detained seven or eight weeks, and consequently had many opportunities of observing the adjacent country, of extending our inquiries, and of enlarging our knowledge of it.

We frequently varied our berth, not only for this purpose, but also for the convenience of getting provisions, and for the benefit arising from the change of air; sometimes lying at North Island, near which happened the unfortunate accident just mentioned. On one side of Angora Point a

[1] 'This man was as remarkable for the ingenuity of his mind as for a thoughtlessness of conduct, which rendered the former of little use to his own welfare. He had seen better days; but the good-humour and merry disposition which he still retained rendered him a favourite with the crew, and few deaths would have occasioned so much as his a detestation against the authors of it.'—Sir G. Staunton, 'Embassy to China.'

wooden monument has been set up to the memory of the late Lieutenant-Colonel Cathcart, who was buried under it. He died in the Straits of Banco, on his way to China, and his body was brought back to be interred at this place.[1] On the upper part of the tomb his arms are carved.

In this climate Fahrenheit's thermometer in the shade was scarcely ever below eighty, or higher than eighty-six degrees at sea, or ninety on shore, but its variations by no means corresponded to the graduations of our sufferings from the heat. The effect of the heat upon the human faculties is not to be measured by its intenseness at any given moment of the day, but by its perseverance during the night.

Whatever the state of the weather may be that occasions water spouts, it would seem they arise from some general cause which affects a considerable part of the atmosphere. We saw several of them, but they were too imperfect and too distant for accurate examination.

The city of Bantam lies at about eighteen miles distance by land from Angora Point; but the gentlemen of my train who had the curiosity to visit it chose to go by water. They were very well entertained there by Mr. Ramond, the Dutch principal officer, but they were disappointed in their expectations of seeing the King, his Bantamese Majesty being then much indisposed and confined to his apartment. They were told that he was about thirty-three years old, had four hundred wives, and was of a good disposition. Though his dominions in Java are pretty extensive, and though he holds a considerable part of the opposite coast of Sumatra in subjection, he himself is absolutely under the harrow of the Dutch. His palace is situated within a fort garrisoned and commanded by their troops, and they have the exclusive right of purchasing the superfluous produce of his dominions; that is to say, what he and his people do not consume themselves. He is High Priest as well as King of his country, and professes the Mahommedan Religion, but mixes with it, by a curious amalgamation of superstition, many of the rites and ceremonies of the ancient Indian Faith.

The water fort of Batavia is built of coral, fished up from the adjoining sea, which has this advantage, that it renders

[1] 'Colonel the Honble. Charles Cathcart was sent as Ambassador from England to China in 1788. He died on the voyage out, and as no one had been appointed to succeed him in his office, in the event of his death, the Embassy came to an end with him.'

THE INHABITANTS OF BATAVIA

it equal to brick masonry, in which cannon-shot is apt to bury itself without splintering or shattering the wall. The country for a great distance from the sea does not produce a single stone; the walls of the town are built of lava.

The city, though extensive and well built, affords no striking appearance as you approach it from the sea, for being situated on a perfect level it is in a great measure hidden (except the dome of the great church) by the broad leaves of the cocoanut and other trees growing in the streets.

The inhabitants of Batavia may be divided into six classes. The native Javanese, the slaves, the freed slaves, the Chinese, the descendants of Portuguese formerly possessors of Batavia, the Dutch and Europeans.

I shall speak of each separately. First, the Javanese, or original inhabitants of the country, have a peculiar colour of complexion that distinguishes them from the other inhabitants of the place. They are neither so swarthy as the Portuguese, nor of so yellow a tinge as the other Malays in general. The faces and features are fuller, their eyes large, and their noses broad and flat. They are all free, and according to the stipulations of their treaty with the Dutch they must not be made slaves. They are mostly of a cowardly, malicious, and revengeful disposition. They are apt to stab or poison on the slightest provocation, and many of them may be hired to commit murder. The common price among themselves is a dollar, and it is said the crime is very frequent. It is not unusual for them, when they have been kindly treated, or obliged by any one, to express their gratitude by offering to kill any of his enemies, and they contrive their measure with such cunning as generally to escape discovery. Although they make so light of assassination of this kind, they never attack openly or dare to face a person who is aware of them. A dozen of them would fly before a single European armed and on his guard. It is this dread that keeps them so much in subjection to the Dutch, who are sensible that to their firearms and artillery they are chiefly indebted for their safety, as the proportion between their numbers is above a thousand to one.[1]

---

[1] 'The resistance which the Dutch have experienced from this people has at all times been trifling. Their spirit, if any they have ever had, seems to have been completely subdued by their Mahommedan conquerors some centuries before their island was discovered

The slaves are very numerous, and the females[1] are more numerous than the males. Every one has so many as he can afford to purchase and maintain. They are brought from all parts of India, but chiefly from the Malay Islands, to the East, and it is remarked that at all times, and at all ages, the original character and habits of the country they come from can be distinctly traced in themselves and their descendants.[2]

The freed slaves, of which the number is not great, are such as have been manumitted from time to time by their masters for various reasons. As soon as they have obtained their liberty they usually hire small spots of ground from the Government and Council, or other servants of the Company who have land to let, and convert them into gardens, where they raise fruit and excellent vegetables for the market. They are the only people who cultivate the betal and areca, so much in use here, so that many of them grow rich and considerable.

The Chinese have been long settled at Batavia, and amount, it is said, to more than one hundred thousand, but I should suppose the number much exaggerated. They are the most active and industrious class of people, and carry on most of the business of the place. They are so much the principal supports of its industry that the settlement could scarcely subsist without them. And the same, I am informed, is the case at Manilla under the Spanish. They live in a quarter entirely by themselves, like the Jews at Amsterdam, and retain the customs, manners, and religious ceremonies,

---

by Europeans. Sunk into the lowest stage of apathy, they seem to be incapable of any great exertion. To the Javanese of condition, the supreme blessings of life consist in stretching himself at full length, or sitting cross-legged on a carpet the whole day long surrounded by women, whilst he draws the smoke through the tube of his hookah.'
—J. Barrow, ' Voyage to Cochin China.'

[1] 'The apprehension of assassination is among the motives for preferring at Batavia female slaves for every use to which they can be applied ; so that the number purchased of them exceeds the other sex.'—Sir G. Staunton, ' Embassy to China.'

[2] 'They [the slaves] have sufficient sustenance, but many of the males among them there, who had formerly, perhaps, led an independent life till made captives in their wars, have been found to take offence against their masters upon very slight occasions, and to wreak their vengeance by assassination.'—*Ibid.*

Æneas Anderson gives instances of the great severity of the Dutch towards their slaves.

character and dress of their original country. They pay considerable taxes, but easily find resources for paying them.[1] They are sober, orderly, and industrious, and make everything thrive under them wherever they go. Every Dutchman at Batavia has his Chinese, who does all his mercantile and other business for him, as the Batavians and others do for the English at Madras and Calcutta. All the Chinese at Batavia are distributed into a number of tribes, or companies, each under the direction or magistracy of a captain of their own nation, who is responsible to the Government for their good behaviour. Those of them who are born in China have all an unconquerable desire to return home and be buried with their ancestors, which gives an additional spur to their natural covetousness and pecuniary exertions. However, the Chinese born here, and who seem to be content to be buried on the spot, seem not at all inferior to the others in their propensity to rapid accumulation.

The fifth class consists of the Portuguese descendants of the first European occupants of Batavia. Although they have lost all commerce and connection with their mother-country, they still continue here (as, indeed, is still the case in many of the old European settlements in India) to speak a corrupt dialect of the Portuguese language, which is also generally understood by the natives, and shows how deep a root the Portuguese power had taken in their regions during its predominance. Their language has survived their sovereignty, and even their religion. For their descendants in Batavia have by the lapse of time dropped into the current profession of the State, and now frequent the Reformed Church, where the dogmas of Calvin and Zwinglius are promulgated in Portuguese. Little did the Pope, who conveyed by bulls these then unconverted regions to King Emanuel, foresee that his grantees and mother-tongue would one day be made the vehicle of heresy and false doctrine instead of the trumpet of Popery and instrument of salvation.

[1] 'The Chinese were heavily taxed on everything, being even compelled to purchase a licence to wear a pigtail. In 1740, many of the Chinese resident in Batavia were most cruelly tortured and massacred, on a pretence that a conspiracy to exterminate the Dutch had been discovered. But the real reason is said to have been the disappointment of the Governor, who, failing to extort a large sum of money from the Chinese chiefs, in revenge accused them of a plot against the Government.'

DUTCH JEALOUSY

The sixth class of inhabitants of Batavia is that of the Dutch[1] and Europeans in general, who have all the power, offices, and employments in their own hands, and exercise authority over the rest, and whose number (which otherwise would soon be reduced to nothing by deaths and departures) is kept up and continued by constant supplies from Europe. They appear sickly, weak, and languid, whilst the other classes are in general healthy, strong, and active. Nevertheless, the Europeans, though so infinitely few in numbers, are, from superiority of mind and effect of combination, the sole masters of the country. The pursuit of wealth being the grand object which attracts the Europeans to this unhealthy place, their attention is incessantly employed in acquiring it, as expeditiously as possible, flattering themselves with hopes of escaping those diseases which would otherwise retain them for ever. We were, therefore, not much surprised at an instance of venality, which, no doubt, if detected, would be rigorously punished. The Dutch Company, always inexorably jealous of these exclusive branches of trade which they possess, have positively prohibited the publication of any charts or maps of those seas or coasts where such trade is carried on. They have, however, an office in Batavia in which all their manuscript charts are deposited, for the inspection and sole use of their sea officers employed in voyages to the Spice Islands, or other intricate and obscure navigation. A gentleman of the Embassy, nevertheless, had an intimation from one of the Dutch Company's servants, who had free access to the office, that for a valuable consideration he would undertake to procure him a true copy of any chart or paper that he wished to have. I hope it is unnecessary to say that this overture was declined. Even if we could suppose that the world was not sufficiently wide for the separate trade of the Dutch and ourselves, or if we were ignorant that fair openings for traffic will always be found in proportion to the skill, industry, and capital of the undertaking, yet such was the handsome reception we met with, and the hospitable treatment we experienced, from the members of the Batavian Government, that we could not admit a thought of the slightest clandestine dealing with any of their servants.

[1] 'That class of men which bears a complete sway over the island is by much the least numerous; it is rare to see a single "right honourable high-born Dutchmàn" condescending to walk the streets. Nothing from Europe,' he observes, 'but Englishmen and dogs walk in Batavia.'—J. Barrow, ' Voyage to Cochin China.'

UNHEALTHY SURROUNDINGS

The Governor and Councillors who compose the Regency reside chiefly in the country round Batavia, but the miasmata arising from the putrid stagnating water in the neighbourhood, and from other causes, render every spot which they inhabit extremely prejudicial, and at last generally fatal, to the health of Europeans. A gentleman, who had resided here for some time, gave us in a few words his sentiments of the place : ' The air,' said he, ' is pestilence, and the water poison.'[1] The country, however, has so pleasing and so novel an appearance, being interspersed and varied with so many magnificent palaces, gardens, avenues, canals, drawbridges, and so formed to captivate the eye, that, as young Staunton very aptly observed, it was a habitation calculated for immortals.

The gentlemen at the head of affairs are, in general, so deeply engaged in their lucrative concerns that we could not well expect to meet with many among them of much science or literature unconnected with commerce, especially as several of them had risen from very inferior stations, and were without the advantages arising from early education. They have, nevertheless, an Academy of Sciences, which published six volumes of their transactions. When they did me the honour of electing me as a member of their body, they sent me a complete set of them ; but as, unfortunately for me, they are all written in Dutch, I am as yet unacquainted with their contents.

Although no place on the globe one would imagine required the aid of good physicians more than Batavia, yet I believe there is scarcely any place on the globe so ill-supplied with them. In other countries they are usually men of liberal education, but here they are mostly adventurers of the lowest class, many of them originally barbers, or of other mean occupations. A nephew of the surgeon of the *Lion*, an ignorant young boy, who had run away from the ship, was eagerly engaged by them, and entered as a practitioner at the great hospital.[2]

---

[1] ' The ditches within the city are many of them stagnant and highly offensive, and the Dutch have the imprudent custom of burying their dead, not only within the city walls, but also in the churches.'—J. Barrow, ' Voyage to Cochin China.'

[2] ' One of the clergymen, and the principal physician of the place, were both said to have originally been barbers. The United Provinces furnish even few military recruits. The rest are chiefly Germans, many of whom are said to have been kidnapped into the service. The Government is accused of the barbarous policy of

Within a mile of the town there is a Hortus Medicus established by Government for collecting and cultivating the plants of the country. Mr. Schowman was the superintendent of this garden, and though the Doctor did not seem to consider him as possessed of abilities at all adequate to his situation, he obtained from him, however, some material information relative to certain plants, and other matters which he was desirous of knowing. Particular inquiry was made concerning the Upas-tree, the marvellous description of which in Dr. Darwin's poem, called 'The Loves of the Plants,' had strongly excited our curiosity. That there had been a surgeon at Batavia of the name of Foersch, the author of the relation cited by Dr. Darwin in his note, we found to be true, but we heard him spoken of as a person of doubtful character, and two gentlemen of the Council declared his account of the Upas to be an impudent falsehood imposed on the public. Mr. Schowman assented to what they said, but nevertheless he some time afterwards told Dr. Gillan that he actually knew, and had in his garden, a tree which he called and believed to be the Upas-tree, although it had not all the extraordinary qualities attributed to it by Mr. Foersch. He said this tree exuded a resin or juice of a venomous nature, that a wound inflicted by any cutting weapon that had been ever so slightly dipped in it was inevitably mortal, that the reason why he had denied the existence of such a tree was because several slaves and servants were attending at the time he spoke, and that he did not choose they should believe such a tree was to be found anywhere, much less that it was then growing in his garden, lest at any time they might be tempted to make an improper use of it. The same reason had made him conceal it from every person at Batavia, except the Governor, and one or two of the Council. This publication of it would certainly be impolitic, and even the production of so dreadful

---

intercepting all correspondence between these people and their mother-country. One of these miserable men availed himself of an opportunity which offered incidentally, of addressing in his native tongue a gentleman of his own country, belonging to the Embassy. He was in the utmost agitation lest he should be observed holding converse with a person not under the Dutch Government's control, and conjured him in a few words of heartfelt anguish to forward a letter he meant to write to his relations in Germany. Unfortunately, he had not then the letter ready, and he had never once afterwards the opportunity of delivering it.'—Sir G. Staunton, ' Embassy to China.'

a poison would be almost considered as reflecting disgrace
upon the country where it grew. Mr. Englehart furnished
Dr. Gillan with a copy of the official paper, written in Dutch,
that had been sent to Holland upon the subject, which,
though intended as a refutation of Foersch's story, and
asserting that the Emperor or Sultan of Java had denied
having any knowledge of such a tree, yet admitted the fact
to be true of his Majesty's having thirteen of his wives
executed by poison, which had been mentioned as a cor-
roborating circumstance in Foersch's narrative. The Dutch
gentlemen at Bantam, residing at some distance from the
immediate seat and refined policy of the Batavian Government, seemed to make no secret of the Upas-tree growing in
the neighbouring mountains; adding, however, that the
Emperor did not wish it to be commonly known, as he was
desirous of preserving the poison for his own purposes.

I forgot to mention that Mr. Schowman had promised
to Sir George Staunton and Dr. Gillan to show them the
Upas-tree in his garden at a convenient opportunity; but
none such having occurred they left Batavia without the
satisfaction of a personal inspection of it. Mr. Schowman
had several nutmeg plants in his garden, which had been
brought from their native soil, the Isle of Banda, and were
in a thriving condition. One of them was grown to be the
size of a small tree, the others were smaller, and in pots of
Banda earth which had been sent along with them from a
belief entertained that the nutmeg could not grow in any
other soil. The earth, when examined, was found to be
volcanic ashes with a considerable portion of iron in them.
Some of the nuts had also been forwarded at the same
time, and these were carefully put up in closed jars with a
liquor around them, which proved to be nothing but pure
water. Some of these nuts have been planted in small pots
of common earth, and are found to grow full as well in it,
as in their natural soil, so that there is little doubt that the
nutmeg may be raised in other places as well as Banda.

But Mr. Schowman's experiments are considered and
authorized only as matter of curiosity, and not at all with
a view to anything further; for, with regard to the clove and
nutmeg, we learned at Batavia a fact of a very extraordinary
and selfish nature, which proves to what unnatural lengths
the narrow jealousies of commerce have carried the Dutch
in this part of the world. I mean the actually subsisting
establishment of extirpators, who are a body of men appointed and employed by the Government, with strict

instructions and ample powers to rout out and extinguish every clove and nutmeg that is to be found in any of the Moluccos within their reach, except Amboyna and Banda, where they are carefully preserved and secured as the exclusive property of the Dutch Company, who are the ingenious contrivers of this project to counteract and defeat the bounty of Nature. But they were near being stifled by their own contractedness, for a few years since a dreadful eruption from the volcano in Banda buried under its ashes all the nutmeg plantations of the island, occasioned an immense loss and damage to the Dutch, and for some time made them apprehensive of that valuable spice being irrevocably lost.

But notwithstanding this monopolizing spirit of the Government, I must not omit that a gentleman belonging to it was of so liberal a turn of mind, that he made a present of a young nutmeg plant in a healthy growing state to Sir George Staunton, who has sent it by good conveyance to His Majesty's conservatory at Kew, where it is to be hoped that it will arrive in safety and in vigour, so that it may be propagated from thence to our West India Islands, as the coffee-tree was in the last century from a single specimen.

The tree which produces the elastic gum is found in Java, and considerable quantities of it are sent to Europe, but seldom in a pure state, being generally more or less adulterated by the vendors, which circumstance we did not know before, but which seems to account in some measure for the seeming contradictions in the experiments of different chemists in Europe, who possibly may have operated upon different mixtures of it.

We saw the bread-fruit, which is about the size of a small melon, and when cut into slices is not unlike (in appearance and porosity) the common English bread, the dough of which had been well fermented; but though we toasted and buttered it, the taste still continued insipid to our palates.

From the low, marshy, and sultry situation of Batavia it is natural to imagine that the number of noxious reptiles should be very great. And it is undoubtedly considerable; but the mischief arising from them cannot be so, for, contrary to the notions entertained by peoples of other countries exempted from such evils, no uneasiness seems ever to be felt here in consequence of an apprehension of them. In the woods may often be observed the webs of the Java spider, which are of so tough a texture that they are not easily snapped asunder, but require to be divided by a cutting instrument. I have, therefore, the less difficulty in supposing practicable the project of Mr. Reaumur, who proposed setting up a cobweb manufactory of gloves and stockings in the South of France, which was so much ridiculed by our English philosophers in France and in England, who had never seen anything of the kind better than the filmy threads of our common spider.

I have already remarked the natural unhealthiness of Batavia, but, still to add to it, the Dutch laid out the city after the mode of their towns in Holland, dividing every street with a stagnant canal, and intercepting the free circulation of the air by bordering each canal with a row of trees thickly planted on each side.

The shops are chiefly kept by the Chinese, and look more like shops of brokers dealing in inferior and second-hand goods than those one would expect to find in such a city as Batavia. The shops of Rio Janeiro exhibited complete assortments of our most curious and valuable manufactures. I suppose the Malays have neither ability to buy, nor taste to admire, such articles. But, nevertheless, the lowest orders of the people here are not obliged (as in many other countries) to lead a life of perpetual labour, but have leisure, disposition, and means to enjoy themselves in positive pleasure, according to their own relish and in their own way.

They are violent and ungovernable in their passions, and though they abstain from fermented and vinous liquors, they are sensual and voluptuous to excess, much addicted to divination and magic; petulant, though indolent, and particularly fond of mimicry and pantomime. One of the Malay entertainments consists principally in the various postures and attitudes of the same actor under different masks. Our tumblers at Hughes's, Astley's, and Sadler's Wells are far inferior to their brethren at Batavia. The practice and exertions of the latter are such as to give an independent involuntary motion to every muscle of the exterior part of the body. And when the contortions are so new, and so extraordinary, as to excite wonder or pleasure in the spectators, the performers immediately feel the effect by the showers of small money which are thrown to them on the stage in great abundance.

I believe I have now almost mentioned everything that I can recollect from my own observation, or from the remarks communicated to me by the gentlemen of the Embassy relative to Batavia and its neighbourhood.

We had arrived in the Straits of Sunda on the 27th of February, and we did not proceed on our voyage northward till the 20th of April.

Three weeks had elapsed from our arrival, and the *Jackall* tender, from which we had parted in coming down the Channel, the first night of departure from Spithead, not appearing, I thought it necessary to purchase another vessel to replace her, and I fortunately found one here that perfectly answered our purpose. It was a small French brig of one hundred tons, European-built, sheathed with copper, mounting six two-pounders, and almost new. I gave five thousand Spanish dollars for her, and changed her French name of the *Nereide* to that of the *Duke of Clarence*, in honour of his Royal Highness. Had I waited a little longer this measure of the purchase would not have been necessary, for within two or three days after the *Jackall*, which we had so long despaired of, appeared in sight.

Sunday, April 21.—This morning we left North Island, and were very well pleased to proceed on our voyage to China, as we had reason to believe the Straits of Sunda extremely unhealthy. We had not lost a man from the time of our departure from England, but we had not been two days at Angora Point before our people grew sickly, and a dysentery began to spread which often baffled all the powers of medicine. Every air was pregnant with putrefaction, and wafted disease and death to the ship. The weather in the different stations where we lay was nearly all the same. It was perhaps somewhat less intensely hot at North Island than at Angora Point, the former being less engaged by the land and more open to the Eastern sea. But the thermometer was seldom below eighty-five or eighty-six in the middle of the day. The sun was almost vertical, the air felt like an oven, in which we were imprisoned. Our limbs were palsied, our voices grew faint, our eyes languid, our skins and our ears were incessantly assailed by myriads of the winged insect tribe, exulting in existence, stinging without mercy, and buzzing without a pause.

When we sailed from North Island we were accompanied by the *Hindostan*, the *Jackall*, and *Clarence* tenders, and by the *Achilles*, an Ostend ship, which we fell in with in the Straits of Sunda.

As the south-west monsoon was now well set in we expected soon to reach the Straits of Banca, but we had calms, winds, and currents so various and unfavourable that for several days we made very little way, and were frequently obliged to come to anchor.

As we passed along the eastern coasts of Sumatra we often saw near the mouths of the great rivers large detached pieces of land, clothed with verdure and trees, sailing by us. These were literally floating islands, torn from the parent shores by the violence of the floods. The roots of vegetables growing upon them being closely matted and interwoven, and loaded with much heavy adhering earth, formed a kind of ballast for steadying the drift and keeping the stems of the trees in a perpendicular position.

Monday, May 6.—On Monday, 6th of May, we considered ourselves as having completely passed through the Straits of Banca. The navigation through them is extremely troublesome. We sounded every inch of our way, and came to an anchor every night. The only Journals of these straits that we had were those of our transient China ships, which ships usually make the best of their way in the same beaten track, if they can, without delaying to make hydrographical observations or discoveries.

The weather was very hot, with violent rain, and at night such constant thunder and lightning as I never met with before. The thunder and lightning of Europe are mere crackers and squibs in comparison of what occurs in these latitudes.

We continue very sickly, although our people have been mostly upon fresh provisions for these two months past. Fevers and dysenteries are the prevalent diseases, and particularly the latter, which increase every day, owing, I conceive, to the want of proper conveniences on board ships of war, as the dysentery is certainly contagious. But it is inconceivable how soon habit reconciles people to almost every accident and misfortune. The death of the nearest triends makes very little impression on the survivors, who from the frequency of losses, and the resignation of seamen to the accidents of their profession, go on as if nothing unusual had happened and seem perfectly resigned to the miseries of their profession.

Thursday, May 16.—We saw Pulo Condore this morning, and about noon came to an anchor in five-fathom water, in a large spacious bay on the south-east side of the island, about four miles distance from the village, which is situated on a fine sandy beach, shaded by a long range of cocoanut-trees, and defended from the north-west sea by a coral reef.

A DESERTED VILLAGE

The village consisted of about forty houses, inhabited by people from Cochin China, who appear as if but recently settled there. They had three or four boats drawn up upon the beach, and there was one lying at a grapnel. They look very meagre and poor, but were tolerably neat and orderly in their houses, and seemed to have a sort of Government established among them, as there was a Chief or Mandarin dressed in a dark-coloured silk habit, who gave directions and spoke with an air of authority. Our Chinese came on shore with the other gentlemen, but could neither understand the speech of the inhabitants, nor make themselves understood by them. However, Mr. Nyang, one of our Chinese, wrote down his meaning, upon seeing which one of the people took his pencil and wrote the answer. Thus an intelligible correspondence was opened, and carried on till at last a woman appeared who spoke Chinese. As we had seen on the island horses, buffaloes, fowls, ducks, limes, cocoanuts, areca, silkworms, cotton, rice, tobacco, timber, trees, water guglets, fish, goats, etc. and eggs, we expected a supply of such of these articles as we wanted, and we told the people so. They promised to have everything ready for us the next morning; but judge of our people's surprise, when they went on shore, instead of finding what they expected, they observed no appearance of a human creature. All was silent and solitary. The people had deserted their houses, and fled in consternation to the hills in the interior of the country. They had left, however, in an exposed place a writing in the Chinese character, which was translated into Latin by Mr. Nyang, and was to the effect that the people of the island were few in number and very poor, and that they felt much apprehension and terror at the arrival of such great ships. They resolved to fly for their lives, leaving all they had behind them, and they supplicated the great people to have pity on them and not burn their cabins, and they concluded by prostrating themselves to the great people a hundred times. Though they had fled from their houses, they had carried nothing off with them but their arms, which consisted of a few spears and muskets and a brass swivel gun. Their houses remained with all their furniture, goods, etc. Our people continued some hours on shore, and, following the paths, walked into the country, where they observed at a distance several of the inhabitants, to whom they made signs, but none could be prevailed on to come near. In the village they had observed before there was a sort of

AN UNFORTUNATE ACCIDENT

temple with an idol, and a tablet with an inscription upon it desiring the prayers of the passengers for the soul of some deceased person. There was a jar in one of the houses containing some very good fish, but they observed no running water. There were several good wells twelve feet deep. There was no vestige to be found of the English fort said to have been formerly erected there.

There were large buffaloes, and several small pretty horses, probably for the purposes of agriculture, for they could scarcely be for any other use in so small an island, not ten miles long and three miles wide. A great many dogs and four or five cats in every house, from whence we conclude the place to be infested with rats and such vermin. No other creatures were to be observed on shore, except a very beautiful venomous snake four feet long.

After waiting several hours, and none of the inhabitants venturing to come down, our gentlemen departed, leaving a letter in Chinese in answer to theirs, explaining to them our reason for touching at the island, telling them who we were (English), and encouraging them to confide in our countrymen, if any such should call there again.

We left everything untouched and just as we found it, not taking away an atom of the most trifling nature, though there were many very tempting articles such as limes, eggs, poultry, etc. We suppose that some ship (an American was one of the conjectures) had touched there, and behaved ill to the people, which rendered the natives suspicious and fearful. They appeared at first to be gentle and civilized. As the Americans resemble us so much, and often hoist English colours in foreign parts, that was the reason why our gentlemen imagined they had been here.

Monday, May 17.—The *Hindostan* parted her cables and drove to sea, the weather being very stormy; we have, indeed, observed that it is generally so near the small islands. Lightning in the evening in every part of the heavens.

On departing from Pulo Condore an unfortunate accident happened on board the *Hindostan*. In heaving up her anchor, the rope which connects the capstan with the cable snapped in pieces. The wooden bars of the capstan, which are about six inches square and sixteen feet long, against which the men lay all their stress, and which serve them as levers to surmount the resistance of the anchor, flew suddenly out of their sockets in every direction, knocking down with irresistible violence every one within their reach. The quarter-deck was instantly strewn with men groaning under their wounds; a large complement of the crew had been employed in this operation. What number might be killed, wounded, or maimed could not for some time be ascertained, but such was the impression upon the Captain, who was a spectator of the accident, that, though there were three surgeons on board, he cried out instantly: 'Attend the fractured limbs in the first place, and inspect the other wounds afterwards.'

The consternation was, indeed, greater than in a day of battle, for which the mind has usually some previous preparation. Happily we did not lose anybody by this accident, and of the few who had their limbs broken, or were hurt in any other manner, all of them recovered.

Sunday, May 26.—Late last night we came to anchor in Turon Bay. Here we met in the road a Portuguese ship from Macao, commanded by one Mansel Houme Cawalho. She had been here some days trading with the Cochin Chinese, exchanging cotton, sulphur, saltpetre, guns, swords, powder, ball, and other military stores for silver, pepper, and sugar. The Captain, being desired by the Cochin Chinese, who were frightened by our appearance, to inquire about us, sent his boat on board, from which we learned that the King of the country was a boy of thirteen or fourteen years old, and resided at a considerable distance off, but that the Mandarin of the town here was a man of rank and consequence, to whom everything was confided, that there were plenty of provisions of various sorts, etc., etc.

Monday, May 27.—This morning the Portuguese Captain and another Portuguese came on board, and desired leave to pay their respects to me. They seemed very inquisitive, and at the same time very talkative. Contrary to what we had been told yesterday by their boat, they said that the place was very poor and in a ruinous state and no adequate supplies to be found for such ships as ours. They, however, offered us their services, and said that if we would give them a list of the things such as we should want, they had brought a person with them who would give us every assistance in his power. We thanked them for their civility, and told them we had already dispatched some of our own people on shore to explore the place and bring us their report. Soon after a boat from the town came alongside of us, commanded by a fellow almost dead drunk, whom they called a Mandarin. He presented to us a paper, which we understood to be a

COCHIN CHINESE FEAST

sort of commission from the chief of the place, empowering him to make inquiries who we were, from whence we came, what was our business, whether friends or enemies, etc., etc. This man, after staggering about on the deck and drinking a few glasses of rum, returned to his boat, was covered over with mats, and carried back to the shore, being considered to have executed the commission upon which he had been sent. His companions gave an account of what had passed, and what they had seen, to a council of Mandarins, who had been assembled in order to receive Mr. Maxwell and Dr. Gillan, whom I had sent to the town early in the morning in order to procure a supply of fresh provisions, which we were in great want of, and to make their general observations on the place and its inhabitants.

These Mandarins appeared to them a very civilized race, as they not only gave them a good dinner, but introduced them to their wives. They had a good deal of conversation with them, and seemed much surprised that the English should know so much of their history and concerns, as appeared in our gentlemen's discourse with them. They were all well dressed in long silk habits, and when they took leave were carried in handsome palanquins to their houses, which were at some distance from the village.

Three guns were fired as a sort of salute on this occasion; from their report they were supposed to be swivels. Mr. Maxwell brought me a complimentary letter from the Governor, and said he did not doubt that we should be able to procure whatever we wanted.

Tuesday, May 28.—Sir George Staunton, Mr. Maxwell, Captain Mackintosh, Dr. Gillan, etc., etc., went on shore. Sir George meant to be incog., but Padre Nyang told the people who he was. A letter was therefore presented to him, inviting him to a feast, but he declined it. Mr. Maxwell, Dr. Gillan, and most of the other gentlemen readily accepted the proposal, and were entertained at two tables with great variety of dishes served in handsome porcelain, which they relished extremely, though somewhat embarrassed in their manœuvres for want of knives and forks, or for want of dexterity in the management of chop-sticks. But however deficient they themselves were in skill of this kind, their entertainers or attendants seemed to be no novices in the use of their hands, most of our gentlemen having their pockets picked during dinner-time. Indeed, there was scarcely anything they had but seemed an object of cupidity to the Cochin Chinese, for what they could not steal they had the impudence to ask for, and pressed particularly for swords, canes, buckles, and everything of a metallic or valuable appearance.

After this medley of hospitality, theft, and begging was over, the curtain drew up and a comedy was represented, but what seemed to have made the greatest impression among the varied amusements of the day was a singular game of shuttlecock, which was played by a numerous party of fellows, who, instead of tossing it with racket or battledore, kicked it backwards and forwards with the soles of their feet, and made it fly to a great height and distance. On occasion of this extraordinary exercise, Captain Mackintosh mentioned the strength, suppleness, and dexterity of the Siamese, particularly in the art of boxing, which with them is not confined to the fists, as an English sailor experienced to his cost; their favourite and most effectual blow is a stroke of the heel, with which poor Jack Tar, to his equal astonishment and mortification, had his jaw-bone broken at the first onset.

In the evening the Governor sent a present of two pigs, two goats, ten ducks, some fowls and vegetables, and in return I gave him six muskets and bayonets, six pistols, and six cutlasses. He had desired an advance of money from Mr. Maxwell to purchase provisions for us, but the proposal was declined.[1]

Thursday, May 30.—This day the market was opened and pretty well stocked, but everything was rated very high. Mr. Maxwell, therefore, and some of the other gentlemen went to a village on the opposite side of the bay, which was pleasantly situated, and where they saw plenty of stock, but could not persuade the people to sell it on any account. It was supposed they were laid under restrictions from the Government. The tents being erected on one of the islands,

[1] 'The Ambassador was visited by several Mandarins with a great train of attendants. They were entertained with wines and liquors of various kinds, which they were very cautious in tasting, till Lord Macartney banished all apprehension by setting them the example. They then drank without reserve what was offered them, but appeared to prefer cherry and raspberry brandy. The dress of these persons consisted chiefly of a black loose gown, of a kind of crape, with silk trousers, slippers, and a kind of turban. A girdle of silver cordage was also tied round their waist. The domestics were clad in a plaid or tartan dress, their trousers were tucked up to the knee, and they wore no shoes or slippers.'—Æneas Anderson, 'Narrative of Embassy to China.'

A LENGTHY VISIT

we sent seventy sick on shore belonging to the *Lion's* crew, among others poor Lieutenant Cox.

Friday, May 31.—Sent several of my guard on shore to the hospital. As Sir Erasmus Gower was preparing to go on shore in order to hasten the people in the ship, a Mandarin came alongside in an eight-oared barge, brought a letter to him, and an invitation to dinner. The market begins to grow better and cheaper, and we expect everything will be set right as soon as we are mutually well understood.

Saturday, June 1.—A principal Mandarin visited me, and announced to me a present, which he said was to be sent to me by the King of Cochin China, viz. : ten buffaloes, fifty hogs, one hundred measures of rice, fifty ducks, fifty fowls, and five jars of samshoe, a liquor like gin.

Sunday, June 2.—The great Mandarin, who had brought me a letter from the King and the present mentioned yesterday, returned to-day with the remainder, and made me an intolerable long visit of two hours and a half, during which time he and the General, his companion, drank a dozen glasses apiece of cherry brandy. They tasted the samshoe, which they said was bad, and was not the same that the King had sent me, but had been changed by the Commissary. They therefore desired to carry it back with them, and said they would send the right sort, and would bastinado and punish the officer who had committed the fraud. I suspected that they were the rogues themselves, and therefore endeavoured to pacify them, and put an end to the matter. They are all beggars, asking for everything they see, handkerchiefs, pillows, papers, hour-glasses, etc. The General told me that he was born near Canton and bred a merchant, and that as such he traded to the island of Hainan, and from thence to Cochin China, and that, being a scholar and understanding many things not much known to the people of Cochin China, he had been appointed preceptor to the young King, who, he says, is fourteen years old and of great parts and promise, being able already to read, write, and shoot with the bow, throw the dart, etc., perfectly well. His dominions, including Tonquin, extend to the frontiers of China, to which he is tributary, paying annually a certain quantity of ivory to the Emperor, which is delivered at Canton.

The country was rich and flourishing till devastated by the civil wars, which began about thirty years ago and are not quite over yet, but peace would soon restore everything to its former prosperity.

VISIT TO THE GRAND MANDARIN

Tuesday, June 4.—This was the day fixed for our visit to the Grand Mandarin, or Governor of the Province, in order to deliver my answer to the King's letter. This answer was written in Chinese, and embellished on the outside with white paper covered with various devices painted by Mr. Alexander, as we had no red paper, which, it seems, is the most respectable colour to be used on such occasions. We proceeded from the *Lion* in a grand marine procession. The two brigs were ordered ahead of us up the river, which is as broad as the Thames at Woolwich, and we followed in eight boats. Sir George Staunton, Sir Erasmus Gower, Captain Mackintosh, and myself went in the twelve-oared barge. Then the yawl came with the band of music in it. The next was the launch carrying fifty of my guard and their officers, Colonel Benson, and Lieutenants Parish and Crewe. The pinnace and the cutter of the lesser yawl came after with Messrs. Gillan, Maxwell, Barrow, Dinwidie, Scott, Kichey, Alexander, etc., etc., and the officers of the *Lion*. Captain Mackintosh's two boats closed the whole with some of the officers of the *Hindostan*. I suppose that in all we composed a body of near two hundred persons, including the boats' crews who rowed with us.

We were met half-way by a number of their finest warboats, which came out dressed with ranges of spears, targets, streamers, etc., in order to escort us, and made a very handsome appearance. On landing I found a body of their troops drawn up to receive us, and a lane formed for us to pass through to the Mandarin's palace, which, though not magnificent, was an extensive edifice. The saloon in which we were received was about seventy or eighty feet long and upwards of fifty feet wide, built entirely of bamboo somewhat in the form and manner of a Gothic Church. The rafters were regularly crossed and interwoven with a neat rice thatch. At the upper end was a large apartment divided into three parts. In the middle was an open alcove, and on each side a chamber where the women were placed, with jalousies or canvases before them, which they often slipped aside, so that we saw their faces and figures very distinctly. They frequently smiled and seemed pleased at the attention with which we observed them. In the alcove was a stage raised about two feet above the ground, and in the recess at the end was placed a gilt cabinet or chest of drawers with two lighted wax tapers upon it, which we were told were intended to represent the King of Cochin China's majesty, and were exhibited there a particular compliment

GEORGE, EARL OF MACARTNEY
From an Engraving by Henry Hudson, *after* M. Brown

To face p. 238

PRESENTS FOR THE KING OF COCHIN CHINA

to me, who was to suppose the King, being too young and too distant to appear there himself, had sent the two candles to blaze in his stead.

The Governor himself received me standing, and having delivered the letter (which I gave him for the King) to his secretary, seated me on an arm-chair on his left hand, which, it seems, is the place of honour in this part of the world. He then squatted himself down on the front of the alcove between two cushions, applied a long pipe to his mouth, and began smoking with great composure. Sir George Staunton sat next to me, and Sir Erasmus Gower and Colonel Benson opposite, and lower down were placed the other gentlemen and attendants. The presents were then brought for the King and delivered in great form to the Governor. They consisted of an excellent plain gold watch by Elliot, a double-barrelled gun complete with pouch, powder-horn, etc., a pair of spring bayonet pistols, a fine steel-handled broadsword, three pieces of fine camblet, red, purple, and yellow. Then the Mandarin who was to carry these presents to the King was introduced in his Court dress, which was a flowered silk nightgown of various colours wrought with various figures upon it. He then made his bows of ceremony, and his attendants carrying the presents before him, he marched off with an air of twice as much importance as he appeared to have when he came in.

This affair, which was considered as the grand State business of the day, being dispatched, we were then to be entertained with the amusements of the place. A Chinese drama, accompanied with music, was performed on a theatre arranged for that purpose at one end of the apartments. The music was both vocal and instrumental, but not very flattering to the ear, being strongly nasal, and somewhat resembling the stilt tune in Psalmody among the Presbyterians in the North of Ireland. The play represented an Emperor and his Empress living in perfect felicity, when on a sudden his subjects revolt, a long war ensues, several battles are fought, and at last the arch rebel, who we were desired to remark was a cavalry officer, as he carried a whip in his hand, overcomes his Sovereign, having with his single hand killed the Emperor and his whole army. The captive Empress then appears on the stage in all the agonies of despair naturally resulting from the loss of her husband, her dignity, and the apprehensions of losing her honour. Whilst she is tearing her hair and rending the skies with her complaints, the conqueror enters, approaches her with respect, addresses her in a gentle tone, soothes her sorrows with his compassion, talks of love and adoration, and, like Richard the Third and Lady Anne in Shakespeare, in less than half an hour prevails on her to dry up her tears, to forget a dead husband, and to console herself with a living one. The piece concluded with their nuptials and a grand procession. During the performance a number of strings and small copper money were laid on the ground at my feet, which I was desired from time to time to throw upon the stage to the actors, as a testimony of my approbation and a reward for the pleasure they afforded me.

We then had a very good dinner served up on the State table for me, Sir George Staunton, Sir Erasmus Gower, Colonel Benson, etc., with knives, forks, spoon, etc., borrowed for the occasion, as I understand, from the Portuguese ship then in the harbour, with Madeira, wine, cheese, and other articles from the same quarters. A long table on each side was served for the gentlemen of my train with equal plenty and convenience. Neither were the servants, nor the sailors who composed the boats' crews, etc., etc., forgetful of themselves, nor forgotten by our entertainers, all being amply feasted and regaled upon the occasion. In about three hours we then rose and took leave, the Governor and Mandarins attending us in order to see my guard manœuvre (who fired three volleys), and to attend to me for my barge. We all then embarked and returned to our ships in the same order that we came. Thus terminated this busy day, in which we flattered ourselves that by our appearance and demeanour we had given a favourable impression of ourselves to the Governor and his Council, and hoped to improve it into a good foundation for further intercourse and commercial purposes. And it was, indeed, the more necessary to inspire them with a good opnion for intention upon this occasion, for we learned that they had conceived strong suspicions to our prejudice, considering us at first to be little better than pirates and freebooters, as we had a very warlike appearance and seemed to have no views of trade, by our purchasing nothing but provisions which we paid for in money, neither selling nor bartering any goods or merchandise in return. Our good friends the Portuguese, notwithstanding their outward civility to us, did not, I believe, take any pains to remove those jealousies, but rather confirmed them by an artful silence, or by expressive innuendoes. For we discovered that, besides the

VISIT TO THE HOSPITALS

hundred and fifty spearmen which paraded near the Governor's house, there were half a dozen elephants, and a considerable number of cavalry in the town, which did not show themselves; besides a large body of foot soldiers in the neighbourhood, that had been ordered down from the country on our first appearance in the bay. We were told that, about three years since, the lawful King of Tonquin, or Nan Nan, which country is now subject to the King of Cochin China, went to Pekin to entreat the Emperor's assistance to restore him to his throne, which he had been some time before expelled from by the father of the reigning Prince. The Emperor in consequence sent a considerable force into Nan Nan for the purpose. But so far from succeeding in their enterprise, they were defeated in several encounters, and at last were almost all cut to pieces. The Chinese general reported to his Court that they had perished by sickness and fatigue. The Emperor considering the distance of the country and the hazard of any further attempt, and desirous at the same time of preserving an appearance of superiority, published an edict, by which he declared that the throned Prince was not worthy of the kingdom, and he therefore conferred it upon the actual possessor, who acknowledges himself his tributary, and pays him annually a certain quantity of ivory, pepper, and other productions of the country, as an evidence of his tenure and homage. This is the principal intelligence that we have as yet been able to collect with regard to the political state of the country, but it must certainly be received as very doubtful and defective, considering the great caution and reserve of the natives, and the frequent misconception and confusion of different interpreters.

Wednesday, June 5.—Sir Erasmus Gower, Colonel Benson, and I went on shore to visit the hospitals that had been fitted up on a charming spot on the peninsula, which we had named New Gibraltar, from its fancied resemblance to that celebrated station in Europe. In the tents erected by the sailors with spars, oars, poles, old sails, and old colours, in so expeditious a manner as to appear almost a magical operation, the sick were conveniently lodged and accommodated. Having finished our business here, we rowed to a pretty village about a mile's distance further to the southeast, and then returned to the ship much pleased with our little expedition.

Thursday, June 6.—Little passed this day worth mentioning but that I sent a compliment on shore to the Governor, with another present of a few muskets, bayonets, pistols, and cutlasses.

Friday, June 7.—This evening Sir Erasmus Gower, Colonel Benson, and I, invited by the fineness of the afternoon and the beauty of the scene around us, made another excursion from the ship in the eight-oared pinnace. We rowed towards the north-west of the harbour, and entered the mouth of a large river, as wide as the Thames of Woolwich, which we had never observed before. It was now sunset, and it was a good three hours' row from the ship. We therefore thought it prudent to put the boat about. The recollection of the pleasing scene we had left engaged our minds and conversation till we safely arrived on board, where we found our friends beginning to grow uneasy at the length of our absence; we found, besides, they had another cause of alarm. It was now near the middle watch, and the cutter was missing. Mr. Jackson, the master of the *Lion*, had gone in her early in the morning, with an intention of making some observations on the tides and soundings of the Faifo River, and had not been since heard of. He had, it seems, mistaken the instructions that were given him, and gone up a wrong branch of it, and being of a suspicious appearance to the natives, was taken prisoner and carried to the nearest village. Of this we had some confused intelligence the next day (June 8th), and immediately wrote to the Governor on shore to claim the boat and the people in her. To this a very civil answer was returned, with assurances that an immediate inquiry should be made upon the subject, and the most friendly proceedings observed.

The fact was that Mr. Jackson and the cutter's crew had been already secured, and were then in custody under the Mandarin's order; but, according to the forms and cautionary Government of the country, he dared not deliver them up to me until he knew the pleasure of the Court, and therefore denied having any previous acquaintance with the matter.

Monday, June 10.—This day I received a letter from the King of Cochin China, whose residence is at thirty miles distance, accompanied by a considerable present, consisting of two elephant's teeth, a large cask of pepper, and several thousand measures of rice, which, far exceeding our wants, I ordered to be set apart and sold at Macao for the East India Company's account.

Tuesday, June 11.—The Governor sent a letter this after-

RELEASE OF THE PRISONERS

noon to acquaint me that the prisoners should be released and delivered in three days.

Wednesday, June 12.—This day Mr. Jackson and his people returned to us in the cutter.[1]

Thursday, June 13.—I returned an answer to the King's letter, and sent him a present in return for the ample supplies he had furnished us with. In the letter I promised to visit him on my way home, and I hope then to complete the friendship so happily commenced between us.

Friday, June 14.—Busied all this day in completing our water, in taking in provisions, and preparing for our further voyage.

Saturday, June 15.—This day we set sail for China from Touron Bay.

[1] 'At four o'clock in the afternoon Mr. Jackson returned with the cutter and his men from their imprisonment, during which period they had undergone the severest sufferings both in body and mind, and no circumstance but their belonging to the British Embassy could have preserved them from being put to death.

'This was not the only unpleasant event that befell us here. We lost a respectable gentleman, Mr. Tothill, purser of the *Lion*, who died on the 12th, after a few days' illness, and was interred on shore, with all possible solemnity and respect.'—Æneas Anderson, 'Narrative of Embassy to China.'

END OF FIRST PART OF DIARY.

CHAPTER X

A JOURNAL OF THE EMBASSY TO CHINA IN 1792-1794

Saturday, June 15, 1793.—This day we sailed on board the *Lion* from Turon Bay, in Cochin China, accompanied by the *Hindostan* and the two little brigs, *Jackall* and *Clarence*.

Wednesday, June 19.—At two o'clock p.m. we saw the mainland of China bearing N.N.E.

Thursday, June 20.—At six o'clock a.m. we came to an anchor off the grand Ladrone.

I sent Sir George Staunton, Mr. Maxwell, and Captain Mackintosh on shore for intelligence. None of the trading-ships of the season being yet arrived, all the gentlemen of the different European factories were still at Macao.

Saturday, June 22.—This afternoon Sir George Staunton returned on board the *Lion*. The information from Macao was that the news of an Embassy from England had been received at Court with great satisfaction, that the Emperor considered it as no small addition to the glory of his reign that its close should be distinguished by such an event, and that orders had been dispatched to all the seaports of China to give the most hospitable reception to His Majesty's ships whenever they should appear on the coast.

At the same time it was perceived that the Embassy had excited great jealousy and apprehension in the minds of some of the Europeans at Macao, particularly of the Dutch and Portuguese. With respect to the former, they were soon quieted by our assurances, and by the letters we brought from Batavia; but with respect to the latter, it was easy to discover that, whatever face they might wear towards us, we had to expect from them every ill office and counteraction in their power.

It is singular enough that, of the Europeans at Macao, none seemed better disposed to us than the Spanish agents, Messrs. Agoti and Fuentes, who not only testified their good-will by several little services, but gave us an essential

LOSS OF AN INTERPRETER

proof of their confidence by sending me a manuscript plan and chart of the city of Macao and the river of Canton, taken upon the spot by M. Agoti himself, the result of several years' observation and labour.

Sir George Staunton left the Missionaries Nyan and Vang on shore, as also one of our interpreters, Padre Cho, who suddenly took fright, and was so impressed with an apprehension of the Government at Pekin that he could not be persuaded to proceed with us. We, indeed, regard the loss of him the less, as his companion, who remains with us, though not so complete a scholar, is a man of much better temper, has a very good understanding and excellent disposition, and is sincerely attached to us.

In the place of Padres Nyan and Vang, we, at the earnest request of the Italian Missionaries of the Propaganda at Macao, to whom we owe some obligations, have consented to give a passage to two others, who had been waiting for an opportunity of proceeding to Pekin and of entering into the Emperor's service there as mathematicians and astronomers.

Friday, June 28.—Lost sight of the *Hindostan* and the two brigs in the dark weather, and sailed for the Quesan or Patchcock Islands, where we expect to fall in with *Endeavour* Brig, Captain Proctor, whom the Company's Commissioners had dispatched some time before, with orders to cruise there for us till the 30th inst.

Sunday, June 30.—We saw nothing of the *Endeavour*, neither could we learn any news of her from the Chinese fishing-vessels, several thousands of which covered the sea all around us.

A Chinese pilot came on board with some of his people, who seemed never to have seen such a ship as the *Lion* before.[1] They examined everything with great curiosity,

[1] 'The sight of a vessel of uncommon construction, as well as size, such as the *Lion* certainly appeared here, put, for a time, almost an end to labour by sea and land. Her decks were so crowded with visitors, and others were waiting with such eagerness to come on board, that it became necessary to dismiss, after a short visit, the first comers, in order to be able to gratify the curiosity of others. Though the ship's crew at length suffered many of them to range unaccompanied and unnoticed through every part of the vessel, this indulgence was not abused. Among them few betrayed awkwardness, rudeness of manners, or apparent vacancy of mind, sometimes observable among other people in the lower classes of life.'
—Sir G. Staunton, 'Embassy to China.'

and observing the Emperor of China's picture in the cabin, immediately fell flat on their faces before it, and kissed the ground several times with great devotion.[1]

Monday, July 1.—At three p.m. we were joined by the *Hindostan*, *Jackall*, and *Clarence*. Ever since we made the coast of China on the 19th of last month the weather has been (excepting one day) always dark, heavy, rainy, moist, or stormy.

Wednesday, July 3.—This day we came to an anchor[2] in Cheusan Roads.

The city of Cheusan is about fifty miles west of us. Sir George Staunton went in the *Clarence* to Cheusan in order to procure pilots from the Governor to conduct us to Tiensing.

Sunday, July 7.—Sir George Staunton returned and brought with him the pilots, who, on being informed of the *Lion*'s draft of water, said that a ship of her size could not proceed further than Mietao, near the city of Tenchoufou, at the entrance of the Gulf of Pecheli, but that all sorts of convenient vessels could be procured at that place to convey us from thence in safety to Tiensing, and the passage could be made in four days. The Gulf of Pecheli is represented by them to be without any good anchoring ground, very shallow, and in many places full of shifting sands.

Sir George Staunton had a good deal of difficulty in procuring the pilots. The Governor of Cheusan, to whom he had applied, told him that his authority extended no further than to furnish us with pilots to conduct us to the adjoin-

---

[1] 'On rising, they appeared to feel a sort of gratitude towards the foreigner who had the attention to place the portrait of their sovereign in his apartment.'—Sir G. Staunton, 'Embassy to China.'

[2] 'Soon after the *Clarence* had anchored, some civil and military officers came on board to inquire the occasion of her visit. With these came as interpreter a Chinese merchant, who knew something of the English language. He explained why a salute from the *Clarence* of seven guns was answered by three only from the shore, by observing the regulations of economy in the Chinese Government permit no greater number. This circumstance led him to mention their rule in saluting—to point their guns always into the air—adding that if such caution had been practised by the English, the accident at Canton, when two Chinese were killed by a shot from an English vessel, would not have happened, which accident ended in the capital punishment of the gunner. The Chinese take it for granted that guns pointed horizontally must be meant for mischief, whatever the pretence.'—Sir G. Staunton, 'Embassy to China.'

SEARCH FOR PILOTS

ing province, where others would in the like manner be supplied, to proceed with us to the next, and so on along the coast till we reached our last port. But as this mode of management did not at all suit us, Sir George requested him, if possible, to find some persons who would take care of our navigation the whole way from Cheusan to Tiensing, without stopping at any intermediate place; adding that if such pilots could not be had at Cheusan, they might, perhaps, be had from Ningpo. Upon this the Governor, fully sensible of the Emperor's orders with regard to the Embassy, and apprehensive that we might address ourselves to his superior Mandarin at Ningpo, exerted himself so effectually that at last two men were found, who, having formerly been owners and masters of vessels in the trade, had frequently been at Tiensing; but it was with the greatest reluctance, and, indeed, under a sort of compulsion, that they undertook the charge.[1] And, after all, considering the little nautical skill they seem to possess, we don't expect much assistance from them, but must trust a good deal to our own.[2]

[1] Barrow, in his account of the Embassy, says that they little expected to have any difficulty in finding pilots. 'The Governor of Cheusan resolved a muster should be made of all persons in that place who had at any time visited the port of Tiensing. Accordingly a number of most miserable-looking men were brought by the soldiers to a sort of hall in a temple, and examined as to their capability for the post of pilot, none being suitable for various reasons, till at length two were brought in, who seemed to answer the purpose better than any we had yet seen. However, it appeared they had not been to sea for many years, and being comfortably settled in trade, had no desire to engage in the service, and begged on their knees to be excused, but without avail. In vain did they plead the ruin of their business by their absence, and the distress it would occasion their wives and families. The Governor was inexorable, and they were ordered to be ready to embark in the course of an hour. Indeed, their tears and entreaties only served to brighten up his countenance, as he felt relieved from a load of anxiety by his success in finding them.'—J. Barrow, ' Travels in China.'

[2] ' While the *Clarence* was in Cheusan Harbour, Mr. Barrow partook too freely of some rather unripe fruit, and had a violent attack of cholera morbus. He says: ' On application being made to the Governor for a little opium and rhubarb, he immediately dispatched to me one of his physicians. With a countenance as grave and a solemnity as settled as ever was exhibited in consultation over a doubtful case in London or Edinburgh, he fixed his eyes upon the ceiling while he held my hand, beginning at the wrist and pro-

Friday, July 19.—We came to anchor this morning in Tchetao Bay, which our pilots had mistaken for Mictao. They seem grossly ignorant and timid, were frightened out of their wits when they observed that on our passage along the coast on shoaling our water we always stood out to sea, and were puzzled beyond measure by our manœuvres, seeing us work to windward without minding weather, tide, or monsoon.[1]

Saturday, July 20.—We got a new pilot from the shore, and in a few hours came abreast of the city of Tenchoufou.

For several days the weather has been very unsettled, sometimes extremely boisterous, and at others almost calm with frequent fogs, the latter always the concomitants of an easterly wind.

In the evening, about three hours after we had let go our anchor, the Governor of Tenchoufou, a Mandarin of high rank, came on board to visit me.

He told me he had orders from his Court to entertain us, to render us all services in his power, and to provide for us proper means of conveyance if we chose to proceed by land from Tenchoufou to Pekin.

---

ceeding to the elbow, pressing sometimes hard with one finger and then light with another, as if he were running over the keys of a harpsichord. This performance continued for about ten minutes in solemn silence, after which he let go my hand, and pronounced my complaint to have arisen from eating something that had disagreed with the stomach !' It is, however, satisfactory to learn that Mr. Barrow's complaint was speedily cured by the arrival of the medicines asked for.

Mr. Barrow also remarks : ' As it is a violation of good morals for a gentleman to be seen in company with ladies, much more so to touch the hands of the fair, the faculty have contrived an ingenious way of feeling a lady's pulse. A silken cord being made fast to the wrist of the patient is passed through a hole in the wainscot into another apartment, where the doctor, applying his hand to the cord, after a due observance of solemn mockery, decides upon the case, and prescribes accordingly.'—J. Barrow, ' Travels in China.'

[1] ' The commanders of the ships were exasperated against the pilots, and these, on their part, were almost petrified with fear. They were confused by the novelty of their situation, and it was in vain to make them endeavour to comprehend the difference in the draft of water between their ships and ours, although they were shown by a piece of rope the depth required. Indeed, their skill in navigation was held very cheap by the lowest seaman on board.'— J. Barrow, ' Travels in China.'

His visit lasted upwards of two hours, during which he talked a great deal, and with as much ease and frankness as if we had been old acquaintances. He is about thirty-five years of age, courteous, intelligent, and inquisitive.

Sunday, July 21.—At noon the Governor of Tenchoufou, who was here last night, sent us a present of four bullocks, eight sheep, eight goats, five measures of white rice, five measures of red rice, two hundred pounds of flour, and several baskets of fruit and vegetables, which was acknowledged by a proper return.

An old man of seventy years of age has been put on board as pilot, who says that the Gulf of Pecheli is always perfectly safe in the months of July, August, and September, so that the *Lion* has nothing to apprehend from the weather for some time to come; that the boats for carrying our baggage and the presents are now ready at the mouth of the river leading up to Tiensing, and waiting for our arrival; that they are large and convenient, and so constructed that there is no danger of our packages being wetted or damaged.

Tuesday, July 23.—We are now in that part of the Yellow Sea called the Gulf of Pecheli, which is remarkably smooth and clear.

This evening we were joined by the *Endeavour* Brig, which the Company's Commissioners had despatched from Macao with letters for us; not knowing of our intention of calling there, they had, a little before our arrival on the coast, ordered this vessel to the northward, in hopes of her meeting us before we got the length of Tiensing.

Thursday, July 25.—This morning at sunrise we discovered at about two or three miles distant a prodigious number of Chinese vessels all around us. Our pilots did not precisely know where we were; we supposed ourselves to be eight or nine miles from the river that goes up to Tiensing, as houses and trees were just discernible from the masthead to the north and south, and we found, when Lieutenant Campbell and Mr. Hüttner[1] returned in the *Jackall* this evening, that we had not been much mistaken. They told us that when they arrived in the mouth of the river some inferior Mandarins had come on board, and finding they belonged to the Embassy, had conducted them on shore, and presented them to two great men, who had been stationed at that place for some time past in expectation of my coming.

[1] Lieutenant Campbell and Mr. Hüttner had been sent on in the *Jackall* to explore.

They were received with many marks of respect and treated with great hospitality. A thousand questions were asked relative to every particular of the Embassy. The number of persons, their ages and qualities, the presents brought for the Emperor, and what they consisted of, the size and force of the *Lion* and the other ships attending us, etc., etc.

The answers to all which were written down by the Secretary in waiting. At their departure they were desired to inform me that everything was ready for my reception, and that as soon as the *Lion* approached the bar two great Mandarins[1] would be sent on board to compliment me. We are now above three leagues distant from the bar.

It appears that the expectations of the Chinese have been raised very high, by the manner in which the Embassy was announced, of the presents which it is to be accompanied with. When Sir George Staunton was at Macao he found, on conversing with the gentlemen there, that they were conceived to be of immense value, and when he mentioned what they were, it was thought that the Chinese would be much disappointed. From these considerations Mr. Brown was induced to add his fine telescope to what we had already brought, and I have this day completed our apparatus with Parker's great lens, which Captain Mackintosh brought out with him on a speculation, and which he has been prevailed upon to part with on very reasonable terms, foregoing all the profit which he had the prospect of deriving from the sale of so valuable and so uncommon an article. As the lens is an object of singular curiosity, I was apprehensive that if it fell into the hands of the Chinese merchants, and were presented through their channel to the Emperor, it might tend towards the disparagement of our fine things, and perhaps be imagined to eclipse them. I therefore thought it advisable, for the public service and the honour of the Embassy, to join it to the other presents; and now being possessed of Mr. Brown's fine telescope and this extraordinary lens, I flatter myself we have no rivalships to apprehend at Pekin from the appearance of any instruments of a similar kind. This evening I sent back Mr. Hüttner in the *Endeavour*, in order to explain to the Mandarins whom he had seen a number of particulars relative to our going on shore, and to make inquiry about several things which it is necessary for us to be previously acquainted with.

[1] The word 'Mandarin' is derived from the Portuguese word *Mandar*, 'to obey.'

A VARIETY OF PROVISIONS

Sunday, July 28.—Several inferior Mandarins came on board, and informed us that everything was preparing for our landing, that a number of boats were already in waiting, and that the remainder would be down to-morrow.

Tuesday, July 30.—The *Endeavour* returned, and brought us all the information we had desired.

Some of the Mandarins, having said that they intended to purchase watches and swords when they came on board, seemed a little disappointed when Mr. Hüttner told them that as we were not merchants we had got nothing to sell.

It would seem, however, from this that they expect presents of the kind, and, unluckily, our baggage where those articles are cannot easily be got at. I must, therefore, I believe, purchase from some of the officers of the *Hindostan* a few small things for the purpose.

Wednesday, July 31.—The wind blowing all day very strong prevented any boats coming from the shore. At noon two Mandarins of high rank attended by seven large junks, laden with a variety of provisions for our ships, came alongside. The profusion of these was so great and so much above our wants that we were obliged to decline accepting the larger part of them. I here insert the list:

20 bullocks, 130 sheep, 120 hogs,[1] 100 fowls, 100 ducks, 160 bags of flour, 160 bags of rice, 14 boxes of Tartar bread, 10 chests of tea, 10 chests of small rice, 10 chests of red rice, 10 chests of white rice, 10 chests of tallow candles, 1,000 water melons, 3,000 musk melons, 22 boxes of dried peaches, 22 boxes of fruits preserved with sugar, 22 boxes of other fruit, 22 boxes of ochras, 22 boxes of other vegetables, 40 baskets of large cucumbers, 1,000 squash cucumbers, 40 bundles of vegetables, 20 measures of peas in the pods, 3 baskets of earthenware or coarse porcelain.

In truth, the hospitality, attention, and respect which we have experienced at Turon, Cheusan, Tenchoufou, and here are such as strangers only meet with in the Eastern parts of the World.

The two chief Mandarins are called Van-ta-gin and Chou-ta-gin. Van and Chou are their family names; Ta-gin is the title annexed to their rank, and signifies Great Man;

[1] 'Numbers of the hogs and the fowls had been bruised to death on the passage, which were thrown overboard from the *Lion* with disdain; but the Chinese eagerly picked them up, washed them clean, and laid them in salt.'—J. Barrow, 'Travels in China.'

Van-ta-gin is a War Mandarin, has a peacock's feather[1] and a red coral flourished button on his cap, which is the second order.[2] Chou-ta-gin, who wears a blue button, which is a degree inferior to the red, is a civilian and a man of letters.[3] After a number of compliments and civilities in the Chinese manner, we proceeded to business, and Chou-ta-gin wrote down from time to time such particulars as he thought necessary.

We have settled everything with them relative to our going ashore, the mode of conveying our baggage and the presents, and the kind and number of vessels for the purpose. I find it will be a work of four or five days at least before we can leave the ship.

These two Mandarins seemed to be intelligent men, frank and easy in their address, and communicative in their discourse.[4]

They sat down to dinner with us, and though at first a little embarrassed by our knives and forks, soon got over the difficulty, and handled them with notable dexterity and execution upon some of the good things which they had brought us.

---

[1] 'It was given by the Emperor, with directions to wear it pendent from his bonnet.'—Sir G. Staunton, 'Embassy to China.'

[2] 'Van-ta-gin, the military Mandarin, was, in the true character of his profession, "open, bold, and brave." He had signalized himself in battle, and received several wounds. He was above middle size, erect, and uncommonly muscular. Though he was no boaster, in his deportment was sometimes perceptible an honest consciousness of his prowess and achievements. But good-nature was conspicuous in his countenance, and his manners testified willingness to oblige. He was cheerful and pleasant in his conversation, banishing all reserve.'—Sir G. Staunton, 'Embassy to China.'

[3] 'Chou-ta-gin, the civil Mandarin, was a man of grave, but not austere, manners. He was not forward in discourse, neither appearing to aim at anything brilliant in himself, nor to be dazzled by it in others. A faithful discharge of his duty seemed to be the sole object of his pursuit. He had been preceptor to some of the Imperial Family, and was considered as a man of learning and judgment.'— Sir G. Staunton, 'Embassy to China.'

[4] 'These gentlemen were received on board the *Lion* with attention and cordiality. Much of the stiffness which generally accompanies a communication through the medium of an interpreter was removed by the good-humour of the parties, and the ardent desire they felt of making out one another's meaning.'—Sir G. Staunton, 'Embassy to China.'

They tasted of our wines of different kinds, and also of our spirits, from gin, rum, and arrack, to shrub, raspberry, and cherry brandy, the latter of which seemed to hit their palate in preference to the rest, and they shook hands with us like Englishmen at their going away. They were much struck with the appearance of the Guard and Marines (which were drawn up on the quarter-deck to salute them as they passed), listened with attention to our music, and departed, I believe, very much pleased with our manner of entertaining them. They were very inquisitive about the presents, and when I explained to them their nature, they seemed to think them very proper, and requested a list of them to be transmitted to Court, which I have promised.

Friday, August 2.—This day the junks came from the shore alongside of the *Hindostan*, and began to take in the articles which are to be carried from on board her. A Mandarin of the third order with a blue button on his cap came with them to superintend the business, and stayed till the vessels were loaded.

Saturday, August 3.—The loading continues, and it is expected to be finished the day after to-morrow. The same Mandarin who attended yesterday returned to-day.

Sunday, August 4.—This day the people worked with great alacrity, the loading was completed, and all the baggage and presents put on board the large junks, to be transhipped into smaller ones, at Ta-cou, in order to be conveyed up the river to Tongsiou (within twelve miles of Pekin), where the navigation discontinues. The Chinese sailors are very strong and work well, singing and roaring all the while, but very orderly and well regulated, intelligent and ingenious in contrivance and resource, each of them seeming to understand and exercise his proper share of the business and labour going forward.

In each vessel were inferior Mandarins, who received the articles and gave accountable notes for them, so that no loss or mistake is likely to happen.

To-morrow we shall proceed on shore; from the very distinguished reception which we have met with, and from every appearance being so much in our favour, I think it will be best to send the *Hindostan* to Cheusan with the *Lion* (which is now so sickly that she must get into the first possible safe port for recruiting her people), in hopes that we may be able to obtain permission for the *Hindostan* to take in a cargo there, by way of a beginning to the expected extension of our commerce in China.

Captain Mackintosh himself comes with us to Pekin, and I propose to dispatch him from thence with the permission (if procured) to join his ship at Cheusan, and to carry our dispatches from thence to England, which we flatter ourselves will then be very interesting.

Monday, August 5.—This day at nine a.m. we left the *Lion* Man-of-War,[1] and embarking in smaller vessels (myself and the gentlemen of the Embassy in the *Clarence, Jackall,* and *Endeavour*, the servants, guards, and other attendants with the baggage, presents, etc., in Chinese junks), proceeded to the mouth of the Payho River, the distance being about eighteen miles. On entering the river we were perfectly astonished and confounded by the inconceivable number of vessels of all sorts with which it was covered.

The troops were drawn up on the southern bank, and made a tolerably good appearance. The Mandarins, Van-ta-gin and Cho-ta-gin, who had dined with us on board the *Lion*, now came to visit us, and pressed us much to accept their invitation to a banquet on shore which had been prepared for us; but being a good deal fatigued, I declined it, and proceeded up the river about a mile further to the yacht provided to convey me to the city of Tongsiou, within twelve miles of Pekin.

This yacht was large, clean, comfortable, and convenient, and here I found the Mandarins Van-ta-gin and Chou-ta-gin to welcome me, and to inquire whether anything was further necessary for my accommodation. Similar care and attention seemed to have been paid to all the other gentlemen.[2]

---

[1] 'On the departure of the Ambassador, the crews of the ships, who had, indeed, been picked men, and had behaved well throughout the voyage, and, in consequence, had lately received marks of his Excellency's satisfaction, most readily obeyed the orders for manning the yards as a mark of respect to him, and gave loud cheers, which, together with the firing a salute of many guns from each of the ships, afforded a new spectacle to the Chinese.'—Sir G. Staunton, 'Embassy to China.'

[2] 'We found the yachts destined to convey us exceedingly convenient—more so, indeed, than any I have ever seen on our canals in England. Their upper works are high, appearing like a floating house. They have three compartments for the accommodation of passengers—the first an antechamber for servants and baggage; the middle, a commodious sitting and dining-room about fifteen feet square; and the third divided into two or three sleeping-rooms. Behind there is the kitchen; and still further aft, small places like dog-kennels for the boatmen. A Chinese sailor requires no room for

CHINESE POPULATION

The river here appeared to be as broad as the Thames at Gravesend.

Great numbers of houses on each side, built of mud and thatched, a good deal resembling the cottages near Christchurch, in Hampshire, and inhabited by such swarms of people as far exceeded my most extravagant ideas of Chinese population. Among those who crowded the banks we saw several women, who tripped along with such agility, as induced us to imagine their feet had not been crippled in the usual manner of the Chinese.

It is said, indeed, that this practice, especially among the lower sort, is now less frequent in the Northern Provinces than in the others. These women are much weather-beaten, but not ill-featured, and wear their hair, which is universally black and coarse, neatly braided, and fastened on the top of their heads with a bodkin.[1]

The children are very numerous and almost stark naked. The men in general well-looking, well-limbed, robust, and muscular. I was so much struck with their appearance that I could scarce refrain from crying out with Shakespeare's Miranda in the 'Tempest':

> 'Oh, wonder! How many goodly
> Creatures are there here!
> How beauteous mankind is! Oh, brave new world
> That has such people in it!'

Tuesday, August 6.—This morning early, provisions for the day were distributed with great order and regularity and in vast abundance among the different departments of the Embassy,[2] and soon after several Mandarins of high rank

---

his luggage, his whole wardrobe being generally on his back.'—J. Barrow, 'Travels in China.'

'The chief distinction, as to ornament, between the Ambassador's and the other yachts consisted in the greater proportion of glass panes which adorned the windows of the former, while the frames of the others were generally filled with a blind of paper.'—Sir G. Staunton, 'Embassy to China.'

[1] 'We saw women in China, though very few, that might pass for beauties even in Europe.'—J. Barrow, 'Travels in China.'

[2] 'Inferior Mandarins attended all the vessels for the distribution of provisions and necessaries for every individual of the suite. A separate table in each yacht was served up in the manner, and occasionally with all the delicacies, of the country, and sometimes also in an awkward imitation of English cookery. With a view to gratifying, as was thought, the English appetite, instructions were

came to visit me, and to inform me that the Viceroy of the Province of Pecheli, whose usual residence is at Pao-ting-fou, one hundred miles distant, was arrived here, having been sent by the Emperor to compliment me on my entrance into his dominions, and to give proper orders upon the occasion.[1] At eight a.m. I went on shore accompanied by Sir George Staunton, his son, and our interpreter, passing from my yacht over a temporary wooden bridge erected for this purpose, covered with mats, and having rails on each side decorated with scarlet silk.

Here we found palanquins prepared for us, which are neat light chairs made of bamboo, covered with satin, and carried by four stout fellows, two of them before and two of them behind.

In these we set out escorted by a troop of horse, for Hy-chin-miao, or the Temple of the Sea God, where the Viceroy had taken up his quarters; and though the distance was near a mile, yet the same men carried us at a pretty smart pace the whole way without resting.

Before the gates of the Temple were several tents pitched of various colours, white, red, and blue (but the latter seemed to predominate), having each a distinguishing pendant, and before them were drawn up several companies of soldiers with sabres in their hands (no firearms), and dressed in a uniform blue stuff or cotton, laced with a broad red galoon. Besides the troop of horse which escorted us there was another body of cavalry attending at the Temple, each cavalier having a bow and a quiver of arrows, but no sword or pistol.

The Viceroy[2] received us at the gate with distinguished

---

given by the Mandarins to roast large pieces, such as pigs, turkeys, and geese, entire. This is a mode of preparing food which did not appear to have been practised in China, and was executed very indifferently by the Chinese cooks.'—Sir G. Staunton, 'Embassy to China.'

[1] 'We have always been taught to believe that the Chinese consider us as barbarians; but we have hitherto no reason to think that they have treated us as such. At all events, it was obvious that the expected arrival of the British Embassy had made no slight impression on the Court of Pekin.'—J. Barrow, 'Travels in China.'

[2] 'He was a man of the most polished manners, tottering with age, but not less dignified than he was venerable. In his reception of the Ambassador he behaved with refined and attentive politeness, but without the constraint of distant forms or particular ceremonies.' —Sir G. Staunton, 'Embassy to China.'

THE EMPEROR'S WISHES

politeness and an air of cordiality, and led us into a great saloon, which was soon filled with his officers and attendants, from whence, after drinking tea, he removed to another apartment, to which we passed through a spacious square court, each side of which was formed by magnificent buildings. The ornaments were so brilliant and so diversified that I at first imagined them to be of wood, painted and highly varnished, but on a nearer inspection I found them to be of porcelain and tiles, of various moulds and colours.

We now entered upon the business.

The Viceroy began by many compliments and inquiries about our health, and talked much of the Emperor's satisfaction at our arrival, and of his wish to see us at Gehol, in Tartary (where the Court always resides at this season), as soon as possible. To these we made the proper return of compliment, and then informed the Viceroy that the train of the Embassy consisted of so many persons, and that the presents for the Emperor and our own baggage were so numerous, and took up so much room, that we should require very spacious quarters at Pekin. That as we found it was the Emperor's wish for us to proceed to Gehol, we should prepare ourselves accordingly, but that we should find it necessary to leave a great part of the presents at Pekin, as many of them could not be transported by land to such a distance without being greatly damaged, if not totally destroyed. We explained to him the high compliment intended by the first Sovereign of the Western World to the Sovereign of the East, by sending the present Embassy, and hoped it would be attended with all the good effects expected from it. That as it was equally my duty and inclination to promote these views to the utmost of my power, I requested the Viceroy would be so kind as to give me such information and advice as might enable me to render myself and my business as acceptable to the Emperor as possible. I also mentioned to him that, as the *Lion* and the other ships that came with me were very sickly, and stood in need of a hospital and of refreshments on shore for the accommodation and recovery of their people, it would be necessary for Sir Erasmus Gower to be furnished with a diploma by virtue of which he might be entitled to those advantages at such ports as he might find it most convenient to repair to on the coast of China, either Mietao, or Cheusan, for the advancing season required his speedy departure out of the Gulf of Pecheli.

It is impossible to describe the ease, politeness, and dignity of the Viceroy during the whole conference, the attention with which he listened to our requests, and the unaffected manner in which he expressed his compliance with them. With regard to the ships, imagining their stores must have been exhausted in so long a voyage, he offered to supply them with twelve months' provisions immediately. I hope this does not forebode his wishes for our speedy departure.

He is a very fine old man of seventy-eight years of age, of low stature, with small sparkling eyes, a benign aspect, and a long silver beard, the whole of his appearance calm, venerable, and dignified.

During the course of this visit I was particularly struck with the apparent kindness and condescension with which the people of rank here speak to, and treat, their inferiors and lowest domestics.

When we returned to our yacht, we found a most magnificent and plentiful dinner prepared for us, which had been sent as a present by the Viceroy.[1]

Wednesday, August 7.—Early this morning Van-ta-gin came to visit me, and said it was the intention of the Viceroy to wait upon me at ten o'clock a.m. He turned the discourse upon the Viceroy's great age and debility of body, which, however, he said, would not prevent him from paying his compliments to me in person, although it would be attended with great inconvenience to him to walk from the shore over the wooden bridge to my yacht; the descent from the bank being very steep, and not very safe for a feeble old man. I immediately saw what he was driving at, and therefore told him that I should be very sorry to be the occasion of the Viceroy's risking either his person or his health for the sake of a visit of ceremony; I was unacquainted with the Chinese customs myself, but as the Viceroy knew them, I was sure he would do, in regard to them, whatever was right, and which the Emperor would most approve of his doing. Upon this, Van-ta-gin said that the Viceroy would come in his palanquin to the end of the bridge, and send in his visiting-ticket to me, and hoped I would consider it the same as if he had come across the bridge in person into my yacht. I repeated what I had said

[1] 'The Viceroy sent a sumptuous repast for the Ambassador and three other dinners, each consisting of twenty-four dishes, to the three gentlemen who had accompanied his Excellency on the visit.'— Sir G. Staunton, 'Embassy to China.'

VISITS OF CEREMONY

before, and told him I left the matter entirely to the Viceroy himself. He seemed to go away very well pleased, and at ten o'clock the Viceroy came in great state with the parade of guards, and a very numerous attendance of Mandarins and officers, who, as soon as his palanquin was set down, all dismounted from their horses and kneeled down to pay him their obeisance. He sent an officer with his visiting-paper, which is a large sheet several times doubled, and painted red, and inscribed with the owner's titles in large characters, and which my interpreter received from him. This business being performed, the Viceroy returned to his quarters in the same form, ceremony, and order with which he came.

This day and the next were chiefly employed in preparing for our departure, and arranging the order of our progress.

In this we were assisted by the different Mandarins appointed to attend us, with regularity, alertness, and despatch that appeared perfectly wonderful.[1] Indeed, the machinery and authority of the Chinese Government are so organized, and so powerful, as almost immediately to surmount every difficulty, and to produce every effect that human strength can accomplish.

The gentlemen of the Embassy, the servants, artists, musicians, and guards, together with the presents and baggage, were embarked on thirty-seven yachts, or junks, each yacht having a flag flying at her mast-head to distinguish her rank and ascertain her station in the procession.

There was, besides, a great number of other boats and vessels of various sorts for the Mandarins and officers who were allotted to our service,[2] and who amounted to near

[1] 'The Mandarins were on every occasion attentive to the accommodation of the passengers. Even the Chinese soldiers and sailors displayed a gentleness of deportment and a willingness to oblige distinguishable from the mere execution of a duty, and which showed that the present strangers, at least, were not unwelcome.'—Sir G. Staunton, 'Embassy to China.'

[2] 'Ample allowance was made of every necessary article to the gentlemen, and likewise to the artificers, soldiers, and domestics in the train of the Ambassador. No slight magnificence was displayed, and no expense seemed to be spared, in the treatment of the Embassy, either as to the number of Mandarins who were appointed to accompany it, and whose salaries were increased upon this particular service, the crowd of inferior Chinese who were engaged to attend upon the occasion, and the many vessels employed in conveying the whole.'—*Ibid.*

one hundred of different degrees, wearing the red, blue, white, and yellow buttons by which their respective qualities are denoted.

Friday, August 9.—This morning I dispatched Mr. Proctor in the *Endeavour* from the river. He was obliged to take back with him the two Macao missionaries, Hanna and Lamiet, without their ever coming ashore.

We found, indeed, that if they accompanied us to Pekin, they would be considered as belonging to the Embassy, and obliged to depart with it, whereas their intention is to enter into the Emperor's service, and to remain the rest of their lives in China, like the other missionaries.[1]

At noon the gongs, or copper drums, began to beat with a most deafening noise, and gave the signal for all being ready for departure. In less than an hour our whole fleet was under sail, and we proceeded up the river with a good breeze and flowing tide at the rate of about five miles per hour.

Sunday, August 11.—This morning we arrived at the city of Tien-sing.

Here the Viceroy had arrived the night before, and here we were met by Chin-ta-gin, a Tartar Mandarin in high office at this place, who was styled the Emperor's Legate, having been deputed, together with Van-ta-gin and Chou-ta-gin, to accompany us from thence to Gehol, the Viceroy's age and infirmities disabling him from any fatiguing service. Our yachts stopped almost in the middle of the town before the Viceroy's Pavilion. On the opposite quay, close to the water, was erected for this occasion a very spacious and magnificent theatre, adorned and embellished with the usual brilliancy of Chinese decorations and scenery, where a company of actors exhibited a variety of dramas and pantomimes during several hours almost without interruption.

Both sides of the river for near a mile in length were lined with the troops of the garrison, all in uniform, accompanied by innumerable flags, standards, and pendants, and by the clangour of various instruments of warlike music. At noon I disembarked with all the gentlemen of the Embassy and my whole train of servants, musicians, and guards. I was received at my landing by the Viceroy and the Legate, and conducted to their pavilion, where as soon as we were seated

[1] 'It may not be ungrateful to the reader to be made acquainted that the perseverance of those pious men was at last rewarded, and they obtained permission from the Emperor to repair to the capital, where they were taken into his service.'—Sir G. Staunton, 'Embassy to China.'

AN UNFRIENDLY DISPOSITION

the conversation began, and continued for some time in the same general strain of mutual compliments and professions as our former one at Hy-chin-miao. We then descended to particulars, and after a very long discussion, during which I easily discovered a perverse and unfriendly disposition in the Legate toward all our concerns, and which struck me the more forcibly when contrasted with the urbanity and graciousness of his superior the Viceroy, it at last was settled that we should proceed upon the river to Tong-siou, a city within twelve miles of Pekin, which would take us up seven days, and consequently carry us to the 18th of August.[1]

From Tong-siou we were to travel the rest of our journey by land, but we should probably be detained at that place for several days, on account of the trouble of removing the presents and baggage out of the boats, of procuring porters and carriages for their conveyance, and a variety of other arrangements necessary to be made for the accommodation of the Embassy previous to our settlement in the Capital. I calculated that thus we should scarcely be able to reach Pekin sooner than the 20th, and that we should at least require ten days to refresh ourselves, to settle my family, to separate the presents, and prepare for our further journey into Tartary, which I supposed we might be able to begin about the 5th September. The planetarium, the globes, the great lens, the lustres, the clocks, and some other articles, I declared my intention of leaving behind at Pekin, and expressed my wishes of taking with me such of the other presents only as were not likely to suffer by a long land carriage. The journey from Pekin to Gehol would not exceed six or eight days at most, so that we might expect to reach the Emperor's Court some time before his birthday, which we understood was to fall on the 17th September.

According to these ideas, which seemed to be approved of, I took my measures, but to my great surprise, soon after the Legate, who now began to come forward with an air of greater importance, took up the subject of our conversation anew, started objections to some parts of the arrangements, and pressed me very urgently to let *all* the presents go to Gehol at once. I told him that nothing could be more

[1] 'In the course of the discussion the Legate betrayed a perverse temper under an exterior of much calmness. His irregular mind seemed tinctured with a jealousy of all foreigners, and, at the same time, with an utter contempt for them.'—Sir G. Staunton, 'Embassy to China.'

agreeable to me than to accommodate myself to his wishes and to his ideas, but that from the nature and mechanism of several of the presents (which I explained to him), it would be impossible to transport them in the manner he wished without irreparable damage. Of my reasons he seemed to have no comprehension, but adhered to his own opinion, and added that he believed the Emperor would insist on having *all* the presents carried to Gehol and delivered at the same time.

I answered him that the Emperor was certainly omnipotent in China, and might dispose of everything in it as he pleased, but that as the articles which I meant to leave at Pekin would certainly be totally spoiled if managed according to his notions, I requested he would take them entirely into his own hands, for that *I* must be excused from presenting anything in an imperfect or damaged state, as being unworthy of His Britannic Majesty to give and of His Chinese Majesty to receive.

This consideration startled him, and, together with the Viceroy's opinion, who perfectly comprehended and felt my reasoning, induced him to recede, and to acquiesce in the first arrangements; but I could not help feeling great disquiet and apprehension from this untoward disposition so early manifested by the Legate. Having now adjusted this matter, we took our leave and returned to our yachts, where a magnificent dinner was sent us by the Viceroy, with wine, fruits, sweetmeats, etc., together with presents of tea, silk, and muslins, not only for myself and gentlemen of my train, but even for all the servants, mechanics, musicians, and soldiers.[1] Although of no great value, they were accompanied with so many obliging expressions and compliments that we received them in the manner we thought

[1] 'The Mandarins of Tien-sing, having sent three parcels of coloured silks, as a present, to be distributed among the Embassy, Mr. Maxwell, by Lord Macartney's order, delivered two pieces of it to each gentleman in his suite. But as the remainder did not allow of a similar division, the lots were all separated and numbered, when the mechanics, servants, and musicians took their chance in drawing them, and except three persons, they all obtained two pieces of the manufacture. The soldiers received each of them half a piece. These pieces were only half a yard wide, and about seven yards and a half in length. The colours were green, mulberry, and pink; but the silk was of a very indifferent quality, and would not, in England, be worth more than eighteen pence a yard.'—Æneas Anderson, 'Narrative of Embassy to China.'

INQUISITIVE VISITORS

most likely to please the person who made them, especially as his whole deportment to us had been so handsome and satisfactory; and as he was to proceed immediately to Gehol, where, no doubt, he would give an account of us to the Emperor, we flattered ourselves from our conduct that it would not be to our disadvantage. During the evening we received many visits from the principal Mandarins of Tien-sing and the neighbourhood. They seemed to examine everything belonging to us—our dress,[1] our books, our furniture—with great curiosity and attention; were very inquisitive, lively, and talkative, and totally void of that composure, gravity, and seriousness which we had been taught to believe constituted a part of the Chinese character.

This evening I received two letters from Mr. Grammont,[2] a missionary at Pekin, offering me his services, and cautioning me against a Portuguese missionary, who, he says, has been appointed interpreter to the Embassy. We received no information of this kind from the Viceroy, the Legate, or Van-ta-gin, or Chou-ta-gin. However, without taking notice of it, or showing that I knew it, I seized the first opportunity to request that we might be allowed, when we arrived at Pekin, to select one of the European missionaries in the Emperor's service to attend us, and assist us in our affairs, and whose language we were acquainted with. They promised to write to the Court on the subject, and said they had no doubt of success.

The crowds of people on shore and in the boats on the river were quite astonishing.[3] Our course is on the main

[1] 'They could not refrain from bursting into fits of laughter on examining the grease and powder with which our hair was disfigured, and sometimes lamented that so much oil and flour had unnecessarily been wasted.'—J. Barrow, 'Travels in China.'

[2] ' J'aurais à communiquer à votre Excellence des choses très importantes, que la prudence ne me permet pas de confier au papier, et dont il est n'ammoins essentiel qu'elle soit instruite, lors de son arrivée à Ge-Ho.

' Quelque court que soit l'intervalle qui me separe aujourd'hui de Votre Excellence, je n'oserois cependant me rendre auprez d'elle sans un ordre exprez' du Gouvernement. . . .

' Les affaires se traitent ici tout autrement qu'ailleurs, et ce qui seroit chez nous raison et justice, n'est souvent ici que déraison et mauvaise humeur.' — Letter to Lord Macartney from Father Grammont.

[3] 'The crowds were immense, not only from the highest ground to the water's edge, but hundreds were actually standing in the

stream N.W., which we are to pursue without stopping, except for a short time to make visits, and to receive the provisions for our tables, which are regularly distributed every day early in the morning.

Monday, August 12.—This morning we arrived at Yongsiun.

There are usually fourteen or fifteen men to each yacht, so that the number now employed by us amounts to upward of five hundred.

The people engaged in this service are comely and strong made, but remarkably round-shouldered, owing, I suppose, to their mode of labour. They appear to be copper-coloured from their constant exposure to the sun; but they are naturally fair, as we observed when they stripped to plunge into the water.

As in summer they go naked from the waist upward, their complexion is, of course, very dark, but in the parts where they are usually clothed this is not so.

We are much troubled with mosquitoes, or gnats, and other insects, among which is a moth of a most gigantic size, not less than a humming-bird, and we are stunned day and night by the noise of a sort of cicada which lodges in the sedgy banks and is very obstreperous.

Tuesday, August 13.—Some of the provisions which were brought for us this morning being found tainted (which was not to be wondered at, considering the extreme heat of the weather—thermometer 88° Fahrenheit), the superintending Mandarins were instantly deprived of their buttons, and all their servants bambooed, before we knew anything of the matter. So sudden and summary is the administration of justice here.[1]

---

water, in order to approach nearer to the vessels which conveyed the strangers. Yet in all the ardour of curiosity the people themselves preserved a great degree of decency and regularity in their demeanour. Not the least dispute seemed to take place among them, and none of the common Chinese who usually wear straw hats kept on theirs while the Embassy was passing, lest they should obstruct the view of the persons behind them, though their bare heads were thus exposed to a scorching sun.'—Sir G. Staunton, 'Embassy to China.'

[1] 'In travelling through the country, a day seldom escaped without our witnessing the applications of the bamboo, and generally in such a manner that it might be called by any other name except a gentle correction. A Chinese suffering under this punishment cries out in the most piteous manner, a Tartar bears it in silence.'—J. Barrow, 'Travels in China.'

ONE OF THE EMBASSY YACHTS
From the Drawing by WILLIAM ALEXANDER *in the British Museum*

A NOISY HONOUR

As soon as we saw Van-ta-gin and Chou-ta-gin we interceded in favour of the degraded delinquents; but though we were heard with great attention, and received very flattering answers, we easily perceived that no indulgence or relaxation of discipline was to be expected on such occasions.

Wednesday, August 14.—This morning we passed by a very beautiful building on the north bank of the river. It is a pleasure house erected for the Emperor's accommodation in his progress through this country. The roof is covered with a sort of yellow tiles, which, when the sun plays upon them, shine like burnished gold.

To-day we had pleasant, cool weather, flying clouds frequently obscuring the sky but never descending in rain. Travelling here would be agreeable enough were it not for the confounded noise of the copper drums, which the people in the forecastle are perpetually rattling upon. This, we were told, is meant as a compliment to do us honour, but I observe that it serves also as a signal of direction to regulate the motions of the accompanying yachts.

Thursday, August 15.—We now observe with pleasure some picturesque blue mountains at thirty or forty miles distance. They contribute a good deal to enliven our prospects, which have hitherto been confined to the level uniformity of the circumjacent country.

We found the river here considerably swelled by the late rains in Tartary, where it takes its rise, and the floods extended so far over the banks that the trackers of our yachts were usually up to their middle in the water.

During the greater part of the passage our conductors, Chin-ta-gin the Legate, together with Chou-ta-gin and Van-ta-gin, visited me almost every day, but this morning they came with an appearance of more formality than usual.

Their business was to acquaint me that the Emperor was much pleased with the accounts which he had heard of us, and that he was disposed to let our arrangements take place as we had proposed; that he had ordered two houses to be prepared for us, one in the city of Pekin, and the other in the country about six miles distance from it, near the Emperor's palace of Yuen-min-yuen. We might choose which we liked best, but they believed we should prefer the one in the country, because of its gardens and its neighbourhood to Yuen-min-yuen.

After we had been presented, and had assisted at the

ceremony of the Emperor's birthday at Gehol, it was intended we should return to the capital, and that the Emperor himself would soon follow us. They added that as our stay in Tartary would be very short, they wished us not to carry the field-pieces and howitzers with us, which, we had told them, made a part of our presents, as there would not be time nor opportunity there to exercise or exhibit them.

They then introduced the subject of the court ceremonies with a degree of art, address, and insinuation that I could not avoid admiring. They began by turning the conversation upon the different modes of dress that prevailed among different nations, and, after pretending to examine ours particularly, seemed to prefer their own, on account of its being loose and free from ligatures, and of its not impeding or obstructing the genuflexions and prostrations which, they said, were customary to be made by all persons whenever the Emperor appeared in public.

They therefore apprehended much inconvenience to us from our knee-buckles and garters, and hinted to us that it would be better to disencumber ourselves of them before we should go to Court. I told them they need not be uneasy about that circumstance, as I supposed, whatever ceremonies were usual for the Chinese to perform, the Emperor would prefer my paying him the same obeisance which I did to my own Sovereign. They said they supposed the ceremonies in both countries must be nearly alike, that in China the form was to kneel down upon both knees, and make nine prostrations or inclinations of the head to the ground, and that it never had been, and never could be, dispensed with. I told them ours was somewhat different, and that though I had the most earnest desire to do everything that might be agreeable to the Emperor, my first duty must be to do what might be agreeable to my own King; but if they were really in earnest in objecting to my following the etiquette of the English Court, I should deliver to them my reply in writing as soon as I arrived at Pekin. They then talked of the length and dangers of our voyage, and said that as we had come to such a distance from home, our King would naturally be anxious for our return, and that the Emperor did not mean to hunt this autumn as usual, but to remove with his Court very early to Pekin on purpose that we might not be delayed.

I told them His Imperial Majesty would judge from the King's letter, and from my representations, what was expected from me at my return to England, and what time would be sufficient to enable me to transact the business I was charged with, and to describe to my Sovereign the glory and virtues of the Emperor, the power and splendour of his empire, the wisdom of its laws and moral institutes, the fame of all which had already reached to the most distant regions.

I was then asked if I had brought any presents to the Emperor from myself, besides those from the King. This question disconcerted me not a little; however, I replied without any hesitation that I had brought a chariot, which was indeed (as it ought to be) much inferior in value to those sent by the King, yet, being of a different form, and remarkably elegant of its kind, I hoped the Emperor would condescend to accept it from me. I added that I flattered myself I should have some other present to offer him at New Year's Day, meaning to impress them with the idea that I expected to be allowed to stay beyond that period; for all along, ever since our departure from Tien-sing, I have entertained a suspicion, from a variety of hints and circumstances, that the customs and policy of the Chinese would not allow us a very long residence among them. In all the different visits and conferences that have passed between us and our conductors, I observe, with great concern, a settled prejudice against the Embassy in Chin-ta-gin the Legate, though often attempted to be concealed by him under extravagant compliments and professions. I have taken great pains to conciliate him; but I suspect he is not of a conciliable nature. With regard to Van-ta-gin and Chou-tagin, I think we have interested them much in our favour. When we have had opportunities of conversing with them in the absence of the Legate, they have scarcely disguised their sentiments of the Emperor's partiality to the Tartars in preference to his Chinese subjects; nor do they seem much to like their colleague the Legate, who is a Tartar, but, being the first in the commission, has the exclusive privilege of corresponding with Court upon our affairs, and whom they consider a sort of crazy and morose man. They said that we seemed very early to have discovered his character, and have admired us much for the complaisance and patient attention of our deportment towards him.[1]

Tuesday, August 16.—This day at half after 6 p.m. we arrived at the suburbs of Tong-siou, where (our navigation

[1] 'The Chinese were invariably more affable than the Tartars.'—J. Barrow, ' Travels in China.'

being now ended) we quitted our yachts and went on shore.

During one of these visits that passed between us and our conductors they turned the discourse upon our dominions in Bengal, and affirmed that some of the English troops from thence had lately given assistance to the insurgents in Thibet. I was very much startled at this intelligence, but instantly told them that the thing was impossible, and that I could take upon me to contradict it in the most decisive manner.

It came out on farther conversation that the Emperor's troops had met with a check on the western borders, which was so unexpected that they could account for it no otherwise than by supposing their enemies to be supported or assisted by Europeans, and they pretended that several persons with hats had been particularly remarked in one of the engagements. I hope that by the manner in which I treated this intelligence any ill impression which such a report might occasion to our prejudice will have been done away. Perhaps it was a feint or artifice to sift me and try to discover our force or our vicinity to their frontiers, and I am the more disposed to think so because a day or two after, on resuming the subject, they asked me whether the English at Bengal would assist the Emperor against the rebels in those parts. As I had told them before that one of the reasons why the story could not be true was the distance of our possessions from the scene of action, their question seemed calculated to catch me, for if, from eagerness or complaisance, I had answered in the affirmative, they would have concluded against my sincerity, because if our troops could come thither to the assistance of the Emperor's troops, they could equally have come to the assistance of his enemies.

Our yachts have been all along the passage most plentifully supplied with provisions, China wine, fruits, and vegetables of various kinds, and served with great sedulity and attention.

At all the military stations we passed (which were very numerous) the soldiers were turned out, with their colours and music, and if at night, with the addition of illuminations and fireworks.

Whatever little articles we seemed to want we were immediately supplied with, and no entreaties could prevail for our being allowed to purchase them.[1]

[1] 'The cost of supplies of every kind that could be wanted the Emperor chose should be entirely borne by himself, upon this grand

The most refined politeness and sly good breeding appeared in the behaviour of all those Mandarins with whom we had any connection; but although we found an immediate acquiescence in words with everything we seemed to propose, yet, in fact, some ingenious pretence or plausible objection was usually invented to disappoint us. Thus when we desired to make little excursions from our boats into the towns, or into the country, to visit any object that struck us as we went along, our wishes were seldom gratified. The refusal or evasion was, however, attended with so much profession, artifice, and compliment that we soon grew reconciled and even amused with it.

We have indeed been narrowly watched, and all our habits, customs, and proceedings, even of the most trivial nature, observed with an inquisitiveness and jealousy which surpassed all that we had read of in the history of China. But we endeavoured always to put the best face upon everything, and to preserve a perfect serenity of countenance upon all occasions.

I therefore shut my eyes upon the flags of our yachts, which were inscribed '*The English Ambassador bringing tribute to the Emperor of China*,' and have made no complaint of it, reserving myself to notice it if a proper opportunity occurs.

Saturday, August 17.—We shall be obliged to remain some days at Tong-siou in order to land our presents and our baggage from the yachts, and to put them in proper order for carriage to Yuen-min-yuen, whither it is meant that we should go directly without stopping at Pekin. The distance from Tong-siou to Pekin is twelve miles, and from thence to Yuen-min-yuen is about seven.

The presents and baggage were lodged in two great pandals built for the purpose in the suburbs near the river. Each of them was two hundred and seven feet long and thirteen feet broad, thirteen feet from the ground to the rafter or wall plate, and thirteen feet from the ground to the middle angle of the roof. The materials were strong bamboos and close matting impervious to the rain.

---

idea—that the whole Empire was as his private property and dwelling, in which it would be a failure of hospitality to suffer a visitor (for such an Ambassador is always considered by the Chinese) to be at the least charge for himself or his train while he continued there. His Imperial Majesty's orders on this subject were very strictly obeyed.'—Sir G. Staunton, 'Embassy to China.'

Between the pandals was a passage or street of forty-two feet wide. The whole was shut with gates at each end, guards posted there, and placards stuck up forbidding any persons from approaching the place with fire. These pandals were erected in a very few hours. Everything belonging to us was landed from thirty-seven vessels in less than one day. Such expedition, strength, and activity for the removal of so great a number of packages, many of which were of enormous weight, awkward shape, and cumbersome carriage, in a few hours cannot, I believe, be paralleled or procured in any other country than China, where everything is at the instant command of the State, and where even the most laborious tasks are undertaken and executed with a readiness and even a cheerfulness which one would scarcely expect to meet with in so despotic a government.

The Chinese seem able to lift and remove almost any weight by multiplying the power: thus they fasten to the sides of the load two strong bamboos; if two are not sufficient they cross them with two others, and so proceed, quadrating and decussating the machine, and applying more bearers, till they can master and carry it with ease.

Our quarters were in the suburbs of the city at a Miao or Temple, consisting of several courts and spacious apartments. Here we were all very commodiously lodged during the time we stayed, and as usual supplied abundantly with whatever we had occasion for.

This Temple or Miao was founded by a munificent bigot some centuries ago for twelve bonzes, and endowed with considerable revenues. The Sanctum Sanctorum forms but a small part of the building, and is solely appropriated to the worship and the images of Fo and his subaltern Deities. The rest is a kind of choultry or caravansera, where travellers of rank are lodged in their journeys through this place upon public service.

My train was so numerous that we took up almost the whole of the Temple; only one bonze remained in it to watch over the lamps of the shrine: all the rest removed to another Temple in the neighbourhood.[1]

[1] The conversion of temples into lodging-houses is attended with some temporal advantages to the priests by the donations that are generally made on such occasions. Most of them being supported entirely by voluntary contributions and trifling legacies, they are thankful for the smallest gifts.

' Little as the priests, or numerous novices that are to be found in the temples, are employed in the duties of their office, or in worldly

VISIT TO THE PANDALS

Sunday, August 18.—Van-ta-gin called upon me this morning at breakfast, and told me that the porters and waggons would all be ready on Tuesday, that our things might begin moving early that day, and be carried away before the following night.

He added that we should set out ourselves on Wednesday morning, pass through Pekin, and proceed to Yuen-min-yuen, where a Colao of high rank was appointed by the Emperor to meet us, together with a European missionary.

He could not inform me of the name or nation of the missionary, but I suspect him to be Bernado Almeyda, the Portuguese whom we had been so often cautioned against.

Van-ta-gin and Chou-ta-gin both came together to visit me in the evening, and brought me the Tartar's excuse for his not accompanying them, saying that he was somewhat indisposed; but it would seem as if his staying away proceeded rather from pride and ill-humour than from real illness. I, however, sent a very civil compliment to him on the occasion expressive of my concern at his illness and my intention to visit him next day.

Monday, August 19.—I went down to the pandals this morning, where I met the Tartar Legate, Van-ta-gin and Chou-ta-gin, and several other Mandarins, who were assembled there to give orders for the operations of the next day.

On this occasion I proposed to amuse them with the exercise of our small brass field-pieces, which were now mounted and prepared for moving with the rest of our presents and baggage.

Though they were remarkably well cast and of a most elegant form, fixed on light carriages, and in every respect completely well served, and fired from twenty to thirty times a minute, yet our conductors pretended to think lightly of them, and spoke of such things as being no novelties in China. I have good reason, however, to suppose there is

---

concerns, they are not less uncleanly in their persons and apartments than those whose time is taken up in providing for the necessities of life. The room in which some of us should have slept was so full of scorpions and scolopendras, and they crept in such numbers into our beds, that we were fairly driven out, and obliged to swing our cots in the open air between two trees. Here we were not much less annoyed by myriads of mosquitoes and the unceasing noise of the chiping cicadoes, which continued without intermission until break of day,'—J. Barrow, ' Travels in China.'

nothing like them in the whole Empire, and that these gentlemen are at bottom not a little mortified by this small specimen of our superiority.

On our return from the pandals, Van-ta-gin and Chou-ta-gin walked up with us to our quarters, and told us that the Emperor's answer was come to our request of having a European missionary to attend us, and that we might choose any of the Europeans in the Emperor's service then at Pekin; that the Emperor was disposed to favour us as much as possible, having already conceived the highest esteem for us, from the accounts he had heard of our appearance, deportment, and conversation ever since our arrival in his dominion.

They then renewed the subject of the ceremonial relative to which they had been perfectly silent for some days. It seems to be a very serious matter with them, and a point which they have set their hearts upon. They pressed me most earnestly to comply with it, and said it was a mere trifle; they kneeled down on the floor and practised it of their own accord to show me the manner of it, and begged me to try it whether I could not perform it. On my declining it, they applied to my interpreter to do it, who, although a Chinese, said he could only act as I directed him; they seem a little disappointed in finding me not so pliant in this point as they could wish. As to themselves, they are wonderfully supple, and though generally considered as most respectable characters, are not very scrupulous in regard to veracity, saying and unsaying, without hesitation, what seems to answer the purpose of the moment. Their ideas of the obligations of truth are certainly very lax, for when we hinted to them any contradictions that occurred, or deviations from their promises in our affairs, they made very light of them, and seemed to think them of trifling consequence.

We then entertained them with a concert of music, which they appeared to be much pleased with, and when they left us repeated the same flattering expressions and compliments which they had set out with in the beginning of their visit.

This night died of dysentery, after a long illness, Henry Eades, a cunning artist in brass and iron, who, hearing of my intention to take with me to China a person in his branch, had strongly importuned both me and Sir George Staunton in London to give him a preference to other candidates. Finding him well qualified, I consented, and had reason to be well satisfied with him, as he was not only

A DUSTY JOURNEY

skilled and ingenious, but a quiet, well-behaved man. As the sea did not seem to agree with him at the beginning of our voyage, I proposed to him to return from Madeira, but unfortunately he determined to persevere.

Tuesday, August 20.—Eades was buried this morning, all the servants, musicians, and guards attending his interment; the funeral service was read upon the occasion,[1] and a volley of small arms was fired over his grave. Vast numbers of Chinese were spectators of the ceremony, and seemed to be a good deal affected by its order and solemnity. After it was over our baggage began to move, and a great part of it was despatched before night.

Wednesday, August 21.—We rose very early this morning and found the palanquins, horses, carriages, and everything ready for our departure. The Tartar Legate Van-ta-gin, Chou-ta-gin, and several other Mandarins of rank waited for us at the great gate, and set off at the same moment that we did.[2]

We stopped at a village half-way between Tong-siou and Pekin to breakfast[3] and to repose ourselves, the day being very hot and the roads very dusty. From thence we reached Pekin in about two hours, and after taking some refreshments of tea and fruit at the palace gate, we proceeded to Yuen-min-yuen, where we arrived about 3

---

[1] 'As no clergyman accompanied the Embassy, I was appointed to read the funeral service of the Church of England on this melancholy occasion.'—Æneas Anderson, 'Narrative of Embassy to China.'

[2] 'The excessive heat of the weather, the dustiness of the roads, the closeness of the carriages, and the slow manner in which we moved along, would have made this short journey almost insupportable but from the novelty of the scene, the smiles, grins, and gestures of the multitude, and, above all, the momentary expectation of entering the greatest city on the surface of the globe.

'Those who had been so unlucky as to make choice of the little covered carriages found themselves extremely uncomfortable, notwithstanding they are the best, the most easy, and genteel sort of carriage that the country affords. Being fixed on wheels without springs, and having no seats in the inside, they are to a European, who must sit on his haunches in the bottom, the most uneasy vehicle that can be imagined.'— J. Barrow, 'Travels in China.'

[3] 'Here we had a most sumptuous breakfast of roast pork and venison, rice, and made dishes, eggs, tea, milk, and a variety of fruits served up on masses of ice.'—*Ibid.*

o'clock p.m., and found the greater part of our baggage already come; the remainder soon followed.[1]

On this journey we were preceded by a great number of soldiers, brandishing long whips in their hands, which they were continually exercising in order to keep off the enormous crowds which incessantly thronged about us, and obstructed the passage.[2]

The house at this place allotted for our habitation consists of several small courts and separate pavilions, and is situated in a little park or garden, laid out, in the Chinese manner, with serpentine walks and a narrow winding river forming an island, with a summer-house in the middle of it, a grove of various trees interspersed with patches of grass ground, diversified with inequalities and roughened with rocks; the whole surrounded with a high wall and guarded by a detachment of troops at the gate.

Some of the apartments are large, handsome, and not ill-contrived, but the whole building is so much out of repair that I already see it will be impossible to reside in it comfortably during the winter. It appears, indeed, to be only calculated for a summer dwelling, though I understand it is the best of the hotels at this place destined (as several more are) for the reception of foreign Ambassadors.[3]

[1] 'Of the Chinese honesty and sobriety and carefulness we received convincing proofs. Of the number of packages, amounting to more than six hundred, of various sizes and descriptions, not a single article was missing, nor injured, on their arrival at the capital, notwithstanding they had been moved about and carried by land and transhipped several times.'—J. Barrow, 'Travels in China.'

[2] 'We found the sides of the roads lined with spectators, on horseback, on foot, in small carriages similar to those we rode in, in carts, waggons, and chairs. In the last were Chinese ladies, but, having gauze curtains at the sides and front, we could see little of them. Several well-looking women in long silken robes, with a great number of children, were in the small carriages. These we understood to be Tartars. We observed that though the soldiers were very active and noisy in brandishing their whips, they only struck them against the ground, and never let them fall on the people. A Chinese crowd is not so unruly as it (a crowd) generally is elsewhere.'—*Ibid.*

[3] The accommodation provided was of a most wretched description. Mr. Barrow remarks that when the official showed the apartment designed for their occupation, he could not forbear observing 'that they seemed fitter for hogs than human beings,' being three or four hovels surrounded by a high wall, although scarcely two

VISIT FROM THE MISSIONARIES

We had been promised that the European missionaries should come to us as soon as we arrived here, but none of them have as yet made their appearance.

Thursday, August 22.—The Tartar Legate came this morning to compliment me on my arrival at Yuen-min-yuen. He said there was a Colao on the road from Gehol particularly appointed to attend to our affairs, and that he would send one or two of the European missionaries to me to-morrow.

As the Legate seemed to be in better humour than usual, I took the opportunity of mentioning the subject of my quarters, which I told him were very handsome, but somewhat out of repair, and rather inconvenient to us Europeans, whose modes of living were different from the Chinese, and that I hoped he would give directions for our removal to Pekin, where I thought we should be more at our ease.

He seemed to agree with me on this point, and said he thought there could be no objection.

Friday, August 23.—This day the Tartar Legate sent to announce his intention of visiting me, and of bringing several of the European missionaries with him. He accordingly arrived at 10 a.m. with Bernando Almeyda Rodriguez[1] and another Portuguese,[2] Poiret,[3] Pansi,[4] and

---

hundred yards from the Hall of Audience and in the palace. The walls were bare, the ceiling broken down, the floors filthy, and no furniture except an old table and two or three chairs.

Mr. Barrow's protests occasioned surprise, and he was informed they were the apartments of Tagin (great men), but as he did not like them, he should be accommodated with others, which proved but slightly better. These were swept out, an operation that had not taken place for many months, and some of their own bedding installed. They, however, had the consolation of good food, as he remarks: 'To make amends for our uncomfortable lodgings, we sat down to a most excellent dinner in the Chinese style. The best soup I ever tasted, their vermicelli excellent, and their pastry unusually light and white as snow.'—J. Barrow, 'Travels in China.'

[1] Bernard Joseph Rodriguez, an ex-Jesuit, aged sixty-nine years, came to China, and entered into the Emperor's service as astronomer and physician. He is a Mandarin of the third class.

[2] 'Antonio della Purificazione, a Franciscan aged about fifty.'—*Ibid.*

[3] 'Louis Poiret, born in Lorraine, but educated at Florence, an ex-Jesuit, aged fifty-eight. He entered the Emperor's service as a painter in 1773.'—*Ibid.*

[4] 'Joseph Pansi, lay ex-Jesuit, aged sixty, a native of Ancona, entered the Emperor's service as a painter in 1773.'—*Ibid.*

Diodati,[1] Italians, Paris,[2] a Frenchman, and one or two others.

The Emperor had, on occasion of the Embassy, distinguished some of these missionaries by his favour, and had conferred white buttons on Poiret and Diodati, and a blue one (which is of higher rank) on Bernado. This latter is the person against whom I had been particularly cautioned from Macao, and from other quarters, as a man of malignant disposition, jealous of all Europeans, except those of his own nation, and particularly unfriendly to the English ;[3] and, indeed, I have seen enough this day to convince me of the truth of the representation.

This man, who was bred a Jesuit, and is upwards of seventy years of age, has been a great many years in China, and now belongs to the College of Mathematics, though of a very limited knowledge in that science. He has some skill in surgery, and having attended the Minister Cho-chang-tong, who is afflicted with a rupture, availed himself of that circumstance to obtain the Emperor's appointment of him to be interpreter to my Embassy.

[1] 'P. Deodati, born at Naples, aged thirty-seven, entered the Emperor's service in 1784 as watchmaker and mechanic.'—J. Barrow, 'Travels in China.'

[2] 'Joseph Paris, a layman aged fifty, entered the Emperor's service as a mechanist and watchmaker.'—*Ibid.*

[3] 'Le gouvernement vient de nommer un missionaire Portugais appelé Joseph Bernado, pour aller a Ge Ho, servir d'interprète à Votre Excellence, et la diriger dans le cérémonial et le costume du pays. L'intérêt sincere que je prends à l'heureux succès de cette ambassade ne me permet pas de laisser ignorer à votre excellence que ce missionaire a deja tenu ici des propos peu favorables à la nation anglaise, et qu'il paroit peu disposé à seconder les vues de votre Excellence. . . . Il est à propos que Votre Excellence connoisse ses bons amis. Le Portugais Almeyda est venu à Peking sous la titre de chirugien ; au défaut de tout autre Portugais, il es entré au tribunal d'astronomie, dont il ignore même les premiers principes. Il y a trois mois qu'il eut le bonheur de guerir une légère incommodité du Ho tchang tang, ministre très puissant à la cour, . . . voilà l'origine de sa fortune ; voilà ce que la enhardi a se procurer l'honneur d'être l'interprète de Votre Excellence, fortune et honneur dont il déchoira bien vite, si, Votre Excellence peut l'empêcher d'être interprète a Ge-Ho. . . . Je prie Votre Excellence de croire que ce n'est point par haine ou par rancune que je lui parle ainsi de ce missionaire. . . . Je n'ai absolument d'autre grief contre lui que ses préventions et ses mauvais propos contre la nation anglaise.'— Letter to Lord Macartney from Father Grammont.

Whether from vanity of being selected for such an office, or from the hope of being able to frustrate its success, I know not, but, unfortunately for him, when he was introduced to me for that purpose, it appeared to the Legate and the other attending Mandarins that he was unqualified for the office, being entirely ignorant of the languages most familiar to us. His mortification upon this occasion he had not sufficient temper to conceal, and almost instantly expressed very unfavourable sentiments of the Embassy to an Italian missionary who stood near him. As they conversed in Latin, he probably imagined I should not understand or overhear him, but his looks and gestures would have been alone sufficient to discover the state of his mind if his tongue had been silent.

At this visit I reminded the Legate of my wishes to remove to Pekin, on which occasion Bernado very impertinently interfered, and advised him against the measure, pretending that it would retard our journey to Gehol and be otherwise unadvisable; but his objections were overruled by a superior authority, although the Legate seemed disposed to admit them.

All the other missionaries seemed shocked at and ashamed of his behaviour, and interposed their endeavours to bring him to a proper composure. During the whole time I remained perfectly calm, and seemed not to perceive or notice his behaviour, but, on the contrary, was pointed in my civilities to him, and at his going away told him, through the channel of a French missionary, how much I regretted my not understanding the Portuguese language, as it deprived me of the advantage of so able an assistant and interpreter.

He came back soon after, and seemed indeed to be a good deal softened, and even gave me assurance of his services and good disposition; but after what I have seen it is necessary to be uncommonly circumspect.

It will be right to cultivate and make use of him, if possible, but it would be egregious folly and dupery to confide in or depend on him.[1]

[1] 'With regard to the intrigues of the Portuguese missionary, Bernado Almeyda ... he lost no opportunity of making misrepresentations to the Chinese Court concerning the English and raising unwarrantable suspicions in the minds of the Chinese. Towards the close of the last war, when it was found expedient to take possession of some Portuguese colonies, this missionary suggested to the Chinese Court that, if the English got possession of Macao, and were once suffered to get footing in the country, China might ex-

About an hour after, Van-ta-gin and Chou-ta-gin returned in order to acquaint us that the Colao Chun-ta-gin, a cousin of the Emperor, who had been announced to us, was come, and that it was now settled for him and Van-ta-gin and Chou-ta-gin to manage all our affairs, without the interference of the Tartar Legate.

In consequence of this arrangement, Van-ta-gin, accompanied by our interpreter and Mr. Maxwell, one of my secretaries, went this evening to Pekin to view the palace intended for my residence, and to give directions for putting it into proper order for our reception.

Whilst they were employed on this business, Chou-ta-gin came to take us to the Emperor's palace of Yuen-min-yuen, or the Garden of Gardens, as the name imports, and to ask our opinion of the fittest apartments to place the globes, the clocks, the lustres, and the planetarium in. This place is truly an Imperial residence; the park is said to be eighteen miles round, and laid out in all the taste, variety, and magnificence which distinguish the rural scenery of Chinese gardening.

---

perience the same fate as Hindostan. Fortunately, this interference took a different turn to what he expected. The intelligence of a hostile force so near the coast of China coming first from a European missionary implied a neglect in the Viceroy of Canton. An angry letter was addressed to him from Court, ordering him to give immediate and accurate information on the subject. The Viceroy, nettled at the officious zeal of the Portuguese, positively denied the fact of any hostile intention of the English, " who, being a brave people, and terrible in arms, had intimidated the Portuguese at Macao, though without reason, as their ships of war came only, as usual, to protect their ships of commerce against their enemies." When this dispatch of the Viceroy reached Pekin, the Emperor was so exasperated to think that the Court had suffered itself to be misled by a European missionary that he ordered Bernado Almeyda to appear before the Master of the Household, and on his knees to ask forgiveness of a crime which, he was told, deserved to be punished with death, and he was dismissed with a caution never to interfere in the state affairs of China.

'The whole of this curious transaction was published in the *Pekin Gazette* of 1803, so that the English gained a considerable degree of reputation by it—so much that the Chinese at Canton (and a great deal depends upon their representations) would have no objection to see the English in possession of Macao, for they cordially hate, even almost despise, the Portuguese, and they speak with horror of the French.'—J. Barrow, ' Travels in China.'

THE PRESENCE CHAMBER

The various beauties of the spot, its lakes and rivers, together with its superb edifices, which I saw (and yet I saw but a very small part), so strongly impressed my mind at this moment that I feel incapable of describing them.

I shall therefore confine myself to the great hall or Presence Chamber of the Emperor. It is one hundred and fifty feet long and sixty feet wide; there are windows on one side only, and opposite to them is the Imperial Throne, of carved mahogany, the logs of which were brought from England, and elevated by a few steps from the floor.

Over the Chair of State is an inscription in Chinese:

'CHING-THA-QUAN-MING-FOO,'

the translation of which signifies:

'VERUS, MAGNUS, GLORIOSUS, SPLENDIDUS, FELIX.'

On each side of the Chair of State is a beautiful argus pheasant's tail spread out into a magnificent fan of great extent.[1] The floor is of chequered marble, grey and white, with neat mats laid upon it in different places to walk upon. At one end I observed a musical clock that played twelve old English tunes, the 'Black Joke,' 'Lillibullero,' and other airs of the 'Beggars' Opera.' It was decorated in a wretched old taste, with ornaments of crystal and coloured stones, but had been, I dare say, very much admired in its time. On the dial appeared in large characters, '*George Clarke, Clock and Watch Maker, in Leadenhall Street, London.*'[2]

This saloon we determined on for the reception of some of our most magnificent presents, which were to be distributed as follows: On one side of the throne was to be placed the terrestrial globe, on the other the celestial; the lustres were to be hung from the ceiling, at equal distances from the middle of the room; at the north end the planetarium was to stand; at the south end Vulliamy's clocks, with the barometer, Derbyshire porcelain vases, and figures, and Fraser's orrery—an assemblage of such beauty as is not to

---

[1] 'A pair of circular fans made of the wing feathers of the argus pheasant, and mounted on long polished ebony poles, stood on each side of the throne.'—J. Barrow, 'Travels in China.'

[2] 'The old eunuch in charge had the impudence to say this clock was the workmanship of a Chinese.'—J. Barrow, 'Travels in China.'

be seen collected together in any other apartment, I believe, of the whole world besides.

At Yuen-min-yuen we were met by the Colao Keen-san-ta-gin, who went round the palaces with us, and entertained us with a collection of fruits and sweetmeats, at which the Tartar Legate assisted; for, to my great surprise, after what I had been told, I found him at my elbow almost every step I took during the evening. I have reason to believe that he does not mean to resign his charge of us; I suspect he has contrived means of settling the matter with the Colao. This will be an unpleasant circumstance, because, as he is a Tartar and has powerful connections at Court, our friends Van-ta-gin and Chou-ta-gin are obliged to pay him great deference, and dare not exert themselves in our favour as much as they are inclined to do. We have, however, found them already very useful to us in many instances.

At eight o'clock Mr. Maxwell returned from Pekin, and reported that he had seen and been all through the palace at Pekin intended for us. It is an immense building, containing eleven courts, and ample room for every purpose we can require.[1]

Saturday, August 24.—Sir George Staunton went to Yuen-min-yuen, and took with him Mr. Barrow, Dr. Dinwiddie, Tiebault, and Petitpierre, and other artists and workmen, to give them directions about arranging the machinery and disposing in their proper places the planetarium, orrery, globes, clocks, lustres, etc.

These gentlemen are to remain at Yuen-min-yuen for this purpose during our journey into Tartary, but it is thought they will not be able to dispatch it in less than six or seven weeks at soonest.

Some of the Chinese workmen, not accustomed to handle articles of such delicate machinery, were interrupted in their attempts to unpack them by our interpreter, who told them that, till put up and delivered, they must still be considered as under our care; upon which the Legate interposed and said, 'No; they are *cong-so*, tributes (*oblata*) to the Emperor,' and consequently we had nothing more to do with them.

Our interpreter replied that they were not tributes (*cong-so*), but presents (*sung-lo*).

[1] 'The pleasure that was this day felt by the whole of the suite of every denomination is not easily described when orders were received to prepare for quitting this horrid place [Yuen-min-yuen] on Monday.'—Æneas Anderson, 'Narrative of Embassy to China.'

EXPENSES OF THE EMBASSY

The Colao put an end to the conversation by saying that the expression of *sung-lo*, or presents, was proper enough.

On his return to quarters our interpreter came to me (as he said) from Van-ta-gin and Chou-ta-gin, and told me that, though the Emperor's allowance for defraying the Embassy was very considerable, yet that it did not equal the expense, and that it was expected that I should make them a very handsome present to supply the difference. I answered that I was very willing to do so, and asked him what he thought they would be satisfied with. Upon recollecting himself a little, he said he believed that five hundred dollars apiece would be a proper sum, which I made no scruple immediately to agree to, as they so strongly professed themselves our friends, as they certainly have weight with the Colao—sufficient, we trust, to counteract the Legate's practices with him to our prejudice—and as if they misbehave we shall have them at our mercy. Besides, being engaged in our business, and having once tasted of our bounty, they are likely to endeavour to deserve further favour by further services; as it is observed of certain beasts of prey that, having once smacked human blood, they never afterwards have a relish for any other.

Sunday, August 25.—Notwithstanding what I have written in the preceding paragraph, our interpreter told me this morning that he was just then come from Van-ta-gin and Chou-ta-gin, who desired him to say that, though they had the highest respect and regard for me, they could not possibly think of accepting any presents of money; that it was true the expense they incurred by their attendance on the Embassy was considerable, but that it chiefly fell upon Chou-ta-gin, who was very rich and well able to bear it; that Van-ta-gin was not rich, and did not therefore contribute to it; but then, he had the principal share of the fatigue of the business. in reviewing and stationing the boats, hiring the porters, horses, and carriages, superintending the provision department, punishing delinquents, etc., whilst Chou-ta-gin did little else than receive the reports, write out the register, and pay the disbursements. All this seems very extraordinary, and I know not how to account for it—first to signify a disposition to take our money, and then to refuse it, at the same time preserving their friendship for us, and actually rendering us every service in their power.

The Chinese character seems at present inexplicable. The Tartar Legate, having delivered to me yesterday a letter, written by Sir Erasmus Gower from Ten-chou-fou, which had come by the Emperor's couriers, I directed an answer to be prepared, and requested to have it forwarded. He asked me what was in Sir Erasmus's letter, and in the answer. I had them both interpreted off-hand, and added with great good-humour that we had no secrets but what he was welcome to know.

Before he went away he mentioned the subject of the ceremonial, and was desirous of practising it before me ; but I put an end to the subject by telling him I had a paper relative to it, which would be ready to deliver to him at Pekin in a day or two.

Monday, August 26.—This morning we removed to Pekin, and are not only comfortably, but magnificently, lodged in the Tartar town in a vast palace consisting of eleven courts, some of them very spacious and airy.

Tuesday, August 27.—Father Raux, a French missionary of the Congregation of St. Lazarus at Paris, a native of Hainault, came and informed me that he had permission to attend us, and that he would wait upon me every day to receive our commands and execute our commissions. He is a tall, corpulent man, of easy manners and conversation, with a great volubility of speech. He understands both the Chinese and Manchoo languages, and seems to be perfectly contented with his lot here. He is well informed, and extremely communicative and fond of talking, so that I imagine it will not be difficult to learn from him everything he knows.[1]

Wednesday, August 28.—Mr. Barrow returned from the Palace of Yuen-min-yuen, and said they had put up in the saloon of the throne Parker's two lustres, had set the globes in their proper places, as also the orrery and Vulliamy's clocks, figures, and vases, and had laid the floor for the planetarium, and that the whole would have a very fine effect. Three of the Emperor's grandsons had been to look at them, and were much delighted with the sight.[2]

---

[1] 'Nicholas Raux, a Lazarite, aged about forty years, came to Pekin in 1785, and entered the service of the Emperor as a mathematician.'—J. Barrow, 'Travels in China.'

[2] 'When the presents were unpacked, not a single thing was missing or injured. Deodato, a Neapolitan missionary whom the Court had appointed to act as interpreter, was an excellent mechanic, and in this capacity was employed in the palace to inspect and keep in order the numerous pieces of European clockwork, mostly of London make. He was extremely friendly and helpful, more especially in explaining the nature, value, and use of the several

They particularly admired the clocks and the vases of Derbyshire porcelain. They, however, asked which we thought, our porcelain or theirs, to be preferable. The answer returned to them was that ours was considered as very precious of its kind, otherwise it would not have been offered to the Emperor; but that the value we set upon theirs was easily to be seen by the great quantities which were every year purchased by our merchants at Canton and sent in our shipping to England; and they seemed to be very well satisfied with this indirect explanation. The great Mandarin attended, and seemed to be much struck with the attention manifested by our bringing several spare glasses for the dome of the planetarium, one of which

pieces of machinery to those Chinese who were appointed to superintend them. They were allowed to remain tolerably quiet while the articles were being unpacked and sorted, only being rather annoyed by the interference and inquisitiveness of an old eunuch with several of the same kind of persons. But no sooner were they taken out of the cases and set up in the room than numerous visitors of all ranks, from princes of the blood royal to plain citizens, came to inspect both the presents and the men who had put them up, who were regarded as much the greatest of the curiosities. The grandsons of the Emperor were almost daily visitors, there being a kind of college in the palace for their education. Though young men from sixteen to twenty-five, the old eunuch who was their aya, or governor, used to frequently put them outside the hall of audience by the shoulders. A great number of Tartar generals and military officers also called. The carriage made by Hatchett seemed to puzzle the Chinese more than any of the other presents. Nothing of the kind had ever been seen at the capital before, and the disputes among them as to the part intended for the seat of the Emperor were most comical. The hammercloth that covered the box of the winter carriage had a smart edging, and was ornamented with festoons of roses. Its splendid appearance and elevated situation determined it at once in the opinion of the majority as the Emperor's seat, but the difficulty arose as to how to appropriate the inside of the carriage. They examined the windows, blinds, and screens, and at last concluded it could be for nobody but his ladies. The old eunuch came to Mr. Barrow for information, but when he learned that the fine elevation box was to be the seat of the coachman, and the Emperor's place within, he asked with a sneer if anyone supposed the Son of Heaven would suffer any man to sit higher than himself, and to turn his back toward him, and he wished to know if the coach-box could not be removed and placed somewhere behind the body of the carriage.'—J. Barrow, 'Travels in China.'

happened to be cracked, and which, without such a precaution, could not be repaired in China.

Thursday, August 29.—This day I put up the state canopy and their Majesties' pictures in the Presence Chamber, and delivered my paper relative to the ceremonial to be transmitted to Gehol. I had a good deal of difficulty in persuading Father Raux to get it translated into Chinese and to put it into the proper diplomatic form, so much is every person here afraid of intermeddling in any State matter without special authority of Government; and he only consented on condition that neither his writing nor that of his secretary should appear, but that I should get it copied by some other hand. Little Staunton was able to supply my wants on this occasion, for having very early in the voyage begun to study the Chinese language under my two interpreters, he had not only made considerable progress in it, but he had learned to write the characters with great neatness and celerity, so that he was of material use to me on this occasion, as he had been already before in transcribing the catalogue of the presents.

In the paper I expressed the strongest desire to do whatever I thought would be most agreeable to the Emperor, but that, being the representative of the first monarch of the Western world, his dignity must be the measure of my conduct; and that, in order to reconcile it to the customs of the Court of China, I was willing to conform to their etiquette, provided a person of equal rank with mine were appointed to perform the same ceremony before my Sovereign's picture that I should perform before the Emperor himself. The Legate shook his head, but Van-ta-gin and Chou-ta-gin said it was a good expedient, and offered immediately to go through the ceremony themselves on the spot; but as they had no authority for the purpose, I civilly declined the proposal. I received a very kind letter and message, together with his portrait, from old Father Amyot,[1] who has been near sixty years in China, lamenting that his age and infirmities prevented him from coming to wait upon me, but expressing the strong interest he takes in the success of my Embassy, and promising me every information, advice, and assistance in his power.

Friday, August 30.—Having now nearly completed the selection of such presents as I judged most eligible to carry

[1] 'Father Amyot died soon after Lord Macartney's departure from Pekin, aged about eighty.'—J. Barrow, ' Travels in China.'

with me to Gehol,[1] I gave notice to the Legate and our other conductors that we should be ready to set out on Monday next, the 2nd of September (which, according to their method of computation, answers to the 27th of the seventh month, their year beginning on the 1st of February), and that I proposed to employ one of the intervening days in viewing the buildings, triumphal arches, and other things most worthy of observation in the city of Pekin. But I found I had miscalculated in this instance, as much as I had done on some former ones of a similar nature, for I was requested to repress my curiosity till after my return from Tartary, as it was improper that an Ambassador should appear in public at Pekin till after he had been presented to the Emperor. On this occasion the question was repeated to me what presents I meant to offer the Emperor from myself, for that, instead of the chariot, which I had mentioned to them before, it would be proper to provide something portable to be delivered into the Emperor's hands by my own at the time of my introduction, no Ambassador approaching him for the first time without one. I told them I was prepared with one, and when my baggage was all unpacked I would show it to them. I was a good deal at a loss what to fix upon, all the principal articles that we had brought having been already inserted in the catalogue and announced to them as presents from the King. Luckily, it happened that Captain Mackintosh had with him some watches of very fine workmanship, which he was persuaded to cede to me at the usual estimate of profit upon things of this kind brought for sale from

[1] 'After the travelling arrangements were settled, the musicians, servants, etc., attended at Mr. Maxwell's apartment to receive the clothes in which they were to make their public appearance at Gehol. A large chest was produced full of clothes; they were of green cloth laced with gold, but their appearance awakened the suspicion that they had been frequently worn. With these habiliments, such as they were, every man fitted himself as well as he could with coats and waistcoats, as there was a great dearth of small clothes. The Chinese may not be supposed to be capable of distinguishing on the propriety of our figure in these ill-suited uniforms, but we certainly appeared in a very strong point of ridicule to each other. The two couriers were furnished with beaver hats, but not a hat was distributed to accompany these curious liveries, which the servants were ordered not to put on till the day when they were to add so much to the entry of the Embassy into Gehol.— Æneas Anderson, 'Narrative of the Embassy to China.'

Europe to Canton. This was the more fortunate, as I had been informed, besides, that not only valuable presents were to be made to the Emperor, but also that his sons and the principal great men in the Ministry expected to be gratified in the same manner. The persons pointed out to me were the Emperor's sons, his eldest grandson, the great General Achong-tong, and Cho-chang-tong and Fou-li-ou, the two favourite Ministers, the President of the Court of Rites, and a few others. I was, however, told at the same time that nothing of this kind was to be offered till my return from Gehol, after the Emperor had seen and accepted the presents destined for him.

When Father Raux came to-day, as usual, to attend me, he brought me a present from his convent of several acceptable articles, some excellent French bread, sweetmeats, and confections, very fine large figs, and a quantity of grapes, both red and white, the latter of a most delicious flavour, and without stones. He told me they were originally brought to the Jesuits' garden from Chama, on the borders of the great desert of Gobi, on the north-western frontier of the Empire, and had much improved by the transplantation. From him I learned more particularly what I had been already told by Van-ta-gin and Chou-ta-gin relative to the state of the Court, and I understand that the Emperor has had twenty-two sons, four only of which now remain alive. He is of so jealous a nature that no person as yet knows with certainty which of them he intends for his successor. He does not allow any of them to interfere in his government, but manages it in a great measure alone, reading all the dispatches himself, and often entering into the minutest detail of affairs. His principal Minister is Cho-chang-tong, a Tartar of obscure origin but considerable talents, whom he has raised by degrees from an inferior post in his guards to his present elevation, having been struck with his comeliness at a review twenty years ago and confirmed in the prepossession by finding his character correspond to his figure. He is in such high favour that the Emperor not long since gave one of his daughters in marriage to this Minister's eldest son, and conferred on him many other marks of distinction. The second favourite Minister is Fou-li-ou, a young Tartar, whose elder brother has by his means also obtained in marriage a daughter or niece of the Emperor and several of the most important employments in the State, having been Commander-in-Chief in the War of Formosa, Viceroy of

Canton, and latterly General of the forces on the Tibet frontier.

The A-cou-i or A-chong-tong, whose exploits are so particularly celebrated in the 'Mémoires sur la Chine,' has a still higher rank of precedence than the Minister whom I have mentioned, but, being much advanced in years, and notwithstanding his great merits, far from being a personal favourite with the Emperor, he now lives a good deal retired, and seldom meddles in public affairs.

The three other Colaos of the first tribunal of state are men of great abilities and of long experience, but, being of Chinese families, possess little influence, though their opinions are highly respected.

Father Raux says that there are above five thousand Chinese Christians in the city of Pekin alone, and he computes the number throughout the whole Empire at a hundred and fifty thousand. He confirmed to me what we read of in most of the histories of China—that it is a common practice among the poor to expose their children. The police send a cart round the city at an early hour every morning, which takes them up and conveys them to a fossé or cemetery appointed for their burial.

The missionaries often attend and preserve a few of these children which appear to them to be healthy and likely to recover.

The rest are thrown indiscriminately, dead or alive, into the pit. But Father Raux assured me very seriously that his brethren always first christened those that appeared to have any life remaining in them, '*pour leur sauver l'ame.*'[1]

---

[1] 'A respectable French missionary, now in London, who was for many years in Tokien, told me that he happened to call on one of his converts just at the moment that a child was born. The infant was delivered to the father, in order to be plunged into a jug of water prepared for the purpose. The missionary expostulated with the man on the heinousness of an act that was a crime against God and nature. The man persisted that, having already more than he could support, it would be a greater crime to preserve a life condemned to want and misery than to take it away without pain. The missionary, finding no argument was likely to divert the man from his purpose, observed that as a Christian he could not refuse him the satisfaction of saving the infant's soul by baptism. During the ceremony, as the father held the infant in his arms, he happened to fix his eyes on the infant's face, when the missionary thought he perceived the feelings of nature begin to work, and protracted the ceremony. When it was ended, he said, " I have

The Chinese, he says, seem to be less jealous of religious conversions than formerly, owing to the discretion of the present missionaries, whose zeal, I presume, is not now quite so ardent as that of their predecessors. Nevertheless, they engage not a little of the attention of Government, and within this twelve months past all their letters, which usually went free by the common post between Pekin and Canton, are constantly opened and examined. The Chinese have, indeed, an indistinct idea of there being at this time great disturbances and rebellions in Europe, and the Legate has often repeated the questions to me on our road whether England was *really* at peace with all the world, as I asserted.

The Bishop of Pekin had permission to visit me to-day in form.[1] He is a Portuguese of about forty years old, of a dignified appearance and conciliating manners, but said to be of false and crafty nature, and to possess no great measure of learning.[2] He, however, speaks Latin with

---

now done my duty in saving a soul from perishing." "And I," rejoined the man, " will do mine by saving its life," and hurried away with the infant to deposit it in the arms of its mother.'—J. Barrow, 'Travels in China.'

[1] 'Alexander Gonea, Bishop of Pekin, aged forty-four, came to China from Lisbon in 1784, and entered into the service of the Emperor as astronomer. In 1787 he was promoted to a seat at the Board, or, as the missionaries translate the Chinese word, the tribunal of mathematics.'—*Ibid.*

[2] 'The difficulty of making the Right Reverend Bishop and his colleagues comprehend the principles upon which the planetarium was constructed, and the phenomena of the heavenly bodies exhibited by it, conveyed a bad opinion of their astronomical and mathematical knowledge, as also that of the president of the Tribunal of Mathematics. The day following the Bishop came, unattended by the Chinese part of the Board, and gave some account of the nature of their employment. The astronomical part of the national almanac was intrusted to him and his colleagues, but the astrological part was managed by a committee of Chinese members. He candidly avowed neither he nor his European brethren were well qualified for the tasks, and hitherto had been more indebted to the *connaissances de temps* of Paris than to their own calculations. The French Revolution having put an end to future communications with that country was a severe blow to them. Fortunately, Dr. Dinwiddie had provided himself, on leaving London, with a set of nautical almanacs calculated for the meridian of Greenwich, which they considered as an invaluable present.'—*Ibid.*

great fluency, and made me a speech in that language of a quarter of an hour long. He was attended by two Portuguese missionaries, and by several others of different nations, and in their presence made me the strongest professions of friendship and attachment; several of them, however, took an early opportunity of advising me not to trust him. I think, indeed, there is some reason, from what I have seen, to believe that the Portuguese have formed a sort of system to disgust and keep out of China all other nations. Between them and the rest of the missionaries there appears to be great jealousy and enmity—*odium plus quam theologicum*. In a conversation with an Italian a few days ago, he told me that all the missionaries except the Portuguese were our warm friends, but that the Portuguese were friends of nobody but themselves. Bernado Almeyda has never come near me since our first meeting at Yuen-min-yuen, but I understand that he has been sent for to Gehol.

Saturday, August 31.—Father Grammont, the French missionary from whom I received two letters at Tien-sing, and also some intelligence since my arrival at Pekin, visited me in the afternoon, and apologized for not having done it sooner, owing, as he said, to a jealousy entertained of him by the Legate on account of his having talked so much of the Embassy, of the power and grandeur of the English nation, of the magnitude of its commerce with, and its importance to, the Chinese Empire. Father Grammont was bred a Jesuit, is now advanced in years, and has been a long time in China.[1] He is certainly a very clever fellow, and seems to know this country well; but as he is said to be of a restless, intriguing turn, it is necessary to be a good deal on one's guard with him.

Saturday, September 1.—Busily employed this day in making preparations for our departure to Gehol, as we are to set out to-morrow. To the occurrences at Pekin, which I have already noted, I must now add that, besides our conductors and the missionaries, we were every day visited by numbers of Mandarins of the higher ranks, some engaged to it by the duty of their station and employment, and others allured by their curiosity, and not a few by my band of music, which performed a very good concert in one of my apartments every evening. Among these visitors was the chief Mandarin of the Emperor's orchestra, who attended

[1] 'Joseph Grammont, ex-Jesuit, aged sixty, came to China in 1769, and entered the Emperor's service as musician and mathematician.'—J. Barrow, 'Travels in China.'

constantly and listened to the performance with all the airs of a virtuoso. He was so much pleased with some of our instruments that he desired leave to take drawings of them. I was willing to give them to him as a present, but he civilly declined my offer, and I found, indeed, they would have been of no use to him. He, however, sent for a couple of painters, who spread the floor with a few sheets of large paper, placed the clarionets, flutes, bassoons, and French horns upon them, and then traced with their pencils the figures of the instruments, measuring all the apertures and noting the minutest particulars, and when this operation was completed they wrote down their remarks, and delivered them to their master. I was told that his intention is to have similar instruments made here by Chinese workmen, and to fit them to a scale of his own.

But what seemed to attract more general notice than anything in the house were the King and Queen's pictures in their royal robes, by Sir Joshua Reynolds, which were hung up opposite the state canopy, in the grand saloon through which we usually passed to the concert room. Indeed, so very great was the crowd of people to see them, as soon as they came to be talked of, that I was obliged to apply to Van-ta-gin to regulate the number and quality of the visitors and the hour of admittance.

Their admiration has been also much excited by the presents and specimens of different manufactures which we have to distribute, and by the various little articles of use and convenience which Europeans are accustomed to[1]—our dressing-tables, shaving-glasses, and pocket instruments—but we have been sometimes sufferers a little on these occasions from the eagerness of their curiosity, and from their awkwardness in handling them. The flexible swordblades, of Mr. Gill's manufactory at Birmingham, they were particularly struck with; and Van-ta-gin, to whom as a military man distinguished by wounds and long service I gave a couple, seemed more pleased with them than if I had offered him any other present of a hundred times the value. I am persuaded that if we can introduce them into China as an article of trade there will be a very great demand for them.

[1] 'Although the Chinese are reduced to the necessity of employing foreigners to regulate their calendar and keep their clocks in order, and . . . receive yearly various specimens of art and ingenuity from Europe, yet they pertinaciously affect to consider all the nations of the earth as barbarians in comparison with themselves.'—J. Barrow, 'Travels in China.'

VAN-TA-GIN

THE WAR MANDARIN WHO ACCOMPANIED THE EMBASSY

By WILLIAM ALEXANDER, 1793. *In the British Museum*

To face p. 290

CHINESE COURT CLOTHING

I know it is the policy of the East India Company to increase principally the export of the coarser woollens, and I have little doubt that in a very few years China will call for more of them than we can easily supply; but I would recommend also the sending out our very finest cloths (for what we call superfine in the invoices are really not the very finest), together with assortments of kerseymeres and vigonias. Those we wore ourselves I observed everybody greatly admired. The Emperor has lately permitted cloth to be worn in his presence in the spring and autumn—that is to say, from the 1st of October to the 20th of November, and from the 1st of February to the 1st of April. Light silk is the dress of summer, and satins or damask, lined with fine furs, of the winter.

It being all settled that we should set out early to-morrow for Gehol, the Colao Keen-sa-ta-gin, attended by two Mandarins of high quality with red buttons on their caps, came late this evening to wish me a good journey, and to repeat that the Emperor was impatient to see us, having particularly remarked and being much pleased with our prudence and circumspection in having desired a separate hospital at Cheusan for the sick people of the *Lion*, and a boundary-line to be drawn in order to prevent the sailors from straggling. The Emperor, he said, highly approved of it, and had given orders that Sir Erasmus Gower should do as he wished, that he might stay there as long as he pleased and go away when he pleased. From all this it is evident that every circumstance concerning us and every word that falls from our lips is minutely reported and remembered.

CHAPTER XI

Monday, September 2.—At 6 o'clock a.m. we began our journey. Young Staunton and myself travelled in a neat English post-chaise which I had provided, and which was drawn by four little Tartar horses not eleven hands high, being, I believe, the first piece of Long Acre manufactory that ever rattled along the road to Gehol. Sir George Staunton, having a touch of the gout, went in a palanquin; the other gentlemen of my train, as also the servants, musicians, artists, guards, etc., were accommodated with horses or carriages in such manner as they preferred. Our whole cavalcade amounted to seventy persons, of which forty composed the guard; the rest, amounting to twenty-one, remained behind, some being employed in putting together and arranging the presents at Yuen-min-yuen,[1] and the others either invalids or attendants necessary to be left behind to take care of the house during our absence.

To carry the presents and our beds and baggage, I dare say, exclusive of horses and carriages, there were at least two hundred porters employed who regularly made the same daily journeys that we did. From my hotel, through the city of Pekin, to the gate are four and a half miles, and from thence to our first stage was five miles to Chingho, a small fort enclosed with a wall, where we breakfasted.

---

[1] 'Some of the gentlemen, with part of the guard and of the servants, remained in Pekin, and Dr. Dinwiddie and myself, with two mechanics, had apartments allotted us in the palace of Yuen-min-yuen, where the largest and the most valuable of the presents were to be fitted up for the inspection of the old Emperor on his return from Tartary.'—J. Barrow, 'Travels in China.'

Mr. Barrow had previously arranged with the Palace officials that he should go to and from the capital whenever he pleased during the absence of the Emperor, and a horse and covered cart was placed at his disposal.

During all this day, the neat husbandry of the country, the industry of the people, the air of business that appears in their faces, the goodness of the road, and the circumstance of travelling in a post-chaise, almost made me imagine myself in England, and recalled a thousand pleasing ideas to my remembrance.

Tuesday, September 3.—From Nant-chut-see, which we left this morning at 5 a.m., we reached the suburbs of Hoai-zeon-shien, a city of the third order (eight and a half miles), in less than two hours, and after breakfasting there, we, in two hours and a half more (twelve miles), came to a palace of the Emperor near Min-yu-shien, a city of the third order also, where we proposed to sleep. The road was much the same as yesterday. The mountains were tumbled about very agreeably, and must have a cheerful appearance when clothed in verdure; at present they are very brown and dusky. Near this place a part of the Great Wall, stretching over a high, steep hill, was visible on our left for about nine or ten miles distant from the road.

This evening a Tartar officer of high rank, and commander of the troops of this district, paid us a visit, and brought us a small present of fruit and sweetmeats. A sensible, gentlemanlike man, and sufficiently informed, as appeared in his conversation, of the pre-eminence of Great Britain in Europe as a civilized, ingenious, and powerful nation. Van-ta-gin, though decorated with the same button and of the same military rank, yet would scarcely venture to sit down in his presence, so great is the respect affected by the Chinese for the Tartars of the Court.

In the course of these last two days both Van-ta-gin and Chou-ta-gin took their turns to come into the post-chaise with me, and were inexpressibly pleased and astonished with its easiness, lightness, and rapidity, the ingenuity of the springs, and the various contrivances for raising and lowering the glasses, curtains, and jalousies. It comes out in conversation that the Legate has never dispatched my letter to Sir Erasmus Gower, and this day he has returned it to me with a trifling excuse for his not sending it. He said it did not appear, from what I had told him, to be of any importance, and in truth it was of very little. What can be the meaning of this? To-morrow he is to leave us in order that he may get to Gehol a day or two sooner, and have things ready there for our reception.

Thursday, September 5.—From You-chin-sa to Cou-pe-kiou, where we stopped to breakfast, are thirteen miles. After breakfast we set out from Cou-pe-kiou in order to visit this celebrated wall which we had heard such wonders of, and after passing through the outermost gate on the Tartar side, we began our peregrination on foot, there being no other method of approach. In less than half an hour, after travelling over very rough ground, we at last arrived at a breach in the wall, by which we ascended to the top of it.

If the other parts of the wall be similar to those which I have seen, it is certainly the most stupendous work of human hands, for I imagine that if the outline of all the masonry of all the forts and fortified places in the whole world besides were to be calculated, it would fall considerably short of that of the Great Wall of China. It is still in some places which I saw quite perfect and entire, and looks as if recently built or repaired, but in general it is in a ruinous condition, and falling fast to decay, very little care being taken to preserve it.

It was not without a little management that we contrived to examine this wall so much at our leisure, for some of our conductors appeared rather uneasy at the length of our stay upon it. They were astonished at our curiosity, and almost began to suspect us, I believe, of dangerous designs. Van-ta-gin and Chou-ta-gin, though they had passed it twenty times before, had never visited it but once, and few of the other attending Mandarins had ever visited it at all. From Cou-pe-kiou are eleven miles to Liou-king-fong, which ends this day's journey. A little incident has happened at this place which strongly marks the jealousy that subsists between the Chinese and the Tartars. A Tartar servant of the lowest class attending at the Palace had, it seems, stolen some of the utensils furnished for our accommodation, and when taxed with the theft by Van-ta-gin and Chou-ta-gin, answered with so much impertinence that they ordered him to be smartly bambooed on the spot. The moment he was released he broke out into the most insolent expressions, and insisted that a Chinese Mandarin had no right to bamboo a Tartar without side of the Great Wall.[1] The punishment was, however, repeated in such

---

[1] 'A Chinese, after receiving a certain number of strokes, falls down on his knees, as a matter of course, before him who has ordered

EXTRACT FROM THE TIEN-SING GAZETTE

a manner as not only to make him restore the stolen goods, but repent of his topographical objection to it. I suspect, however, that there was some sort of ground for his distinction, but that the commission of our conductors was sufficiently extensive to overrule it, and supersede it by any local immunities. Van-ta-gin could not help saying to our interpreter on this occasion: '*A Tartar will always be a Tartar.*'

Chou-ta-gin tells me he has every reason to believe that my proposal relative to the ceremonial will be approved of.

Friday, September 6.—Our journey to-day was very short, it being only thirteen miles from Liou-king-fong to Ching-chang-you, where we mean to sleep. It was remarkably sharp this morning; the farther we advance among the mountains we find the weather grow colder.

The country here has a very Alpine appearance, much resembling Savoy and Switzerland.

This evening our interpreter amused us with an extract from one of the Tien-sing gazettes, which seem to be much on a par with our own newspapers for wit and authenticity. In an account given there of the presents said to be brought for the Emperor from England the following articles are mentioned: Several dwarfs or little men not twelve inches high, but in form and intellect as perfect as grenadiers; an elephant not larger than a cat, and a horse the size of a mouse; a singing-bird as big as a hen, that feeds upon charcoal, and devours usually fifty pounds per day; and, lastly, an enchanted pillow, on which whoever lays his head immediately falls asleep, and if he dreams of any distant place, such as Canton, Formosa, or Europe, is instantly transported thither without the fatigue of travelling. This little anecdote, however ridiculous, I thought would not be fair to leave out of my journal.

Sunday, September 8.—This morning we set out from Cola-cho-you, which is twelve miles from Gehol, and we stopped at Quon-ur-long, two miles short of Gehol, in order to dress and marshal the procession for my public entry.

---

the punishment, thanking him in the most humble manner for the fatherly kindness he has testified towards his son in thus putting him in mind of his errors. A Tartar grumbles, and disputes the point as to the right a Chinese may have to flog him, or he turns away in sullen silence.'—J. Barrow, 'Travels in China.'

It was arranged in the following manner, and made a very splendid show :

> One hundred Mandarins on horseback.
> Lieutenant-Colonel Benson.
> Four light Dragoons.
> Lieutenant Parish.
> Drum.   Fife.
> Four Artillerymen.
> Four Artillerymen.
> A Corporal of Artillery.
> Lieutenant Crewe.
> Four Infantry.
> Four Infantry.
> Four Infantry.
> Four Infantry.
> A Sergeant of Infantry.
> Two Servants ⎫
> Two Servants ⎪
> Two Servants ⎪
> Two Servants ⎬ in a rich green-and-gold livery.
> Two Couriers ⎪
> Two musicians ⎪
> Two musicians ⎭
> Two gentlemen of the Embassy ⎫ in a uniform of
> Two gentlemen of the Embassy ⎬ scarlet embroidered
> Two gentlemen of the Embassy ⎭ with gold.
> Lord Macartney   ⎫
> Sir George Staunton and son ⎬ in a chariot.
> A servant in livery behind.

We were near two hours from Quon-ur-long to the palace prepared for us at Gehol, which is spacious and convenient. All the luggage, presents, etc., etc., were already arrived before us.[1]

Our journey upon the whole has been very pleasant and, being divided into seven days, not at all fatiguing. At the end of every stage we have been lodged and entertained in the wings or houses adjoining to the Emperor's palaces. These palaces, which occur at small distances from each other on the road, have been built for his reception on his annual visit to Tartary. They are all constructed nearly upon the same plan.

[1] 'The presents brought to Gehol were two hundred pieces of narrow coarse cloth, chiefly black and blue ; two large telescopes ; two air-guns ; two fowling-pieces, one inlaid with gold, the other with silver ; two pair of richly inlaid saddle pistols ; two boxes, each containing seven pieces of Irish tabinets ; two saddles and riding harness, richly ornamented ; two large boxes of fine British carpets.'
—Æneas Anderson, ' Narrative of Embassy to China.'

The common road from Pekin to Gehol is, in general, pretty good for the last two days, but I must observe that there is another road parallel to it, which is laid off for the sole use of the Sovereign, no other person being permitted to travel upon it, a circumstance of Imperial appropriation which I do not recollect even in Muscovy or Austria. As the Emperor is expected to return to Pekin in the latter end of this month, the repair of this road is already begun, and we calculated that in the hundred and thirty-six miles from Pekin to Gehol above twenty-three thousand troops were employed upon it. Almost close to the road, at various distances, are towers or military posts, each post having from six to fifteen soldiers attached to it, who all turned out as we passed along, and fired a salute for us from three small chambers of iron fixed vertically in the ground, while a brass gong rattled upon the parade and a yellow flag fluttered upon the battlements.

The garrison of Gehol during the Emperor's residence is about a hundred thousand men.

Gehol, Sunday, September 8 (*continued*).—Soon after we arrived at this place the Legate came and gave me back my paper about the ceremonial, and said that if I delivered it myself to the Minister I should receive the answer.

Our interpreter also came, and told me from Van-ta-gin and Chou-ta-gin that the Emperor had seen my entry and procession from one of the heights of this park, and was much pleased with them, and that he immediately ordered the first Minister and another Colao to wait upon me. In the meantime Van-ta-gin and Chou-ta-gin themselves arrived, and told me that as there would not be sufficient room in my apartment for all the first Minister's suite, he, the first Minister, hoped I would excuse him from coming to me in person, and that it would be the same thing if I would be so good as to come to him; they added that the first Minister had received a hurt in his knee, which rendered it inconvenient and painful to him to move much about. It being very hot weather, and the servants being very much hurried and fatigued with the operations of the day, and our baggage, etc., not being yet unpacked or put into order, I excused myself with a civil compliment, but told them that if there was any business necessary to mention immediately, Sir George Staunton should attend the first Minister in the evening.

They then informed me that the Tartar Legate had been censured by the Emperor for some misrepresentation with regard to the Embassy, and had been already punished by a degradation of three ranks. The Emperor, having heard that I had his picture in my cabin on board the *Lion*, asked the Legate whether it was like him, upon which it came out that the Legate had never been near the *Lion*, which he had been ordered to visit. It was said that he was afraid of the water, and therefore would not venture, not suspecting that his omission would be discovered.[1]

Soon after several Mandarins of high rank came to visit me,[2] some of them wearing yellow vests, which are marks of particular favour from the Emperor.

The Minister having signified a desire this afternoon of seeing Sir George Staunton, he immediately went with his son and our interpreter to the Minister's house, which is about a mile from my hotel, having passed through a great part of the town of Gehol in his way to it. There he found the Legate at the door, who conducted him to an apartment, where the Minister was sitting, attended by four other Colaos, all having red buttons on their caps, and two of them dressed in yellow vests. On Sir George Staunton's return I found that the Minister's objects were to know the contents of the King's letter to the Emperor (of which a copy was accordingly promised to be given by him), and to contrive means of avoiding, if possible, the compliment to His Majesty, in return for my compliance with the Chinese ceremony, as proposed in my paper, which it was apparent the Minister had seen before the Legate had given it back to me. Sir George now delivered it to the Minister officially from me.

Monday, September 9.—The Legate, Van-ta-gin, and Chou-ta-gin came this morning to urge me to give up the reciprocal compliment I demanded, but I dwelt upon the propriety of something to distinguish between the homage

[1] 'The peacock's feather, which he wore as a sign of his master's favour, was exchanged for a crow's tail, the sign of great disgrace; and the consideration of his age and his family alone saved him from banishment.'—J. Barrow, 'Travels in China.'

[2] 'During the visit the attendants were very busily employed in examining the dress of the English servants, the lace of which they rubbed with a stone to certify its quality, and then, looking at each other with an air of surprise, they shook their heads and smiled—a sufficient proof that they clearly comprehended the inferior value of the trimmings that decorated the liveries of the Embassy. They appeared to be a polite and pleasant people, and of an agreeable appearance.'—Æneas Anderson, 'Narrative of Embassy to China.'

of tributary Princes and the ceremony used on the part of a great independent Sovereign. I understand privately that the Emperor is not acquainted with the difficulties that have arisen on the subject, but that when he is the matter will probably be adjusted as I wish.[1]

Tuesday, September 10.—This day the Legate, Van-ta-gin, and Chou-ta-gin renewed the conversation of yesterday relative to the ceremony, in the course of which I told them it was not natural to expect that an Ambassador should pay greater homage to a foreign Prince than to his own Sovereign, unless a return were made to him that might warrant him to do more. Upon which they asked me what was the cere-

---

[1] 'From the time the Ambassador began to make conditions his table was abridged, under an idea that he might be starved into an unconditional compliance. Finding this experiment fail, they had recourse to a different conduct, and became all kindness and complaisance.'—J. Barrow, ' Travels in China.'

' Though it cannot be supposed that such a conference as was this morning held between the British Ambassador and the Mandarins would be communicated to the general attendants on the Embassy, yet we could not resist the spirit of conjecture on the occasion. The following circumstance which took place this morning did not serve to dissipate that disposition to forebode ill which prevailed among us. The Ambassador ordered Mr. Winder to intimate to the servants that in case they should find in the course of the day any deficiency in their provisions, they should not complain to the people who supplied them, but leave them untouched, and intimate the grievance to his Excellency, who requested, for very particular and weighty reasons, that this order might be punctually observed. It excited no small degree of astonishment that we should be ordered to prepare ourselves for ill-treatment in the article of provisions, of which we had hitherto been served, and had so little reason to complain. Our treatment in this respect had been not only hospitable, but bounteous in the extreme. However, when dinner came, instead of that abundance with which our tables had hitherto been served, there was not now a sufficient quantity of provisions for half the persons who were ready to partake of them. The emotions of everyone . . . were very unpleasant upon the occasion. We felt . . . the Embassy was treated with disrespect. We had our feelings as Britons, and felt the insult. . . . The meagre meal was therefore left untouched, and complaints were preferred to his Excellency. Mr. Plumb, the interpreter, was requested to communicate the cause of discontent to the Mandarins, nor was the remonstrance without an immediate effect. Five minutes after it was made each table was served with a variety of hot dishes, not only in plenty, but in profusion.'—Æneas Anderson, ' Narrative of Embassy to China.'

mony of presentation to the King of England. I told them it was performed by kneeling upon one knee and kissing His Majesty's hand. 'Why, then,' cried they, 'cannot you do so to the Emperor?' 'Most readily,' said I; 'the same ceremony I perform to my own King I am willing to go through for your Emperor, and I think it a greater compliment than any other I can pay him.' I showed them the manner of it, and they retired seemingly well satisfied. In the afternoon Chou-ta-gin came to me alone, and said that he had seen the Minister, and had a long conference with him upon this business, the result of which was that either the English mode of presentation (which I had shown them in the morning) or the picture ceremony should be adopted, but he had not yet decided which.

I said nothing. Soon after the Legate arrived, and declared that it was finally determined to adopt the English ceremony, only that, as it was not the custom in China to kiss the Emperor's hand, he proposed I should kneel upon both knees instead of it. I told him I had already given my answer, which was to kneel upon one knee only on those occasions when it was usual for the Chinese to prostrate themselves. 'Well, then,' said they, 'the ceremony of kissing the Emperor's hand must be omitted.' To this I assented, saying, 'As you please, but remember it is your doing, and, according to your proposal, it is but half the ceremony, and you see I am willing to perform the whole one.' And thus ended this anxious negotiation, which has given me a tolerable insight into the character of this Court, and that political address upon which they so much value themselves.

Wednesday, September 11.—At half-past 9 a.m. the Legate, Van-ta-gin, and Chou-ta-gin came to my house to attend me to the Minister or chief Colao. His palace is very spacious, and consists of several courts, through which we passed before we arrived at his apartment, which is small and has nothing magnificent in furniture or appearance. He received us with great affability, and seemed, as Sir George Staunton told me, quite a different sort of person from what he appeared a few days go. He is a handsome, fair man about forty to forty-five years old, quick and fluent. On his right hand was the Fou-li-ou, a handsome, fair man also, of about thirty years old, and on his left two old Chinese Colaos, one the President of the Court of Rites and the other the President of the Tribunal of Finance, and at the end of all was another great man in a yellow vest, but who did not seem of equal authority with the others.

I began by saying that, being now recovered from the fatigue of my journey, I was happy to have an early opportunity of waiting upon him and expressing my wishes to present the King's letter to the Emperor as soon as possible, every difficulty being now obviated.

I said that in the meantime I had made many inquiries about the Emperor's health, and was rejoiced to hear that it was so good as to promise long life to him, and consequently much happiness to his subjects, and that it would give sincere pleasure to the greatest Sovereign in the West to hear such good news from the greatest Sovereign of the East. The Minister made some compliments in return, and said that, on account of the very great distance from which the Embassy had been sent, and of the value of the presents, some of the Chinese customs (which had hitherto been invariably observed) would now be relaxed, and that I might perform the ceremony after the manner of my own country, and deliver the King's letter into the Emperor's own hands. So now these preliminary difficulties are over, and Saturday next, being a grand festival at Court, is fixed for the day of my introduction. In the course of this conversation, which lasted a considerable time, he asked me several questions relative to our voyage—where we had stopped on the way, and for what purposes. Having mentioned our putting in at Turon Bay, in Cochin China, for water, he observed to me that that country was a tributary and dependance of China. He inquired how far England was from Russia, and whether they were good friends together, and whether Italy and Portugal were not near England and tributary to it. I explained to him the distance between England and Russia in Chinese measure, and repeated that we were at present at peace with all the world, and with the Empress of Russia as well as with others, but that there did not seem to be the same cordiality at present as formerly, on account of the King of England (who is a lover of peace and justice, and a friend of the distressed) having once interfered to repress a spirit of encroachment shown in some of her measures with regard to Turkey. As to Italy and Portugal, they were not tributaries of England, but, from the same motives of general justice and equity before mentioned, the King of England had often afforded them protection and shown them marks of his friendship. When I arose to go away the Minister took me by the hand, and said he should be happy to cultivate my acquaintance, and hoped to have frequent opportunities of seeing me familiarly at Yuen-min-yuen, as the bustle and hurry of business and the festivals of the Emperor's Anniversary must necessarily engage the greater part of his time whilst the Court remained at Gehol.

In the afternoon our friends Van-ta-gin and Chou-ta-gin visited us, and repeated a great many flattering things which they assured us the Minister had said of us, and that he had made so favourable a report to the Emperor that he was quite impatient for Saturday.

Then the Tartar arrived, and brought us a present of fruit and sweetmeats from the Minister, with a compliment similar to that brought by Van-ta-gin and Chou-ta-gin. We employed the rest of the day in getting the presents put in order.

Thursday, September 12.—And this day they were sent to the Palace to be viewed. Soon after the Legate came to visit me, and brought another present of fruit and sweetments, but seemed much out of sorts.

Friday, September 13.—Van-ta-gin and Chou-ta-gin called on us to say the presents were much approved of,[1] but that it was wished that somebody might be sent to show them how the telescopes were to be put up and used; upon which

[1] 'Among the presents was a collection of prints of the English nobility and distinguished persons. The Emperor was so pleased with it that he sent it immediately to Yuen-min-yuen for translation into the Chinese and Manchoo languages. The Tartar writer got on pretty well, but was not a little puzzled with the letters *b*, *d*, and *r* that so frequently occurred in the English names. The Duke of Marlborough was Too-ke-Ma-ul-po-loo, and Bedford was transformed into Pe-te-fo-ul-te. The rank also was written down, and here a serious difficulty occurred with the Duke of Bedford's portrait, taken from a painting made of him, when a youth, by Sir Joshua Reynolds. I told the Chinese to write down 'Ta-gin,' or Great Man of the second order, to which he observed that it must be the father who was a Ta-gin, and laughed heartily at the idea of a man being born a legislator by hereditary right, as it required many years of close application to enable one of their own countrymen to pass his examination for the lowest order of State offices. As, however, the descendants of Confucius continue to enjoy a nominal rank, and as the Emperor can also confer an hereditary dignity, they considered the Duke might be of this description, and wrote down his rank accordingly. But they positively refused to give him the title of Great Man, or Ta-gin, saying their Emperor was not so stupid as not to know the impossibility of a little boy having attained the rank of a great man.'—J. Barrow, 'Travels in China.'

THE AMBASSADOR'S ATTIRE

Dr. Gillan and our interpreter went and taught the eunuchs how to join them together, to adjust the day and night glasses, and to manage the rack-work. Notwithstanding their complete ignorance, these gentry pretended to understand, at half a word, all the machinery of these instruments, but Dr. Gillan did not leave them till he thought he made them really masters of it. To-morrow being the grand festival at Court, and the day appointed for our first presentation, we are busily employed in getting ready for the occasion.

Saturday, September 14.—This morning at 4 o'clock a.m. we set out for the Court under the convoy of Van-ta-gin and Chou-ta-gin, and reached it in little more than an hour, the distance being about three miles from our hotel. I proceeded in great state with all my train of music, guards, palanquins, and officers and gentlemen of the Embassy on horseback. Over a rich embroidered velvet I wore the mantle of the Order of the Bath, with the collar and diamond badge and a diamond star.[1]

Sir George Staunton was dressed in a rich embroidered velvet also, and, being a Doctor of Laws in the University of Oxford, wore the habit of his degree, which is of scarlet silk, full and flowing. I mention these little particulars to show the attention I always paid, where a proper opportunity offered, to Oriental customs and ideas. We alighted at the park gate, from whence we walked to the Imperial encampment, and were conducted to a large, handsome tent prepared for us on one side of the Emperor's. After waiting there about an hour his approach was announced with drums and music,[2] on which we quitted our tent and came forward upon the green carpet.

---

[1] 'Lord Macartney's dress was of spotted mulberry velvet, with a diamond star and his ribbon, over which he wore the full Order of the Bath, with the hat and plumes of feathers which always form a part of it.'—Æneas Anderson, ' Narrative of Embassy to China.'

'It does not seem that the dress of a foreign Ambassador was considered of much importance by the Chinese. The Dutch, on the occasion of their third Embassy to the Court of China in 1795, wishing to excuse themselves from going to Court on account of their dusty and tattered clothes, the Master of the Ceremonies observed it was not their *dress*, but their *persons*, which the Emperor was desirous of seeing.'—J. Barrow, ' Travels in China.'

[2] 'The Emperor was preceded by a number of persons busied in proclaiming aloud his virtues and his powers.'—Sir G. Staunton, ' Embassy to China.'

He was seated in an open palanquin, carried by sixteen bearers, attended by a number of officers bearing flags, standards, and umbrellas, and as he passed we paid him our compliment by kneeling on one knee, whilst all the Chinese made their usual prostrations.[1] As soon as he had ascended his throne I came to the entrance of the tent, and, holding in both my hands a large gold box enriched with diamonds in which was enclosed the King's letter, I walked deliberately up, and ascending the side-steps of the throne, delivered it into the Emperor's own hands, who, having received it, passed it to the Minister, by whom it was placed on the cushion. He then gave me as the first present from him to His Majesty the Ju-eu-jou or Giou-giou, as the symbol of peace and prosperity, and expressed his hopes that my Sovereign and he should always live in good correspondence and amity. It is a whitish, agate-looking stone about a foot and a half long, curiously carved, and highly prized by the Chinese, but to me it does not appear in itself to be of any great value.

The Emperor then presented me with a Ju-eu-jou of a greenish-coloured stone of the same emblematic character; at the same time he very graciously received from me a pair of beautiful enamelled watches set with diamonds, which I had prepared in consequence of the information given me, and which, having looked at, he passed to the Minister. Sir George Staunton, whom, as he had been appointed Minister Plenipotentiary to act in case of my death or departure, I introduced to him as such, now came forward, and after kneeling upon one knee in the same manner which I had done, presented to him two elegant airguns, and received from him a Ju-eu-jou of a greenish stone nearly similar to mine. Other presents were sent at the same time to all the gentlemen of my train.[2] We then

[1] 'The Emperor was clad in plain dark silk, with a velvet bonnet, in form not much different from the bonnet of Scotch Highlanders; on the front of it was placed a large pearl, which was the only jewel or ornament he appeared to have about him.'—Sir G. Staunton, 'Embassy to China.'

[2] 'The Emperor inquired whether any person of the Embassy understood the Chinese language; and, being informed that the Ambassador's page, a boy then in his thirteenth year, had alone made some proficiency in it, he had the youth brought up to the throne, and desired him to speak Chinese. Either what was said or his modest countenance or manner was so pleasing to his Imperial Majesty that he took from his girdle a purse, hanging from it, for holding

THE APPROACH OF THE EMPEROR OF CHINA TO RECEIVE THE BRITISH AMBASSADOR

From a Drawing by WILLIAM ALEXANDER *in the British Museum*

To face p. 304

A SUMPTUOUS BANQUET

descended from the steps of the throne, and sat down upon cushions at one of the tables on the Emperor's left hand; and at other tables, according to their different ranks, the chief Tartar Princes and the Mandarins of the Court at the same time took their places, all dressed in the proper robes of their respective ranks. These tables were then uncovered and exhibited a most sumptuous banquet.[1] The Emperor sent us several dishes from his own table, together with some liquors, which the Chinese call wine, not, however, expressed from the grape, but distilled or extracted from rice, herbs, and honey. In about half an hour he sent for Sir George Staunton and me to come to him, and gave to each of us, with his own hands, a cup of warm wine, which we immediately drank in his presence, and found it very pleasant and comfortable, the morning being cold and raw.

Amongst other things, he asked me the age of my King, and being informed of it, said he hoped he might live as many years as himself, which are eighty-three. His manner is dignified, but affable and condescending, and his reception of us has been very gracious and satisfactory. He is a very fine old gentleman, still healthy and vigorous, not having the appearance of a man of more than sixty.[2]

---

arecanut, and presented it to him.'—Sir G. Staunton, 'Embassy to China.'

'The Emperor, it was said, received the credentials of the Embassy with a most ceremonious formality. All, however, that we could learn, as a matter of indubitable occurrence, was the notice His Imperial Majesty was pleased to take of Master Staunton, the son of Sir George Staunton. He appeared much struck with the boy's vivacity and deportment, and expressed his admiration of the faculty which the young gentleman possessed of speaking six languages. The Emperor presented him with his hand with a very beautiful fan and several small bags and purses, and commanded the interpreter to signify that he thought highly of his talents and appearance.'—Æneas Anderson, 'Narrative of Embassy to China.'

[1] 'The tables were small, but on each was a pyramid of dishes or bowls piled upon each other, containing viands and fruits in vast variety. A table was placed for His Imperial Majesty before the throne, and he seemed to partake heartily of the fare that was set before him. Tea was also served. The dishes and cups were carried to him with hands uplifted over the head.'—Sir G. Staunton, 'Embassy to China.'

[2] 'At the age of eighty-three he had the appearance and activity of a hale man of sixty. His mind was extremely active, and he was prompt and resolute. He was kind and charitable towards his

The order and regularity in serving and removing the dinner was wonderfully exact, and every function of the ceremony performed with such silence and solemnity as in some measure to resemble the celebration of a religious mystery.[1] The Emperor's tent or pavilion, which is circular, I should calculate to be about twenty-four or twenty-six yards in diameter, and is supported by a number of pillars, either gilded, painted, or varnished, according to their distance or position.

---

subjects, on many occasions remitting taxes and administering relief in periods of distress. But he was often vindictive and relentless towards his enemies, and his impatient, irascible temper led him to act with injustice and too great severity. It once was the cause of a severe and lasting affliction to himself. And his mind is said to have never recovered from the gloom and melancholy consequent upon his action.

'About the middle of his reign he made a circuit through his Empire, and at the town of San-tchoo-foo (celebrated for its beautiful women) the Emperor was captivated with a girl of extraordinary beauty and talents, whom he intended to carry back with him to his capital. The Empress, on hearing this news through one of the eunuchs, became so depressed and unhappy that she put an end to her life by hanging herself. The Emperor, on receipt of the news, was greatly distressed, and hurried to Pekin. One of his sons was doubtful as to what clothing he should appear in before his father. Ought it to be deep mourning for his mother, which might be construed as an insult to his father? Or should he appear in robes of ceremony, which would be disrespectful to the memory of his mother? In this dilemma he consulted his schoolmaster, who, in true Chinese fashion, advised him to put on both. The Prince followed this advice, but, unfortunately, covered the mourning with the ceremonial habit. Tchien-lung, who was deeply lamenting the fate of his Empress, to whom he appears to have been sincerely attached, on perceiving his son at his feet without mourning, became so exasperated and enraged at the supposed want of filial respect that he gave the young man a violent kick which caused his death.

'None of his four surviving sons ever possessed any share of the confidence and the authority which in later years he bestowed on his First Minister, Cho-chang-tong. He seems to have entertained an extreme jealousy of his natural heir.'—J. Barrow, 'Travels in China.'

[1] 'No conversation among the guests, no bustle among the attendants. The commanding feature of the scene was the solemnity and silence with which the whole business was conducted.'— Sir G. Staunton, 'Embassy to China,'

The material and distribution of the furniture within at once displayed grandeur and elegance. The tapestry, the curtains, the carpets, the lanterns, the fringes, and the tassels were disposed with such harmony, the colours so artfully varied, and the light and shade so judiciously managed, that the whole assemblage filled the eye with delight, and diffused over the mind a pleasing serenity and repose undisturbed by glitter or affected embellishments.

The commanding feature of the ceremony was that calm dignity, that sober pomp of Asiatic greatness, which European refinements have not yet attained.[1]

I forgot to mention that there were present on this occasion three ambassadors from Tatze or Pigu and six Mahommedan ambassadors from the Calmucks of the south-west, but their appearance was not very splendid. Neither must I omit that, during the ceremony, which lasted five hours, various entertainments of wrestling, tumbling, and wire-dancing, together with dramatic representations, were exhibited to the tent, but at a considerable distance from it.

Thus have I seen ' *King Solomon in all his glory*.' I use this expression, as the scene recalled perfectly to my memory a puppet show of that name which I recollect to have seen in my childhood, and which made so strong an impression on my mind that I then thought it a true representation of the highest pitch of human greatness and felicity.[2]

---

[1] 'During the ceremonies His Imperial Majesty appeared perfectly unreserved, cheerful, and unaffected.' — Sir G. Staunton, ' Embassy to China.'

[2] ' Soon after the Ambassador's return home, he received from the Emperor presents of silks, porcelain, and tea for himself and all the gentlemen of his suite. The silks were of a grave colour such as were worn by men. Some were woven into patterns of dresses, with the four-clawed dragon or Imperial tiger, and some with the Chinese pheasant. The porcelain consisted of detached pieces, slightly differing in form from those which we generally exported. The tea was made up into balls of different sizes by means of a glutinous liquid. This species of tea is highly prized in China, but the English preferred that to which they had been accustomed.'— *Ibid.*

' A second cargo of presents arrived from His Imperial Majesty. They consisted of large quantities of rich velvets, silks, and satins, with some Chinese lamps and rare porcelain. To these were added a number of calabash boxes of exquisite workmanship.'—Æneas Anderson, ' Narrative of Embassy to China.'

Sunday, September 15.—The Emperor, having been informed that, in the course of our travels in China, we had shown a strong desire of seeing everything curious and interesting, was pleased to give directions to the first Minister to show us his park or garden at Gehol. It is called in Chinese Van-shou-yuen, which signifies the paradise of innumerable trees.

In order to have this gratification (which is considered as an instance of uncommon favour) we rose this morning at three o'clock, and went to the Palace, where we waited, mixed with all the great officers of state, for three hours (such is the etiquette of the place) till the Emperor's appearance. At last he came forth borne, in the usual manner, by sixteen persons, on a high open palanquin, attended by guards, music, standards, and umbrellas without number, and observing us as we stood in the front line, graciously beckoned us to approach, having ordered his people to stop. He entered into conversation with us, and, with great affability of manner, told us that he was on his way to the pagoda, where he usually paid his morning devotions; that, as we professed a different religion from his, he would not ask us to accompany him, but that he had ordered his first Minister and chief Colaos to conduct us through his gardens, and to show us whatever we were desirous of seeing there.

Having expressed my sense of this mark of his condescension in the proper manner, and my increasing admiration of everything I had yet observed at Gehol, I retired; and whilst he proceeded to his adorations at the pagoda, I accompanied the Minister and other great Colaos of the Court to a pavilion prepared for us, from whence, after a short collation, we set out on horseback to view this wonderful garden. We rode about three miles through a very beautiful park, kept in the highest order, and much resembling the approach to Luton in Bedfordshire; the grounds gently undulated and chequered with various groups of well-contrasted trees in the offship. As we moved onward an extensive lake appeared before us, the extremities of which seemed to lose themselves in distance and obscurity. Here was a large, magnificent yacht ready to receive us, and a number of smaller ones for the attendants, elegantly fitted up and adorned with numberless vases, pendants, and streamers. Where any things particularly interesting were to be seen we disembarked, from time to time, to visit them, and I daresay that in the course of our voyage we stopped at forty or fifty different palaces or pavilions.

THE EMPEROR'S PAVILIONS

These are all furnished in the richest manner, with pictures of the Emperor's huntings and progresses; with stupendous vases of jasper and agate; with the finest porcelain and japan, and with every kind of European toys and sing-songs; with spheres, orreries, clocks, and musical automatons of such exquisite workmanship, and in such profusion, that our presents must shrink from the comparison and *hide their diminished heads.* And yet I am told that the fine things we have seen are far exceeded by others of the same kind in the apartments of the ladies and in the European repository at Yuen-min-yuen. In every one of these pavilions was a throne, or Imperial state, and a Ju-eu-jou, or symbol of peace and prosperity placed at one side of it, resembling that which the Emperor delivered to me yesterday for the King.

It would be an endless task were I to attempt to give a detail of all the wonders of this charming place. There is no beauty of distribution and contrast, no feature of amenity, no reach of fancy which embellishes our pleasure grounds in England, that is not to be found here.

At our taking leave of the Minister he told us that we had only seen the eastern side of the gardens, but that the western side, which was the larger part, still remained for him to show us, and that he should have that pleasure another day. Of the great men who accompanied us on this tour the principal were, 1st, The Minister, or great Colao; 2nd, The Fou-liou, or Second Minister; 3rd, His brother, formerly Viceroy of Canton, but lately named Viceroy of Sechuen; and 4th, Sun-ta-gin, a young man of high quality—all Tartars, and, if I may use the expression, Knights of the Yellow Vest.

Sun-ta-gin had, not long since, been employed upon the frontiers of Russia, to accommodate the disputes with that nation; and knowing that I had been formerly the King's Minister at St. Petersburg, he talked to me a good deal about his own mission. He said that he had negotiated at Kiachta with a great Russian General, who wore a red ribbon and a star like mine, and they very soon understood each other and concluded their business. He was particularly pointed in his civilities to us, seemed very intelligent, and asked many proper questions relative to the riches and power of Russia. It would seem as if he was selected on purpose to try the extent of my knowledge, or of my sincerity, by comparing my answers with his own notions upon the subject.

During the whole course of the day the First Minister, or Colao, paid us very great attention, and displayed all the good breeding and politeness of an experienced courtier, though I am afraid I can already perceive that his heart is not with us, for, on my mentioning to him this morning, as we rode along, that the creation of such a paradise as Gehol in so wild a spot was a work worthy of the genius of the great Cam-shi, he seemed to be quite astonished how I came to know that it was undertaken by Cam-shi, and asked me who told me so. I said that, as the English were a wise and learned nation, and acquainted with the history of all countries, it was not to be wondered at that they should be particularly well informed of the history of the Chinese, whose fame extended to the most distant parts of the world. Notwithstanding this compliment was a natural and a flattering one, he did not seem to me to feel it so; and I suspect that at the bottom he rather wonders at our curiosity than esteems us for our knowledge. Possibly he may consider it as impertinent towards them and useless to ourselves.

The Fou-liou or Second Minister's deportment towards us was very gracious. Not so that of his brother, which was formal and repulsive. I mentioned above that he had been Viceroy of Canton, and it would appear that he has not been an inattentive observer of European manners and character.

I could not avoid remarking it this morning, for, happening to be next to me at the moment, I approached the Emperor, and perhaps not thinking me quick enough in my motions, he pulled me by the sleeve, and at the same time, though with an air of complaisance and respect, touched my hat with his hand to indicate his wishes that I should take it off on the occasion—a thing that could scarcely have occurred to any of his brother courtiers, as the salutation of the hat is entirely a European custom, and only used by Europeans, the Asiatics never uncovering their heads, even in the presence of their most elevated superior.

Well aware of his connections and consequence, I was desirous of conciliating him to our interests, and endeavoured to soothe his vanity on the points where he was thought most accessible. I told him that I had often heard of his reputation as a warrior, and therefore I hoped that the exercise of my guard and their military evolutions, with the latest European improvements, might afford him some pleasure and entertainment. But he declined the proposal with great coldness and a mixture of unreasonable vanity, saying that nothing of that kind could be a novelty to him, though I have my doubts whether he ever saw a firelock in his life; at least, I am sure *I* have never yet seen anything above a matchlock among all the troops in China. But another incident in the course of our tour more strongly marked his indisposition towards us. The Minister having informed me that an account was just received of the arrival of the *Lion* and the *Hindostan* at Cheusan, I seized the opportunity of requesting that Captain Mackintosh (in whose ship the greater part of the presents for the Emperor had been brought), having paid his obeisance to the Emperor, might be permitted to proceed, and join his ship at the port where she now lay, but Fou-chang-tong interposed, and said that it was improper, and against the laws of China, for strangers to be permitted to travel about in such a manner through the provinces of the Empire. Nor could any reasoning of mine, though conveyed to him in the gentlest and most flattering terms, induce him to relax his opinion, or draw even a smile from him for the rest of the day. Whether whilst at Canton he may have met with some unintentional slight, or whether —which is more probable—he may have remarked (for he is certainly a man of capacity) and felt, with regret and indignation, that superiority which, wherever Englishmen go, they cannot conceal from the most indifferent observer, I know not. Finding this moment so unfavourable, I declined pressing the matter further, but requested the Minister to allow me a short conference with him, either the next day or the day following. I found, however, that, though infinitely gracious and civil in his manner and expression, I could gain no ground upon him. He excused himself on account of the approaching ceremony of the birthday, and the load of business on his hands requiring dispatch before the departure of the Court from Gehol, and repeated to me, as he had done in his first conference, that he hoped to have frequent opportunities of seeing me at Yuen-min-yuen and cultivating my friendship there. I therefore take it for granted it has been a settled point from the beginning to do no business with me at Gehol. I, however, before we parted, persuaded him to consent to receive a short note, which I said I should take the liberty of sending him in a day or two. This is now my only resource, and I must, therefore, set about it without further delay.

Monday, September 16. — Having now twice paid our obeisance to the Emperor, we conceived, from what had been told us before we left Pekin, that we might go freely about and walk abroad without constraint and impediment. To avoid anything, however, that might commit my character, I continued within doors; Sir George Staunton and some other gentlemen made a little excursion into the country to-day; but they were followed the whole way by a number of Mandarins and soldiers, who, though they never attempted to direct their motions, still attended them at no great distance.

Thus I see that the same strange jealousy prevails towards us which the Chinese Government has always shown to other foreigners, although we have taken such pains to disarm it, and to conciliate their friendship and confidence. Perhaps our conductors are apprehensive that, from the novelty of our appearance and the singularity of our dress, we may be subjected to rude curiosity, and that some disturbance might arise for which they must be responsible, it being, as I am informed, a maxim of the Chinese Government never to excuse an officer for any accident that may happen in his department.

This morning Cho-chan-tong, the First Minister, sent for Dr. Gillan, and without hesitation explained to him all his ailments—his rupture, his rheumatism, etc., etc.—and desired the doctor's opinion of his case. The doctor is now preparing it, and has promised me a copy.[1]

I received a visit this afternoon from a genteel young Tartar, decorated with a smooth red button and a peacock's feather of two eyes. His Manchoo name is Poo-ta-vang, his Chinese one Mou-liou. He affects to be well informed of the geography and history of his country. He told me that the present Emperor is descended from Co-be-li, or, as we call him, Kubla-Khan, a son of Gengis Khan, who, in

[1] 'Dr. Gillan accompanied the messenger to the Colao's house, where he found assembled some of the principal persons of the faculty then at Court, who were attending with no little anxiety upon their illustrious patient. The Colao desired the Doctor's explanation of the nature of his ailments, together with the methods of relief and cure which he proposed, to be put down in writing. He made him a present of a piece of silk, and was pleased to say that his ideas appeared clear and rational, though they were so new and distant from the notions prevalent in Asia that they seemed as if they came from the inhabitant of another planet.'—Sir G. Staunton, 'Embassy to China.'

the thirteenth century, conquered China, and whose family (called the dynasty of Yen-tchao) held it under the Mongul yoke for near one hundred years, till dethroned by the dynasty of Ming. The Monguls, who then fled in the country of the Mantchoo, intermarried and mixed with them, and from one of these alliances sprung the Bogdoi Khans,[1] who invaded China in 1640, and have reigned over it ever since. Poo-ta-vang says that all the Tartar Princes who dined with us in the Emperor's tent are persons of great consequence, have numerous clans dependent upon them, and can bring large bodies of troops into the field. They are often called upon in time of war, and have their respective stations, rank, and duty assigned to them under the grand banners of Tartary. Their lands, or fiefs, were formerly hereditary by primogeniture, and are properly so still; but it is now necessary for the eldest son, on the death of his father, to receive a sort of investiture from the Emperor, who, if no objection arises, never refuses it. They seem like the honours of the *Casas Titulares* in Portugal. These Tartar Princes usually marry the daughters and nieces of the Imperial family, and hold a certain rank at Court in consequence of the alliance. They are obliged to come every year to attend the Emperor's birthday, and then return home, being seldom detained, or employed in China in offices that require much literature, as their education is usually directed to military pursuits.

Their weapons are chiefly the scimitar and the bow and arrow, in the exercise of which they are remarkably expert. They seemed a good deal surprised when I once told them, in answer to their enquiries, that we had left off the use of the bow in Europe, and fought chiefly with firearms in its place. The bow is the Emperor's favourite instrument of war; and I observe that he is always represented in the pictures as shooting at stags, wolves, and tigers with arrows, and never with a musket.

Poo-ta-vang says that Moukden, or Chin-yan-tsin, as the Chinese call it, the Emperor's Tartar capital, which is about two hundred miles off, is larger than Pekin,[2] and that the Emperor has immense treasures there. Scarcely any

[1] Lord Macartney remarks in a note: 'N.B.—I do not find, upon enquiry from others, that this genealogy is quite unequivocal.'

[2] 'According to the best information given to the Embassy, the population of Pekin was about three millions. In the last century the Jesuit Grimaldi estimated it at about sixteen millions.'—Sir G. Staunton, 'Embassy to China.'

Chinese have ever been at Moukden, or, indeed, many miles beyond Gehol.

Tuesday, September 17.—This day being the Emperor's birthday, we set out for the Court at 3 o'clock a.m., conducted by Van-ta-gin, Chou-ta-gin, and our usual attendants.[1] We reposed ourselves for above two hours in a large saloon at the entrance of the palace enclosure, where fruit, tea, warm milk, and other refreshments were brought to us. At last notice was given that the festival was going to begin, and we immediately descended the stairs into the garden, where we found all the great men and Mandarins in their robes of state, drawn up before the Imperial pavilion. The Emperor did not show himself, but remained behind a screen, from whence, I presume, he could see and enjoy the ceremonies without inconvenience or interruption. All eyes were turned towards the place where His Majesty was imagined to be enthroned, and seemed to express an impatience to begin the devotions of the day. Slow, solemn music, muffled drums, and deep-toned bells were heard at a distance. On a sudden the sound ceased, and all was still; again it was renewed, and then intermitted with short pauses, during which several persons passed backwards and forwards, in the proscenium or foreground of the tent, as if engaged in preparing some *grand coup de théâtre*.

At length the great band struck up with all their powers of harmony, and instantly the whole Court fell flat upon their faces before this invisible Nebuchadnezzar. 'He in his cloudy tabernacle sojourned the while.' The music was a sort of birthday ode or State anthem, the burden of which was '*Bow down your heads, all ye dwellers upon earth; bow down your heads before the great Kien-long, the great Kien-long.*' And then all the dwellers upon China earth there present, except ourselves, bowed down their heads, and prostrated themselves upon the ground at every renewal of the chorus. Indeed, in no religion, ancient or modern, has the Divinity ever been addressed, I believe, with stronger exterior marks of worship and adoration than

[1] 'The appearance of the suite was exactly the same as on the first day of audience, and we returned, in an equal state of embarrassment and fatigue, at one o'clock. A very large quantity of presents soon followed us, consisting of the same kind of articles as had been already sent, but of different colours and patterns. There were, however, added a profusion of fruits and confectionery.'—Æneas Anderson, 'Narrative of Embassy to China.'

were this morning paid to the phantom of his Chinese Majesty.

Such is the mode of celebrating the Emperor's anniversary, according to the Court ritual.[1]

We saw nothing of him the whole day, nor did any of his Ministers, I imagine, approach him, for they all seemed to retire at the same moment as we did. Of them, the first, or great Colao, Cho-chan-tong, the Fou-liou, the Fou-liou's brother Fou-chan-tong, and Sun-ta-gin, with other great men who attended us two days since in our visit

[1] 'On the Emperor's birthday [at Yuen-min-yuen] all the Princes and officers in the palace assembled in their robes of ceremony in the great hall to make obeisance to the throne. Before it were placed on the floor, on three small tripods, a cup of tea, of oil, and of rice, as an acknowledgment of the Emperor being the proprietor of the soil, of which these are three material products.

'Two mornings after, every one appeared much upset in the palace; the old eunuch in so sullen a mood that he could not be induced to speak, and different groups of officers assembled in the courtyard, all looking as if something very dreadful had occurred, or was going to occur. Deodati also appeared with a no less woeful countenance, and said that the Embassy was lost, ruined, and undone. Lord Macartney had refused to comply with the ceremony of prostrating himself nine times before the Emperor, like Ambassadors of tributary Princes, unless one of equal rank with himself should go through the same ceremony before the portrait of the King of England; and that, rather than do this, they had accepted his offer to perform the same ceremony as to his own Sovereign. Although little was thought of this affair at Gehol, the great officers of State in Pekin, in the Tribunal of Ceremonies, were mortified, perplexed, and alarmed at an event unprecedented in the annals of the Empire. The Emperor, when he began to think more seriously over the subject, might possibly impeach before the criminal tribunal those who had advised him to accede to such a proposal, on reflecting how much his dignity had suffered by the compliance. Also that the records of the country might hand it down to posterity as an event tarnishing the lustre of his reign, being nothing short of breaking through an ancient custom, and adopting one of a barbarous nation in its place.

'Every one remained in much ill-humour for several days, showed it by materially affecting the table, both as to number and quality of dishes. It wore off, however, after a time, although the Princes who had been daily visitors now kept entirely away; and the old eunuch, when put out of his way, used to apply the epithet of "proud, headstrong Englishmen."'—From J. Barrow's 'Travels in China.'

to the eastern garden, now proposed to accompany us to the western garden, which forms a strong contrast with the other, and exhibits all the sublimer beauties of Nature in as high a degree as the part which we saw before possesses the attraction of softness and amenity.

In the course of this day's tour, as in the former one, we were entertained with a collection of *petits pâtés*, salt relishes, and other savoury dishes, with fruit and sweetmeats, milk and ice-water, and as soon as we rose from table a number of yellow boxes or drawers were carried in procession before us, containing several pieces of silk and porcelain, which we were told were presents to us from the Emperor, and we consequently made our bows as they passed. We were also amused with a Chinese puppet-show, which differs but little from an English one. There are a distressed Princess confined in a castle, and a knight-errant, who, after fighting lions and dragons, sets her at liberty and marries her, wedding-feasts, jousts, and tournament.

Besides these there is a comic drama, in which Punch and his wife, Bandimeer and Scaramouch, perform capital parts.

This puppet-show, we were told, properly belongs to the ladies' apartments, but was sent out, as a particular compliment, to entertain us. One of the performances was exhibited with great applause from our conductors, and I understand it is a favourite piece at Court.

I could not help admiring the address with which the Minister parried all my attempts to speak to him on business this day, and how artfully he evaded every opportunity that offered for any particular conversation with me, endeavouring to engage our attention solely to the objects around us, directing our eyes to the prospect, and explaining the various beauties of the park and buildings. I, nevertheless, found an occasion to remind him of his promise to peruse the note, which I meant to send him, and told him that it would be ready to-morrow. It was now near 3 o'clock, when, he said, he must take his leave of us, at the same time expressing his concern that affairs of consequence required his attendance; but he added that he left us under the care of the Colao Sun-ta-gin, who would accompany us to the grand pagoda at Pou-ta-la, and the others in its neighbourhood. The Fou-liou and his brother went away with the first Minister.

Pou-ta-la is an immense edifice, and, with the offices belonging to it, covers a vast deal of ground. In the chapel we found all the monks or lamas busily engaged in their devotions, dressed in yellow vestments, with books in their hands, and chanting their liturgy in a kind of recitative, not unlike our cathedral service, and not disagreeable to the ear. The paraphernalia of religion displayed here—the altars, images, tabernacles, censers, lamps, candles, and candlesticks—with the sanctimonious deportment of the priests, and the solemnity used in the celebration of their mysteries, have no small resemblance to the holy mummeries of the Romish Church as practised in those countries where it is rich and powerful. In the middle of the chapel is a small space railed off and elevated by three steps above the floor, which presents three altars richly adorned, and three colossal statues, one of Fo, one of Fo's wife, and the other of some great Tartar divinity, whose name I forget, all of solid gold. Behind these altars is the sanctum sanctorum, which is dimly lighted by an expiring lamp, seemingly placed there for the purpose of inspiring religious horror or exciting pious curiosity. As we approached it, the curtain, which had just before been drawn a little aside, was suddenly closed, as if on a sudden alarm, and shut out the shrine from our profane eyes. This pagoda is dedicated to Pou-ta-la, one of the transmigrations of Fo; for Fo, like Brahma, the supreme divinity of the Hindoos, has condescended, from time to time, to leave the heavenly mansions, and to become incarnate among men and beasts in this earthly world below. Hence he is represented in his temple as riding upon dragons, rhinoceroses, elephants, mules, and asses, dogs, rats, cats, crocodiles, and other amiable creatures, whose figures he fancied and assumed, according to the lama mythology, for the edification and instruction of Tartars. There are, in some of these pagodas, a thousand of these monstrous statues, all most horribly ugly, and so ill-represented, and so unlike anything in heaven or earth, or in the water underneath the earth, that one would think they might be safely worshipped even by the Jews without incurring the guilt of idolatry. There are also niches filled with the images of saints and bonzes without number, fully sufficient to match the longest catalogue of the Romish calendar. The Emperor, it is affirmed, thinks that he is not only descended in the right line from Fo himself, but, considering the great length and unparalleled prosperity of his reign, entertains of late a strong notion that the soul of Fo is actually transmigrated into his Imperial body.

Nihil est quod credere de se non possit, etc., etc.,[1] so that the unbounded munificence he has displayed in the erection of these pagodas may be looked on as not quite disinterested; for, according to this hypothesis, there has been nothing spent out of the family.

Wednesday, September 18.—We went this morning to Court, in consequence of an invitation from the Emperor, to see the Chinese comedy and other diversions given on the occasion of his birthday. The comedy began at 8 o'clock a.m. and lasted till noon. The Emperor was seated on a throne beside the stage, which projects a good deal into the pit; the boxes are on each side, without seats or divisions. The women are placed above, behind the lattices, so that they can enjoy the amusements of the theatre without being observed. Soon after we came in the Emperor sent for me and Sir George Staunton to attend him, and told us, with great condescension of manner, that we should not be surprised to see a man of his age at the theatre, for that he seldom came thither, except upon a very particular occasion like the present; for that, considering the extent of his dominions and the number of his subjects, he could spare but little time for such amusements. I endeavoured in the turn of my answer to lead him towards the subject of my Embassy, but he seemed not disposed to enter into it farther than by delivering me a little box of old japan, in the bottom of which were some pieces of agate and other stones much valued by the Chinese and Tartars, and at the top a small book, written and painted by his own hand, which he desired me to present to the King, my master, as a token of his friendship, saying that the old box had been eight hundred years in his family.[2]

[1] 'There is nothing which he is not able to believe of himself.'

[2] 'The Emperor, presenting the casket, said: "Deliver this casket to the King, your master, with your own hand, and tell him, though the present may appear to be small, it is, in my estimation, the most valuable that I can give, or my Empire can furnish. It has been transmitted to me through a long line of my predecessors, and is the last token of affection I had reserved to bequeath to my son and successor as a tablet of the virtues of his ancestors, which he had only to peruse, as I should hope, to inspire him with the noble resolution to follow such bright examples; and, as they had done, to make it the grand object of his life to exalt the honour of the Imperial throne, and advance the happiness and prosperity of his people." Such were the words delivered by the Emperor on the occasion as communicated by Mr. Plumb, the interpreter.'—Æneas Anderson, 'Narrative of Embassy to China.'

He at the same time gave me a book for myself, also written and painted by him, together with several purses for arecanut. He likewise gave a purse of the same sort to Sir George Staunton, and sent some small presents to the other gentlemen of the Embassy. After this several pieces of silk and porcelain, but seemingly of no great value, were distributed among the Tartar Princes and chief courtiers, who appeared to receive them with every possible demonstration of humility and gratitude.

The theatrical entertainments consisted of great variety, both tragical and comical; several distinct pieces were acted in succession, though without any apparent connection with one another. Some of them were historical, and others of pure fancy, partly in recitative, partly in singing, and partly in plain speaking, without any accompaniment of instrumental music, but abounding in lovescenes, battles, murders, and all the usual incidents of the drama.

Last of all was the grand pantomime, which, from the approbation it met with, is, I presume, considered as a firstrate piece of invention and ingenuity. It seemed to me, as far as I could comprehend it, to represent the marriage of the Ocean and the Earth. The latter exhibited her riches and productions—dragons, elephants, tigers, eagles, and ostriches, oaks, pines, and other different trees. The Ocean was not behindhand, but poured forth on the stage the wealth of his dominions, under the figures of whales, dolphins, porpoises, leviathans, and other sea-monsters; besides ships, rocks, shells, and corals—all performed by concealed actors, who were quite perfect in their parts, and performed their characters to admiration.

These two marine and land regiments, after separately parading in a circular procession for a considerable time, at last joined together, and, forming one body, came to the front of the stage, when, after a few evolutions, they opened to the right and left to give room for the whale, who seemed to be the commanding officer, to waddle forward, and who, taking his station exactly opposite to the Emperor's box, spouted out of his mouth into the pit several tons of water, which quickly disappeared through the perforations of the floor. This ejaculation was received with the highest applause, and two or three of the great men at my elbow desired me to take particular notice of it, repeating at the same time *Hoha, hung, hoha!* ('Charming, delightful!')

As the entertainment lasted some hours, and there was

an uninterrupted communication between the Court boxes where we were and the others, several of the principal Mandarins took the opportunity of entering into frequent conversation with us, and from what passed I have certainly derived much matter for observation and reflection.[1] It did not escape me that most of the Mandarins were Tartars, scarcely any real Chinese coming near us, but among those that addressed us most familiarly I remarked two, who appeared to have a more confident and disengaged manner than the rest, and who asked us whether we could speak Persian or Arabic.

It seems they are Mussulmen, and chiefs of those hordes of Calmucks who, not long since, on occasion of some discontent or misunderstanding with Russia, migrated in great numbers from the coasts of the Caspian Sea to the frontiers of China, and put themselves under the Emperor's protection. He gave them a very favourable reception, and has decorated these two leaders, or *mirzas*, with transparent blue buttons and peacock's feathers to their caps as an earnest of his accepting their submission and allegiance.

A little before 1 o'clock p.m. we retired, and at 4 returned to Court, to see the evening's entertainments, which were exhibited on the lawn in front of the great tent or pavilion where we had been first presented to the Emperor. He arrived very soon after us, mounted his throne, and gave the signal to begin. There were wrestling, dancing, tumbling, and posture-making, which appeared to us particularly awkward and clumsy from the performers being mostly dressed according to the Chinese costume, one inseparable part of which is a pair of heavy quilted boots, with the soles of an inch thick. The wrestlers, however, seemed to be pretty expert, and afforded much diversion to such as are admirers of the *palæstra*.

There were many other things of the same kind, but I saw none at all comparable to the tumbling, rope-dancing, wire-walking, and straw-balancing of Sadler's Wells; neither did I observe any feats of equitation in the style of Hughes's and Astley's amphitheatres, although I had been always told that the Tartars were remarkably skilful in the instruction and discipline of their horses. Last of all were the fireworks, which in some particulars exceeded

[1] 'Between the acts many of the spectators went into the Ambassador's box to see and converse with him. Most of them were Tartars, few original Chinese being invited to Gehol.'—Sir G. Staunton, 'Embassy to China.'

AN IMPOSING SPECTACLE

anything of the kind I had ever seen. In grandeur, magnificence, and variety they were, I own, inferior to those of Batavia, but infinitely superior in point of novelty, neatness, and ingenuity of contrivance. The whole concluded, as at Batavia, with a volcano or general explosion and discharge of suns and stars, squibs, bouncers, crackers, rockets, and grenadoes, which involved the gardens for an hour after in a cloud of intolerable smoke. Whilst these entertainments were going forward, the Emperor sent to us a variety of refreshments, all which, as coming from him, the etiquette of the Court required us to partake of, although we had dined but a short time before.

However meanly we must think of the taste and delicacy of the Court of China, whose most refined amusements seem to be chiefly such as I have now described, together with the wretched dramas of the morning, yet it must be confessed there was something grand and imposing in the general effect that resulted from the whole spectacle, the Emperor himself being seated in front upon his throne, and all his great men and officers attending in their robes of ceremony, and stationed on each side of him, some standing, some sitting, some kneeling, and the guards and standard-bearers behind them in incalculable numbers. A dead silence was rigidly observed, not a syllable ejaculated nor even a laugh exploded during the whole of the performance. Before we left the Court, Van-ta-gin told me that all the ceremonies and diversions at Gehol were now finished, and that, as the Emperor had fixed the time for his departure for Yuen-min-yuen to be on the 24th instant, it would be proper for us to set out some days before him. He therefore proposed to me the 21st, and hoped it would not be inconvenient. So we must get ready accordingly.

I have now just received the translation of my note to the First Minister, in which I request that Captain Mackintosh, having safely delivered all the presents brought in the *Hindostan*, and paid his obeisance to the Emperor, may be allowed to repair without delay to Cheusan, to resume the care of his ship there; that his purser may be allowed to purchase a cargo of tea, or such other produce as that port and its neighbourhood can furnish; and that the officers may have leave to dispose of their private trade, in case they should have any. I have also recommended to send a European missionary with Captain Mackintosh, who may (if thought proper) conduct the two mathematicians who had come to Tacou in order to enter into the Emperor's service, but were still on board the *Hindostan ;* and I have repeated my desire to have a free communication with Canton for the purpose of epistolary correspondence. But, after all, I am now under some difficulty about the transmission of my note. I cannot trust the Legate, and none of the missionaries have as yet had leave to come near us since we have been at Gehol. Neither would it be proper to send it by a common messenger, if such could be procured and depended on. Van-ta-gin and Chou-ta-gin say they cannot venture to interfere in the matter, as it is solely in the Tartar's department. *Il faut y penser.*

Thursday, September 19.—This morning very early my interpreter contrived to elude the vigilance of all our attendants, and to make his way to the First Minister's house. His undertaking, however, was not a little difficult, for, being dressed in the European habit, it was not without some obstruction, and even insult, from the populace that he was able to pass. The Minister not being visible, my paper was delivered to Ma-lou-ye, one of his secretaries, who promised to deliver it and to obtain a speedy answer. The interpreter offered him a handsome present in money for this service ; but he declined accepting it, saying, however, when he returned to Pekin he should not be averse to receive from me some little European article as a mark of my favour. Late this evening the Legate, Van-ta-gin and Chou-ta-gin came here together. The Tartar took out of his pocket a paper, which he said was in answer to my note of this morning to the Minister, and read to me the contents, which were as follows :

' That Captain Mackintosh, having come with me, could not be allowed to separate, but must go away at the same time with me; that his ship might sell at Cheusan what goods she had brought, and take in a loading there in return, for which she should be exempt from any duties. That the two European mathematicians should be allowed to come to Pekin, and enter into the Emperor's service, and that the Minister would give proper directions for the purpose without our interference.'

I requested a copy of the paper from the Legate, but he refused it, and in the whole of this conference showed himself as much indisposed to us as ever.[1]

[1] 'The Legate, though degraded by the Emperor, was protected by Cho-chan-tong, the Chief Minister, and retained his authority and offices, still having the principal care of the Embassy. His disposition towards the English was not softened, as they, however

DEPARTURE FROM GEHOL

But what gives me much more serious concern is, that I apprehend a decided disinclination towards the Embassy in a more important quarter. A council, I find, was lately held on our subject, to which the First Minister had called the attendance, not only of the late Viceroy of Canton, Foo-chan-tong, but had brought the former Hou-poo of Canton out of prison (where he had long lain under sentence of various crimes) and consulted him at the Board. The particulars of what passed there I have not been able to learn, but I cannot avoid auguring the worst from the convention of such a divan.

Friday, September 20.—The Emperor's presents for the King, consisting of lanthorns, pieces of silk and porcelain, balls of tea, some drawings, etc., were finally packed up this morning in the presence of the Mandarins. I order ' George III., Rex.' to be marked on each box to prevent any mistake or confusion. They do not appear to me to be very fine, although our conductors affect to consider them as of great value.

We have been busied all this day in making preparations for our journey of to-morrow. I understand from Van-ta-gin and Chou-ta-gin that, as we are now less encumbered than we were before, we shall be only six days upon the road instead of seven. The Tartar Legate came and made us a visit to-day, but had nothing more to mention to us relative to the business of yesterday. He said he should accompany us to Pekin, and hoped to visit us at the different stages where we meant to stop at.

Saturday, September 21.—This morning at 7 a.m. we set out for Pekin from Gehol, much in the same manner and order as we had travelled before to Gehol from Pekin. The weather has been cold and windy, though not unpleasant in the sun. This day died Jeremy Reid, one of my guard, belonging to the Royal Regiment of Artillery. His disorder was occasioned by a surfeit of fruit, the man having eaten no less than forty apples at a breakfast ![1]

---

innocently, had been the cause of his disgrace.'—Sir G. Staunton, ' Embassy to China.'

' The last stage of public degradation (in China), which amounts to a sentence of infamy, is an order to superintend the preparation of the Emperor's tomb, which implies that the person so sentenced is more fit to be employed among the dead than the living.'—J. Barrow, ' Travels in China.'

[1] ' In the beginning of the journey, one of the Ambassador's guards died of a surfeit, as was supposed, of fruit. His death

DEATH OF A GUNNER

Sunday, September 22.—This morning we buried Reid, the gunner who died yesterday, and we proceeded to our present stage (Chin-chan-you), being eighteen miles, where we have dined and shall stay to-night. The Legate made us a short visit this evening.

Monday, September 23.—Our journey to Con-pe-kiou this day has been twenty-four miles. For upwards of an hour before we reached it we had a very fine view of the great wall in front of us and on each side of us. Some of the gentlemen of the Embassy were desirous of paying another visit to it, in order to examine it with greater accuracy than formerly; but the passage or breach where they had mounted before having been stopped up during our absence with stones and rubbish,[1] and consequently now rendered impracticable, they were obliged to look out for another

---

happened in one of the Emperor's palaces, but such is the extraordinary delicacy of the people in everything relating to their dread Sovereign that it was contrary to rule to have allowed any person to breathe their last within the Imperial precincts. The conductors, therefore, of the Ambassador directed the corpse of this European to be carried from thence in a palanquin as if still alive, and his death was announced at some distance upon the road.' —Sir G. Staunton, 'Embassy to China.'

[1] 'The breach through which those travellers had passed was filled up . . . to prevent their passage. The . . . attendants seemed to be embarrassed between the fear of offending guests they were ordered to respect and the dread of being responsible for suffering strangers to have too near an insight of the country.'—Sir G. Staunton, 'Embassy to China.'

A lengthy description of the Great Wall is given in the Journal, which, much condensed, runs as follows:

'The Wall is built of a bluish-coloured brick, drained and raised upon a stone foundation. As measured from the ground on the side next Tartary it is about twenty-six feet high in the perpendicular. At the bottom the walls [composing the Great Wall] are five feet thick, and diminish gradually as they rise, being one foot and a half at the top. The space between the walls is filled up with earth and rubbish, and paved with bricks, and is eleven feet clear, so that there is room for tow coaches or five horsemen abreast. The Great Wall is strengthened and defended by some square towers at one hundred and fifty to two hundred feet distance. I entered one, which projected eighteen feet from the rampart on the Tartar side; there is no projection on the Chinese side. All their writings agree that this Wall was built above two hundred years before the Christian era.'

place of access, which, having discovered, they were enabled to gratify their curiosity a second time.

Thursday, September 26.—We set out this morning at 4 o'clock a.m., and arrived about noon at my hotel in Pekin[1] (twenty-seven miles), having performed the journey from Gegol in five days and a half.

We were lodged and entertained at the Emperor's houses on our return, in the same manner and with the same attentions as in our former journey. Van-ta-gin and Chou-ta-gin continue their friendly disposition towards us, and on every occasion do us all the good offices in their power; but the Legate still preserves the same vinegar aspect without relaxation.

Pekin, Friday, September 27.—We were all this morning employed in arranging the remainder of the presents to be sent to Yuen-min-yuen.[2] Our conductors seem pressing

---

[1] 'The return of the Ambassador and his suite to Pekin was a joyful event to such of the companions of the voyage as he had left behind. They had lived in that interval a retired and secluded life. Many of the missionaries were desirous of their society, and some of the Fathers called upon the English every day; but this aroused the jealousy of the Chinese, and it was quickly determined by the officials that little opportunity should be afforded for communication between the old and new Europeans there.'—Sir G. Staunton, 'Embassy to China.'

'The gentlemen left in the city were less agreeably situated than those at Yuen-min-yuen. At the outer gate of their lodging a guard was stationed, with orders to allow no one to pass, and all their proceedings and movements were strictly watched. Sometimes they were a little relieved by occasional visits from the European missionaries, but they were invariably accompanied by some of the Government officials, in the capacity of spies, notwithstanding they could not comprehend one single word of the conversation held. The Chinese watches the actions, and even the motions of the eyes, and makes his report accordingly.'—J. Barrow, 'Travels in China.'

[2] 'In the principal room of the Ambassador's apartments the State canopy brought from England was put up. It was made of flowered crimson satin, with festoons and curtains enriched with fringes of gold. On the back part of it the arms of Great Britain appeared in the richest embroidery; beneath it was spread a beautiful carpet, on which were placed fine chairs of the same materials as the canopy, and fringed with gold. The centre chair was elevated two steps above the rest. At the other extremity of the room, opposite the canopy, were hung the portraits of their Britannic Majesties.'—Æneas Anderson, 'Narrative of Embassy to China.'

for us to finish this business, which, added to our own observations and intelligence from others, induces us to imagine that it is not intended we should pass the winter here.

Saturday, September 28.—The greater part of the presents are delivered, and my interpreter is gone to Yuen-min-yuen, in order to assist the gentlemen and artists (whom I left there) to translate and explain everything relative to the machinery and management of the planetarium, orrery, globes, clocks, etc.,[1] so that the missionaries and others, who are to have the charge of them, may be able to keep them in order after our departure.

The Legate visited me to inform me that the Emperor was to arrive on Monday next, and that it was the custom for Ambassadors, as well as the great Mandarins of the court, to go and meet him on the road at a place about twelve miles off. He therefore proposed to me, seeing that I was much indisposed with the rheumatism, that, in order to lessen the fatigue, I should sleep at my former quarters at Yuen-min-yuen, which were half-way, and proceed the next day to attend the Emperor. Though in very great pain at the moment, I told him I should exert myself to the utmost on such an occasion, and hoped I should be able to travel to-morrow.

Sunday, September 29.—I kept myself quiet till the afternoon, and then set out for this place (Yuen-min-yuen), where I now am, very much fatigued, and going to bed to recruit for to-morrow's expedition.

Monday, September 30.—This morning at 4 o'clock we were all in motion, and arrived at our ground in less than two hours. We were conducted into a large saloon, where refreshments were prepared for us, and then proceeded to the spot where the Emperor was to pass and to take notice

[1] 'A Chinese, even in the higher ranks, has no idea of a man's learning, if he be ignorant of the art of discovering events by means of numbers.

'I was very frequently applied to at Yuen-min-yuen, by persons in office, to know if I could tell them their fortune, and it was difficult to persuade them I had any knowledge of the astronomical instruments intended for the Emperor, after professing my ignorance in casting a nativity.'—J. Barrow, 'Travels in China.'

'Each town is supposed to be under the protection of certain stars or constellations, of which last the Chinese reckon twenty-eight. Their astrologers publish annually in almanacs the lucky and unlucky days for every possible human undertaking.'—Sir G. Staunton, 'Embassy to China.'

of our attendance. Our station was on a high bank on the left of the road; on each side of us, and opposite to us, were several thousands of Mandarins, household troops, standard-bearers, and other court officers, lining the way for several miles, as far as our eyes could reach. The Emperor himself soon made his appearance, carried in a kind of sedan chair,[1] and followed by a clumsy state chariot upon two wheels without springs, which must be so rough and disagreeable a machine that I think he will be delighted with a transition to the elegant easy carriages we have brought for him.[2]

We paid him our compliment as he passed,[3] and he sent me a message importing that, as he understood I was not well, and as the cold weather was approaching, it would be better for me to return to Pekin immediately than to make any stay at Yuen-min-yuen. The Minister Cho-chan-tong soon followed the Emperor, and gave me a very gracious salute as he passed by, but he did not stop a moment, as I imagined he would do from what the Legate had said yesterday.

As soon as the cavalcade was at some distance, and the crowd a little dispersed, I returned to Yuen-min-yuen, and, after resting myself a short time, came to Pekin, where I arrived this afternoon, extremely tired and very much out of order.

Tuesday, October 1.—This day the gentleman and artists who had been employed in the arrangement of the plane-

[1] 'The sedan chair was covered with bright yellow cloth, and adorned with windows of plate-glass. It was carried by eight bearers; eight others walked close by, in readiness to relieve the former.'—Sir G. Staunton, ' Embassy to China.'

[2] But this was not the case, as Barrow, in his ' Travels in China,' says: ' In one of the buildings they [the Dutch] saw the several presents deposited which had been carried the preceding year by the Earl of Macartney. They were stowed away with no great care among many other articles. . . . It seems the elegant carriages of Hatchett, that were finished with so much care, and objects of admiration even in London, were here carelessly thrown behind one of their mean and clumsy carts, to which they pretended to bestow a preference.'

[3] ' This morning the Emperor passed on his return; they went out to see him, and all fell and worshipped, except certain strangers, who, being obstinately resolved to do no greater homage to any sovereign than what is required by their own, bent one knee only to the ground.'—J. Barrow, ' Travels in China.'

tarium, lustres, globes, etc., at the palace of Yuen-min-yuen returned there to finish that business, and to put up Parker's great lens, which I had procured from Captain Mackintosh, and which seemed to strike the Chinese in a most particular manner; and yet, so ignorant are they in matters of this kind, that they asked Mr. Barrow whether he could not make such another for them; and when he told them that it was made by the artist who had executed the lustres, and whose sole profession was to compose works of glass and crystal, and that there was not such another lens in the world beside, they shook their heads as if they doubted his veracity; but, having asked Dr. Gillan the same question apart, and receiving a similar answer, they seemed to be somewhat satisfied. They, however, requested that it might be fixed in its place immediately; and when they were informed that it would require some time, they expressed the utmost astonishment, and were scarcely made to comprehend how it could admit of any delay, as they said it was the Emperor's order to have it done instantly, for he was impatient to see it, and our gentlemen might have a hundred, two hundred, or any number of hands that they chose to call for, to assist them.

The Legate, indeed, testified no less surprise upon a former occasion, on being told that it would take several weeks to combine all the different movements of the planetarium, imagining that labour, not skill, was the only thing necessary, and that putting together so complicated a machine as a system of the universe was an operation almost as easy and simple as the winding up a jack. By this intercourse with the palace a new channel of communication and intelligence has been opened, which we have already derived some advantage from. This is the more fortunate, because none of the missionaries, except Father Kosielski,[1] have been allowed to frequent us since we returned from Gehol.

It seems that, before our arrival and the presentation of the King's letter, some of the Emperor's Ministers had given it as their solemn opinion that we should be desired to depart at the end of our forty days, which period is pretended by the Chinese to be the term fixed by the law of the Empire for the stay of a foreign embassy.

To obviate this notion in time, and to rectify some other

[1] 'Romoaldo Kosielski, Pole, aged forty-four. Entered the Emperor's service as astronomer 1783.'—J. Barrow, 'Travels in China.'

mistakes, I sent a note to the Minister (Cho-chan-tong) expressing my thanks to the Emperor for his gracious permission that Captain Mackintosh's ship should load at Cheusan, but repeating that, as nothing could be done but under the inspection of Captain Mackintosh himself, for whose discretion and good conduct I would be responsible, I hoped he might be allowed to rejoin his ship at Cheusan without delay; that, with regard to myself, I proposed to return to Europe by way of Canton, for which place I should ask the Emperor's permission to set out as soon after the new year as the season would allow, as I expected the Kings' ships would be then arrived at Macao, in order to convey me home. The Minister's answer to this note is a desire to see me at Yuen-min-yuen to-morrow morning.

Wednesday, October 2.—This morning, though much indisposed, I went to Yuen-min-yuen, and found the Minister sitting with Fouliou and the Fouliou's brother Fou-chan-tong, but no other Colaos attending. He began by delivering me some letters by the post from Cheusan. One of them was for Captain Mackintosh from his first mate, and there were two of them from Sir Erasmus Gower for myself. On asking me what news they brought, I immediately told him the contents, which were that the *Lion* was preparing to leave Cheusan with all expedition, but that the *Hindostan* could not depart till her commander should join her. I then freely put into his hands the letters themselves, in order to remove from his mind any doubt he might entertain of the authenticity of my information to him. He said he hoped the *Lion* was not gone, for he imagined that, after so long an absence from home, I must be very desirous of returning to it; and that the Emperor, upon first hearing that I was ill and that I had lost some of my people by death since my arrival in China, remarked how much foreigners were liable to suffer from the cold winters of Pekin, and had expressed his apprehensions that we should run great risks of injuring our health if we did not set out from it before the frost set in. The Minister added that, as to the feasts and ceremonies of the New Year, which, he observed, I had mentioned in my note, they were nothing more than a repetition of the amusements I had already seen at Gehol. To this I answered that I had been accustomed to cold climates, and was, therefore, not much afraid of feeling inconvenience from that of Pekin, especially as I had taken precautions to guard against its ill-effects. After a few more words upon this subject, I begged to recall to his recollection the flattering hopes he had given me when at Gehol that I should have frequent opportunities of seeing him at Yuen-min-yuen, the earliest of which I wished to take, in order to explain to him fully my sovereign's instructions to me, and to enter into negotiation upon the points contained in them; that as yet I had barely opened my commission, but it was the King's wish that I might be allowed to reside at his (the King's) expense constantly at the Emperor's Court, according to the custom in Europe, for the purpose of cultivating and cementing a firm friendship between two such powerful monarchs. I said that, with this view, I had been directed to propose that the Emperor would please to send a reciprocal Embassy to England, the care of which I would undertake to have managed in such a manner as I was sure would be highly satisfactory, as I should have ships with every accommodation prepared for the purpose of conveying it to England and bringing it back to China in safety, with every possible mark of honour and respect. I then explained to him in general terms the favours I had chiefly to ask, endeavouring to state them in such a manner, and in such terms as to take away any appearance of demand and merely to convey a sense of propriety in themselves, unattended with the slightest inconvenience of any kind whatsoever to China; and an assurance to him that they would be received as strong marks of benevolence and friendship towards the Prince who had sent me to request them, and whose subjects would always endeavour to render themselves deserving of the Emperor's favour and protection.

The Minister, with his usual address, avoided entering into discussion of any of these points, which I had taken so much pains to lay before him, and turned the discourse upon the state of my health, assuring me that the Emperor's proposal for my departure arose chiefly from his anxiety about it, for that otherwise my stay could not but be agreeable to him.

Although from the course of the conversation, and from the deportment of the Minister and his two assessors, I was led to draw an unfavourable inference relative to my business, yet, when I rose to take my leave, nothing could be more gracious or more flattering than the expressions which he made use of to me upon the occasion, in so much that my interpreter congratulated me on the fair prospect of my negotiation, and said that he expected the happiest issue from it. Nevertheless, since my return home, I have received two different communications, by which I am informed that the Emperor's answer to the King's letter is already prepared and sent to be translated into Latin from the Chinese. This, I find, is an infallible indication of the Court's intentions and as a signal for us to take our leave. I am afraid there is good ground for my apprehensions, as Van-ta-gin and Chou-ta-gin, who have just been here, tell me that I shall have a message from the Minister to meet him to-morrow at the palace. They say that the Emperor's letter for the King will *probably* be then delivered to me, (for they pretend not to know *certainly* that it will), in which case they advise me to ask permission to depart without delay. I suppose they have been directed to hold this discourse to me; but they appear much dejected, for, besides the loss of such advantages from us they might expect should we obtain the objects of the Embassy, they have now little hopes of the advancement and preferment at Court which they had conceived hopes of from being selected to attend us.[1]

Thursday, October 3.—The Legate came early this morning to acquaint me that the First Minister and several other Colaos were to assemble at the palace of the city, and hoped that I would meet them there in ceremony as soon as I could be ready. Being ill in bed when he came, and scarcely able to rise, I do not remember ever having received a more unpleasant message in my life. However, I got up immediately and gave directions, in consequence of this summons, to prepare everything for the occasion. It was not long before I set out, but I need not have been so punctual, for we were kept waiting near three hours before the Minister and his coadjutors were in proper order for our reception. At last we were conducted through several spacious courts, and over several magnificent bridges, to the foot of the great stairs of the Imperial Hall, where I found a line of yellow silk arm-chairs, representing the majesty of China and containing the Emperor's letter to the King. After making our usual reverences, we proceeded to the hall, the chair and letter being carried up in great state before us.

The Minister explained to me the meaning of all this formality, and told me that the letter, which was now un-

[1] Their fears, however, were not realized. Barrow says: 'We had the satisfaction to hear that immediately on their arrival in Pekin they were both promoted.' This was after the departure of the Embassy on its return to England.

covered, would be sent to my house in the same pomp, but he did not tell me what was in it. He then pointed to some tables upon which were arranged in great regularity a number of bundles with yellow wrappers over them, and said they were the remainder of the Emperor's presents to the King, and also there were some presents for myself and for all the persons who had come with me from England.

All that had now passed was not only without the Minister's usual graciousness of manner, but with a degree of constraint and stiffness that appeared to me not natural, but assumed for the occasion. I soon, however, discovered his real disposition towards us by his decisive refusal of some magnificent presents which I had made him, and which I had every reason from himself to imagine he had accepted, as he informed me into whose charge they should be delivered. The other Colaos were equally steady in their refusals, and had declined what I sent.

I was now almost fainting with fatigue, and therefore requested the Minister's leave to retire, but first reminded him of the points I had mentioned to him yesterday, which I had my Sovereign's command to solicit (although not particularly specified in his letter), and requested that he would allow Sir George Staunton to continue the subject with him, as I was unable to speak longer. He said I might send him a note of my requests, but he said it in such a tone as gives me no great hopes of success from it, especially as he chose to be quite silent on the subject of my former note, which, from the manner of our parting yesterday, I had reason to think he would have mentioned to me to-day.

Soon after my return home this afternoon, the Emperor's letter to the King was brought to my house in great ceremony, accompanied by sixteen mandarins of rank and their attendants. The presents followed it, and those for the King were immediately packed up in boxes, and marked as before.

It is now beyond a doubt, although nothing was said upon the subject, that the Court wishes us to be gone,[1] and if

[1] 'It was reported in the palace, by the Chinese, that the Emperor, having considered the business as completed between the two Courts, expressed his surprise that the English Minister should wish to make an unnecessary stay at Pekin, and not be eager to return to his own country. His Imperial Majesty was also said to be alarmed at the number of sick persons in the retinue of the Embassy.'
—Æneas Anderson, 'Narrative of Embassy to China.'

we do not take the hints already given, they may possibly be imparted to us in a broader and coarser manner, which would be equally unpleasant to the dignity of the Embassy and the success of its objects.

That no time might be lost or advantage taken, I have dispatched the note to the Minister which he had desired me this morning to send to him. It consists of six principal articles extracted from my instructions, and compressed into as narrow a compass as possible.

The first is a request to allow the English merchants to trade to Cheusan, Limpo, and Tiensing.

Second, to allow them to have a warehouse at Pekin for the sale of their goods, as the Russians had formerly.

Third, to allow them some small, detached, unfortified island in the neighbourhood of Cheusan as a magazine for their unsold goods, and as a residence for their people to take care of them.

Fourth, to allow them a similar privilege near Canton, and some other trifling indulgences.

Fifth, to abolish the transit duties between Macao and Canton, or at least to reduce them to the standard of 1782.

Sixth, to prohibit the exaction of any duties from English merchants, over and above those settled by the Emperor's diploma, a copy of which is requested to be given to them, as they have never yet been able to see it for their unequivocal direction.

Friday, October 4.—Yesterday Father Amyot, who had sent me the earliest notice of the Emperor's letter to the King being prepared, and several other pieces of important intelligence, and who seemed watchful over our interests and anxious for our success, found means of letting Sir George Staunton know (for I was very ill, and obliged to go to bed) his sentiments on the state of our affairs here at this juncture for my speedy information. He is of opinion that the Chinese consider Embassies as mere temporary ceremonies, sent on particular occassion only, none of those from Europe having been of any considerable duration, and the last from Portugal, though very well received, of less than six weeks; that they have as yet no favourable ideas of treaties with distant Powers, but that they might be rendered sensible of them if applied to and solicited without precipitation, and managed with caution and adroitness, for nothing was to be expected as attainable on the sudden.

He thinks that the Embassy would have met with fewer difficulties at its outset if it had arrived before the Government had been alarmed by the news of great trouble in Europe, the inhabitants of which are indiscriminately considered by them as of a turbulent character; but, nevertheless, that my Embassy has been so brilliant, and has made such an impression in the country, as in the end must be productive of very happy consequences, notwithstanding any different appearances at present. He advises that ground gained by sending an Embassy from the King to the Emperor should by no means be lost, but be followed up by an intercourse of letters between them, which the annual ships might convey, and which might be still improved, and perhaps carried to the most desirable effect by a person resident at Canton, with the King's Commission, in order to ensure him free access to the Viceroy, and to enable him to appear at Court, and negotiate with authority, in case he should be invited to attend there on occasion of the accession of a new Emperor, or any other solemnity. He desired me to be told that he was afraid my illness was occasioned by disappointment here; but that I ought not to give way to feelings of that sort, as both those who had planned the Embassy and undertaken it might well forego the satisfaction of momentary promises in favour of the more solid and permanent advantages which must gradually follow from it. In conclusion, his judgment was, that it would be for our interests, at present, to signify my wishes to return home as soon as I could conveniently set out.

This is nearly the sum of the good Father's opinion and advice, though mixed with many other observations and ideas relative to the late subversion in France, which are needless to insert here, but which strongly mark the horror which it has inspired, and which may probably prove advantageous to us. But I do not require many arguments at present to induce me to follow my own sentiments, which, since the receipt of Mr. Irwin's letter, strongly lead me to depart, both on account of the propriety of the measure in itself and the beneficial service which, if the *Lion* be not gone, I may possibly be able to render to the company in case, when I arrive at Canton, I should find Mr. Irwin's apprehensions realized of a war with the French Convention.

Nevertheless, having been selected for this Commission to China, the first of its kind from Great Britain, of which considerable expectations of success had been formed by many, and by none more than by myself, I cannot help feeling the disappointment most severely. I cannot lose sight of my first prospects without infinite regret. The consciousness of doing all in a man's power to do in the exercise of public employments is an ultimate consolation against most evils that can happen; but it requires no ordinary strain of philosophy to reconcile him at once to the immediate failure of success in a favourite undertaking, be the remote consequences ever so flattering. In Father Amyot's letter to me, before I set out for Gehol, he desired me not to be disturbed or discouraged by any untoward accidents, and to be assured that, in the end, the objects of the Embassy might be attained by patient perseverance and unruffled attention; and his opinion seems not to be changed by what has happened since. From living half a century in this country, possibly from well-grounded knowledge and experience, he is become a very warm admirer of the Chinese nation, and has taken much pains, and, in some instances, not without success, to remove several false ideas entertained in Europe of their character, customs, and policy. I have been but so short a time in the country, and he has been so long in it; I have seen so little of it, and he has seen so much; he is, besides, a man of such probity and universal charity that his opinion is entitled to considerable respect from me. Nevertheless, from the great difference and veneration which the Chinese have long paid to his acknowledged virtue and abilities, he may have insensibly contracted too great a partiality for them, and may view their Government through a flattering medium. His apostolic zeal, too, which is a predominant feature in his character, may tend to render him sanguine. He knows that without a better intercourse between Europe and China, or a miraculous interposition from above, the Gospel is likely to make but slow progress in this part of the world; and he knows that if the trade of China were once properly opened to us, it would wonderfully facilitate the business of conversion, and those of his own faith would still have the vineyard to themselves, for he has no jealousy of the English interfering with them in the proselyte branch.

At this time it is a prevailing opinion among the missionaries, and such whose minds are solely employed upon religious objects, that the crisis of Catholicism is at hand, and that the Church of Rome is to rise triumphant and universal from all the troubles and convulsions that now assault and distract it. These considerations naturally lead the good father to contribute his endeavours, and to wish us not to relinquish an object which certainly no other power is more likely to attain. He, possibly, is afraid that I may imbibe hasty prejudices, and that my vanity may be wounded by finding that our appearance and address, which we had reckoned so much upon, had availed us so little here, and he is therefore solicitous to set me right, and prevent my going wrong.

Whether the difficulties we have met with arise chiefly from the particular humour and jealousy of the Court, or from the *immutable* laws of the Empire, which they talk so much of, must be left to time to determine; but from the observations which it has fallen in my way to make, I should rather imagine that the personal character of the Ministers, alarmed by the most trifling accident, the aversion they may naturally have to sudden innovation, especially at the Emperor's late period of life, and some recent events ill understood, joined, perhaps, to a paltry intrigue, have been among the chief obstacles to my business; for most of the principal people, whom I have had opportunities of knowing, I have found sociable, conversable, good-humoured, and not at all indisposed to foreigners. As to the lower orders, they are all of a trafficking turn, and it seemed at the seaports where we stopped that nothing would be more agreeable to them than to see our ships often in their harbours. With regard to their *immutable* laws, what laws are *really* so I know not; but I suspect the phrase has no very precise meaning, and is only made use of as a shield against reason and argument, for we know that they have broken through some of their laws that were declared to be unalterable. The recent instance of the ceremony in my own case is one, not to mention others, which the accession of the present dynasty to the throne must have often rendered necessary. I have written down these reflections as they arise in my mind; how far they are just it is not in my power at this moment to ascertain, but at all events it appears to me that the wisest measure for the public service and my own character is to retire with as good a grace as I can, and to signify my intentions to do so without delay.

The more distant object of my mission must be for future consideration, and depend on circumstances, on my finding the *Lion* still at Cheusan, and on such further news as I shall learn at Canton.

Dispatched a note to the first Minister, in which, after a

SPEEDING THE EMBASSY

few compliments, I acquainted him that, as soon as I should receive a written answer to the requests of my former note, I wished to have the Emperor's leave to depart, and to proceed to Cheusan, from whence it was possible that Sir Erasmus Gower was not yet sailed, and for whom, in that hope, I enclosed a letter desiring him to wait for my arrival; but that, in case Sir Erasmus should have sailed, it would be necessary for me to proceed to Canton, as the *Hindostan*, which must remain till Captain Mackintosh joined her, could not accommodate half my train and baggage; and I concluded, as I began, with the customary compliments and professions.

Late this evening the Legate came to inform me that the Minister had dispatched my letter for Erasmus Gower, and that my desire of taking leave and of proceeding to Cheusan was agreed to; and to prevent any likelihood of our being surprised by bad weather, the Emperor had fixed the 7th instant for the beginning of our journey, and given orders that every honour and distinction should be paid us on the road. He added that I should receive the answers to my requests when I took leave of the Minister, who would come into the city on the morning of my departure for the purpose of delivering it to me, and of wishing me a prosperous return home.[1]

Saturday, October 5.—So this matter is now settled. Van-ta-gin and Chou-ta-gin tell me that the Emperor has appointed two very great men, Sun-ta-gin and I-shon-ta-gin, to conduct us. The latter I remember to have seen at

[1] 'The Emperor himself came to the palace, and after he had taken a view of the presents, His Majesty was pleased to order eight ingots of silver to be given to each person.

'The Emperor is about five feet and ten inches high, and of a slender but elegant form. His complexion is relatively fair, though his eyes are dark; his nose is rather aquiline. His countenance presents a perfect regularity of features, which by no means announce the great age he is said to have attained. His person is attractive, and his deportment, accompanied by an affability without lessening the dignity of the Prince, evinces the amiable character of the man. His dress consisted of a loose robe of yellow silk, a cap of black velvet with a red ball on the top, and adorned with a peacock's feather. He wore silk boots embroidered with gold, and a sash of blue silk girded his waist. This description of the Emperor was given by the six English artificers who were employed in fitting up and arranging the presents when he came to view them.'—Æneas Anderson, 'Narrative of Embassy to China.'

Gehol; the former is my acquaintance who had been on the frontiers of Russia, and who accompanied us on our visit to the garden of Gehol and the pagodas of Pou-ta-la and its environs.

The Legate is to go no further with us than to Tien-sing, but Van-ta-gin and Chou-ta-gin say they are not yet informed how far they are to attend us, but they suppose not beyond the limits of their province.

Sunday, October 6.—The Legate, Van-ta-gin, and Chou-ta-gin came early this morning in order to assist us in our preparations for our departure to-morrow,[1] and also to give directions for whatever accommodation we may require. They say all will be ready to a minute, so that we may set out as soon as I receive notice of the Minister's being prepared for the ceremony of my taking leave. I understand that there is a considerable number of great people at Court who have expressed their being much pleased with us, and who wished that we had continued here longer.

[1] 'Lord Macartney sent his own state carriage as a present to the Grand Colao, who refused to accept it. It was then redemanded to be unslung and packed up, but no answer was returned. So short was the period allotted us to stay, and so much was to be done in it, that there was no time to make further enquiries concerning the fate of this chariot.

'On our arrival at Tong-siou, we could not help feeling a considerable degree of astonishment at seeing the chariot opposite the house appointed for the reception of the Embassy.'—Æneas Anderson, 'Narrative of Embassy to China.'

CHAPTER XII

Tong-siou, Monday, October 7.—This day at noon[1] we set out from my hotel at Pekin on our road to Cheusan. In my way through the city I stopped at the Minister's pavilion, where I found him ready to receive me, attended by the Fou-liou, the Fou-liou's brother's Fou-chan-tong, and several Colaos of distinction, all dressed in their robes of ceremony. He pointed to a table covered with yellow silk, on which were placed two large rolls; one of them, he told me, contained the Emperor's answer to my paper of requests, the other a list of all the Emperor's presents.[2] I said I hoped the answer was favourable to my wishes, as it might contribute in some degree to soften the regret which it was natural to feel on leaving the place of His Imperial Majesty's residence. He seemed as if surprised with the courtliness of such an address, considering the circumstances of the moment, and, feeling himself embarrassed to make a suitable return, changed the subject, and among other things said he hoped our tables had been properly served during our stay. He then mentioned the Emperor's nomination of Sun-ta-gin to conduct me to Cheusan, as a matter which, I suppose, he imagined would be agreeable to me. The Minister had a smile of affected affability on his countenance during the greater part of the time, but I thought the Fou-liou and his brother looked

---

[1] 'The hurry and confusion of this day is beyond description. The portraits of their Majesties were taken down, the canopy absolutely torn from the wall, and given to some of Lord Macartney's servants. The state chairs were presented to some of the Mandarins.'—Sir G. Staunton, 'Embassy to China.'

[2] 'The tubes of bamboo-wood covered with yellow cloth were placed upon a table containing rolls of yellow paper resembling vellum.'—*Ibid.*

confoundedly sour at us. I have reason to suspect that there is some mystery in this appearance, and that a Court intrigue, which may be still on foot, relative to the affairs of the Embassy, has occurred and occasioned a disunion or difference of opinion among these great personages.

Before we took our leave a Mandarin of the Fifth Order, decorated with a white transparent button on his cap, was called forward, who immediately kneeled down, and continued in that posture till the Emperor's letter and the list of the presents were fastened on his back by broad, yellow ribands tied round both his shoulders. As soon as this operation was performed, he rose and, thus accoutred, mounted his horse, and rode before us the whole way to this place (Tong-siou), where he delivered his charge into my hands in the same humble posture that he had received it. From the time we quitted the Minister, it took us near two hours before we arrived at the last gate of the eastern suburbs of Pekin.

The hotels of the great are mostly situated in retired, narrow streets. The one I inhabited was near the city wall, and had not been long built. It is supposed to have cost near £100,000, and was erected by a former Hou-pou of Canton, who has been degraded for his crimes, and has long lain under sentence in prison. As all his fortune was forfeited to the Crown, my hotel made part of the confiscation, and we were told by one of the missionaries that the wits of Pekin had been much diverted with its being allotted for our residence, and said it was but a fair retribution, as the house had been built by the Hou-pou out of his extortions from our countrymen at Canton.

The civil officer, or Mandarin, of this place, a Mantchou Tartar (Van-ta-gin, the military commander, is a Chinese), has just been here to pay me a visit and offer his services. Mentioning to me in conversation that the waters were now very low and daily decreasing, he took occasion to observe how attentive and considerate it was in the Emperor to fix an early day in the season for our departure. A few days later the river would have become too shallow to float our yachts, and it would be excessively inconvenient and uncomfortable to go in small boats or to travel by land. This is certainly true, and shows how soon the Court lesson reached this gentleman, and how aptly he had already learned it.

Our conductors inform us that the yachts and everything else will be ready for our embarkation to-morrow morning.

Tuesday, October 8.—This morning I walked down to the waterside, and found it would be some hours before the final arrangements could be made for our setting out. I went on board my own yacht, and some of the others, and observed with pleasure the same care and attention for our accommodation down the river that we had experienced before in ascending it.

Wednesday, October 9.—We made but little progress last night, as the waters were low, and the yachts frequently got aground.[1] This has happened two or three times again to-day. The weather is cold during the night and early in the morning, but grows very warm towards the middle of the day.

Thursday, October 10.—This afternoon Van-ta-gin came to tell me that Sun-ta-gin had just received a letter from the Emperor, the contents of which he wished to communicate to me, and soon after I saw his yacht approaching very fast; I therefore desired Van-ta-gin to tell him that as soon as he came alongside I would pay him a visit. I accordingly went on board his yacht, and immediately began by reminding him of his former civilities to me at Pou-ta-la and the gardens of Gehol, and renewing my acknowledgments of them, and then I expressed how happy I felt from his being appointed the superintendent of our present voyage. He received me with every possible mark of consideration, expressed the highest satisfaction at having been chosen upon the occasion to accompany us, and then read to me the Emperor's letter, the purport of which was that he (Sun-ta-gin) should take us under his particular care, and render everything agreeable to us in the course of our voyage. That he should conduct us to Cheusan, and see us safe embarked on board our ships, if they should still be there; if not, that he should proceed with us to Canton. I discovered from him, however, that my letter for Sir

[1] 'Whenever the wind was contrary, or it was found necessary to track the vessels against the stream, a number of men were employed for this purpose. The poor creatures were always pressed into this disagreeable and laborious service, for which they received about sixpence a day so long as they tracked, without any allowance being made for them for returning to the place from whence they were forced. They often deserted by night, disregarding their pay, and the soldiers, in order to procure others, used to proceed to the nearest village, taking the inhabitants by surprise, and forcing them out of their beds to join the yacht.'—J. Barrow, 'Travels in China.'

Erasmus Gower, desiring him to wait for me at Cheusan, had not been sent. They suspected I know not what, and had therefore suppressed it. I told him that Sir Erasmus, having performed the King's orders to land the Embassy in China, would certainly proceed upon other service, unless he heard reasons from me to detain him; I therefore requested him not to lose a moment in having my letter dispatched. He said he would immediately write to Pekin upon the subject, and did not doubt that it would be done. I then took my leave, and in about half an hour he came on my yacht to return my visit. Here the conversation became less formal. He talked to me a great deal about the Russians, who, he said, though fierce and barbarous, were by no means a bad people. Understanding from me that I had resided three years in Russia as the King's Minister, he expressed much surprise, and asked me what I could be doing there so long. I explained to him the laws and customs of European nations with regard to their mutual intercourse, and told him that the Sovereigns of Europe usually kept Ambassadors constantly residing at each other's Courts for the purpose of cultivating reciprocal friendship, and preventing misunderstandings. He answered me that it was otherwise in China, which never sends Ambassadors *to* foreign countries; that Ambassadors *from* foreign countries were only occasionally received, and, according to the laws of the Empire, allowed but forty days' residence, although on particular occasions it might have happened that the term was extended to eighty days. He mentioned some other niceties relative to the etiquette of the Court, and entered a good deal into the manners and customs of China, which, he said, he knew were different from ours; but they could not be broken through without inconvenience, and perhaps mischief, to the State, and that, therefore, foreigners should not be surprised or dissatisfied at them. I expressed my concern on account of the ignorance I had been kept in with regard to many things which he now told me, adding that I had endeavoured to do, as were equally my duty and my wishes to do, everything which I imagined could render me agreeable to the Emperor and his Ministers, and that if anything were omitted, it was not my fault, as I had been so much restrained in my intercourse with the European missionaries who had lived long in China, and could consequently have assisted me with information and instruction. His answer was that of a complete courtier, assuring me that our

TRACKERS FOR THE YACHT CONVEYING THE AMBASSADOR

From a Drawing by WILLIAM ALEXANDER *in the British Museum*

behaviour had been such as showed we required nothing of the kind, but entitled us to every favour and regard that the laws of the Empire could authorize, that he did perfect justice to my sentiments and declaration, and would not fail to transmit them faithfully to Court.

After he went away Van-ta-gin and Chou-ta-gin remained with me a great part of this evening. In the course of conversation, they said that, including all the yachts, baggage-boats, and those of the attending Mandarins, there were forty vessels employed in our present expedition, and upwards of a thousand persons attached to this service. That the Emperor allows five thousand taels per day (each tael equal to 6s. 8d.) for defraying the expense of it, and if that sum should fall short it must be levied on the provinces we pass through. That fifteen hundred taels per day were allotted for the expense of our residence at Pekin, and that they were scarcely sufficient. Although the maintenance of the Embassy must have undoubtedly been very considerable, I can by no means conceive it in any degree adequate to so large an amount. That it has been fully charged to the Emperor is highly probable, but between the money charged and the money actually expended I understand there is usually a very material difference; for although the Emperor's warrant may be signed for a great sum, yet the checks of office, as they are called, are so numerous and so burdensome, that before it arrives at its last stage it is almost sweated to nothing.[1] I remember Chou-ta-gin telling me one day, as an instance of this, that an inundation in the course of last year had swept away a village in the province of Chan-tong so suddenly that the inhabitants could save nothing but their lives. The Emperor (who, from having formerly hunted there, was well acquainted with the place) immediately ordered one hundred thousand taels for their relief, out of which the first Li-poo took twenty thousand, the second ten thousand, the third five thousand, and so on till at last there remained no more than twenty thousand for the poor sufferers. So that we find the boasted moral institutes of China are not much better observed than those of some other countries, and

[1] 'One of the missionaries informed me in Pekin that those who had the luck to be appointed to manage the concerns of a foreign Embassy considered it as one of the best windfalls in the Emperor's gift, the difference between the allowances and the actual expenditure being equivalent to a little fortune.'—J. Barrow, 'Travels in China.'

that the children of Confucius are composed of the same fragile materials as the children of Mammon in the Western World.

Friday, October 11.—This day we made very little way. The river was in some places so shallow that our yachts were often dragged along the bottom by mere bodily force. One of them being somewhat larger than the others, and more heavily laden, was not able to proceed,[1] and Mr. Maxwell, Captain Mackintosh, and Dr. Gillan were obliged to remove into smaller boats and divide the baggage.

Sunday, October 12.—This day I paid another visit to Sun-ta-gin, who told me that by the latest accounts from Cheusan our ships were still there. He said that as, on account of the shallowness of the water, our progress was very slow, we might have time to amuse ourselves by going on shore, if we chose it, and viewing the country on the banks,[2] only taking care not to lose sight of our vessels. His attention and civility continuing so pointed, and his good opinion and esteem so unaffectedly expressed, I had the less difficulty in engaging him to converse freely upon the subjects which are now most interesting to me. I renewed the topic of my former conference with him, and endeavoured to impress him with high ideas of the compliment meant to be paid to the Emperor by the King's sending an Embassy from so great a distance, with such distinguished marks of regard and consideration. I said I had hoped to find frequent opportunities of fulfilling the

[1] 'One of our barges got aground in the middle of the night. The air was piercing cold, and the poor creatures belonging to the vessel there busy until sunrise in the midst of the river, using their endeavours to get her off. The rest of the fleet had proceeded, and the patience of the superintending officer at length being exhausted, he ordered his soldiers to flog the captain and the whole crew, which was accordingly done in the most unmerciful manner. And this was the only reward for the use of the yacht, their time and labour for two days.'—J. Barrow, ' Travels in China.'

[2] ' One day an officer of high rank took it into his head to interrupt them in their usual walk, and dispatched nine or ten of his soldiers, who forced them in a rude manner to return to the vessels. Our two conductors, Van-ta-gin and Chou-ta-gin, being made acquainted with the circumstances, gave to each of the soldiers a severe flogging. The officer received a severe reprimand and forty strokes of the bamboo as *a gentle correction.* Our two Chinese friends were particularly pressing that the insulted gentlemen should be present at the punishment of the officer, and with great difficulty were persuaded that such a scene would not afford any gratification.'—*Ibid.*

purposes of it, which were to testify the sincere interest my Sovereign took in the Emperor's welfare, to improve the connexion between them, and to recommend the King my master's subjects in China to protection and favour. To this he replied with quickness, that the Emperor had lately given fresh orders to treat the English and other Europeans at Canton with indulgence and liberality.[1] I told him I had no doubt of the Emperor's good disposition toward us, and that he should always find the gratitude of our merchants in the respect and obedience which they would pay to his orders; but that they wished to be precisely informed what those orders, that related to them, really were, which hitherto had not been the case, as for twelve years past several new duties had been levied on them without their being able to learn the reason; that these duties were every year increasing, and that, if not soon regulated, the English commerce, which is now carried on in sixty large ships annually, must be relinquished and given up, as unable to bear so heavy burdens. It was therefore become an object of such consequence that I could not but hope proper steps would be taken thereupon. He answered me that certainly there would, but that the duties and taxes could not be fixed *absolutely*, because they must necessarily vary from time to time, according to the exigencies of the State, or of the particular provinces where they were levied. I observed to him that they should be reduced to their former level as soon as the extraordinary occasion was past, but that ever since the year 1782 they had been regularly augmenting at Canton, and were now become an intolerable grievance. He confessed that the duties at Canton had been increased of late years on account of the wars of Tonquin and Tibet, but that as there was peace at present they would certainly be diminished. I

[1] 'The Abbé Raynall says: "When the Europeans first appeared upon the coast of China they were admitted into all the ports. Their extreme familiarity with the women, their haughtiness with the men, and repeated acts of insult and indiscretion, soon deprived them of that privilege; now they are only suffered to put in at Canton. The magistrates, wearied out with their perpetual complaints, would no longer hear them, but through the channels of interpreters who were dependent on the Chinese merchants. All Europeans were ordered to reside in one particular part of the town that was allotted to them; none were exempted but such as could procure a person who would be answerable for their good behaviour. The restraints were made still more grievous in 1760."'—From Lord Macartney's Notes.

expressed to him the pleasure I felt in receiving this information, together with what he had mentioned before of the Emperor's orders in favour of the English, from so high an authority and in so agreeable a manner, and I begged leave to request the continuance of his good offices in our affairs. It is much to be regretted that as the first Minister was determined not to give me such opportunities as I sought for conversing upon business with him, he had not appointed Sun-ta-gin to attend to us from the beginning instead of the Legate, as possibly we might have been able by his means or through his channel to enter into negotiations, whereas the Legate did everything in his power to obstruct and disappoint us. I just hinted this to Sun-ta-gin, who said that possibly it might have been so, but that I should find him now as ready to convey our sentiments and explain them to the Minister as he could have been then. Through all his discourse there is such an air of candour, frankness, and amity that if I am deceived in him he must be the most consummate cheat in the world.

Sunday, October 13.—This day we arrived at Tien-sing, where we were served with a most sumptuous provision for our tables, excellent mutton, pork, venison, and poultry of all kinds, fruits in great variety—peaches, plums, apples, pears, grapes, chestnuts, walnuts, and several others quite new to me. I should not have mentioned this entertainment particularly had it not been intended as a personal compliment from Sun-ta-gin himself, for, in general, we have always been supplied in great abundance. And here I cannot avoid remarking a singular proof of attention shown to us in this journey The Chinese seldom use milk in any part of their food (it being appropriated entirely to the nourishment of the calves), but, observing that we had been much accustomed to it, and that we always mixed it with our tea when we could get it, they have taken care that we shall not want that article on the road, for they have brought with us a couple of cows, in a boat fitted up on purpose, by which means we shall have a constant supply of milk all the way—an accommodation of no inconsiderable value to English travellers.[1]

[1] 'Milk, cheese, and butter are little known to the Chinese, and when it is found that the gentlemen of the Embassy wished to be supplied with the first of those articles, it was necessary to take some pains to find out a person who understood the management of cows, and who, with two of those animals, was put into a barge with proper nourishment to accompany the yachts.'—Sir G. Staunton, 'Embassy to China.'

How are we to reconcile the contradictions that appear in the conduct of the Chinese Government towards us ? They receive us with the highest distinction, show us every external mark of favour and regard, send the First Minister *himself* to attend us as cicerone for two days together through their palaces and gardens; entertain us with their choicest amusements, and express themselves greatly pleased with so splendid an Embassy, commend our conduct, and cajole us with compliments. Yet, in less than a couple of months, they plainly discover that they wish us to be gone, refuse our requests without reserve or complaisance, precipitate our departure, and dismiss us dissatisfied; yet, no sooner have we taken our leave of them than we find ourselves treated with more studied attentions, more marked distinctions, and less constraint than before. I must endeavour to unravel this mystery if I can. Perhaps they had given way to impressions which they could not resist, but are ashamed to confess; perhaps they begin to find their mistake, and wish to make some amends for it.

Monday, October 14.—The weather was remarkably cold this morning, but grew excessively hot towards noon. These sudden vicissitudes begin already to affect the health of our people, and several of the guard are growing sickly. Their living in the midst of such plenty without much restraint or exercise may, however, contribute also to their complaints.

Thursday, October 17.—Passed by several large burying-grounds,[1] from which I conclude we are not far from some large town or city. The population seems prodigious, and we are told it increases the farther we go southward. To-day we observed a great many women mixed with the men, but few of them handsome. They labour in the fields at harvest and other country business just like their husbands.

Monday, October 21.—This morning I paid a visit to Sun-ta-gin, and had a very long conference with him. The Emperor's letter to the King made a principal subject of it. The secretary who had penned the last letter, and who was now in the train of Sun-ta-gin, was present, and endeavoured to excuse that part of it which I complained

[1] 'The expense attending a Chinese funeral is more extravagant than an Englishman can well conceive.

'A Hong merchant kept his mother nearly twelve months above ground, because it was not convenient to him to bury her in a manner suitable to his supposed wealth and station.'—J. Barrow, 'Travels in China.'

of, in which it is said that the requests made in the Ambassador's note of the 3rd of October were supposed to have come rather from him than from the King. According to the explanation given me, it is a sort of political conundrum, a Court artifice to elude an ungrantable demand, for Chinese urbanity does not admit a supposition that one sovereign can desire of another what is possible to be refused. It is, therefore, concluded that the request has never been made, that the Ambassador has been guilty of an error in the delivery of his message, and to have asked from his own head what had never entered into that of his master.

This mode of interpretation, however respectful it may be pretended to the King, is certainly not very flattering to his representative; but I was willing to understand the matter in their own way and let it pass so. When I mentioned to Sun-ta-gin my surprise at finding myself supposed, in the letter, to be desirous of introducing the English religion into China, he said that they had taken it for granted we were like the other Europeans, who, it was well known, had always been industrious and active in propagating their faith. To this I replied that, whatever might be the practice of some Europeans, the English never attempted to dispute or disturb the worship or tenets of others, being persuaded that the Supreme Governor of the Universe was equally pleased with the homage of all His creatures when proceeding from sincere devotion, whether according to one mode or another of the various religions which He permitted to be published; that the English came to China with no such views, as was evident from their merchants at Canton and Macao having no priests or chaplains belonging to them, as the other Europeans had; and that, so far from an idea of that kind entering into my mind or my commission, I had not in my whole train any person of the clerical character, and that it was only such persons who employed themselves, or were employed, as the instruments of conversion; that it was true, as stated in the letter, the English had been anciently of the same religion as the Portuguese and the other missionaries, and had adopted another, but that one of the principal differences between us and them was our not having the same zeal for making proselytes which they had. I added, however, that I could not but be surprised at its being known in China that we had formerly been of the same faith as the missionaries, and that I supposed it must have come from the missionaries themselves. He answered that no such thing was inserted in the letter—at least in the Chinese and Tartar

GRIEVANCES AT CANTON

copies—and that if it was to be found in the Latin it must arise from the blunder or malice of the translator.

I continued my observations on the letters, and said that in the first the Emperor had chiefly dwelt upon the request of an English Minister being allowed to reside constantly at Pekin (which was not complied with), but that he had avoided touching particularly on the other points of my mission, confining himself to a general assurance that the English merchants should be treated with kindness and favour; and that, in the second letter, besides imputing to me the strange religious project which I had already mentioned, he seemed to accuse us of an unfair design to obtain exclusive privileges, which I totally disavowed. It was true, I admitted, that we had only asked for ourselves, but that, however grateful we should be for any favours granted to us, we by no means presumed to desire that his bounty should not be extended to others. I renewed the subject of the grievances complained of at Canton, which, I observed, were so disguised in the Emperor's letter that it was not surprising that they should be disregarded; but that they were of the most serious consideration to us, and if not speedily remedied that the trade of Canton would fall to decay, than which nothing could be more prejudicial to China. Sun-ta-gin begged me to lay aside the uneasiness I seemed to feel from the perusal of the letters, which, he declared, were not meant to convey anything unfavourable or unpleasant to the Embassy or myself, but he wished to remind me that the laws and usages of China were invariable, and that the Emperor was so strictly observant of them that no consideration could ever induce him to infringe them. He was, therefore, upon his guard against the slightest appearance of innovation, and had declined any immediate compliance with the particular requests we had made; but that we were not to infer from thence a disinclination in him towards us or our concerns, for that, notwithstanding any surmises of others, he entertained very kind intentions with regard to us, and that the English at Canton would soon find the good effects of them. He said that from the mechanism of their Government a great deal must be left to the discretion and recommendation of the Viceroys, whose conduct might not possibly be always unexceptionable, but that, as a particular mark of attention to us, Chan-ta-gin, a Mandarin of high rank and allied to the Emperor, was just appointed Tson-tou, or Viceroy, of Canton, a man of **remarkable benignity to strangers, and whose justice and** integrity displayed in his late government of Che-kiang had pointed him out as the fittest person for this new employment. That orders had been sent to him to make the most minute inquiries at Canton into such vexations and grievances as may exist there, and, as soon as he has maturely considered them, to rectify everything amiss by the most effectual exertion of his authority. That this would probably take some time, and the good consequences could scarcely be felt until the ensuing season, when, upon proper notice being given to him of the arrival of our ships, every reasonable indulgence will be allowed them. To these agreeable declarations I was not backward in expressing how satisfactory they were to me; but I insinuated to him that to render them completely so to my Sovereign a third letter from the Emperor, confirming the flattering hopes now given me, would be very desirable, as it would remove every doubt that might arise from others, and that it was the more necessary as, from the singular variation in the translation from the original in one particular instance, it was not unreasonable to imagine some other mistake or insertion might be found there. Sun-ta-gin seemed sensible enough of the value I put upon obtaining a third letter, but said it could make no difference whatsoever as to the public advantages in consideration, and that he was afraid, if I had taken leave, a new dispatch would be incompatible with the etiquette of the Court. He told me that it appeared to him that the Emperor was every day more and more pleased with the compliment of the Embassy, and he added that the assurances which he had given me of the Emperor's favourable intentions were by no means to be taken as effusions of his own friendship, or the compliments of his office, but as the literal words (which they really were) of the Emperor's dispatches to him, and that when I came to converse with Chan-ta-gin, whom I should find at Han-chou-fou, he would confirm all he had mentioned in the fullest manner. I find that scarcely a day passes without Sun-ta-gin's receiving and dispatching letters, so that it would seem we form no small object of Court solicitude. The Chinese couriers are so expeditious that, I am told, it is no uncommon thing to convey a letter fifteen hundred miles in ten or twelve days.[1]

[1] 'The dispatches to and from the Emperor were carried by a man on horseback, in a flat bag or basket, tied round his body. At the bottom of the bag were bells suspended, to announce his

INDULGENCE AND FAVOUR

Thursday, October 24.—This day we passed through three sluices. Received a message from Sun-ta-gin that he had received a letter from the Emperor, and would communicate the contents when convenient to me. I was taken very ill this morning, and have not stirred out of bed all day, but I hope to be well enough to-morrow to see him.

Friday, October 25.—Sun-ta-gin told me that the Emperor was very much pleased with the accounts he was enabled to give him of our prosperous journey, and had sent me a testimony of his benevolence (a cheese and some sweetmeats) with a gracious repetition of kindness and regard.

We had a good deal of desultory conversation upon the general subjects of our last meeting, during which he took occasion to say that we should find it an easy matter to set everything to rights with the new Viceroy of Canton, who was so reasonable and so just that I might depend upon it he never would countenance the most trifling oppression. He again declared that greater indulgence and favour were intended to be shown to the English than they had ever experienced before, and seemed anxious to impress this opinion upon me. If the Court of Pekin is not really sincere, can they possibly expect to feed us long with promises?

Saturday, October 26.—Continued our course on the canal, which is now supplied from a very extensive lake on our left hand.

Monday, October 28.—I have observed for some days past that there are eighteen trackers and one driver uniformly attached to each yacht.[1] The regulation had been sometimes departed from before, so I suppose the police here are more strict. The districts through which the canal passes are obliged to furnish the people for this service, as the post-masters in France and Germany are bound to supply a certain number of horses for travellers. The wealthiest farmer in China would be obliged to perform the work himself if he did not provide a substitute.[2]

---

approach at every stage, where he and his horse were to be relieved. This distance between the stages was about ten or twelve miles.'—Sir G. Staunton, 'Embassy to China.'

[1] 'The condition of those employed about the vessels was one of poverty. With the greatest thankfulness they received the offals of our allowance, and the tea-leaves which we had used were fought after by them with avidity, and boiled up for their beverage.'—J. Barrow, 'Travels in China.'

[2] 'The trackers employed upon the Pay-ho at the entrance of the Ambassador into China, and hitherto on his return, were clad

Tuesday, October 29.—A lively breeze sprang up from the south-west this morning, which makes the feel of the air uncommonly pleasant. A fine grey marbled sky, which from time to time discloses such a proportion of the sunbeams as to render the hue of the weather more cheerful. Sun-ta-gin came to say that he had received a letter acquainting him that the *Lion* and the smaller vessels had sailed away from Cheusan on the 16th instant, so there remained only the *Hindostan* to convey us to Macao. I told him she was totally incapable of accommodating us, being built for trade, and not calculated for passengers. From our manners and habits of life we required a good deal of room; and that a general sickness was the inevitable concomitant of a crowded ship. He said he would immediately write these particulars to Court, and did not doubt that he should receive such orders thereupon as would be perfectly agreeable to us. He proposed that, if we proceeded to Canton through the inland provinces, we should send away our heavy baggage by the *Hindostan*. To this I made no objection, as I wished to travel with as little encumbrance as possible; but I could not avoid reminding him of my letter to Sir Erasmus Gower, and observing that if it had been forwarded as I requested, the inconvenience we now felt from his departure would have been prevented. He seemed perfectly conscious of this, and rather confused at my mentioning it, as he knew very well the unfavourable inference that might be drawn from the omission. Thus, from the suspicious character of the Court which is so disposed to imagine some deep design in almost every proceeding of a European, we are now very seriously disappointed. Sir Erasmus Gower, hearing nothing from me, and knowing nothing of the state of things in Europe, is gone to the eastward, and will not return before May. Our valuable China ships must sail home without a convoy, which, should we have a French war, would be attended with very great danger.

Thursday, October 31.—Sun-ta-gin made me a visit this morning, and repeated to me what he had mentioned some

---

in the plain blue cotton garments, and sometimes in the tattered remnants of the poorest peasantry. They now appeared in a new and regular uniform, edged with red, and a smart bonnet with a flat red button on the top of it, all of which passed from one set of trackers to another. This new dress was more consistent with the appearance of the yachts and barges in every other respect.'—Sir G. Staunton, ' Embassy to China.'

days before, that the Emperor had strongly expressed in his last dispatch his satisfaction at the accounts which had been transmitted to him of our deportment and conversation, and the more he reflected on the circumstances of the Embassy the better he was pleased with it, being now convinced that it had not been sent from any improper view or mischievous curiosity, but solely to do him honour and solicit commercial privileges and protection. He added that the new Viceroy of Canton was fully impressed with the Emperor's sentiments, and that he was to allow our merchants to have free access to him, in order to lay before him their complaints in person instead of sending them to him through the channel of Hong merchants. I said I was infinitely sensible of the Emperor's goodness, and nothing could render it more valuable than some paper or writing to the purpose of what he had said which I might have to show my Sovereign, who, whatever credit he might be disposed to give to his Ambassador, would pay much more attention to anything of that sort from the Emperor himself. But to this he answered that the Emperor had his own method of doing business, and nobody presumed to prescribe to him a different one; that it was his style to give general assurances, not specific promises, and that it was not at all unlikely we might find the former turn out more to our advantage than the latter could do. He told me that he had already mentioned in one of his dispatches my wishes to have a third letter, and that he should be glad that they were gratified, adding, however, that he had no answer as yet upon the subject.

Friday, November 1.—Since passing the last sluice yesterday the canal has widened very much, and is now as broad as the Thames at Putney.

Saturday, November 2.—This morning we fell down the canal into the Hoang-ho, or great Yellow River, which, where we crossed it, was about three miles wide and very muddy.[1] We then struck into another canal,

---

[1] 'Before our barges launched into the stream of the Yellow River, which rolled in a very rapid torrent, certain ceremonies were conceived to be indispensably necessary. It was deemed expedient that an oblation should be made in every vessel of the fleet to the genius of the river. The animals sacrificed on the occasion were different in different yachts, but generally consisted of a fowl or pig. The blood, with the feathers and hair, was daubed upon the principal parts of the vessel. On the forecastle of some were placed cups of wine, oil, and salt ; in others tea, flour and salt ;

and are now proceeding to the southward in our way to Yang-chou, where it is intended to stop for some days.

Tuesday, November 5.—We arrived at Yang-chou, which is a considerable trading town, and expected to stop here, but Sun-ta-gin has altered his intentions and means to go on to Han-chou-fou.

Wednesday, November 6.—At daybreak we fell into the Yang-tse River, commonly called the Kiang-lo, which was about a mile and a half wide at the place where we crossed it. On the southern shore stands the town of Tchien-chien, which is large, well situated, well built, and well inhabited, but the walls seem much out of repair and going fast to decay. A garrison of at least two thousand men all turned out to show themselves, with colours and music, and appointed as if going to be reviewed.

Thursday, November 7.—Proceed this morning to Tchan-chou-fou, and pass through a very noble bridge of three arches, the centre one so high that my yacht had no occasion to lower her masts in going under it.

Tchan-chou-fou is a city of the first order, and was formerly very considerable, but is much declined.

We passed through three small lakes at one place, by the side of a very long bridge of one hundred arches.[1]

Sun-ta-gin has shown me a letter just received from Court, by which he is directed to put the Embassy, as soon as we arrive at Han-chou-fou, under the care of the new Viceroy of Canton, who is soon to set out for that place, and to conduct us thither. Captain Mackintosh is to join

---

and in others oil, rice, and salt. The cups and slaughtered animals remained there, the Captain standing over them on one side, and a man with a gong in his hand on the other. On approaching the rapid part of the stream, at the signal given by the gong, the Captain took up the cups, one by one, and flung their contents over the bow of the vessel into the river. The libation performed, a quantity of crackers and squibs were burnt, with uplifted hands, while the gong was struck, as the vessels swept along the current. The ceremony ended by three genuflexions and as many prostrations.'—J. Barrow, 'Travels in China.'

[1] 'I lament exceedingly that we passed this extraordinary fabric in the night. It happened to catch the attention of a Swiss servant, who, as the yacht glided along, began to count the arches, but finding them increase in number much beyond his expectation, and at the same time in dimensions, he ran into the cabin calling out with great eagerness: "For God's sake, gentlemen, come upon deck, for here is a bridge such as I never saw before; it has no end."'—*Ibid.*

THE NEW VICEROY

his ship at Cheusan,[1] and I told Sun-ta-gin that I should send on board with him the presents and all the baggage which we should not have occasion for in the remainder of our journey, also a part of my guard and of my other attendants. He seemed to receive this information with pleasure, and said he should himself go as far as Limpo, on the way from Cheusan to Han-chou-fou, to give orders that the *Hindostan* might have every indulgence and assistance necessary for her dispatch, and that he should then return to Pekin to render an account of his commission to the Emperor, and he was happy to say that we had enabled him to give a very agreeable and satisfactory one. He desired me to tell Captain Mackintosh that if, from the shortness of time or from any other difficulties, he was disappointed of a cargo at Cheusan, he should nevertheless have the same privileges when he came to Canton that were promised for Cheusan, and that, as a particular compliment for the Embassy and on account of the ship's connexion with it, she should be exempted from the payment of any measurage or other duties.

Saturday, November 9.—We stopped this morning at a village without the walls of Han-chou-fou, and found that the new Viceroy of Canton had come up in his yacht to confer with Sun-ta-gin, and that he would soon be alongside of mine to welcome us on our arrival here. Whether I was prejudiced in his favour or not by the accounts I had heard of him, I thought his appearance much to his advantage. He is perfectly well bred, and the whole of his manner candid and gentleman-like. He confirmed to me everything Sun-ta-gin had said upon business, and particularly mentioned the Emperor's instructions to him to pay the greatest regard to the English at Canton, who, on every occasion, he said, should have free access to him in person or by letter. He then asked me some questions about my passage from England and the length of the voyage back, and said it was very flattering to the Emperor to have an Embassy sent to him from so great a distance; that the Emperor had charged him to repeat his satisfaction from

[1] 'It was settled that Colonel Benson, Dr. Dinwiddie, and Mr. Alexander were to accompany Captain Mackintosh to Cheusan, and four servants and two mechanics to take care of the stores. The rest of the suite were to accompany His Excellency overland, and I was of that number. The Ambassador ordered ten dollars to be given to the owners of each junk for respective crews.'—Æneas Anderson, 'Narrative of Embassy to China.'

it, and to deliver to me an additional present for the King, consisting of some pieces of gold silk, some purses taken from his own person, and—what was of very high value— the *paper of happiness* inscribed by the Emperor's own hand, which is known to be the strongest mark a Sovereign of China can give to another Prince of his friendship and affection. A paper was also sent to me of a similar import, as a testimony of his approbation of the Embassy and an earnest of his proposed attention to its objects. The Viceroy then said that he hoped, in four or five days, everything would be ready for us to proceed, and that he expected much pleasure from seeing us and conversing with us frequently in the course of the voyage. As for Captain Mackintosh, etc., Sun-ta-gin would take care of them, but he was afraid the Captain would not find it easy to get a loading either at Limpo or Cheusan. Upon this I begged leave to send for Captain Mackintosh, to whom he then explained the difficulties he was likely to meet with. The Viceroy told him that the merchants there were not accustomed, like those of Canton, to trade with Europeans and to purchase English goods; that they were probably not at present provided with such articles as Captain Mackintosh might want; and that whatever they sold to him they would expect to be paid for in ready money. He mentioned some other objections, which I endeavoured to obviate, but, observing so many impediments and thinking it better not to urge further a business which we plainly saw they wished us to decline, and which it was in their power to defeat, we gave it up with a good grace upon the Viceroy's repeating the assurances given before of the *Hindostan* being exempted from the payment of measurage and duties at Canton.[1]

Sunday, November 10.—The Tson-tou, or Viceroy, paid me a visit, and repeated in still stronger terms than yesterday the assurances and declarations of the Emperor's favour, and of his own particular good wishes and disposition towards us.

Monday, November 11.—This afternoon I received a letter from Sir Erasmus Gower, dated at Cheusan the 15th of October, which, through the singular jealousy and sus-

[1] 'I presume that every nation has a right to regulate its trade, and make such laws for that purpose as appear best to it, however hard they may seem to press upon foreigners. The country is to take care of itself, and what it considers as its own interest, in the first place; if strangers are dissatisfied, they need not trade with it. This argument may, like almost every good one, be pushed too far.'—From Lord Macartney's Notes.

FAREWELL VISIT FROM SUN-TA-GIN

picion of the Chinese Government, had been kept from me until now. From this letter I have received news of the *Lion's* people being very sickly, and of the surgeon and his first mate not being likely to recover. That the ship was in such want of medicines, particularly of bark and opium, that it became necessary to have a speedy supply of both, and therefore he (Sir Erasmus Gower) was returning for that purpose to the mouth of the river at Canton, but should proceed again from thence to the northward without delay. Having mentioned to the Viceroy that Sir Erasmus Gower was probably now in Macao Roads, and that it was possible a letter from me might reach him if dispatched immediately, he has promised to send it this night by a special messenger to Mr. Brown at Canton, who will know how to forward it.

Wrote my letter to Sir Erasmus, telling him that I was upon my road to Canton, and requesting him to remain off Macao till he either saw me or heard from me again.

Tuesday, November 12.—The Viceroy made us another visit, and improves upon us every time we see him.

Wednesday, November 13.—Received a farewell visit from Sun-ta-gin, who seemed to be quite melted at parting from us. Among other things, he said to me, in a strain of liberality scarcely to be expected in a Tartar or a Chinese, that, as all distant countries must necessarily have different laws and customs, we should not be surprised that theirs varied from ours, that we owed each other mutual indulgences, and he therefore hoped I should not carry with me to Europe any impression to the disadvantage or disparagement of China.

He possesses an elevated mind, and during the whole time of our connexion with him has on all occasions conducted himself towards us in the most friendly and gentleman-like manner. This kind of behaviour is not only agreeable to his natural character, but I believe he thinks it will be agreeable to his Court, as no part of it can be concealed or misrepresented; for, notwithstanding his high rank and situation, such is the caution and circumspection of this Government, that two considerable Mandarins (one of whom was the secretary who penned the Emperor's letters to the King) were always present at our conferences. Sun-ta-gin declined accepting the presents I offered him, but expressed himself in a very becoming and unaffected manner.

Before I quit this subject I must not omit that our discourse together sometimes turned upon Russia, of which he endeavoured to speak as of a country they had no apprehensions from. He said that whenever disturbances happened on the frontiers they were usually occasioned by disorderly people whom, when complained of, the Court of Russia always disavowed, and delivered to be punished as soon as they could be taken hold of, and that at bottom the Russians were not a bad sort of people, though very ignorant and unpolished.[1] It appears not only from Sunta-gin, but from several others whom I have conversed with, that the Chinese are no strangers to the Czarina's character, nor to the manner of her mounting the throne.

Thursday, November 4.—This morning we proceeded from Han-chou-fou on our journey to the southward. I travelled in a palanquin through the city, which I found still larger and more populous than I at first imagined. The environs of the town are very beautiful, embellished by an extensive lake, a noble canal with several inferior ones, and gentle hills cultivated to the summit, interspersed with plantations of mulberries and dwarf fruit-trees, sheltered by oaks, planes, sycamores, and camphors. On one side of the lake is a pagoda in ruins, which forms a remarkably fine object: it is octagonal, built of fine hewn stone, red and yellow, of four entire stories besides the top, which was mouldering away from age. Very large trees were growing out of the cornices; it was about two hundred feet high. It is called the Tower of the Thundering Winds, to whom it would seem to have been dedicated, and is supposed to be two thousand five hundred years old.

After travelling about six miles from the east gate through this charming scene, we came to a broad tide-river, where we found the yachts ready for our embarkation. These vessels have cotton or canvas sails and something of a

---

[1] In one of his notebooks Lord Macartney draws the following comparison between the two nations: 'The common Chinese, like the common Russian, is only half civilized. The Chinese gentleman is as much civilized as a man can be who never has conversed with any but those of his own nation. The Russian gentleman has usually travelled, but if he has not, is much inferior to the Chinese gentleman.

'The Chinese not having seen others is apt to think highly of himself in comparison of others; he is therefore perfectly at home wherever he is, and is as unembarrassed and free the first time he sees a stranger as if he had known him all his life; but when he has seen him and felt him he shrinks a little back, and is mortified in finding what he did not expect.'

AN AMIABLE VICEROY

European air, being sharp both fore and aft. Although their bottoms are quite flat, they sail well and draw very little water, not more than ten inches even when laden with two tons and a half weight. At the different stations on the road the troops always turned out to salute us, which they frequently did by falling down on their knees, but there was a large body of five hundred to a thousand drawn up to receive us at the waterside, dressed and armed in their best manner, who made a very handsome appearance. They seemed, indeed, to look more like soldiers than any I had seen in China before, and to show a marked admiration of my guards as they marched along to embark, noticing every particular—their dress, their arms, the cadence of their movements, their quick and slow steps, their erect figures, their manly air and military mechanism.

Friday, November 15.—This morning at daybreak I found we had advanced up the river above the reach of the tide; it is still very broad, not less than half a mile across. Yesterday we sailed, but now we are towed.

I made a visit to the Viceroy, at which Van-ta-gin and Chou-ta-gin were present. It was intended these two latter gentlemen should leave us at Han-chou-fou; but as they were well known to the Viceroy, and as he observed that they were agreeable and accustomed to us, he desired them to come on and accompany the Embassy to Canton. Very little was said in this conversation relative to our affairs. I thought it better to avoid entering upon that subject abruptly, and to wait for more favourable opportunities of introducing it, many of which must occur in the long journey now before us. I left it to him to lead the discourse as he liked, which, though chiefly upon general topics, he artfully contrived to intermingle with many expressions of compliments to me and profession from himself.[1]

Sunday, November 17.—The Viceroy returned my visit, and began of his own accord to talk to me of the trade carried on between Great Britain and China, of which he owned he was but imperfectly informed. He therefore

[1] 'From the Viceroy's station as Governor of two great provinces, and from his kindred to the Emperor, no subject was entitled to more profound forms of respect; but his meek mind seemed to shun all show of superiority. He insisted on both Van-ta-gin and Chou-ta-gin sitting in his presence ... nor was the Chinese interpreter under any constraint before him.'—Sir G. Staunton, 'Embassy to China.'

desired me to explain to him the principal points in which I wished his assistance when we came to Canton. When I had done this he requested me to give it to him in writing, which I told him should be done as soon as possible. He said his reason for asking it was that he might read it at his leisure, in order to be master of the subject, for he was determined to do what was equitable and proper, to grant what was reasonable and to deny what was not so. He was sensible that some changes of conduct towards us would be right, both for the sake of justice and the reputation of his country. But he confessed that, though his affinity to the Emperor and his rank in the State afforded him strong ground to stand upon, yet he had measures to keep and delicacies to observe, for he was well aware of the counter-action he might expect at Canton from those who may perhaps be interested in the continuance of those very grievances we suffered. That he had heard of the prejudices entertained against us by some of the great people at the Court, particularly Foo-chan-tong, his predecessor, who would not be much pleased to see him adopt a new system the reverse of his own. But there was another thing which he would candidly mention. He said he knew the refusal that had been given by Cho-chan-tong to the requests of the Embassy, and the disappointment resulting from it. It was therefore to be apprehended that the English might be led from thence to infer an unfavourable disposition in the Court towards them which it really had not, and to conduct themselves in such a manner as to defeat any indulgences meant to be granted to them, and consequently render him culpable for any representations he might make in our favour. For this reason he requested me to satisfy him fairly how I considered matters ought to stand relative to this point. I told him I should answer him with the utmost frankness, and own that, from the reception my requests had met with, I naturally concluded the Court of Pekin to be indifferent, if not unfriendly, to Great Britain; and that I should have represented it so in my dispatches home if Sun-ta-gin had not taken such pains to impress me, as he declared he had the highest authority to do, with the Emperor's favourable sentiments towards us and our concerns, and if he, the Viceroy himself, had not confirmed that at the first conference I had with him in the presence of Sun-ta-gin. That the solemn assurances then given to me by him and Sun-ta-gin had not only prevented me from writing in the manner that I had intended, but induced me to inform my Court that, notwithstanding what had passed at Pekin, I had since that time received so many kind messages and promises from thence that I could not doubt of a very serious attention being paid to my representations. That thus the matter now stood, and that it rested with him to determine whether I had deceived my own Court or not. It was from what he should do, not what I should write, that they would form a judgment. Soon after the Viceroy left me he sent presents of fans, tea, and perfumes to me, and all the gentlemen of the Embassy.

This evening Van-ta-gin brought two genteel young men with him on board my yacht, and presented them to me as the Ambassadors from the King of the Lieu-kieu islands, now on their way to Pekin. Regularly once in two years this prince sends such ambassadors to Emoi, in the province of Fo-kien (no other part being open to these strangers), from whence they proceed by this route to carry their master's homage and tribute to the Emperor. They speak Chinese well, but have a proper language of their own, whether approaching to the Japanese or Corean I could not well comprehend. They told me that no European vessel had ever touched their island, but if they should come they would be well received. There is no prohibition against foreign intercourse; they have a fine harbour capable of admitting the largest vessels not far from their capital, which is considerable in extent and population. They raise a coarse kind of tea, but far inferior to the Chinese, and have many mines of copper and iron; no gold or silver mines have as yet been discovered among them, which may in some measure account for these islands being so little known.

The dress which these Ambassadors wore I particularly remarked. It is a very fine sort of shawl made in their own country, dyed of a beautiful brown colour and lined with a squirrel skin, or *petit-gros*. They wore turbans very neatly folded round their heads; one was of yellow silk and the other of purple. They had neither linen nor cotton in any part of their dress that I could perceive. The fashion of their habit was nearly Chinese. They were well-looking, tolerably fair complexions, well-bred, conversible, and communicative. From the geographical position of these islands they should naturally belong to the Chinese or the Japanese. They have chosen the protection of the former, and when their Sovereign dies his successor receives a sort of investiture or confirmation from Pekin. It would seem that the Japanese give themselves no sort of concern about their neighbours.[1] Concentrated and contented in their own Empire, they seldom make excursions beyond their own coasts, and are equally averse that their coasts should be visited by others. If circumstances will permit, I think it may be worth while to explore these Lieu-kieu islands.

Tuesday, November 19.—The river is nearly of the same breadth to-day as yesterday, but very unequal in its depth ; in some places not less than ten or twelve feet, in others so shallow that we were often suddenly stopped in our progress. It is quite wonderful to see the strength of the Chinese boatmen, who, by main force, often dragged or lifted over sands and gravel almost dry the yachts we travelled in, some of which were heavy-laden and seventy feet in length by twelve feet in the beam. The banks of the river and the views are wild, but not unpleasant, the grounds varied by cultivation in the valleys and by plantations on the hills, which are neither high nor steep. The people have a boorish, rustic aspect, and are less polished than any we have yet met with. I am just informed by Chou-ta-gin that the Viceroy has received a dispatch from Court with an account of Sir Erasmus Gower's arrival in Macao Roads on the 31st of last month, so that a letter from Canton to Pekin and from thence to this place, including every delay, has been transmitted in less than twenty days, so good a look-out do the Chinese keep on their coasts, and so watchful have they been of the motions of our ships of war.

Wednesday, November 20.—This evening we arrived at the end of our first navigation from Han-chou-fou, and to-morrow we are to cross overland to You-san-chou, where we are to embark again.

[1] That Japan did occasionally hold communication with other Powers is apparent from the following. Among Lord Macartney's papers is a copy of a confidential letter to Lord Grenville from Mr. Whitworth, English Minister and Envoy at St. Petersburg, dated May, 1792, in which he speaks of the jealousy of Russia with regard to British influence, and the trouble taken to cut off all communication between the Japanese at the Russian Court and himself. Mr. Whitworth concludes his letter by remarking : ' Unless it [Japan] listens to the counsels of those who may warn them of their danger, it will probably sooner or later share the fate of all those weak States who already feel the ill-effects of such a neighbourhood. . . . They [the Russians] certainly build much on the advantages which they expect to derive from that country, and they consider Great Britain as the only Power capable of thwarting them.'

THE VICEROY'S APOLOGY

Soon after we came to an anchor the Viceroy visited me, and made me an apology for our accommodation, saying that it was not so good as he wished it to be on account of the road being very little frequented. Our accommodation has, nevertheless, been very good, and I told him I thought so, and that had it been less good, yet as it was exactly the same as he had himself, I could not be discontented.

He seemed still somewhat apprehensive, whether from his own reflections, or from those of his superiors, that I must feel some dissatisfaction at bottom, as I certainly do, in not having succeeded in the points I had solicited, and that consequently my representations home might be the occasion of future trouble or mischief. He was, however, much pleased when, on his renewing the subject of our former conversation, I repeated to him exactly what I had said to him a few days before. But, still doubtful of my sincerity, I found he was desirous of putting it to a test, by his asking me whether I would authorize him to tell the Emperor that the King my master would always continue in friendship with him, and in testimony of it would write to him, and send an Ambassador again if the Emperor were willing to receive him. I said that, though what I solicited was refused, yet in every other respect I had no reason to complain, as the Embassy had been very honourably received and entertained, and that the Emperor had sent presents to the King as marks of his friendship in return for those sent by the King for the Emperor. That, therefore, I had no doubt that the King might go as far as to write to the Emperor to acknowledge the receipt of the presents, and the marks of distinction conferred on the Embassy. As to matters of business, they stood on a different ground. The King's original idea was to have an Ambassador usually resident in China, and if I had found my staying at Pekin had been agreeable I should have remained there a considerable time, but that frequent or temporary Embassies from so great a distance were attended with much trouble and expense to both Courts. Nevertheless, I thought another Minister might be sent to China if there was good ground to expect that such a measure would be requited by adequate advantages;[1] but that my state of health and

---

[1] Lord Amherst's Embassy to Pekin took place in 1816. The China trade had been suspended two years previously, and the ships of the Company detained at Chumpee. Lord Amherst was not well treated, and failed in carrying out the objects of his mission,

many other circumstances rendered it impossible for me to think of undertaking a second Embassy. He then asked me if the King were to send here another Minister, how soon it would be ; but that he did not mean to propose to me a repetition of so great and splendid an Embassy as mine, which he was sensible could not be equipped without great charge and inconvenience. I told him it was not in my power to say how soon or to calculate any time, the space between England and China being so vast, and sea voyages being so precarious. Before he went away he assured me he had received the greatest satisfaction from the different conversations he had had with us, and should immediately write to the Emperor, who would be highly pleased in every respect with his accounts of us. I gave him the paper which he had desired a few days ago, containing a short sketch of the points I wished to obtain at Canton, also a letter to be forwarded to Sir Erasmus Gower, and he then returned to his yacht. But in a few minutes afterwards he came back, and said that, as he was going to send a dispatch to Court, he thought it would be more agreeable to the Emperor if accompanied with a few words from me to him (the Viceroy) in the Chinese style, of general compliment and acknowledgment of the Emperor's attention to us, and anxiety for our welfare. I thanked him for the suggestion, and told him I should not fail to follow it. Every time we see this gentleman he gains upon our good opinion, and I do not despair

---

which was undertaken merely to secure and consolidate the ordinary commercial intercourse between England and China. No additional privileges, such as the opening of new ports, were asked or expected. His failure was due to no fault on his part, but the feeling of the Chinese Court at that time was strongly against foreign connexions of every kind, and the Emperor then reigning much less favourably disposed towards foreigners than his predecessor.

His hasty and capricious rejection of the Embassy seems to have been due to mismanagement on the part of the Mandarins ; and the Emperor apparently regretted his action in the matter, as, a few days after it, he published a sort of apologetic explanation, and degraded several of his Ministers.

T. G. Staunton (the 'little Staunton' mentioned in Lord Macartney's journal) accompanied Lord Amherst's Embassy, and was of opinion that, 'notwithstanding its apparent failure, it has been productive of solid advantages to the commerce of this country.' Also, 'that nothing could have occasioned the precipitate dismissal of the Embassy but the peculiarly untoward character of the Emperor.'

of the Company's receiving many advantages by his means. It is true that he has art and address, and an air of candour to disguise them with, but he has prudence, sagacity, and a sense of character.

Thursday, November 21.—At 10 o'clock a.m. set out on our journey by land, and dined at the half-way house, which marks the boundaries of the provinces of Che-kiang and Kiang-si. We then came on to this place, Yu-san-chien, having performed the whole journey of twenty-four English miles in less than nine hours. The mode of travelling is on horseback, in a covered palanquin, or an open chair. Our gentlemen had the choice of their conveyance; but as the weather was uncommonly pleasant most of them preferred riding. We found this transition from the water to the land very agreeable, and were highly delighted with the face of the country we passed through.

I must not omit that the Viceroy, observing our curiosity about everything relative to natural history, allowed us to collect seeds and fossils as we came along, and to take up several tea-plants in a growing state with large balls of earth adhering to them, which tea-plants, I flatter myself, I shall be able to transmit to Bengal, where I had no doubt that by the spirit and patriotism of its Government an effective cultivation of this valuable shrub will be undertaken and pursued with success.

I delivered to the Viceroy the note of compliment, which he had suggested to me the idea of, to be transmitted with his letter to Pekin. Observing the character of the writing to be remarkably neat, he inquired who had transcribed it, and when I informed him that it was little George Staunton, he would scarcely believe that a boy of twelve years old could have already made such a progress. Nor was he perfectly satisfied till he had actually seen him add, at the bottom of the paper in Chinese characters, that it had been written by him.

Sunday, November 24.—Last night we continued our voyage, but so dense a vapour had risen in consequence of the late rains and overspread the atmosphere, that, though the river widened and deepened considerably, our navigation seemed often attended with danger. Our vessels frequently struck upon the shelves, and sometimes ran foul of each other with a sudden crash, thus contributing not a little to the dismal character of the night, which was still, moist, cold, and comfortless. The mist grew every moment darker and heavier, and so magnified the objects around us that no wonder our senses and imaginations were equally deceived and disturbed, and that temples, turrets, and pagodas appeared to us through the fog, as we sailed along, like so many phantoms of giants and monsters flitting away from us, and vanishing in the gloom.

Thursday, November 28.—We have now changed our yacht for vessels of a larger size, and are proceeding in them. The small ones were very pleasant and convenient, but had not sufficient room for the proper stowage of our baggage.

Friday, November 29.—We stopped all last night at a village about four miles from Nan-chan-fou, where the Foo-yen, or Governor of the province, paid us a visit, and brought us presents of tea and tea-cups, some beads, pieces of silk, and red Nankin. I returned his compliment with a pair of pearl watches, an assortment of hardware, knives, scissors, wine, and brandy.

Saturday, November 30.—The river still continues wide, but, in general, very shallow. The shores are flat and sandy, and in the wet season the whole country must be under water to a vast extent. No trees or houses to be seen but on a few elevated spots. The weather cold, no sun.[1]

The Viceroy, accompanied by Van-ta-gin and Chou-ta-gin, paid me a long visit this evening. They came at eight o'clock, and stayed till this moment. It is now midnight. The Viceroy was uncommonly civil and sociable, and talked freely upon a great variety of things. He asked me several questions relative to Canton, to the value and amount of our trade there, and that of other nations; and, what surprised me, he seemed to know already the difference between the country ships from India and the ships of the Company. He suspects great peculation among the public officers at Canton, and that the Emperor is much defrauded in his revenue there. I answered him with a proper reserve, saying that, as I had never been at Canton, I could not speak with precision, but that when I arrived there I would endeavour to procure for him any information in my power that he wished to have. He requested that I would, and at the same time desired Chou-ta-gin, who is the man of letters and business, to take notes of what I should mention to him.

[1] 'After sailing a few days up the River Chen-tang, the weather became wet and gloomy. The travellers had been long enough from England to see a day passing in November without any appearance of the sun, and to be surprised at it.'—Sir G. Staunton, 'Embassy to China.'

FIRE IN A FOB

Having occasion to light his pipe, and his attendants being absent, I took out of my pocket a small phosphoric bottle, and instantly kindled a match at it. The singularity of a man carrying fire in his fob without damage startled him a good deal; I therefore explained to him the phenomenon, and made him a present of the bottle. This little incident led to a conversation upon other curious subjects, from which it appeared to us how far the Chinese (although they excel in some branches of mechanics) are yet behind other nations in medical or chirurgical skill and philosophical knowledge. Having often observed numbers of blind persons, but never having met a wooden leg or a deformed limb here, I concluded that good oculists were very rare, and that death was the usual consequence of a fracture. The Viceroy told me I was right in my conjecture. But when I told him of many things in England, and which I had brought people to instruct the Chinese in if it had been allowed, such as the reanimating drowned persons by a mechanical operation, restoring sight to the blind by the extraction of the glaucoma, and repairing or amputating limbs by manual dexterity, both he and his companions seemed as if awakened out of a dream, and could not conceal their regret for the Court's coldness and indifference to our discoveries.

From the manner of these gentlemen's inquiries, the remarks which they made, and the impressions which they seemed to feel, I have conceived a much higher opinion of their liberality and understanding. Whether in these two respects the Minister be really inferior to them, or whether he acts upon a certain public system, which often supersedes private conviction, I know not. But certain it is that, in a conversation with him at Gehol, when I mentioned to him some recent inventions of European ingenuity, particularly that of the air balloon, and that I had taken care to provide one at Pekin with a person to go up in it, he not only discouraged that experiment, but most of the others, which from a perusal of all the printed accounts of this country we had calculated and prepared for the meridian of China. Whatever taste the Emperor Cam-hi might have shown for the sciences, as related by the Jesuits in his day, his successors have not inherited it with his other great qualities and possessions. For it would now seem that the policy and vanity of the Court equally concurred in endeavouring to keep out of sight whatever can manifest our pre-eminence, which they undoubtedly feel, but have not yet learned to make the proper use of. It is, however, in vain to attempt arresting the progress of human knowledge.

I am, indeed, very much mistaken if all the authority and address of the Tartar Government will be able much longer to stifle the energies of their Chinese subjects. Scarcely a year now passes without an insurrection in some of their provinces. It is true they are soon suppressed, but their frequency is a strong symptom of the fever within. The paroxysm is repelled, but the disease is not cured.

Thursday, December 5.—The sun shines out this morning, which, after so long an absence, is a very welcome and cheerful appearance. High hills rise on each side of the river, planted and cultivated with trees and grain on terraces, and embellished with small, neat villages perched on ledges of rock wherever the projection could sustain a superstructure.

Stopped this evening at Kian-chou-fou, a large, walled city of the first order. On our arrival before the town we had a profusion of military honours. I may here remark once for all that at every place on the way where troops were stationed they always turned out for us, unfurled their colours, sounded their music, and saluted with their guns, which number is never exceeded on such occasions. They also frequently sent us little presents of fruit and other refreshments.

Monday, December 9.—The weather is still delightful; but the country more barren than any we have observed in our progress. In this province the women of the lower sort, whom we saw, have their feet generally of the natural size, and go without shoes or other covering of that sort. They are mostly ill-favoured, and, except by wearing their hair and having rings in their ears, are scarcely distinguishable from their husbands. They are so strong and accustomed to labour that it is said many Chinese come into Kiang-si from the other provinces to improve their fortune by marrying what they call a working wife.

At 9 p.m. we arrived at this place (Nan-gan-fou); here the Viceroy showed me a paper or edict from the Emperor addressed to him, of which I am to have a copy. As it was explained to me it seems conceived in very friendly terms, saying that if the King should send a Minister again to China he would be well received. But in such case it is desired that he should come to Canton, which implies a sort of disapprobation of our having gone up the Gulf of Pe-che-li. Nevertheless, I would not, for any consideration, that we had not, as by these means we are masters now of the geography of the north-east coasts of China, and have acquired a knowledge of the Yellow Sea, which was never before navigated by European ships.

The Viceroy told me that he had sent my letters to Canton at the time I delivered them to him. He had not yet received any news from thence about the *Lion*, which makes me very apprehensive that Sir Erasmus Gower may be gone away.[1]

Tuesday, December 10.—This morning we set out by land from Nan-gan-fou, which is a large walled city situated on the side of a steep hill rising abruptly from the left shore of the river. We travelled up in the same manner as in our former expedition, some in palanquins and some on horseback, according to the conveyance they liked best.[2]

The whole distance from Nan-gan-fou to Nan-chou-fou is about thirty-three miles, and we performed the journey in nine hours, the time of baiting included. The horses on this road are remarkably small, but hardy and nimble; they have not handsome forehands, but are otherwise well shaped, with limbs as clean and slender as those of a stag. To the southward of this place the people seem less civilized than on the other side of the mountain.

Wednesday, December 11.—The city of Nan-chou-fou is very extensive and wonderfully populous. We were upwards of an hour in passing from our entrance at the first gate to our quarters, which were in a spacious public edifice

---

[1] About this time Lord Macartney received a letter from Sir Erasmus Gower, of which the following is an extract:

'*Macao, November* 22.—Having related many untoward accidents that have befallen us, I must add that the disappointment has had such an effect upon my mind that I have been very ill, and am now so weak that it is with difficulty I can move about, my spirits, strength, and appetite quite exhausted; however, I hope to get recruited while at Manilla.'

[2] 'In about half an hour we got clear of the city, when every exterior object was lost in attending to the peculiarities of our appearance. The gentlemen of the suite, with the merchants, soldiers, and servants, were all on horseback. Many . . . were . . . indifferent riders, and some . . . obliged to ride for the first time. The horses were very frolicsome and ungovernable, so the diversion which occurred from cries of alarm . . . served to amuse the tediousness of travelling. I had chosen a horse which was very wild and mettlesome, and so restive and unmanageable that I wished to make an exchange, but was obliged to abide by my choice, such as it was.'
—Æneas Anderson, ' Narrative of Embassy to China.'

with a large hall in the centre of it, where the provincial candidates for literary degrees (which alone qualify for civil offices in China) are examined and received. Here most of the gentlemen of the Embassy slept; but, as my yacht was ready prepared, I preferred settling myself in it at once.

This day we left the city of Nan-chou-fou, and proceeded on our voyage.

The river below the bridge is very shallow, and the navigation becomes every day more difficult.[1] The banks are of a loose sand, which the least swelling of the waters washes into the channel and forms into spits and ridges which scarcely any industry can remove. Our present boats are therefore small, but we are to change into larger at Chao-chou-fou, where the river begins to deepen. From Nan-chou-fou the passage to Canton is usually made in seven or eight days; but we shall probably be longer, in order to give time to the Viceroy to get there a little before us to prepare for our reception. He has been constantly with us till now ever since we left Han-chou-fou. When he took leave of us to-day he told us that he had written to the Emperor in such terms upon our subject that he was persuaded we should leave China, not only without dissatisfaction, but with essential proofs of the Emperor's favour. I said that his indulgence to the King my masters' subjects at Canton would be the most essential and acceptable favours he could possibly confer upon me. I have now good reason to know that Van-ta-gin and Chou-ta-gin have sincerely endeavoured to promote our interests. The Viceroy appears to have much confidence in them, and to treat them with great respect and regard.

Saturday, December 14.—Proceeded to-day from Chao-chou-fou and came to this place (Quan-yong-gan). Here we mean to pass the night, that in the morning we may have

[1] 'In our navigations from Nan-chou-fou, the boatmen were usually wet up to their knees twenty times a day, and sometimes almost the whole day, dragging our yachts along, and often actually lifting them by mere bodily force over the shallows that occurred so often in the course of the rivers which we travelled upon.

'I doubt whether the labour of a negro in our West Indies be near so constant, harassing, toilsome, or consuming as that of the Chinese boatmen. They seem to work night and day with very little intermission; and every exertion they make is accompanied by such vocal efforts, such a screaming symphony as would alone exhaust a European more than any manual employment.'—Lord Macartney, 'Journal of Embassy to China.'

THE TEMPLE OF PUSA

an opportunity of visiting the neighbouring Miao, or Temple of Pusa, who is said to have been a near relation of Fo, and is much in vogue among the devotees of this province.

Sunday, December 15.—My curiosity being much excited by the accounts which I had heard of the Temple of Pusa, I rose at an early hour and embarked in a small shallop in order to avoid interruption or encumbrance. The morning was remarkably fine, the sun rose with uncommon brilliancy, and the whole face of Nature was lighted up with cheerfulness and beauty. Before we had proceeded many hundred yards we were attracted to the left by an arm of the river, which, after stretching itself considerably from the main stream, had bent and elbowed itself into a deep cone or basin, above which enormous masses of rocks rose abruptly on every side, agglomerating to a stupendous height, menacing collision. The included flood was motionless, silent, sullen, and black. The ledge where we landed was so narrow that we could not stand upon it without difficulty. We were hemmed round with danger, the mountains frowned on us from on high, the precipices startled us from beneath. Our only safety seemed even in the jaws of a cavern that yawned in our front. We plunged into it without hesitating, and for a moment felt the joys of a sudden escape. But our terrors returned when we surveyed our asylum. We found ourselves at the bottom of the staircase hewn in the rock, long, narrow, steep, and rugged. At a distance a feeble taper glimmered from above, and faintly discovered to us the secrets of the vault. We, however, looked forward to it as our pole star. We scrambled up the steps, and with much trouble and fatigue arrived at the landing-place. Here an ancient bald-headed Bonze issued from his den, and offered himself as our conductor through this subterraneous labyrinth. The first place he led us to was the grand hall or refectory of the convent. It is an excavation forming nearly a cube of twenty-five feet, through one face of which is a considerable opening that looks over the water and is barricaded with a rail. This apartment is well furnished in the taste of the country with tables and chairs highly varnished, and with many gauze and paper lanthorns of various colours, in the middle of which was suspended a glass lanthorn of prodigious size made in London, the offering of an opulent Chinese bigot at Canton. From hence we mounted by an ascent of many difficult steps to the temple itself, which is directly over the hall, but of much greater extent. Here

INTERIOR OF THE SANCTUARY

the god Pusa is displayed in all his glory—a gigantic image with a Saracen face, grinning horribly from a row of gilded fangs, a crown upon his head, a naked scimitar in one hand, and a fire-brand in the other. But how little, alas! is celestial or sublunary fame. I could learn very few particulars of this colossal divinity. Even the Bonzes, who live by his worship, scarcely knew anything of his history. From the attributes he is armed with, I suppose he was some great Tartar prince or commander of antiquity; and if he bore any resemblance of his representative he must have been a most formidable warrior, and probably little inferior in his day to the King of Prussia or Prince Ferdinand in our own. A magnificent altar was dressed out at his feet, with lamps, lanthorns, candles and candlesticks, censers, and perfumes, strongly resembling the decorations of a Romish chapel. On the walls were hung numerous tablets inscribed in large characters with moral sentences and exhortations to pious alms and religion.

Opposite to the image is a wide breach in the wall, down from which the perpendicular view requires the finest nerves and the steadiest head to resist its impression. From the chapel we were led through several long, narrow galleries to the rest of the apartments, which had all been wrought in the rocks by invincible labour and perseverance into kitchens, cells, cellars, and other recesses of various kinds. The Bonzes having now learned the quality of their visitors, had lighted an additional number of torches and flambeaux, by which means we were enabled to see all the interior of the Souterrain, and to examine into the nature of its inhabitants and their manners of living in it. Here we beheld a number of our fellow-creatures, endowed with faculties like our own ('some breasts pregnant with celestial fire'), buried under a mountain and chained to a rock, to be incessantly gnawed by the vultures of superstition and fanaticism. Their condition appeared to us to be the last stage of monastic misery, the lowest degradation of humanity.

At my departure I left among this wretched community a small donation, which was, however, so far above their expectations that I think it not unlikely they will insert a new clause in their litany, and heartily pray that the Chinese Government may adopt a more liberal policy, and open the country to the free inspection and curiosity of English travellers.[1]

[1] Upon lately reading this account of the Temple of Pusa to one or two gentlemen who had visited it as well as myself, I find that,

Monday, December 16.—The river now flows between two rows of high, steep, green hills, broad, smooth, and deep. On the side of one of these hills I observed a black patch of very considerable extent enclosed within a pale, and found upon a nearer approach that it was a great mass of coal emerging above the surface; and I understand that all this part of the country abounds with this substance, although very little use is made of it by the Chinese.

The weather for these two days has been very sharp, with a clear, frosty air.

We stopped at Tchian-yuan, and Van-ta-gin and Chou-ta-gin passed the whole evening with me.

Having observed many barren and wild mountains at different distances in the course of our journey from Pekin, and particularly in this neighbourhood, I took occasion to ask them some questions on the subject, and I learned from them that all uncultivated or desert lands are supposed to belong to the Sovereign. But any person, on giving notice of his intention to the nearest magistrate, may cultivate them if he chooses, and thereby acquire the property of them, for there is no such thing in China as a waste or common depending upon a manor or lordship for the purpose of feeding the game or the vanity of an ideal paramount. But, in truth, I believe there is scarcely an acre of cultivable land in China that is not cultivated.

Van-ta-gin and Chou-ta-gin gave me the following

---

though they agree perfectly in all their recollection of the principal features of the place, they think them rather heightened and surcharged. This I think it fair to take notice of; but at the same time I must add that I wrote the above description immediately on my return to my yacht, merely for the purpose of aiding my recollection, and certainly without any intention of imposing on myself or others. Scarcely any two travellers, however, see the same objects in the same light, or remember them with the same accuracy. What is involved in darkness to the optics of one man is often arrayed in the brightest colours to those of another.

An impression vanishes or endures according to the material that receives it. I have, therefore, often thought what amusement and instruction might be derived from a perusal of the journals kept (if such have been kept) by the different persons belonging to my Embassy. Even the memorandum of a *valet de chambre* might be of some value.*

---

* Æneas Anderson, whose narrative of the Embassy has been often quoted from, was a body-servant to Lord Macartney. He was assisted in the work of editing his Journal by Mr. Coombes.

THE EMPEROR'S MANNER OF LIFE

particulars of the Emperor's usual course of life, when not engaged in hunting or in other excursions.[1]

He rises at three o'clock a.m., and then goes to his private pagoda to worship Fo. He then reads the dispatches of the different officers, who, from their stations, are permitted to write to him directly. At seven o'clock a.m. he breakfasts, after which he amuses himself about his palace and gardens with his women and eunuchs.[2] He then sends for the First Colao, or Chief Minister, with whom he transacts the current business, and then has a kind of levée, which is attended by all the Colaos and great Mandarins who have the *entrée*. He dines usually at three o'clock p.m., and then goes to the theatre or other diversions of the day, after which he retires and amuses himself with reading till bedtime, the hour of which is never later than seven o'clock in the evening.

The female establishment is one Empress (now dead), two queens of the first rank, six queens of the second rank, and one hundred concubines. He has sons by the late Empress, and has others by his Queens and concubines, also several daughters, who are married to Tartar Princes and other Tartars of distinction, but none of them to Chinese. He is a man of great parts, learning, and application, religious and charitable; affable and affectionate to his subjects, vindictive and relentless to his enemies; much elated with his greatness and prosperity, and impatient of the slightest reverse or mischance; jealous of his power, suspicious of his Ministers, and when angry not easily to be appeased. He has never admitted any of his sons to the smallest share of his confidence or authority, although some of them are upwards of forty years old. Nor is it known or presumed whom he intends for his

[1] 'On rising, the Emperor had a draught of cordial to fortify himself with, and about 7 a.m. he partook of a breakfast of tea, wines, and confectionery.'—J. Barrow, 'Travels in China.'

[2] 'There are two kinds of eunuchs, one emasculated only, the second kind, or black eunuchs, have lost every trace of manhood. The first class are instructed with the work of the gardens, and the superintendence of the palaces and buildings. The second class work in the interior of the palaces. They paint their faces, and study their dress. They are detested and feared by the Princes who reside in the palace, and the court officials. They are capricious, and often rise to high favour with the Emperor, as they and the women of the court are the Emperor's only companions in his leisure hours.'—*Ibid.*

THE EMPEROR TCHIEN-LUNG

From a Drawing by WILLIAM ALEXANDER *in the British Museum*

successor.[1] Min-yul-ye, his eldest grandson, is a man of capacity, has been employed in affairs, and is supposed to be much in his favour.

Some years since the Emperor had pretended that he was weary of the throne, and fixed a time for his retiring from it; but as the period approached he began to think it better to defer his resignation to a more distant day. At present it stands for 1796, but it is by no means certain that it will then take place.[2] He is naturally of a healthy constitution and of great bodily strength, and, though upwards of eighty-three years old, is as yet but little afflicted with the infirmities of age.[3] These particulars relative to this great personage I have set down as I received them from my two friends, who have given them to me, I am persuaded, according to the best of their knowledge and opinion. From their rank and situation they have certainly had good opportunities of obtaining intelligence and of forming their judgments.

Tuesday, December 17.—The river grows very broad and meets the tide here, being thirty miles above Canton. The mountains on each side are about seven or eight miles distant. We stopped at San-chou-hien, where the State yachts were in waiting to convey us to Canton. But as the Viceroy's preparations for our reception are not yet quite completed, I understand that we shall not arrive there till Thursday.

Wednesday, December 18.—Early this morning we passed by the town of Fou-sang, which is a very considerable one. Arrived before noon at a garden-house belonging to the

[1] 'The Emperor Tchien-Lung resigned the throne of China to his fifteenth son, Kia-king, in February, 1796, and he died three years later, aged 89.'—J. Barrow, 'Travels in China.'

[2] 'He [the Emperor] had a strong sense of the importance of religious duties, and regularly performed them every morning. He religiously observed the vows made at the commencement of his reign, that it should please Heaven to grant him a complete cycle (sixty years) of government; he would resign the throne in favour of his successor on its completion. He built and endowed many temples in Tartary, and, owing to the success of his reign, in later years entertained the idea that Fo had become incarnate in his person.'—*Ibid.*

[3] Barrow describes the Emperor as having at eighty-three the appearance of a hale man of sixty, and says he was fully persuaded his uninterrupted health was due to his habit of early rising and early retiring to rest.

Chinese Hong merchants of Canton, where we found Messrs. Browne, Irwin, and Jackson, the Company's Commissioners, together with Mr. Hall, the secretary. They had come up from Canton to meet us, and brought with them our letters and packets from Europe, which after a fifteen months' absence were singularly acceptable. By these we have learned the state of affairs between Great Britain and France. It remains to consider how far the motions of the Embassy are to be regulated by it. The Commissioners inform me that my letters had been forwarded to Sir Erasmus Gower, and that the *Lion* is now lying below the second bar. They presented to me the Hong merchants, who had come from Canton on purpose to pay their respects to the Embassy.[1]

To-morrow we make our entry into Canton.

I cannot omit remarking that, in the course of our navigation from Nan-chou-fou, we have had an uncommon profusion of military honours lavished upon us everywhere as we passed along, which I attribute to the Viceroy's having given directions for the purpose as he preceded us. As the Chinese consider the province of Canton to be the most obnoxious to invasion from the sea, the military posts in it are very numerous. There seemed to be an affected reiteration of salutes wherever we appeared, in order, I presume, to impress us with an idea of the vigilance and alertness of the troops, and to show that they were not unprepared against the enemy. Nevertheless, as they are totally ignorant of our discipline, cumbersomely clothed, and armed only with matchlocks, bows and arrows, and heavy swords, awkward in the management of them, and of an unwarlike character and disposition, I imagine they would make but a feeble resistance to a well-conducted attack. The circumstance of greatest embarrassment to an invader would be their immense numbers, not on account of the mischief they could do to him, but that he would find no end of doing mischief to them. The slaughter of millions

---

[1] 'Chinese merchants will cheat whenever opportunity offers, because they are supposed to. An exception is to be made in the case of those merchants who, acting under the immediate sanction of the Government, have always been noted for their liberality and accuracy in their dealings with the Europeans at Canton. They are called Hong merchants, in distinction to a common merchant, and might not unjustly be compared with the most eminent of the mercantile class in England.'— J. Barrow, 'Travels in China.'

ARRIVAL AT CANTON

would scarcely be perceived, and, unless the people themselves soon voluntarily submitted, the victor might indeed reap the vanity of destruction, but not the glory or use of dominion.

Thursday, December 19.—At eleven o'clock a.m. we set out in the State barges for Canton, and, at an hour after one, were landed at the great stairs of the island house, which had been prepared for our reception.[1] From the stairs we walked upon a stage of fifty or sixty yards long, covered with carpets, till we reached the place where it united with terra firma. Here we were received by the Viceroy, the Foo-yen, or Governor, the Hou-pou, or Treasurer, and the principal Mandarins of rank in this neighbourhood, all dressed in their robes of ceremony. We were then conducted into a very large apartment, with double semicircular rows of arm-chairs on each side. The Viceroy and his assessors took their stations opposite to us, and a conversation began, which lasted about an hour. It chiefly turned upon the incidents of our journey from Pekin and the arrival of the *Lion*, which the Viceroy requested might come up to Wampo. We then adjourned to the theatre, on which a company of comedians (who are reckoned capital performers, and had been ordered down from Nankin for that purpose) were prepared to entertain us. Here we found a most magnificent Chinese dinner spread out upon the tables, and a display of the presents given upon this occasion. The Viceroy conducted the whole ceremony with the greatest dignity and propriety, dis-

[1] 'Although the British Factory was in every sense more comfortable than the most splendid palace that the country afforded, yet it was so repugnant to the principle of the Government for an Ambassador to take up his abode in the same dwelling with merchants, that it was thought expedient to indulge their notions in this respect, and to accept a large house on the opposite side of the river, which was furnished with beds in the European manner, and fitted up with glazed sash-windows, and fire-grates suitable for burning coal.'—J. Barrow, ' Travels in China.'

' Lord Macartney and suite went on shore and took possession of the residence . . . provided for the use of the Embassy. This temporary habitation . . . was far superior to any we had seen in our long journey through this country. Nor was it among the least agreeable circumstances of our present situation that we saw once again a domestic arrangement which partook of the habitual comforts of our native soil.'—Æneas Anderson, ' Narrative of Embassy to China.'

tinguishing us by the most pointed marks of respect and regard (things quite new and astonishing to the Chinese here, who are totally unused to see foreigners treated with any attention), and evincing in every instance the high consideration the Embassy was held in by the Government.

Our quarters are in an island, opposite to the English Factory, which is situated on the mainland in the suburbs of the city of Canton. The river that divides us is about half a mile broad. These quarters consist of several pavilions or separate buildings, very spacious and convenient, and some of them fitted up in the English manner with glass windows and fire-grates, which latter, at this season, although we are on the edge of the tropic, are very comfortable pieces of furniture. Our habitations are in the middle of a large garden, adorned with ponds and *parterres*, and with flowers, trees, and shrubs, curious either from rarity or beauty. On one side of us is a magnificent Miao, or Bronze Temple, and on the other a large edifice, from the top of which is a very fine view of the river and shipping, and the city and the country to a great extent.

Friday, December 20.—The theatre, which is a very elegant building with the stage open to the garden, being just opposite my pavilion, I was surprised when I rose this morning to see the comedy already begun and the actors performing in full dress. It seems it was not a rehearsal, but one of their regular formal pieces. I understand that whenever the Chinese mean to entertain their friends with particular distinction, an indispensable article is a comedy —or rather, a string of comedies which are acted one after the other without intermission for several hours together. The actors now here have, I find, received directions to amuse us constantly in this way during our time of residence. But as soon as I see our conductors I shall endeavour to have them relieved, if I can do it without giving offence to the taste of the nation or having my own called in question.[1]

[1] 'On our arrival we found a company of comedians hard at work, in the middle of a piece which had begun at sunrise, but their squalling and their shrill, harsh music were so dreadful that they were prevailed upon, with difficulty, to break off during dinner, which was served up in a veranda directly opposite the theatre.

'Next morning, however, about sunrise, they began again, but at the particular request of the Ambassador and the whole suite, they were discharged, to the no small astonishment of our Chinese conductors, who concluded that the English had very little taste for elegant amusements.'—J. Barrow, ' Travels in China.'

In case His Imperial Majesty Tchien-lung should send Ambassadors to the Court of Great Britain, there would be something comical, according to our manners, if my Lord Chamberlain Salisbury were to issue an order to Messrs. Harris and Sheridan, the King's patentees, to exhibit Messrs. Lewis and Kemble, Mrs. Siddons, and Miss Farren during several days, or rather nights, together, for the entertainment of their Chinese Excellencies. I am afraid they would at first feel the powers of the great buttresses of Drury Lane and Covent Garden as little affecting to them as the exertions of these capital actors from Nankin have been to us. We have found here five Indiamen almost ready to sail for England.

Saturday, December 21, Sunday, December 22, Monday, December 23.[1]—These three days have been chiefly taken up in receiving visits from the Viceroy, the Foo-yen, or Governor, the Hou-pou, or Treasurer, the Song-pin, or Governor of Chao-chou-fou, and several other great Mandarins, some of whom I find are come from a considerable distance to see us. The great public honours and respect paid here to the Embassy cannot fail, I think, to have a very good effect upon the people in favour of our factory. In these visits I explained at length the different grievances of our trade. The Hou-pou was averse to any alterations, and wished everything to remain as he found it. The Viceroy thought every reasonable alteration should be made, and they debated together with great earnestness for a considerable time. The subject was renewed again and again, and I should hope, from the Viceroy's professions and assurances, that we have got the better of the Hou-pou.

We have also been employed in consulting and settling with the Commissioners the destination and departure of the ships, and in preparing our letters for England.

[1] 'At Canton, our two worthy conductors met an old acquaintance, who was governor of a city in Pekin. He gave to them an evening entertainment in a splendid yacht, to which I was privately invited. On entering the great cabin, I found the three gentlemen each with a young girl by his side, very richly dressed. I was welcomed with a cup of hot wine from each of the ladies, who first sipped by way of pledging me. During supper the girls played on the lute and sang several airs, but there was nothing very captivating in the vocal or the instrumental part of the music. We passed a most convivial evening, free from any reserve or constraint, but on going away I was particularly desired by Van-ta-gin not to take any notice of what I had seen.'—J. Barrow, ' Travels in China.'

After maturely considering all the circumstances before me, I have now, however painful to me, been obliged to dismiss from my mind many flattering ideas which I had entertained at the commencement of my Embassy, of distinguishing it by some happy discovery, some signal and brilliant success, in the prosecution of our political and commercial interests in these distant parts of the world. I have given up my projected visit to Japan, which (though now less alluring in prospect) had been always with me a favourite adventure as the possible opening of a new mine for the exercise of our industry and the purchase of our manufactures. All these ideas I have resigned at present, and adopted the measures which appear to afford the most probable substantial advantages to the public. It is, therefore, determined that the *Bombay Castle*, the *Brunswick*, the *Minerva*, the *Chesterfield*, and the *Bellona* shall proceed immediately for England. The other ships (probably thirteen) will proceed, when ready, under the convoy of His Majesty's ship the *Lion*. Thus, by the speedy departure of the five ships, not only their demurrage will be saved, but if they arrive safe, the Court of the Directors will be the earlier enabled to judge of their China resources. By the *Lion's* convoying the remainder, an immense property will be secured from danger in these seas, and, I trust, reach England in safety.

Tuesday, December 24.—Our interpreter[1] came and mentioned to me the different persons who expected to receive presents from the Embassy. I have desired Mr. Barrow to select and deliver them, and to put whatever remains into the hands of Mr. Browne, according to the Company's instructions, and to take a receipt for the same.

Wednesday, December 25.—This day being Christmas Day, we all went over and dined with the British Factory.

Thursday, December 26, *Friday, December* 27, *Saturday, December* 28.—I have had some conversation with the principal Hong merchants of this place. Pan-ke-qua is

[1] 'On the conduct of Lee (Ly), our Chinese interpreter, any praise that I could bestow would be far inadequate to his merit. Fully sensible of his perilous situation, he never at any time shrunk from his duty. At Macao he took an affectionate leave of his English friends, with whom, though placed in one of the remotest provinces of the Empire, he still continues to correspond. Lord Macartney has had several letters from him, the last in 1802.'—J. Barrow, 'Travels in China.'

DISTINCTION BY BUTTONS

one of the principal, a shrewd, sensible, sly fellow. Chi-chin-qua is the next in point of consequence, but not inferior in point of opulence. The latter is a younger man and of a franker character. To me he affected much regard for the English nation, and declared without reserve his willingness to try experiments in trade with any new articles our Factory desired him. Mr. Irwin and Mr. Jackson were present when he said this to me. Pan-ke-qua wears a white opaque button on his cap, and Chi-chin-qua wears a crystal one, which is a degree superior to Pan-ke-qua's, but I soon learned the reason. Pan-ke-qua is more prudent and less ostentatious. Chi-chin-qua owned to me that he had also a blue button; but that, though he always wears it at home in his own family, he never appears with it abroad, lest the Mandarins in office should visit him on that account, making use of it as a pretence to squeeze presents from him, naturally supposing that a man could well afford them who had given ten thousand taels[1] for such a distinction. These different ranks of buttons are sold here to the wealthy merchants, but confer no official authority. When I say sold, I do not mean that the Government sells them, but the suitor certainly buys them by the large presents which he makes to the great men at this extremity of the Empire who have interest enough at Court to procure them.

Monday, December 30, *Tuesday, December* 31.—The accounts which we have heard of the commotions in Cochin China have been now confirmed to us by good authority. We are informed that the King of Donai (the southern region) had attacked the King of Tonquin, or Nangan, as the Chinese call the reigning Prince in the neighbourhood of Turon Bay, which we had visited, and that the town of Taifo had been taken and plundered. The King of Nangan himself had fled to the northern part, and the whole country was in the utmost confusion.

Wednesday, January 1, 1794.—This morning the Viceroy visited me in great ceremony, and said he had received a letter from the Emperor,[2] the contents of which he was

[1] Each tael is equal to 6s. 8d.

[2] 'Your King has sent you out on a very long voyage, thro' vast extents of sea, to evince his benevolent disposition by offering presents to His Imperial Majesty, which giving the greatest satisfaction to the Emperor, he bestowed the highest encomiums upon you, at the same time entertaining and rewarding you in the most sumptuous manner. . . . As for your intimation of your meaning to return with another Royal letter, to offer presents to the Emperor . . . His Imperial

ordered to communicate to me. It contained, as usual, a repetition of the Emperor's satisfaction from the Embassy, his good disposition towards the English, and promises to them of his future favour and protection. These seem to be expressed in stronger terms than the former, and the Viceroy himself was particularly courteous and caressing. He told us he had already issued two proclamations, denouncing the severest punishments against any persons who should attempt to injure Europeans, or practise extortion in dealing with them. (I here delivered to the Viceroy a more particular account of the grievances at Canton.)[1] These proclamations are published, and it is hoped it will have a good effect.

This being New Year's Day, we all went over and dined with our Factory.

Thursday, January 2, to Tuesday, January 7.—As none of the gentlemen of our Factory had ever been within the city of Canton, except the Commissioners, when they went to deliver the Chairman's letter announcing my intended Embassy, I had a strong curiosity to see it. I entered it at the great water-gate, and traversed it from one end to the other. It covers a great extent of ground, and is said to contain a million of inhabitants. This account may possibly

---

Majesty will certainly permit their being presented to him, and amply reward you, in order to show his knowing how to treat strangers with becoming dignity and esteem. According to this declaration you will . . . inform His Britannic Majesty, that what you came to ask was not refused in consequence of the Emperor's indisposition towards you, but merely as being incompatible with the Chinese customs, and consequently not in the Emperor's power to grant; neither has he at any time doubted of your good and benevolent intentions. This, we hope, will be satisfactory to your King: and yourselves may expect from us, whenever you return, the choicest presents. We desire that this our edict be clearly explained to the Ambassador, that not only himself, but also, as we certainly hope, the King may be pleased."—Extract from a Translation of the Letter from the Emperor of China.

[1] Restraints, which already were heavy, had been made more grievous in 1760. 'The Court, being informed by the English that trade laboured under great difficulties, sent commissioners from Pekin, who were bribed by the parties accused. Upon the reports made by these partial men, all the Europeans were confined in a few houses where they could only trade with such merchants as had an exclusive privilege. This monopoly has lately been abolished, but the other restraints still continue the same.'—From Abbé Raynall's 'History,' Lord Macartney's Notes.

be exaggerated, but the population everywhere in China is so vastly disproportionate to what we have been accustomed to observe in Europe that it is difficult for us to determine upon any rule or standard of our own to go by. I can, therefore, only repeat upon this point what I have learned from the best informed of the natives. The streets are narrow and paved with flag-stones, much resembling those of Han-chou-fou. No wheel carriages are admitted, nor did I see any horses in the town except those which my servants rode upon. It is full of shops and trades, and has in general a gloomy appearance, except in two or three large open squares, where the Viceroy and other great men reside.

All the people seemed very busily employed, chiefly in making silk boots or straw bonnets, in the working of metals, and the labours of the forge, and most of them wore spectacles on their noses. The ordinary troops here, instead of a blue uniform and red lace as elsewhere, are clothed in red with a blue lace. I am informed that several persons have been punished for petty extortions practised against some strangers here, notwithstanding the late proclamations. But there are many other things that depend a good deal on ourselves, which, I think, would be more likely to secure us than proclamations and punishments. We, no doubt, labour under many disadvantages here at present, but some of them we have it in our own power to remove. Instead of acting towards the Chinese at Canton in the same manner as we do towards the natives at our factories elsewhere, we seem to have adopted a totally opposite system. We keep aloof from them as much as possible. We wear a dress as different from theirs as can be fashioned. We are quite ignorant of their language (which, I suppose, cannot be a very difficult one, for little George Staunton has long since learned to speak it and write it with great readiness, and from that circumstance has been of infinite use to us on many occasions). We, therefore, almost entirely depend on the good faith and good-nature of the few Chinese whom we employ, and by whom we can be but imperfectly understood in the broken gibberish we talk to them. I fancy that Pan-ke-qua, or Mahomet Soulem, would attempt doing business on the Royal Exchange to very little purpose if they appeared there in long petticoat clothes, with bonnet and turbans, and could speak nothing but Chinese or Arabic. Now, I am very much mistaken if, by a proper management, we might not gradually and in some few years be able to mould the China trade (as we seem to have done the trade everywhere else) to the shape that will best suit us. But it would certainly require in us great skill, caution, temper, and perseverance, much greater, perhaps, than it is reasonable to expect. I dare say there are many hasty spirits disposed to go a shorter way to work, but no shorter way will do it. If, indeed, the Chinese were provoked to interdict us their commerce, or do us any material injury, we certainly have the means easy enough of revenging ourselves.

The Portuguese,[1] who, as a nation, have long been really exanimated and dead in this part of the world, although their ghost still appears at Macao, hold that place upon such terms as render it equally useless and disgraceful to them.[2] It is now chiefly supported by the English, and on the present footing of things there, the Chinese can starve both it and those who support it whenever they please. If the Portuguese made a difficulty of parting with it to us on fair terms, it might easily be taken from them by a small force from Madras, and the compensation and irregularity be settled afterwards. Or with as little trouble, and with more advantage, we might make a settlement in Lantao or Cow-hee, and then Macao would of itself crumble to nothing in a short time. The forts of the Bocca Tigris might be

[1] 'The first Portuguese who came to Canton in 1518, Peres, was sent Ambassador to Pekin. All was well for some time, but the Portuguese misbehaved in the ports, the Chinese fitted out a fleet, and beat and banished them. Peres died in prison at Pekin.

'Some years after, however, the Chinese were reconciled, and granted them a settlement at Macao in recompense of help received against a pirate, who took possession of Macao and some isles, and besieged Canton.

'The Portuguese pay no duties to the Chinese on goods imported at Macao, but they pay a tax on the measurement of all their vessels.'
—From Abbé Raynall's 'History,' Lord Macartney's Notes.

[2] 'Macao is hardly of any account as a port . . . of foreign trade. Although Macao is, *de facto*, . . . a colonial possession of Portugal, the Chinese Government persistently refused to recognize the claim of the Portuguese to territorial rights. This diplomatic difficulty prevented the conclusion of a commercial treaty between China and Portugal for a long time, but an arrangement was come to in 1887. China confirmed the occupation and government of Macao by Portugal, and Portugal engaged never to alienate Macao and its dependencies without the consent of China.'—'Encyclopædia Britannica.'

CHINA TRAFFIC

demolished by half a dozen broadsides. The river would be impassable without our permission, and the whole track of Canton and its correspondencies annihilated in a season. The millions of people who subsist by it would almost instantly be reduced to hunger and insurrection. They must overrun the country as beggars or as robbers, and wherever they went would carry with them misery and rebellion. In such distraction, would Russia remain inactive ? Would she neglect the opportunity of recovering Albazin and re-establishing her power upon the Armour ? Would the ambition of the great Catherine, that has stretched beyond Onalaska to the eastward, overlook the provinces and partitions within grasp of her door ?

Such might be the consequences to this Empire if we had a serious quarrel with it. On the other hand, let us see what would be the consequences to ourselves. It is possible that other nations, now trading or expecting to trade with China, would not behold our success with indifference, and thus we might be involved with much more formidable enemies than Chinese. But I leave that consideration aside, and proceed to others.

Our settlements in India would suffer most severely by any interruption of their China traffic, which is infinitely valuable to them.

To Great Britain the blow would be immediate and heavy. The demand from Canton for our woollens alone cannot now be less than from £500,000 to £600,000 per annum, and there is a good reason to believe that, with proper care, it may in some years be stretched to a million. We should lose the other growing branches of export to China of tin, lead, copper, hardware, and of clocks, watches, and similar articles of ingenious mechanism. We should lose the import from China not only of its raw silk—an indispensable luxury in our silk fabrics—but of another indispensable luxury, or rather, an absolute necessary of life—tea. We should also in some measure lose an excellent school of nautical knowledge, a strong link of marine power, and a prolific source of public revenue.

These evils, it would seem, must infallibly follow from a breach with China. Whether in time other markets might not be found or created to make amends, I am not yet sufficiently acquainted with this part of the world (and still less with the disposition of the Court of Spain) to hazard a decision ; but it is not impossible that, though prodigious inconvenience and mischiefs would certainly be felt at the moment from a rupture, means might be discovered to reverse or repair them. But all these inconveniences and mischiefs which I have stated as objects of apprehension may happen in the common course of things without any quarrel or interference on our part. The Empire of China is an old, crazy, first-rate Man of War, which a fortunate succession of able and vigilant officers have contrived to keep afloat for these hundred and fifty years past, and to overawe their neighbours merely by her bulk and appearance. But whenever an insufficient man happens to have the command on deck, adieu to the discipline and safety of the ship. She may, perhaps, not sink outright; she may drift some time as a wreck, and will then be dashed to pieces on the shore; but she can never be rebuilt on the old bottom.

The breaking-up of the power of China (no very improbable event) would occasion a complete subversion of the commerce, not only of Asia, but a very sensible change in the other quarters of the world. The industry and the ingenuity of the Chinese would be checked and enfeebled, but they would not be annihilated. Her ports would no longer be barricaded; they would be attempted by all the adventurers of all trading nations, who would search every channel, creek, and cranny of China for a market, and for some time be the cause of much rivalry and disorder. Nevertheless, as Great Britain, from the weight of her riches and the genius and spirit of her people, is become the first political, marine, and commercial Power on the globe, it is reasonable to think that she would prove the greatest gainer by such a revolution as I have alluded to, and rise superior over every competitor.

But to take things solely as they are now, and to bound our views by the visible horizon of our situation, without speculating upon *probable* events (which seldom take place according to our speculation), our present interests, our reason, and our humanity equally forbid the thought of any offensive measures with regard to the Chinese, whilst a ray of hope remains for succeeding by gentle ones. Nothing could be urged in favour of a hostile conduct, but an irresistible conviction of failure by forbearance.

The project of a territory on the Continent of China (which I have heard imputed to the late Lord Clive) is too wild to be seriously mentioned, and especially if all can be got quietly without it that was expected to be got with it. By my Embassy the Chinese have had, what they never had before—an opportunity of knowing us—and this must lead them to a proper way of thinking of us and of acting towards us in the future. If, when the dispute happened in the year 1759, a Royal Ambassador had been sent to the Court of Pekin, I am inclined to think the affair would have taken a very different turn. They would certainly have received the Embassy with respect, possibly, indeed, with less honours and distinction than mine, on account of the difference between compliment and complaint; and though they might then have granted no favours, yet the caution of the Government would at least have guarded them from injustice.

At present, after reflecting upon all the incidents of the Embassy, the complexion of the Court of Pekin, and the footing of our Factory at Canton, I cannot but be of opinion that nothing is more likely to contribute essentially to the promotion of our interests than having a King's Minister, or a Company's Minister with a King's Commission, always resident at Canton, totally unconcerned with trade of any kind, and clearly known to be so. The first object is to preserve the ground we have lately gained. It is no small advantage arising from the Embassy that so many Englishmen have been seen at Pekin, from whose brilliant appearance and prudent demeanour a most favourable idea has been formed of the country which sent them. Nor is it any strain of vanity to say that the principal persons of rank who, from their intercourse with us, had opportunities of observing our manners, temper, and discipline very soon dismissed the prejudice they had conceived against us, and by a generous transition grew to admire and respect us as a nation and to love us as individuals. Gained by our attentions, we found them capable of attachment; though in public ceremonious, in private they were frank and familiar. Tired of official formalities, they seemed often to fly to our society as a relief, and to leave it with regret. Dispositions like these an able Minister would not fail to improve. By his intercourse with the Viceroy, the Fo-yen, and the Hou-pou, he would be able to excuse irregularities and clear up mistakes. He would discover the proper seasons for advancing or receding, when to be silent with dignity and when to speak with confidence and effect. But, above all, the King's Commission would authorize him to write to, and entitle him to be heard by, the Court of Pekin itself—a circumstance probably alone sufficient to awe the Regency of Canton and keep them within the bounds of justice and moderation. These opinions I have formed, and these conclusions I have drawn, from what experience I have had of this country, from what observations I made upon the characters of the people that were within my reach to converse with, and the Emperor's letter to the Viceroy.[1]

I am aware that a measure of this kind may seem to interfere with the Company's servants of Canton, but it ought to have no such operation. It should neither lessen their emoluments nor their consequence, but have a contrary effect. I believe that nothing has contributed more to render our merchants at Lisbon and St. Petersburg respectable and important than the residence of His Majesty's Minister at those ports to maintain our commercial rights and protect them from wrong. The Chinese, it is true, are a singular people, but they are *men* formed of the same materials and governed by the same passions as ourselves. They are jealous of foreigners; but are they jealous of *us* without reason? Is there any country on the globe that Englishmen visit where they do not display that pride of themselves and that contempt of others which conscious superiority is apt to inspire? Can the Chinese, one of the vainest nations in the world, and not the least acute, have been blind and insensible to this foible of ours? And is it not natural for them to be discomposed and disgusted by it? But a better knowledge of the better parts of our character will calm their disquiets, weaken their prejudices, and wear away their ill-impressions. Every day we shall have fewer enemies and rivals to injure us in their opinion. The French, who had long flourished here, have given up the trade and disappeared, and other nations also must either soon abandon it or be content to carry it on, as the Dutch and Americans do, with little credit and little advantage.

Having now no particular business to detain the Embassy longer at Canton, and unwilling to trespass further on the hospitality of the Court of China, at whose expense we have been entertained ever since we landed in the Empire (they not permitting us to maintain ourselves, though often pressed by me, and entreated to let us do so), I told the Viceroy of my intention of going to Macoa, and of waiting there until our ships should be ready to sail for England under the *Lion's* convoy. To prevent his taking umbrage, or imagining I was not perfectly pleased with my reception and residence here at Canton (which have certainly been as honourable and agreeable to me as possible), I put my removal chiefly upon the state of my health, which has

[1] Enclosed in my despatch from Canton to Mr. Secretary Dundas, of the 23rd last month.

been much impaired, and which it is thought the sea air would be favourable to. I fixed with him the time of my departure for to-morrow, and as I proposed to embark from the wharf of the Factory, I invited him to breakfast with me there, in order that I might have the opportunity (which he had before promised me) of introducing and recommending the Company's Commissioners to him, to the Fo-yen, and the Hou-pou in the most public and the most distinguished manner. He was particularly inquisitive about the nature of these gentlemen's office and their rank. I endeavoured to explain the matter to him as well as I could ; but there is no making the Chinese understand the wide difference there is between an English merchant and a merchant of any other nation.

Wednesday, January 8.—This day at ten o'clock a.m. we set out from our quarters and crossed the river to the English Factory, where I was met by the Viceroy,[1] the Fo-yen, the Hou-pou, and the other principal Mandarins. I presented the Commissioners, to whom they gave a very gracious reception, with liberal promises of access and attention. This ceremony being finished, we all sat down together to the collation prepared for us, which our Chinese friends did ample justice to; some of them seeming to relish much the good things set before them, and nothing more than our sweet wine and cherry brandy.

At 1 p.m. Sir George Staunton, Sir Erasmus Gower, Lieutenant-Colonel Benson, and I took our leave of them, and embarked on the *Lion's* barge. The other gentlemen went in the pinnaces and boats of the Indiamen, which their Captains had obligingly brought up from Wampo for this occasion, with pendants flying, and the crews all dressed in uniform, so that our procession down the river was very numerous and splendid. Van-ta-gin and Chou-ta-gin, together with the Song-pin of Chao-chou-fou, a man of

---

[1] 'Sun-ta-gin remained friendly to the English, and during the short period of six months in which he held the office of Viceroy of Canton, he invited the chief British authorities there to several conferences and entertainments, and generally evinced a friendly disposition.

'It was unfortunate that this opening was not followed up, for Sun-ta-gin, immediately after his recall from Canton, was promoted to a post of high confidence about the person of the Emperor (Kea King), the duties of which he continued to discharge until within a few months only of the arrival of Lord Amherst's Embassy.'— T. G. Staunton, 'China Trade.'

high quality, with a red button and peacock's feather on his cap, and of a sociable, pleasant humour, accompanied us in a State yacht, and dined with us on board the *Lion*. And here our friends Van-ta-gin and Chou-ta-gin took leave of us. They shed tears at parting, and showed such marks of sensibility and concern as could proceed from none but sincere and uncorrupted hearts. If I never could forget the friendship and attachment of these two worthy men, or the services they rendered us, I should be guilty of the deepest ingratitude.[1]

Thursday, January 9.—Received this morning a most liberal present of fruit and vegetables of all kinds in twenty large baskets, sent us by Van-ta-gin and Chou-ta-gin as a farewell token of their remembrance. Their respective duties and employments now call them away to very distant provinces, and they are not likely to see any of us again. Of this little attention I, therefore, confess myself the more sensible. But I consider it in two ways as equally intended to be a mark of their public consideration for us attaching to their character as men of high station in this country, and of particular regard to us as their private friends of another.

Chou-ta-gin is a man of letters and capacity. He stands high in the opinion of the Viceroy, whose universal reputation, joined to his connexion with the Imperial family, will probably elevate him one day to the first situation at Court. I have more than once talked with Chou-ta-gin on the subject of office and preferment, and from his prospects of advantage being enlarged by what he has seen here, his pretensions heightened by his connexions with us, and his ambition dilated by the patronage of the Viceroy, I think it not at all improbable that he may soon be sent here in a high employment. The place of Hou-pou, which is usually of three years' duration, seems to be the object of his present views. *Honores mutant mores*, and it is possible that promotion might have the same effect upon him as upon his predecessors; but as he is of an age before which a man's principles have usually been settled and his character decided, I have reason to believe that if he ever obtains the

[1] 'It is impossible to speak of these two worthy men in terms equal to their desert. Kind, condescending, unremitting in their attentions, they never betrayed one moment of ill-humour from the time we entered China till they took their final leave at Canton. These two men were capable of real attachments. At parting they burst into tears, and showed the strongest marks of sensibility and concern.'—J. Barrow, 'Travels in China.'

CHOU-TA-GIN

THE CIVIL MANDARIN WHO ACCOMPANIED THE EMBASSY

By WILLIAM ALEXANDER, 1793. *In the British Museum*

appointment we shall receive the most essential advantages by it. But from the very circumstance of his connexion with us, our address to him and management of him would require the more care and dexterity.[1]

Friday, January 10.—We fell down the river below the first bar, and anchored for the night.

Wednesday, January 15.—This day at 10 a.m. I went on shore at Macao with all the gentlemen of the Embassy, and was received at landing by the Governor, Don Manuel Pinto, and the Disembargador, Don Lazaro de Silva Ferreira, who is the principal civil officer of the place. A company of foot, mostly negroes and mulattoes, but commanded by European officers, were drawn up in military order on the quay, and endeavoured to make as good an appearance as they could. Their undersize, motley complexion, and shabby regimentals impressed us, however, with no very high ideas in their favour.

We were very handsomely entertained at dinner by the Governor, who is a well-bred reasonable man of about forty years old, and has the rank of Lieutenant-Colonel in the Portuguese service. His wife, a native of Goa, is of an agreeable figure, and did the honours of her house extremely well. The Disembargador has parts, observation, and address, and speaks very good French.

Most of the gentlemen of the Embassy are lodged at the English Factory. My quarters are at a house in the upper part of the town, rented by Mr. Drummond, who has been so good as to lend it to me during his absence. It is most delightfully situated, and has a very pleasant romantic garden adjoining to it of considerable extent. The tradition of Macao says it was formerly the habitation of the celebrated Camoens, and that here he composed his 'Lusiad.'

At this place we propose to stay till our homeward-bound ships, now thirteen in all, are ready to sail (which it is calculated will be in less than six weeks), and then proceed on the *Lion* as their convoy to England.[2]

[1] 'We had the satisfaction to hear that immediately on their arrival in Pekin they were promoted.

'Chou-ta-gin is at present in a high situation at Court; but Van-ta-gin, the cheerful, good-humoured Van, has paid the debt of nature, having fallen honourably in the service of his country.'— J. Barrow, 'Travels in China,' written in 1806.

[2] 'At this place Mr. Plumb quitted the service of the Embassy. He was very amenable and obliging in his conduct. He was offered a suitable provision if he would return to England, but though

I now close my China Journal, in which I have written down the transactions and occurrences of my Embassy, and my travels through this Empire, exactly as they passed and as they struck me at the time.

To these I have added in the Appendix a few papers relative to some particulars which I was desirous to be informed upon. They could not be inserted in their proper places, as it was frequently a long time after I had made my inquiries that I could obtain the answers, and when I did obtain them I was obliged to follow them up with further inquiries for explanation.

Should any accident throw this Journal under the eyes of a stranger unacquainted with me and the country I am quitting, he might possibly imagine that I had indulged myself too much in local description and political conjecture. But nothing could be more fallacious than to judge of China by any European standard. My sole view has been to represent things precisely as they impressed me. I had long accustomed myself to take minutes of whatever appeared of a curious or interesting nature, and such scenes as I have lately visited were not likely to obliterate my habits or to relax my diligence. I regularly took notes and memorandums of the business I was engaged in and the objects I saw, partly to serve for my own use and recollection, and partly to amuse the hours of a tedious and painful employment. But I will not flatter myself that they can be of much advantage or entertainment to others.

---

he appeared to part from his European friends with regret, he naturally preferred to return to ... his family and friends.'—Æneas Anderson, ' Narrative of Embassy to China.'

SELECTIONS FROM APPENDIX TO JOURNAL

If I venture to say anything upon the manners and character of the Chinese, I must begin by confessing that I am very far from being a competent judge of them. Though assisted by an honest and able interpreter, though possessed of many advantages from the intercourse which my station afforded me with persons of the first rank and abilities, yet I am sensible that it was impossible to avoid falling into frequent mistakes. From my not knowing the language, from sometimes misconceiving those who did, from misinterpreting looks and gestures where our hands and our eyes were to perform the office of our tongues and our ears, I may have formed wrong judgments and have deceived myself. But as I do not mean that others should be deceived, I fairly own my disadvantages, and give previous notice of the nature of the information that may be expected from me. It will chiefly be the result of what I saw and heard upon the spot, however imperfectly, not of what I had read in books or been told in Europe. It should be never absent from our recollection that there are now two distinct nations in China—the Chinese and the Tartars—whose characters essentially differ, notwithstanding their external appearance be nearly the same. They are both subject to the most absolute authority that can be vested in a Prince, but with this distinction—that to the Chinese it is a foreign tyranny, to the Tartar a domestic despotism. The latter consider themselves as in some degree partakers of their Sovereign's dominions over the former, and that imagination may, perhaps, somewhat console them under the pressure of his power upon themselves—like the house servants and house negroes belonging to a great landlord in Livonia or planter in Jamaica, who, though serfs themselves, look down upon the peasantry and field negroes as much their inferiors.

If opinions were solely to be formed of China and its inhabitants from the accounts of the first travellers and even of the later missionaries, they would often be inadequate or unjust. For those writers, although they probably did not mean to deal in fiction, yet, when they do tell the truth, they do not always tell the whole truth, which is a mode of narration that leads to error almost as much as falsehood itself.

When Marco Polo, the Venetian, visited China in the thirteenth century, it was about the time of the conquest of China by the Mongol Tartars, with Kubla-khan at their head. A little before that period the Chinese had reached their highest pitch of civilization; but not having improved, or having rather gone back, at least, for these hundred and fifty years past, whilst we have been rising in arts and sciences, they are actually becoming a semibarbarous people in comparison with the present nations of Europe. Hence it is that they retain the vanity, conceit, and pretensions that are usually the concomitants of half-knowledge; and that, though during their intercourse with the Embassy, they perceived many of the advantages we had over them, they seemed rather surprised than mortified, and sometimes affected not to see what they could not avoid feeling. In their address to strangers they are not restrained by any bashfulness or *mauvaise honte*, but present themselves with an easy, confident air, as if they considered themselves the superiors, and that nothing in their manners or appearance could be found defective or inaccurate.

Their ceremonies of demeanour, which consist of various evolutions of the body, they consider as the highest perfection of good breeding and deportment, and look upon most other nations who are not expert in this polite discipline as little better than barbarians. Nevertheless, having once shown off and exhausted all these tricks of behaviour, they are glad to relapse into ease and familiarity, and never seem so happy as when indulging in free conversation with those whom they do not distrust; for they are naturally lively, loquacious, and good-humoured. They were certainly much surprised to find us so mild, sociable, and cheerful.

The Court character is a singular mixture of ostentatious hospitality and inbred suspicion, ceremonious civility and real rudeness, shadowy complaisance, and substantial perverseness. This prevails through all the departments connected with the Court, although somewhat modified by the personal disposition of those at their head. But as to that genuine politeness which distinguishes our manners, it cannot be expected in Orientals, considering the light in which they regard the female world.

Among the Chinese themselves, society chiefly consists of certain stated forms and expressions, a calm, equal, cold deportment, studied hypocritical attentions, and hyperbolical professions.

Where women are excluded from appearing, all delicacy of taste and sentiment, the softness of address, the graces of elegant converse, the play of the passions, the refinements of love and friendship must of necessity be banished. In their place gross familiarity, coarse pleasantry, and broad allusions are indulged in, but without that honesty and expansion of heart which we have sometimes observed to arise on such occasions among ourselves. Morality is a mere pretence in their practice, though a common topic of their discourse.

Although the difference of ranks be perhaps more distinctly observed in China than in any other country, yet I often observed that the Mandarins treat their domestic servants with great condescension, and talk to them with good-nature and familiarity. But in return an unremitted attention and obedience are expected and never withheld.

A Chinese family is regulated with the same regard to subordination and economy that is observed in the government of a State. The paternal authority, though unlimited, is usually exercised with kindness and indulgence. According to Chinese ideas, there is but one interest in a family; any other supposition would be unnatural and wicked. An undutiful child is a monster that China does not produce.

The houses of the better sort exhibit a certain show of grandeur and magnificence, and even of taste and elegance in their decorations; but at the same time discover—at least, to our eyes—evident marks of discomfort and inconvenience. There is a want of useful furniture. They have, indeed, lanterns of gauze and paper, and horn and diaphanous gum, most beautifully coloured and disposed; and they have tables, couches, and chairs loosely covered with rich carpeting, with gold and silver damasks, and other silks. But they have no bureaux, commodes, lustres, or looking-glasses. They have no sheets to their beds, neither does their bedding itself seem well adapted or agreeable. They do not undress themselves entirely, as we do, when they go to rest, but lay themselves down upon alcoved benches, which are spread with a single mat or thin mattress, and adjusted with small pillows and cushions. Their apartments are not well contrived or distributed, according to our ideas of utility and propriety, having seldom any doors that shut with locks or proper fastenings, but in lieu of them screens and curtains, which are removed or drawn back as occasion requires. In the cold weather they are warmed by flues under the floor, for there are neither stone fireplaces nor fire-grates in the rooms ; but sometimes braziers filled with charcoal are brought in and occasionally renewed.

The people, even of the first rank, though so fond of dress as to change it usually several times a day, are yet in their persons and customs frowzy and uncleanly. Their outward garment of ceremony is richly embroidered with silks of different colours (those of the highest class with golden dragons), and their common habit is of plain silk, or fine broadcloth ; but their drawers and waistcoats are not very frequently shifted. They wear but little linen or calico, and what they do wear is extremely coarse and ill-washed, the article of soap not being employed by them. They seldom have recourse to pocket-handkerchiefs, but spit about the rooms without mercy, blow their noses in their fingers, and wipe them with their sleeves or upon anything near them. This practice is universal, and, what is still more abominable, I one day observed a Tartar of distinction call his servant to hunt in his neck for a louse that was troublesome to him.

At their meals they use no towels, napkins, table-cloths, flat plates, glasses, knives, nor forks, but help themselves with their fingers, or with their chop-sticks, which are not kept very cleanly. Their meat is served up ready cut in small bowls, each guest having a separate bowl to himself.

Seldom more than two sit together at the same table, and never above four. They are eaters of garlic, and strong-scented vegetables, and drink mutually out of the same cup, which, though sometimes rinsed, is never washed or wiped clean. Their chief drink is tea, or liquors distilled from rice and other vegetables, of different degrees of strength, according to their taste, some of which are tolerably agreeable and resemble strong Madeira.

They almost all smoke tobacco, and consider it a compliment to offer each other a whiff of their pipes. They also take snuff, but in small quantities, not in that beastly profusion which is often practised in England, even by some of our fine ladies.

Although so much prejudiced in favour of their own customs and fashions, they could not after some time withstand the superiority of ours in a variety of instances. The lightness, neatness, and commodiousness of my post-chaise, in which I travelled to Gehol, they were quite delighted with; but the fearlessness and celerity and safety with which my postilions drove it along almost petrified them with astonishment.

Our knives, forks, spoons, and a thousand little trifles of personal conveniency, were singularly acceptable to everybody, and will probably become soon of considerable demand, although the Government is certainly averse to all novelties, and wishes to discountenance a taste for any foreign article that is not absolutely necessary; but luxury is stronger than law, and it is the prerogative of wealth to draw from abroad what it cannot find at home. One great advantage of the Embassy is the opportunity it afforded of showing the Chinese to what a high degree of perfection the English nation had carried all the arts and accomplishments of civilized life; that their manners were calculated for the improvement of social intercourse and liberal commerce; that, though great and powerful, they were generous and humane, not fierce and impetuous like the Russians, but entitled to the respect and preference of the Chinese above the other European nations of whom they have any knowledge. This favourable impression of the English character may be confirmed and improved in them by a continuance of our own attention and cautious conduct. The restriction and discipline of our seamen at Canton are among the proper regulations for this purpose, not to mention some other arrangements that will naturally be made there, in consequence of the ground we now stand upon.

The common people of China are a strong, hardy race, patient, industrious, and much given to traffic and all the arts of gain, cheerful and loquacious under the severest labour, and by no means that sedate, tranquil people they have been represented. In their joint efforts and exertions they work with incessant vociferation, often angrily scold one another, and seem ready to proceed to blows, but scarcely ever come to that extremity. The inevitable severity of the law probably restrains them, for the loss of a life is always punished by the death of the offender, even though he acted merely in self-defence, and without any malice aforethought. Superstitious and suspicious in their temper, they at first appeared shy and apprehensive of us, being full of prejudices against strangers, of whose cunning and ferocity a thousand ridiculous tales had been propagated, and perhaps industriously encouraged by the Government. A Chinese boy, who was appointed to wait upon young George Staunton, would not for a long time trust himself to sleep in the house with our European servants, being afraid, he said, that they would eat him. The Chinese, however, at all the seaports where we touched were quite free from these foolish notions, and I flatter myself that the Embassy will have effectually removed them in all the provinces through which it passed.

The lower sort most heartily detest the Mandarins and persons in authority, whose arbitrary power of punishing, oppressing, and insulting them they fear, whose injustice they feel, and whose rapacity they must feed. The Mandarins themselves are equally at the mercy of their superiors, and are punishable by confiscation and even by death, not only for their own offences, but for what others may do amiss within the jurisdiction of their department. The Ministers and Colaos, too, are liable to any indignity which the caprice of the Emperor may chance to dictate. The bamboo is one of the grand instruments of discipline, from which no rank or elevation is exempt or secure. The Emperor's nearest relations, even his own sons, are subject to it, and there are two of them now living upon whom it is known to have been inflicted. But this is an argument of obedience which will probably one day refute itself.

Although the Emperor, as the father of his people, affects and professes impartiality, and wishes to have it understood that he makes no distinction between Tartars and Chinese, neither Tartars nor Chinese are imposed upon by the pretence. After a short residence in the country, I found no difficulty in distinguishing a Tartar from a Chinese, although their mode of dress and forms of behaviour are precisely the same; but there was always something (I know not well how to describe it) that indicated the difference in a moment.

As my knowledge of the female world in China was very limited, I have little to say upon the subject; but it may not be improper to say that little.

The women of the lower sort are much weather-beaten, and by no means handsome. Beauty is soon withered by early marriage, by hard labour, and scanty fare. They have, however, a smart air, which arises partly from their manner of tying up their hair on the crown of their heads, and interspersing it with flowers and other ornaments.[1] In the neighbourhood of Pekin I met some ladies of the higher ranks in their carriages, who appeared to have fair complexions and delicate features. They were all painted, as, indeed, are many of the inferior classes.

The Tartar ladies have hitherto kept their legs at liberty, and have not submitted to the Chinese operation of crippling the feet, though it is said that many of their husbands were desirous of introducing it into their families. I made many inquiries relative to this strange practice, but with little satisfaction. Chou-ta-gin admitted that no very good reason could be given for it. Its being an ancient custom was the best he could assign, and he confessed that a religious adherence to ancient customs, without much investigation of their origin, was a principal feature in the Chinese character. He added, however, that it possibly might have taken rise from Oriental jealousy, which had always been ingenious in its contrivances for securing the ladies to their owners; and that certainly a good way of keeping them at home was to make it very troublesome and painful to them to gad about.[2]

[1] 'The women had painted faces, wore a blue cotton frock, reaching nearly to the knees like that of the men, and a pair of wide trousers, red, green, or yellow, extended to below the calf of the leg, where they were drawn close, the better to display their cramped, unnatural feet and swollen ankles. Bunches of gaudy artificial flowers were stuck in their hair. The best dressed men wore a sort of velvet cap, a short jacket, with wide sleeves made of cotton cloth, black, blue, or brown silk quilted petticoat, and black satin boots. The common people wore large straw hats, blue or black cotton frocks, wide cotton trousers, and thick, clumsy shoes, sometimes made of straw. A single pair of drawers constituted, indeed, the whole clothing of a great portion of the crowd.'—J. Barrow, 'Travels in China.'

[2] 'Marco Polo takes no notice of this singular fashion, although he makes frequent mention of the beauty and dress of the women.

'The Ambassadors of Shah Rokh, the son of Tamerlane, in 1419, remark, "There were many taverns, at the doors of which sat a number of young girls of extraordinary beauty," but say nothing of the unnatural smallness of the women's feet.

'Neither do the two Mahommedans who travelled in China in the ninth century mention it.'—*Ibid.*

It is inconceivable from whence arises the dissatisfaction at our natural form that seems to be felt by the whole human species, from the politest nations of Europe to the most barbarous islanders of the South Seas. Boring the ears, painting the face, dusting and plastering the hair with powder and grease, are equally fashionable in London and Otaheite; but this perverseness and disfiguration are not confined to ourselves, but extended by us to inferior creatures.

A noble lord of my acquaintance in Ireland contrived to put out all the eyes of Argus, and extinguish the brilliant plumage of his peacocks, and to propagate in their stead a breed of whites, greys, and cream colours. The good wives of Dorking have added a supernumerary claw to all the chickens of their hatching; and our jockeys, by their docks and crops, their fan tails, short tails, and no tails at all, make their horses as little like what God made them as can possibly be imagined. We find beauty in defects, and we create defects where we do not find them.

I by no means wish to apologize for the Chinese custom of squeezing their women's petitoes into the shoes of an infant, which I think an infernal distortion. Yet so much are people subject to be warped and blinded by fashion, that every Chinese above the vulgar considers it as a female accomplishment not to be dispensed with. Nay, a reverend apostolic missionary at Pekin assured me that, in love-affairs, the glimpse of a little fairy foot was to a Chinese a most powerful provocative. Perhaps, after all, we are not quite free from a little folly of the same kind ourselves. We have not yet, indeed, pushed it to the extreme which the Chinese have done, yet are we such admirers of it that, what with tight shoes, high heels, and ponderous buckles, if our ladies' feet are not crippled, they are certainly very much contracted, and it is impossible to say where the abridgment will stop. It is not a great many years ago that in England thread-paper waists, steel stays, and tight-lacing were in high fashion, and the ladies' shapes were so tapered down from the bosom to the hips that there was some danger of breaking off in the middle upon any exertion. No woman was thought worth having who measured above eighteen inches round at the girdle. At present a contrary mode prevails; Prior's comeliness of side is exploded, and protuberance is procured wherever it can be fitted. But the Chinese ladies, like other Asiatics, never alter the costume of their dress; and I suppose that gowns they now wear are much of the same cut as those of their ancestors before the Flood. But though the habit is the same, they are perhaps a little more changeable and coquettish than their ancestors were in the choice and disposition of their ornaments.

The shift is of silk netting, the waistcoat and drawers are usually of silk, and trimmed or lined with furs in cold weather. Over all they wear a long satin robe, made full and loose, which is gracefully gathered round the waist and confined with a sash. They adorn and set off their hair with ribbons and flowers, with bodkins, mock pearls or real ones below a certain size; but wear neither powder nor pomatum, diamonds nor feathers. Many of the mysteries of a European toilet they have never heard of, though perfectly versed in all those of their own, to which they devote no small portion of their time. They have not yet been initiated in the secrets of the captivation by false pretences and love swindling, or of eking out a skeleton figure by a cork rump, a muslin bosom, and a buckram stomacher; for though they reckon corpulence a beauty in a man, they think it a most palpable blemish in their own sex. They, therefore, pay particular attention to the slimness of their shape, and have the art of preserving it in all its ease and delicacy without effort or compression.

Though a Chinese has properly but one wife at the head of his family, the number of his concubines depends on his opulence and discretion. So far, in this point, Chinese and European manners seem pretty much alike; but they differ widely in another. The mistresses of a Chinese live in tolerable harmony together in the same house, and even under the authority of the wife, who adopts and educates their children; and these children inherit from the father equally with her own.

I have been the less reserved in what I have said upon this subject, because I was willing to convey an impartial idea of some things in China which, to our local vanity and prejudice, appear monstrous or incredible. Nor was I sorry to have this opportunity of remarking how little right we have to despise and ridicule other nations on the mere account of their differing from us in little points of manners and dress, as we can very nearly match them with similar follies and absurdities of our own.

Religion.

The project of an alliance between Church and State does not seem to have entered into the contemplation of the politicians of China. Perhaps the pride of despotism disdained the support of religion, or the wisdom of Government rendered the aid of superstition unnecessary. The Europeans who visited the country first were astonished to find a general toleration of religious worship and opinions prevail, and to observe Lamas and Bonzes, Parsees, Jews, and Mahommedans living in peace together, and believing as they pleased; a state of society as yet uncommon in Europe, and at that time little expected to be found in Asia. It is, therefore, not improbable that Christians would have enjoyed the same indulgences had it not been for the rashness of the missionaries. The pious zeal of these good fathers outran their discretion, and they seemed desirous of anticipating the promised call of the Gentiles, without patiently waiting for the day of the Lord. The jealousy of the State was naturally alarmed, and measures were adopted to repress an innovation which, if not regulated, might soon become dangerous; but if it were found innocent, might be afterwards allowed. And now, notwithstanding the disturbances at different times, occasioned by their apostolic labours, and the persecutions which have raged against the Christians in China, they are neither forbidden the profession nor restrained in the exercise of their religion at Pekin. They enjoy a perfect toleration, and are capable of holding offices in the State; nothing more is required of them than not to interrupt the public tranquillity by working at conversions and fishing for proselytes. In these regulations they apparently acquiesce, and conduct themselves with much more prudence and circumspection than their predecessors.

Some few of their neophytes may, perhaps, be adult persons, but the greater part are foundlings, or children purchased from indigent parents. They send some of the most promising youths to be educated in the Chinese community at Naples. Those of them whom I had occasion to know the best appeared to be persons of acute understandings, of gentle manners, and sincere piety, zealous for the propagation of their faith, but possessing little energy or powers of persuasion.

Although it is affirmed that there are at present about

CHRISTIANITY IN CHINA

one hundred and fifty thousand Christians in China, the number, at the same time, is confessed to be much smaller than it was a century or two ago; but I much question whether many of those who were called Christians could fairly come under that description. The first Evangelical adventurers there highly magnified their own merits, and the success of their labours. There appear to be, indeed, several unfavourable circumstances to the rapid growth of Christianity in China. The prohibition or restriction of sensual gratifications in a despotic country, where there are so few others, is difficult to be relished; confession is repugnant to the close and suspicious character of the nation, and penance would but aggravate the misery of him whose inheritance is his labour and poverty his punishment. Against it is also the state of society in China. A religion which requires that women should at stated times communicate to priests in private their thoughts and actions must be particularly distasteful to a Chinese husband, who had not himself been suffered to see his wife till the day of his marriage, and who but seldom suffers her afterwards to see even her near relations of another sex. A religion like that of Mahommed can only be extended by violence and terror, for the natural stubbornness of men does not readily give way to novel impressions; but the mild spirit of the Gospel is most readily infused through the means of gentleness, persuasion, and imperceptible perseverance. These are the proper instruments of conversion, and peculiarly belong to the fair sex, whose eloquence on such occasions gives charms to devotion and ornaments to truth. The earliest stages of Christianity received no small support from female agency and example, and for what show of religion still appears in our churches we are surely not a little indebted to the piety and attendance of the women.

The missionaries at Pekin, with the exception of one or two of the youngest, appear perfectly reconciled to their situation, and to live as contentedly and happily as they probably would do in any other place. Among them the Italian and French are best informed, the most learned, and the most liberal in their sentiments; but their coadjutors, the Portuguese, still retain a considerable share of ancient bigotry and rancour. They all wear the Chinese dress, acquire the language of the country, and in outward appearance are scarcely to be distinguished from the other inhabitants.

There is properly no established religion in China, none

to which any monopoly of particular privileges is attached, none that excludes the professors of another from office and command. The employments of the State are open to all subjects, whether they pray in a Miao or a Pagoda. Of those deputed by the Emperor to attend my Embassy, the Legate followed the doctrine of the Lamas; Van-ta-gin was a disciple of the Bonzes; and Chou-ta-gin a Confucionist.

The Tartars, for the most part, profess the Court religion, which is the worship of Fo, according to the doctrine and discipline of the grand Delai-Lama, the Pope or Patriarch of Lhassa in Thibet, of whom so many fables have been related, and sometimes credited, in Europe.

The mass of the people worship a deity by the name of Fo, but he is understood to be by them a different personage from the Fo of the Court, although he is reported to have come from the westward, as well as his namesake, and to have preached his revelation at a very remote period of time, long before the Christian era.

The higher ranks of the Chinese and those of good education are, many of them, what in England we courteously call the free-thinkers and philosophers; the rest are mostly disciples of Confucius, of whom there are two sects.[1]

Lay Europeans as well as missionaries, assuming the dress and manners of the Chinese, and desirous of entering into the Emperor's service at Pekin, would, I believe, be received and naturalized without much difficulty. I saw nothing at Canton to hinder any Englishman who would wear the Chinese habit and speak the Chinese language from becoming one of themselves if he chose it, and of becoming even a Hong merchant if possessed of a sufficient stock of money and address. It is true he could not easily quit the country and return home without a particular permission. Several missionaries, however, have found means of procuring it, and are now actually resident in Europe. But whilst we are startled with such difficulties in China, how can we forget that, at this hour, no person whatever can depart from Russia without a formal passport from the Chancery? An attempt to escape from such a restriction would be highly criminal, and incur a most rigorous punishment. Every foreigner whatsoever, even the most respectable English merchant at St. Petersburg, is subject to this regulation as much as the meanest peasant in the Empire.

In speaking of the religions of the Chinese, I ought to

[1] Barrow naively remarks anent Confucius that 'his religious notions and morals do him great credit.'

THE TARTAR CONQUEST

have mentioned the Tao-tses, or Immortals, who are the most ancient of all the superstitions, being, as it is pretended, some thousand years antecedent to the revelation of Fo; but as they are not at present very numerous, it was the less necessary to be particular on their subject. For the same reason I have not noticed the various subdivisions of the other religions which are from time to time branching into new sects and fraternities, like the Methodists, Seceders, Swedenburghers, Moravians, and Muggletonians of England.

Government, Justice and Property, Science, Trade, etc.

The ancient constitution of China differed essentially from the present. Although the Emperor was in truth despotic, the power and administration of the State resided in the great councils or tribunals. It was a government by law, and when attempts were made by their Princes to render it otherwise, as often happened, rebellion was the consequence, and expulsion the penalty. Hence, according to history, the regular succession of the Crown was many times broken through, new Sovereigns elected, and the former constitution restored. The present family on the throne is the twenty-second distinct dynasty whose hands have swayed the sceptre of China.

The Government, as it now stands, is properly the tyranny of a handful of Tartars over more than three hundred millions of Chinese. Various causes have contributed to this wonderful phenomenon in the political world.

When the Tartars entered China, the country had long languished under a weak administration, had been desolated by civil wars and rebellions, and was then disputed by several unworthy competitors. The Tartars first took part as auxiliaries, but soon became principals, and by valour and perseverance surmounted every obstacle to their own establishment. The spirit of the Chinese was subdued by the weight of calamity, and the less reluctantly submitted to a foreign usurpation. The conquerors were conducted by a leader of a calm judgment as well as of a resolute mind. Chinese preceptors were appointed to conduct the education of the young Tartar Princes. The Chinese language was preserved, the established forms of office and administration were retained, and the external manners of the vanquished were assumed by the victors. All these contributed at first to impose upon the people, and to reconcile them to the new Government. From hence also has arisen a vulgar mistake that the Tartars had indiscriminately and sincerely adopted all the maxims, principles, and customs of the Chinese, and that the two nations were now perfectly amalgamated and incorporated together. So far as respects the habit and head-dress, they are certainly assimilated, but it is not the Tartar who has conformed to the Chinese costume, but the Chinese who has been obliged to imitate the Tartar. The nature and character of each continue unchanged, and their different situations and intrinsic sentiments cannot be concealed under any disguise. Superiority animates the one, depression is felt by the other. Most of our books confound them together, and talk of them as if they made only one nation under the general name of China; but whatever might be concluded from outward appearances, the real distinction is never forgotten by the Sovereign, who, though he pretends to be perfectly impartial, conducts himself at bottom by a systematic nationality, and never for a moment loses sight of the cradle of his power. A century and a half has not made Tchien-lung a Chinese. He remains at this hour, in all his policy, as true a Tartar as any of his ancestors.

The Viceroys of the provinces and the commanders of the armies and the great officers of State are almost all Tartars.

The detail of business, indeed, and the laborious departments are chiefly carried on by Chinese, as being more regularly educated, more learned, and more patient than the Tartars. In all the tribunals of justice and finance, in all the courts of civil or military administration, an equal number of Tartar assessors is indispensably necessary to be present in order to watch over and control the others. A Chinese may preside at the board and pronounce an opinion, but the prompter and manager is a Tartar, who directs and governs the performers. These regulations and precautions sufficiently disclose the Sovereign's real opinion of the tenure of his Empire, and how little he depends upon the affection and loyalty of his Chinese subjects. Considering the circumstances, the government must be a task of inconceivable vigilance and toil, and yet it is a task that has hitherto been performed with wonderful ability and success. Whoever is the Atlas destined by the Emperor to bear this load of empire when he dies is yet unknown;

but on whatever shoulders it may fall, another transmigration of Fo into the next Emperor will be necessary to enable him to sustain it on its present balance ; for, although within the serene atmosphere of the Court everything wears the face of happiness and applause, yet it cannot be concealed that the nation in general is far from being contented. The frequent insurrections in the distant provinces are ambiguous oracles of the real sentiments of the people. The predominance of the Tartars and the Emperor's partiality for them are the common subjects of conversation among the Chinese whenever they meet together in private. There are certain mysterious societies in every province, who, though narrowly watched by the Government, find means to elude its vigilance, and often hold secret assemblies, where they revive the memory of ancient independence, brood over recent injuries, and meditate revenge.

Though much circumscribed in the course of our travels, we had opportunities of observation seldom afforded to others and not neglected by us. The character of the inhabitants, and the effects resulting from the polity and principles of the Government, naturally claimed my particular attention. In my researches I often perceived the ground to be hollow under a vast superstructure. The Chinese are now recovering from the blows that had stunned them ; they are awaking from the political stupor they had been thrown into by the Tartar impression, and begin to feel their native energies revive. The volume of the Empire is now grown too ponderous and disproportionate to be easily grasped by a single hand, be it ever so capacious and strong. It is possible, notwithstanding, that the momentum impressed on the machine by the vigour and wisdom of the present Emperor may keep it steady and entire in its orbit for a considerable time longer, but I should not be surprised if its dislocation and dismemberment were to take place before my own dissolution.

In the ancient accounts of China the administration of justice, the strict impartiality, and the equal security afforded to all men by the laws, are mentioned in such high strains of eulogy that we are tempted to suppose this was the spot where the last footsteps of Astrea were imprinted. So long a period has elapsed since that time that the marks are a good deal effaced, and seem to be wearing out every day. My friend Chou-ta-gin endeavoured to impress me with an idea of the equity and regularity of the courts where he presided, and as I entertain a very favourable opinion of him, I dare say that few of the others are better ordered or more pure; but it escaped from him in conversation that considerable presents were often made by the suitor to the judge. I explained to him as well as I could the nature and principles of our jurisdiction, which rendered the acceptance of presents as unnecessary and improper. To this he answered that the circumstance of presents in China ought not to be misinterpreted, and that the offering and receiving them formed a part of their ceremonies, and were an established usage from which no mischief was to be feared, and assured me that perquisites of office had seldom any influence on the determination of a cause. Perhaps he did not wish to deceive me, for there are some favourite points on which men are apt to deceive themselves; but I have strong ground to suspect the general course of justice to be very much otherwise.

I had been informed that a delinquent was sometimes allowed when sentenced to be bambooed to hire another person to undergo the punishment in his place, but the fact was strongly denied. Neither did I find it now to be true, though possibly it may have been so in former times, that a son might substitute himself for his father's punishment.

The order and administration of the gaols are said to be remarkably good. The debtor and felon are confined in separate places, and not permitted to approach each other, but the case of a debtor in other respects is extremely cruel. Although he should resign every farthing of his property, yet, if it be insufficient to discharge the whole of his debt, and his relations cannot or will not make up the deficiency, he is condemned to wear a neck-yoke in public for a certain period. If his insolvency be incurred by gaming, he is liable besides to corporal punishment. The Emperor's debtors, if fraudulently such, are strangled; if such only by common misfortunes, their wives and children and property of every kind are sold, and themselves banished into the wilds of Tartary. But though this may be strictly the letter of the law, the Emperor always makes a merit of forgiving those who, from unavoidable misfortunes, have nothing left to pay.

As in China the interests of the Emperor are always the first consideration, no property can be secured against his claims. In cases of delinquency, confiscation is inevitable.

If a man dies without a will, his lands, etc., are equally divided among his sons, reserving a proper dower for the widow, which varies according to the province where she chooses to reside. The daughters have nothing, but are maintained until they marry by their brothers ; and if there be no brothers, by their next inheriting relation.

Rank in China is generally supposed to be the reward of merit and service, and it frequently is so ; but there appears to be one glaring partiality in the distribution of it. A Chinese seldom attains the highest degree till very advanced in life, but I have seen Tartars already possessed of it at the age of five- or six-and-twenty.

In all the public acts and papers a Mandarin is invariably styled according to the order of his button, and if he should be degraded to an inferior one he is obliged to write himself : Mandarin, formerly of the class ——, but now degraded to the —— class. This mode of punishment is considered rather a fatherly kind of correction than as a mark of much severity, and the culprit, after a certain term of contrition and probation, is usually restored to his former dignity.

In respect to science, the Chinese are certainly far behind the European world. They have but a very limited knowledge of mathematics and astronomy, although from some of the printed accounts of China one might be led to imagine that they were well versed in them. Doctor Dinwiddie gave a few lectures and exhibited some experiments at Canton to the English Factory, which were constantly attended by the Chinese merchants, who seemed highly delighted with them, and showed the strongest desire of further instruction. Had Dinwiddie remained at Canton and continued his courses, I dare say he might have soon realized a very considerable sum of money from his Chinese pupils alone. The Mandarins at Pekin manifested very little disposition of this kind. It was observed that most of the great men who went to see the globes, the planetarium, the barometer, and pendulums put up at Yuen-min-yuen affected to view them with careless indifference, as if such things were quite common and familiar to them, and the use of them well understood. They could not, however, conceal their sense of the beauty and elegance of our Derby porcelain when they saw the ornamental vases belonging to Vulliamy's clocks.

As it is generally supposed that the art of printing is of great antiquity among the Chinese, I must not pass it by without some notice. Their printing, such as I saw, is merely the impression of a wooden cut, or rather, perhaps, from an embossing or carving in alto-relievo upon a flat board or tablet, which, when wetted with ink and impressed by the paper, delivers a reversed copy of itself. From the size of the paper and the tediousness of execution, it would seem that new publications are not very frequent, and that knowledge is not so rapidly disseminated in China as in England by reviews, magazines, and such other periodical oracles of taste and literature.

The weekly gazettes published in most of the great cities of the Empire are, I believe, struck off in their common method of block-printing.[1]

Whether printing as practised by us be an original European invention, or whether the first hint of it was received by way of Tartary from China, I will not presume to determine; but it is certain that the art was not known in Europe till one hundred and fifty years after Marco Polo's return from China. As he did not impart the discovery, I conclude he was ignorant of it, and that such books as he may have seen there he mistook for manuscripts; and indeed, to the eye of a stranger, they have much of that appearance.

For near forty years past our knowledge of the commerce of China has been confined to Canton.

The profits of the Hong merchants upon their foreign trade must be very great to enable them to bear the expense of the numerous and magnificent presents which they make to the superior Mandarins at Canton, who, in their turn, send a part of these presents to the Emperor and his Ministers and favourites at Gehol.

By what I saw, and by the reports concerning the things I did not see, I am led to believe what I have been assured of—that the Emperor possesses to the value of two millions sterling in various toys, jewellery, glass, musical automatons, and other figures, instruments of different kinds, clocks, watches, etc., etc., all or most of them made in London.

The trade of the Dutch, French, Americans, Danes, and Swedes with China is so much declined, and so likely in a few years to be almost annihilated, that it is the less necessary for me to dwell upon the subject. The Danes and Swedes have, in a great measure, given it up, and will, I believe, send but few more ships to Canton. Many years must elapse before it can revive in France. The Americans,

[1] 'The press in China is as free as in England, and the profession of printing open to every one, which is a singular circumstance, and perhaps the only instance of the kind in a despotic Government.'— J. Barrow, 'Travels in China.'

TRADE WITH RUSSIA

with all their contrivances and industry, are not likely, as I am well informed, to pursue it with much advantage; and as for the Dutch, the affairs of their company in these parts of the world are in so deplorable a condition that it scarcely is possible to contemplate them without compassion, or to approach them without shrinking. They afford an awful lesson for our instruction.[1]

The trade between Russia and China, which had been long interrupted, is now open again. The returns to China are made chiefly in furs, leather, and woollen cloth, the latter mostly German, with a small quantity of English superfine. In my road to Gehol, I met with several camels laden with these woollens; and so ignorant in matters of trade were many of the Chinese, that they believed them to be the manufacture of Tartary, just as several English articles which I saw at Pekin were supposed to be the production of Canton.

Conclusion.

Before I set out upon my Embassy to China, I perused all the books that had been written about the country in all the languages I could understand. With everybody from whom I had hopes of information I endeavoured to converse, and where that could not be done I corresponded with them by letter. Having thus stored up in my mind all the materials within my reach, I shut my books, and as soon as I arrived in the Yellow Sea I began a different course of study upon the same subject. Instead of reading the accounts of others, I turned to the originals themselves, and lost no opportunity in my power of perusing and considering them.

The intercourse of the Chinese with foreigners is, however, so regulated and restrained, and the difficulty of obtaining correct information so great, that the foregoing papers must not be received without reserve, nor regarded as otherwise than as merely the result of my own researches and reflections.

For I am sensible that, besides being defective in many points, they will be found to differ a good deal from the accounts of former travellers; but I am far from saying

[1] 'The Dutch, discovering their views too soon, in China, about a century ago, were massacred.'—Abbé Raynall's 'History,' Lord Macartney's Notes.

that the errors may not be in me rather than in them. I may have seen neither so well nor so much as they did, but whatever I did see or could learn from good authority I have made it a point most faithfully to represent and report. The picture may seem harsh, cold, or ill-coloured, but the fancy of the painter has intruded nothing into the piece that did not appear to him in the original from which he drew.

He meant neither to embellish nor disfigure, but solely to give as just a resemblance as he could.

CHAPTER XIII

WHEN Macartney arrived in London on September 5, 1794,[1] he was gratified to find that during his absence he had not been forgotten, the King having bestowed on him the title of Earl of Macartney in the county of Antrim on March 1 previously.

He found, however, his wife much occupied and in great trouble, her mother being hopelessly ill of a lingering and painful malady. Lady Portarlington was at that time unable to undertake the long and tiring journey to England, and to her Lady Macartney wrote fully and frequently of all that occurred.

'Lord M. wants me very much here. He only arrived at this house [3, Curzon Street] last Friday to dinner, but is, thank God, perfectly well.'

Lady Bute died shortly after,[2] to the great grief of her daughters, Lady Macartney alone finding consolation in religion, and the thought that the mother she so adored, after many trials and much suffering, was at length at rest. She thus mentions her husband's sympathy: '. . . Lord Macartney, too, is very kind. I have never been able to stay with him above three days at a time since he arrived.'

[1] '*Wednesday, September* 3, 1794.—At five o'clock p.m. we anchored safe, after a long and curious voyage, at Spithead, and soon felt the inexpressible satisfaction of once more treading the terra firma of our native country.'—Æneas Anderson, 'Narrative of Embassy to China.'

[2] Lady Bute died on November 6, 1794. Lord Bute had predeceased her about two and a half years, as he died on March 10, 1792, some months before Lord Macartney's departure for China.

The winter following passed quietly at home, but in the summer of 1795 Macartney was sent on a confidential mission to Louis XVIII., then resident at Verona. This had to do with the probabilities of Louis' accession to the throne of France on the death of his nephew, and Macartney had orders to reside near his person and watch events, especially the dealings of the other Courts of Europe in the matter. Louis, on his side, was extremely anxious that the English Court should openly recognize him as King of France, and assist in placing him at the head of the Royalist party in that country. Barrow merely touches upon all this, observing that the undertaking was 'of a delicate and confidential nature, the particulars of which there are many reasons for not disclosing at present.'

On Macartney's journey to Italy he passed through Anspach, whose Margrave had lately abdicated.

'The country already shows evident marks of incipient decay. The people and villages have an impoverished air, . . . and the roads are swarming with importunate beggars of both sexes. Whilst the Margrave resided in his dominions he was extremely beloved by his subjects, but since his abdication of his inheritance they never mention his name without rage and indignation, nor do they seem to be much better satisfied with their new master.'

He arrived at Verona early in the morning on August 6, after a somewhat hurried journey, in the course of which he rested only every second night, and 'met with all the usual distresses of a traveller, such as bad roads, bad inns, bad horses, and bad weather.'

'*August* 6, 1795.—Arrived at Verona at 7 a.m. At 10 sent a note to the Maréchal de Castries . . . to say I was just come, and would wait upon him when convenient. . . . He came to me himself in half an hour. Our conversation was not long, as he naturally was desirous to attend His Majesty as soon as possible on the occasion, but during the short time it lasted he expressed himself very properly on the occasion of my mission, of which the King had been informed a few days before by the common post in a letter from the Duc de Harcourt. . . . In about two hours' time he returned . . . and informed me that, if not inconvenient to me after the fatigue of my journey, His Majesty would be glad of my company to dine with him at four o'clock. . . . I accordingly accompany'd the Marshall at the appointed hour, who presented me to the King, by whom I was received in a very gracious manner. . . . I said that, tho' I had not, for reasons of which he was already apprized, brought any credential letters, yet I was authorized to express the King, my master's, compliments of condolence on the death of the late King, and that I hoped the time was not far off when I should also be able to express my compliments of felicitation on his re-establishment upon the throne under happier auspices. He said it was impossible to say what he felt upon the many essential marks of kindness and friendship from the King of Great Britain. . . . After about a quarter of an hour . . . dinner was announced, and in the passage His Majesty presented me himself to all the persons of the company. . . Among them was the Prince de Nassau, . . . now in the service of Spain, whither he was to proceed this night by way of Genoa. By his opportunity I wrote a few lines to my Lord Bute at Madrid to mention my arrival here, and the report that I had met with at Augsburgh of a peace being signed at Basle between France and Spain.[1] . . . M. de Nassau . . . said he gave little credit to it, altho' he owned that some time ago there had appeared a disposition in the Court of Spain to treat with the Convention, but that the death of Louis XVII. had occasioned a change of sentiment, . . . and that Spain would now . . . wait to see what was likely to arise from the event of the young King's demise. He seems to be an able man, speaks with an appearance of good information and good sense, but rather with too much the tone of an adventurer for a person of his rank. He seems to be uncommonly zealous in the cause of the exiled Princes, to whom he has long been particularly known.'

To this letter Lord Bute returned a lengthy reply in cipher, in the course of which he said :

[1] 'I confess to you no one was ever more duped throughout the whole business of the Peace, amused with fair speeches, communications, etc.; although from the first I knew of the negotiation, I flattered myself that the results of the campaign would have proved too favourable to admit of such a business, and that the Minister himself was too wise to conclude a treaty before it was ascertained.'
—Private Letter to Macartney from Lord Bute.

'The news of the Peace produced as much astonishment at this Court as it possibly has done in other parts of Europe ; so much so, that we are inclined to believe the Minister was rather disposed to temporize than to conclude it.[1] . . . You know the character of the Duke d'Alcudia—young, idle, ignorant, though with a great portion of common sense, but, until the present occasion, extremely open, frank, and sincere, exceedingly partial to the old Spanish system of hatred to the French, and desirous of uniting with England. . . . Upon the death of the King of France the Duke seemed keen for acknowledging Monsieur, and insisted upon my informing the Court of England of the determination, and his master's desire that we should do the same. . . . I cannot conclude without mentioning that the present language of this Court is, to a degree, virulent against England. Far from disarming, they appear to increase their navy, and I do not see the possibility of avoiding a rupture. . . . What do you say, my dear Lord, to the Spaniard, who, having publicly renounced his claim to the Monarchy of France, by acknowledging the Republic, as publicly rewards his Minister for the glorious act by a title unknown before in this country, Prince of the Peace ?'

On August 7 M. de Castries visited the British Envoy, in order to discuss the contents of the dispatches brought by the latter. He also gave him a copy of King Louis' proclamation, a document entirely of the French King's own composition, which M. de Castries hoped would be perfectly agreeable to the English Court,

'being founded upon my Lord Grenville's note to the Duc de Harcourt, and breathing that spirit of clemency and conciliation as could not fail to produce a proper effect upon the majority of the French nation.'

M. de Castries then went on to press for the recognition of the King by Great Britain, saying it would produce a most powerful impression in France. He knew for certain

[1] The Court of Spain kept their intentions of making peace with the French Convention so secret that none of their own Ministers in this part of the world had any suspicion of it, insomuch that it was their tone to treat it as a mere Jacobin story, for several days after it was known by almost everyone else to have been already signed.'—Private Dispatches to Lord Grenville from Verona.

NECESSITY FOR CAUTION

the Empress of Russia to be in favour of it, and that the recognition of Louis XVIII. by those countries

'would operate most forcibly in favour of the King's cause, and give almost as much courage and energy to his friends as if the recognition were more general.'

Lord Macartney pointed out the reasons why the British Court thought differently upon the matter, and added that the more he saw of affairs, the more persuaded he was of the necessity for caution and restraint of the King's impatience, as a premature recognition could not fail to be extremely embarrassing to all parties, and more especially to the King himself.

M. de Castries further complained of the continual references from Vienna to London and London to Vienna, and lamented that, in consequence, many precious moments were lost, and the critical point of action could not be seized. Macartney replied, directly a Royalist party was formed in any part of France that could support itself with effect the English recognition would follow without delay. To this M. de Castries not unnaturally observed that acknowledgment from the Court of Great Britain would the better enable such a party to subsist and maintain itself. Lord Macartney then turned the conversation upon the King's residence, which he thought seemed 'not a very eligible or pleasant one'; but M. de Castries answered that, all things considered, he was by no means dissatisfied with it or the conduct of the Venetian Republic towards the King, and questioned Macartney upon the likelihood of pecuniary assistance from England. To this the latter made answer that he hoped to give a satisfactory reply,

'but added, with a less serious air, how confoundedly poor we were grown from the enormous expenses attending our exertions for the cause in almost every part of the world, . . . and that at this moment there was less opportunity left to the King, my master, of doing what his own generosity and liberality would make him desirous of towards this most Christian Majesty.'

After the departure of his visitor, Macartney set himself to study King Louis' proclamation, which he found very different from what he could have wished, in spite of its being well written in parts. It also differed greatly from the sketch put into his hands by Lord Grenville previous to his departure from London. He described the document as

'rather the declamation of a pulpit from a preacher to his sinful congregation, than a plain impressive discourse from a father to his faulty children, from a King to his subjects, where mutual errors were to be admitted, to be pardoned on one hand and rectified on the other.'

Macartney learnt with concern that copies of this composition had already been sent to the Comte d'Artois and the Prince of Condé, and would have been despatched even sooner but that the King could not actually spare the fifty louis d'or necessary to enable the messenger, M. de Hautepool, to perform the journey. That event having taken place ten days previous to Macartney's arrival at Verona, the proclamation was most probably by that time printed and disseminated in France.

On August 8 Macartney had a private interview of nearly three hours' duration with the King, in which he endeavoured to discover the true state of his mind and his real sentiments. Louis expressed his regret that any past action on his part or that of his brothers should have given cause for discontent to the King of Great Britain, whose views he was anxious to conform to. He repeated what M. de Castries had said as to the readiness of the Empress of Russia to acknowledge him, and

'was persuaded that, if Great Britain would do so too, the other Powers would follow without delay. He seemed to think that till that seal was put upon him by us his importance and regal existence was incomplete, . . . and that neither the Prince of Condé's army would be properly organized nor Marshall Clairfait's be quickened into the activity which it was capable of.'

The King further said there was a Royalist party in La

LORD MACARTNEY

From the Drawing by BARTOLOZZI *in the British Museum*

To face p. 418

Vendée, which had been in existence for two years. He spoke of his manifesto, saying he had drawn it up himself as soon as the news of the death of his nephew had been confirmed, and spoke of the proclamation 'with a degree of partiality as to induce me to believe him the real parent of the offspring.'

It being by then beyond recall, its criticism became a matter of much delicacy, especially as the King seemed persuaded it was composed according to the spirit of Lord Grenville's note to the Duc de Harcourt. On Macartney pointing out some matters which seemed to be brought forward in a different manner to what his Government thought best, Louis in reply regretted the British Envoy had not arrived earlier, as he might have concerted with him some alterations in the paper, but added that he had framed his discourse from his knowledge of the people he was to speak to, 'and drew the French character, and compared it with the English in a very masterly manner and with a good deal of wit and pleasantry.' He looked upon the ancient constitution of France with veneration, but assured Macartney that if he ascended the throne he intended to devote himself to the reform of abuses. He also seemed quite desirous of a perfect amnesty, with the exception of the regicides, and even with regard to them said, though he could not permit them to remain in France, he would allow them to remove with their possessions to America, which country, he supposed, was the only one they could wish to go to, or where they could expect to be received.

Macartney had many more confidential interviews with Louis. In these the King spoke constantly of his wish to be in action at the head of his adherents in La Vendée—'*de jouer le tout pour le tout*'—and did not take at all kindly to the British proposal that he should proceed to Rome or Gibraltar on his departure from Verona. To go there, he said, would take him still further from where he wished, and ought to be, and would give an improper impression to his subjects, more especially as it had been mentioned in several papers that he had renounced his throne in consideration of receiving compensation for it. He concluded by saying:

'My lord, you have certainly fulfilled your instructions, and I have expressed to you my feelings upon them. I cannot possibly . . . think of Rome. It was proposed by Spain long since as being nearer to her than Verona, and at a time when she gave me hopes of soon receiving me, . . . and yet I could not then bring myself to the measure.'

The King's principal advisers, the Maréchal de Castries and Baron de Flachelande, were of the same opinion, and strongly pressed Macartney to recommend to Lord Grenville the advisability of Louis going to Cuxhaven, and being met there by a British ship to convey him to La Vendée. To them Macartney replied that if the King would not go to Rome for the short time that was proposed, instead of England directing his conduct, he was directing hers. They entreated him not to view the matter in that light, and to have some regard for the feelings of the King. At length it was arranged that Louis should remove from Verona to Swabia, as soon as a suitable residence could be found neither too close to the Prince of Condé's army nor too distant from it, where he was to remain till further instructions from England. They then renewed the subject of the money, and seemed disappointed that Macartney expressed himself as only authorized to make an advance of £8,000. To Lord Grenville he wrote as follows:

'The appearance of everything about the King indicates many symptoms of great distress. His table, which is so serious a matter to a Frenchman, is scantily and inelegantly served. His servants are few and shabbily dressed, and even in his own private apartments there seems a want of proper furniture. He is lodged about half a mile without the first gate of the city, at a villa which he has hired. It is neither large, handsome, nor convenient. . . . There is, however, a pretty garden belonging to it, the prospect of which alone is a considerable resource to a Prince, who passes a great part of his time in his closet, and for several months has never stirred beyond the enclosure.

THE KING'S CHARACTER

Indeed, from the great corpulence and unwieldiness of his figure, he is little able to take much exercise of any kind.

'He certainly has a good understanding, a respectable share of literature, and appears to be particularly well versed, not only in the history of France, but in that of other nations, as far as connected with it. He talks Italian tolerably well, understands the English language, and speaks his own with great correctness and volubility. His manner and address are affable and pleasing, and his deportment to those about him gracious, and even familiar, without departing from his dignity, which is still apparent through his eclipse. Nor is he by any means defective in judgment when not biassed by the prepossessions of his education, and even these are in a considerable degree diminished or softened by misfortune and reflection. Adversity seems to have improved and not exasperated him. He is by no means a bigot, as has been supposed. He is not even at bottom devout, but imagines that decency and propriety require a certain exterior conformity to the rules and ceremonies of the worship he professes, and performs all the duties which are enjoined by it. He never fails to hear Mass every day, or to observe the stated fasts of his Church, always abstaining from flesh meat on Fridays and Saturdays. It is affirmed that he never showed any turn towards practical gallantry, and that his attachment to Madame de Balby was merely a tie of long acquaintance and habit, without the smallest link of a more electric nature. He is susceptible of private friendship, and steady in his observance of it, and his courtiers and attendants approach him and serve him with respect, zeal, and affection. He writes regularly once a week to his Queen; but, what appears to me somewhat singular, I have never heard her name once mentioned, either by him or by anybody about him. She still resides at Turin, comfortably provided for by her father, lives a very retired life, and seldom sees anyone but a Madame de Courbillon, formerly her *femme de chambre*, who, like most favourites, is universally disliked by all those who are not so, or have not the same qualities to recommend them.

'The principal persons of business about the King are the Maréchal de Castries, the Baron de Flachelande, and the Bishop of Arras. The Maréchal is a man of honour and understanding, very capable of business, and fond of it. He is much broken by age and long service, reduced in point of health, and deeply affected by the calamities which have overwhelmed his country.

'The Baron de Flachelande is an old officer, turned of sixty, but of a strong and vigorous constitution, of quick parts, and a frank, military manner, opinionative, intriguing, and full of resources. He is much in his master's favour, and I should think deservedly so from his talents, services, and attachment.

'The Bishop of Arras is an ecclesiastic who enjoyed a great reputation and great benefices in France, of a lofty and ardent spirit, with a head much turned to politics. I am disposed to imagine he had no small share in the King's manifesto.[1]

'The other principal persons whom I have seen about the King . . . are all men of fair character, well bred and correct in their behaviour, not a roué or declared profligate among them. They all speak a language becoming their situation and circumstances, and I particularly observed that in mentioning the members of the present Government in France the term *sans culottes* never once fell from any of their lips.

'The gentlemen around the King's person, having, like other courtiers, nearly the same designs for favour and distinction, and, however unequal in desert, yet considering themselves equal in pretensions, are mutually jealous and envious, although they still live together upon terms of apparent kindness and cordiality.'

At Verona Lord Macartney met the Comtesse de Crenneville, sister of Lord Erroll, who, having been obliged to fly from France during the Revolution, in which she lost her only son, was advised to try the baths at Pisa for the recovery of her health and nerves. To her Macartney gave a letter of introduction to Mr. William Wyndham, British Minister there.

Towards the end of August arrived a letter, in her own handwriting, from the Empress of Russia to the King of France, congratulating him on his accession to that title.

---

[1] The Bishop of Arras, later on, declared to Macartney that he had had no hand in the manifesto, being absent when it was drawn up, and added it was entirely composed by the King and his secretary, there being some things in it which he should have wished to omit.

In this communication she informed him that her Ministers in London and Vienna had instructions to press both these Courts for a speedy recognition of him, and that she had strongly urged the latter to put the Prince of Condé's army on such a footing that the King himself might command it. At the same time arrived the news that a manifesto, supposed to be declaratory of the King's intentions, had been fabricated at Paris by his enemies, and circulated with great industry.

Lord Macartney, ever fond of sight-seeing, went for a short trip to Padua and Venice about this time. On his return the Maréchal de Castries told him they were suspicious of the real views of the Court of Vienna, and afraid of its making peace with the Republic, as Spain had done. They were also disturbed with regard to the future of the King's niece, Madame Royale, whom they wished should be at her uncle's disposal when set at liberty, instead of proceeding to Vienna, according to the projects of the Austrian Court. Louis was desirous that his niece should join him, wherever he might be, at first, and then proceed to Rome to remain under the care of her two aunts. This very natural demand had been made as soon as the intentions of the French Convention with regard to Madame Royale were known. It had been twice repeated, and as often evaded, if not explicitly refused by the Emperor, from what motive they were at a loss to discover, various conjectures being made, none of them very favourable to the honesty or moderation of the House of Austria.

Henry IV. had united in his person the kingdoms of France and Navarre, the latter being inherited in the female line through his mother. The States of Navarre had never confirmed the act of Louis XIII. for the alteration of the nature of the succession, and Louis XVIII., in order to prevent any doubts or unpleasant discussions upon the subject, was anxious to arrange a marriage between Madame Royale and his nephew, the Duc d'Angoulême, eldest son of the Comte d'Artois. The King's ostensible reason for desiring to see his niece was that he wished to see the only surviving member of his brother's family to satisfy himself with regard to the care that had been taken of her health and education. But to these desires the Emperor turned a deaf ear, and, it was strongly suspected, harboured designs of marrying the Princess to one of his own brothers, by that means attaching to the House of Austria whatever rights or claims she might derive as an only daughter of France.

Money and diamonds (to the value of 800,000 livres) which had been seized upon M. de Semonville in the Milanese territory were being held by the Austrian Emperor for the benefit of Madame Royale, as heir to her late father and mother. But this was not all, as Macartney wrote to Lord Grenville :

'It is farther imagined that the Emperor has it in view at a fit moment to resign the Netherlands to his brother, the projected husband of this Princess, which measure might, it is hoped, be rendered palatable both to France and England, to the latter as not leaving them in French hands, and to France as not putting them in dangerous ones. The Emperor is not, however, to be suspected of much disinterestedness in such a sacrifice, his scheme being to obtain a more valuable consideration in exchange, no less than the Great Duchy of Tuscany, the settlement of which he would wish to have annulled in his own favour, not solely as an advantage to himself, but as a punishment to his brother, whose conduct for a considerable time neither he nor any of the coalesced Powers can have seen without the highest displeasure, and whom, therefore, he would reduce to the state of an Austrian provincial governor, to be stationed in such part of his dominions as he might think fit. . . .

'I should imagine few difficulties would arise to our claims of indemnification out of Europe. No French Royalist can conceal from himself the rights we have acquired in this war to carve for ourselves such portion of the French West Indies as may be most suitable to our immediate interests and our future security. Perhaps greater impediments might be apprehended from a few selfish planters of our own colonies than from a negotiation with the French Monarchy. . . . As to the French East Indies, I know not how far it may be wished to add them to the Empire we have in Asia already, but as they are not very tenable against us in case of a war, and the charge of maintaining them is, in any case, enormous, I should imagine that a considerable part of them would not be thought a very important sacrifice. . . .

'I must not omit to mention . . . an important passage in one of my conversations with the King. Complaining of the slowness of the Court of Vienna, he dropped that it was perhaps owing to his silence with regard to what might be expected from him in case of success. I seized the opportunity of saying that he must be sensible how natural it was for a Power that expended its blood and treasure in his service to look towards some compensation. "I understand you perfectly," he replied, "and there can be no doubt of it, but that compensation must be settled by negotiation and discussion at a future day, and my friend may then rely upon finding me perfectly disposed to act with justice and equity." . . .

'The inertion of the armies on the Rhine, the conduct of M. de Vins in the Riviera di Genoa, the perfidy of Spain, and the duplicity of other Powers, have made such an impression here that the King told me a few days ago his whole hopes and dependence rested solely on the good faith and exertions of Great Britain and Russia. He has no doubts whatever that, if the Court of London enable his brother to proceed to La Vendée in the manner at first intended, that he will maintain himself and his party there during the winter, but thinks that his own presence on the spot would be of double efficacy. The letters from Charette and the other Royalists in that part of France certainly hold out to him the strongest encouragement.'

Macartney did not at all care for his employment at the exiled Court. He found one of the most unpleasant circumstances arising from it was the number of applications from impecunious French gentlemen, who had, or thought they had, just claims on the English Government on account of real or pretended services. In vain did he disclaim having the slightest ability or influence that would be of any service in the prosecution of their demands. They persevered in their applications, and teased him without mercy.

The following letter from Sir William Hamilton was written shortly after he had heard that Lord Macartney, with whom he was on very friendly terms, had arrived at Verona on his diplomatic mission :

'NAPLES,
'*August* 25, 1795.

'It was with much satisfaction that Lady Hamilton and I heard of your being actually in Italy, as we are persuaded you will not leave it without giving us the pleasure of seeing your Lordship at Naples. We hope also that Sir George Staunton is with you. . . . Your coming to Verona gives me hopes that our Ministry are better acquainted with the affairs of France than we are here, and have good reason to expect a sudden turn in our favour from the vigorous measures now carried on in Brittany and Normandy. It is surely unfortunate that Spain should just choose this moment to make a separate peace, but I am happy to find that the Courts of Vienna and Naples are not inclined to follow the example of Spain. . . . Your Lordship will find Emma much improved in every respect, and upon so respectable a footing that the new Russian Minister, who seems to be *alert* enough, has placed his wife under Emma's direction.

'I have the honour to be, my dear Lord, with Emma's grateful love for the goodness your Lordship was pleased to show her in England,

'Your most aff[ct] humble servant,
'W. HAMILTON.'

It seemed a matter of no little difficulty to find a suitable retreat for poor Louis, and various polite excuses arrived from the Margrave of Baden with reference to the exile's sojourn in his territory. He declined to comply with the proposal unless the consent of the Emperor of Austria was first obtained. Rottenburg was then suggested as a place of residence, but to this suggestion the Emperor returned a flat refusal.

Upon the first hint of a peace between France and Spain, Louis had dispatched an Envoy to Madrid to ascertain the truth of the rumour, press for his recognition, and endeavour to obtain a more regular payment, and, if possible, an increase in the amount of the pension promised by the Spanish Government. The Envoy returned at the end of

September, conveying a letter from the King of Spain addressed simply to his brother, Louis XVIII. In it an attempt was made to excuse the peace on account of the particularly distressed condition of the country and the general discontent of the Spanish nation, arising from its great loss of men during the war, and from the total failure of public credit. As this argument was pleaded in apology for want of punctuality in paying the stipulated allowance, so was it used as a still stronger reason against making any addition to it. They further refused to allow the services of the corps of four thousand French emigrants in Spain, but assured Louis that when he was restored to his throne, he should have an immediate renewal of the *acte de famille* and all former friendship.

Louis complained bitterly to Macartney of the manner in which he had been treated, and said that if the state of Spain really rendered his abandonment necessary, the Court should, in common humanity, have given him a timely hint of the possibility of their being forced to withdraw from his interest. As far as their future friendship went, he should not want it, but prefer that of those who had shown it in his adversity. At the same time he expressed his personal affection for the Spanish King, and attributed the whole of the proceedings to a Court intrigue of the Queen and her Minister, the 'Prince of Peace,' at which new title he could not forbear smiling.

No place north of the Alps seemed open to poor Louis, and in October Macartney wrote to Lord Grenville :

'I had an affecting conversation with the King yesterday, before we went to dinner, when he lamented to me his unfortunate situation, from which, through the Court of London's solicitude for his personal safety, and through the Court of Vienna's inhospitality, he saw little prospect of relief. The kindness of the one and the coldness of the other were equally inauspicious to him. . . . I endeavoured to console him with assurances of my Court's kindest dispositions, and of their desire to do the best for his interests, . . but . . at the same time repeating that they must be the best judges of what was practicable or expedient.

I doubt, however, whether he can long remain in his present state of stagnation here, for besides . . his eagerness to be in action, those . . most attached and solicitous for his fame, . . . well knowing what impression even a slight display of exertion in so high a personage would produce, . . urge the necessity of a speedy enterprise, and junction with his brother in La Vendée, who they are apprehensive may eclipse him.'

Towards the end of November the little Court heard rumours that Madame Royale had been delivered over by the French Commissaries to the Prince and Princess de Gavre, sent by the Emperor to receive her, and that she was then on her road to Vienna by way of Innspruck. The Count d'Avary was dispatched by Louis to meet her, with orders that, if not allowed an interview with her, he should endeavour to speak to Madame de Tourzelle, a French lady, who, having had the charge of her early education, was to be permitted to attend her. Louis spoke bitterly of the impertinence and unkindness of the Austrian Court not having sent him a notification of the liberation of his niece. He said he was so extremely anxious to see the only remaining member of his unfortunate brother's family that he had intended himself to go to Innspruck for the purpose of meeting her. He was only deterred from this purpose by an apprehension of the affront of being denied access to her when he should have reached there.

By this time Lord Macartney was heartily tired of the mission, which was not at all to his taste, and wrote to Sir George Staunton that he trusted it would not be long before he was relieved. He had far more to do than what he imagined when he came there, but must continue to go on with it, as he did not love doing things by halves. His situation was neither pleasant nor lucrative, and considering the places he had filled elsewhere, not very eminent. He spoke well of Louis to Sir George, saying :

'He has as good an understanding, perhaps as much information, and certainly more virtue than any of the five Kings in the executive Directory of Paris, and adversity seems to have wrought the proper effect upon his mind.

He speaks of the principal persons concerned in the Revolution without any appearance of rancour, and of the Revolution itself with a degree of calmness and dispassion that one could scarcely expect. I own my favourable sentiments of him. I have seen him almost every day for these five months past, stripped of all those trappings which dazzle, and have only to say that if I am imposed upon, he is the most consummate hypocrite that ever was born in purple. . . .

'I saw young Lord Holland at Florence, who is a remarkably clever and agreeable young man. He is a little of a democrat, but few people argue so *right* as he does on the *wrong side* of a question. I don't think him likely to return soon to England, and I hope he will not, as he is in a course of much greater improvement where he is than he could possibly be at White's or Brooke's. He is a great friend and favourite of Fontana, who gave us the most satisfactory lecture in anatomy of four or five hours that I ever heard. Our museum in Great Russell Street is quite a paltry collection in many essential parts when compared either to that of Florence or Bologna.'

Madame Royale did not pass through Innspruck when expected, and the Comte d'Avary returned to Verona after three weeks' fruitless waiting. Many rumours as to her ill-health were circulated, it being also said her movements were to be kept secret, as the Republican authorities feared there might possibly be demonstrations of affection or loyalty on the part of the people during her journey through France. Report also said she was to be sent to Madrid instead of Vienna, and that strict orders had been given to her keeper, the Prince de Gavre, that she was not to be allowed to speak to any French person, without exception, on her journey south. The report as to Madrid being her destination was unfounded, and in January, 1796, news arrived that the Princess had reached the Austrian dominions.

'On Sunday last we received an account here that, after all the delays and *pourparlers* relative to the exchange of Madame Royale, she has been at last released and delivered to the Prince de Gavre on the 26th December. She is expected to arrive at Vienna this day [January 9th], but

Madame de Tourzelle, who is a sister of the Duc de Havre, and for whom leave had been asked by the Emperor to accompany her, was not allowed that indulgence. It is said, with what truth I know not, that the Court of Vienna first desiring that lady's attendance arose from a suspicion of the sincerity of the French Government, which it was imagined might attempt to palm upon them a sham Princess or fictitious personage properly instructed for the purpose. Madame de Tourzelle, therefore, who had been constantly with her Royal Highness from her infancy, was pitched upon as an infallible witness to prove her identity. Some difficulties occurring with respect to Madame de Tourzelle, another lady, Madame de Sourcy, equally capable, from her former situation at Versailles, of detecting such a counterfeit, was accepted in her place, and is the only French woman in Her Royal Highness's train. Soon after the Princess passed the frontier, she sent back to the French Government all her wardrobe, carriages, and every atom of accommodation which they had provided for her. Several emigrants, who had placed themselves on her road through Germany, write word that they had seen her in her coach and at the windows of the inns where she baited. They all say that she is beautiful in her person, and appeared to be in perfect health. In spite of the prohibition of any French persons being allowed to speak to Madame Royale, the Vicomte de Mory, an officer formerly attached to the Prince of Condé's service, found means of approaching her and of entering into conversation with her; but, being observed by the Prince de Gavre, was interrupted and directed to keep at a distance. Her great-uncle, the Elector of Treves, also met her on her road through his own Bishopric of Augsburgh, and, notwithstanding the general order, was permitted to sup with her. I have reason to suspect that all that the Comte d'Avary could have said to her from the King, her uncle, had he seen her at Innspruck, has long since been very safely conveyed to her, so that many of the precautions taken by the Court of Vienna to prevent intercourse with her were perfectly useless, as well as being liable to misconstruction. She is represented as having a good understanding and a decisive character.'

'*January* 31.

'The King conceives that the present rulers of France will find it impossible to keep their ground many months, but he does not expect that his own restoration would be an immediate consequence of their destruction. It is probable, he thinks, that other experiments of government may be tried at Paris before such an event takes place ; but he appears to be fully persuaded that the general state of the public mind in France of at least three-fourths of the people is now in his favour, and that if it could by any means be contrived to convey him and his brother to their partisans in Brittany and Poictou, the most reasonable hopes of success might be entertained.

' Those about the King are equally convinced with him that peace is at a great distance. Though much provoked by the usage which the Prince of Condé has met with, and the consequent disappointment of revolt in the south-western provinces, they appear still more xasperated at the petticoat politics of the Court of Vienna in its monopoly of Madame Royale, who, they complain, has been smuggled from her family by a contraband traffic with the French Republic, for they express themselves convinced that the other coalesced Powers could have had no share or knowledge of the transaction. Madame de Sourcy was separated from the Princess soon after her arrival in Vienna, and no French person is now allowed to attend her. The Bishop of Nancy, who is at present charged with the French King's affairs there, has not yet been permitted to see her. Means had, however, been found to convey to her, before she left Paris, the King, her uncle's, sentiments with regard to her, and his wishes that she should hold herself disengaged, in order that she might marry her cousin, the Duc d'Angoulême. She was at the same time apprised of the Emperor's project to dispose of her to one of his brothers, so that she is perfectly on her guard as to the conduct that may be proper for her to hold at Vienna. The King has received a letter from her, written soon after her arrival there, which is worded with singular propriety, and shows that her education has by no means been neglected. She is sensible of her situation, and was aware that the contents of her letter might be seen by others than the person to whom it was addressed, . . as . . it was forwarded to this place by the common post under a mere official envelope. It is taken for granted here that her Royal Highness has *trop d'esprit et trop de sentiment* not to prefer the chance of being one day Queen of France to the reality of being an Archduchess and Vicereine of a skirt or two of Poland. . . . The jewels, etc., seized upon Semonville, and now in possession of the Emperor, are looked upon by him as her property, and she has besides such rights and pretensions as may derive from her being an only daughter of France. These latter, indeed, would not appear at present to be of much value, but favourable circumstances might some time or other give them considerable importance.

'Monsieur the Comte d'Artois has been sent to reside at Holyrood House, in Scotland, in order to secure his person against arrest for debt, and there he must remain till means are found for enabling him to go at large. It was proposed that the King of Sardinia, his father-in-law, should invest him with a diplomatic character, which would, by the statute of Queen Anne, fully answer the purpose; but this was flatly refused by the Court of Turin. Recourse has been since had to the Empress of Russia to grant a credential of this kind to Monsieur, and I think I know that great Lady too well to doubt of her agreeing to it. It will be a fine decoration to the diplomatic archives of Muscovy to enrol a presumptive heir of the French monarchy, a sprig of Charlemagne's crown, in her list of Ambassadors. She will scarcely let slip the opportunity of sticking such a feather in her Imperial cap. The King said I must be sensible that such a measure could not be very pleasant to him, but that he was compelled to it by the immediate pressure of his affairs, and by the local embarrassment and acute position of his brother, to whom the enjoyment of personal liberty was absolutely necessary. . . . Great Britain had most generously supported his cause, and afforded him an asylum; but as the intervention of certain laws deprived him of all the benefits intended, he saw no other way to get free of the difficulty but by obtaining a diplomatic character for the security of Monsieur, which, however extraordinary with regard to him, was not liable to any fair objection from others.

'. . . Ever since the death of Louis XVII. the King's residence here has been assuming more and more the air of a Court, not, indeed, . . . in point of equipage or expense, for he has only one carriage and a very moderate table (at which . . . scarcely any stranger ever appears, except myself, who seldom dine there above once in the week), but by the numerous correspondences, the arrival and dispatch of couriers from time to time, and the ministerial attendance of different persons who formerly held high offices under the Monarchy. . . .

'The number of French in this city and other parts of the Venetian territory is already very considerable and seems to be increasing. Such a collection of emigrants . . . has of late given some umbrage to the subsisting Government of France, and occasioned a representation against it to the Republic. I believe, in truth, that the movement of the Directoire relative to this matter is a mere French parade without any expectation of a very serious attention being paid to it. They must be sensible that it is better for them that the King should remain quietly at Verona than remove to a more active scene, as his motions, being well watched and known, he is likely to do them less mischief here than anywhere else. . . . The King, however, seems heartily tired of his present stagnant condition, . . and desirous of removing to some other residence. It certainly can be neither pleasant nor decorous to remain in the territory of the Venetians, who have not only received a public Minister from the French Convention, but deputed from themselves a man of the highest quality as their own Ambassador to it. Where to find a suitable asylum seems a difficulty that none of the coalesced Powers have yet agreed to remove.'[1]

Macartney obtained leave of absence in February, and proceeded to Naples, where he remained a short time, returning from thence by Rome and Florence.

'CASERTA,
'*March* 9, 1796.

'We regret much that it was not in your power to give us a little more of your company. . . . The Royal family here talk of you incessantly, and regret . . that your stay was so short. But both the King and Queen thought that they perceived in your Lordship's countenance that you left them with regret, which has flattered them greatly. Emma says she will write to you herself before you leave Rome.'

'*March* 26.

'The King and Queen of Naples and three of the Princesses are ill of the measles in this city. . . . When the business of sending infantry from hence shall be finally settled . . I will let you know. . . . You will have heard that the Great Duke has refused their passage through his dominions, but I can tell you that the King of Naples has told his son-in-law that whenever the safety of Italy should require it, he should nevertheless march his

[1] Extracts from private letters to Lord Grenville and others.

troops through Tuscany. . . . By this your Lordship will see that, as to politics, there is no great harmony between these two Courts; but as the Great Duchess was always the favourite daughter of the King of Naples, that family have existed as strong as ever. . . .

'. . . The late melancholy news from the Riviera of Genoa has sunk our spirits exceedingly. . . .'[1]

In the beginning of April Lord Macartney returned to his duties at Verona, where he found the little Court very much the same as he had left it. But almost immediately after his return the Venetian Government in very plain terms signified to Louis that his conduct not being agreeable to them, they requested he would depart as soon as possible, the asylum of their State ceasing from the moment he received the notification. To this unexpected discourtesy the King replied:

' Je partirai, mais j'exige deux conditions, la première, qu'on me présente le livre d'or, où est inscrit ma famille, pour enrayer le nom de ma main; le seconde, qu'on me rende l'armure, dont l'amitié de mon aïeul Henri Quatre a fait present à la République.'

The day following the same Venetian nobleman who had been deputed by the Senate to deliver the notification to the King arrived to protest against the *manner* of his reply, being sent for that purpose by the Podestà of Venice. Louis, however, refused to modify it, and said:

' J'ai répondu hier à ce que vous m'avez dit de la part de votre Gouvernement. Vous m'apportez aujourdhui une protestation de la part du Podestà. Je ne la reçois pas. Je ne recevrai pas celle du Senat. Je partirai en effet dès que j'aurai les passeports que j'ai envoyé chercher à Venise, mais je persiste dans ma réponse d'hier. Je me la devais. Je ne puis oublier que je suis Roi de France.'

Macartney deeply regretted the manner in which the matter had been carried out, and wrote as follows:

' I cannot but sincerely regret that the Republic did not think fit to communicate to me, as Minister of a friendly

[1] Extracts from letters from Sir William Hamilton.

State, her wishes for the King of France's speedy removal. I should have been happy to have used my good offices upon the occasion, and I have little doubt that I should have . . . accomplished their object for them without any ill-humour, especially as I know that for a long time past it has been the King's most earnest desire to change the place of his residence. But, unfortunately, the Republic has adopted another mode of proceeding, and the matter must now take its course.

'The King's language upon this occasion is considered by those about him as a sublime effusion and a noble assertion of his dignity, and by those to whom it was addressed as an unseasonable rhodomantado. It has, however, had the effect (that rhodomantados usually have upon weak persons) of frightening and embarrassing the Republic, already sufficiently terrified by the French Directory, . . . into the step taken. . . . And yet it would not appear, considering the immediate prospect of affairs and her position and circumstances, that she has a great deal to dread from the arms of France at present; but she might have much to apprehend from her influence and intrigues at a future day, for the memory of injury, much less of insults suffered under misfortune, is seldom effaced by prosperity and the power of revenge that may attend it.

'The firmness of His Majesty's tone and the turn of his answer were, I believe, little expected, for the Duc de la Vauguyon was much solicited to obtain an alteration. It was wished that the King should signify *only* his intention to go away without talking about the *livre d'or* or Henry the Fourth's armour.

'. . . It is conjectured here that the resolution taken to urge the King of France's departure from hence was in consequence of a requisition from Paris. If this be true, it forms a striking contrast to what lately happened at Rome during my stay there, when the Pope treated with a dignified contempt worthy of an old Roman the impudent and ridiculous proposals that were made to him by the French Directory.[1]

[1] The four propositions made to the Pope, in March, 1796, by the French Directory were as follows:

1. That the Pope should recognize the Republic and then Government of France.

2. That he should for ever give up and quit claim to all right and title to the city and territory of Avignon, and the county of Venaissin.

'The King is extremely impatient to leave this place. He is now putting his affairs in order as fast as he can, and does not mean to delay a moment after he receives the Emperor's passports, without which there is no exit for him from this State. He immediately wrote for them, but the departure of his messenger was delayed for some hours by a refusal of horses from the Post Office, where an order of Government was pleaded in justification of it; so that he has been obliged, I suppose, to use another mode of conveyance. I should have sent this letter by an express of my own, but I did not care to expose myself in my situation to a similar denial, which might lay me under the necessity of making a complaint, a thing I am always averse to wherever it can possibly be avoided. . . .

'At my return here from Naples I was informed that several extracts had appeared in German Gazettes from a publication entitled "Lord Macartney's Embassy to China." . . . Before I left London there was a book published upon the subject under the name of Æneas Anderson. You will please observe the said Æneas Anderson was a servant in livery attending upon the Embassy, and, of course, you will judge of its authenticity, and what sort of materials it was likely to be composed of. I have never seen it, but I have been told that it was a mere bookseller's job to gratify the public curiosity. The only work upon that subject that has my sanction is now in the press under the digestion of Sir George Staunton. . . . I propose leaving this place in four or five days without any intention of returning to it.'[1]

On April 21, 1796, at three o'clock in the morning Louis set out from Verona *en route* for Germany. Horses were engaged for Volarmi, the first post stage leading from Verona to the Tyrol, and the Duc de la Vauguyon, whose figure was much of the same height and corpulence as the King's, took his place in the travelling carriage with two other gentlemen, and ordered the postilions to drive on. Louis himself stepped into a light Berlin, accompanied by

---

3. That he should grant a free exportation of the productions of his dominions into France, together with all other privileges allowed to British subjects.

4. That he should transmit to them the statue of Apollo Belvedere with an inscription at the foot of it, expressing that it was a present from the Pope to the French Republic.

[1] Extracts from letters to Lord Grenville and others.

the Comte d'Avary, and took the road through Castel Nuomo to Brescia, Bergamo, Belinzona, and the St. Gothard. His intention was to proceed through Switzerland and join the Prince of Condé in the Brisgau. Everybody being well muffled up, and favoured by the darkness, the departure was successfully accomplished without the real destination of the Royal traveller being discovered; the reason of the King's wish for secrecy as to his real movements being that he feared his creditors or other adversaries might seek to place impediments in his journey, and make it difficult to leave the country.

To Lord Grenville, Macartney wrote as follows:

'Of the King's prudence in this point there can be so far no question, but that of crossing the Alps at all before he was perfectly sure of an eligible abode on the other side of them may not, perhaps, be so evident, and will probably be judged of like most other risks, only by the event. I took the liberty of representing to him the objections that offered themselves to my mind, . . . but his inveterate aversion to reside in the Papal dominions, his doubts of the Duke of Parma's disposition, the state of the war in Italy, the propriety and necessity of approaching as near as possible to his own kingdom, and his firm persuasion that at least Great Britain and Russia would feel no other part was so becoming him as that which he had chosen, were circumstances that I found it in vain to combat. Nothing remained for me but to give such other advice and assistance as I imagined might be of the most benefit to him in the difficulties he was likely to encounter. He told me he had written to the King of Great Britain, and also to the Empress of Russia and His Imperial Majesty, to explain to them the state of his mind as affected by the suddenness of the late event here, and to explain to them the reasons which impelled him towards the army of Condé. How far he may find a situation there agreeable to himself or to the Court of Vienna . . . I have not at present sufficient information to guide my conjectures. I know, however, that some time after Madame Royale's arrival at Vienna, and her declaration there upon the subject of marriage, the French King wrote a very conciliatory letter to the Emperor, expressive of his sense of that Prince's kindness and attention to his niece, and he at the same time gave such a turn to the whole as to mark very strongly how much he wished that whatever little jealousies or treacheries might have arisen should be considered as entirely excused and forgotten. The answer is said to have been frigid and reserved, and the moment of mutual cordiality between the two correspondents appears to be still at a long distance.'

Five days later Macartney set out for England, and on his arrival found the following letter awaiting him:

'MY LORD,

'I am very happy in obeying the commands I have just received from the King to signify to your Lordship his pleasure that you attend the Levée to-morrow for the purpose of being presented to His Majesty in consequence of the British Peerage which he has thought proper to confer upon you. I beg your Lordship's acceptance of my best congratulations on this accession of dignity, at which I the more particularly rejoice, as it reflects no less lustre upon the discernment of the Great Prince who confers it than upon the services of the meritorious subject whom it is intended to distinguish.

'I have the honour to be, etc., etc.,

'PORTLAND.'

Thus, on June 8, 1796, Macartney attained his wish of a seat in the English House of Lords, under the title of Baron Macartney of Parkhurst in Surrey.

From Louis, who had a genuine regard for him, Macartney received the following letter shortly after his return to England:

'*A Riegel ce* 18 *Juin*, 1796.

'J'attendois avec impatience, my dear Lord, de vous sçavoir arrivé en Angleterre, pour vous écrire, vous parlé de mes regrets de ne plus vous avoir auprès de moi. . . . Mon voyage . . . est très heureusement passé. . . . Je me suis flatté un moment que nous allions passer le Rhin et vous juger de la douce satisfaction que j'en ressentois ; ce n'étoit pas une carrière d'exploits que j'envisageois . . . mais . . . le moyen de parler de plus près à mes malheureux enfans, . . . de les réunir autour de moi, je voyais en moi l'égide des fidèles qui m'auroient suivi, car j'aurois été le premier, et qui est-ce qui tire sur son père. Les malheurs de l'Italie ont tout dérangé, mais nous ne sommes qu'au mois de Juin et par conséquent nous avous bien du temps devant nous.

'Je sçais, my dear Lord, les démarches que votre gouvernement a faites à mon sujet ; je n'en suis pas surpris, vous connoissez mon opinion à son égard, mais je n'y suis pas moins sensible. On ne ma pas laissé ignorer non plus ce que vous avez dit de moi à Londres, je voudrois le mériter mais tout en me rendant justice, je vous avoue que je suis fier, de vous avoir inspiré assez d'amitié pour vous faire tenir ce language à un homme qui n'a jaimais trahi sa pensée.

'Adieu, my dear Lord, croyez je vous prie que mon estime et mon amitié pour vous dureront autant que ma vie.
'Louis.'

To this letter Macartney replied as follows :

'LONDON,
'25 *July*, 1796.
'SIRE,
'Je suis infiniment sensible à l'honneur que votre Majesté a daigné me faire en m'écrivant. . . . Qu'il eut été heureux pour l'Europe et le monde entier, que les bonnes intentions de ma cour eussent été secondée. Les bons effets d'une telle mesure auroient été prodigieux. . . . J'eus l'honneur de dire à votre Majesté à Verona, que l'on me proposoit ici une mission que j'esperois pouvoir refuser, mais depuis que je suis de retour, on m'a fait des instances si fortes qu'il m'est impossible de me dispenser d'y acquiescer. Mon plus grand regret est de me trouver obligé par là de m'éloigner encor plus de votre Majesté et de n'être pas dans le cas de me transporter auprès d'Elle aussitôt que les heureuses circonstances qui pourroient se presenter me le permettroient.

'J'ai l'honneur, etc., etc.,
'MACARTNEY.'

A few days later Macartney received from the Comte d'Avarez an account of the attempt made on the life of Louis XVIII. on July 19, 1796, at Dillingen. It took place about 10 p.m. on a moonlight evening. The King, having worked for several hours after dinner, was fatigued and hot. It being a warm night, the windows of the room were open, and he sat near one of them. Suddenly the report of a gun coming from the shelter of a neighbouring haycock was heard. The ball hit the King on the top of his head, and he fell to the ground covered with blood. His terrified attendants feared at first that he was mortally wounded, but the injury proved to be not a serious one.

D'Avarez terminates his letter with an eloquent tribute to the King's courage, saying, in conclusion : ' Il est impossible de montrer plus de sang froid, de douceur et d'intérêt pour ses serviteurs éperdues que le Roy ne la fait dans cette occasion.'

CHAPTER XIV

WHILE Macartney was absent in Italy, and without consulting his inclinations in the matter, the Minister for the Colonies had nominated him Governor and Captain-General of the Cape of Good Hope, which had surrendered to the British in September, 1795. Mr. Dundas fully appreciated the value of this acquisition to the colonial possessions of Great Britain. He realized the importance of framing suitable regulations for the administration of its future government, and the necessity for obtaining a full and accurate account of the real resources of this new addition to the Empire, its capabilities as a colonial settlement being hardly less important than its position as a military and naval post for the defence and support of British India.

Macartney was not in good health, and did not feel himself at all equal to the undertaking—in fact, would willingly have refused to take up the office. He went to Court with this idea in view the day after his arrival in England; but the King spoke in flattering terms of the appointment, and seemed so desirous for Macartney's acceptation of it that he was unable to refuse compliance. The precarious state of his health, however, rendered necessary the stipulation of one condition—namely, that he should be allowed to resign the government to the next in command, without waiting to be superseded from home, whenever he should find it necessary to return. In this, as in every other respect, Macartney's wishes were consulted as much as possible. Mr. Dundas willingly resigned to him a great part of his patronage as Secretary for the Colonies. He allowed him to take out his former secretary, Mr. Maxwell, and Mr. Barrow,[1] both of whom, as will be remembered, had accompanied the expedition to China, giving them liberal salaries and acquiescing in their promotion. The Governor's salary was fixed at £10,000 a year, and an additional sum of £2,000 was added as an allowance for his table. This latter amount was settled upon him by the King as a pension for the rest of his life in consideration of his long, faithful, and exemplary services.

It would appear by the following letter from his old friend Thomas Coutts, the famous banker, that, being, as usual, somewhat hard up, he had endeavoured unsuccessfully to obtain an advance upon his salary:

'. . . I am very sorry I cannot reply in the manner I would wish, and in other times would not have hesitated about it for a moment. . . . Most of the bankers, I have reason to believe, have for two years past declined all advances of money to their best friends; and though I believe my House has been the last to adopt such measures, we have at last been compelled to it. Other circumstances, as well as the exorbitant interest to be made of Navy bills and other floating securities, have operated completely to employ all the idle money people were in use to keep in our hands. The general distress from the war has clipped our wings so much that we are obliged to be on our guard; and the arrear on the Civil List, I believe, has been as severe on me as on any other, as I have so many friends concerned in it.'

Lord Macartney sailed from Portsmouth in the *Trusty* man-of-war during the month of January, 1797, and landed in the evening of May 4 at the Cape of Good Hope,

'under every mark of honour that it was possible to offer to His Majesty's representative. In the morning at ten o'clock the courts of justice, the Burgher Senate, the clergy,

[1] Mr. (afterwards Sir John) Barrow, author of the 'Life of the Earl of Macartney,' and Secretary to the Admiralty, was born of humble parentage, but rose rapidly in life through his cleverness and industry. When a boy he was exceedingly fond of the study of mathematics. On one occasion he had been puzzling over a problem of conic sections for two days and nights; the third night he fell asleep, and in his dreams continued the work, with the result that next morning he was able to sketch out the correct solution.

ROOM AT MESSRS. COUTTS' BANK, SHOWING THE WALL-PAPER BROUGHT BY
LORD MACARTNEY FROM CHINA

To face p. 442

CAPE OF GOOD HOPE

and principal inhabitants having been convoked in the Government House in the garden, his Lordship caused his commission to be read and took the oath. At eleven o'clock all the principal officers of the guard waited upon the new Governor, and on the same day, in presence of all the most respectable persons in the colony, Major-General Craig was invested in due form with the order of the Bath.'[1]

His administration of Cape Colony seems to have been conducted on the same lines of economy and justice which had distinguished him in former positions of a similar kind, and the country advanced rapidly in prosperity. The revenue was nearly doubled without the addition of a single tax, and the value of property increased in proportion. The confidence of the inhabitants was secured by this, and the attention and just decisions which the Governor gave in all cases of appeal. He kept on excellent terms with the commander of the King's forces, although he was, in fact, the Commander-in-Chief, and the line of authority distinctly defined. He got on well with his inferiors, as he 'most cautiously avoided small interferences, though he was ever in his place, when it was necessary, the head of all.'[2] He also always insisted that the soldiers should not receive their pay in paper money, which ever gave rise to discontent, owing to the fluctuations of exchange.

Lady Anne Barnard,[3] whose interesting and confidential letters to Mr. Dundas give an entertaining account of Cape society at that time, mentions Lord Macartney's success as Governor there.

'You will be pleased to see how wisely, temperately, and agreeably General Dundas conducts himself in his situation, and how well he and Lord M. are together.[4] I see, also,

[1] From scroll day-book during the government of Lord Macartney at the Cape.
[2] Lady Anne Barnard's letters, edited by W. H. Wilkins.
[3] Lady Anne Barnard, daughter of James, fifth Earl of Balcarres, was the wife of Mr. Andrew Barnard, who accompanied Lord Macartney to the Cape as Secretary for that colony.
[4] Later on Lady Anne wrote that General Dundas eminently disliked Lord Macartney while he stayed at the Cape, though he was awed by his superior abilities.

great satisfaction with the manners of our Lord, who was expected to be cold and dignified, fond of his own opinion, and stiff in maintaining it. Such was the public notion of him : he certainly has wished to impress it differently, and has succeeded. He promotes society, and is markedly attentive to the individuals who compose it, lays down rules with wise firmness, but no mixture of pride, and is (I may say), as far as things have come, beloved. I shall only quote you the words of one smallish man, as it contains more than his own feelings. " I am so glad," said he, " to find myself a gentleman now. I had begun to fancy myself a blackguard, but I look up to myself now, from the manner Lord M. treats me." '

In October, 1797, a mutiny broke out in the naval squadron stationed at the Cape, at that time anchored in Simon's Bay. The flagship took the lead, and was rapidly followed by all the others. After a few days' riot and confusion order was restored by Admiral Pringle,[1] but on the return of the fleet to Table Bay, where they were joined by ships from St. Helena, fresh disturbances of a more serious nature broke out. The Governor took prompt and decisive measures to suppress the rising, the mutineers were brought to order, and the whole affair subsided. Macartney wrote to Mr. Dundas that, after a careful investigation of the second mutiny, he could not discover a shadow of a grievance to be pleaded in extenuation of it, and thought it proceeded from a wish on the sailors' part to follow the example of their fraternity elsewhere. The mutiny referred to was that which broke out in the fleet in May, 1797, commonly called the Mutiny at the Nore. It was eventually quelled by judicious concessions and Lord Howe's personal influence with the seamen.

But Lord Macartney now began to find the strain of carrying on the government of the Cape too much of an effort in his increasingly delicate condition. He wrote to Sir George Staunton in December, 1797 :

[1] Lady Anne Barnard considered the sailors really had some grievances ; one of their chief complaints being that they were given no vegetable food.

'I flatter myself that I shall be allowed to return home next summer. Indeed, my health has so much declined, and the attacks of gout are so frequent of late in my head and stomach, that I feel almost incapable of attending to business as formerly. . . . I have done with politics for ever when I set foot on board to leave this place. . . . I should have wished to close my career with the arrangement of the colony, but I feel myself to be totally unequal to such a task, and shall certainly, if I live, return home in the course of the autumn.'

His physical condition improved in the next few months, and he wrote again in July, 1798 :

' My health has for this month past in general been a good deal better, though now and then I feel such sudden short strokes of gout in my head and stomach as alarm me much. Unless I should have a regular fit soon it is not unlikely that I may tip off in one of these spasms, and, in truth, I think it would be better so than in a lingering mode. . . . I think the Cape would be worth any price to the Company. . . . The arrangement and future government of these countries will require some delicacy and address for a time. . . . Very few of the Dutch here. . . have ever been in Europe, and our manners seem already to have effaced most of the original impressions. You and I have seen at Grenada the impossibility of English and French ever assimilating together. It is otherwise with regard to English and Dutch. The latter have a different feeling towards us, and, if well managed, may amalgamate with us easily enough ; but a Frenchman cannot bear our preponderance in the mass, and evaporates immediately if he cannot pervade. Whatever may happen, I am persuaded that nine-tenths of the people would rather see an English than a Jacobin flag fly here. They are, however, most of them, honest enough to own that they would rather see a Dutch one than either, although, at the same time, they admit that the Cape never was in so prosperous and flourishing a state as since we have been in possession of it. . . . It is pretty clear to most of them that Holland is no longer a nation, and the most interested among them are now speculating how to choose their country when a peace takes place, for few doubt of the Cape being then ceded to us. If we keep it, I don't believe any will migrate from hence that are worth retaining.'

Lord Mornington[1] and his brother, the Hon. Henry Wellesley,[2] had stopped at the Cape on their way to India in 1798, and the former appears to have been charmed with Lord Macartney's manners.

'He finds them more pleasing in some respects than he looked for. Ability and knowledge he expected, but there is a mildness and consideration of everybody, with a sort of parental affection to those immediately attached to him, which he [Lord Mornington] did not expect in the degree he finds it. Wines of strong body and high flavour are sometimes ameliorated by time, and become more gracious to the taste than when new.'[3]

In the early autumn of 1798 Lord Macartney wrote to Lord Mornington, then Governor-General of Bengal :

'Lord and Lady Clive passed a few days here on their way to Madras, and Lord Teignmouth stayed near a month with us on his return to England. I wrote you that my Lord Hobart had arrived here . . . at the end of April, and left us on the 9th May. I understood that he had not been very well pleased at his recall, but on perusing your letter, which I delivered to him, his countenance cleared up, and he seemed to be in very good humour all the time he remained here. Indeed, one of our Cape misses[4] seems to have contributed a good deal to it, and if the scandal of the place may be credited, her attentions were very amply returned by him. The latest accounts from England are of the 29th April. The projected invasion seemed to have totally engrossed the minds of all ranks of people. . . . Ireland continued still in the same disturbed state, notwithstanding the numerous executions which were found necessary ; and it appeared that no sooner was insurrection quelled in one county, but it broke out in another. It has, I think, made the tour of almost the whole kingdom, and I hope will now stop ; but it has been of a very serious nature indeed, and a number of persons of a rank much

[1] Afterwards Marquess Wellesley.
[2] Afterwards Lord Cowley. He accompanied his brother to India as private secretary.
[3] Lady Anne Barnard's letters, edited by W. H. Wilkins.
[4] Lady Anne Barnard said the Dutch ladies loved dancing, and flirting still more ; and the young ones did not seem to share their fathers' dislike of English officers.

above common rioters are known to have been concerned. I understand that the county of Antrim, where my principal estate lies, is, from being the most seditious, become one of the quietest parts of the north.

'I do assure you . . . nothing but ill-health and a despair of better could impel me to quit my situation here; but the frequent indispositions I have suffered since you left us, and the gout, which still hangs heavily upon me, render me totally unequal to the exertions required, . . . and I must soon resign my task to a more active successor. . . . To what a state has *patriotism* reduced poor Ireland! But I trust that the next accounts will tell us of Lord Cornwallis's success there. "A union, a union," was for many years the burthen of old Cassandra Downshire's song, but he sang to so little purpose I doubt the strain is not likely to be renewed. If it were I should be disposed to join in the chorus.'[1]

About this time Lady Anne Barnard wrote as follows to Mr. Dundas:

'Never saw I such a succession of Governors . . . the sea has been quite covered with them for the last six months. Happy shall I be if it sees nothing of the departure of our own dear Governor, Lord Macartney, for some time yet. I have ever thought he would stay till the beginning of the year 1799, and I believe I shall be proved a witch. I wish I could give him a right fit of the gout and lodge it in his toe; it jumps about his stomach and head, and sometimes affects his spirits, but never the force and firmness of his mind, which, when called upon, can rally and rise above pain. It is wonderful to hear how he can jest and talk away with memory and fancy at a time when (his company gone) he can hardly support himself.'

At length Macartney's health broke down so completely that he was compelled to resign his Governorship, and make arrangements for a speedy return to Europe. He wrote a long private letter to Mr. Dundas, giving notice of his intention to do so and the reason for it.

' . . . I came in under very great doubts, as you know, of being able at my time of life and in my state of health to answer the expectations your partiality formed of me;

[1] Wellesley Papers.

and I am now sure . . . I fall very short of my own wishes. This place demands a younger and a more active man, with greater vigour of body and elasticity of mind. . . . My situation here is in every other respect so agreeable to me that I should not be desirous of removing from it if I could flatter myself that a man at my time of life were likely to improve, either in his constitution or faculties. . . . I am now sixty years old, . . . and of late—particularly within the last few weeks—I feel myself declining fast. I am at this moment afflicted with the gout in my head and stomach. . . . I have the piles, if not a fistula, and am not without apprehension of a stone in my kidneys. To this I am to add an increasing weakness in my eyes, which makes me more melancholy than all the rest. You will pardon me, my dear sir, for troubling you with these matters, which I should not venture upon did I not value your good opinion so highly that I cannot bear an idea of your imagining me capable of declining any public service at all in my power to perform. . . .'

Lady Anne Barnard wrote to Mr. Dundas on November 10, 1798 :

' Sorry I am at the departure of our own dear Governor, who this day leaves the Garden House and takes up his residence with us during the short time which will be necessary to get all arranged for his leaving the colony. If he felt he could have stayed longer with safety to himself I am convinced he would, but the gout hangs constantly over him, never fixing itself properly, and often making him feel himself hardly more than the tenant of the hour.'

A few weeks later she again mentions Macartney's indomitable spirit :

' One of the last times I was in company with Lord Macartney he danced a reel remarkably well to the Scots bagpipes, with Lady Anne Dashwood, Mrs. Campbell, and a Brigade Major. Perhaps you think this is a cross-reading or conundrum, but no such thing—it is true. He was in excellent spirits, and paid a compliment to the piper and the reel of Tulloch, which neither the General nor the transported piper will soon forget. I dare not add what I believe is true, too, that I fear the little twinge in the toe next day whispered to His Excellency that he had been rash.'

DEPARTURE FROM CAPE TOWN

On November 20, 1798, Lord Macartney left the Cape. He embarked at noon, and,

'after having taken a paternal and warm leave of all the principal civil and military officers, was by them attended to the waterside, under every possible mark of public honour that could be shown to so distinguished, so meritorious, and so respectable a magistrate, bearing the universal attribution of having, during his government, unremittingly attended to the general welfare and the prosperity of the colony.'[1]

Major-General Dundas, the next in command, was left as Lieutenant-Governor in his place, with enjoyment of the full salary of £10,000 a year. Although Macartney had a right to half the salary until the new appointment from home was made, he did not avail himself of it, his invariable rule being that all his appointments should cease from the day he gave up office.

Here, as in India, he considered it advisable to leave on record a declaration that he had never accepted any presents, with the exception of some trifles, such as fruit and venison, which it was out of his power to refuse. He also added that he had never engaged in trade or commerce for his own benefit, and had received nothing save his salary and the use of the house and slaves appointed for the Governor.

Two days after Macartney's departure from Cape Town a disastrous fire occurred, which consumed the stables of the cavalry, the naval stores, and the stores of the Commissary-General. The fire, which was said to be the work of incendiaries, was only stopped by pulling down a house; the south-west wind which was blowing at the time greatly increased the violence of the flames.

General Dundas carried on the government of Cape Colony until the arrival of Sir George Yonge, who was sent out from England as successor to Lord Macartney. Yonge was disliked, and his administration soon became unpopular for various reasons, amongst others the decrease in the

[1] Scroll day-book during the government of Lord Macartney at the Cape.

revenue and increase in the expenses. He was recalled in 1801, being, according to one of Macartney's correspondents, ' very, very low in the estimation of both Dutch and English.'[1] General Dundas succeeded him as Governor, and immediately appointed Mr. Barrow, who had been a good deal at variance with Sir George Yonge, as his secretary. Among Macartney's letters are many dealing with the business affairs and social gossip of the Colony, in which he appears to have continued to take a friendly interest.

A certain Van Ryneveldt, one of the Government officials, wrote requesting that he would interest himself in the introduction of vaccination in Cape Colony.

' In a former letter I endeavoured to represent the dreadful apprehension this colony is exposed to on account of the small-pox, and, understanding lately that the cow-pox is being attempted in England, I beg again to press to your lordship's humane consideration our sad situation should the small-pox, unfortunately, ever be amongst us, and to entreat your good offices that the cow-pox might be introduced here, if found successful in England, as a substitute for small-pox.'

In a later letter the same correspondent remarks :

' Dr. Titler is just arrived from England, and has brought with him the matter of the cow-pox. He is authorized by Government to try the matter upon four slave children.'

Shortly after Lord Macartney's return home, he and Lady Macartney settled at Corney House, Chiswick, of which they acquired a lease for their joint lives from Sir C. W. Boughton Russell. Corney House, which was pulled down in 1832, stood close to the river and Chiswick Church. It must not be confounded with the present building of the same name, the site of the original house and gardens being now included in the ground occupied by Messrs. Thorneycroft's well-known torpedo-boat works and the new portion of the cemetery.

Corney House originally belonged to Sir William (after-

[1] Lady Anne Barnard describes Sir George Yonge as ' a very, very weak old soul, full of good intentions, disposed to conceive that he is the man to make this a fine and flourishing colony.'

LIFE AT CORNEY HOUSE

wards Lord) Russell, a distinguished military character,[1] to whom Queen Elizabeth paid a visit at Chiswick on October 2, 1602. The property descended to his grandson, Edward, youngest son of Francis, first Earl of Bedford, and since then has passed through various hands. In 1802 Sir C. W. Boughton Russell sold it to Viscountess Bateman, who left it to Lady Caroline Damer, subject to the lease for life to Lady Macartney.

Chiswick was at that time quite in the country, and Lord Macartney and his wife were very fond of the place, and for the last six years of his life spent a good deal of their time there.

During that period he suffered terribly from continual and severe attacks of gout, which compelled him to decline the presidency of the Board of Control, offered him by the Addington Cabinet; but in the intervals, when free from pain, he enjoyed as much as ever the society of his friends. In his house were always to be found people of distinction in art, literature, and the social world. All shades of political opinion were also welcome, it being well known that Lord Macartney's mind was free, as it always had been, from party feeling of any kind.

In December, 1799, he received the following letter from Louis XVIII., thanking him for his congratulations on the marriage of Madame Royale and the Duc d'Angoulême:

'J'ai reçu, my dear Lord, avec un veritable plaisir votre lettre du 1er Novembre. . . . J'ai appris avec joie, mais sans étonnement vos succès et la conduite aussi ferme que prudente que vous avez tenue dans une circonstance critique.[2] . . . Je suis touché jusqu'au fonds du cœur de ce que vous me dites au sujet de mon frère et du mariage

[1] 'Stow, speaking of his (Lord Russell's) heroic achievements at the battle of Zutphen, says: "He charged so terribly that after he had broke his lance, he, with his curtleax, so plaid his part that the enemy reported him to be a devil, and not a man; for where he saw six or seven of the enemies together, thither would he, and so behaved himself with his curtleax, that he would separate their friendship." '—Lysons, 'Environs of London,' published 1795.

[2] The naval mutiny at the Cape.

de mes enfans. . . . Quand au mariage vous avez été témoin des premiers transports de ma joye lorsque ma nièce, ou pour mieux dire, ma fille, est sortie de captivité, de mes premiers efforts pour unir ces chers enfans. Je n'ai qu'un regret, c'est que vous ne soyez pas témoin de ce bonheur qu'on ne peut me ravir, car ils sont heureux, autant qu'ils le puissent être.

'La crise du moment est forte, mais peut on d'espérer du salut de l'Europe, en voyant l'union qui regne entre votre auguste et vertueux Monarque et le généreux Paul Ier. Il étoit bien jeune lors de votre mission en Russie, mais n'importe, je suis sûr que vous éprouvez une véritable satisfaction d'avoir connu celui que la Providence semble si visiblement avoir destiné a finir les malheurs du genre humain.

'Adieu, my dearest Lord! Vous connoissez mon amitié pour vous.

'LOUIS.'

In 1801 died Sir George Staunton. He had a paralytic seizure shortly after his return from China, which prevented him from ever again being able to accept any public office. The British Government had wished to send him to China in 1796 as Minister Plenipotentiary, in consequence of an express invitation from the Chinese Court, but the state of his health rendered this quite out of the question. He gradually grew weaker and more helpless, and died on January 14, 1801.

Lord Macartney was left one of the executors of his will. He wrote as follows to G. T. Staunton, who, in consequence of his knowledge of the Chinese language, had obtained a writership at Canton two years previous to his father's death.[1]

'*November*, 1800.

'. . . Lady Staunton seems to be very well in health at present, but I am sorry to say her spirits are not

[1] A writership in China was a most valuable piece of East Indian patronage, being usually reserved for the connexions of the Directors; and young Staunton's appointment was not popular. He was not particularly happy during his first two years in China, partly owing to that circumstance, and partly to the peculiar method of his education.

DECLINING HEALTH

as good as we could wish. We cannot, indeed, expect that they should be, as she has the daily view of your dear father's declining state before her eyes. His intellects remain as perfectly clear as ever, but I . . . observe a gradual decay of his bodily health every time I see him. Lady Macartney joins me in a thousand thanks for the fine tea which you have been so obliging as to send us.'[1]

Young Staunton returned home for two years after the death of his father. Lord Macartney obtained permission for him to do so, and wrote to announce it, at the same time mentioning the business arrangements which had been made.

' . . . I shall be ready to give to Lady Staunton every advice and assistance, should she have occasion for any, in order to promote your interests or regulate her proceedings. I flatter myself that your father's disposition of his fortune will be agreeable to you. . . . Wishing you a pleasant voyage . . . and assuring you of my earnest desire to supply to you, as far as in my power, the place of your excellent father, I remain, . . .

' Your most sincere friend,
' MACARTNEY.'[2]

In December, 1802, Lord Macartney presented young Staunton to the King and Queen, and secured his election into the Literary Club.

Sir George Staunton was buried in the north aisle of Westminster Abbey, and a monument, designed and carried out by Chantry, was erected to his memory. It particularly commemorates the firmness, coolness, and prudence displayed by him during the negotiations for the treaty of peace concluded with Tippoo Sahib in 1784.

During the autumn of 1805 Macartney grew perceptibly weaker. For several months the gout hung about him without advancing to a decided fit. He suffered from nausea, entirely lost his appetite, and refused all kind of nourishment.

The state of affairs in Europe weighed upon his spirits, and the death of Pitt, whose disinterestedness and un-

---
[1] ' Memoirs of Sir G. L. Staunton.' [2] *Ibid.*

sullied integrity he profoundly admired, affected him deeply.

Those about him feared that he was near the end, but some of the physicians attending him were hopeful until three days before his death. The day that they pronounced the case to be quite hopeless, he had been able to read the whole of the Budget brought forward by the new Chancellor of the Exchequer, whose performance, he considered, showed him to be a promising young man.[1]

About eight o'clock on the evening of March 31, 1806, while resting his head on his hand, he appeared to fall gently asleep, and passed away without a sigh or struggle.

On the same evening at Lissanoure, Ellen MacGloughlin, one of the housemaids at the Castle, was startled by meeting Lord Macartney on the staircase leading to the room he habitually occupied when in residence there. He spoke, telling her to get some of the rooms ready, and passed on. She naturally thought it a very curious proceeding on his part to arrive without any notice, and finding no one else in the Castle had seen him, hurried to the agent's office to relate what had occurred. The agent wrote down the date and hour, and a few days later the news arrived from London that Lord Macartney had died just about that time.[2]

The following obituary notice appeared in the *Morning Post* of April 2, 1806 :

' This highly distinguished and most respectable nobleman died on Monday evening at his house in Curzon Street, in the 69th year of his age, after a life chiefly devoted to the

[1] Henry Petty-Fitzmaurice, afterwards third Marquis of Lansdowne. Petty became Chancellor of the Exchequer at the age of twenty-five. Finding the exigencies of war made fresh taxation necessary, he introduced a new property tax on March 28, 1806. This scheme raised the existing tax of 6½ to 10 per cent., at the same time cutting down and strictly regulating the exemptions. It was carried after considerable opposition.

[2] This story was told to the writer by a relation who, in her youth, had often heard it from Ellen MacGloughlin, then an old woman living in a cottage on the estate.

service of his country. To trace his conduct through the many arduous and trying situations in which the public service called for his exertions would furnish an example of integrity, ability, and wisdom which all may desire, but few hope to attain. His loss must, therefore, be not less regretted as a statesman than it will be by a wide circle of friends as a character in private life eminently endowed with social virtues and rare and splendid acquirements.'

By his express wish Lord Macartney was buried quietly in the riverside churchyard of Chiswick, near by the country residence of his last years, in the improvement of which he had taken a great deal of pleasure. His tomb lies close beside the pathway through the old cemetery, not far from the grave of the painter Hogarth. It is of oblong, box-like construction, and on one side of it the following inscription, now much obliterated, was engraved :

SACRED TO THE MEMORY OF

THE RIGHT HON[BLE] GEORGE EARL OF MACARTNEY,

PRIVY COUNCILLOR, KNIGHT OF THE HON[BLE] ORDER OF THE BATH, ETC.

A Nobleman

endowed by nature with the most extraordinary talents, which he cultivated with a degree of assiduity and perseverance hardly ever equalled. The greater part of his life was devoted to the public service. He filled a variety of high and important situations in different parts of the world, with the most unsullied honour, the strictest integrity, and with great credit and advantage to his King and country. His private virtues were such as to demand universal esteem and admiration. His liberality and generosity were unbounded. His superior knowledge, sweetness of temper, amenity of disposition, lively, entertaining conversation, rendered him the delight of his friends, and an ornament to society.[1]

The fact of his burial in Chiswick Churchyard is thus recorded in the parish register :

' The noble George Earl of Macartney, aged 69 years, buried April 9, 1806.'

[1] A copy of the above inscription was found among Lady Macartney's papers.

The following account of the funeral is taken from the *Monthly Magazine*, May, 1806:

'A hearse and four, two mourning coaches, and the private coach of the Marquis of Hertford, constituted the whole funeral procession. The privacy observed upon the occasion was so great that not even his lordship's old friend and companion in India, Sir William Duncan, was allowed an opportunity to pay a last tribute of respect to the memory of the deceased.'

A cenotaph with a Latin inscription composed by the Rev. George Henry Glass, Rector of Hanwell, was erected to the memory of Lord Macartney in Lissanoure parish church.

Macartney left everything to his wife for her life, and full power to dispose of many of his personal belongings and papers as she thought fit. On her death the Irish and Scotch properties were to go to his niece and adopted daughter, Elizabeth Hume, with the stipulation that the son who inherited them from her should assume the arms and surname of Macartney. The title became extinct. From Elizabeth Hume, Lissanoure has descended to her great-grandson, Carthanach George Macartney, now the present owner of it.

Lady Macartney survived her husband for twenty-two years, and when she died, in February, 1828, was buried beside him. Her house was a home to all her youthful relatives, and she was universally beloved by them for her never-failing kindness and goodness. On the south-west end of the tomb at Chiswick the following inscription, now partially effaced by time and weather, can be seen:

JANE COUNTESS OF MACARTNEY,
SECOND DAUGHTER OF JOHN EARL OF BUTE BY MARY
WORTLEY, HIS WIFE.

From early youth
an example of the most fervent piety unalloyed by the slightest tinge of superstition or enthusiasm. She fulfilled the precepts of loving God above all things, and her neighbours as herself. Her young relations found her a mother, and all who needed it a friend. She died at Corney House, in this parish, the 28th Feb^y, 1828, aged 85.

Trotter, pinxit

ELIZABETH HUME

NIECE AND ADOPTED DAUGHTER OF LORD MACARTNEY

From the Portrait in the possession of C. G. MACARTNEY, ESQ.

Lord Macartney had scholarly tastes and possessed a fine library. It remained untouched for years after his death, but, with many of his manuscripts, was brought to the hammer in 1854.

The printed books were principally on historical and topographical subjects, such as were usually to be found in libraries of the time, with others relating to the histories of those countries which had been the scene of his diplomatic services. The numerous and important manuscripts elicited a spirited competition. Among them were two folio volumes of letters and documents addressed to Sir G. Doming, British Ambassador to the Netherlands 1644 to 1682. This sold for £152. There were two holograph letters of Andrew Marvel, and a collection of original manuscripts and autograph letters relating to Francis Atterbury, Bishop of Rochester;[1] and Hobbes' 'Leviathan,' a curious manuscript, said to be the identical one presented to Charles II. Numerous papers and letters relating to the Chinese Embassy, and Russia, were also sold, together with copies of the correspondence which took place with regard to the affairs of India, between Macartney, Warren Hastings, and various others.

It has been justly remarked of Lord Macartney that no public servant ever left office with purer hands, and this, considering the time he lived in, was no common attribute. His conduct was invariably upright and disinterested, and while extremely generous with his own money, he was almost parsimonious with that of the country, as, in some cases, he did not take what was justly due to him, in order to relieve the public expenditure. This was notably the case in India, where, so desirous was he of discountenancing the spirit of extravagance then prevalent, that he really hardly had what was necessary for his comfort and convenience.

---

[1] Bishop Atterbury, born 1662, was a man of great learning and ability, a fine writer, and a most excellent preacher. In 1722 he was imprisoned in the Tower on suspicion of being concerned in a plot in favour of the Pretender. He was banished the following year, and died at Paris in 1732.

A staunch upholder of the British Constitution, he was an enemy to despotism of any kind, and, fearless of consequences, acted up to his principles on every occasion.

Macartney owed his success in the world of men and matters entirely to himself. The son of a country gentleman in the North of Ireland, he started in life without the advantages of noble birth and family connexions. He had great determination and a talent for success, but, above all, was notable for his strict integrity and well-balanced mind, which qualities gained him the confidence of men of all shades of political opinion. Throughout his long and active life of manifold interests, with an extensive acquaintance among the leading characters of various administrations and oppositions, he managed to keep himself totally unconnected with any party in politics. He deplored that system of government, and wrote thus on the subject in one of his note-books:

'Party spirit seems the most distinguishing spirit of the British nation. Other countries, on some occasions, suspend their interior divisions, but England admits of no holidays in this particular. Peace or war makes no difference, and Party displays her standard at all times and in all places. . . . I happened some time ago to inquire in a common conversation the character of two of my friends in a certain town in the West of England. I was answered that Tom was a very honest man, but that Jack was a rascal. I was at a loss to account for this decision, which I knew to be directly the reverse of the truth, and upon inquiry discovered that the most satisfactory reason was that at an election Tom wore a blue cockade in his hat and Jack a yellow one. It is not easy to account for this extraordinary turn among us. . . . I have often imagined we might attribute it to the influence and grossness of our diet, or the inclemency of our climate. The first is apt to make us saturnine and choleric, and the latter to occasion gloominess and melancholy. Besides that, in England every man being at liberty to think as he pleases, is apt to form a little system for himself, and to condemn, if not to hate, every one who acts contrary to it. Almost every Englishman is a slave to some particular dogmas either of religion or

VIEWS ON IRELAND

politics, is proud of propagating them, . . . and no less ready to defend them. This produces argument . . . and rancour.

' . . . And yet are we not particularly distinguished for our good nature and generosity, and . . . are the finest of mankind in our friendships, and the most inveterate in our enmities ? . . . And are we not apt to think all our excellence confined to ourselves ?

' This is so much the case that our first term of reproach to a foreigner is the name of his country; and I have often seen a man, otherwise charitable, refuse an alms to a wretch because he asked it in the dialect of a particular country.'

Lord Macartney was a warm advocate for the union of Ireland with Great Britain, and urged it strongly at the time of the disturbances in America. If this were not effected, he regarded as necessary the restrictions upon its commerce.

' If you grant a free trade to Ireland whilst a separate kingdom, I am much mistaken if she does not give as much trouble to Great Britain as ever America did. For the people are naturally of lofty, independent spirit, and will become doubly so as they grow rich, which will be the sudden consequence of an open commerce.'

He desired as much independence as possible, and recommended a federal union upon the best terms that could be settled.

' Let Ireland govern itself according to its own fancies for some time. It will return from vagaries and soon follow its true interests.'

As leader of the Ministerial side in the Irish House of Commons, Macartney was noted for his good temper and firmness in dealing with the Opposition, led by Henry Flood, Dr. Charles Lucas, and others. He took a good deal of pains drawing up an account of what he observed of the state of Ireland during the time of his employment there.

' I was much commended, but very little regarded, and I have since had the regret of seeing that country totally misunderstood, and growing every day more difficult to govern or to please.'

OPINION OF LORD NORTH

Of the various Ministers with whom he had to do at different times, Macartney seems to have preferred Lord George Germaine, and most disliked Lord North. Of the latter he wrote:

'During Lord North's administration of five years, America has been most shamefully neglected. There is no doubt that long since a prudent, steady minister might have terminated the dispute, without injuring the colonies or disgracing the mother-country; . . . but we have the melancholy reflection of having neither conciliated affection nor maintained authority. . . . The Minister, instead of taking a decided part, has been tottering between . . . a constant see-saw of menaces and flattery, advancing and receding, enacting and repealing. Having no feeling himself, he has not an idea of the feelings of others. If you apply to him, he either insults you with his answer or mortifies you with his disregard.'

The most difficult period of Macartney's public life was, undoubtedly, the time of his government in India. Russia tried his tact and perseverance, Grenada his energy and courage, Ireland his temper and powers of management, but India was the touchstone of his merits, and he was proof to the test. He took no credit for the purity of his conduct, and remarked that it was not to be supposed his motives arose from any more heroic virtues than those which actuate the generality of mankind.

'I . . . confess I have a stronger passion than the love of wealth; to reinstate India in its former glory would give me more pride and satisfaction than I should be able to derive from ten times the fortune of Mr. Hastings. It is, in fact, a bad calculation in the accounts of the world to sacrifice reputation for any increase of fortune. Such is the opinion of one upon this subject who has had it twenty times in his power to make a large fortune, and never has had it in his thoughts.'

He had a supreme contempt for the ordinary methods practised in India to obtain wealth.

'Notwithstanding the indignation I feel, I am really sometimes diverted with some of these woodcocks, who

FATHER GRAMMONT'S VIEWS

thrust their bills into the ground, shut their eyes, and then think nobody sees them.'

He used to say that a man who had not been in India knew mankind but by halves, and he who had been there knew mankind, alas! but too much.

Macartney's Embassy to China has sometimes been spoken of as a failure, for he was unable to obtain permission for the permanent residence of a British Ambassador at the Court of Pekin, and failed to conclude the commercial treaty which had been hoped for. This would have constituted a new departure, which Chinese prejudices, at that time, were too strong to allow of. But his mission was followed by a longer interval of commercial tranquillity, and freedom from annoyance, than had ever been before experienced. It may also be questioned how far China would at any time have opened up her ports, and concluded treaties, had she not been practically compelled to do so.[1]

After the return of the Embassy, assertions were also made that an unconditional compliance on the part of the Ambassador with the ceremonies the Chinese were anxious he should perform would have been productive of better results. This view was supported by a letter from Father Grammont, one of the French missionaries, who gave that among several reasons for the non-success of the expedition.

'Never was an Embassy deserving of better success . . . and yet, strange to tell, never was there an Embassy that succeeded so ill. . . . These gentlemen, like all strangers who know China only from books, were ignorant of the manner of proceeding, and of the customs and etiquette of the Court. To add to their misfortunes, they brought with them a Chinese interpreter still less informed than themselves. . . . They came without any presents for the Minister of State and the Emperor's sons. They refused to go through the usual ceremony of saluting the Emperor,

[1] 'It has been justly observed of Macartney's Embassy to China that the Ambassador was received with the utmost politeness, treated with the utmost hospitality, watched with the utmost vigilance, and dismissed with the utmost civility.'—Beckles Willson, 'Ledger and Sword.'

without offering any satisfactory reason for such refusal. They presented themselves in clothes that were too plain and too common. They did not use the precaution to fee the several persons appointed to the superintendence of their affairs, and their demands were not made in the tone and style of the country. Another reason of their bad success, and in my mind the principal one, was owing to the intrigues of a certain missionary, who, imagining that this Embassy might be injurious to the interests of his own country, did not fail to excite unfavourable impressions against the English.'[1]

Some of these views were, later on, disproved by the complete failure of the third Dutch Embassy in 1795, who had made use of all the hints contained in Father Grammont's letter. They cheerfully submitted to every ceremonial required by the Chinese, even kow-towing to the Emperor's name painted on a cloth. Their credentials were remodelled by the Government at Canton, and they had an interpreter from that city appointed to attend them. In return they were treated in a most contemptuous manner, being ill-lodged, ill-fed, and at the end dismissed without having been once allowed to open their lips on business. They were not permitted to see any of the European missionaries, with the exception of one, who was allowed to make them a visit of half an hour, the day before their departure, accompanied by ten or twelve officials.

Van Breams, the chief of the expedition, complained that he lost five inches in the circumference of his body owing to exposure and want of proper food. Being rather corpulent, and not very expert in performing the Chinese ceremony, at their public introduction his hat fell to the ground, upon which the old Emperor began to laugh.

'Thus,' said Van Breams, 'I received a mark of distinction and predilection such as never Ambassador was honoured with before. I confess that the recollection of my sufferings from the cold, in waiting so long in the morning, was very much softened by this incident.'[2]

[1] Stow Collection Manuscripts.
[2] 'Travels in China,' J. Barrow.

LORD AMHERST'S EMBASSY

The second English Embassy to China, under Lord Amherst, took place in 1816, and failed also to carry out its objects. This was not due to any fault on the part of the head of it, but to the adverse disposition of the reigning Emperor.

Lord Macartney had a steady and loyal attachment to his Sovereign, which never wavered, whether he was in or out of place, favoured, or apparently neglected. He considered the private character of the King was no concern of his subjects. . . . 'It is merely his public function we are to consider, and to render it useful to the people, either enlarging or abridging it, as the public service requires it.'

Macartney enjoyed the society of ladies, but, according to his sister-in-law, considered every woman, no matter what her age or appearance, liked to hear of her beauty to the last. Lady Louisa also found fault with him for laughing at the 'blue-stocking' Mrs. Montagu, although he professed great admiration for her powers of mind and learning, and wrote thus to her friend Miss Clinton :

'Even among the men who diverted themselves most with her (Mrs. Montagu's) foibles were some who, when serious, would avow a high opinion of her abilities. Of this number was my brother-in-law, Lord Macartney, who piqued himself upon carrying compliments beyond the moon, and maintained that they were always acceptable to every woman without exception, although he paid them in a manner so glaringly ironical, and took so little pains to look decently grave, that one wondered how the bait could possibly be swallowed by anybody who had the use of a pair of eyes. I have heard him laugh peal upon peal as he repeated behind Mrs. Montagu's back the fine speeches he had made, or intended to make. Yet when the laugh was over he would conclude with, "After all, she is the cleverest woman I know; meet her where you will, she says the best thing in the company." '[1]

With regard to Mrs. Montagu, Macartney wrote to the *chère amie*, to whom so many of the letters from Grenada were addressed :

[1] Lady Louisa Stuart's 'Letters to Miss Clinton.'

'Her understanding, her wit, her learning you know better than anyone. But her house, her furniture, her dress are *gauche* to the last degree, points in which it is not permitted either to the most superior or the most trifling woman to fail in. But her case, I fancy, is this, though born a genius, she was bred a scholar and not a lady. Her penetration discovers the graces in others. Her good sense shows her the want of them in herself. She aims at what she cannot attain, she endeavours to practise what she was never taught, and seems now to be at best a grown gentlewoman learning to be a fine lady.[1] With all this criticism, I admire and I respect her; I value her virtues, but I can't avoid seeing her ridicules, and lamenting the inconstancy and imperfection of human nature in those where inconsistency and imperfection were least to be expected. She is a woman of great worth and very extraordinary parts, and I can perceive all her foibles without detracting an atom from her talents and virtues, which are considerable. . . . Pray have you seen the young "Emile," her nephew?[2] I tremble for the cookery of his education. Mrs. M. will not be satisfied with anything short of perfection, so you see she will never be satisfied with her nephew, for if she tries to make him good for everything, he will be good for nothing. He is making the grand tour, and were he to go abroad at

[1] 'To the world at large Mrs. Montagu's devotion to society in extreme old age excited much sarcasm. Her love of finery, which Johnson had excused as a pardonable foible, did not diminish. Samuel Rogers, who came to know her in her latest years, regarded her as "a composition of art," and "as long attached to the trick and show of life." '—' Dictionary of National Biography.'

[2] Matthew, son of Mrs. Montagu's brother, Morris Robinson. She brought the boy up and provided for him, and he was her constant companion after her husband's death. Matthew Robinson took the surname of Montagu in June, 1776. The following letter to Lord Macartney was written by him:

'PORTMAN SQUARE,
'*May*, 1800.

'Mrs. Montagu's early habit of retiring, together with the weak state of her eyes, render it necessary for me to thank your lordship for the very liberal manner in which you have ministered to the comfort of her existence. I do not intend to take out of her hands a duty which she is only capable of performing, but must leave it to her to acknowledge in an adequate manner her sense of this very kind and valuable proof of your friendship. I am obliged to write in the midst of company, and am fearful that I shall have expressed myself in a confused manner.'

A GOOD FRIEND

present he would pass everywhere as the nephew of Mrs. Montagu. When young Panton was in Italy, his Governor always presented him as "Le frère de la Duchesse d'Ancaster." An old Swiss who was tired of this definition of the pupil, peevishly called out one day: "Que diable, Monsieur, est ce que votre ours est comme Melchisédech qui n'avait ni père ni mère?"'

Lord Macartney was a good friend, and always ready to do a kindness, being both generous and compassionate. Among his well-kept and methodically arranged correspondence are numerous applications and letters of thanks for favours received. Though he never possessed a superfluity of money, he was open-handed, as far as he could be, when applied to by anyone in distress.

Among the letters is one from a lady, asking advice on the management of a troublesome husband; and another from Lady Templetown, anxiously inquiring what he thought of a certain Captain Orr, and whether he considered she and her husband would be justified in receiving Captain Orr's addresses for their daughter.

'The happiness of a very amiable young woman is, I believe, at stake, yet her affection not so committed as to occasion disappointment of a *serious nature* on either side. You may be well assured your name shall never be made use of, but your opinion of this gentleman would be very satisfactory.'

The reply to this confidential communication does not appear.

Macartney was considered an exceedingly good classic scholar, and retained to the last his love of books and knowledge of literature. His wonderfully retentive memory enabled him to make the most of his powers of observation and discernment, which were considerable. He was a man of strong mind, but gentle temper and disposition, qualified by an exceedingly keen sense of humour, which had a decided tendency to be satirical. Inflexible when convinced of being in the right, in spite of great quickness of apprehension, he made up his mind but slowly, seldom departing from his first intention save for a very good reason.

His self-control was very great, and in one of his letters to the *chère amie* before alluded to he told her it was his custom never to allow his mind to dwell continually on anything unpleasant. When a disagreeable impression, which he desired to forget, constantly recurred, he visualized ' a field of daffodowndillies,' and kept his thoughts persistently directed to it.

Macartney had great pride, and a good deal of conceit, but this arose rather from a contemptuous opinion of others than from a vain one of himself. He was above self-interest of any kind, was high in his notions of the authority of government, but moderate in the execution of it. Ambition, as before observed, was the keynote of his life. Money was at all times an object of low consideration in his eyes; but he desired to serve well his King and country, and to hand down his name untarnished to posterity. This he has most certainly succeeded in doing, and his character may be very fitly summed up in the motto of the Macartney arms: *Mens conscia recti.*[1]

[1] ' A mind conscious of right.'

INDEX

ADDINGTON Cabinet, 451
Albatross, capture of, 199; unfortunate end of, 200, 201
Alexander, William, artist, 238, 355 *note*
Alexander, Rev. Nathaniel, afterwards Bishop of Meath, 170 *note*
Ambassadors, to China, 342; from the Lieu-kieu islands, 361; Chinese objections to Resident, 461
America, war with, 103, 459, 460; proposed asylum for French regicides, 419
Americans, 95; use of English colours, 233; trade with China, 388, 410
Amherst, Lord, Embassy to China, 363 *note*, 463
Amsterdam Island, first sight of, 202; description of, 207-209
Amyot, Father, 284; views of, 333-336
Ancaster, Duchess of, 51, 465
Anderson, Æneas, servant to Macartney, 373 *note*, 436; extracts from his account of the 'Embassy to China': *notes*: entertainments, 182, 183; young ladies, 185; an exorbitant laundry bill, 189; Viceroy's dress, 192; *billets-doux*, 194; the Royal Batavian Hotel, 213; a fit of the gout, 218; visit from Mandarins, 236; return of the prisoners, 243; a present of silk, 262; funeral service, 273; entry into Pekin, 273; a horrid place, 280; dress for entry into Gehol, 285; presents brought to Gehol, 296; gold lace, 298; Britons' feelings, 299; Lord Macartney's dress, 303; the Emperor and G. T. Staunton, 305; presents from the Emperor, 307; Emperor's birthday ceremony, 314; an ancient box, 318; the State canopy, 325; a report, 332; description of the Emperor of China, 337; Lord Macartney's carriage, 338; overland journey, 355; ungovernable horses, 369; agreeable circumstances, 377; a Chinese interpreter, 391; terra firma, 413
Andrew Marvel, 457
Anglo-Irish, grievances of, 55
Angoulême, Duc de, 423, 431; marriage of, 451
Anspach, Margrave of, 414
Antrim, county of, 1, 3, 413; *custos rotulorum*, 171; sedition, 447
Appendix to China Journal, 393-412;
Arcot, Nabob of, creditors of, 117, 118; neglect to fulfil engagements, 124; difficulties with, 125; offers money to Macartney, 130; affairs of, 130, 131
Arras, Bishop of, 421, 422
Artillery, 296; death of a gunner, 323
Artois, Comtesse d', 113
Artois, Comte d', 418, 423; financial difficulties, 432
Atterbury, Francis, Bishop of Rochester, 457
Auchinleck, Mac-Cartney of, 2
Austrian Emperor, projects of, 423, 424, 431; a flat refusal, 426
Avary, Comte d', 428; a fruitless journey, 429, 430; accompanies Louis XVIII., 437; account of attempt on the King's life, 439, 440

Balaquier, Elizabeth, 163; marriage of, 166
Bambooing, Chinese punishment, 264, 294, 408
Bangalore, sufferings of English prisoners, 127, 128
Barbadoes, 96, 104

INDEX

Barnard, Lady Anne, 443; letters to Mr. Dundas, 443, 446, 447, 448

Barrow, Mr., afterwards Sir John, 442 *note;* expedition up the Peak of Teneriffe, 186; scientific attainments, 198, 206; illness of, 247 *note;* arranges the presents, 280, 282, 328; accompanies Macartney to the Cape, 442

Barrow, Mr., afterwards Sir John, extracts from ' Autobiographical Memoir ' : Mrs. Crewe and her son, 178 *note;* Dr. Dinwiddie, 181 *note;* Dr. Gillan and Mr. Maxwell, 184 *note;* Colonel Benson, 203 *note*

Barrow, Mr., extracts from ' Voyage to Cochin China '—*notes:* Entertainment at Madeira, 182; a dangerous expedition, 184; St. Jago, 187, 188; Ambassador's house at Rio, 190; ladies at Rio, 196; sealhunters, 205; a Batavian banquet, 213, 214; dress of Batavian ladies, 216; Javanese, 221, 222; Batavia, 224, 225.

Barrow, Mr., extracts from ' Travels in China '—*notes:* Pilots, 247, 248; Chinese doctors, 248; rejected provisions, 251; yacht accommodation, 255; Chinese women, 255; barbarians, 256; English hairdressing, 263; differences between Chinese and Tartars, 264, 267, 294, 295; dirty temples, 270, 271; a sumptuous breakfast, 273; Chinese honesty, 274; a good dinner, 275; missionaries, 275, 276, 282, 284, 285, 288, 289, 328; an intrigue, 277, 278; the Emperor's presence chamber, 279; an impudent eunuch, 280; inspection of presents, 282, 283; infanticide, 287; astronomical calculations, 288; Chinese vanity, 290; Yuen-min-yuen, 292; peacocks' feathers, 298; starvation, 299; great men, 302; dress of Ambassadors, 303; Emperor of China, 306, 374; ' proud Englishmen,' 315; public degradation, 323; Chinese watchfulness, 325; astrology, 326; Hatchett's carriages, 327; trackers, 341, 351; peculation, 343; Chinese justice, 344; funerals, 347; ceremonies on entering the Yellow River, 353, 354; an endless bridge, 354; eunuchs, 374; Chinese merchants, 376; British factory, 377; Chinese entertainments, 378, 379; Ly the interpreter, 380; Van-ta-gin and Chou-ta-gin, 390, 391; Chinese dress, 399; press in China, 410

Batavia, 211, 212; governor, 212, 213; society, 214-217; horticultural garden, 226; unhealthiness, 229

Bateman, Viscountess, 451

Bedford, Duke of, 302 *note;* Francis, first Earl of, 451

Belfast, 3

Bengal, Government of: Reinforcements for Sir Eyre Coote, 122; indignation against Nabob of Arcot, 124; letter from, 131; disapproval of negotiations, 143, 144, 146; action in regard to treaty with Tippoo Sahib, 146

Bengal, tea-plants for, 365; offer of Governor-Generalship to Macartney, 151; appointment of Lord Cornwallis, 159; Lord Mornington Governor-General of, 446

Benson, Colonel, 203; accompanies Macartney, 238, 240, 242; accompanies Captain Mackintosh, 355 *note*

Berkeley Square, 50

Blacket, MacCartney of, 2

Blaquière, Colonel, Irish Secretary to Lord Harcourt, 88; differing opinions, 91, 92, 93

Bolton, Duchess of, 5

Brazil, account of, 192-195

Bristol, Earl of, 50, 56

Bruce, Edward and Robert, 2; General, 134

Buckinghamshire, Earl of, 14; opinion on Russian Ministers and politics, 15; popularity in Russia, 17; Macartney's letter to, 35

Burgoyne, Sir John, 133, 136; unsatisfactory behaviour, 138; abuse of Macartney, 139; arrest of, 139, 140, 155

Burke, Edmund, 8; a lost letter, 39; Sir George Saville's speech, 72; high words in the House, 74; his intimate friend, 83; speech on election of Governor of Madras, 118; pamphlet on French Revolution, 172

Burke, William, relationship to Edmund Burke, 8 *note;* letter from Macartney, 37-39

Bute, John, Earl of, 49; daughters' marriages, 51; indisposition, 79; death of, 413 *note*

Bute, John, Earl of, afterwards first Marquis, 415; letter from, 416

INDEX 469

Bute, Countess of, 76; uneasiness, 112, 113; letters from, 69 *note*, 155; indisposition, 164; advice to her daughter, 169; death of, 413
Buttons, distinction by, 381, 409

Calmucks, 320
Camoens, Luis de, 391
Campbell, Lord Frederick, 58
Cam-shi, Emperor, 310, 367
Cape Colony, Government of, 442-449
Cape of Good Hope, Macartney appointed Governor, 441; his arrival, 442; his departure, 449
Cape Town, fire at, 449
Canton, English subjects at, 172, 173; letters from, 219; grievances of traders at, 345, 349, 360; disgraced Hou-pou of, 340; peculations at, 366; arrival of Embassy at, 377; suburbs of, 378; visit to city of, 382, 383
Canton, Viceroy of, 176, 278 *note*, 310, 323, 350, 351, 353; description of, 355; favourable disposition, 356, 359, 364; conversations with, 359-361, 363-369; reception by, 377, 378; professions and assurances, 379; visit of ceremony, 381; farewell to, 389
Carlow, Lady, 153; letters from, 154; letter to, 155 *note*
Caroline Matilda, Queen, of Denmark, 85, 86
Carnatic, invasion of, by Hyder Ali, 120; coast of, 122; finances, 125; Macartney's authority, 132; revenues of, 149, 158
Castries, Maréchal de, 414, 416, 417, 418, 420, 421
Cathcart, Lord and Lady, 82; Colonel the Hon. Charles, 220
Catherine, Czarina of Russia, 13; Macartney's first public audience of, 16; Macartney's description of, 23, 24; attitude towards the Treaty of Commerce, 32, 33; liking for Macartney, 35; Chinese knowledge of, 358; ambitions of, 385
Celtic chiefs, 2
Charles II., King of England, 457
Charlotte, Queen, of England, portrait of, 48, 290; Russian ear-rings, 82; drawing-room, 84, 85, 159, 160; accompanies the King, 85, 167; G. T. Staunton presented to, 453
Chatham, Earl of, 56; moves resolution in House of Lords, 76, 77

Cheusan, search for pilots, 246, 247; request for leave to obtain cargo at, 333, 355
China, Empire of, possible break-up of, 385, 386, 407
China, Empress of, 306 *note*, 374
China, Journal of Embassy to, 180-392; English in, 172, 173, 174; first sight of, 244; coast of, 246; commerce with, 253; Emperor of, 174, 179; Court dress, 291; Court etiquette, 321, 342, 350; land tenure in, 373; Government of, 406, 407; laws and administration of justice, 407, 408; rank, 409; religion, 402-405; science, 409
Chinese, authority of Government, 259, 312; athletic performances, 320; watchfulness, 269, 312, 325 *note*; view of Embassies, 333; prejudice, 367; soldiers, 376, 383; vanity, 388, 394; subjection to Tartars, 293, 393, 394, 405-407; character, 394, 395, 397, 398; houses and clothing, 395, 396, 397; couriers, 350; distrust of strangers, 174, 345, 384, 398, 411
Chinese, in Batavia, 222, 223, 229; in Cochin China, 232, 234; merchants, 246, 250, 347 *note*, 353, 376, 380, 410; dramatic performances, 214, 239, 240, 307, 318, 319, 378; hospitality, 251, 255; ceremonies of demeanour, 258, 259, 394, 395; sailors, 253; population, 255; women, 255, 347, 368, 395, 398, 399, 401, 403; cookery, 255 *note*; method of lifting weights, 270; honesty, 274; Court ceremony, 298, 299, 300, 304, 314
Chinese Ministers, 298; 300, 301, 309, 310, 315; avoidance of business conversation, 311, 316, 330; interview with, 329; easily alarmed, 336
Chiswick, 450, 451; Macartney's tomb, 455; Lady Macartney buried there, 456
Chittoor, loss of, 125
Chou-ta-gin, civil Mandarin, 251, 390; dines on board the *Lion*, 252, 253, 390; accompanies the Embassy, 260, 263; 265, opinion of the Tartar Legate, 267; visits the English Ambassador, 271, 278; deference to the Tartar Legate, 280; inexplicable behaviour, 281; ceremony of Kow-tow, 284; travelling in a post-chaise, 293; at the Great Wall, 294; dispenses justice, 294,

344; Court ceremonial again, 295; visits from, 297-302, 322; good offices, 325; promotion of, 331, 391 *note*; departure of Embassy, 337, 338; conversation with, 343; accompanies the English Ambassador, 359; visit from, 366; Viceroy's confidence in, 370; describes the Emperor Tchien-lung and his family, 374; a festive evening, 379 *note*; a sad farewell, 390; religious views, 404; ideas on administration of justice, 407, 408
Christianity in China, 402, 403
Christians in China, 287
Clive, Lord, 386; Lord and Lady, 446
Coal in China, 373
Cochin China, King of, 234, 237, 242; visit to the Grand Mandarin, 238-240; conquest of, 241; commotion in, 381
Coke, Lady Mary, extracts from diary of: Macartney's marriage, 50; visit to Lady Jane Macartney, 51; political gossip, 53, 56, 57; capture of Grenada, 112, 113; Macartney-Stuart duel, 163, 164
Condé, Prince of, 418; army under, 420, 423
Confucius, 344, 404
Conway, Right Hon. Henry Seymour, letters to, 40-45; letters from, 45, 46
Cook, Captain, voyages of, 183, 187
Coote, Sir Eyre, action in regard to Mr. Whitehill, 117, 118; co-operation with Macartney, 123; opposition to investment of Negapatam, 124, 144; apoplectic seizure, 125; despotic ideas, 128; differences with Macartney, 128, 129, 132; death of, 135
Corney House, 450, 456
Cornwallis, Lord, 159, 447
Coutts, Thomas, 442
Crannog, 4
Crenneville, Comtesse de, 422
Crewe, Mrs., 84 *note*, 178 *note*; Lieutenant, 178 *note*, 238
Curzon Street, Macartney's house in, 165, 454

Danes, trade with China, 410
Dashkoff, Princess, 19, 83
Dashwood, Lady Anne, 448
Dawson, Lady Caroline, 51, 52
Dawson Court, 164, 165
Debtors in China, 408

Dervock, village of, 171
Dinwiddie, Dr., 181, 280, 292 *note*, 355; lectures and experiments, 409
Dorsetshire, Crichel House, 166
Dundas, General, 443, 449, 450
Dundas, Mr., afterwards Lord Melville, Minister for India, 153, 158; Minister for the Colonies, 441; letters to, from Lady Anne Barnard, 443, 446, 447, 448; letters to, from Macartney, 447, 448
Dutch settlements in India, 122, 123, 124; claim in Straits of Sunda, 211; hospitality at Batavia, 213-217; inhabitants of Batavia, 224, 225; commercial jealousy, 227, 228; at Macao, 244; trade with China, 388, 410, 411; at the Cape, 445; Embassy to China, 462
Dysentery, 230, 231; death of member of Embassy from, 272

East India Company, a President for Madras, 116, 117; appreciation of Sir Eyre Coote's services, 135; offer Governorship of Bengal to Macartney, 157; grant annuities to Macartney and Sir George Staunton, 159; expenses of Embassy to China, 175; send commissioners to announce the Embassy, 176; present from King of Cochin China, 242; trade with China, 291
Elizabeth, Queen, of England, 451
Embassy to China, journal of, 180-392; departure of, 179; impression made by, 334; honours and respect paid to, 379; results of, 387; departure from Canton, 388; non-success of, 461
Embassy to and from Great Britain, 330, 333, 334, 344; maintenance of the, 343; suggestions for another, 363, 364
England and Englishmen, 458
England, King of, letter to Emperor of China, 298, 301, 304; form of presentation to, 300; Emperor's inquiries for, 305; presents for, 304, 309, 318, 323; 'paper of happiness,' 356; wish for resident Ambassador in China, 363; Macartney's loyalty and attachment to, 463, 466
English Government, orders to Macartney, 149
Erroll, Lord, 422
Estaing, Comte d', 103, 106; attacks Santa Lucia, 107; peremptory

INDEX

summons to Macartney, 108; terms for capitulation, 109; dishonourable conduct, 110, 111; Mr. Staunton's visit, 115
Eunuchs, 374

Family life in China, 395, 401
Fireworks, at Batavia, 215; in China, 321
Flachelande, Baron de, 421, 422
Fleets, engagement between French and English, 126
Flood, Henry, 459
Florence, 12 *note*, 429, 433
Fo, Chinese deity, 270, 317, 374, 404
Fox, Charles James, early training, 11; letters from, 12 *note*, 16 *note*; speech against Sir G. Saville's motion, 72; disapproval of Warren Hastings, 148; letter to, from Macartney, 144, 145; comments on the King's Speech, 157, 158
Fox, Stephen, Macartney's acquaintance with, 11; his extravagance, 76
France, Constitution of, 419; attitude of Government towards Louis XVIII., 433
French Directorate, 435; fleet, 122; in India, 123, 136; officers, 128; Consul at Santa Cruz, 185; trade with China, 388, 410; King, 416; Court at Verona, 420-422
Funchal, 181
Funerals of members of the Embassy, 273, 324; expenses of, in China, 347 *note*

Gallitzen, Prince, 18
Gavre, Prince de, 428, 429, 430
Gehol, 257, 277; arrangements for journey to, 285; journey to, 292-296; road to, 297; Embassy at, 300, 301, 303; Imperial Gardens, 308-310, 316; departure of Embassy from, 323
Geneva, 9
George III., King of England, 15; speech at opening of Parliament, 48; Lord Bute's influence with, 49; reception of the Remonstrance, 75, 76; levées, 84, 85, 169; interposes his authority, 90, 162, 163, 164; Lady Staunton presented to, 159, 160; State visit to St. Paul's, 167; portrait of, 48, 290; wish for Macartney's appointment to the Cape, 441; grants pension to Macartney, 442; G. T. Staunton presented to, 453
Germaine, Lord George, letter to, 109, 110; Macartney's liking for, as Minister, 460
German goods in China, 411
Gillan, Dr., 184; visits the convent at Rio Janeiro, 194, 196; surgical skill, 200, 208; exploration of Amsterdam Island, 205, 206, 209; the Upas-tree, 226, 227; Cochin-Chinese entertainment, 235, 238; telescopes at Gehol, 303; medical visit to the chief Colao, 312; Yuen-min-yuen, 328; move from yacht, 344
Good Hope, Cape of, 195
Gower, Sir Erasmus, commander of the *Lion*, man-of-war, 180; at Madeira, 182; at St. Jago, 187; at Rio Janeiro, 189; Tristan d'Acunha, 197; Amsterdam Island, 203, 209 *note*; at Batavia, 211, 212, 218; Cochin China, 237-242; in China, 257; letter from Ten-chou-fou, 282; at Cheusan, 291; no letter received, 293; Macartney receives letters from, 329, 356, 357; letter forwarded, and suppressed, 337, 342; departure from Cheusan, 352; arrival in Macao roads, 362; letter from, 369 *note*
Grafton, Duke of, Secretary of State for northern department, 29, 30, 31; First Lord of the Treasury, 58, 59, 61, 67
Grammont, Father, letters to Macartney, 263 *note*, 276 *note*; views on the Embassy, 461, 462
Great Britain, King of, 415, 418
Great Wall of China, first sight of, 293; inspection of, 294; second visit to, and description, 324
Grenada, island of, Macartney's arrival and first impressions, 96, 97; salary of Governor, 101; residence of Governor, 102; exciting times, 103, 105, 106; inhabitants' address to Macartney, 112; captured colours, 115; French and English in, 445, 460
Grenville, Lord, dispatch to, 416, 418; Macartney's letters to, 420-422, 424, 427, 429-433, 435, 436, 437, 438
Greville, Mrs. Fulke, 84
Guildhall, entertainment at, 80
Halifax, Earl of, 76, 80
Hamilton, Emma, Lady, 426, 433
Hamilton, Sir William, 176, 425

INDEX

Hamilton, Sir William, letters from, 426, 433, 434
Hanwell, Rector of, 456
Harcourt, Duc de, 414, 419
Harcourt, Lord, Lord-Lieutenant of Ireland, 87; arrival in Ireland, 88, 89; opinions as to his ability, 89, 90, 92, 93
Hastings, Warren, 117; dislike of Macartney, 130, 146; letters from Macartney, 132 *note*, 146, 147, 148; objection to treaty with Tippoo, 148; correspondence with Macartney, 457; his fortune, 460
Hatchett, carriages made by, 283 *note*, 327 *note*
Henri IV., King of France and Navarre, 423; his armour, 434, 435
Hertford, Marquis of, 456
Hervey, Lady, 49
Hindostan, East Indiaman, 175; loss of anchors, 184; arrival at Amsterdam Island, 203; arrival at Batavia, 211, 212; accident to, 233, 234; sails for China, 244, 245, 246; cargo for, 253, 355, 356; at Cheusan, 311, 352
Hobart, Lord, 446
Hobbes' 'Leviathan,' 457
Hogarth, tomb of, 455
Holland, Lady, marriage, 10; mentioned by Charles Fox, 12 *note*; letter to, from Macartney, 21-24
Holland, Lord, 10, 11; letter to Macartney, 13; opinion of Macartney, 14; his son, Stephen Fox, 76; health and temper, 79; return to England, 80
Holland, Lord, grandson of first Lord Holland, 429
Holland, nation of, 445
Howe, Lord, 444
Huddleston, Mr. J., appointed third Commissioner, 140; treaty with Tippoo, 143; question of allowance to, 152
Hughes, Vice-Admiral Sir Edward, 120, 122; departure from Madras, 129, 130
Hume, Elizabeth, birth of eldest child, 166; visit to London, 167, 168; Macartney's heiress, 456
Hume, Rev. Travers, 166, 167
Hüttner, Mr., tutor to G. T. Staunton, 177 *note*, 249, 250, 251
Hyder Ali, 117; war with, 121, 122; captures English guns, 123; Dutch treaty with, 124; repulsed by British troops, 125; treatment of English prisoners, 126, 127, 128; death of, 133

India, Macartney in, 116-157, 457, 460, 461
Indian Empire, importance of, 145; Princes, 121
Indians in Brazil, 194
Innspruck, 428, 429
Inquisition, in Madeira, 183; in Brazil, 193
'Ireland, An Account of,' extracts from, 54, 61, 62, 63, 70
Ireland, North of, 5, 458; visits to, 69, 91; Lady Macartney's dislike of, 168, 169, 170, 171; political parties, 61; undertakers and patriots, 62; Augmentation Bill, 64; difficulties of Government, 70; Macartney's views on, 459
Irwin, Mr. Andrew, 99

Jackall, brig tender to the Embassy, 180; lost to sight, 183, 196; reappearance of, 230; sails for China, 244, 246, 249
Jackson, the Right Hon. Richard, 66, 67, 68; letter to Lady Louisa Stuart, 170
Jackson, Mrs. (Anne O'Neill), 170 *note*
Japan, projected visit to, 176, 380
Japanese, 361; at the Court of Russia, 362 *note*
Java, Island of, 218; Sultan of, 220, 227
Javanese population, 221; spiders, 228
Jesuits in China, 276, 286, 289, 367
Journal of Embassy to China, 180-392
Junks, Chinese, 253, 254, 259; Ambassador's gift to crews of, 355 *note*

Kalmucks, 307
Keith, Sir Robert, 14
Kia-King, Emperor of China, 364 *note*
King, Rev. J. G., author of 'Rites and Ceremonies of the Greek Church in Russia,' letters from, 81-84
Kow-tow, ceremony of, 266; Chinese anxiety for ceremonial of, 272, 282, 284; Ambassador's objections, 298, 299, 300, 301; Ambassador's refusal to perform it, 315 *note*
Kubla Khan, 312, 394

INDEX

Laguna, 185, 186

Lansdowne, third Marquis of, 454 *note*

Leinster, Duke of, 59, 92; opposes Lord Townshend's measures, 63, 70

Lens, Parker's great, 250, 328

Line, crossing the, 96, 189

Lion, man-of-war, 180; at Madeira, 182, 184, 185; at St. Jago, 187; at Rio Janeiro, 189, 195, 196; at Amsterdam Island, 205, 209 *note*; at Batavia, 212, 218; off Cochin China, 238, 242; death of purser, 243; China, 244, 245, 249, 250; sickness on board, 253, 257, 291, 357; Mandarins dine on board, 254; at Cheusan, 291, 311; Tartar Legate's omission to visit, 298; leaves Cheusan, 329, 352; convoy to East Indiaman, 380, 391; farewell dinner on board, 390

Lissanoure, 1, 4; description of, 5 Lady Macartney's first visit, 69; her dislike of the place, 167; Macartney's interest in the place, 170, 171; a last appearance, 454; cenotaph in parish church, 456

Lonsdale, Lady, 52

Lottery tickets, 79, 81

Louis XVII., King of France, 415, 432

Louis XVIII., King of France, 414, 423; mission to, 413-440; proclamation, 418; conversations with Macartney, 419, 420, 425; description of, 420-422; wishes respecting Madame Royale, 423; letter from King of Spain, 427; opinion of state of affairs in France, 430; letter from Madame Royale, 431; Court at Verona, 432, 433; reply to Podestà of Venice, 434, 435; letters to Macartney, 438, 439, 451, 452; attempt on life of, 439, 440

Lowther, Sir James, afterwards Lord Lonsdale, 54, 56

Lucas, Dr. Charles, 459

Luton Park, 69, 308

Macao, 244, 245, 249; return of missionaries, 260; Sir Erasmus Gower at, 357; Portuguese possession, 384; visit to, 391; Governor of, 391

Macartney family, 1, 2

Macartney, Black George, 'Soveraigne' of Belfast, 3, 4; Carthanach George, 456

Macartney, George, Earl of, birth, 1, 4; father and grandfather, 4; childhood, 5; school bills and outfit, 6, 7; proceeds to London, 8; visit to Voltaire, 9; friendship with the Holland family, 10, 11; manners and appearance, 11; first stands for Parliament, 12; Lord Holland's letter to, 13; knighted and appointed Envoy-Extraordinary to the Court of Russia, 15; first audience of the Czarina, 16; friendship with Panin, 17, 18, 19; opinion of the Russians, 19, 20, 21; letter to Lady Holland, 21-24; love affair, 24, 25; a difficult negotiation, 27, 28, 32; painful situation, 33; remodels treaty, 34; letter to William Burke, 37; letters to Mr. Conway, 40, 42; letter to Mr. Stanley, 40; Czarina's farewell gift, 46; letter from King of Poland, and Order of White Eagle, 47; appointment as Ambassador to Russia, 47; refusal of the office, 48, 53; moderate demands, 48; marriage, 49, 50; relations with his wife, 52, 53; elected member for Armagh, 54; Chief Secretary for Ireland, 56; Spanish Ambassadorship, 56, 57, 65; letters from Lord Townshend, 57-66; visit to Scotch relations, 64; residence in Dublin Castle, 69; letters from friends, 66-93; firmness and good humour, 70; installed K.C.B., 86; Toome Castle, 87; Lord Townshend's admiration, 90; appointed Governor of Grenada, 94; Irish peerage, 94; voyage to West Indies and arrival, 95, 96; debts, 94, 101; first impressions, and Mr. Staunton, 97; visit to Tobago, 100; salary, 101; first attack of gout, 101; Governorship of Jamaica, 103, successful government of Grenada, 105; gallant defence of the island, 108, 109; loss of possessions, 110; prisoner of war in France, 110, 115; address from inhabitants of Grenada, 112; candidature for Governorship of Madras, 116, 118; appointment, 119; letters to Mr. Staunton, 119, 120; government of the Carnatic, 122, 123; successful military operations, 124; letter from Edmund Burke, 125, 126; differences with Sir Eyre Coote, 128, 129; refusal to accept bribes,

INDEX

130, 131; recall and arrest of General Stuart, 134, 136; letter to Sir John Burgoyne, 139 *note*; letters to Mr. Staunton, 141, 142, 143; peace with Tippoo Sahib, 140, 141, 142, 143, 144; letter to Lady Macartney 144; letter to Charles Fox, 144, 145; efforts to conciliate Warren Hastings, 146, 147; resignation of Governorship of Madras, 149; ill-health, 149, 151; visit to Bengal, and offer of Governor Generalship, 150, 151, 157, 158; duel with Mr. Sadleir, 151, 152; departure from India, 152; request for English peerage, 158; duel with General Stuart, 160-164; life in Curzon Street, 165, 166; letters to Sir G. Staunton, 168, 169, 171, 172; life in Ireland, 170, 171, 172; appointed Ambassador to China, 174, 176, 178, 179; journal of voyage from England to China, 180-244; visits to various Governors, 181, 182, 185, 188; arrival at Rio, and visit to the Viceroy, 189-191; observations on Brazil, 193-196; observations on Amsterdam Island, 207-209; visit to Batavia, 212-230; visit to Cochin China, 232-243; account of Embassy to China, 244-392; visits from Mandarins, 248, 250, 251, 252, 253; first impressions of China, 255, 263, 264; diplomatic conversations, 257, 258, 268, 277; discussion as to the presents, 261, 262, 267, 280; the subject of Kow-tow, 266, 272, 284, 299, 300; at Yuen-min-yuen, 274-282; meetings with missionaries, 277, 282, 286, 288, 289; journey to Gehol, 295-297; visit to the chief Minister, 300, 301; first reception by the Emperor, 303-307; second reception by the Emperor, 308; visits to Imperial Park at Gehol, 308, 316; intercourse with the Chinese Ministers, 309, 310, 311, 313, 316, 329-332, 339, 340, 341-347, 348-357, 360, 361, 363, 364, 366, 367, 370, 379, 381, 382; celebration of the Emperor's birthday, 314, 315; third reception by the Emperor, 318, 319; departure from Gehol, 323; return to Pekin, 325; passing of the Emperor, 327; ill-health, 326, 331, 332; disappointment, 334-336; journey from Pekin to Canton, 339-377;

visits from Hong merchants, 380, 381; visit to city of Canton, 382, 383; reflections upon China and Chinese, 383-388; departure from China, 389, 390; Appendix to journal, remarks on the Chinese, their laws, customs, and habits, 393-412; return to England, and Earldom, 413; mission to Louis XVIII. at Verona, 414-438; letters to and from Louis XVIII., 438, 439, 451, 452; Governor of Cape Colony, 441-449; ill-health, 445, 447, 448, 451, 453; indomitable spirit, 448; departure from Cape Town, 449; lease of Corney House, 450, 451; executor of Sir George Staunton's will, 452, 453; death, and post-mortem appearance, 454; funeral and tomb at Chiswick, 455, 456; love of books and library, 457, 465; character and leading ideas, 457-466

Macartney, Lady, marriage, 50; visit from Lady Mary Coke, 51; character and appearance, 52, 53; deafness, 56; mentioned by Lord Townshend, 58, 60, 69; likeness to her father, 79; ear-rings made from the Great Stone, 82; household orders and hopes of motherhood, 92, 93; accompanies her husband to the West Indies, 94, 98; voyage home and loss of possessions, 111; her anxiety, 112, 113; letter from Macartney, 144; reasons for not going to India, 153; Macartney's confidence, 153; letter to her husband, 155 *note*; letters to her sister Lady Carlow, 155, 156, 157; presents Lady Staunton at Court, 159; farewell letter from Macartney, 162, 163; illness and anxiety, 163, 164; move to Curzon Street, 165; letters to her sister Lady Portarlington, 167, 168, 413; dislike of Lissanoure, 169, 170, 171; death of her mother, Lady Bute, 413; residence at Corney House, 450, 451; death and burial, 456

MacCarthy More, The, 1

Mackenzie, Lady Betty, 50, 53, 56

Mackintosh, Captain, commander of the *Hindostan*, 203, 204, 238; sent on shore for intelligence, 244; articles for sale, 250, 285; arranges to go to Pekin, 254; wishes to leave Gehol, 311, 321, 322; discretion, 329; move from yacht, 344; leave to trade and join ship at Cheusan, 355, 356

INDEX

Macpherson, Mr., letters to, 129 *note*, 151; visit from Mr. Staunton, 132
Madame Royale, 423; Austrian plans for, 424; release from captivity, 428; journey to Austria, 429-431; description of, 430; circumspect conduct, 431; marriage, 451
Madeira, 180-183
Madras, 116, 117; Macartney appointed Governor, 119; his arrival, and condition of affairs, 120, 121; destructive storm, 129; death of Sir Eyre Coote, 135; Government and Sir J. Burgoyne, 139; Government,strained relations with Warren Hastings, 132, 147
Mahomedans, 307, 403
Mahomet Ali, 149
Malay slaves, 216, 222; population, 218, 219; entertainments, 229
Mandarins, derivation of word, 250 *note*; behaviour of, 269; yellow vests, 298, 301; meet the Emperor, 326; dislike of lower orders to, 398
Marco Polo, 394, 399 *note*, 410
Marines, 253
Marlborough, Duke of, 302 *note*
Mary, Queen, of England, 3
Maxwell, Mr. Acheson, 163, 184; pursuit of game, 198, 206; search for provisions, 235, 236; sent on shore for intelligence, 244; goes to and from Pekin, 278, 280; move from yacht, 344; accompanies Macartney to the Cape, 441
Meath, Nathaniel Alexander, Bishop of, 170 *note*
Merchants, Chinese Hong, 347 *note*, 353, 376, 380, 410; English, 389
Midhurst, Borough of, 12, 13
Milk in China, 346
Missionaries, Chinese, 245; Italian, 245, 260, 277, 403; French, 263, 277, 282, 284, 286, 287, 289, 403; Portuguese, 263, 288, 289, 403; in China, 402-404
Missionary, Bernado Almeyda, 271, 276, 277, 289; Polish, 328
Mitchell, Sir Andrew, letters to, 18, 36, 37
Montagu, Lady Mary Wortley, 49; Mrs. Elizabeth, 463, 464; Matthew, nephew of Mrs. E. Montagu, 464 *note*, 465
Monthly magazine, 456
Morning Post, 454
Mornington, Lord, 446; letter from Macartney, 446, 447
Moths and mosquitoes, 264
Mutiny at the Nore, 444

Naples, King of, 433, 434
Naples, missionary college at, 175, 402; Court of, 426; Macartney's visit to, 433
Naval mutiny at the Cape, 444
Navarre, union of, with France, 423
Navigation Act, 29, 30, 32
Negapatam, successful attacks on, 124, 128
Netherlands, 424, 457
Nizam ud Dowleh, Nabob, letter from, 121, 122
North, Lord, gaining ground, 73; Irish affairs, 76, 77; reported resignation, 78-83; letter to Lord Townshend, 87 *note*; Macartney's opinion of, 89, 460; absentee tax, 93; a confidential mission, 115
Northumberland, Duchess of, 52
Nuns in Maderia, 185, 186; in Rio Janeiro, 193, 194, 196
Nutmeg plants, 227, 228

Orange, Princess of, 72
Orchestra,Emperor of China's, 289,290
Orloff, Gregory, 16, 18; Panin's relations with, 30, 42
Orotava, 186

Panin, his ability, 15; friendship for Macartney, 18, 19, 38, 39; projects for Russia, 26, 27, 28; indignation with Great Britain, 31, 36; ordered to cancel treaty, 32; his inflexibility, 34, 44; farewell speech to Macartney, 36; letter from, 46, 47
Panin, Mademoiselle, wedding of, 35
Pantomime, Chinese, 319
Papers and painting in China, 410
Parkhurst, 50, 167
Party spirit, 458
Patchcock Islands, 245
Paul, Grand Duke, 35
Paul I. of Russia, 452
Payho, River, 254, 255
Pecheli, Gulf of, 246, 249, 257; Viceroy of, 256-263
Pekin, English at, 174; accommodation for Embassy, 257, 280; distance from Tongsion, 269; first arrival at, 273; Macartney's wish to reside there, 277, 278; *Gazette*, 278 *note*; Embassy at, 282; buildings in, 285; Christians in, 287; Bishop of, 288; population of, 313 *note*; second arrival at, 325; cold weather, 329; final departure of Embassy, 339; wits of, 340; Court of, 351

INDEX

Peter III. of Russia, 23 *note*
Pigot, Lord, 117, 136, 163
Pilots, Chinese, 245, 247, 248
Pisa, 422
Pitt, William, opinion of Macartney's conduct in India, 158, 160; death of, 453
Poland, King of, 47
Pondicherry, 120
Ponsonby, Mr., Irish Speaker, 63, 65, 68; opposition to Government, 70, 93
Pope, the, 435
Population in China, 383
Porcelain, 283, 307 *note*
Portarlington, Lady, 51, 413; letters from, 164, 165; letters to, 167, 168
Portland, Duke of, 155 *note*; letter from, 438
Portugal, Queen of, 195; Embassy to China, 333
Portuguese in Brazil, 190-194; in Batavia, 223; in Cochin China, 234, 240; at Macao, 244, 278 *note*, 384; missionaries, 263, 288, 289, 403
Poutala, Pagoda of, 316, 317
Presents for the Chinese Emperor, 176, 250; transhipment of, 253; discussion with Tartar Legate, 257, 261, 262; from Macartney, 267, 285, 304; accommodation for, 269, 270; arrangement of, 280, 282, 337 *note*; Chinese expectation of, 286; account of, in *Tiensing Gazette*, 295; brought to Gehol, 296 *note*, 302; for the English Embassy, 361, 366, 377; to officials at Canton, 380; made by Chinese to their Emperor, 410
Priests, Chinese, 270, 371, 372
Prisoners, address to Macartney, 145, 146
Puppet show, 316

Queen of France at Versailles, 113; exiled, of France, 421
Queen of Naples, 433
Queen of Spain, 427
Queen's County, 164, 165

Remonstrance, the, presented to George III., 74, 75, 76
Reynolds, Sir Joshua, 8, 12, 290
Revolution, French, 422; Burke's pamphlet on, 172
Rio Janeiro, 189-196; Viceroy of, 191; shops at, 229
Rochester, Bishop of, 457

Rome, asylum for French King, 419, 420; asylum for Madame Royale, 423; Macartney's visits to, 433, 435
Royal Road from Pekin to Gehol, 297
Rumbold, Sir Thomas, 117, 118
Russell, Lord, 451
Russia, a first-class Power, 13; necessity of alliance with, 14; Macartney's mission to, 15-48, 460; society in, 19-25; Empire of, 44; Chinese dealings with, 309, 358; Chinese ideas of, 342; passports, 404; trade with China, 411
Russia, Empress of: dealings with Louis XVIII., 417, 418, 422, 432; and the Comte d'Artois, 432

Sadleir, Mr. A., 134; differences with Mr. Staunton, 140, 141; peace with Tippo, 143; duel with Macartney, 151, 152
St. Jago, Island and Governor, 187; poverty of inhabitants, 188
St. Paul, Island of, 200, 207
Sandwich, Earl of, Secretary of State for Northern Department, 12, 14; letter from, 17 *note*; letters to, 19 *note*, 26 *note*, 28 *note*
Santa Cruz, 183, 184, 185
Sardinia, King of, 432
Saville, Sir George, speech in House of Commons, 72
Schonberg, Duke of, 4 *note*
Sea-lion, 199, 200
Sea-serpent, 201, 202
Seal-hunters, 203, 204, 209
Sects in England, 405
Shakespeare, quotation from 'The Tempest,' 255
Shannon, Lord, 63, 68
Shirley, Mr. H., 19, 82
Small-pox, 450
Sovereigns of the East and West, 257, 284
Spain, King of, 427
Spain, peace between French Republic and, 415, 416, 423, 426; perfidy of, 425, 427
Stanley, Right Hon. Hans, appointed Ambassador to Russia, 34; Macartney's letter to, 40; resignation of appointment, 47
Staunton, George Leonard, afterwards Sir, first acquaintance with Macartney, 97; birth and family, 98; taking of Grenada, 108, 109; loss of possessions, 110; prisoner of war in France, 113, 115; appointed

INDEX

Indian Secretary to Macartney, 119; letter to Macartney, 132; arrest of General Stuart, 136, 137; letters to Macartney relative to negotiations for peace with Tippoo Sahib, 141, 142, 143; Macartney's praise of, 144, 145; advice to Lady Macartney, 156; made a baronet, 159; Macartney's duel with General Stuart, 162, 163; letters to and from Macartney, 168, 169, 171, 172; Secretary to Chinese Embassy, 174; search for interpreters, 175, 176; ideas on education, 176, 177; letter from Macartney, 178; at Madeira, 180; at Teneriffe, 184, 186; at Rio Janeiro, 189, 195; projects for exploration, 198; a ghostly appearance, 202; at Tristan d'Acunha, 203, 205, 207; at Batavia, 212, 227, 228; in Cochin China, 238, 240; in China, 244, 245, 250, 256; procures pilots, 246, 247; journey to Gehol, 292; visit to principal Minister, 298; dress for attendance at the Chinese Court, 303; reception by the Chinese Emperor, 304, 305; an excursion, 312; represents the Ambassador, 332; departure from Canton, 389; letters from Macartney, 428, 429, 445; work on China, 436; death of, 452; monument in Westminster Abbey, 453

Staunton, Sir G. L., extracts from 'Embassy to China'—*notes*: A runaway nun, 186; seal-hunters, 209; a murdered seaman, 219; slaves in Batavia, 222; military recruits in Batavia, 225; visitors to the *Lion*, 245; Chinese customs, 246; Chou-ta-gin and Van-ta-gin, 252; English crews, 254; Chinese yachts, 255; food, 256, 258; Mandarins, 259; Macao missionaries, 260; Tartar Legate, 261, 322; Chinese curiosity, 264; cost of Embassy, 268; Emperor's dress, 304; banquet, 305, 306, 307; the Colao's ailments, 312; population of Pekin, 313; theatrical performance, 320; Great Wall, 324; return to Pekin, 325; astrology, 326; the Emperor's sedan chair, 327; departure from Pekin, 339; cows, 347; the Emperor's dispatches, 350; dress of the trackers, 352; Viceroy of Canton, 359; wet weather, 366

Staunton, Mrs., afterwards Lady, 98; letter from France, 113-115; presentation at Court, 159, 160; objections to her son going to China, 177; illness and death of her husband, 452, 453

Staunton, G. T., birth of, 115 *note*; education, 176, 177; in China, 256, 292; knowledge of Chinese language, 284, 365, 383; accompanies Lord Amherst's Embassy, 364 *note*; note from 'China Trade,' 389 *note*; death of his father, 452; Macartney's letters to, 452, 453

Stuart, General, 133; indignation at recall, 134; dismissed from the service, 135, 136; arrest, and subsequent indignation, 136, 137, 138; schemes for revenge, 160; challenges Macartney, 161; duel with Macartney, 162-164

Stuart, Lady Jane, 49, 50

Stuart, Lady Louisa, 51, 153; opinion of Macartney, 53, 165, 166; letters from Lady Carlow, 154; letter to Lady Carlow, 155 *note*; letter from Mr. Jackson, 170; letter to Miss Clinton, 463

Stuart, Lord William, 182

Sturt, Mrs., 166

Sturt, Humphrey, 166

Sunda, Straits of, 197, 211, 230

Suntagin, 309, 337; Macartney's conversations with, 341, 344-351, 355, 356; high character, 357

Swedes, trade with China, 410

Tartar conquest, 405

Tartar Legate, 260; unfriendly disposition, 261, 262, 267, 271, 322, 325; introduces European missionaries, 275, 277; officiousness of, 280; ceremony of Kow-tow, 282; neglect to send letter, 293; degradation of, 298; surprise of, 328; assists at departure of Embassy, 338; endeavour to obstruct, 346; religion, 404

Tartar divinities, 317, 372; government, 368; ladies, 399; Princes, 312, 313, 374; education of, 405; religion, 404

Tartars, ascendancy in China, 393, 405-407; partiality of Emperor of China for, 267, 286, 309, 320, 398, 406, 407; Chinese respect for, 293; punishment of, 294;

Tartary, 257, 266; Chinese Court there, 296; capital of, 313

INDEX

Tchien-Lung, Emperor of China, portrait of, 246; orders as to the Embassy, 247, 271; presents for, 250, 257, 262, 267, 280, 285, 286; birthday of, 261; customary obeisance to, 266, 284; troops checked in Tibet, 268; favourable impression of Embassy, 272; favours to European missionaries, 276; family, and favourite Minister, 286; approval of conduct of English sailors, 291; witnesses approach of the Embassy, 297; first reception of the Ambassador, 304-307; descriptions of, 305, 306 note, 337 note; State banquet, 306, 307; second reception of the Ambassador, 308; favourite weapon, 313; celebration of his birthday, 314, 315, 318, 320, 321; divine descent, 317, 407; presents to the Embassy, 319, 332; presents to George III., 318, 323, 332; return to Pekin, 326, 327; orders, 328, 345; apprehensions, 329; letter to King of England, 331, 332; fixes date for departure of Embassy, 337; answer to paper of requests, 339; letters from, 341, 347, 348, 349, 351, 381, 382 note; allowance for expenses of the Embassy, 343; satisfaction with the Embassy, 353, 364, 382; marks of friendship, 363, 368; description of, 374, 375; Tartar descent, 406; fate of his debtors, 408; is seen to laugh, 462

Tea-plants, 365
Temple of the Sea-God, 256, 257; at Tongsiou, 270; of Pusa, 371, 372, 373 note; at Canton, 378
Templetown, Lady, 465
Tenchoufou, city of, 248
Teneriffe, Island of, 183, 187; Governor, 185; expedition up the Peak, 184, 186
Thames, compared with the Payho River, 255; compared with the canal to Yellow River, 353
Theatrical performances, 378, 379
Tibet, insurgents in, 268; frontier of, 287; Delai-Lama, 404
Tien-sing, city of, 247, 249; *Gazette*, 295; entertainment at, 346
Tippoo Sahib, negotiations for peace with, 140; arrogance and cruelty, 142; treaty with, 143, 144, 146, 453
Tongsiou, 253, 254, 267; distance from Pekin, 269; departure from, 273

Toome Castle, 87
Tower of the Thundering Winds, 358
Townshend, Lord, Lord-Lieutenant of Ireland, 56; letters to Macartney, 57-61, 64, 65, 90; military schemes, 67; letter to Lord North, 70 note; recall of, 87; second marriage, 88 note; departure from Ireland, 89; denunciations against, 92; respect and friendship for Macartney, 90, 162
Trade with China, 410, 411
Treaty of Commerce with Russia, 26-29; various opinions on, 29-31; mentioned by George III., 48
Treaty of Commerce with China, 461
Treves, Elector of, 430
Trinity College, Dublin, 7
Tristan d'Acunha, Island of, 197, 200, 201
Tunbridge, 155, 156, 208
Tuscany, Grand Duchy of, 424; Grand Duke and Duchess of, 433, 434
Tyrconnel, Earl of, 55
Tyrone, Earl of, 59, 61

Ulster, 3, 171
Universal fashions, 400
Upas-tree, 226, 227

Vanta-gin, war Mandarin, 251; dines on board the *Lion*, 252, 253; accompanies the Embassy, 260, 263, 265, 325; his opinion of the Tartar Legate, 267; visits the Ambassador, 271, 278, 366; deference to the Tartar Legate, 280; inexplicable behaviour, 281; Birmingham sword-blades, 290; visits from, 297-302; Kow-tow, 284; travelling in a post-chaise, 293; the Great Wall, 294; Court ceremony again, 295, 322; dispenses justice, 294, 344; promotion, 331, 391 note; conversation with, 343; accompanies the Ambassador, 337, 338, 359, 341; introduces 'two genteel young men,' 361; Viceroy's confidence in, 370; description of the Emperor Tchien-Lung, 374; a festive evening, 379; a sad farewell, 390; death of, 391 note; his religion, 404
Velloor, investment and relief of, 125
Venice, Republic of, 417; trip to, 423; Republic of, request Louis XVIII. to withdraw from their territory, 434

INDEX 479

Verona, Macartney's arrival at, 414, 418; French King's residence at, 420; French Court, 432, 434; French King's departure from, 436, 437
Versailles, 113
Vienna, 417; Court of, 425, 426, 427; residence for Madame Royale, 428, 429; her arrival there, 431
Voltaire, 9, 10

Waite, Mr. T., official at Dublin Castle, letters from, 66-68, 87-89, 91, 92
Wales, Princess of, 49, 84, 85
Wellesley, Hon. Henry, 446
West Indies, 94-111; French in, 424
Westminster Abbey, monument to Sir Eyre Coote, 135; monument to Sir George Staunton, 453
Weymouth, Lord, 66, 67, 71
Whitehill, Mr., sometime Governor of Madras, 117, 118
Whitworth, Charles, afterwards Lord Whitworth, British Minister at St. Petersburg, 362 *note*

Wilkes, John, 73
William III., King of England, 3
Wurtemburg, Duke of, 10
Wyndham, Mr. W., British Minister at Pisa, 422

Yachts, Chinese, 254, 255 *note*, 308, 366; number provided for the Embassy, 265; trackers for, 264, 341 *note*, 344, 351; provisions, 268; inscription on flags of, 269; strength of boatmen, 362
Yang-tse River, 354
Yellow River, 353 *note*, 354
Yellow Sea, 249, 369
Yonge, Sir George, 449, 450
Yuen-min-yuen, distance from Pekin, 269; arrival at, 273; accommodation there, 274, 275; 'Garden of Gardens,' 278; the Emperor's presence-chamber, 279; arrangement of presents, 280, 292, 326, 328; celebration of the Emperor's birthday, 315 *note*; return to, 326

Made in the USA
Lexington, KY
19 February 2013